SINATRA

IN HOLLYWOOD

Also by Tom Santopietro

The Importance of Being Barbra
Considering Doris Day

SINATRA
IN HOLLYWOOD

Tom Santopietro

Thomas Dunne Books
St. Martin's Press ♒ New York

BIO
Sinatra
Frank

THOMAS DUNNE BOOKS.
An imprint of St. Martin's Press.

SINATRA IN HOLLYWOOD. Copyright © 2008 by Tom Santopietro. All rights reserved. Printed in
the United States of America. For information, address St. Martin's Press, 175 Fifth Avenue,
New York, N.Y. 10010.

www.thomasdunnebooks.com

www.stmartins.com

Photographs courtesy of Photofest

Library of Congress Cataloging-in-Publication Data

Santopietro, Tom.
    Sinatra in Hollywood / Tom Santopietro.—1st ed.
        p.   cm.
    Includes bibliographical references, filmography, and index.
    ISBN-13: 978-0-312-36226-3
    ISBN-10: 0-312-36226-9
    1. Sinatra, Frank, 1915–1998. 2. Singers—United States—Biography. 3. Motion picture
actors and actresses—United States—Biography. I. Title.
    ML420.S565S26   2008
    791.4302'8092—dc22
    [B]   2008024941

First Edition: November 2008

10   9   8   7   6   5   4   3   2   1

In memory of my father,
Olindo Oreste Santopietro, M.D.,
and our great night seeing Frank in concert at Carnegie Hall

Contents

Acknowledgments

With gratitude and thanks to the following friends and colleagues for their help, suggestions, and support: the Erickson family; Jeanine Basinger; Savannah Jahrling; Janet and Carol Strickland; Peter Joseph, Harriet Seltzer, Joan Higgins, and Kevin Sweeney at St. Martin's Press; Diana Varvara; Alan Markinson for his intrepid sleuthing of hard-to-find Sinatra films; Ron and Howard Mandelbaum at Photofest for their great help with photos; Mimi Lines; Ruth Mulhall and clan; Rheba Flegelman; Don and Anne Albino; special thanks to Lynnette Barkley, Brig Berney, and Jan Heise, charter members of the Sinatra Cinema Club, for their encouragement and willingness to sit through *Johnny Concho* as readily as *From Here to Eternity.*

Most especially, thanks to my editor and publisher, Tom Dunne, for his guidance and patience.

Parts of the analysis of the film *Young at Heart* appeared in my book *Considering Doris Day* (St. Martin's Press, 2007).

March 25, 1954

MARCH 25, 1954: Total silence envelops the star-studded audience inside the RKO Pantages Theatre in Hollywood, California, as actress Mercedes McCambridge begins to read the names of the five nominees for Best Supporting Actor in a Motion Picture at the 26th Annual Academy Awards ceremony: Eddie Albert—*Roman Holiday,* Brandon de Wilde—*Shane,* Jack Palance—*Shane,* Frank Sinatra—*From Here to Eternity,* Robert Strauss—*Stalag 17.* Pausing briefly and opening the envelope, McCambridge exclaims:

"And the winner is—Frank Sinatra in From Here to Eternity."

Upon hearing those long-coveted words, Frank Sinatra does what every Oscar winner has ever done—he exhales. As the applause turns into cheers, he kisses both of his dates for the glittering occasion—daughter Nancy, thirteen, and son Frank, ten—and bounds up the aisle to excitedly accept his award. Taking the stage and grasping the golden statue, Frank Sinatra pronounces himself "deeply thrilled and very moved." Briefly cracking wise— "And I'd just like to say, however, that they're doing a lot of songs here tonight, but nobody asked me"—Frank professes his love for the crowd, expresses his thanks, and strides offstage, where, Oscar clasped firmly in hand, he runs the gauntlet of photographers. Flashbulbs pop and hundreds of photos are snapped. Frank Sinatra is back on top of the show business world.

Never mind the two studios that had dropped Frank's contract, the back-to-back flops of *Double Dynamite* and *Meet Danny Wilson,* and the three years spent in the wilderness of turned backs and unreturned phone calls. Tonight's a new night—and in that marvelously phony "Hooray for Hollywood" fashion always at its white hottest on Oscar night, everyone wants to congratulate Frank. Everyone wants a piece of the comeback *Variety* almost instantly termed "the greatest comeback in theatre history." And after backs are slapped, hands shaken, and hugs exchanged, Frank Sinatra, Mr. "Center-of-the-Action," does something quintessentially Sinatra—he walks out. Leaves all the festivities, the glittery Governors Ball, where everyone in Hollywood could pay homage, and walks the streets of Beverly Hills. Alone. As if no one else could understand the true distance of his journey.

Reflecting on the night years later, Frank mused, "I couldn't even share it with another human being. I ducked the party, lost the crowds, and took a walk. Just me and Oscar. I think I relived my entire life as I walked up and down the streets of Beverly Hills." In an entire adult lifetime spent onstage and now onscreen, through all the cheering crowds and boozy camaraderie with friends, Frank Sinatra never could outrun the loneliness that had haunted him since his solitary childhood. Loving parents? Yes. Parents who were always there? Most decidedly not. And as Frank grew up, and the desire—no, need—to perform grew, the reverent attention of the crowds provided consolation for his lonely nature. The years rolled on, and stardom arrived, but records and public performances no longer sufficed; Frank Sinatra had made a willful decision that the worldwide fame and immortality afforded by Hollywood movies would be the ticket, and tonight, Oscar night, he had proved it to every last person in America.

Through sheer force of talent and willpower, Frank Sinatra had fulfilled his dream of movie stardom, won Hollywood's top honor, and reminded everyone in filmland—hell, everyone in the world—that he had officially arrived as a top-flight dramatic actor. This was no mere singing-and-dancing routine alongside Gene Kelly. This was powerful dramatic work—"a whole new kind of thing," as he said in his acceptance speech—and there'd be plenty more of it to follow if Frank had anything to say about it. And he did.

Rattling off no fewer than seventeen major motion pictures in the next six years alone, Frank Sinatra served notice over and over again that he was a very big and important film actor. A movie star. One of the immortals.

But nothing was ever simple with Frank Sinatra, especially when it came to Hollywood. In his own words: "I made some pretty good pictures . . . and I tried a few things that turned out to be mistakes. . . ."

Right on both counts.

Well, Did You Evah (Care)?

"Well, Did You Evah!" sung by Frank Sinatra
and Bing Crosby in *High Society*

Frank Sinatra is beyond talent. It's some sort of magnetism that goes in higher revolutions than that of anybody else in the whole of show business. There's a certain electricity permeating the air. It's like Mack the Knife was in town and the action is starting. —BILLY WILDER

The trouble with me is that I get impatient. I've always been that way. You know, I might do some great things if only I could learn not to be impatient. —FRANK SINATRA

WHEN FRANK SINATRA DIED on May 14, 1998, nearly every press account of his storied career referred to him as "the greatest popular vocalist of the twentieth century." There were no qualifiers. Just an emphatic statement with the words "the greatest." Period. End of discussion. As to his film legacy, however, the verdict was much more uncertain. Yes, even the most critical of commentators admitted, he was sensational in *From Here to Eternity* and *The Manchurian Candidate,* but those were, in the minds of many, exceptions. The verdict remained that Sinatra didn't try very hard, slumming his way through dozens of movies because he simply didn't care.

Which leads to the two crucial questions: First, was Frank Sinatra a good actor? The answer is not exactly—because he actually was a great actor who, when given the right material, proved himself an artist capable of elucidating the human condition with a depth and range every bit the equal of his work in the recording studio. Second, just how seriously did Frank Sinatra take his film career? The answer? Very. Yes, he was the first to joke about cringe-worthy films like *Double Dynamite* and *The Kissing Bandit,* but contrary to popular, and knee-jerk, reaction, he cared, and cared big-time. For starters, he was willing to plumb the darkness in a variety of ways, which not only didn't interest other singing actors like Bing Crosby, but also did not speak to other nonmusical Hollywood A-list stars. As Sinatra's dramatic range grew, reaching its peak in the 1950s, he had only one serious competitor for the plum dramatic film roles of that decade: Marlon Brando, a man widely hailed as *the* American film actor of the twentieth century. From *On the Waterfront* and *Guys and Dolls* on to *The Man with the Golden Arm,* Sinatra and Brando traded off the prime roles of the decade. Sinatra outhustled and outbid Brando for the rights to *The Man with the Golden Arm,* and that is the action of an actor who cares very much indeed.

Frank Sinatra prized the body of work he'd leave behind, evincing a keen interest in his film legacy, which resonated not just in interviews, but in personal encounters as well. In singer Michael Feinstein's fulsome tribute to Sinatra entitled "You're Sensational," Feinstein writes of a meeting with Sinatra: "His passion for his films was extraordinary, because it was almost as if he was reliving their production as he talked." (Feinstein's tribute forms an ironic counterpoint to his comments in his autobiography of seven years earlier, wherein he bluntly wrote: "As I listened to Sinatra, he got more and more on my nerves. Mind you, I am well aware that this is a minority opinion and I freely acknowledge Sinatra's *vocal* talent—a great natural instrument—but his message continues to elude me.")

Just how important was his screen legacy to Sinatra? So much so that when he made a guest appearance on *The Tonight Show* and host Johnny Carson asked him to detail the "highlight" of his career, Sinatra stated: "Obviously, winning the Academy Award for *Eternity* and then . . . being a part of a film called *The Man with the Golden Arm,* which I thought was a milestone in the picture business." Like so much about Sinatra the actor, the answer is unexpected and thought-provoking. Sinatra mentioned his films, not the brilliant Capitol concept albums with Nelson Riddle or the smash hit singles and multiple Grammy Awards.

In the days before television, home video, or the Internet, Sinatra knew that movie stardom could ensure his immortality and reach the widest possible audience worldwide, providing a visual record of all his powers, dramatic and musical. One of the reasons why Sinatra reached out to Hollywood, spending untold time and passion on his film career, and calling California home from 1944 onward, is that the state of mind prevalent in Hollywood fit the construct of the Sinatra personality perfectly: Hollywood was the ultimate home of that most American of pastimes, self-reinvention. The boy crooner from tough little Hoboken would now become Frank Sinatra, Hollywood movie star.

Frank embraced Hollywood and, like so many others, would do anything in his power to make sure that the world of his upbringing would never be a part of his life again. Hoboken was dead for Sinatra, but the sense of struggle that world bred in him lingered for the rest of his life—it was as if he could not ever fully let go of it. Hollywood fit Sinatra because in a town that always demanded more, Frank himself always wanted more, both professionally and personally. If people thought of him as a singer, well, he'd show them: he'd also become an actor, and a damn good one. Sinatra continually eyed the next main chance, the prize over the horizon, and the professional and personal choices that ensued in his quest to create a new type of all-media career fed each other and ensured an unending drama, one that fascinated the world for nearly six decades.

In the 1940s, at the height of America's infatuation with the movies, approximately eighty-five million Americans attended the movies at least once a week. (In the twenty-first century, with a national population more than double that of 1945, movie attendance is less than half what it was in the 1940s.) With that huge audience waiting to be conquered, Frank Sinatra arrived in Hollywood a man on a mission. Longtime valet George Jacobs, who spent over ten years working for Sinatra, observed Frank in all his workaholic manifestations, and in his 2003 memoir about life with Sinatra tellingly noted: "Although movies were a crapshoot compared to music, where Mr. S was undisputedly numero uno, cinema was the Everest Frank Sinatra felt compelled to conquer. . . . Some dreams, like movie stardom, were beyond the bottom line."

The dream of movie stardom made perfect sense to Frank Sinatra, not only because of his extraordinary self-confidence, but also because even in the early stages of his singing career, he was able to beautifully delineate the deepest of feelings precisely because he was always, instinctively, acting: "I do believe that singing on one-nighters all of those years, without my really understanding it, I was acting, acting out songs, and I began to become comfortable as a performer on screen." Onscreen, with a cocked eyebrow here, a catch in the voice there, Sinatra communicated on a gut level with his ever-growing audience. He heard lines musically, both the rhythms and the emphases that changed meaning, and it's why he developed into a first-rate dramatic actor. In the words of Buddy Adler, producer of *From Here to Eternity,* "He has the most amazing sense of timing, and occasionally he'll drop in a word or two that makes the line actually bounce."

Contrary to popular legend, Sinatra didn't just wing it in Hollywood. At the start of his film career, he visited sets, observed directors, and studied the actors. It's not just that Sinatra wanted to succeed. He *had* to succeed: "I went around to all the different sets in the studio, and watched the different people work, all the veterans. I'd stand up on a ladder way in the back and picked up pointers from these people. I still have never been to a dramatic coach; I suppose I should have. I almost regret that I didn't." Note Sinatra's choice of words: I *almost* regret that I didn't. Almost. In the end, Sinatra trusted his instincts as an actor and remained convinced that overanalysis would ruin his work.

And yet, study he did, with a thoroughness that would have pleased many a Method acting coach. In his own words: "I always try to remember three things as a movie actor. First, you must know *why* you are in the movie, understand all the reactions of the man you are playing, figure out *why* he's doing what he is doing. Secondly, you must know the script. . . . I keep a script in my office, my car, my bedroom, by the telephone, even in the john. And I read the whole script maybe fifty or sixty times before shooting even starts. . . . Thirdly, you must learn and listen to the lines of others; it's no good just learning your own. . . . I have my own technique that I've evolved from discussing acting with some of my chums, like Spencer Tracy and Bogie when he was alive. . . . Once we've begun shooting I rarely open the script. If two good actors in a scene listen intently to what the other is saying, they'll answer each other intelligently. Actors who go only by the lines never seem to be listening to the other actor, so the scene comes out on the screen as if you can see the wheels going around in their heads."

Reading a script fifty times? These are not the words of a man who took the business of acting lightly or who was oblivious to the needs of his fellow actors. Yes, Sinatra did in fact strongly prefer to deliver only one take. Even there, however, it was a method of acting which evolved because his instinctive talent really did function better on a first take, not because he disdained his art. As director George Sidney (*Anchors Aweigh* and *Pal Joey*) stated: "Sinatra's first take is better than anyone else's fifteenth take."

In essence, Sinatra on film ran the gamut of emotions and roles enumerated in one of his hit recordings of the 1960s, "That's Life." The song actually reflected Sinatra to a far greater degree than did Paul Anka's "My Way." (After all, how accurately could those lyrics reflect Frank's own life if he began singing the famous opening words—"And now the end is near"—as a very healthy fifty-two year old, thirty years before he died?) The famously alliterative lyric of "That's Life" rattles off a list of life roles that Sinatra seems to have inhabited both onscreen and off: (I've been a) "puppet, a pauper, a pirate, a poet, a pawn—and a king." In Frank's own, nearly identical words—"I've been up and down in my life more than a roller coaster on the Fourth of July." No wonder he could sing "That's Life" with such feeling—he had indeed been "up and down and over and out . . . picked himself up and got back in the race." His wildly exciting, frequently depressing, and all-encompassing life experience is what allowed Frank to access the most complicated of emotions onscreen, informing his portrayals with an extraordinary depth of emotion. Yes, he made a lot of second-rate movies that wasted his talents, but he also restlessly and relentlessly searched for a wide range of vehicles that could fully express his protean talents: the boy next door of *Anchors Aweigh* evolved into the pathetic Maggio of *From Here to Eternity,* who morphed into the tortured Bennett Marco of *The Manchurian Candidate,* before finally sliding into the world-weary Edward Delaney of *The First Deadly Sin.* So wide-ranging was Sinatra's extraordinary acting ability that he remains the only film star in history who carved out separate ongoing onscreen careers as the star of musicals, comedies, dramas, and thrillers. What is more, he remains the only actor audiences ever accepted in such disparate genres without hesitation.

Frank Sinatra struck a chord with the moviegoing public because his persona on film reflected so much of the America he embodied: he was outgoing and had the "world on a string," yet also proved tender and often afraid. If America in the 1950s and 1960s was afraid of the Communists, afraid of ceding its position as the world's number-one power, then Sinatra reflected that dichotomy onscreen; he was confident and brash, yet very often vulnerable, both in song and with women. Such a dichotomy wasn't just acting—it was the essential Sinatra shining through. It's as if Sinatra feared the entire edifice

could come crashing down at any minute, and the relentless activity of filming, even when he knew the material was inferior, kept that fear at bay both
onscreen and off. As ex-wife Mia Farrow perceptively observed: "They have
it all wrong, they don't really know him. They can't see the wounding tenderness that even he can't bear to acknowledge—except when he sings. Maybe if
they look at the earliest photos of Frank . . . if they really looked at that face,
almost feminine in its beauty, they'd see exactly who it was that Frank Sinatra
the tough guy has spent his life trying to protect." Underneath all that brash
behavior, away from the fun-filled nightclub gigs and the center-of-the-action
persona he projected around the globe, life was never easy for Sinatra, or at
the least, never easy for extended periods of time. In Frank's own highly self-
aware words: "Nothing anybody's said or written about me ever bothers
me—except when it does."

Nor, for that matter, was it easy for those close to him, so overwhelming
were his personality and needs. Sinatra battled loneliness, onscreen and off,
but it was more than mere loneliness; his was a loneliness that seemed poised
to topple into heartbreak, exposing a wounded tenderness underneath the
bravado that registered beautifully in close-up. It proved to be both mesmerizing and more than a little unsettling. As daughter Tina wrote in her autobiography: "Raised a Catholic, Dad figured he had it coming when he was
miserable. His perpetual unease was part and parcel of his nature—and, I
maintain, an integral part of his art."

Frank Capra, extraordinary filmmaker and onetime director of Sinatra,
wrote in his autobiography *The Name Above the Title*: "There is heartbreak
in Sinatra's pleasure-go-round: heartbreak that could find release in total
commitment to a spiritual ideal." It's a spiritual dimension to Sinatra on film
that convinced Capra that Sinatra would be the perfect choice to play St.
Paul, the persecutor of early Christians who ultimately became Christ's first
and most powerful missionary. The professional scoffers made hay of the very
idea, and the film never came to pass, but wise old pro that he was, Capra was
on to something. On film—and record—Frank Sinatra projected this dichotomy of pleasure and heartbreak, and a large part of Sinatra's power on
film lay in the fact that he registered as nothing short of the king of ambivalence. (It's yet another reason why one wishes that Sinatra had recorded more
songs by Stephen Sondheim, the poet laureate of ambivalence.) Sinatra's own
complexity resonated with audiences around the world because, unable to

articulate their own feelings of ambivalence, they felt better for seeing them expressed onscreen.

If Sinatra the vocalist provided the soundtrack to the momentous events of the twentieth century—his version of "Fly Me to the Moon" was played during the Apollo space flight—his visual persona was of no less importance. Sinatra the actor flashed across Hollywood screens for a full four decades, a run matched by very few stars, and by no others who maintained a similarly high profile, indeed a legendary career, in another medium. (Bing Crosby had a longer run as a top box office attraction, but his string of starring vehicles was neither as long-lasting nor as varied as Sinatra's.) It was Sinatra the actor, forty feet high on the motion picture screen, who fleshed out a literal picture of the star to audiences around the world, making him a living, breathing icon with an actual physical presence. If the communal nature of attending a movie theater as part of a mass audience informs the public's response to stars, helping to determine the very few who evolve into genuine icons, then Sinatra became an icon precisely because in his onscreen evolution from boy next door to seen-it-all detective, audiences recognized their own journey from youth to maturity and, finally, old age. In Sinatra's seemingly endless quest for self-expression and meaning, his journey on film started out full of youth and unfettered belief, and ended up as the personification of "what's it all about?" and "is that all there is?" It was a journey that resonated with audiences precisely because in their need to share a common memory, they saw themselves in Sinatra. As critic John Lahr wrote in his 1997 book *Sinatra: The Artist and the Man,* "In time, of course, Sinatra seized more than power; he infiltrated the Western world's dream life."

Sinatra was, and always had been, a volcano of coiled energy ready to explode at any moment, and it is therefore no accident that his greatest performances on film, as Maggio in *From Here to Eternity,* Frankie Machine in *The Man with the Golden Arm,* and Marco in *The Manchurian Candidate,* all featured men not completely in control of themselves, men whose extreme passions were greater than their ability to control those very same passions. In effect, those men, like Sinatra himself, all waged a valiant, yet ultimately doomed battle against disillusionment. In the eloquent words of Donald Clarke: "The greatest loneliness is in disillusion, which is one reason why we need art. Sinatra has been fighting against disillusionment all his life." So, too, did his most indelible screen characters.

With a near overabundance of acting, as well as singing, talent, Sinatra never stopped exploring what it meant to be an American male in the twentieth century, and for all of the second-rate vehicles onscreen, he appeared in no fewer than a dozen films that stretched the boundaries of manhood as the new millennium approached. While Pete Hamill has written that "A Sinatra film never reached down into the darkness the way the songs did. He never cheated on the songs," that assessment is actually only partially true; as a rule he dug down further on record, but in a list of first-rate films which included everything from *Suddenly* and *From Here to Eternity* to *The Manchurian Candidate,* Sinatra indeed dug down into the darkness of his characters and etched brilliantly realized men of ungovernable passions.

If America towered over the world like a colossus in the aftermath of World War II, Frank Sinatra himself bestrode Hollywood, amassing the kind of power through his all-media career, heretofore unknown amongst Hollywood actors. Driven to create his own world, one that he could control, Sinatra actually succeeded in doing so, so strong was his talent. Like all true movie stars, Sinatra overlaid his own enormous personality onto the roles he assumed, in the process reflecting American mores in all their glory and dishonor. In his very complexity, the power laced with extreme vulnerability, a palpable goodness tangled up with wrongheaded actions, and a myopic self-interest mixed with extraordinary generosity, the onscreen Sinatra functioned as nothing less than an emblem of his own country, a vision of America that reached every corner of the globe throughout the twentieth century.

Hoboken

"We Hate to Leave," sung by Frank Sinatra
and Gene Kelly in *Anchors Aweigh*

In Hoboken, when I was a kid, I lived in a plenty tough neighborhood. When some-body called me a "dirty little Guinea," there was only one thing to do—break his head. When I got older I realized you shouldn't do it that way. I realized you've got to do it through education. —FRANK SINATRA

If England's future wars were at one time won on the playing field of Harrow, then Hoboken's future wars were won on the vacant lots, alleys and hostile neighborhoods in which he grew up. In addition to being a skinny kid with soulful looking eyes, he had the further disadvantage of an adoring mother who insisted on dressing him in "sissy" clothes. This was tantamount to carrying a red cape in front of wild bulls!
—SOUVENIR PROGRAM, FRANK SINATRA CONCERT TOUR, 1976

Sinatra told the truth no matter what. He is probably the last famous person who didn't give a damn what you thought. He would tell you what he was thinking. And nobody ever told Frank Sinatra what to say, except maybe his mother.
—BILL ZEHME, *NEWSWEEK*

BORN ON DECEMBER 12, 1915, in Hoboken, New Jersey, Frank Sinatra made one hell of an entrance into the world: the delivery of the ex-tremely large baby—thirteen pounds seven ounces—stuck in the breech position, necessitated the use of forceps. The resulting punctured ear-drum, and severe scarring to his left cheek, ear, and neck, were the least of the problems; so traumatized by the breech birth was the inept doctor delivering the baby, that he pronounced the boy dead. It was Frank's maternal grandmother, Rose Garaventi, who saved the day, plunging her new grandson under the faucet's cold water. Sinatra entered the world fighting, and he left it the same way, his final words a whispered, "I'm losing." It was always a struggle for Frank Sinatra, even at the height of his success, but damn, what a struggle it was.

Mother Dolly Sinatra's difficulty in delivering Frank ensured that he would be an only child, a state of affairs unusual in early-twentieth-century immigrant cultures and particularly so in Italian-American families. Without siblings, and with both parents working extremely long hours at multiple jobs, young Frank spent a great deal of time by himself. It was in these early years that Sinatra's lifelong sense of otherness took hold. Such a feeling of isolation not only fed his sense of standing apart, but also seemingly helped form his self-identity as an outsider, an outlaw of sorts, like his screen heroes, the cowboys and gangsters he avidly watched. In actuality, it appears that part of Sinatra's enduring fascination with mobsters may have been because these tough guys were both powerful and in many ways the exact opposite of Frank: even as a young boy, he must have realized they did not live with mothers like Dolly, a woman who ruled the roost with a volatility that ranged from curses to smothering affection and back again. Similarly, while the adult Frank Sinatra may have proved a take-no-prisoners artist in the recording studio and on the film set, a ferocious businessman who loved winning at the art of the deal, in his private life, he would, according to first wife Nancy, simply "follow the path of least resistance."

It may have been Frank's grandparents who first broke with tradition by defecting from the old country and coming to America, but it was Sinatra himself, the first generation born in America, who always seemed to feel like the interloper, to most strongly feel the sting of the then-prevalent anti-Italian insults. Frank's World War II generation expected more, initially believing in the melting pot myth of a classless "we're all Americans together" society more fully than did their parents and grandparents. When confronted with the reality of discrimination, their ensuing disappointment cut all the more deeply, and in Frank's case, was never to be forgotten.

What made Sinatra's journey different from that of his parents and grandparents was the fact that he was born in New Jersey, not Italy. This made him a new type of Italian—an Italian-American, whose connection with the old country was entirely secondhand, learned only through stories and anecdotes of the old life. Whether the northern Italy of mother Dolly's Garaventi family, or the Sicily of father Martin's family, Italy always remained at a remove for Frank. His entire worldview was American: his attitude, stance, talk, and talent all spoke American, but an Americanese filtered through an outsider's sensibility, that of a non-WASP in a world controlled by WASP society. Yet even with an outsider's sensibility, Frank Sinatra would never allow himself to feel limited. Frank's grandparents may have remained old country in outlook for their entire lives, and even parents Marty and Dolly's world was shaped and limited by Hoboken and surrounding environs. But Frank's worldview? Even if unarticulated while Sinatra was still a youth, it was already crystal clear: Today, Hoboken. Tomorrow, Manhattan. After that? Why not Hollywood and the whole damn world.

In effect, in the five generations of the Sinatra family in America, the cycle of the immigrant's journey was rendered utterly complete: Frank's grandparents emigrated from Italy to the United States, but as Frank himself pointed out, for all intents and purposes never left the old country in outlook or spirit. Frank's parents, Dolly and Marty, lived virtually their entire lives in America, evolving into true Italian-Americans for whom life presented far more opportunities than they could ever have known in Italy, yet remaining Americans whose worldview was shaped and limited by Hoboken. Sinatra himself wanted the world, and he'd make damn sure he got it. Hoboken was jettisoned as soon as practicable. Frank's children never lived in Hoboken, and while they may have heard tales of their father's youth while they were growing up, they never experienced gritty Hoboken firsthand. As happens with nearly all immigrant families, by the time Frank's grandchildren were born, the straight line to the immigrant's life in Hoboken had disappeared— granddaughters A.J. and Amanda and grandson Michael were Californians who just happened to be of partial Italian heritage. The wards and local politics of Dolly Sinatra's Hoboken might as well have existed on the moon, for all their direct connection to her great-grandchildren. It is the ultimate irony of the journey that what the oldest generation mourns as irrevocably lost is precisely what they have spent their lives striving to overcome and forget.

Pete Hamill, who has written perceptively about Sinatra's roots in Hoboken, points out that the lonely, well-dressed, and noticeably skinny Francis Albert Sinatra came in time to represent a blend of both his parents: Dolly (born Natalia), the gregarious, warm, take-no-prisoners mother, whose parents emigrated from Genoa in northern Italy, coupled with quiet, nearly somber father Martin, whose parents, John and Rosa, had come to America from the Sicilian coast town of Agrigento. If Sinatra wallowed in periods of moodiness where no one could reach him, that was an inheritance from his father; indeed, Frank once referred to his father with the words "I loved him, but the man was the loneliest guy I ever knew." Dolly, on the other hand (who came to America at the age of two), proved to be exactly the opposite. She was tough but in the limited time she spent with her son, spoiled him and made him believe, in his daughter Tina's words, that "he could do no wrong."

Frank inherited one key personality trait from his mother that allowed him to achieve worldwide success and renown yet at the same time caused great hurt to both strangers and loved ones: He wanted to help others, tried to do the best he could for those he cared about, but in the end, he would always do what was best for himself—the career came first. Always. Writes Tina, "In that he was his mother's son."

Dolly Sinatra completed eighth grade, a remarkable achievement for any young immigrant girl in the early days of the twentieth century, and one that stood her in marked contrast to her basically illiterate husband. Dolly's education, coupled with a determination to make her mark in America, allowed her to branch out of the stiflingly parochial immediate surroundings of her neighborhood. If son Frank helped to define a new type of Italian-American, one famously proud of his ethnic heritage, in effect, Dolly was actually the first Italian-American (as opposed to Italian) in the family, assimilating into the community to a larger degree than did Marty or especially her own parents. Dolly's parents had, in fact, disapproved of her marriage to Marty, whose Sicilian roots they found inappropriate and beneath their rank. Dolly didn't care, an attitude she passed along to her even more Americanized Italian-American son. Said Frank decades later, "One thing about Dolly. She never looked back very much. She was alive today and looked forward to tomorrow. That was her. The thing about my grandparents was they never really got over leaving the old country."

With the boundless supply of energy she passed along to her son, Dolly charged through life a woman on a mission—a quest to establish a position of prominence in Hoboken. She ran a candy store, worked as a midwife (also performing abortions), and rose through the echelons of the local Democratic party as a ward leader who could be trusted to deliver votes; it was Dolly, with her political connections, who helped Marty land his job as a fireman, a pioneering Italian in a profession then dominated by the Irish. Along with Marty, she ran a neighborhood saloon that had started life as a speakeasy during Prohibition and evolved into a well-known watering hole called Marty O'Brien's. The ever-practical Sinatras utilized this name under which Marty Sinatra boxed in those days of anti-Italian prejudice, as a means of easing the path toward acceptance. It was a name change never forgotten by the proudly Italian Francis Albert.

Given his parents' multiple jobs, young Frank inevitably spent more time with his grandmother and aunts than with his own parents. It was a familial structure whose psychological underpinnings influenced Sinatra's performing career and personal life throughout the decades. Indeed, in critic John Lahr's view, for Sinatra the artist, the "stillness, attention and unequivocal adoration that weren't there in his mother, were there with his rapt listeners." As a result, Frank Sinatra was a lonely little boy, developing a feeling of standing alone, which pervaded his entire life. Said one close friend, "They fly in his plane, eat his food, drink his whiskey, get fantastic gifts, are entertained internationally; and with all the friends, he has always been a complete loner." So bone-deep was this sense of standing alone that when daughter Nancy made him an extremely proud grandfather with the birth of her first daughter (Angela Jennifer Lambert) on May 22, 1974, he quickly told Nancy that he hoped she'd have another child. As an only child whose parents were always busy working, he elaborated that his own boyhood had been "very lonely for [me]. Very lonely." At that moment of genuine joy for his daughter, the old feelings of otherness bubbled to the surface, and therein lies a key to his voracious appetite for work; it's why he recorded dozens and dozens of albums, acted in an astonishing sixty-one films, kept up a grueling schedule of concert dates, raised millions for charity, partied relentlessly, stayed up until all hours, and slept a mere four hours per night. Sinatra didn't just want to be in the center of the action—he needed not to be alone.

Such loneliness informed his singing; as Pete Hamill has aptly pointed out in his book *Why Sinatra Matters,* Sinatra's songs are all about his loneliness after losing the girl or his unfettered joy at landing the girl and thereby banishing loneliness. This feeling of "aloneness"—or as the title of one of his masterly concept LPs put it, *Where Are You?*—never left Sinatra. He attained a level of success only dreamed of by others, residing at the very epicenter of show business while idolized by millions, yet ofttimes careened wildly through a life without moorings, awash in too much booze and too many cigarettes. Avidly watched on movie screens worldwide, cheered and honored by adoring strangers, he could, even amongst loved ones, disappear into an impenetrable sphere of loneliness.

He was, and always would be, a solitary man, which is why it made perfect sense that Frank Sinatra celebrated his Oscar win by walking the streets alone. Sinatra had to connect with people through his art, but ultimately, he seemed to feel, no one else could understand his path or the toll it took upon his psyche. In his own famous words, "Being an eighteen-karat manic-depressive and having lived a life of violent emotional contradictions, I have an overactive capacity for sadness as well as elation."

If consistent emotional nourishment wasn't present for young Frank at home, then he would—and did—eventually find it with audiences throughout the world. So personal was Sinatra's style of performing that it evolved into an expression of more than just his own emotions; it was as if he were feeding off the collective emotions of his audience. At times the interplay between star and audience became dizzying in its complexity, a less desperate version of Judy Garland's connection with her live audience. Was Sinatra providing consolation to the audience through his triumphant but hard-luck life, or was the audience consoling him, assuring him that he would never be alone?

This unending need was why Sinatra couldn't last more than a few years in his early-1970s retirement, and why he continued to perform into the 1990s, even when his voice had lost much of its power and range. Most important, it was why his most memorable film portrayals involved characters who were outsiders, their defining trait a nearly palpable sense of loneliness. Think Maggio in *From Here to Eternity,* the addict Frankie Machine in *The Man with the Golden Arm,* Marco in *The Manchurian Candidate,* and all the detective loners he portrayed at the end of his film career. Frank Sinatra felt those characters in his bones, and movie audiences responded to the authenticity of his portrayals. The movie roles may have been different from Sinatra in the particulars, but they were alike in the most basic ways. Like Frank himself, they were all men of the night. Indeed, Sinatra the movie star functioned as the virtual personification of the night; one never pictures him strolling in the sunshine. In the mind's eye, he is always a solitary figure tracking the rain-slicked city streets or drinking away his despair on the corner stool at a dive of a bar. In the history of Hollywood, there may never have been a darker male icon than Frank Sinatra.

The little boy who loved watching tough guys like James Cagney and Edward G. Robinson in the movies, who acted like a punk on the streets of Hoboken, merged this sense of otherness with a growing idolization of crooner and actor Bing Crosby, to eventually create a unique singing and acting talent: the tough yet extremely vulnerable loner. His was a new kind of urban male, one who could sing a beautiful ballad in one film and then, in a movie such as *From Here to Eternity,* rip into a domineering bigot of a commanding office with a doomed gallantry that was both physical and emotional. The tough-yet-vulnerable loner came to define both Sinatra's screen legacy and his larger-than-life public persona throughout the decades. Audiences continually wondered, "How can a man so gifted and generous also be so difficult and dangerous?" Or, as one wag would have it, "He's St. Francis of Assisi with a shoulder holster." Sinatra had the talent to make this startling new combination work in a way never equaled since, finding just the right blend of tough and tender. Or, as he himself said, "If what you do is honest and you make it, you're a hero. If what you do is crooked and you make it, you're a bum. Me—I grabbed a song." To say the least.

While Frank charted his own rather idiosyncratic path through childhood and adolescence, he may have lacked for parental attention but suffered no lack in material terms: "I never wanted for anything but we did not have an abundance of anything." Much has been made of the fact that young Frank, although not rich, had more money than other boys in the neighborhood, ambling through the streets of Hoboken turned out in dapper clothes and acquiring the nickname Slacksey O'Brien. (Note that the nickname was not the alliterative Slacksey Sinatra but rather represented another co-opting of Martin's Irish boxing nom de plume.) Somehow, in tales of this well-dressed boyhood, the implication is made that young Frank bought his friends. That wasn't the case, but the family did acquire enough money so that in 1930 when they moved to a three-bedroom apartment, Frank had his own bedroom for the first time. The following year, the Sinatras bought a three-story home, complete with that symbol of upward mobility: a finished basement. (Dolly Sinatra, a house-proud Italian woman, kept an immaculate home, and when Ava Gardner first visited Frank's parents, she was immediately struck by two aspects of the house: the spic-and-span cleanliness as well as the placement of crucifixes in nearly every room.)

It wasn't until 1953 that Marty and Dolly moved to nearby Fort Lee, New Jersey, into a new home Frank had purchased for them. Theirs was the American dream made good, but it was the Hoboken version of the American dream: barely comprehensible to the elder Sinatras and Garaventes, it was embraced by Dolly and Martin, but certainly could never be enough for Frank.

Sinatra may have found his time singing with the Harry James band to be "the first time in [his] life [he] was with people who thought the sky was the limit," but life with the band simply provided affirmation of his own burning desires. Even as an adolescent, Frank possessed ambition in his bones. It was an ambition formed at least in part by the then-dawning age of radio. Italian immigrants, especially those of his grandparents' generation, may have been suspicious of the outside world, allowing only friends and the occasional neighbor to draw near, but for the younger generation, like Frank's, radios allowed the outside world to come right into their very living rooms. Such accessibility shaped the dreams of Sinatra and his entire generation because dreams of a world outside Hoboken, exemplified by nearby yet oh-so-distant Manhattan, now seemed possible. As Frank told writer Pete Hamill, "The radio was like a religion. They were even shaped like cathedrals."

Just as important to Sinatra's development as an artist was the nature of the radio itself, an intimate medium that encouraged a personal communion between the vocalist and the audience listening at home. Sinatra's hyperpersonal style of singing was made for the radio; just like his contemporary Doris Day, Sinatra possessed the ability to make each listener think he was singing directly to them. Both Sinatra and Day had roots in live radio broadcasts, and throughout their rise to worldwide fame on recordings and in movies, they both maintained the illusion of a personal connection to audience members that they had forged in their apprenticeship on radio.

As he progressed through adolescence, Sinatra began to harbor a near-desperate need to escape from Hoboken and the atmosphere at home that proved simultaneously loving and distant. It was tough for a sensitive adolescent like Frank; when expectations were not met, verbal altercations ensued. Frank and his mother were each other's biggest fans, but they scrapped until the day Dolly died, neither strong-willed character giving an inch. Frank's relationship with his mother was certainly the longest and most formative emotional relationship of his life, and it's no surprise that Dolly was perhaps the one person who could ever frighten Frank. Even as a fully grown man, the king of all he surveyed in the entertainment world, Frank spoke of his mother in terms recognizably adolescent in nature: "She was a pisser . . . but she scared the shit outta me. Never knew what she'd hate that I'd do."

Father Marty, quieter than Dolly, nonetheless commanded Frank's respect, and it hurt the fledgling singer enormously that Marty characterized his choice of career as one that would make him "a bum." Indeed, when Sinatra was just starting out as a singer, Marty began to sarcastically hail him as Mr. Big Shot, at one point booting the young Frank out of the house. While Dolly was always much more forthright in her praise of Frank and his achievements, Marty found it hard to offer his praise, perhaps because, as his granddaughter Tina wrote, "he was so unsure of the larger world and of his son's place in it." In this circumscribed worldview, Marty was clearly a product of his times and his virtually nonexistent education, which could only have served to heighten Frank's determination to escape the constricting world of his hometown.

Growing up in Hoboken, Frank saw the petty hoodlums on the street exulting in their power; he may have been fascinated by these "bad boys" and their refusal to play by anyone else's rules, but although he would maintain a lifelong fascination with such under-the-radar characters, he also felt certain that a different sort of glory awaited him across the Hudson in Manhattan. Contrary to Marty's wishes, there would be no career in engineering, and Sinatra's iron-willed determination to achieve show business success resulted from a burning desire to prove he was anything but a bum. Even as a youngster, Frank Sinatra liked the sound of the applause when he would sing a song in his parents' saloon. Never mind that Dolly led the applause; singing in a noisy bar still made the lonely Frank Sinatra the center of the crowd's scrutiny and, finally, the center of his parents' attention. Standing alone in the spotlight allowed Frank Sinatra to appease the contradiction at the very core of his personality: he was alone on the stage, in a world of his own creation, yet remained inextricably linked with everyone in the crowd.

Who, the young Sinatra seemed to reason, had time or use for school? Certainly not he. Attending A. J. Demarest High School only forty-seven days, he couldn't wait to leave that prison of "useless" knowledge and regulations, and dropped out. Although Sinatra would grow to be a voracious reader throughout his entire adult life, at ease discussing the relative merits of Hemingway and Fitzgerald, any consideration of literature lay well in the future. For now, Frank's impatience manifested itself in a string of spectacularly unsuccessful jobs. He worked catching rivets at Teijent and Lang shipyard but quit in short order. Unloading boxes at Lyons and Varnahan book publishers, he barely lasted through a paycheck or two, a scenario also repeated during his short stint at United Trust Lines. It didn't matter what the job entailed; it never could have stuck, because music was what he loved, not some damn job at the shipyard.

Frank wanted to sing, and it's all he wanted to do. With a determination that characterized his entire professional life, he proceeded to start doing just that. A lack of support from his parents? Too damn bad. He'd show them. That, of course, was harder to do while finances dictated he still live at home, a state of affairs that in turn only increased his frustration and desire to get out.

The dreams fueled by radio and by movie screens weighed upon the young Frank, simultaneously making Hoboken seem ever more oppressive yet also holding out the promise of a freer, more exciting, and powerful life as exemplified by nearby New York City. Unlike young men stuck on the plains with amorphous visions of glory in their heads, Manhattan's all-too-tangible form was readily available, a stone's throw across the Hudson River. Long after Sinatra became a star of the first order, he reflected, "There really was nothing to lose. . . . Yes, you might fall on your ass. But so what? You could always work on the dock. What was important was to *try*."

Sinatra had to try because he honestly could not help himself. He had fallen under the spell of singing. He eventually developed an unparalleled ability to communicate that love to audiences throughout the world, and his wish to do so never deserted him. To the end of his performing career, Sinatra would oftentimes end his concert with a simple and heartfelt, "Thank you for letting me sing for you."

Having first performed in his parents' saloon, Frank began to take on singing jobs in various Hoboken bars and clubs and with the help of his parents, bought a portable public address system, as well as his own arrangements. A smart businessman even as a seventeen-year-old, Sinatra very logically reasoned that "if the local orchestras wanted to use my arrangements, and they always did, they had to take the singer, Sinatra, too."

At that early stage of his career, the influence of Bing Crosby upon Sinatra was enormous; it's not just that Sinatra admired the way Crosby sang. It's that Crosby's success made Frank believe that he, too, could succeed as both vocalist and movie star. After all, Crosby, for all his pleasant looks, was not a classically handsome man; if Frank had a scarred neck and worries about a receding hairline, well, Crosby had jutting ears and sported a hairpiece. Over the years, their differences and similarities evolved into a low-key, pleasantly competitive, and unspoken version of "anything you can do, I can do better."

The crucial difference in their approach, of course, came in how they sang. Crosby was so self-contained that it was as if he were singing to himself. Watch him singing "True Love" to Grace Kelly in *High Society*—he's barely acknowledging her presence as he sings to the horizon. It's a performance in marked contrast to Sinatra's erotic murmur of "You're Sensational," sung directly to Kelly in the same film. Sinatra wanted and needed to make a direct personal connection with the audience. The loneliness pouring out of Frank informed his art all along the way, both in the recording studio and on film.

At his best, Sinatra was in a performing delirium, the audience taking pleasure from the longing and aching, the pain he expressed through his art. Audience members intuitively understood that Sinatra "got it"—he knew what it was like to stand alone, to feel the bone-deep loneliness that is inevitably a part of the human condition. When experiencing a 3 A.M. of the soul, the time when an average Joe feels that no one else understands, well, that same average Joe knew that Frank did. We're born alone and we die alone, so set 'em up, Joe. Bing could be comforting, both on disc and on-screen, but there was no mistaking the subtext—he didn't want to know about anyone else's wee small hours of the morning.

Using Crosby as a springboard, Sinatra continued to evolve his singular vocal style throughout his teenage years. "What I finally hit on was more of the *bel canto* Italian school of singing. . . . I'm much more of a singer than a crooner." He developed a singing voice markedly different from his speaking voice—when the singing began, the Hoboken accent disappeared. In his own words, "So I started becoming, in some strange ways, bilingual. I talked one kind of English with my friends. Alone in my room, I'd keep practicing the other kind of English."

The dichotomy is one of many Sinatra shares with his female counterpart in all-media stardom, Barbra Streisand. Even as a mature woman, when Barbra Streisand speaks, the inflections of her native Brooklyn are still on prominent display. Put her within range of a microphone, however, and when the music begins, the staccato ethnic-inflected speech patterns disappear, and out pour warm, rounded, perfectly enunciated syllables. As proved to be the case with Streisand decades later, Sinatra's distinct speaking and singing voices are in evidence from the very first recordings onward.

By his own admission, Sinatra began to approach singing as a professional when he left home at the age of seventeen. The problem lay in the fact that, unable to scratch out a living as a singer, he briefly had to move back into his parents' home. Having met and fallen in love with Nancy Barbato in the summer of 1934, and in rather dire need of money, he went to work for her father as a plasterer. The end result was no different from before: terrible at his job, Sinatra quit, seemingly just before being fired. However, the relationship with Nancy remained intact, thriving for one basic but all-important reason: Nancy Barbato believed in Frank Sinatra. When he took her to a Bing Crosby concert in Jersey City, famously telling her afterwards, "Someday that's gonna be me up there," she did not scoff. She believed him.

Such belief forged an unbreakable connection between Frank and Nancy. Although famously divorced in 1951 after Sinatra fell in love with Ava Gardner, they remained friends, not just for the sake of their three children, but also because of their genuine affection for each other. Anyone doubting that lifelong bond need only look at the footage of the 1965 CBS News profile *Frank Sinatra: Off the Record*; fourteen years after their divorce became final, Nancy, along with daughters Nancy and Tina, sits ringside, whether in Jilly's Restaurant or at Frank's performances. Nancy Barbato Sinatra knew Frank *when*— before he was a star, an icon, or the king of show business—and if anyone knew the "real" versus the "reel" Frank Sinatra, it was Nancy Barbato. A smart woman, she is the only person who can claim to have known Frank Sinatra intimately for his entire adult life, and her insight into the man shows that

Seventeen-year-old Nancy Barbato and eighteen-year-old Frank Sinatra in Jersey City, summer 1934.

keenly. It was Nancy who fully understood that underneath the tough exterior lay a man who never wanted to disappoint anyone close to him, yet was doomed to do so repeatedly.

Nancy and Frank shared roots as Italian-Americans from Hoboken, but given Sinatra's personality, a lasting union would have proved nearly impossible—Ava Gardner or not. On the one hand, Sinatra personified the prevailing Italian ethos of protecting family at all costs. With all his wives, he maintained the stereotypical Italian immigrant attitude that, as the man of the house, he was the boss. He flew into towering rages with Ava not only because of her free spirit, which simultaneously attracted and infuriated him, but also because she would not subordinate her career to his. Similarly, the marriage to Mia Farrow never recovered from Mia's decision to fulfill her contractual obligation to the producers of *Rosemary's Baby* rather than accede to his demand that she leave that film in order to join him in shooting *The Detective*. On the other hand, if Frank sensed a woman becoming too possessive—such as when first wife Nancy tried to pin him down to a regular and regulated lifestyle—his independent streak and distrust of authority in any form would rear their heads, and he would disappear.

Plugging away on the local circuit, learning his craft as he worked, Sinatra received his first break. He followed a gig at the Union Club in Hoboken by scoring an engagement at the Rustic Cabin and forming a quartet with the Three Flashes. Major Bowes, who ran the 1930s radio version of *American Idol*, approved of the four young men, booked them onto his famous radio show, *Major Bowes and His Original Amateur Hour,* and in the process renamed them the Hoboken Four.

Although no known film footage exists of Sinatra's appearance on the *Amateur Hour,* there is a fascinating "re-creation" of that appearance on the 2005 DVD release *The Original Amateur Hour.* A compendium of *Amateur Hour* winners from the 1930s through the 1970s, the two-disc set, hosted by onetime contestant Pat Boone, features vintage footage of a sixteen-year-old Ann-Margret, a latter-day appearance by Connie Francis, and most notably, an audio track of Sinatra's appearance played over a collection of stills. The stills show a dewy-eyed Sinatra in the full flush of youth, surrounded by his fellow Hoboken "singing and dancing fools"; as the photographs flash by, the audio track features the youthful Sinatra confidently stating, "I'm Frank—I'll speak for the group. We're looking for jobs—how 'bout it?" Even at that early stage, there was no question who was calling the shots in the group.

As the Hoboken Four sing a close-harmony version of "Shine," the camera closes in on photographs of the boys with Major Bowes himself and pans across the contestant forms filled out by the group; on those forms, the group is known as "Frank Sinatra and the 3 Flashes," listing the contact location as Sinatra's home address of 841 Garden Street, Hoboken, New Jersey. The nature of the act? "Singing-Dancing-Comedy." That 1934 appearance found the almost-nineteen-year-old Sinatra and his three costars being paid $12.50 each for a grand group payday of fifty dollars.

It was Frank's performance on the *Major Bowes Amateur Hour* radio show that, in fact, led to his first movie appearance. Audiences eager to provide a highlight reel for Sinatra's Cinderella-like rise to fame, and for the talent that burst out and ensured instant stardom, can supply their own fanfare here— the thundering symphony orchestra, the fresh-faced kid who wowed everyone, the camera gliding in for the startling close-up of the soon-to-be-famous blue eyes. Well, they can supply it any way they want, but it ain't the truth, because forget Hollywood, forget the MGM sixty-piece orchestra, forget the sumptuous, elegant sets—Frank Sinatra made his film debut in a two-bit black-and-white short filmed on a budget of about $1.98. It was the Bronx, not Hollywood. But it was a start.

It was also the occasion for a paycheck of ten dollars per day. Filmed in 1935 and shown in theaters as *Major Bowes Amateur Theater of the Air,* the film actually consisted of six shorts, all of them made by Biograph Productions at its Bronx studios. Produced and directed by John H. Auer, the six no-budget short films were shot in one week—and they look it. Sinatra appeared in two of the six films: In *The Nightclub,* he is said to play a waiter, although it is difficult to tell where he even is. There is no mistaking his participation in *The Big Minstrel Act,* however, which features an unfortunate turn as a blackfaced member of the chorus. Decked out in an outfit of spats, top hat, and bow tie (fourth from the right in the seated chorus), Sinatra does not really register. He couldn't, given the short running time and the embarrassing nature of the material.

His later unease over his blackfaced appearance in the film finds an interesting "knowing" corollary in 1960's *Ocean's Eleven*; in that Rat Pack epic, Sinatra, Dean Martin, and Peter Lawford apply dark camouflage makeup to their faces after robbing five Vegas casinos. As Sammy Davis Jr. drives the garbage truck that will take them to the hidden loot, he takes one laughing look at his fellow thieves dabbing on blackface, and wisecracks, "I knew this color would come in handy someday."

Referring to *The Big Minstrel Act* in later years, Sinatra recognized his youthful mistake: "We didn't realize that we were hurting anybody at the time, until the mid-forties when the NAACP made us all aware. We were insensitive." Sinatra spoke strongly against racial discrimination at a time when very few entertainers did so, which is why it is disconcerting to view his 1956 television interview with Edward R. Murrow, and observe him casually introducing his household help—two grown men from the Philippines and Japan—with the phrase, "They're good boys."

Major Bowes Amateur Theater of the Air actually premiered at Radio City Music Hall in October of 1935, and it made absolutely no impression—an inauspicious start to what evolved into a storied Hollywood career. It was to be six years before Sinatra appeared on film again. In the meantime, however, the Hoboken Four proved to be so popular, Major Bowes invited them to become a part of his *Amateur Hour* tour, a cross-country trek that featured a mind-numbing thirty-five shows per week. Sinatra's pay for the work? Sixty dollars per week—or a little less than two dollars per show. Partially due to the resentment of the three other singers (Pat Principe, James Petrozelli, and Fred Tamburro) toward Sinatra's hold on young girls in the live audiences, and mostly because he was far too ambitious to settle for being one member of a quartet, Sinatra quit the tour.

Returning to life in New Jersey and the ever-beckoning Oz of Manhattan, Sinatra commenced singing, for free, on both WAAT Jersey City and the popular WNEW in Manhattan. He was going backwards financially, but forward rapidly—in terms of knowledge. Garnering arrangements, studying other singers in nightclubs, and, crucially, acquiring the vocal coach John Quinlan, Sinatra began to gain the professionalism that came to embody his thorough approach to singing. He developed a mastery of the microphone, learning to create the personal mood so crucial to his success as a singer. The microphone's amplification allowed Frank to act out the lyrics of his songs in a subtle way that resonated with the audience. It made possible an intimate manner of performing heretofore impossible; without the aid of microphones, singers like Al Jolson bellowed, both by inclination and temperament, in order to reach the most distant members of the audience. The invention of the microphone was an advancement tailor-made for Sinatra's inherently dramatic approach to song lyrics.

Leaving nothing to chance, Sinatra utilized the family connection of cousin Ray Sinatra, a member of NBC's resident orchestra, in order to gain a featured spot on air. The pay was next to nothing—seventy cents per week at the beginning—but it was a fifteen-minute daily spot on the radio, and it led to his 1938 job as singing emcee at the Rustic Cabin in Englewood Cliffs, New Jersey. Yes, the Rustic Cabin found Frank singing only for tips, working with a blind pianist, and even moving the piano himself, but he was singing five nights a week on WNEW's live broadcast of *Dance Parade with Bill Hein and His Headliners,* and he was acquiring a name, no matter how small. Finances dictated that he still live at home with his parents, but all his scraping led up to *the* break—the storied visit to the Rustic Cabin by trumpeter Harry James.

James, who was just then leaving Benny Goodman's band to form one of his own, was on the hunt for a male vocalist; his wife, singer Louise Tobin, had heard Sinatra on the WNEW *Dance Parade* and encouraged her husband to see Sinatra live at the Rustic Cabin. Suitably impressed by what he heard, James encouraged Sinatra to audition in New York City and, when that audition proved successful, signed him to a two-year contract at seventy-five dollars per week. Frank Sinatra was on his way. He didn't know the destination, but he was going to be a success. Of that he felt certain. Most important of all, he was on his way out of Hoboken. For good.

Boy Singer

"As Long as There's Music,"
sung by Frank Sinatra in *Step Lively*

I walked up [to Benny Goodman] and said "Every time I see you, Ben, you're con-
stantly noodling [the clarinet]. Why do you do that constantly?" He said, "Because if
I'm not great, I'm good." That stuck in my head. —FRANK SINATRA

RANK SINATRA, AN AMERICAN-BORN son of immigrants, a new kind of Italian-American, had, like any true immigrant, now left his native land of Hoboken behind. Twelve years later, he was to leave behind wife Nancy, but in 1939, that marriage was brand-new, as was a contract with Harry James and a residence in Jersey City. Jersey City may have been only 2.7 miles away from Hoboken, but as far as Frank was concerned, it meant a new town and a new start. As Frank Sinatra would find out through the years, however, while the Hoboken environment that had formed his essential character may have been jettisoned, its lingering influences and mind-set could never be fully left behind, no matter how many years he spent in Hollywood.

The never-ending journey away from Hoboken had begun, and Sinatra's career started to gather momentum. He cut his first recordings with the James band, appeared with them at the 1939 New York World's Fair, and acquired the confidence of a steamroller. Even when his original, seminal recording of "All or Nothing at All" sold only eight thousand copies on first release, that confidence remained undiminished. Well, Frank seemed to reason, so what if it took those other dummies a while to catch on—they'd come around. And they'd find him exactly as he was—no alteration of looks, and no modifying of his name; when Harry James suggested changing Frank's name to the wildly inappropriate Frankie Satin, Sinatra knew it was a bad idea, or as he bluntly related: "I said 'no way, baby. The name is Sinatra. Frank fucking Sinatra.'"

The climb to fame well-begun, Sinatra had exactly two thoughts: Faster. Bigger. How to make that happen? Leave James for the premier band of the day, Tommy Dorsey, at a salary of $125 per week. The gentlemanly James (in contrast to Dorsey, who would later battle with Sinatra) threw out Sinatra's two-year contract after only six months. About to join stern taskmaster Dorsey, Sinatra had a momentary bout of doubt as he left the James band in the wintry Buffalo of January 1940: "I stood in the snow with my two bags and the bus was pulling away. . . . I'm in tears as I see the red lights going away. And I figure to myself I ain't never gonna make it and I'll never get home and it'll be terrible. I'm going to die up here in the Buffalo snow."

Frank Sinatra was afraid, and in his declaration of the fear and his determination not to give in to it lay the elements that solidified his connection with his male fans decades later. In the Sinatra worldview, "Fear is the enemy of logic. There is no more debilitating, crushing, self-defeating, sickening thing in the world—to an individual or to a nation." Sinatra acknowledged the fear that all men feel at one point or another but won't admit aloud; even more strikingly, he willed himself past this fear, and his male fans in particular loved him for it.

Momentary lapse into self-doubt aside, Frank the vocalist thrived as a member of Dorsey's band, Tommy himself evolving into Sinatra's single biggest musical influence. Captivated by Dorsey's seamless trombone playing, Frank modeled his own style of singing after Dorsey's playing, building up his own breath control literally by staying underwater as long as possible: "What did I learn from T-Bone Dorsey? Well, just about everything I know about phrasing and breath control. In fact I may be the only singer who ever took vocal lessons from a trombone. Old TD could blow that thing a whole week on one tank of air and I latched on to his secret." Studying how Dorsey's smooth play seemed to eschew any need for taking breaths (the trick was a pinhole in the side of the instrument), Sinatra evolved the creamy vocal style that characterized his earliest and purest singing, leading to an increased star status and the interest of Hollywood. Just as Sinatra's acting style was to evolve from a tentative take on boy-next-door roles into full-fledged dramatic explorations of urban angst in films such as *The Man with the Golden Arm,* his vocal stylings, which influenced his acting enormously, grew from the youthful sound with Harry James to the deeper, more personalized approach developed during his time with Dorsey. Stated Will Friedwald in his definitive study of the Sinatra vocal legacy *Sinatra! The Song Is You*: "If Harry James instilled in Sinatra a greater feeling for jazz, Dorsey imparted to the young singer something more meaningful than his own prodigious technique: The concept of stating a melody so that it could instantly be recognized, yet at the same time personalizing it so that it sounded like a creation completely by or for the performer."

Frank Sinatra was now surrounded by the best musicians in the country, ranging from Bunny Berigan and Sy Oliver to his equal-in-volatility roommate Buddy Rich; the learning curve was steep, for the lifestyle as well as the music. Sinatra may have seen tough-talking wiseguys on the screen, or swaggering down the streets of Hoboken, but in the Dorsey band he was surrounded by the real thing: boozing, skirt-chasing men whose lifestyle registered as the polar opposite of that found in settled family life. It was these men who made Sinatra realize that a totally different way of life was possible. It was a tough life—even the biggest-name bands endured slogs through one-night stands, endless bus rides, cheap hotels, and greasy spoons. But it was also a life that delivered freedom. Big-time.

Sinatra had his first, albeit minor, hit with the Dorsey band on "Polka Dots and Moonbeams," and his first major hit with 1941's "I'll Never Smile Again" (backup vocals by the Pied Pipers, to whom Sinatra was known as Sinatch). The sheet music market was dying, records were taking over, and a new era in modern pop music was dawning. When Frank Sinatra recorded "I'll Never Smile Again" with Dorsey, the *Billboard* magazine pop music charts had just been inaugurated, bringing with them an increased nationwide awareness of fan favorites, veteran and newcomer alike; it was the new boy in town, Frank Sinatra, whose smooth phrasing, style, and sound fit the times. Analyzing Sinatra's vocal take on "I'll Never Smile Again," William Ruhlmann writes, "The slow tempo, the prominent vocals that turn up right at the beginning of the song, the restrained band parts, and most of all

Brilliant, volatile musical trio in the days with Tommy Dorsey's big band: Frank, roommate Buddy Rich, Dorsey

Sinatra's feel for the lyric, all mark 'I'll Never Smile Again' as a precursor to the vocalists' era that would follow the big bands. . . . From now on, people would come to see Sinatra as much as to see the band." Which was a state of affairs that suited Frank just fine.

As the band's nascent attraction for the public, Frank Sinatra was positioned to lead the way, and the new father (daughter Nancy Jr. having been born on June 8, 1940) began to draw big crowds. Yes, men seemed willing, in a rather offhand fashion, to accept him, but it was women who came to form the core of his fan base, women who began to squeal at the undeniable sexual heat his vocals generated. It was presumed, therefore, that it was women who would come to movie theaters to see Sinatra when Dorsey signed on for a starring appearance in 1941's *Las Vegas Nights*. After a six-year wait, Sinatra at long last went before the cameras again, this time in Hollywood, not the Bronx.

Okay, it was another unbilled performance, one for which he was paid exactly fifteen dollars per day, but it was still Hollywood, and it was Paramount, an A-list setting if ever there was one. The only problem was the film itself, a C-list event no matter how you look at it. Directed by Ralph Murphy, the film presents a Las Vegas that never could have existed—even in 1941, let alone in the new millennium. Says leading man Bill Stevens (Phil Regan), "We haven't locked a door in Vegas in twenty years." Right.

Then again, why bother to lock the doors when this "last frontier town" is presented as an oasis of immaculate streets, one wherein Bill Stevens leads a posse of his fellow singing cowboys in a rousing chorus of "I Gotta Ride" as they amble down the strip on horseback, belting out this campfire tune at the top of their lungs. Good thing there's no traffic on those Vegas streets, with nary a car in sight; the cowboys simply ride their mounts into the hotel and the horses clomp right up to the bar.

There's a lot of low-budget nonsense about the singing Jennings Sisters trio, a group presented as a discount-store version of the Andrews Sisters, and the evil businessman who attempts to fleece them out of their valuable Vegas property. Before the film drags its way through ninety minutes of forced high jinks from Bert Wheeler and several talking horses, there are exactly two items of note:

1. These old films were miracles of insensitivity to minorities, with *Las Vegas Nights* featuring an African-American waiter who grins delightedly as one of the Jennings Sisters warbles her ode to "the old South," as well as an Asian houseboy, who, of course, can't speak English that anyone understands.
2. The real star of the film is Tommy Dorsey, who leads the band in several numbers and gamely attempts several "dramatic" scenes with dialogue. Even when playing himself, Dorsey never loosens up on camera—a one-dimensional performance mirrored by Buddy Rich's nonstop grinning. As for Sinatra, he is granted approximately sixty seconds of screen time, singing "I'll Never Smile Again." (Sinatra was also filmed singing the Frank Loesser and Louis Alter song "Dolores," but the song was cut from the film.) He looks even younger than his twenty-six years, and his brief appearance therein presents the clearest evidence on film of Dorsey's influence on his vocal style. On both "Song of India" (introduced with a nice, very smooth tracking shot as the camera enters the club before settling onto the band) and "I'll Never Smile Again," Sinatra spins out his phrases into a seamless Dorsey-like flow. However, it's all over so quickly, it's tough to get a real sense of Frank. He sings for thirty

seconds and is accorded one brief close-up, whereupon the camera cuts away from this great song to a less-than-fascinating vignette of cowboy Bill and girlfriend Norma (Constance Moore) discussing the virtues of Nevada's status as the land of no taxes. The song then finishes up with another thirty seconds of Frank in long shot. His singing partners, the Pied Pipers (with soon-to-be best-selling female vocalist Jo Stafford), reappear in several more numbers, and Buddy Rich blasts away with his own solo, but it's over and out for Frank after that one truncated vocal.

Unbilled or not, however, Sinatra did receive his first-ever film review from George Simon in *Metronome* for that single sequence: "He sings prettily in an unphotogenic manner."

George Simon may have had only the first three words of his review stated correctly, but there still wasn't much more of Frank to see when he and Tommy next appeared together in 1942's *Ship Ahoy,* a black-and-white MGM musical starring Eleanor Powell and Red Skelton. Shot during November and December 1941, the film, directed by Edward Buzzell, was in production when the Japanese attacked Pearl Harbor on December 7, a fact that may have "inspired" the screenwriters to include a stereotypical Japanese villain, complete with bad eyesight, amongst the Axis saboteurs who trick entertainer Tallulah Winters (Eleanor Powell) into inadvertently aiding their cause. Still "just" a member of Tommy Dorsey's big band, Sinatra did not receive solo billing, the screen credit listing only "Tommy Dorsey and his Orchestra." Frank Sinatra was still only one of the boys in the band to the Hollywood studios.

It's bandleader Dorsey himself who opens the wacky film, playing the end of his theme song, "I'm Getting Sentimental over You," that mellow ballad quickly followed by drummer Buddy Rich and trumpeter Ziggy Elman soloing on the decidedly nonmellow "Hawaiian War Chant." Good thing Dorsey et al are on hand, because the musical numbers are the one touch of zip that director Edward Buzzell is able to inject into the remarkably flaccid proceedings.

In one of those "zany" musical plots that occurred only during World War II, Eleanor Powell whirls across the screen as Tallulah Winters, a tap dancer who is tricked into carrying a magnetic mine to Puerto Rico on her travels with the Tommy Dorsey band. Accompanied by sidekick Virginia O'Brien, Eleanor must not only withstand the traitorous villains, but even more dan-

Ship Ahoy (1942). *Tommy Dorsey's the star; Frank's shunted off to the left. Not for long.*

gerously, the scenery-chewing antics of both love interest Red Skelton and his sidekick Bert Lahr. No surprise, then, that it is not until thirty minutes into the film that Sinatra makes his first appearance, singing "The Last Call for Love."

In the usual style of the big bands, there is no elaborate introduction of Frank: he simply steps up to the microphone, folds his hands in front of his body, sings "The Last Call for Love," cedes the song to the band soloists, and then finishes the song himself. (Sinatra also recorded "Blue Skies" for the film, but the scene was cut.) This is a very young Sinatra—oddly handsome with his jutting ears—whose underwater training had definitely paid off, because the vocal lines flow so effortlessly that it is, in fact, difficult to discern where he is even taking breaths. Tune over, Frank disappears—or rather, is shoved aside by the production number "I'll Take Tallulah," wherein Eleanor Powell, who was a truly sensational dancer, taps both poolside and on the diving board and cartwheels over the water, all the while accompanied by chorus girls wearing swimsuits with matching high heels. What, one wonders, did Sinatra make of these fantasyland goings-on?

As the plot grinds on with further romantic and spy-filled complications, compensation ensues in the form of the Dorsey Orchestra playing "How

About You," followed by Frank delivering another first-rate vocal on "Poor You." The only problem with the latter song is that Frank's vocal unfortunately segues into Red Skelton's serenading of Eleanor Powell; Skelton, an acquired taste, had his share of fans, but they came to see him clown, not vocalize, and it's a waste of a golden opportunity to hear the young Sinatra at his vocal peak. Then again, at that point in time, no one—except Frank himself—expected the young band singer to become FRANK SINATRA, the icon.

One can understand the hesitation—make that utter indifference—on the part of Hollywood studios at the time to invest much energy into developing the film career of Frank Sinatra. He was perceived as a somewhat talented singer who doubled as the idol of bobby-soxers, and Hollywood wisdom dictated that as soon as the bobby-soxers grew a little older, they would move on to other interests and leave the mildly talented New Jersey singer behind. The entire notion of the multimedia superstar career—a decades-long run of triumphs on records, in person, and on movie screens—was just being invented by Bing Crosby. Sinatra was not yet thought of in such exalted terms. There were only hints of the brilliant depth and characterization he would bring to his singing during the golden 1950s Capitol Records years, and certainly no one yet harbored any expectations of great acting. Instead, Hollywood seemed to reason, let's make what we can out of this flash in the pan. In other words, no one got it. Only Frank figured that if Bing Crosby could be a movie star, then so could he.

So it was that for two minutes in *Ship Ahoy,* the viewer is simply granted a song delivered by a young man possessed of a great voice, a nice, easygoing screen presence, and the impressive ability to overcome having to deliver a ballad while dressed in the "Bal Caribbean" costumes best described as Mongolian cruise wear; audiences who were still awake at that point in the proceedings were treated to the eye-popping sight of both Frank and Tommy Dorsey sporting outfits accessorized with fur collars and what appear to be Christmas tree ornaments.

Sinatra's final contribution to the film is a reprise of "The Last Call for Love"; he does not appear onscreen, and the song is heard only in the background with dialogue and breaking dishes intruding on the vocal. As the film wraps up, Eleanor, who has already sallied forth as a dancing matador, saves the day by tapping out the top-secret spy information; Eleanor taps, and presto-chango—the federal agents find the mine and save the day. Yep, four screenwriters and ninety-five minutes later, that's the solution to a case of international espionage. . . . There is a final vocal to "On Moonlight Bay," but the screen is filled only with a long shot of the Pied Pipers—no close-up on Frank. *Ship Ahoy* did not exactly constitute a major film break for Frank, but it did garner him a notice in *Variety,* which, while turning a thumbs-down on the film itself, noted that Dorsey's tromboning and Buddy Rich's drum work, along with "Frank Sinatra's singing, latter doing 90% of the vocalizing in the film and doing it well, stand out. . . ." It was a start.

Having been wooed by Columbia Records, specifically producer Emanuel Sacks, to record on his own, Sinatra sensed that the time was right to leave Dorsey; the ever-competitive and ambitious Frank wanted to leave quickly and thereby establish his solo credentials before any of his fellow big band vocalists like Perry Como (then with the Ted Weems Band) beat him to the punch. (Analyzing her father, Tina Sinatra wittily—and perceptively—wrote, "Had he been a healthier, less tortured man, he might have been Perry Como.") Having scored a number-one hit with "There Are Such Things," as well as three other top-ten hits amongst the eighty-three songs he had recorded with Dorsey in two years, Sinatra was ready to bolt. There were records to be made—he had already cut his first solo recordings in January of 1942 for Victor's low-budget Bluebird label—and, Frank reasoned, who knew what might lie ahead in Hollywood. Just one problem remained, and it was a large one: his contract with Dorsey.

Unlike James, who freely let Sinatra leave his band to join Dorsey, when Dorsey heard that Frank wanted to leave the band and work on his own, he insisted on enforcing the draconian provisions contained in Frank's contract. Sinatra could leave, all right, but he'd have to pay the 33 percent commission due to Dorsey for any and all solo appearances, plus an additional 10 percent to Dorsey's agent, making for a staggering commission of 43 percent. It was tantamount to slavery, but so desperate had Sinatra been to leave James for Dorsey that he signed the hopelessly one-sided contract, 43 percent commission and all. It was left to Manie Sacks to hire entertainment lawyer Henry Jaffe in order to extricate Sinatra from the agreement. Jaffe informed Dorsey that if he didn't release Frank from the contract, he ran the risk of losing his NBC radio contracts. Dorsey refused, agreeing to release Sinatra only after top agent Jules Stein of MCA consented to pay Dorsey a seventy-five-thousand-dollar buy-out fee. (Some commentators peg the figure at sixty thousand.) With the end in sight, Sinatra sang a few more dates with Dorsey, leaving the band for good on September 3, 1942. Dorsey's last comment to Sinatra? "I hope you fall on your ass."

Jaffe and Stein's negotiations on behalf of Sinatra were later mythologized in the public imagination as the work of Mafia members who demanded that Dorsey release Sinatra—or else. It is indeed a myth—one that members of the public seem to prefer, in all its drama, to the more prosaic reality that tough negotiations by Sinatra's representatives and Dorsey's hunger for a seventy-five-thousand-dollar payoff actually solved the problem. As the whispers turned to murmurs of undue pressure being exerted upon Dorsey by several of Frank's "friends," the legend of Sinatra and the mob took hold, never to disappear.

Why the persistence of the rumors? Well, for starters, Sinatra was photographed on several social occasions throughout the years with well-known organized-crime figures. Given Frank's already famous volatile temper, an association with violent men fit the public's burgeoning idea of his questionable background. Sinatra, both in person and especially onscreen, carried an inherent sense of danger with him. Audiences never knew what he would do next; it was that very unpredictability that made him so effective on film. At the same time, the sense of danger that crime figures exuded seemed to appeal to Sinatra's own notion of power. His continued friendships with such figures may also have been bolstered by the fact that amongst these uneducated men, Sinatra felt no deficiency in his own education. Indeed, with his voracious reading habits, Frank was far better educated than were these acquaintances. When in their company, Sinatra was not looked upon as ignorant, nor was any moral judgment forthcoming about his own explosive temper.

It must be remembered that Sinatra became familiar with those men from his days in nightclubs—so, too, did fellow Italian-American singers Tony Bennett and Dean Martin. He enjoyed being around men of power, however questionable that affinity, but that's a far cry from being in business with them. Rumors of involvement with the mob haunted Sinatra for fifty years. In the end, the release of his FBI file showed that after undergoing the scrutiny of law enforcement officials to a greater degree than any other entertainer in history, he was never formally charged in a single case. (In 1979 and 1980, Sinatra himself requested his file under the Freedom of Information Act.)

Without help from the mob, but with the assistance of some very powerful and high-priced Hollywood bigwigs, Frank Sinatra had now secured his long-sought freedom from Tommy Dorsey. What to do? He decided to try his luck in Hollywood, hoping to land a singing job on NBC radio. When the radio job did not materialize, he ended up making do with a cameo appearance in the downright nutty feature film *Reveille with Beverly*. Sinatra finished filming his cameo in *Reveille with Beverly,* and then lightning struck—or maybe it was more an earthquake, because on December 30, 1942, he opened at the Paramount Theater in New York City to hordes of screaming teenage girls. Originally booked as a special added attraction with the Benny Goodman band, with this one appearance Sinatra achieved true legendary show business status. This was the modern age of instant coast-to-coast communication, and the throng of hysterical girls was, in effect, heard around the country.

Comedian Jack Benny, who introduced Sinatra onstage later, recounted in nicely understated fashion: "And then I said 'Well, anyway, ladies and gentlemen, here he is, Frank Sinatra.' And I thought the god-damned building was going to cave in. I never heard such a commotion, with people running down to the stage screaming and nearly knocking me off the ramp. All this for a fellow I never heard of." Or, in the immortal words of Benny Goodman when he first heard the ear-shattering screams for Sinatra, "What the fuck was that?"

Well, to answer Mr. Goodman's elegantly phrased query, that was the introduction of sex into popular music. Frank Sinatra seduced an audience, both consciously and unconsciously, combining sex and overwhelming feelings of emotion with romance and compassion. In his personal life, Sinatra required the love of one utterly devoted woman, but professionally, he seemed to need the love of the entire world. In the screaming bobby-soxers he nearly found the whole world, because word of the Sinatra hysteria soon spread around the globe. And if it was good enough for girls in New York, well, then, it became good enough for girls everywhere. Sinatramania was born.

Bobby-soxers screamed because Frank injected sex into the music, treating the pop songs with the same importance that his teenage fans attached to them. For teenage girls who felt no one understood the depth of their feelings—well, now someone did, and he happened to be a sexy and macho yet vulnerable young man. The combination proved irresistible. Yes, the crazed response had been helped by press agent George Evans, who had earned his pay and then some by planting girls who would scream on cue. What had started out as a manufactured hysteria, however, quickly evolved into the real thing. In essence, the bobby-soxers who reacted to the emotionally wounded Sinatra simultaneously wanted to mother him and sleep with him. Boyfriends were going off to war, but Frank Sinatra was on the home front, and married or not, he fit the needs of girls on the cusp of womanhood. Sinatra was really expressing in song what his young fans felt themselves but were not yet able to articulate. Young girls swooned to the words of "I'll Never Smile Again," and lying underneath it all was their feeling that they'd make Frankie smile, all right—if they had the chance.

The hyperemotional response was aided by the fact that Frank Sinatra was not just some passing teenage fancy. He had already grown into a serious, mature artist who understood the power of beautifully crafted pop songs. In Sinatra's hands, three-minute songs became individual plays, complete with rising action, conflict, climax, and resolution. In the words of singer Connie Haines, one of the Pied Pipers, "Frank believed in the *words* like an actor. He delivered the message." It's an approach he perfected ten years later on film and with the brilliant concept albums for Capitol Records. In 1942, all the key elements of the fully mature artist were in place.

Just how strongly did the Paramount Theater appearance reverberate across the country? Consider the fact that Sinatra's cameo in *Reveille with Beverly* had garnered little notice in the pre-Paramount days; rereleased after the screamathon at the Paramount, the film turned into a smash hit, eventually grossing $3 million, a good portion of which seemingly came from the Sinatra-obsessed bobby-soxer Rosemary Clooney, who later admitted to seeing the film no fewer than seventeen times.

One can be sure that the success of the rerelease didn't lie in the film's inherent greatness, because even sixty years later, it's slightly difficult to do justice to just how nutty its plot is. Suffice it to say, the film revolves around a tap-dancing disc jockey played by Ann Miller. It's utter nonsense, albeit amusing, but it both presents the very young Frank Sinatra at the height of his bobby-soxer appeal and serves as a very welcome visual record of the big bands at the height of their popularity. Interestingly, Sinatra received only a thousand dollars for his one-song appearance in the seventy-eight-minute film, and the budget for the entire film totaled a mere $350,000 (of which, approximately $9.98 appear to have made their way to the screen). This was definitely the land of B musicals, and Sinatra had accepted the cameo role only after a strike had forced the closing of all the recording studios. The money wasn't great, but it beat nothing at all, so the still East Coast–based Sinatra headed off to Hollywood to film his cameo with Columbia Pictures.

Right off the bat, the viewer knows that the actors are not going to count for very much in the bargain-basement production, simply by virtue of the billing: the big bands, led by the top-billed Bob Crosby, are all given credit before any of the actors are mentioned. It's Duke Ellington, Count Basie, and Bob Crosby who are the real points of interest. The story—and the term is here used loosely—centers on KFEL radio station employee Beverly Ross (Ann Miller), who dreams of a job as a disc jockey. When pompous morning disc jockey Mr. Lewis becomes sick, his unpopular classical music program is replaced by *Reveille with Beverly*—an early-morning show that's "a hot one with plenty of jive." Beverly spins records to wake up the nearby soldiers at army camp, and the program skyrockets in popularity. There is a great deal of nonsense about two soldiers exchanging identities and both liking Beverly, each GI appearing to embody that miraculous Hollywood wartime invention: soldiers who possess unlimited leave time. Approximately every four minutes, the soldiers go to Beverly's home for dinner, an event that is almost worthwhile for the glimpse it affords of the hilariously unrealistic-looking victory garden in her backyard.

The first two-thirds of the film is actually genial goofy fun for the window it provides into how Hollywood ofttimes presented the years of World War II on film. There are plenty of jokes about ration cards and air raid wardens, the women work as riveters in a factory that manufactures planes, and the unified American stance toward total victory is presented as unequivocal. It's only toward the end of the film that the B movie origins make it fairly unwatchable, with the last fifteen minutes almost literally presented as a filmed radio show. The camera is plopped in front of the stage—one angle and one angle only— while the performers woodenly tell their jokes. The material is so labored that the repeated shots of an audience of soldiers convulsed in laughter are hard to fathom. Are they watching the same thing we are?

However, before the musical's bumpy conclusion, there are top-notch performances by the Duke Ellington Orchestra performing "Take the A Train," and a surprisingly effective Freddie Slack Orchestra, with a nifty vocal by Ella Mae Morse on "Cow Cow Boogie." It's an interesting example of how the sound of America in those years—the crisp, swinging, straight-forward sound of the big bands—mirrored the equally straightforward ethos of the times. There was no problem that couldn't be solved with a lit-tle elbow grease and a rolling up of the sleeves. Hands on hips, eyes on the horizon, this was America at war, and the good guys, the Americans, were going to win.

And where did Frank Sinatra fit in? Approximately halfway through the film, a saddened Beverly spins a Frank Sinatra record for consolation, and as the disc spins on the turntable, the screen is filled with the sight of a very young Frank entering through a pair of curtains, decked out in top hat, white tie, and tails. Singing Cole Porter's "Night and Day" in velvet-smooth tones, Frank strolls amid the all-female orchestra, which features no fewer than twelve pianists and violinists. This was Sinatra at his popular best. He may not have looked like a traditional matinee idol, but he was young, handsome in an offbeat way, and in weaving a spell with the luxuriantly romantic Porter lyrics ("Night and day, you are the one—'neath the moon and under the sun"), he was making love to teenagers, to young married women with hus-bands overseas—hell, to all the women in the audience. Sinatra on film made love through song just as Fred Astaire made love to Ginger Rogers through dance. Song over, mission accomplished, Frank strolls right back through the curtains, never to be seen again.

What does remain to be seen, however, is the film's entertainingly wacko finale with Ann Miller tapping up a storm in her skimpy armed-forces uni-form, backed by a chorus of servicemen. Beverly pivots, spins, and whirls around the stage, dancing all around a V FOR VICTORY carved in the floor, which promptly bursts into flames as she taps by. Well, of course—isn't that the way it is for all disc jockeys?

Reviewers generally dismissed the picture as the threadbare filmed radio program it was, mentioning Sinatra's participation but not covering him in any depth. One exception, in a review both hilarious and noteworthy for its remarkably wrongheaded analysis of Frank's vocal style, described him as

> a slight young man given to violent sport jackets. He sings, yes—with an almost studied affectation of zombie mannerisms. His voice is pleasant enough—a kind of moaning baritone with a few trick inflec-tions that involve going off-key at turning points in the melody . . .

each time he so much as turns his dead-pan head or flickers an eye-lid, the adolescent set goes absolutely nuts! . . . When he is finished, they are emotionally spent.

The reviewers didn't seem to care much about Frank, but the youngsters did, and the lines at the box office upon the film's reissue meant one thing: Hollywood now cared as well. It was time for Frank Sinatra's first starring role. So Hollywood did what it usually did—it hedged the bet. Frank Sinatra would play himself. After all, no one yet had any idea whether Frank Sinatra could really act. They were about to find out. Fast.

The Boy Next Door

"The Charm of You,"
sung by Frank Sinatra in *Anchors Aweigh*

And then I showed up onscreen, wearing fourteen pounds of hair.
—FRANK SINATRA, COMMENTING ON *HIGHER AND HIGHER*

When asked if he preferred singing to acting, Sinatra once commented, "I started out as a singer; the acting was in between. But I'd prefer not to classify or pigeon-hole things because there's a lot of acting in my singing, and my singing has helped my acting." —THE SINATRA TREASURES

AFTER THE SUCCESS of Frank's appearance in *Reveille with Beverly*, his agents at General Artists Corporation negotiated a seven-year contract with RKO that guaranteed him twenty-five thousand dollars for the first movie, a cumulative pay raise of 100 percent for each subsequent picture, and an out clause allowing him to make one movie each year at a studio other than RKO. (The terms of the RKO contract caused Sinatra's 1943 cameo, singing "The Song Is You" in the March of Time's film *Music at War,* to be deleted. Sinatra actually filmed the song at Hunter College in New York City, singing to a group of Waves; shortly before the film's release, however, RKO filed suit to stop distribution of the film, claiming that Sinatra's cameo violated his RKO contract. The court granted an injunction stopping the distribution of the film, which necessitated the deletion of Sinatra's song and the retitling of the new, shorter film to the rather strange *Upbeat in Music.* In the end, the short, minus Sinatra, was distributed in December of 1943.)

Sinatra was big business—and big press—by the end of 1943; he had performed his first solo nightclub act at the Riobomba Club in New York City, seen Columbia's rerelease of "All or Nothing at All" turn into a hit this time around, landed eight singles in the top ten, and performed on two radio series (*Your Hit Parade* and *Broadway Bandbox*). Most famously of all, he had been classified 4-F by the army when summoned before the Judson County, New Jersey, draft board for his physical on December 11, 1943. Sinatra's exemption garnered considerable press attention and great controversy, with many claiming he had received preferential treatment. At the time, Sinatra stated, "I feel badly about being turned down. I'd told my friends I preferred to get in and that I preferred the Army or the Marines." Sinatra did indeed have a punctured eardrum as a result of his difficult birth, a physical defect that excused him from service, but the controversy proved strong enough that it arose both in the 1940s, when claims of favoritism made the rounds, and also fifty years later, with the public release of the FBI's 1944 inquiry into the exemption. The 1998 release of those records reveals that the doctors classified Sinatra 4-F because of the perforated eardrum, which Frank stated caused him "running ear" and "head noises." The doctors also took note of his claim that he was "neurotic, afraid to be in crowds and would want to run when surrounded by people. . . . Been very nervous for four or five years." Yes, it does seem strange to read that Frank Sinatra was afraid of crowds—the man spent his life performing for very large audiences, but all those who find his 4-F status highly suspicious also choose to ignore the fact that there were valid physical reasons for his exemption. What's most interesting in the released files is that the army doctors claimed Sinatra was "not acceptable material from a psychiatric viewpoint," choosing to utilize the legitimate ear injury as a means of ensuring that "the diagnosis of severe psychoneurosis was not added to the list." Instead, a notation of emotional instability was made to avoid "undue unpleasantness for both the selectee and the induction service."

All this controversy is documented in the FBI dossier on Sinatra, which clocks in at a hefty one thousand pages; what's of greatest interest regarding the dossier's 1940s information is that at least 25 percent of the reports detail Sinatra's "left wing" political leanings. In the worldview of J. Edgar Hoover and the FBI of the time, left wing equaled Communist—ironic, given that Sinatra was anything but Communistic in his pursuit of the financial rewards his career offered. Whatever the reason, the 4-F status was to rear its head and plague Sinatra at various times throughout the years, with the press bringing up his nonservice whenever relations between the ever-contentious star and the media took a turn for the worse.

With many A-list Hollywood stars like James Stewart, Clark Gable, and Henry Fonda off to war, the time was propitious for a new male star to make a splash. Whatever the reason, Sinatra was not in the service, and after his four "warm-up" cameo appearances, the time was ripe to film his first major role, playing himself in the December 1943 release *Higher and Higher*. Make no mistake about it—Frank Sinatra wanted to be a movie star, and it wasn't just because of Bing Crosby's example. It was also because Sinatra, smart businessman that he always was, knew that Hollywood stardom meant a path to a great deal of money in a short space of time; Hollywood allowed him to receive a lump-sum payment up front, without waiting for dicey record royalties. If Frank's voice disappeared or his vocal popularity waned, then the acting could still continue and pick up the slack. If the time was now right to begin pursuing acting in earnest, then *Higher and Higher* seemed like the right vehicle to officially launch a screen career; how much trouble could he get into playing himself? After all, Bing Crosby had made his feature film debut playing himself in Paramount's 1929 *The Big Broadcast*. Besides, favored musical arranger Axel Stordahl was on hand to handle the musical chores (along with Gene Rose). The time had come.

Filming on *Higher and Higher* began in August 1943, with the film's official release in December of the same year. The opening credits, which scroll upward while superimposed upon a cloud-filled background, seem to promise the third-billed Sinatra (after Michèle Morgan and Jack Haley) as a sort of heavenly presence—well, the filmmakers were nothing if not literal in their adherence to the title. Of further note in the credits is the information that while the original Broadway score for the material featured songs by Rodgers and Hart, the songs for the film were composed by Jimmy McHugh and Harold Adamson. It was, to say the least, a very strange musical choice; talented as Jimmy McHugh was, who in their right mind throws out almost an entire Rodgers and Hart score? Adding insult to injury, the powers-that-be retained only the "Disgustingly Rich" ditty and threw out the beautiful ballad "It Never Entered My Mind." Then again, six years later, MGM was to jettison a good deal of the terrific Leonard Bernstein/Comden and Green score for *On the Town* in favor of lesser tunes composed by Roger Edens. Hollywood, it seemed, had its own peculiar ways.

Produced and directed by Tim Whelan, with a screenplay by Jay Dratler and Ralph Spence, *Higher and Higher* opens with the musical number "It's a Most Important Affair," which notably features a very young, very skinny Mel Tormé shining shoes in the Drake household. Turns out that Mr. Drake (Leon Errol) may have a house full of servants, but the staff hasn't been paid for seven months, and the bank is foreclosing on the house. It is then decided amongst the staff (led by Jack Haley as Mr. Drake's valet, Mike) that Millie (Michèle Morgan), the lowliest and least skilled of all the servants, will be passed off as Drake's daughter in order to marry a rich man and restore Drake's fortune. Good thing that Mrs. Drake conveniently disappeared fifteen years ago with her daughter, a plotline that is never explained or solved. That *Fantasy Island* disappearance, of course, is just about as likely as the fact that in this never-never land, upon hearing the news of the planned deception, the other servants are only too happy for Millie (whom they were berating only seconds earlier for her clumsiness) and begin to sing and dance around the dining room table, all the better to express their joy. Evidently, it hadn't crossed anyone's mind that forcing the lowest-ranking maid to marry someone she doesn't yet know, let alone love, just to save her boss and fellow servants might be expanding her work duties a tad too much. One era's harmless plot contrivance is another's version of prostitution. . . .

Having taken its own sweet time to set up this silliness, the film waits a full twenty-seven minutes before the doorbell rings, Mickey the maid (Marcy McGuire) answers the door, and the caller simply states, "Good morning; my name is Frank Sinatra." At which point, Mickey proceeds to faint into his arms. Well, Hollywood seemed to figure, if the bobby-soxers fainted at Frank's live concerts, why couldn't they pass out on film just as well?

What becomes immediately apparent in Sinatra's first scene is that he possessed a face made for the camera. With its creases and planes, the protruding ears, the high cheekbones, and above all the piercing blue eyes that expressed icy toughness and genuine vulnerability with equal ease, the Sinatra visage fascinated. He was relatively short, at five feet seven and a half inches (although press releases, presumably with the star's approval, listed him at five-ten), and given his then downright thin physique, it was fortunate that the camera did, in fact, add ten pounds. Frank Sinatra was one skinny young man—"lean" would be giving him credit for more weight than he possessed—but somehow on film the entire package worked.

In that first scene, a very soft-spoken Frank is bringing flowers to Millie, the next-door neighbor to whom he has waved but never spoken. With Dooley Wilson (Sam in *Casablanca*) on hand to play the piano, Frank casually sings the love song "I Couldn't Sleep a Wink Last Night" (Academy Award nomination for Best Song). Who gives a damn that he's singing to a woman whom he has never met? A full orchestra magically sweeps up in the background, and Frank Sinatra lays down a melting, sex-filled vocal that rivets not just Michèle Morgan, but the entire audience as well. Fortunately, director Whelan, who elsewhere bogs down in a plethora of medium-range shots, saves his best staging for this beautiful song, filming in a single long take, and thereby heightening the emotion as the camera moves smoothly between Sinatra and Michèle Morgan. Sinatra seems instinctively to have understood the power of the camera, and he makes the close-ups register. The vocal is amazingly understated; there is no belting to the balcony's last row. As he fixes Michèle Morgan with his eyes, crooning a lullaby in a sensuous manner, it's clear the apprenticeships with the big bands (as well as his own solo appearances) have taught him well; it's his first sizable role on film, but he is already capable of delivering the full meaning of the song, utilizing his body as well as his voice. Sinatra inherently knew how to move onscreen— the sudden intake of breath followed by a slow smile—it all exuded sex on the screen as easily as it did onstage, but with a heightened impact, given the power of forty-foot-high close-ups. Like any real movie star, he fills the frame but is never desperate to pull focus. The audience—and the camera— come to him.

In this, his very first starring role, Frank Sinatra already understood that onscreen, less is more. The acting skills are as yet undeveloped, but he already has a star's presence, exerting a fascination over audiences that allows them to overlook the fact that when trying to tell Mike that Millie really does love him, Frank actually appears awkward. It's not that he lacks conviction in the lines, but rather that he appears physically ill at ease. He can't quite figure out how to relax onscreen when not singing, and he clumsily twists his hands to such an extent that the viewer is aware that character and actor alike are uncomfortable. And yet, the physical uneasiness just doesn't matter, because the instinctive understanding of how to sing on film, how best to convey layers of emotion, is already nigh onto perfect.

Playing himself, Frank here establishes the film archetype that was to define his movie image in one form or another through his first nine starring roles, until 1951's *Meet Danny Wilson* (wherein he played a much darker version of himself). Here was a nice young man, soft-spoken, courteous, and shy with women. Seems he possessed a rather nice singing voice as well. . . . Just as important, with this very first featured role, Sinatra plants the origins of his screen persona: never a rich boy or man, Frank is a striver, ofttimes in show business, one who'd like to get rich but never starts off that way. Trading on his urban speech patterns and his well-known Hoboken roots, Frank's persona allowed movie audiences to identify with him. Time after time, Sinatra portrayed a man of humble origins who wanted to better himself, and it's a key reason why Sinatra resonated so strongly with the emerging middle class in the immediate aftermath of World War II. He might register as an urban ethnic male with his nose pressed up against the window, but his characters (and Sinatra himself) would not, in effect, be denied a place at the table. Frank Sinatra was never presented on film as a member of the upper classes, because his audiences wouldn't buy it, and neither would he. It was his singing that made him elegant, the perfect enunciation nearly aristocratic in nature, but never the speech patterns. It was Frank's singing that leveled the playing field. Take one look at him breezing through Newport aristocracy as photographer Mike Connor in *High Society,* and you realize that he is the audience's surrogate; cracking wise at the sheer scale of the riches, Mike Connor likes what he sees but isn't fooled by it for one minute. He's a breath of fresh air, and when he launches into any of his terrific Cole Porter songs, this brash but likeable working stiff makes the whole stodgy joint come alive. It's his voice that allows him to seduce the aristocratic Tracy Lord in the person of Grace Kelly. One chorus of "You're Sensational," and she's a goner.

In the contrast between Sinatra's singing and acting voices, in the contrast between his tough and tender screen personalities lay a key reason why Frank Sinatra became an enormous movie star: he functioned as the onscreen embodiment of the contradictions and complexities that are part and parcel of the human condition, particularly that of American men in the second half of the twentieth century. The knowledge that Sinatra the man could move in a flash between solicitude and deep anger, from charming to boorish, informed audience response to his onscreen persona, just as that same figure onscreen could vacillate between a casual, indeed indifferent, response to the material at hand and the intense, passionate commitment of an artist in full cry.

Higher and Higher may represent Frank Sinatra's first significant film role, but it's as if everyone involved already realizes he's the real deal; his talent and celebrity are well-enough established that the screenplay humorously positions him as a worthy rival to Bing Crosby—

MR. DRAKE: Who was that singing down there? Bing Crosby?
SANDY BROOKS (played by Mary Wickes, in one of her first wisecracking sidekick roles): Bing Bang Sinatra.
MR. DRAKE: Well, he'll never get anywhere.

It's a nice in-joke, which registers precisely because it was clear he would be getting somewhere, and fast.

Later in the film, Frank rides up to the Drake house on his bicycle, a pipe clenched in his mouth à la Bing Crosby (this bit of business was definitely not a stretch—the very young Frank in Hoboken having emulated Bing's yachting cap and pipe). According to Daniel O'Brien's *Frank Sinatra Film Guide,* this visual is all that remains of the screenwriters' original idea to have Sinatra and Crosby ride past each other on bicycles, stick out their tongues in mock disrespect, and then continue on their separate ways. Either Crosby's schedule didn't allow him to participate or he demanded too much money, but as a result, the Sinatra/Crosby feature film debut would have to wait until 1956's *High Society.*

Instead, audiences are treated to a dependably dopey script, but one wherein Sinatra's vocals redeem everything else in the film, whether on the languid "The Music Stopped" or most particularly on the first-rate "A Lovely Way to Spend an Evening." The audience may hear only a fragment of that beautiful song, but it's so damn good that you forget the rest of the claptrap. When Mickey asks Frank, "How would you make a girl fall in love with you?" Frank smoothly tells her, "I'd sit her down on a bench like this, and say—(beginning to sing) "This is a lovely way to spend an evening." When Sinatra sings on film, even in this first genuine solo, the attention to his partner, the tentative smile, the smooth yet powerful voice—it all registers as total seduction.

The ability to project genuine emotion is made even clearer in Sinatra's reprise of "When It's Love You're on Your Own," a song that previously functioned as a near-comic servant-group sing-along led by Dooley Wilson and Mel Tormé. When Sinatra sings it to Michèle Morgan as he advises her about her love for Jack Haley, the reprise may last only thirty seconds, but his singing supplies the real emotion totally lacking in the film's protracted farce of mistaken identities.

Even when not singing, Frank Sinatra possesses a true star's presence: he photographs well (cinematography by 1939 Academy Award nominee Robert De Grasse), sounds great, and, not so incidentally, wears clothes beautifully. Throughout his life, Sinatra was always impeccably attired both onstage and off, with very careful attention paid to the details of his clothes. Onstage Frank Sinatra utilized his custom-tailored tuxedos as a sign of respect for the audiences. He was dressed up because he was the best, and he was telling the audience that he would put forth his best effort. In fact, writing a letter in *Newsweek* to the recently deceased Sinatra, Shirley MacLaine posited that Frank's impeccable appearance was, in essence, a prop: "It was almost as though your power lay in presenting yourself to perfection because your

Frank's first starring role, playing himself, in Higher and Higher *(1943). Singing to Michèle Morgan and Barbara Hale, he's already a star, if not yet an actor.*

inner power tumbled about in turmoil." Whether onscreen or offstage, Frank felt like a star, and wanted to look the part. Even when dressed casually, his clothes were always beautifully tailored and immaculately clean. Frank Sinatra even walked like a star—head up, eyes surveying all in front of him, a major presence even in repose.

Unfortunately, the movie's plot absurdities seem to multiply and become even more labored as the film limps toward the finish line. Millie's wedding is about to begin, the guests are all assembled, but she—like all brides—is, of course, in the attic . . . looking for "something old" to wear. Fortunately the screenwriters are on hand to craft a realistic nuanced solution to that dilemma: True love Mike finds her, and while the guests wait, they dance the minuet. In the attic . . .

Mike ends up trapped in the cellar and stumbles into a secret room that holds an heirloom harpsichord that can restore Mr. Drake's fortune. One-two-three, Frank is now found starring on a radio broadcast from the secret room (which has been turned into a popular tavern) and sings "I Couldn't Sleep a Wink Last Night." He's all set to marry rich debutante Katherine, and Millie, alongside true love Mike, is happy as a clam to be washing dishes in the tavern.

The last image of the film shows Frank singing a reprise of "The Music Stopped" as he stands on upwardly spiraling clouds. It's a startling image, which led no less an observer than James Agee to call it "an effect which can only be described in the terms of an erotic dream." Which may have been precisely the point, because the studio certainly knew that Sinatra was the draw here; he may have been third billed, but his face was by far the largest on the film's window cards and posters, the top of the posters bannered from side to side with THE SINATRA SHOW in large capital letters.

Reviews were mixed on the film, although generally favorable to Sinatra, with the notable exception of one written by Bosley Crowther, chief critic for *The New York Times*. Crowther, who would veer wildly between praise and near contempt for Sinatra throughout the decades, here let loose: Referring to the film as *Lower and Lower,* he bluntly stated, "Frankie is no Gable or Barrymore and the movie registers as a slapdash setting for the incredibly unctuous renderings of the Voice." The prevailing attitude, however, seemed best summed up in John L. Scott's *Los Angeles Times* review: "The crooner certainly doesn't fulfill the cinema's traditional idea of a romantic figure, which may be a break for him eventually. He . . . appears more at ease than we expected and should find a place as a film personality with careful choice of subjects. Crosby did, didn't he?"

Just as *Higher and Higher* began playing on screens across the country, son Franklin Wayne Emmanuel Sinatra was born on January 10, 1944. At the same time, in a signal of his intent to pursue a serious film career, Frank moved wife Nancy and his two children to California. Sinatra had his eyes set on a big-time Hollywood career, so why stay on the East Coast? He wanted to live near the center of the action and, to that end, purchased a home on Toluca Lake in the San Fernando Valley. And it wasn't just any home either—this was the former home of a genuine movie star, Mary Astor of *The Maltese Falcon* fame.

Forever referred to as Frank Sinatra Jr., Franklin Wayne is not technically a junior, having actually been named after both Sinatra's political idol Franklin Delano Roosevelt, and his agent, Emanuel "Manie" Sacks. For her part, Nancy Jr.—who in time came to function as her father's biggest cheerleader, successfully compiling books lavishly chronicling her father's legend—may have overlooked some of his worst movies and behavior in her enthusiasm and role of loving daughter, but in many ways, she came to write in remarkably clearheaded fashion about the unique place her father held in American life. From the vantage point of decades later, she said of her childhood, and of her father's dizzying climb to film stardom at the time: "Already I was being prepared for having to share him with the rest of the world. It was the start of one of the themes of my life: a father who was always going away."

Sinatra was clearly a loving, proud, but ofttimes absent father, with child-rearing basically left in the hands of first wife Nancy. Nancy chose to ignore the rumors of her husband's wandering eye, most notably as concerned actress Marilyn Maxwell, and her up-and-down marriage to Frank continued through the birth of daughter Tina on June 20, 1948. Ultimately the marriage proved unable to survive either Ava Gardner or Frank's meteoric rise. What's most interesting about the family dynamic is not just the closeness of father and children—there were no signs here of the sadly troubled relationship typified by Bing Crosby and the sons by his first marriage. Rather, the significance lies in how remarkably clear-eyed all three children became about their father. It may be a function, in Nancy Jr.'s words, of having to share their father with the world, but these children, like their mother, could see their father without blinders on. If it wasn't Nancy Jr. wishing for a father who would stop the adolescent pranks and act more like a traditional father, it was son Frank, working as his father's conductor and delivering dry-eyed DVD commentaries of cultural touchstone films such as *Ocean's Eleven*. Like Nancy Jr., Frank Jr. loved his father, but throughout the years there was distance enough to cause Junior to refer to his father most often as "Sinatra"—it wasn't Dad, or Pop, or Frank, but Sinatra. As in the icon.

As for daughter Tina, the child most temperamentally similar to her father, she eventually took on the role of producer, filming the well-received 1992 *Sinatra* miniseries for network television. In that capacity, she performed the difficult juggling act of working for and with her father and approving a final script that not only acknowledged the huge talent but also provided a rather straightforward look at the extramarital affairs and the bouts of temper. Indeed, Tina's long-term problems seemed to stem not from her father but rather from his fourth wife, Barbara Marx. As a result, the second half of Tina's autobiography, *My Father's Daughter,* fashions an extraordinarily negative portrayal of the final Mrs. Sinatra, with Tina pulling no punches. Tina Sinatra always spoke her mind—as the title said, her father's daughter.

Such working relationships with his children lay twenty-five years in the future, however. For now, Sinatra was busy establishing Los Angeles as his professional and personal home. It wasn't just Hoboken he was leaving behind; it was New York City and the entire East Coast, and in his determination to conquer Hollywood, he hit the ground running. In the course of this one year, Sinatra appeared on radio with both *Your Hit Parade* and *The Frank Sinatra Show,* charted two singles in the top ten, returned to New York City long enough to cause the infamous "Columbus Day riots" of bobby-soxers at the Paramount Theater, and filmed *Step Lively,* a new film version of the Broadway play *Room Service,* at RKO. Considering the quality of the production, the film was definitely the least of Sinatra's achievements that year.

The first film version of the Broadway play *Room Service,* released in September 1938 and starring the Marx Brothers, had not proved to be successful, so RKO, in an only-in-Hollywood piece of logic, decided to remake the John Murray/Allen Boretz stage farce as a musical with Frank Sinatra. Not to put too fine a point on it, the second time around did not prove to be the charm. *Step Lively* may have provided Sinatra with top billing for the first time, and the Tim Whelan–directed film consisted of A-list people from top to bottom—songs by Jule Styne and Sammy Cahn, orchestrations by Axel Stordahl—but it was all a case of much frantic effort to little avail.

The frenetic story centers around the efforts of producer Gordon Miller (George Murphy) to produce a new musical on Broadway. He's stone-cold broke, lives in a luxury hotel with ever-mounting bills, and because he's penniless, he must rehearse the Broadway musical numbers—where else?—in his penthouse hotel room. The film actually opens in impressive fashion, with a nicely staged musical number involving all the hotel employees, fluidly filmed in a long tracking shot and so smoothly executed that it leads one to believe that a lively musical comedy lies ahead. Wrong. That number is the one and only non-Sinatra-inspired moment of quality in the film, so it is a relief when seven minutes into the film, playwright Glenn Russell arrives onscreen in the person of Frank. Seems he is a serious playwright, who has written a decidedly awful play titled *Godspeed.* Funny thing—turns out playwright Glenn Russell can also sing a little, and good thing, too. His serious play stinks, and it's in his role as a "singing Shakespeare" that he saves the day.

But before this happy show biz ending that Frank's singing ensures, there is an awful lot of labored farce to sit through. George Murphy, as fast-talking Broadway sharpie Gordon Miller, is onscreen more than any other character but succeeds in doing nothing so much as provoking irritation. He never stops talking and never stops moving, yet arrives absolutely nowhere. An inspired farceur he ain't. There is better support from Walter Slezak as sympathetic hotel manager Joe Gribble (referring to the cast, he squawks, "They're not human beings—they're actors"), but whatever meager charms the film possesses all come courtesy of Sinatra himself. The material almost defeats him, but in the end, his talent somehow manages to trump the third-class goings-on.

In a nod to Sinatra's appearance and persona, there are in-jokes aplenty about playwright Russell being skinny, and in fact, no amount of lighting or costuming can hide the fact that he is rail-thin. Yet, somehow Sinatra's oddly appealing demeanor works for him, not against. Sitting at a table in the nightclub, he very softly begins to croon the lightly swinging song "Come Out, Come Out, Wherever You Are," and like any true musical star, he makes each person in the nightclub—and by extension in the movie audience—feel like he is singing directly to them. The song also functions as a production number for Christine Marlowe—smoothly played by Gloria DeHaven—wherein she sings the title lyric in an onstage bubble bath, before leaving the bath with nary a trace of bubbles or water anywhere. DeHaven is actually a pleasant match for Sinatra, and the two stars appear to have established a nice friendship onscreen and off, leaving aside Sinatra's demand that the close-in-height DeHaven stop wearing a large hat that made her appear taller than he.

Disappearing bubbles, production numbers in bathtubs—it's no nuttier than a plotline that features the female pianist becoming so excited over this particular playwright's singing that she starts to levitate out of her seat. Applying the logic of this screenplay by Warren Duff and Peter Milne, one can only imagine what kind of reaction Tennessee Williams would have engendered if he had been able to carry a tune.

Once again, in this, his second starring film, Frank Sinatra is directed by Tim Whelan, photographed by Robert De Grasse, and is playing a naïf. He speaks very softly, albeit with a noticeable New Jersey accent, and manages to maintain a straight face when producer Miller pronounces that "the best way to become a successful dramatic playwright is through musical comedy." He is still shy and uncertain around women, but it's a shyness that evaporates as soon as he begins to sing. When he becomes stuck in a phone booth with tough dame Miss Abbott (Anne Jeffreys), their bodies pressed up against each other in those very tight quarters, Miss Abbott starts to kiss him; as their faces conveniently disappear below camera range, playwright Russell is so overwhelmed with the sexual heat that he has only one option: That's right, he begins to sing "Where Does Love Begin?" The music starts and—lo and behold—this innocent playwright immediately sounds like a man of the world, a lothario who knows the exact score when it comes to women.

After endless, loud, and ultimately exhausting farcical complications, which involve duping the backer into putting up additional money for the show, the film arrives at the moment that seems to have aroused more press interest than any other in the movie: Frank Sinatra's first bona fide onscreen kiss, with love interest Gloria DeHaven. It's the moment that the public had been waiting for, and once again there is only one possible denouement to the moment—a song. Frank begins to sing "Some Other Time," the balcony doors open, and the audience is plopped into the middle of a giant production number. In fact, two production numbers follow, the second of which constitutes the first "you gotta see it to believe it" moment in a Frank Sinatra film musical:

channeling a Middle Eastern potentate by way of Burbank, George Murphy portrays a tap-dancing swami surrounded by chorus boys sporting glittery harem pants and turbans that spray water. It was all a long way from Hoboken.

Sinatra plows gamely ahead during this nonsense, and his acting is slowly improving. Required to fake being drunk, his acting of "acting" inebriated is, well, sorta, kinda okay. Even if he is not yet fully assured onscreen, he is acquiring a sense of rhythm to his line readings, and nicely carries off a funny bit requiring him to test his voice by warbling the opening lines of Bing Crosby's signature song, "Where the Blue of the Night Meets the Gold of the Day." Two films completed, and both poked fun at the rivalry between Crosby and Sinatra—Crosby's first legitimate rival had arrived.

After all the leaden setups, in its closing moments, the film finally gets down to business, as Frank Sinatra, pinspot on his face and surrounded by girls, begins to sing "As Long as There's Music." In other words, someone finally came to their senses and said, "Let Sinatra be Sinatra." The song begins in visually stunning fashion, the pinspot on Frank's face irising out to reveal a Sinatra clad in white tie and tails. Positioned in the lower right-hand portion of the frame, Frank raises his arm and an array of lights emanates from the upper left portion of the frame, enabling Gloria DeHaven to walk down an invisible set of stairs to join him. It's a great start, one reminiscent of deluxe MGM musicals, but from here on out, it's all downhill, just like Gloria descending the stairs in full Ziegfeld girl mode. The song turns into a dance between George Murphy and his partner, all of it shot from a great distance and thereby robbing the moment of any emotional impact. There's no emotional release to be found. Not by a full-body long shot. Only a second-class film would actually end, as this one does, with Sinatra, Murphy, and DeHaven blithely stating, "That's all," directly to the camera. It's the closing line to the Warner Bros. cartoons of the time; in other words, a cartoonish, albeit live-action, musical film here steals from a superior bona fide cartoon.

Canny man that he was, Sinatra clearly knew that this material was not only silly but also a waste of his time, and ever-impatient, he found it impossible to put up with the lengthy waits required by lighting setups. Even by Sinatra's short-tempered standards, however, it was startling to read his comments to United Press reporter Hal Swisher, made while filming his next movie, *Anchors Aweigh*: "I don't want any more movie acting. Pictures stink. Most of the people in them do, too. Hollywood won't believe I'm through, but they'll find out

I mean it." It was all duly reported in *The New York Times,* complete with Sinatra's claim that he would be devoting his time entirely to his radio work.

The vow didn't last long, not only because Frank fervently claimed he had been misquoted, but also because the power of weekly radio shows was starting to diminish. Frank Sinatra needed movies, required them as a performing outlet and as a means of reaching global audiences in his unending drive to express himself. The pattern had here been set for actor Sinatra's run-ins with the press, but in the short term, all was forgotten and forgiven. Before long, movies were to need Sinatra in a big way, and all because of another little concert appearance at the Paramount Theater in New York City beginning on October 11, 1944.

An event now firmly entrenched in American mythology as the forerunner of Beatlemania, Sinatra's appearance at the Paramount was without precedent in mass media American culture, and even today rates amazement on the part of pop culture students. In those far-off days before widespread network television, cell phones, the Internet, and iPhones, Sinatra's engagement set off cultural shock blasts around the world. Returning to the Paramount in October of 1944, Sinatra caused a near riot amongst his bobby-soxer fans, the hysteria so widespread that the concerts became known as the "Columbus Day riots." It was all much larger than a matter of the crowd's nonstop screaming during the concerts. This time around, ten thousand fans gathered outside the Paramount Theater, with estimates of another twenty thousand teenagers running wild in Times Square.

Girls were desperate to see their idol in person, but part of the reason that the scene reverberated across the country was that Sinatramania represented a first unleashing of teenage power, the crystallization of just what could happen when music collided with hormones and tens of thousands of teenagers. The music might have been utterly different from rock and roll, but the exercise of shared power was remarkably the same. It was, in effect, a prequel to Woodstock, but this time minus the earlier press agent–aided hysteria. Sinatra was THE VOICE, and as described in *The New Republic,* the scene was "an electric contagion of excitement . . . a phenomenon of mass hysteria that is seen only two or three times in a century." Such an outpouring occurred again with both Elvis Presley and the Beatles, but Sinatra was the first, the pioneer when it came to inciting (mostly female) teenage hysteria. Police were called out to control the mobs—in short, it all represented a press agent's dream.

The height of Sinatramania in 1944.

This was really a case of the right star at the right time, because Frank Sinatra could not have become the star he was and remained throughout his career if not for the mass media explosion of the twentieth century. Newspapers and radio reports instantly spread the word about the Columbus Day riots, ensuring that Frank Sinatra became a household name, one so familiar to the general American public that he garnered his own list of nicknames (most notably Swoonatra). America in the 1940s still consisted of a largely homogenized culture; the same middle-class audience listened to the same radio programs and went to the same Hollywood movies. There was no fragmentation of the audience as happened in the late twentieth century with the invention of new entertainment outlets. Sinatra became the king of show business because of his staggering all-around talent, his achievements on-screen and on record driving interest in his personal life so that the talent and fame formed a continuous loop.

In Sinatra's heyday, talent and notoriety coexisted. It was, in the words of T. H. Adamonski, "consensual American culture," an era that no longer exists

and can no longer exist. The forces that allowed Ed Sullivan to present different morsels of culture to the same mass television audience have vanished,
shattered by the marketplace of the electronic age. It's why Barbra Streisand
reigns as the last mass media star in the Sinatra tradition; twenty-seven years
younger than Frank, she arrived just under the wire, before the rules changed
forever. In the twenty-first century, however, fame is its own reward, a means
and end unto itself. Today, it is a talent for running afoul of the law that ensures acres of newsprint and a six-figure paycheck for appearing at a party.

With his enormous talent, Frank Sinatra would still be a big star if he were
starting out today. But he'd be a different kind of star. The days of worldwide
icons who could maintain stardom for fifty years are gone forever.

Unlike the most notorious entertainment figures in the twenty-first century,
it really was all about the work for Frank Sinatra, and as American involvement in World War II entered its fourth year, he appeared in two short-film
morale boosters: *The Road to Victory* and *The All-Star Bond Rally.* (The wartime Sinatra can also be briefly seen in the archival footage that makes up
the 1989 documentary *Entertaining the Troops.*) The first of those short films,
the Warner Bros. release, *The Road to Victory,* was directed by LeRoy Prinz and
crammed an all-star cast—including Bing Crosby, Cary Grant, and Dennis
Morgan—into the propaganda film's very short running time of ten minutes.
This film, which promoted the Fifth War Loan, was actually a shortened version of *The Shining Future,* originally produced for Canada's (Sixth) Victory
Loan. That longer version had included Benny Goodman and Sinatra's old
boss Harry James, but their songs were eliminated when the film was shortened
to the one-reel *Road to Victory.* Sinatra's contribution was a snappy version of
the quintessential 1940s tune "(There'll Be A) Hot Time in the Town of
Berlin." Playing himself with no attempt at characterization or plot development freed Sinatra, and he sounds in top form, loose and free on camera.

This quick appearance was followed by another short release, *The All-Star
Bond Rally,* produced by Twentieth Century-Fox for the Office of War Information and the Treasury Department, filmed in 1944 and released in May of
1945. Clocking in at nineteen minutes, *The All-Star Bond Rally* forms a very
interesting time capsule of the Hollywood studios' morale-boosting version
of patriotism. With Bob Hope as emcee—"Buy extra bonds—buy more and
more and more to make victory complete"—the film trots out one 1940s icon
after another. Box office superstar Betty Grable is on hand to sing, tap, and

jitterbug her way through "I'll Be Marching to a Love Song." Radio stars "Fibber McGee" and "Molly" re-create their famously bickering couple, and Bing Crosby settles in for a relaxed visit. It may not be a road picture, but it might as well be, because after Crosby says a few words, Hope, his crooked grin in place, mutters, "They're even giving the extras lines to read now."

As for Sinatra himself, the noteworthy aspect of the short lies in its reunion of Frank and the Harry James big band. In a nicely understated introduction, Hope intones, "Here's Harry James and his boys—and also a fella who used to work with him—Mr. Smooth himself—the old Collapso singer—Frank Sinatra." Striding onstage, Sinatra plants himself front and center, the James band on his left, dozens of additional strings on his right, and launches into a terrific version of his famous hit with the band, "Saturday Night (Is the Loneliest Night in the Week)." In a double-breasted suit and tie, Sinatra looks the part of a star. This is no boy singer center stage for three minutes while his boss conducts the orchestra. This is a star, commanding the spotlight and sure of himself. Arms and legs akimbo, in an early version of the stance to be made famous—or is that infamous—in his rendition of "Ol' Man River" from *Till the Clouds Roll By,* Sinatra is utterly in charge. He sounds in top form, confidently sailing through as the obligatory poke at the Sinatra–Crosby rivalry is presented via a close-up of an earmuff-wearing Crosby yawning elaborately at the end of Frank's song. Bing may close the short with the wartime ditty, "Buy Buy Bonds," but it's Frank's brief appearance that registers more strongly than anything else in the film.

Frank had done his patriotic duty, but now it was time for the main event: his debut at the biggest, plushest studio in Hollywood, Metro-Goldwyn-Mayer. Sinatra's involvement with MGM actually came about after studio chief Louis B. Mayer saw Sinatra perform at a benefit concert and particularly liked the way Frank sang "Ol' Man River." As Sinatra related the story, "I guess the way I sang it made him cry. . . . L.B. turned to an aide and said 'I want that boy.' When he said 'I want that boy,' he got that boy."

The net result was that Frank's new agents at MCA negotiated a $1.3 million contract with MGM (approximately $15 million in 2008 monies), guaranteeing five years at $260,000 per year ($3 million in 2008), with a fivefold pay increase over his RKO paycheck. With a guaranteed payment of $130,000 for the very first film, this contract, structured to run concurrently with his already-existing RKO contract, gave Sinatra the opportunity to make one film per year outside of MGM, and also made provisions for his continued work in radio and recordings, as well as granting him publishing rights to music in certain films. The contract even called for no fewer than twelve weeks' vacation per year.

According to Kitty Kelley in her Sinatra tell-all, *His Way,* the contract also granted Sinatra a less stringent "morals" clause than the rather draconian measures usually found in MGM contracts. Standard morals clauses of the time guaranteed that the actor in question would conduct himself with "due regard to public conventions and morals," agreeing not to act in any fashion that would "degrade him in society or offend the community or ridicule public morals or decency or prejudice the producer." It was all standard language for 1940s Hollywood studios, but particularly important at MGM, where studio head Louis B. Mayer insisted that his stars conform to his fairy-tale whitewashed vision of one big, homogenized, happy family. Loosening the stringently structured morals clause was one smart move by Frank's agents, because over the years, between his womanizing and his scrapes with the press, Sinatra kept the MGM press agents working overtime. Frank Sinatra, neophyte film actor, had landed himself one plush deal.

MGM contract in place, the Frank Sinatra of 1945 continued his all-media assault on the American consciousness by conducting an orchestra for the first time, hosting two separate radio series (*Songs by Sinatra* and *The Frank Sinatra Show*), and placing three singles in the top ten of the charts. All of this, however, paled in comparison to his major film release of the year, *Anchors Aweigh.* In beginning work at MGM, Sinatra was, in effect, leaving the black-and-white Kansas of RKO and entering the Technicolor world of Oz at MGM. It was time to show his stuff. Which is exactly what Frank Sinatra proceeded to do—and then some.

MGM represented the World Series for makers of movie musicals: the talent was bigger, the risks were greater, and the possible payoff was without equal. No other studio came close to the deluxe standard set by MGM's famed musical Freed Unit, which existed as a nearly separate kingdom under the leadership of producer Arthur Freed. In addition to producers Freed and Joe Pasternak, MGM had corralled the industry's best musical talents in screenwriter-lyricists Comden and Green, orchestrator Conrad Salinger, and vocal arrangers Saul Chaplin and Roger Edens. Utilizing a concerted team effort, the Freed Unit turned out fully integrated musical films, wherein dialogue, songs, and dance all blended into one seamless whole. Indeed, the Freed Unit laid the groundwork for the fully integrated Broadway-concept musicals of Jerome Robbins (*West Side Story,* 1957) and Michael Bennett (*A Chorus Line,* 1975).

Surrounded by such top-flight talent, Sinatra knew he could relax and concentrate on his work, confident in the support he would receive. Yes, he couldn't control it all as he could in the recording studio, but in terms of musical film production, this was as good as it ever would be, and Sinatra knew it. What a very different musical film career Frank Sinatra would have had if stuck under contract at a studio not conducive to the making of musical films. Would Paramount have churned out equivalently great Sinatra musicals? Not likely.

On *Anchors Aweigh,* Frank Sinatra worked with a team that was A-list from top to bottom: costar and choreographer Gene Kelly, director George Sidney (later to direct Frank in *Pal Joey*), and songwriters Jule Styne and Sammy Cahn. It's worth noting that although Styne and Cahn came in time to be regarded as Hollywood songwriting royalty, they were relatively unknown as film composers at this point, and producer Joe Pasternak fought Sinatra about his insistence upon using the duo. When Sammy Cahn told Frank that such loyalty was appreciated but he didn't want to jeopardize Frank's chances with the film, Sinatra simply stated, "If you're not there Monday, I'm not there Monday." With the Styne/Cahn compositions orchestrated by Sinatra stalwart Axel Stordahl, a screenplay by Isobel Lennart (who would provide excellent screenplays for *Funny Girl* and *Love Me or Leave Me,* but decidedly less inspired scenarios for Sinatra with *It Happened in Brooklyn* and *The Kissing Bandit*), and art direction by Cedric Gibbons, Frank Sinatra could not have asked for a better team of collaborators.

In this splashy Technicolor musical, Frank's first "sailor suit" movie, Sinatra actually received top billing, followed in order by Kathryn Grayson and Kelly. Most felicitously of all, *Anchors Aweigh* teamed Frank for the first time (of three) with Gene Kelly, a partnership that resulted in a friendship based on a mutual respect for each other's talent. Sinatra maintained a lifelong gratitude toward Kelly for his expert tutelage regarding moviemaking in general and screen dancing in particular. Indeed, Frank often spoke of Kelly as the man who helped him to believe in himself as a film actor, pulling him through early uncertainty about his own abilities. So complete is Sinatra's image of absolute power and confidence that it is still rather startling to read about his own strong self-doubts of that time:

> Because I didn't think I was as talented as some of the people who worked there, I went through periods of depression and I'd get totally embarrassed. It was Gene who saw me through. We became a team only because he had the patience of Job and the fortitude not to punch me in the mouth because I was so impatient. Moviemaking takes a lot of time and I couldn't understand why. He managed to calm me when it was important to calm me because we were doing something that we wanted to do. I couldn't dance exactly like he danced so he danced down to me.

Filmed and released at the height of American patriotism during World War II, *Anchors Aweigh* opens with shots of U.S. Navy bands being led by pianist and conductor José Iturbi as Clarence "Brooklyn" Doolittle (the twenty-eight-year-old Sinatra playing an eighteen-year-old) and Joseph Brady (Kelly) are awarded Silver Star medals. Clarence and Joe proceed to sarcastically inform their shipmates in song "We Hate to Leave" as they head for shore and the pleasures of four days' leave. Once again, Sinatra's character is a naïve rube, a young hick who usually spends his time on leave in libraries, but this time out, he simply begins to follow Joe around an amazingly clean and friendly Hollywood, and the plot wheels are set in motion.

Running into five-year-old Donnie (Dean Stockwell, an actor whose future Mafioso roles lay a long way from this innocent never-never land), Clarence and Joe take the boy home to his guardian, Aunt Susie (Kathryn Grayson). Turns out Susie can sing a little (kind of like Sonja Henie can skate a little in her enjoyably crackpot ice epics) and is appearing as an extra in a film being conducted by José Iturbi. In the meantime, and in a decidedly long stretch, the operatic and very white-bread Susie sings in a nearby Mexican restaurant as Susita, her ensuing "ethnic" warbling registering with all the authenticity of Dame Joan Sutherland starring in the Jennifer Lopez story.

Fortunately, the film is back on terra firma when all involved return to Susie's home and former choirmaster Clarence sings Donnie to sleep. Sinatra sings so tenderly to the little boy, in such a beautiful yet masculine voice, that he makes not only Donnie fall asleep, but Brady as well. Even at this early stage, and even in Sinatra's innocent rube roles, he was extremely paternal in song, authoritatively assuring children and adults alike that he understood and would protect them. In a very nice touch, which grounds the film in a sweet yet non-cloying fashion, Clarence gently closes Donnie's mouth as he falls asleep, only to have the little boy's mouth open right up again. This charming sequence is the first ever demonstration of how effective Sinatra could be on film with children, a facet of his persona seen again years later in *A Hole in the Head*. For all his tough-guy come-on, Sinatra's gentleness with children shone through readily.

This engaging sequence is followed by the absolutely terrific number "I Begged Her," in which dialogue about an evening out with women leads seamlessly into Frank and Gene's song-and-dance turn extolling their time with the ladies. Here the uptempo number begins with a fast tap duet between the two men, one making it abundantly clear that Sinatra's innate sense of musicality translated into dancing skills as well. If Kelly is a terrific dancer who also sings, and Sinatra is a terrific singer who also dances, Frank here registers as a very good dancer indeed. Yes, the sequence is filmed largely in long shot, the better to hide the difference between Kelly's and Sinatra's respective dancing abilities, but Sinatra's dancing here is fluid, natural looking, and sharp enough to lift the film to the heights of the very best screen musicals when he flashes the footwork in tandem with the ever-athletic Kelly. Frank and Gene really do form a superb team, both men possessing abundant charisma and star power, their different screen personas forming a pleasing contrast: Kelly's determined high spirits help Frank become a more fun-filled and winning performer than heretofore glimpsed onscreen, and Sinatra's then-prevalent soft, naïve screen persona helps to tone down Kelly's occasionally overexuberant mien. The number finishes with a bang as the two men bound from bed to bed in their dormitory room, the trampoline effect instilling in viewers the feeling that both men are about to take flight from the sheer giddiness of it all.

Years later, Sinatra recalled: "We rehearsed *Anchors Aweigh* here for six days a week—for eight weeks—before our first foot of film was shot on a soundstage. No way was I a dancer. Boy did we work—we all did." In a measure of just how much hard work went into such musicals, the "I Begged Her" number required a total of seventy-two takes shot over the course of several weeks. Knowing he had much to learn and had been handed a golden

Terrific first pairing with Gene Kelly in Anchors Aweigh *(1945). Said Frank: "It was Gene who saw me through."*

opportunity, the Frank Sinatra of 1944 was still willing to rehearse, albeit grudgingly—it was on this film that he earned the moniker One-Take Charlie. Sinatra may have preferred one take, but he knew Kelly was the boss and he did, in fact, put up with numerous takes. At that point, Sinatra had an infinite capacity for hard work on set, and in the words of Gene Kelly, Frank's dancing progressed "from lousy to adequate" by working harder than anyone else he'd ever encountered.

In fact, *Anchors Aweigh* registers as such lighthearted fun in the early musical sequences that it's unfortunate when the film begins to simply run on too long; since costar Grayson had to be given her due, there is an extended sequence where she sings "Jealousy" at the Mexican resturant while decked out in a dress rather unfortunately decorated with giant sunflowers. It's a demonstration of MGM's odd idea of "culture," as if they figured "give 'em a taste of exotic foreign music, especially if José Iturbi can be thrown into the mix as well." The very pretty Kathryn Grayson really could sing, and she proved herself a capable actress in *Kiss Me, Kate* and *Show Boat,* but there's no real sense of lightness here, and her segments seem wan in comparison with the exuberance winningly displayed by Sinatra and Kelly.

Frank Sinatra here gives evidence of what a fine actor he would eventually develop into, because even with the ever-increasing press reports of Frank's frequenting of nightclubs and his eye for the ladies, audiences then, and now, believed him as a rube who describes his job on the gun crew as "keen" and exclaims "gee whiz" in moments of high emotion. (According to Daniel O'Brien's *The Frank Sinatra Film Guide,* relative newcomer to film Sinatra arrived at the initial production meeting with an entourage of no less than eight men, which means the naïve act was just that—a solid acting job.)

Sinatra's beautiful solo at the restaurant table, the gently Latin-flavored "What Makes the Sun Set," registers in such hopeful, even vulnerable terms that it instantly makes the waitress serving him fall head-over-heels in love. Since this waitress (Pamela Britton) conveniently hails from Brooklyn and speaks with a thick Brooklyn patois ("I'm the kind of girl a guy brings four bottles of beer to"), the audience happily knows exactly where this romance is heading.

Before that happy ending can be reached, however, there is a rather leaden and disruptive sequence depicting Iturbi playing the piano and conducting a recording session, a lump in the middle of the film that prevents it from claiming its rightful place on the short list of all-time movie musical classics. Audiences can be forgiven for asking themselves exactly why Iturbi was playing himself in the middle of this Technicolor romp, because he registers a similar expression of bemusement himself, as if to say, "What the hell—it's a paycheck."

The Iturbi-led bit of force-fed culture is forgotten in light of the next sequence, when Joe visits little Donnie in school. As Joe begins to tell a story to the navy-besotted Donnie and his little friends, the film fades into the justly famous four minute sequence of Gene Kelly dancing with Jerry the Mouse. Okay, it has nothing to do with the rest of the film, but with musical talent like Kelly's at its peak here, logic can fly out the window and even Scrooge himself would manage a grin or ten. Blending live action with animation, the sequence finds Brady in a magical kingdom populated with cartoon animals, where he proceeds to teach King Mouse Jerry how to dance. Tap-dancing with the mouse, leaping, spinning, and hurtling across the screen in his jazz-inflected all-American, all-exuberant style, Kelly is nothing short of dazzling. It's a great sequence of inspired filmmaking and justifiably received a fresh round of acclaim when excerpted in MGM's 1974 *That's Entertainment!* It's a terrific achievement even by the standards of the new millennium, but considering the technical limitations of 1945, it's downright stupendous. This technical wizardry was achieved by filming Kelly in his solo dance and then animating the mouse to match him frame by frame. As film scholar Jeanine Basinger relates in her *Pyramid Illustrated History of the Movies: The Films of Gene Kelly,* the two figures were then optically linked, requiring two months of work and ten thousand painted frames.

After that extraordinary display, the film hits another dead spot when the audience must sit through a full seven minutes of fourteen pianists rehearsing in the Hollywood Bowl, a sequence that has nothing to do with the plot and seems to exist simply as another chance for MGM to provide Middle America with a little class, whether they want it or not.

The audience is better served, and then some, when Frank Sinatra, alone at a piano in the cavernous and completely empty Hollywood Bowl, sings "I Fall in Love Too Easily." It's a beautiful romantic ballad, and with Sinatra at the peak of his vocal beauty here, the song also functions in the fashion of all great musical numbers: it furthers our understanding of the character. Singing the song in a gentle lovelorn voice, Clarence comes to realize that waitress "Brooklyn" is the girl for him. He finally gets up the gumption to kiss her—twice—and then asks her to marry him. In an amusing reversal of the normal roles, sweet Clarence leans in and puts his head on her shoulder, and she puts a protective arm around him.

"I Fall in Love Too Easily" is a seminal moment in the Sinatra filmography because it represents the first full-scale blending of Sinatra the actor and Sinatra the star. It's not just that Frank sounds great and acts the hell out of the song. It's that Sinatra is doing what all true movie stars do: he functions as the direct visual and aural personification of what the moviegoing audience itself is feeling—here the tenuous and often heartbreaking nature of love in wartime—codifying the despair yet providing a relief and release for that very feeling of sadness. Whether it was lonely soldiers overseas or lovelorn women on the home front, that audience didn't despair even though Frank was singing of love and loss. Rather, the audience was actually uplifted because their own inner feelings were now on display, exemplified and articulated by a true artist in a manner beyond their own capabilities.

Great as Sinatra is in *Anchors Aweigh,* it's the third-billed Kelly who emerges as the driving force and unquestioned star of the film, singing, dancing, and choreographing with an assist from Stanley Donen. In his most spectacular number, Gene woos Kathryn Grayson in a full-fledged production number. Flinging himself around a soundstage set designed as a Spanish village, Kelly blends his signature mix of the athletic and sexual, peaking just this side of the overblown. There is no singing, no dialogue, just extraordinary dancing set off by the flowers, sword, and swirl of capes. It's actually a remarkably sexual number: Kelly throws a rose to Grayson, who slowly places it between her breasts, whereupon Kelly pushes his sword into his red cape and slowly draws it out again. It doesn't exactly take Sigmund Freud to figure out what's going on here (and in a family musical, no less), but it's also a sequence that fully demonstrates why MGM made the best musicals and why Frank Sinatra and MGM were mutually fortunate to be aligned during their respective peaks: star, music, direction, camerawork, choreography, and art direction all blend together for one top-notch number. At the climax of this scene, Kelly leaps from building to building with the aid of nothing more than an enormous piece of material, landing on the balcony, where the white-clad Grayson waits demurely. It's all silly—and all pretty damn great.

Frank singing, Gene dancing—of course, it'll end happily. Clarence and Brooklyn are happily united, Joe and Susie kiss, and Susie passes her José Iturbi–conducted screen test with flying colors. Everything nicely wrapped up, the film spins to its happy ending with everyone warbling that well-known tender ballad of enduring love, "Anchors Aweigh."

Swamped with popular and critical acclaim, *Anchors Aweigh* was nominated for an Academy Award as Best Picture of the Year, won the Oscar for Georgie Stoll's Musical Scoring and claimed additional nominations for Best Actor (Kelly), Best Song ("I Fall in Love Too Easily"), and Best Color Photography. Forgotten for now was Hollywood's outrage over Sinatra's statement that "Pictures stink." Hit movies have a way of making movies stink a whole lot less, and the brouhaha blew over. Instead, the general reaction was best summed up in Louella Parsons's bottom-line assessment: "Sock artists, sock tunes and sock dances."

The highly successful July 1945 release of *Anchors Aweigh* was almost immediately followed by the September 11 release of the RKO ten-minute short about prejudice, *The House I Live In.* The very idea behind the film was

Sinatra's own, in tandem with producer/director Mervyn LeRoy (director of the classic gangster film *Little Caesar*). Everyone involved in the production donated their services, all profits from the film were funneled to social service agencies, and even budget-minded RKO studios agreed to a rent-free use of its studio sets and soundstages for the one day of shooting.

The House I Live In opens with a remarkably young-looking (almost thirty-year-old) Frank, here playing himself, recording the lovely ballad "If You Are But a Dream" in a studio. At that point in time, the long, flowing vocal line employed by Sinatra was a near object of beauty—tender yet utterly masculine. Axel Stordahl (who chose the title song by Lewis Allan and Earl Robinson) conducts a flawless take after which Frank grabs a five-minute smoking break in the alley by the stage door. Walking out the door, Frank encounters a group of ten young boys, all chasing another youngster, who escapes by hopping onto a windowsill. Frank's arrival has saved the boy from the group beating which would have ensued because, in the words of one of the bullies, "We don't like his religion and don't want him in our school."

These school yard bullies, needless to say, have no chance against Frank, who quickly states, "You must be Nazis." When the boys protest loudly, Frank tells them, "Religion makes no difference except to Nazis or someone stupid. . . . God didn't create one people better than another. I'd be a first-class fathead if I thought like that." The boys have started to listen to Frank—the scared boy is still on the windowsill, but Frank is piling on the verbal ammunition in an obvious yet convincing fashion: "There are one hundred different ways of talking and going to church, but they're all American."

How to convince the boys? Frank moves in with a wartime analogy as he tells the tale of the Americans bombing the Japanese battleship *Haruna.* "It takes guts, know-how, teamwork. . . . The pilot of that ship was Colin Kelly, an American and a Presbyterian. You know who dropped the bombs? Myron Levin—an American and a Jew. You think they should have called the bombings off because they had different religions?" Admonishing the boys to "think about it—use your good American heads," Frank prepares to walk back into the recording studio but is stopped when the boys ask him what he does. "I sing," he replies, and in answer to their disbelieving protests, he proceeds to do just that. How could the Nazis or any religious prejudice have any chance against Frank's singing? It's no contest at all in this sweet film.

Frank launches into the title song, first asking the musical question, "What is America to me?" and then answering:

The children in the backyard . . .
All races and religions
That's America to me.

Having now spoken and sung his rebuke to prejudice, Frank walks back into the recording studio as the chief bully picks up the books dropped by the tormented boy, and all the boys walk off together as "America the Beautiful" plays in the background.

It is easy to scoff at this simplistic ten-minute sermon (written by Albert Maltz), which solves all religious prejudice in a few lines of dialogue and one intense aria, but that does the material a disservice. It is very difficult to pull off impassioned belief—especially when viewed through the prism of irony so prevalent in 2008. But 1945, at the end of "the Good War," represented the last time America believed in those platitudes fully and freely, and people wholeheartedly accepted such sentiments. This film expressed a heart-on-the-sleeve affirmation of America, one all the more stirring in the wake of the

The House I Live In *(1945). A naïve but heartfelt Oscar-winning short film attacking prejudice.*

then recently discovered unspeakable atrocities of the concentration camps in Europe. *The House I Live In* symbolized a country where concentration camps could never arise—at least that's how Americans liked to think of the United States (somewhat lost in that belief was the wartime existence of the internment camps for Japanese-Americans). Frank Sinatra himself believed in those sentiments.

With the latter-day picture of the Reagan-supporting Republican Frank Sinatra so strong in people's minds, it is easy to forget that he was an outspoken liberal in an era when (unlike in the twenty-first century) stars and politics did not mix publicly. He was determined to use his position and influence to film this short, and he did so. Hard as it is to believe, in the 1950s during the height of the hysteria about Communism, this sweet film speaking out against religious prejudice was mentioned as proof of Sinatra's Communist sympathies. As to Sinatra's take on the ridiculous-seeming but disquieting claim that he was a Communist: "I'm always for the little guy, and if that makes me a Communist, then I'm red through and through."

Frank Sinatra's political idol at this time was überliberal President Franklin Delano Roosevelt; it was no accident that on Sinatra's 1956 *Person to Person* television interview with Edward R. Murrow, one of the first things Sinatra did on camera was to proudly show off the framed signed photograph of FDR hanging in a place of honor. (It was only after showing off FDR's photo that Sinatra displayed his two Oscars.) Sinatra believed in the Allan lyrics to "The House I Live In," and that fervent belief informed his performance of the song.

Just how much Sinatra identified with the lyrics of the song is borne out by the fact that he re-created the film on his *Frank Sinatra Show* (for television) in 1950, intoning on camera, "That's a fine piece of material. I wouldn't mind doing that every week." He then proceeded to record the song again for the 1964 patriotic Reprise release "America, I Hear You Singing," included it in *Sinatra: The Main Event*, his live 1974 television concert and recording, and even released a duet version with Neil Diamond on the 1994 album *Duets II*. So deeply embedded did the song become in the American consciousness that in 1998 it was inducted into the Grammy Hall of Fame.

The short film proved to be so effective that Sinatra was awarded a special Academy Award at the 1946 ceremonies, an award he shared with producers LeRoy and Frank Ross. In a very odd presentation at the March 7, 1946,

Academy Awards, George Murphy introduced Sinatra with, "A lot of people were talking about 'Who owns Sinatra.' " Given that there were already rumors of Sinatra's ties to organized crime, it's an extremely strange question, one Murphy answers himself: "People of this great country—139,000,000—own Sinatra. You have a great moral obligation to them which you've accepted." One can only imagine what Sinatra thought of that bizarre introduction. Regardless, he was thrilled to accept a first Academy Award for this idealized version of America.

More to the point, it was Frank's vision of America that won the Oscar—Italian-American Francis Albert Sinatra's vision, not L. B. Mayer's or Darryl Zanuck's or Harry Cohn's. No name change, no nose job, no phony background to comfort the heartland of America. Marty and Dolly's boy was up on the silver screen, winning awards in all his tough, urban, Italian, Hobokenesque glory. He was living large on the screen for every damn paesano who'd ever been called a dago—and he'd be the only one doing any name-calling now. The name was Frank Fucking Sinatra, and he'd make sure not one damn person forgot it.

A Paesano Onscreen

"La Ci Darem la Mano,"
sung by Frank Sinatra with Kathryn Grayson in
It Happened in Brooklyn

Then I discovered at—what? Five? Six? I discovered that some people thought I was a dago. A wop. A guinea. You know, like I didn't have a fucking name.

—FRANK SINATRA

FRANK SINATRA WAS NOW an Academy Award–winning movie star, and his emergence onscreen provided Italian-American audiences starved for role models with a new kind of screen icon: far from embracing assimilation, he proudly emphasized his very Italian heritage. He changed the very image of Italian-Americans onscreen, and altered the manner in which Italians viewed themselves, a state of affairs that represents artistic power of the highest order. Frank Sinatra as movie star allowed Italian-Americans to see one of their own on the screen—one who, far from being the butt of jokes (as on radio's *Life with Luigi*), was actually in control of the situation. (Proud Italian Sinatra hated *Life with Luigi,* which starred J. Carrol Naish—and his stereotypical accent. Decades later, looking back at the paucity of Italian role models, Sinatra characterized himself as a teenager who listened to that very show, yet he would, in his own words, "hate myself for laughing at the goddamned thing.")

If, as statistics have it, roughly five million Italians emigrated to America from 1880 through the beginning of the First World War, then during the next decades, these five million new citizens were hungry for role models, and in Frank Sinatra they found one—mostly for better, and sometimes definitely for worse. As Italians began to make slow inroads into American society from the 1930s onward, there were very few role models to choose from. Put aside the priests and the criminals, and who the hell was around? Which Italian-Americans even had a media presence, a status to which one could aspire?

Pete Hamill has written about the importance of Fiorello La Guardia and Joe DiMaggio as role models for millions of Italian-Americans in the 1930s and 1940s, but La Guardia had a Jewish mother and was a Protestant to boot. DiMaggio may have been the biggest baseball star in the major leagues during his tenure with the New York Yankees, and in later years had a connection to 1950s-style Hollywood glamour via his marriage to Marilyn Monroe, but genuine hero that he was, DiMaggio was still an intensely private man, one so self-contained that he seemed cut off from his own emotions. He was, even to his most devoted admirers, remote and nearly untouchable. Looking further, Amadeo Giannini founded the Bank of America, but bankers, with their buttoned-down corporate responsibility, have never been natural role models for young men and women.

In reality, the problem ran even deeper, because in those very different "melting pot" times, even potential role models downplayed their identities as Italian-Americans. Salvatore Guaragna composed one remarkable hit song after another—"Lullaby of Broadway," "I Only Have Eyes for You," "42nd Street," but Guaragna's father had found it necessary to change the family name to the determinedly nonethnic Warren. As a result, the Italian-American community's identification with composer Harry Warren was nonexistent. (Ironically, it was this purposefully bland, WASPy-sounding name that seemed to hold Warren back from achieving the name-recognition level he so deserved. Gershwin, Irving Berlin, Hoagy Carmichael—those were names to remember. Even the one top-tier WASP composer among the group, Cole Porter, had a rather memorable name. But Harry Warren? Eminently forgettable.)

Italians, when they were visible in the press at all in the early decades of the twentieth century, were relegated to the role of criminal or exotic, dangerous outsider. Onscreen, the situation was exactly the same, even while playing the hero. Rudolph Valentino may have been the biggest movie star around during the silent screen era, but he was pigeonholed by audiences as a sheik who belonged in the desert. Offscreen, he was labeled a powder puff and subjected to newspaper taunts about his masculinity. By way of contrast, when Frank Sinatra hit the big screen in all his unabashed Italian-American glory, a very different kind of screen hero was born.

If all immigrants, especially in the early and poorly educated decades of the twentieth century, were suspicious of government, trusting only in family and the closest of friends, in Italian-Americans those suspicious tendencies loomed particularly large. In the day and age of Sacco and Vanzetti, Italians were suspect, their very names a seeming code for "dirty foreigners." Italian-Americans usually kept a low profile, hunkering down with family and friends, but not Sinatra. Maggio in *From Here to Eternity* may have been the first character Frank played who had a distinctly Italian surname, but audiences were always aware of Sinatra's ethnic identity. Unlike Edward G. Robinson (born Emanuel Goldenberg) or Danny Kaye (born David Daniel Kaminsky), Sinatra did not play down his ethnic roots by changing his name, nor did he exist in a big-screen vacuum as a vaguely urban young man. He popped off the screen in all his Italian-American glory, and audiences proudly accepted and idolized him as a result.

What made Sinatra not just a successful actor, but also a bona fide movie star, however, was the fact that his support cut across a broad swath of American society, encompassing a variety of ethnic groups. The reason for such success was simple, but basic to his appeal: especially in the post–World War II years, Sinatra's ethnicity, combined with his cocky attitude, made him a uniquely American and new type of screen star.

Frank Sinatra—crooner, movie star, proudly Italian in a time when ethnic pride was virtually nonexistent—was always identified by the audience as "one of us." Even while amassing unprecedented power onscreen and off, Sinatra still seemed to exemplify the common man, an ethnic twentieth-century American male who reached the "top of the heap" through talent, yet never forgot his roots. His speech and mannerisms may have become more refined, but a tension underneath always seemed to exist, an element of the scrappy underdog willing to take on the powerful, willing to strike a blow for individual freedom. This tension ensured constant audience interest, and it informed the best of his onscreen film roles: Maggio in *From Here to Eternity* takes on the military power structure in the person of Sergeant Fatso Judson, while Marco in *The Manchurian Candidate* takes on the Washington political establishment. These men fight for what they believe in. Audiences ignored Sinatra's increasing power and wealth, forgiving him whatever excesses they perceived, not only because of his talent, but most notably because of their identification with him.

With his relatively hardscrabble background, Sinatra became an idol of the post–World War II emerging middle class; trading in crowded city apartments for the promised land of suburbia, the majority of these men and women were negotiating the shores of Middle America for the first time, and they knew that Sinatra had made the same journey of reinvention in which they were now engaged. No wonder Sinatra loved F. Scott Fitzgerald's *The Great Gatsby*. It wasn't just that he and Jay Gatsby shared a fevered self-invention; it's that, like Gatsby, underneath the tough-guy exterior Frank always maintained his sense of wonder, and audiences responded to the tender-and-tough dichotomy. Indeed, Sinatra actually helped to shape the Greatest Generation's notion of upward mobility and sophistication as they headed to Levittown, and it's no accident that Sinatra's boozy, chain-smoking lifestyle was considered the very symbol of sophistication in the postwar years.

It was only in the last twenty years of Sinatra's life, when his place in the conservative Republican firmament seemed utterly comfortable and complete, that the "little guy's" struggle was no longer evident in his persona. Sinatra's rightward turn seemed to be the action of a man unsure of, indeed dismayed by, the world around him. He became a remote deity—admired, still idolized in some quarters, but no longer idealized. In the words of Ralph J. Gleason in *Rolling Stone* magazine: "I don't believe any more that he is one of us. He is one of *them* now, singing from the other side of the street. . . ." Of course, time does that to every rebel.

In reality, Sinatra's increasingly conservative point of view mirrored that of many aging Americans—it's just that somehow people expected different from Frank. He was now protecting his position as a member of the world of privilege; he sported increasingly conservative clothes, his politics were staunchly Republican, and his friends now resided in the highest bastions of the conservative political and social scenes. It was, in the words of Sinatra observer Tommy Thompson, as if Sinatra were trying "to cloak himself in respect and dignity enough that any man, even a President, would answer his invitation."

It seems likely that Sinatra's lack of education influenced his desire for power and his wish to be treated as an equal by those highly educated men who held positions of influence in the highest reaches of government. Well, his reasoning seemed to run, if he interacted on a level playing field with such men, then the lack of education didn't matter, and the key to such a leveling of the playing field was power. Writing about the then nearly sixty-year-old Sinatra in the October 1974 article "Understanding Sinatra," Thompson further wrote that "one key to Frank is that he relishes power. He revels in it more than any public figure I can think of. Perhaps his reasoning is that this entitles him to sit as an equal at the table of other kings—those of industry, medicine, politics, and government."

In so many ways throughout Sinatra's life, it was all about the power. In his art, he perfected the power of captivating a nightclub audience to the point of utter silence, or inducing near breathlessness in a movie audience as he underwent withdrawal in *The Man with the Golden Arm*. In his personal life, the power could manifest itself in the ability to seduce a seemingly unattainable woman—Ava Gardner. Sinatra fed off this power because it seemed to provide the legitimacy he so strongly desired. Whether in the form of love or prestige, the search for some kind of validation fueled his restlessness. Such a yen for power was mirrored in his legendary gift-giving, as he showered family, friends, and sometimes strangers with expensive gifts, never expecting (indeed, never wanting) anything in return. In the words of Ruth Conte—the ex-wife of frequent Sinatra costar Richard Conte, herself an actress turned psychotherapist—this gift-giving was "a kindness that was also an assertion of power."

Over the years, Sinatra came to live in a world he had created himself, created in part to control it. Everyone wants to control their world, but Sinatra was able to do so because of his talent: the talent ensured success, which ensured financial reward, which ensured power. In the realm of the entertainment world, Frank Sinatra was one of the very few actors or singers who had ever amassed money sufficient to be considered "fuck-you money." And that is exactly what Frank Sinatra said, in differing ways, to members of the press, as well as to those in the public, who condemned his lifestyle. There was just one little not-so-secret component to it all: even when tut-tutting over Sinatra's wild ways, many secretly thrilled to the tales, living vicariously through Frank's exercise of a personal power to which many aspired but few grasped.

Such amassing of power and money lay decades in the future of Sinatra's film career, just as did the embrace of the conservative establishment. In the early days of his films, Sinatra was anything but unsure and dismayed by the world around him. He was up on the screen in Technicolor glory, living the American dream, an outsider breaking through. Italians wanted to see one of their own, a fellow paesano who had triumphed over the odds. Indeed, immigrants of all stripes who felt that the odds were stacked against them enjoyed Sinatra's rise. Frank Sinatra represented a defiantly non-WASP screen image, an anomaly in Hollywood's golden age. Of course, Sinatra himself thoroughly appreciated the irony of the Jewish moguls running the studios positioning fair-haired WASPs as the "true" and ideal Americans. Desperate to prove their own essential "American-ness" and their ability to blend in, the moguls presented white-skinned Protestants as media ideals. In the view of the studio chiefs, it couldn't get any better than Andy Hardy. Now, there was a real American family, and one most certainly not Italian.

As a result of that worldview, in his films Frank Sinatra would now be swathed in heavenly white as he crooned an African-American anthem of survival, appear in all-American baseball flannel, or even materialize in a full-length black cassock as an ever-compassionate priest. It was all in the service of characters whose last names never ended in a vowel. Just one problem— good performance or bad, great film or turkey, it was Frank Fucking Sinatra who kept popping out, stirring up trouble, growing as an actor, and exuding star quality all over the damn joint. In other words, a mogul's nightmare and a wary but fascinated public's new screen legend.

All Over the Map

"The Song's Gotta Come from the Heart,"
sung by Frank Sinatra and Jimmy Durante in
It Happened in Brooklyn

It looks as though Mr. Sinatra—and "the kids" are growing up.
—BOSLEY CROWTHER, *NEW YORK TIMES* REVIEW OF *IT HAPPENED IN BROOKLYN*

The trouble with Frankie is, he'll never stop doing what he thinks is right.
—SCREEN ALBUM, FALL 1947

IN THOSE FAR-OFF DAYS when stars still appeared in short films, Sinatra followed up his back-to-back triumphs in *Anchors Aweigh* and *The House I Live In* with a quick appearance in MGM's three-minute 1945 *Special Christmas Trailer,* in which he sang "Silent Night." Distributed to MGM's Loew's theaters during the month of December 1945, the short proved to be simply another piece in the endlessly restless Sinatra's Olympian list of multimedia appearances.

Concurrent with his movie roles and concerts, he also continued to host numerous radio series, starring in no fewer than six of them during the 1940s. There were two separate stints as the male vocalist on *Your Hit Parade,* a 1943 series called *Broadway Bandbox,* a 1944 radio program simply titled *The Frank Sinatra Program,* a 1945–47 run of *Songs by Sinatra,* the network show *Light Up Time,* and the aptly named *To Be Perfectly Frank.* Throw in the fact that he also undertook appearances on the dramatic radio series *The Rocky Fortune Show,* released an early LP titled *Voice of Frank Sinatra,* placed five top-ten songs on the charts, and had the number-one song in the country with "Five Minutes More," and one is left with exactly one reaction: When the hell did this guy sleep? No wonder Sinatra reputedly survived on four hours of sleep per night—he didn't have time for any more rest.

Voted the Most Popular Film Star of 1946 by *Modern Screen,* Sinatra's next appearance confirmed his appeal. Amidst a cavalcade of Metro's biggest stars, it was Frank who was featured in the climax of the Jerome Kern biopic *Till the Clouds Roll By,* singing "Ol' Man River." This brief appearance, certainly the best known of all his cameo film roles, is an odd one, to say the least—awful and memorable in equal measure. Sixty years after its initial release, the appearance still gets under the viewer's skin.

Till the Clouds Roll By, a 1946 release, stands as a quintessential whitewashed Hollywood biography of a well-known composer, in this case Jerome Kern (who died during the filming). Facts are glossed over, a pink cotton candy gauze appears to overhang the entire film, and the movie really represents nothing more than an attempt—successful if only in terms of the box office receipts—to parade the musical talents of as many MGM stars as possible. The behind-the-scenes talent was extraordinary—the film was produced by Arthur Freed, directed by Richard Whorf (with some sequences directed by Vincente Minnelli and George Sidney), and employed the musical talents of Lennie Hayton (musical supervisor and conductor), Conrad Salinger (orchestrations), and Kay Thompson (vocal arrangements). The problem lies in the fact that by employing the more-is-more approach of utilizing as many stars as possible, they've overstuffed the film. It's the dodo bird of MGM musicals—it moves but never flies.

In reality, the film plays like nothing so much as a "let's spot the star singing a well-known tune" revue. Passing along in quick succession are June Allyson, a very young Angela Lansbury singing and dancing twenty years before she hit Broadway and musical stardom as Mame, a loose-limbed (and first-rate) jitterbugging Van Johnson, and a surprisingly wan Cyd Charisse. According to the lights of this screenplay, Kern (Robert Walker) appears to have been a veritable saint his entire life. There isn't much attempt at period accuracy, and several of the stars are hampered by substandard choreography (musical numbers staged by Robert Alton). June Allyson sings and dances to

the title tune in what appears to be a forerunner of the four-years-later *Singin'*
in the Rain, but the number is clumsily staged. Coming off best in the proceedings are Judy Garland, singing a wistful "Look for the Silver Lining," as
Follies star Marilyn Miller, and particularly Lena Horne as Julie, in an excerpt
from *Show Boat.* Just as Frank Sinatra was born to play Billy Bigelow in
Carousel, Lena Horne was seemingly born to play the tragic Julie in *Show*
Boat, and her moving renditions of "Can't Help Lovin' Dat Man" and "Why
Was I Born?" show how much grit and genuine feeling she would have
brought to MGM's 1951 version of *Show Boat.* (MGM, fearful of a Southern
boycott of the film if the African-American Horne played the lead, tapped
Horne's good friend Ava Gardner to play the role. Gardner performed ad-
mirably, but Horne's presence is missed.)

And where, exactly, does Frank Sinatra fit into the proceedings? As the
film lumbers toward its climax, it is clear that the eleven o'clock spot is being
reserved for Kern's most famous song of all: "Ol' Man River" from *Show*
Boat. And singing this song specifically written for an African-American
male? That's right, Italian-American Frank Sinatra.

Show Boat's score has justifiably been hailed as a work of genius, and
nowhere is that more evident than in the kingpin number, "Ol' Man River."
Yes, it is a song by two white men about the African-American experience,
but in its simple yet heartfelt lyrics and majestic building choruses, it is a song
of undeniable power. In a matter of four minutes, there is insight into the
African-American experience and the bitter lasting legacy of slavery: "I'm
tired of livin' and scared of dyin'." In its very specificity, the song resonates
most powerfully when sung by an African-American artist, just as the song's
composer and lyricist intended. Indeed, *Till the Clouds Roll By* opens with
five songs from *Show Boat,* including "Ol' Man River," sung by an African-
American male (Caleb Peterson) in a rather statically staged presentation.
Kern and Hammerstein wrote character-specific songs, and here the character was a hardworking, exhausted, yet resilient African-American male. What
then to make of Frank Sinatra's appearance?

Well. It's wildly inappropriate, ludicrously overstaged, and yet somehow affecting. The power of a great artist, even when stuck in a hopeless situation . . .

As the kettledrums beat and the camera glides in, the audience finds a
white-suited Frank Sinatra standing on top of a pedestal, in front of what

*The famous—and infamous—
"Ol' Man River" in* Till the
Clouds Roll By *(1946).*

appears to be a one-hundred-piece orchestra and backing choir. And here it
becomes evident that the MGM art department, courtesy of Cedric Gibbons,
has gone a little cuckoo. Frank Sinatra is standing on a white pedestal, in front
of a white-garbed all-Caucasian orchestra positioned in front of a solid-white
MGM-style wedding cake set, all curving stairs and rounded corners, set off
by a pink backdrop. It's like a giant vat of vanilla cake frosting, an ethereal,
heavenly atmosphere (evidently, according to MGM, heaven is all white),
which takes the film's title all too literally. It leaves the viewer with one key
question: Given the mournful tone of Hammerstein's lyrics, why the hell is the
(white) singer dressed up in a white tux? What the hell is going on here?

And yet. Frank Sinatra may be wrong for the song, but he sure as hell delivers. His voice resonates with force—it is more powerful than in his late
1930s big band days—and most important, he invests the song with real passion. In fact, it is a passion for the material that no other star in the entire
gummy enterprise has displayed—there's a reason why MGM closed the film
with Frank's rendition. When he reaches the climactic words, "Git a little
drunk and you lan' in jail," his voice slides down the scale on the word "jail"
and seamlessly glides into the powerful phrase, "Ah gits weary an' sick of

tryin','" to great effect. There may have been extra resonance to Sinatra's rendition, given his well-known and highly liberal political views at the time, and he did, in fact, refuse to sing the original version of the lyric, which used the word "darkies." Sinatra believed in the liberal sentiments with his heart and soul, and he believed in the power of musical geniuses like Hammerstein and Kern, always granting credit to composers and arrangers in his concerts.

In fact, part of Sinatra's eventual conversion to right-wing Reagan supporter may have been due to the late-1960s dismissal not just of Sinatra's own vocal style, but of the value of brilliant composers like Kern and Gershwin. It all represented a state of affairs guaranteed to make such a man unsure of his life's work and his very place in American society. As Sinatra's one legitimate male singing rival, Tony Bennett, remarked in an atypical bitter moment: "[In the '60s it was decreed that] you had to write your own material . . . all of a sudden Cole Porter wasn't good enough." It's a mind-set that persisted until a slow reevaluation of the classic American songbook began with rock star Linda Ronstadt's 1983 release of her Sinatra-inspired album of standards titled *What's New.*

Till the Clouds Roll By proved an enormous financial success upon release. Critical response, however, was more mixed, with *Life* magazine proclaiming Sinatra's appearance the worst moment in any 1946 film: "a high point in bad taste." *Variety* was more evenhanded in its assessment of the film's two versions of "Ol' Man River"—"Both versions are creditably done and are calculated to meet any divergence of audience preference in the singing of 'Ol' Man River.'" Clearly the Sinatra appearance rankled, and even sympathetic chronicler Pete Hamill admitted, "He is at his most ludicrous in the film clip [from *Till the Clouds Roll By,* 1946] where he sings 'Ol' Man River' in a white tuxedo. . . ." Well, no—it's not his most ludicrous. That would have to be something like *Double Dynamite* or *The Kissing Bandit,* films and performances totally bereft of all passion and commitment. In the end, the most interesting comment of all came from composer Kern himself: "My idea with that song . . . was to have a rabbity little fellow do it—somebody who made you believe he was tired of livin' and scared of dyin'. That's how you do it, Frankie.'" Hmmm . . .

The success of the lavish *Till the Clouds Roll By* makes it doubly odd that Sinatra's next film role, in 1947's *It Happened in Brooklyn,* was a very cheap-looking black-and-white affair, produced at top-drawer MGM, no less.

Perhaps MGM didn't have the confidence that without Gene Kelly or dozens of costars Sinatra could draw at the box office on his own. Whatever the reason, *It Happened in Brooklyn* remains a film both indifferently directed (by Richard Whorf) and produced (by Jack Cummings, nephew of studio head L. B. Mayer). Constituting the second teaming of Sinatra and Kathryn Grayson, this paean to the borough of Brooklyn included some excellent Styne/Cahn songs (with top-notch musical support in the form of orchestrations by Axel Stordahl), but it featured an inferior screenplay by the usually reliable Isobel Lennart, one so limp in concept and execution that it nearly manages to submerge the film's one indisputable asset: the great Jimmy Durante.

Evidently in the minds of MGM screenwriters, Hoboken, New Jersey, was the same place as Brooklyn, because once again Frank plays a character (Danny Miller) who not only hails from Brooklyn, but also can find true love only by settling down with the Brooklyn-born nurse (Gloria Grahame) who has taken care of him in England. It's obvious from the very first scene, even before Kathryn Grayson appears, that Gloria is the gal for Frank. With her offbeat sex appeal and straightforward manner, she makes sense when teamed up with Sinatra, a lot more sense than does Ms. Grayson.

Of course, it takes the entire movie for Danny to figure this out, but what's to be expected from a Sinatra musical where his first full-fledged solo is a love song about . . . the Brooklyn Bridge. How much does he love the Brooklyn Bridge? Well, he carries a picture of the bridge in his wallet. Oh. It's just a variation on the old boy-meets-bridge, boy-loses-bridge, boy-finally-wins-back-bridge, and all-ends-happily story. Yes, it really is that wacky a movie. Since it seemed to be an unwritten rule of all World War II movies that one of the characters hail from Brooklyn—preferably a street-smart, wisecracking but lovable "ethnic" type—the screenwriters here must have figured, *Why not just make that ultimate symbol of Brooklyn, the bridge itself, an actual character.*

The movie begins at the end of World War II, with Yank-in-England army man Danny Miller (Frank here trades in his sailor suit for an army uniform) moping around as he is about to be demobbed. No-nonsense Nurse Gloria Grahame (who never seems to acquire a name, which gives you an idea of how much screen time she garners) chastises Miller to start smiling and stop whining about how much he misses his beloved Brooklyn Bridge. With that kind of carrying on, why, she's ashamed he's from her home borough. (Brushed aside is the fact that in reality Danny would be ecstatic at leaving the army.) Determined to try harder, Frank begins to play the piano and sings "Whose Baby Are You?" overheard by a very rich elderly duke (Aubrey Mather), grandfather to Jamie Shellgrove (Peter Lawford). The duke decides that what his rich, upper-crust grandson needs is—of course—a shot of Brooklyn. Doesn't every titled aristocrat want his grandson to "be more hep"?

So Frank returns home to the States and sings his song to the bridge. It's a tribute to Sinatra that the audience doesn't burst out laughing—he may be the only singer capable of pulling off such nonsense. Styne and Cahn's "Brooklyn Bridge" song was actually shot on location two years before the groundbreaking location filming of *On the Town,* and it is filmed very nicely indeed, with Danny traversing the length of the bridge as ships glide by underneath and the New York City skyline atmospherically frames the scene. It's all staged very fluidly, but in musical film parlance, the main character's all-important character-defining "I want" song—that which defines the character and what quest he is on—here revolves around a man loving a bridge. What exactly is at stake? The answer—not much.

Shortly thereafter Danny "meets cute" with high school music teacher Anne Fielding (Kathryn Grayson). Danny is instantly smitten, but this Goody Two-shoes doesn't seem like a particularly good match for Danny. Fortunately, the uninspired pairing ceases to matter, because at this point, the audience is also introduced to school custodian Nick Lombardi, in the person of the great Jimmy Durante. Durante is so winning a personality that he lifts the film to another level and it doesn't really matter what is happening onscreen when Jimmy is in high gear. He's not acting; he's just Durante being Durante, which is plenty in and of itself. (Said Sinatra, "Durante can upstage anybody, me included.") Waiting for Durante's next outrageous—and lovable—piece of schtick, the audience doesn't even spend too much time thinking about the fact that Frank Sinatra appears to be skinnier than ever (in the production number "I Believe," he is depicted as being so skinny that he can't make a see-saw move) or that the high school boy working out in the gym appears to be working out in a pair of tap shoes—with nary a pause, he interrupts his workout for a big production number.

The greatest portion of the movie takes place in Durante's dingy apartment housed in the school's basement—which, of course, is where all high school custodians live. It's not just Durante's run-down apartment that's shabby: the whole film registers as the cheapest musical of Frank Sinatra's entire feature film career, looking as if L. B. Mayer cashed in a leftover fifty-dollar war bond in order to fund the production.

Fortunately, the film does include two moments of genuine musical inspiration, which helps to alleviate the gloom. The first arrives when Frank sits down to play and sing the beautiful Styne and Cahn ballad "Time After Time" (the actual piano playing was supplied by the then-seventeen-year-old André Previn), and the result is pretty damn great. Sinatra, looking a little less fresh-faced than in *Higher and Higher,* is still in terrific voice, and the match of great singer and great song nearly redeems the entire silly affair.

Redeeming the silliness and providing the second outstanding musical moment is also precisely what Jimmy Durante succeeds in doing, as he injects fun and even a bit of pathos into the story line. Nick is actually a bit of a sad sack, a school janitor taken for granted by all except for former student Danny. He is sweet, kind, and oddly interested in the movie *Goodbye, Mr. Chips*: Nick's apartment even features a picture of Robert Donat in the title role. Go figure. The audience actually feels for this character, but with Durante's larger-than-life persona, there is always a healthy injection of fun to undercut any maudlin tendencies. His faux English accent mocking Peter Lawford's high falutin' speech is particularly enjoyable, but best of all is "The Song's Gotta Come from the Heart," a terrific number wherein Durante plays the piano, sings solo, and then ducts with Frank to terrific effect. Sinatra and Durante had worked together quite often on radio, and their mutual affection shines through on film. Imitating Durante in voice, walk, and trademark gesture of adjusting his necktie, Frank is obviously having a great time with Jimmy. It's certainly no accident that Sinatra's recording of "How About You," on his seminal *Songs for Swingin' Lovers* LP, changed part of the lyric to read: "I'm mad about good books, can't get my fill—And James Durante's looks give me a thrill."

"The Song's Gotta Come from the Heart" is a great moment in the Sinatra film oeuvre, one later excerpted to tremendous effect in *That's Entertainment!* It's so good, in fact, that one can even accept the logic behind the number: that janitor Nick has now given the lacking-in-confidence Danny a jolt of belief so strong that Danny instantly scores a job as a song plugger at a music store. The only problem with the scenario is that after four bars of music from these two, anyone with half a brain would rush the duo, not to a Brooklyn music store, but straight to Broadway, where they'd be the toasts of the town in a New York minute.

It Happened in Brooklyn *(1947). Second-rate movie but sensational duet on "It's Gotta Come from the Heart" with the great Jimmy Durante. Said Frank about Jimmy: "Durante can upstage anyone, me included."*

At this point in the story, the Sinatra/Durante duo must give way musically to the second-billed Kathryn Grayson, whose character of Anne Fielding must build up confidence for her own audition by singing an excerpt from *Don Giovanni* at a conveniently nearby rooftop Italian restaurant. Frank even joins in at one point, acceptably singing his phonetic version of the Italian aria. It's not that Grayson is bad; rather, it's that the movie comes to a halt while MGM plays cultural nanny to Middle America.

Just when the culture really starts flying fast and furious, the film takes us back to the music store for two pop music sequences. The first finds song-plugger Danny singing and playing "It's the Same Old Dream," a nicely lilting song, which Sinatra first sings as a creamy ballad, followed by the onscreen teenage kids swinging the song (vocal dubbed by the Starlighters), before ending with a reprise from Frank. What's interesting about Sinatra's vocal here is that it really does register as the quintessential example of his late 1940s ballads on film, the still fresh-voiced Frank unleashing his long flowing vocal line on a billowing string-heavy Stordahl orchestration. Anyone wondering why Frank Sinatra became such a pop sensation needn't look any further than this one song for evidence. The musicality, the intelligence, the attention to the lyrics and the story they tell—it's all here, front and center. Of course, this high point is rather quickly undercut by the second music-store sequence, which finds the aristocratic Jamie Shellgrove playing boogie-woogie piano, after which he sings and dances his way through the record store. Since Peter Lawford moves gingerly, sings mildly off-key throughout the entire song, and appears to have no inherent feel for music, his version is—what else?—a rousing success with the kids.

Danny is on his way, and since boogie-woogie has evidently now successfully invaded the British aristocracy, there's just one musical problem left to solve: Anne has given up on her own music career because she was once told that she had a "cold" voice. Gee, if only she had the chance to give a concert, she'd sing "Lakme," whereupon—abracadabra—we're into an extended opera sequence wherein Kathryn Grayson appears in dark-hued body makeup and sports what looks like a pagoda on top of her head. This all-singing, no-dialogue excerpt lasts a full (and very long) five minutes, and at last, all careers successfully managed, Jimmy Durante appears on the scene to straighten out everyone's romantic complications. Since, as Jimmy explains, "if you're in love with someone, you notice the little things that no one else does—her eye color, her height, the color of her nail polish," Danny comes to realize that it's Jamie and Anne who are meant for each other, while he happily runs off in search of Nurse Gloria Grahame—Brooklyn boy to mate with Brooklyn girl.

Frank Sinatra delivers a fully capable performance in the film, and the movie actually showcases one interesting variation of his film persona; during the course of the film, he begins to emerge from his shell and project a more worldly image. He gains employment as a song plugger and helps organize and run the charitable concert to benefit Anne's student. He is no longer presented solely as a hick who moons after the girl he loves. When at film's end he sets off in pursuit of Brooklyn dame Gloria Grahame, the action seems to signal a growth in Sinatra's acting opportunities, pointing the way to a new and more mature film identity.

Sinatra himself may have proved credible, but aside from the inspired duet with Durante and the beautiful "Time after Time," there is something a little dispirited about the whole proceedings. The film doesn't just look cheap—there's a corresponding air of lethargy hanging over the affair. Says Kathryn Grayson's Anne Fielding early in the film: "There aren't any nice days in

Brooklyn." Whew—guess her thwarted opera career has made this high
school music teacher more than a tad bitter. Maybe Sinatra's well-documented
dissatisfaction during production spread a pall over the filming. In an all-too-
typical example, production memos reveal that on September 12, he was
called for rehearsal with director Jack Donohue at 10:30 A.M., didn't show up
until 12:30 P.M., and left at 2:45 P.M. That's unprofessional behavior on any
level, and behavior Sinatra would never have tolerated from anyone else. He
also stopped filming for several days to fly to New York and help out his friend
Phil Silvers by performing with him after Silvers's partner Rags Ragland died.
This gesture represents a terrific and spontaneous act of friendship by Sinatra,
one for which he wanted no compensation from Silvers—and also cost the studio money, formed a breach of contract, and proved insensitive to the needs of
his fellow actors.

Sinatra received a lot more press for his offscreen activities than for anything connected with the dreary *It Happened in Brooklyn* when, at the time
of that film's release, the long-whispered rumors of his supposed mob connections hit the newspapers in a major way. Negative in the extreme and
laced with long-lasting repercussions, this press coverage all resulted from
an extremely ill-advised trip to Cuba with reputed mobster Joe Fischetti. To
this day, it is rumored that Sinatra delivered $2 million in cash to Lucky Lu-
ciano on that trip, but although Frank certainly knew Luciano, simply as a
practical matter, one wonders how a man as slight as the 1947 Sinatra could
lift a suitcase stuffed with $2 million in small bills. For that matter, how
could the cash even fit into the one briefcase with which Sinatra was photographed?

The resulting mob insinuations rapidly gathered force when printed in the
newspaper column of Scripps Howard columnist Robert Ruark, a right-wing
journalist who detested Sinatra. Most incriminating of all was a photograph of
Sinatra getting off a plane in Havana with Joe Fischetti. The visual cues in the
photograph told a public eager to believe the worst all that they wanted to
know. One look at the two Italian-Americans, both wearing dark glasses and
carrying attaché cases, and the still-prevalent anti-Italian prejudice blew this up
into a case of Sinatra being married to the mob. It's unclear whether Sinatra
knew in advance that Lucky Luciano himself would be in Havana at what
turned out to be a very large mob gathering, but in Ruark's purple prose, "Mr.
Sinatra, the self-confessed savior of the country's small fry by virtue of . . . his

movie shorts on tolerance and his frequent dabblings into the do-good depart-ment of politics seems to be setting a most peculiar example for his hordes of pimply shrieking slaves. . . ."

Sinatra defended himself with a simple, "I was brought up to shake a man's hand when I am introduced to him without first investigating his past," but as Pete Hamill pointed out, between Ruark's column and the photo, the damage had already been done. Decades down the road, all Sinatra would say about that ill-fated trip was, "It was one of the dumbest things I ever did."

More damage was inflicted upon Sinatra's public image when he and long-time press adversary Lee Mortimer had an encounter outside the Hollywood nightspot Ciro's, pushing and fighting in the early morning hours of April 9, 1947. Claiming that Mortimer had called him a dago and that "for two years he's been needling me," Sinatra hit Mortimer, an attack that resulted in Sina-tra being arrested the next day in the middle of rehearsing a song at CBS stu-dios. (It's an arrest with one amusing sidelight: the "grinning" Sinatra acknowledged that he did not have enough cash with him to make bail, with the money ultimately being put up by sympathetic bystanders.) In the end, Sinatra paid Mortimer nine thousand dollars in damages, settled out of court, and the charges were dropped, with Mortimer publicly acknowledging, "I have received satisfaction for the injury done to me. Sinatra has publicly stated I did not call him the vile names he stated I called him."

The repercussions from the altercation were to reverberate for decades, however. Mortimer may have been, as Sinatra called him, the only press mem-ber with whom he had a "physical bout in my lifetime," but as Pete Hamill accurately noted in *Why Sinatra Matters,* "it was a critical mistake to belt him. Newspaper people who despised Mortimer suddenly started getting much tougher about Frank Sinatra; as contemptible as Mortimer was, he was part of their Guild, not Sinatra's." The conservative press throughout the country jumped on the case, and the scuffle with Mortimer provided a perfect excuse to attack Sinatra's liberal political beliefs, complete with implications that he was a Communist sympathizer. Such coverage painted him into a corner, the public in effect being forced to choose between Sinatra the mafioso and Sinatra the Communist. Clearly those were not the best of times presswise for Frank.

As Sinatra's troubles carried over into 1948, the only bright spot on the horizon came with the birth of daughter Tina on June 20 of that year. On the

Family photo, July 1949, taken shortly before the marriage breakup.

professional front, however, his relations with the press continued to sour, and he was battered by the poor reception accorded his films released that year, *The Miracle of the Bells* and *The Kissing Bandit.* Sinatra may not have been thrilled with the strange *Miracle of the Bells,* but it proved to be a helluva lot more interesting than the truly terrible *Kissing Bandit.* A Technicolor farce wherein Frank plays a bumbling Hispanic would-be bandit in 1840s California, *The Kissing Bandit* began filming right after the final broadcast of *The Frank Sinatra Show* on CBS radio; Frank may have been top billed in the film, and he did have the services of top-drawer cinematographer Robert Surtees, but it was all for naught. *The Kissing Bandit* is, in a word, awful.

Does *The Kissing Bandit* really rate as Frank Sinatra's worst-ever film? Well, the funniest answer to that question was provided by Sinatra himself, decades after the film's release, when his first grandchild was born. Overjoyed at becoming a grandfather, Sinatra added that he had asked Nancy to promise him that she would never let granddaughter A.J. see *The Kissing Bandit.* Good call by Frank.

Opening with some beautiful shots of the Stanislaus National Forest in Sonora—the cinematography providing the only touch of class in the entire project—the film goes on to introduce one cartoonish Hispanic character after another, all of them complete with Frito Bandito accents. Sinatra himself fares horribly in the second-rate screenplay by Isobel Lennart and John Briard Harding. Making his entrance headfirst through the front wall of a rundown inn after losing control of his horse, Ricardo the Kissing Bandit slowly raises himself off the floor, and the audience sees Frank Sinatra for the first time. He is dazed and wondering where he is, a question every viewer older than five will be asking themselves as well. Turns out that far from being the macho, dashing Kissing Bandit that his legendary father personified, Ricardo is a timid easterner who just wants to run an inn complete with "window-boxes filled with pretty flowers." Some concept: Frank Sinatra, playing a would-be Hispanic bandit in nineteenth-century California, speaks with a noticeably thick New Jersey accent but is presented as a college graduate from Boston. He appears in fancy dress, his first words are "How do you do?" and he faints when he hears that his father was the real Kissing Bandit. Yep, it's grade Z right from the get-go.

Screenplay and star alike doom this movie. Frank has absolutely no feel for the material, and he looks trapped, desperate for a way out. Sinatra is an urban creature—he looks completely at home in any city. His cocky walk, the edgy speech patterns—this is a man who has grown up on the streets, and in all his films up to that point, his urban persona had been accommodated in one form or another, be it New York City in *Higher and Higher* and *Step Lively,* or Hollywood in *Anchors Aweigh*. With his skinny frame swathed in MGM costume designer Walter Plunkett's nutty MGM version of Western wear, Sinatra looks like 1840s California is the last place he wants to be.

As it is, Ricardo's first "job" as a bandit finds him outfitted in a glittery caballero outfit that makes him look like a male figure skater all set to glide around the rink to Ravel's "Bolero." He is not helped by first-time director László Benedek, who appears completely out of touch with both the setting and the requirements of farce. (Evidently Benedek, who fared better with Marlon Brando in *The Wild One* six years later, was replaced by George Sidney early on in shooting.) So heavy-handed is the approach employed by both the director and composers (Léo Arnaud, George Bradley, and André Previn) that when Ricardo sees love interest Teresa (Kathryn Grayson) for the first time, the

The awful Kissing Bandit *(1948). Said Frank:"I hated reading the script, hated doing it and, most of all, hated seeing it. So did everyone else."*

soundtrack blasts cartoon-type music that all but says *boing*. (It's hard to believe that the film really did employ seven arrangers, including Previn.)

It's a sign of how backwards this musical is that while Kathryn Grayson begins singing within fifteen seconds of her first appearance, top-billed, popular recording star Frank Sinatra does not sing a note until thirty-six minutes into the film. And what does Frank sing about? Afraid to kiss Teresa, Ricardo musically wonders "What's Wrong with Me?" A full-length motion picture is here centering around the question of why the Kissing Bandit won't kiss—this is terminally dopey by anyone's standards. The one note of reality injected into the movie comes in the form of Ricardo's horse, Gonzales, who is far smarter than any of the characters in the film; he takes off for home at the first sight and sound of trouble. Maybe Gonzales was the forerunner of Mr. Ed, the star of the 1960s television series about a talking horse, but it's not a good sign when the horse is the smartest one onscreen.

For his second solo, Ricardo serenades Teresa at night, strumming his guitar underneath her balcony. Sinatra looks ridiculous in yet another cuckoo glittery outfit, but when he sings "If I Steal Your Heart," he sounds terrific, and those three minutes of song provide the only genuine human emotion to be found in the entire film. Any hopes of the film finally hitting its stride are quickly undercut by the next musical number, however, wherein the mandatory spitfire Bianca (Broadway dance stalwart Sono Osato) serenades Ricardo in an attempt to make him forget Teresa. It's a plan hatched by Ricardo's well-intentioned pal Chico, played by J. Carrol Naish complete with fake nose, ridiculous bushy black wig, and offensively stereotyped accent.

As it is, when Bianca's serenade does not cut the mustard, she pulls out the heavy artillery and begins a frenzied "Whip Dance" of seduction, complete with swirling skirts and crackling bullwhips. Osato may be talented, but the dance, as choreographed by the esteemed Stanley Donen, goes absolutely nowhere, registering only as loud enough to make the "Barn Dance" in *Seven Brides for Seven Brothers* seem like "Swan Lake" by comparison.

The ineptitude on display continues with the arrival of the evil count, who has journeyed to California in order to check on the collection of taxes. Sporting both a permanent sneer and an ensemble of glittering purple hat, lavender cape, and matching gloves, the count forces any sensible viewer to ask, "Was the Wild West really this fey?" It's the sort of film in which Ricardo and Chico win a nonsensical slapstick fight with the count, secure him to a chair with rope, and then tell the governor's aide, "You can't disturb the count—he's all tied up." They then proceed to repeat the joke word-for-word, just in case the audience isn't speedy enough to grasp such rapier wit.

Kathryn Grayson—who seems made for Technicolor, with her dark hair, full red lips, and larger-than-life voice—has more verve here than she did as the wan music teacher in *It Happened in Brooklyn,* but for a musical made at MGM, the songs included here sure are second-rate. Indeed, Grayson's operetta-like warbling is followed up with a very clumsy introduction to the song "Siesta," wherein all the characters fall asleep so that Frank Sinatra, the foremost interpreter of the great American songbook, can actually sing the words

I'm talking to you, fly—
Why don't you shoo, fly

No wonder Sinatra hated the movie.

Realizing during production that they had a giant turkey on their hands, MGM executives ordered another production number shoehorned in, a supposedly lusty dance of seduction titled "Dance of Fury," featuring Ricardo Montalban, the great Cyd Charisse, and Ann Miller (terrific tapper, but not exactly someone whom one associates with the Wild West). It's all for naught, with a lot of flaring nostrils and two great female dancers trying to whirl up some passion while wrapped in what seem to be Western versions of the orange-and-red Burger King uniforms.

Finally, after yet another Kathryn Grayson solo and an exceedingly dopey fight between Ricardo and the count (in which it becomes clear that according to MGM, such duels were settled by tossing flower pots at each other), Kathryn Grayson and Frank Sinatra are united. After three feature films together, she and Frank finally kiss, she faints, and as a final insult, the soundtrack plays cartoon *boing* music yet again as the film mercifully ends.

The release of this Technicolor dud was delayed one full year until November of 1948, by which time Sinatra's next two films, *The Miracle of the Bells* and *Take Me Out to the Ball Game* had already finished production. The delay did nothing to diminish critical disdain for *The Kissing Bandit,* with *Los Angeles Mirror* critic Justin Gilbert dismissing Sinatra with a quick thumbs-down: "While his songs aren't bad, his acting is." In later years, Sinatra himself tersely summed up the terrible film and his lackluster performance in blunt terms. "I hated reading the script, hated doing it and, most of all, hated seeing it. So did everyone else."

At this point, Frank probably felt relieved to escape the fantasyland of MGM musicals for a serious dramatic role back at RKO, *The Miracle of the Bells.* Filmed after *The Kissing Bandit,* but released in March 1948, eight months before that debacle hit movie screens nationwide, *The Miracle of the Bells* was produced by legendary industry pioneer Jesse Lasky. The end result was one of the strangest films of Sinatra's entire career.

Just how offbeat a movie it is registers in director Irving Pichel's opening shots, which find the leading lady's coffin being taken off the train in her depressed blue-collar hometown. And Frank Sinatra is playing the parish priest. Uh-oh. Well, the reasoning seemed to be, if Bing Crosby won an Oscar for *Going My Way,* then surely Sinatra would have the chance to show his acting chops in his first nonsinging role. Narrated by top-billed Fred MacMurray in his role as press agent Bill Dunnigan, the film depicts the rise and death of actress Olga Treskovna (Alida Valli), who has been brought back to her broken-down coal-mining town for burial. Haunted by his inability to tell Olga that he loved her while she was alive, Dunnigan is determined to give Olga the funereal send-off she wanted.

Flashing back to Dunnigan's first meeting with aspiring actress Olga when she was dancing in burlesque, the screenplay depicts an ambitious young woman eager to escape her hometown, the sort of down-at-its-heel burg where the oily funeral director also runs a bar right next door to the mortuary. Dunnigan, instantly smitten, believes in Olga; sounding like his fast-talking character in Billy Wilder's *Double Indemnity,* MacMurray quickly tells her, "I never saw a face like yours, baby." Subsequent flashbacks reveal that Olga has landed a job as stand-in for the star of a movie about Joan of Arc, and when the diva in question throws a campy fit and stalks off the set, Bill hatches a plan for the unknown Olga to take over as star. Says Bill to Olga, "Be quiet, baby. I'm incubating." Not exactly the sort of talk one normally hears when discussing Joan of Arc.

Olga's subsequent illness and death are slowly revealed in further flashbacks, but in the meantime, a proper funeral must be planned, and that is where Father Paul of Saint Michael's Catholic Church comes onto the scene, in the person of Frank Sinatra. Sinatra was third billed in the film (for the first time since *Higher and Higher*), a result of both dwindling box office returns from the likes of *It Happened in Brooklyn* and an increasingly hostile press for his offscreen cavorting. (In order to counteract Frank's bad press, RKO trumpeted the fact that he was donating his hundred-thousand-dollar salary to the Catholic Church.)

Sinatra's third billing makes sense in terms of actual time onscreen, because in the first fifty-four minutes of the film, he is in only one brief scene. Limited screen time or not, what Sinatra does deliver here is actually a very interesting characterization, which for the first time suggests untapped acting ability.

From the standpoint of the twenty-first century, so strong is the public's Rat Pack, "My Way" perception of the Sinatra public persona, that it's easy to assume the moviegoing audience in 1948 had a difficult time believing in Frank Sinatra as a priest. (Amusingly enough, an ABC radio poll taken during 1947, the year that *The Miracle of the Bells* was filmed, named Sinatra as the second most popular living person, wedged between Bing Crosby and Pope Pius XII!) Contrary to legend, however, Sinatra here turns in quite a good performance. Speaking very softly and with both conviction and gentleness, Sinatra does, at least vocally, strike one as a comforting priest. Nearly crooning some of his lines, he is actually soothing, and the religious message plays far more effectively in his decision to underplay throughout and eschew overt displays of emotion. Yes, there's a bit too much chair swiveling in his first scene discussing funeral arrangements with MacMurray, an activity that seems to denote a slight bit of nervousness, but nonetheless, the viewer finds himself ready to accept Sinatra in the role. Indeed, whatever the audience's reaction, it must have been a convincing act in person; in a widely reported incident—or press agent's invention—when the non-English-speaking mother of Sinatra pal George "Bullets" Durgom visited the set, she supposedly mistook Sinatra for an actual priest and kissed his ring. Not wanting to disappoint the woman, Sinatra never let on who he really was.

As the film progresses, one begins to understand why Sinatra remained Frank Capra's first choice to star in his proposed film about Saint Paul. Spencer Tracy may have spoken of how comfortable he felt in a priest's vestments, and Bing Crosby achieved his greatest popular successes with his turns as a priest in *The Bells of St. Mary's* and *Going My Way* but it is Sinatra who—oddly or not—most convincingly sounds like a priest, who most accurately seems to convey the complexities inherent in a man of the cloth.

The problem here lies in the fact that just as Father Paul begins to develop into an interesting flesh-and-blood character, he disappears for another twenty-five minutes as the movie flashes back to Hollywood. Dunnigan convinces studio chief Marcus Harris (Lee J. Cobb) that he should give Olga a chance: "Can she act?! Can Joe Lewis fight?!" As exemplified by this unfortunately typical dialogue, the film plays more like a heavenly version of *A Star Is Born* than like a religious picture, uneasily juggling a switch in tone between Olga's rise to Hollywood stardom and an inspirational film. In fact, to Bill Dunnigan, it's all the same; in his view, the twelve apostles were like twelve press agents who "sold the biggest story that ever happened to the whole world—without benefit of newspapers or radio."

Back in full press-agent mode, Dunnigan begins to sound like a not-entirely-trustworthy newspaperman right out of *The Front Page,* which is not

Frank as a priest, no less.
The Miracle of the Bells
(1948): odd but curiously
affecting.

surprising, considering that Ben Hecht was coauthor of the screenplay along with Quentin Reynolds and DeWitt Bodeen (the latter reportedly contributing Sinatra's dialogue). Pitching the story of Olga, the church bells, and her hardscrabble upbringing to hard-boiled newspapermen, Dunnigan lays on the fevered press-agent prose: "Her father was born with a gift for song and laughter." This sequence actually encapsulates all the problems with the screenplay. The film is investigating interesting ideas—the selling of religion and miracles, for starters—yet it undercuts the effectiveness with caricatured dialogue. Hecht simply appears to have been more at ease writing for the worlds of *Scarface* and *Spellbound* than for a film whose worldview, clear-eyed as it purports to be about religion, is best viewed without any irony or sense of cynical distrust.

When Frank Sinatra does appear onscreen, he is, in fact, allowed one song, and it's certainly a long way from the world of *Anchors Aweigh*. The song in question is a touching a capella version of "Ever Homeward" (written by Styne and Cahn, based on a Polish folk melody) and is sung while Father

Paul is walking in the cemetery with Dunnigan: "Ever homeward, ever homeward, now the journey's over." The song represents one of the very few times in Sinatra's film career that he sang live on film, the other (terrific) example being "High Hopes" in *A Hole in the Head*. Sinatra detested the process of lip-synching to a previously recorded vocal, necessary though it usually proved to be from a technical standpoint. In Frank's view, such prerecording robbed the performance of spontaneity: "I never sing a song exactly the same way twice, so when I come to mime, I find it very hard."

As the film lumbers along toward the climactic moment of Olga's funeral, the most unusual twist in the story occurs: the statues of Mary and Jesus begin to move, right before the start of Olga's funeral. The assembled congregation convince themselves that they have witnessed a genuine miracle, but Father Paul returns to the movie to provide a more earthly explanation: extensive mining of the earth has caused the two pillars to shift position. Forget the mystical otherworldly explanations, says Father Paul: "The [real] miracle of the Olgas of the world is that the world might see, through her toil and sacrifice, the beauty that there was in the tired and lonely hearts of her people." It's a nice sentiment, but in trying to be all things to all people, *The Miracle of the Bells* ends up not being terribly successful as anything. As for Sinatra, contrary to its reputation, the film offers evidence of his increasing acting talents. His gentle demeanor on display throughout serves the role well, and he is quietly affecting when simply stating, "I know what makes a saint and I also know what makes a beautiful human being. Such a one lies now at our feet." Those are not easy words to wrap one's mouth around—just try saying "such a one" out loud—yet Sinatra actually convinces here.

The critics, however, were not convinced, and the film opened to mostly terrible reviews, with *Cue* magazine bluntly declaring: "The picture can be reasonably described as nauseating." One notable exception was Philip K. Scheuer in the *Los Angeles Times,* who did notice that "Sinatra wisely doesn't attempt to 'act' at all. His portrayal has the virtue of simplicity," but it was Hollywood gossip columnist Hedda Hopper who pithily summed up the prevailing view in the most succinct fashion, calling the film "A hunk of religious baloney."

Sinatra did himself no further favors by telling producer Lasky that he would not attend the film's premiere in San Francisco, and when contractually forced to attend, proceeded to purposely run up enormous hotel bills.

Evidently the saintly demeanor ended as soon as the cassock came off. What made the situation even worse for Frank was the simple fact that the lackluster reception for *The Miracle of the Bells* was followed at the end of the year by the even worse box office receipts for *The Kissing Bandit.* MGM executives were uneasy over Sinatra both onscreen and off, RKO was none too happy with *The Miracle of the Bells,* and with two studios voicing displeasure, Frank had every reason to feel anxiety over his screen career.

Perhaps it was the unfortunate one-two-three combination of *It Happened in Brooklyn, The Miracle of the Bells,* and *The Kissing Bandit,* but 1948 found Sinatra appearing in the strangest film of his career, a ten-minute short film titled *Lucky Strike Salesman's Movie 48-A.* That's right, Frank Sinatra participated in a film produced by the American Tobacco Company, singing "Embraceable You" with the Lucky Strike Quartette. How "Embraceable You" was thought to fit nicely into a film that regales the audience with the growing, harvesting, and buying of tobacco is anyone's guess. Well, it was a paycheck.

The solution? Back to the protective assistance of Arthur Freed and Gene Kelly, for the nostalgic baseball musical *Take Me Out to the Ball Game.* If not quite so much fun as *Anchors Aweigh* or the soon-to-be-filmed landmark *On the Town, Ball Game* still registered as a snappy, entertaining musical, and served to reestablish Frank's bona fides onscreen.

Beginning with the rip-roaring title tune (which is oddly reminiscent of Kelly's and Donald O'Connor's three-years-later "Fit as a Fiddle" duet in *Singin' in the Rain*), *Take Me Out to the Ball Game* presents a (top-billed) Frank Sinatra who has gained back his confidence, even if just temporarily. Freed from the constraints of roles as priest and kissing bandit, real-life sports fan Sinatra seems emotionally and physically liberated by the sheer physicality of the role.

Producer Arthur Freed had originally intended to have the film directed by Warner Bros. movie-musical legend Busby Berkeley, and although Berkeley retained final billing credit as director, it is largely acknowledged that Kelly and Stanley Donen directed much of the film. At the time of filming, Berkeley was dealing with a number of personal and financial problems, which prevented his working at full capacity, and certainly his choreography (which tended to be camera-driven tableaux of chorus girls in ofttimes startling formations) could not have been the inspiration for the exuberant

Kelly-led production numbers herein. (Berkeley does, however, appear to have directed the Esther Williams swimming pool sequences.)

Ball Game actually came to life as a result of creative dissatisfaction, when Gene Kelly refused to star in a movie about two sailors (Kelly and Sinatra) turning an aircraft carrier into a floating nightclub. Shooting down that idea—one so threadbare that it reads like the sequel to *Ship Ahoy*—Kelly and Donen sketched out a two-page outline of ballplayer/vaudevillians in the early days of professional baseball. For their troubles, the fledgling screenwriters received twenty-five thousand dollars when they sold the idea to Arthur Freed. The resulting film may have adhered to an early twentieth-century setting, but thirty seconds of viewing tells anyone and everyone that this movie was made at MGM in the 1940s, so distinctive is the Freed unit production stamp. It may not be *Singin' in the Rain,* but it's a lot of fun and, fortunately for Frank Sinatra, a long way from the lugubrious *The Miracle of the Bells.*

The formulaic but pleasant script by Harry Tugend, George Wells, and Harry Crane presents Sinatra (Dennis Ryan) and Kelly (Eddie O'Brien) in another variation of their *Anchors Aweigh* personas: Sinatra is once again the timid, bashful rube, and Kelly the wolfish man about town. Sinatra's comic timing has improved markedly by now—he is more at ease with the onscreen jokes—and here, baseball uniforms are substituted for sailor suits. Just like all professional ballplayers, Frank and Gene work as vaudevillians in the off-season. . . . Well, what the hell, the vaudeville setting allows the film to race out of the blocks right from the get-go, with Frank and Gene clad in straw hats and red-and-white pin-striped suits, dancing up a storm as they belt out the title tune in a vaudeville theater. Baseball and vaudeville—what could be more all-American than that? Now, this was a scenario to L. B. Mayer's liking, and the opening number sets the tone for the red, white, and blue patriotic color scheme that suffuses the film.

Frank Sinatra is here engaging in some real hoofing, tapping, leaping, and appearing full of vim and vigor. The number is presented in lengthy takes (as is Kelly's later solo "The Hat Me Dear Old Father Wore"), evidence of genuine dancing ability on display—no stop-and-start minutely edited bits and pieces here. Gene Kelly may still be "dancing down" to Sinatra somewhat, but he sure isn't slumming. Gene and Frank register as a bona fide song-and-dance team, and that is high praise indeed considering Kelly's legendary status. Costar Betty Garrett's comment that "Frank worked hard on all the dances; he had a natural grace and moved easily" is borne out in spades.

Yes, the musical does, in fact, trade yet again on Frank's nearly shopworn persona of naïf, but that persona is undercut as soon as Frank begins to sing. Dialogue naturally flowing into the song "Yes, Indeed," Frank's knowing vocal instantly establishes an entirely different, confident character. When the boys (and here they act like boys out for a good time) arrive at spring training, they break into a dance on the ball field, and with the fluid camerawork tracking in and out on the dancing duo, the film, like its stars, exudes a sense of total confidence.

Comic relief is introduced in the person of Nat Goldberg (Jules Munshin), and in a very nice precursor of the terrific "New York, New York" opener in *On the Town,* the three gents sing about their ball-field prowess in "O'Brien to Ryan to Goldberg," a hymn of praise to, of all things, a double play. Well, if Frank could sing a love song to a bridge, why not to a double play? There's some great physical clowning and hoofing here, and a perfect blend of singer (Sinatra), dancer (Kelly), and clown (Munshin) puts across the nimble number.

Hoofing up a storm with Gene Kelly in Take Me Out to the Ball Game *(1949).*

Esther Williams, now introduced as K. C. Higgins, the new (and unexpectedly female) owner of the Wolves ball club, presents a more-than-capable character. It's a role that goes a long way toward proving that she was capable of a great deal more than just swimming in the MGM pool. K. C. Higgins is one heckuva Renaissance woman, one who can run a ball club, field hot grounders, give batting tips to Gene Kelly, and after a team dinner, change clothes and whad'ya know, take a dip in the pool while singing the title song. It's no wonder that Frank's character of Dennis Ryan falls hopelessly in love with her.

Nervous, bashful Dennis is making all the inappropriate gestures, but then Comden and Green come to the rescue. When K.C. asks, "How can you tell it's the right girl?" Dennis glides into the lyric, "I'll hear heavenly music, I'll hear bells ringing," and as he continues to sing "She's the right girl for me," his character is, for a change, in charge. It may be Sinatra's only solo in the film, but it's a nice one and lands solidly with the audience. And what happens next? Well, of course, Frank and Esther engage in—no, not sex, just some baseball practice.

(Sinatra, as usual at this point in his career, sounds in such great voice that it's too bad his solo on "Boys and Girls Like You and Me" was cut after filming. Originally written for the Broadway musical *Oklahoma!* the Rodgers and Hammerstein song did resurface as a special feature on the DVD release.)

Song over, Danny reverts to schlemiel mode, and it becomes clear that it's Eddie and K.C. who are made for each other. Kelly is so athletic that he shinnies up to her balcony perch without a hitch, and between her swimming and his gymnastics, they're like a two-person MGM Summer Olympics team. (The film does present an amusing montage of Danny trying to eat heartily and thereby gain weight, only to find himself skinnier than ever—Sinatra's bony frame was always good for a gag or two in these early musicals.)

The film does slow in several of the romantic sections, and there is some needless vaudeville mugging before the game—once it's mildly amusing; twice it's a bore. However, just when the pace threatens to slacken completely, Betty Garrett arrives on the scene as Shirley Delwyn, a no-nonsense dame who instantly fixes her gimlet-eyed gaze on hapless Danny. After a big fight on the field between opposing ballplayers, Shirley, clad in full-length gown, hat, and matching parasol, simply takes matters into her own hands.

She marches onto the field, slings Danny over her shoulder, and carries him off the field. She chases him from locker room to the far-off bleachers, all the while singing the witty comic ode "It's Fate, Baby, It's Fate." This is great fun, playful in the best sense, and Danny might not yet realize it, but in Betty Garrett's witty performance, Shirley has reeled him in—hook, line, and sinker.

A train montage accompanied by flashing newspaper headlines helps to push the film along at a suitably fast pace, before the action settles in for the big clambake and two first-rate production numbers. The first is the smoothly delivered all-company song-and-dance patriotic tribute "Strictly U.S.A." The second is an outstanding Gene Kelly dance number titled "The Hat Me Dear Old Father Wore," a tour de force that starts out in high gear, slows down for a reverie-like middle section, and finishes up with a slam-bang romp all over the nautical setting. It's a great example of how Gene Kelly utilized dance exactly as Frank Sinatra used song; they were actors who dramatized and conveyed emotion through their respective art forms, constructing dances and songs as three-act plays wherein they set the scene, introduced the conflict, heightened emotion to a climax, and finally arrived at a resolution. *Take Me Out* is not the art that *An American in Paris* aspired to be, but it's great fun.

Granted, it's all about as realistic as the vaudeville routine that the boys conveniently perform before the start of the play-off game. No matter, all is resolved happily, the game is won, and as Frank runs the bases at film's end, one's reaction is "Hey—he's pretty damn fast." Just like the film itself. In fact, it ultimately ends with a coda wherein a charming song-and-dance reprise of "Strictly U.S.A." finds the two couples clad in red, white, and blue, all of them singing and dancing to in-joke lyrics referring to the respective Sinatra and Kelly "rivals," Bing Crosby and Fred Astaire.

In this number, Frank is once again really hoofing, and no matter how hard he had to rehearse, he appears effortless alongside the great Kelly—there is an appealing natural grace about Sinatra in motion, smiling, singing, and generally charming the audience. Although not a blockbuster, the film was a hit, and by and large, reviews for both the film and Frank were favorable, the *Hollywood Reporter* pronouncing, "Sinatra sings and gags his way through a most pleasant role." A few brickbats were tossed as well, *Time* magazine stating, "*Take Me Out to the Ball Game* is a lazy Technicolored cine-musical," an indication of how the critics didn't really grant the film its due—the one thing the film is *not* is lazy, not with Kelly (and Sinatra) whirling around onscreen. It's a pleasant, undemanding movie musical that has been unfairly forgotten over the years, perhaps hidden in the large shadow cast by Frank's next musical, the uneven but exciting and innovative *On the Town*.

Although *On the Town* is certainly a very enjoyable musical, the passage of nearly sixty years since its original 1949 release has made clear the fact that its importance lies in its pioneering use of location filming more than its variable quality. *On the Town* may not have actually been the very first musical to film numbers on location—Fred Astaire, for one, filmed his golf number in *Damsel in Distress* on an actual golf course, not to mention Frank's own paean to the Brooklyn Bridge in *It Happened in Brooklyn*—but the exhilarating "New York, New York" number at the start of the film ensured that *On the Town* would be remembered as the first musical shot outside of a studio.

Kelly himself recalled, "I really believed it would be a milestone. . . . Everything we did in the picture was innovative from the way we flashed the time of day across the screen as if it were a news flash . . . to the way we cut the picture which was pretty revolutionary for its time. . . . The fact that make-believe sailors got off a real ship in a real dockyard, and danced through a real New York was a turning point in itself." Kelly was right: thirty-five years before the revolution of MTV, the quick-cutting of the musical numbers set a new standard for the pace of screen musicals. With the passage of time, this revolutionary editing seems especially groundbreaking, as does the location work. Lugging the then-cumbersome camera equipment all over the chaotic streets of Manhattan (hordes of New Yorkers followed Sinatra wherever he appeared on location), the filmmakers still managed a fast and fluid opening number that has yet to be surpassed. Codirectors Kelly and Stanley Donen broke new territory here, building upon Jerome Robbins's Broadway production of the same material to craft a dancecentric film that featured modern-day characters dancing within real New York City streets. And as a full-fledged dance musical, where exactly did that leave Frank?

For starters, it left Sinatra, in what was to be his last outing as a dancer, second-billed after Kelly, and very much in Gene's shadow in terms of the structure of the film. At the same time, it actually proved helpful to Sinatra's screen legacy, delighting audiences and landing as a solid box office hit.

In fact, Frank would have registered even more strongly if the film had been more faithful to the lines of the hit Broadway original, but although the

Broadway book writers, Comden and Green, were retained for the screenplay, the terrific jazz-inflected score by Leonard Bernstein (with Comden and Green lyrics) was bowdlerized. Such a wholesale ransacking reportedly occurred because producer Arthur Freed simply did not like the score, and additional songs were supplied by crackerjack arranger Roger Edens. Although Edens was an extraordinary musician who greatly aided the development of screen musicals, the film suffered by jettisoning so much of the original score. (That said, Edens and Lennie Hayton did win Oscars for Best Scoring of a Musical Picture.)

Even more startling is the report that upon seeing the show on Broadway, the hyperpatriotic L. B. Mayer found this most all-American of shows to be "smutty" and "Communistic." Mayer, in fact, seemed to have become most exercised over Jerome Robbins's decision to utilize an interracial couple in a dance sequence; his reaction is particularly interesting in light of the fact that MGM had actually invested $250,000 in the Broadway production, obtaining the film rights in the process. As a result of that investment *On the Town* rates as the first Broadway play sold to Hollywood as part of a preproduction deal.

The gutting of the original score unquestionably weakened the film, lessening Sinatra's impact in the process. The most egregious deletion for Sinatra was the last-minute decision not to include "Lonely Town," a beautiful, slightly mournful ballad that exposed the melancholy flip side of the urban valentine, and one that also served to heighten interest in and understanding of Frank's character. Originally conceived as a number combining Kelly's dancing and Sinatra's singing, the sequence was inexplicably cut by Arthur Freed. Any doubts about how seriously Sinatra took his film career are dispelled by the fact that thirty-five years later, the memory of the omitted number still rankled him greatly: discussing his movie musical work with singer and pianist Michael Feinstein, Frank told Feinstein that the number would have been great, "But that f——ing Arthur Freed got in the way." In fact, only four songs from the original score were utilized in the film: "New York, New York," "Miss Turnstiles Dance," "Come Up to My Place," and "A Day in New York Ballet." Fortunately, the best song in the score—"New York, New York"—is not only retained, but starts off the film with an exhilarating shot of adrenaline that is among the greatest moments in musical film history.

The brilliant "New York, New York" number in the groundbreaking On the Town *(1949).*

As the film opens with a shot of the New York City skyline at 5:57 A.M. (the exact time scrolling across the bottom of the screen in ticker tape fashion), the camera pans in on a navy ship docked by the wharf. A beefy construction worker slowly walks by, lazily swinging his lunch pail in perfectly matched rhythm with his stride. Breaking the silence of the serene early-morning calm, the burly foreman surprises by singing the film's opening lines, "I feel like I'm not out of bed yet," in a beautiful quasi-operatic voice. This vocal introduction is filmed in a single long take by Kelly and Donen, whereupon the whistle blows at 6 A.M. and sailors explode off the ship, dressed in their whites and ready for twenty-four hours' leave on the town. The camera zooms in for a close-up of Frank Sinatra (Chip), Gene Kelly (Gabey), and Jules Munshin (Ozzie), and as the reunited stars of *Take Me Out to the Ball Game* belt out "New York, New York," while sprinting through beautifully photographed locations (ranging from Wall Street and Central Park to the Statue of Liberty), the nonstop motion peaking in an exhilarating circular pan of the trio on top of the Empire State Building. (Munshin was so phobic about heights, having to stay on hands and knees for even an elevator ride, that he could not rehearse the ending, and made it through this sequence only by means of a safety rope tied underneath his sailor suit.) As the rhythmically propulsive Bernstein melody crescendoes with the three sailors gleefully proclaiming, "It's a wonderful town," from their perch far above Manhattan, one realizes that it doesn't get any better than this. Great stars, great number, great locations—bliss for any movie lover, musical fan or not. (Overlooked in the all-around exhilaration of the number was the fact that censors actually demanded that the original lyric be changed from "a helluva town" to "a wonderful town"—it's the latter sanitized version heard in the film.)

Expensive location filming was extremely rare in the late 1940s, and cost-conscious MGM executives allowed the directors only five days of shooting in New York City, which Kelly and Donen cannily managed to stretch out to eighteen days. The opening number aside, the remainder of the film was shot in the studio, and the exhilarating sense of freedom in this opening sequence could not be equaled again. After the New York City locations, the studio sets registered as noticeably phony-looking.

A bit of in-joke humor—Ozzie sarcastically asks Gabey, "Who you got waiting for you in New York—Ava Gardner?"—launches the film into a fast-paced boys-meet-girls musical comedy. Actually, it's a bit of a variation on that formula, because, contrary to the usual plot strictures, although all three couples pair off quickly, they never actually lose each other romantically: the plot is simply a romp around New York City as Gabey chases after "Miss Turnstiles," Ivy Smith (Vera-Ellen), whom he mistakenly believes is a rich and famous celebrity. Within the context of a plot that takes place in only twenty-four hours, the chase serves to propel the film at a gallop.

It's not just Gabey and Ivy who provide the enjoyment here—the other two couples prove to be equally entertaining. As soon as the aggressive but lovable female cab driver Brunhilde Esterhazy (the terrific Betty Garrett) sets her eyes on "skinny runt" Chip (Sinatra), he is a goner. In a role that easily could have toppled over into a caricatured, off-putting, overly aggressive female, Garrett is winning and attractive, terrific as singer, dancer, and comedienne. As in *Take Me Out to the Ball Game,* she makes a great team with Sinatra.

Rounding out the feminine trio is rich anthropologist Claire Huddesen (Ann Miller), who takes one glance at Ozzie (Jules Munshin), decides he looks just like prehistoric man—*Pithecanthropus erectus,* to be precise—and proceeds to belt out "Find Me a Primitive Man" while she tap-dances up a storm in and around a full-scale dinosaur reproduction. Just as Esther Williams surprised in *Take Me Out to the Ball Game,* Ann Miller surprises here, utilizing a terrific belt voice that would do Ethel Merman proud (and made Miller the toast of Broadway in her second-act stage career starring in *Mame* and *Sugar Babies*). This is one anthropologist who dresses for success, coming to the museum clad in a green frock, which just so happens to separate down the front in order to show off the plaid lining—and, not so coincidentally, her gams. The three sailors and their girls may destroy the dinosaur, but this wacky number is sheer fun.

Frank Sinatra is here playing another semi-hick (he covers his eyes when they stumble into a nude still-life drawing class), and while it stretches credulity to accept Frank Sinatra's Chip as hailing from Peoria, Illinois, the film is so much fun that it does so in a most pleasant way. Although the libidinous Hildy only wants Chip to "Go to My Place," as she tells him in a zippy Comden/Green lyric, Chip wants to tour the city and see the sights. The difference in Sinatra's character this time around, however, is that he ultimately does land at Hildy's place, where he enthusiastically kisses her, only to be interrupted by Hildy's plain Jane roommate Lucy Schmeeler (Alice Pearce) a sneezing, coughing, nasal embodiment of every sailor's nightmare date. Make that a 1940s sailor nightmare: there's something a little off-putting in the relentless gags at Lucy's expense. She's goofy, but a nice girl, and there's more than a touch of chauvinism in all the merriment at her expense.

A Sinatra solo finally arrives on the top of the Empire State Building, where Chip serenades Hildy with the humorous song "You're awful—awful nice to look at...." Sinatra and Garrett, two genuine all-around talents, make an appealing pair, and the viewer scarcely notices that the then thirty-four-year-old Sinatra, with his receding hairline, looks substantially older than any young sailor ever would. (The still-skinny Sinatra even needed to have his sailor suit padded in the rear because there simply was not enough of him to fill out the suit.)

Just as the dance of seduction in *Anchors Aweigh* foreshadowed moments in the climactic *American in Paris* ballet, so, too, does Kelly now lay the extensive groundwork for that same ballet here, with the "Day in New York" set piece wherein he and Ivy dance the story of their meeting, loving, and losing each other. Utilizing the terrific Bernstein music that is alternately bluesy and romantic, Kelly and Vera-Ellen range in style from ballet to jazz, sexy and wistful by turns, telling a full-blooded story in dance. With the red spotlight backlighting their two figures as their bodies intertwine at the ballet barre, Kelly and Vera-Ellen are downright erotic. (The other two couples are represented by look-alike ballet dancers, none of the other four stars being up to the demanding Kelly choreography. Frank Sinatra was a man of extraordinary talents, but ballet dancing was definitely not one of them.)

Yes, the ballet does come across, in part, as a rather unnecessary recapping of the story we have just watched, but it is done with such exceptional skill and style that we really don't mind. Gene Kelly is here pushing the boundaries of the American film musical forward, and combined with his assured direction and the landmark location shooting, the film represents a crowning achievement for him, paving the way as the first in his triple crown of musicals, to be shortly followed by *An American in Paris* in 1951 and *Singin' in the Rain* in 1952.

The film stumbles as it reaches its climax: the scene of police chasing the fast-driving Hildy to Coney Island is attenuated, and the scene of the girls successfully talking their way out of trouble with the police is downright silly. However, the movie circles back effectively to its beginning frames as the same burly stevedore strolls by the quiet wharf manfully singing, "I feel like I'm not out of bed yet." The three couples share a hurried embrace before the boys return to their ship, whereupon, 6 A.M. whistle blowing, another trio of sailors leaps off the ship singing of the glories awaiting them in "New York, New York, a wonderful town." It's a nice bookend to the film, but the sequence leading up to this reprise also represents a true missed opportunity by the filmmakers.

The Broadway version of *On the Town* climaxed with a brilliant Bernstein/ Comden and Green song, "Some Other Time," one that combined a lovely wistful melody with plaintive, nearly elegiac lyrics expressing resignation and hope in equal measures for couples parting in wartime: "Where did the time go. Oh well, we'll meet up—some other time." In the hands of such master songwriters, one three-minute pop song summed up the entire national mood in 1944, and in terms of popular songs, only "Sentimental Journey" spoke as eloquently of wartime love and loss. The screenplay could easily have been manipulated to allow Sinatra's character the opportunity to sing this song, because the chance to hear Frank Sinatra singing such heartfelt lyrics was the chance of a lifetime, but the filmmakers blew it. The war may have been four years over by the time of filming, but the inclusion of that song would unquestionably have granted the film an additional layer of poignancy.

The actual production of *On the Town* was particularly noteworthy for two reasons. The first is that Sinatra had reverted to a state of extreme impatience on set, refusing to wait while locations were lit and relit due to the vagaries of New York City weather. According to published reports, Frank calmed down only when friend and mentor Gene Kelly lost his patience with him: "Front-office suits could go hang but Sinatra couldn't bear losing the respect of fellow pros."

The second, and much more damaging, bit of fallout from production came from Frank's joke about Louis B. Mayer and his riding accident. Sinatra greeted news of the mishap with the wisecrack, "He didn't fall off a horse, he fell off Ginny Simms." Simms, who may or may not have been Mayer's love interest, was a singer and actress of ability and some renown. When word of the put-down reached Mayer, his limit had been reached: fond though he was of Sinatra in many ways, he would no longer overlook the on-set impatience, the spotty record at the box office, and the now-ongoing affair with Ava Gardner that so consumed the press.

Mayer was hurt personally, and he was also fed up from a business standpoint. Underneath all the glamour and excitement of golden age Hollywood lay the fact that MGM was a business, a sometimes quirky yet nonetheless remarkably efficient business, which churned out a fantasy product where the bottom line was always money. Frank Sinatra was not only a pain in the neck, but he was also costing Mayer money. Net result: good-bye, Frank.

According to daughter Nancy, although Sinatra himself told Mayer, "I wish I could take that back," Mayer was unmoved: "That's not a very nice thing to do. I want you to leave here, and I don't ever want you to come back again." Louis B. Mayer terminated Frank Sinatra's MGM contract on April 27, 1950, four months after the release of *On the Town.* In Sinatra's retelling of his termination: "My face dropped. I knew I was sunk." Frank was paid eighty-five thousand dollars on the remaining one year of his contract, and the MGM public relations machine softened the blow by reporting, "As a freelance artist, he is now free to accept unlimited, important personal appearance, radio and television offers that have been made to him."

At the time of the release of *On the Town,* however, Frank's termination lay months in the future. For the moment, MGM had a big hit on its hands, with the film breaking box office records at Radio City Music Hall and garnering rave reviews, most of them, understandably enough, focusing upon Kelly. In a representative review, *Time* magazine announced,

> *On the Town* brings airy imagination and solid showmanship to the kind of movie that needs it most: the musical . . . by combining a fluid cinematic approach and slick Broadway professionalism, Co-Directors Gene Kelly and Stanley Donen have turned out a film so exuberant that it threatens at moments to bounce right off the screen.

After the December 30, 1949, release of *On the Town,* Sinatra continued to work on radio with the series *Light Up Time* and *Meet Frank Sinatra,* but now in trouble with two major film studios and ever restless, Sinatra shifted his focus to the new medium of television. Households across America were now buying sets by the tens of thousands, and the move to television was a logical one, but there was just one problem: Sinatra and series television were a bad match right from the start.

Sinatra's first television series, *The Frank Sinatra Show,* ran on CBS, from October 1950 through April 1952. Frank simply never appeared fully at ease on his own television series, his edgy, impatient personality conveying a pent-up energy on the verge of exploding, more than a warm easygoing presence one wanted to invite into a living room every week. He may have signed a five-year contract for $250,000 a year, but the series never really settled into its groove—neither the star nor the show ever relaxed. Unlike in his feature film appearances, Sinatra sometimes graced the small screen without his toupee, but while the one-hour episodes (some of which actually clocked in at forty-five minutes) found the star in fine voice, he was not an inviting figure like Perry Como or, decades later, Dean Martin. Sinatra would go on to score brilliantly with television specials such as 1965's *A Man and His Music,* programs where he could conceptualize sequences and use the medium as an extended nightclub session. On a weekly basis, however, he was incapable of supplying the comfort food America wanted in the post–World War II era. The cold war was gathering force, and the somewhat-justified audience perception that Frank was making clever "inside" remarks and leaving the audience out of the joke did not endear him to the viewing public. Indeed, the very nature of television itself worked against Sinatra's intimate performing style on the weekly shows. There is a distance between the performer and the

viewer at home in his or her living room, and as Wilfrid Sheed smartly as-
sessed the situation, "A TV set cannot whisper 'I love you' the way a radio
can. With the box, one is aware of technicians in between."

Occasionally there were flashes of genuine wit—witness one fascinating
and amusing bit of comic byplay on the February 3, 1951, telecast. Then in
the midst of his torrid affair with Ava Gardner but not yet divorced from wife
Nancy, Sinatra is asked by guest June Hutton (Axel Stordahl's wife) exactly
who would be receiving his valentine that year. Knowing that both the studio
and television audiences were very much aware of the affair with Gardner,
Frank momentarily pauses and, with a grin on his face, wisecracks, "Bulova,
of course." It's a funny plug for his sponsor, one made more memorable in
Sinatra's follow-up to the audience: "Fooled you!" Such good-natured bits of
humor were somewhat few and far between, however, and in a harsh but
rather accurate critique of the series as a whole, *The New York Times* sniffed
that "Sinatra walked off the TV high end but unfortunately fell in the shallow
end of the pool."

Sinatra did not fit the small screen—it couldn't contain him—and coupled with the lackluster box office returns of the two feature films released
during his tenure on television (*Double Dynamite* on Christmas Day 1951
and *Meet Danny Wilson* a scant one month later), Sinatra's career was sliding
precipitously. Frank had not yet hit upon the new vocal style he would subsequently forge at Capitol Records, and with his bobby-soxer fans growing
older and marrying, his records sales fell dramatically. Coupled with a personal life plastered all over the tabloids, this downward spiral was only has-
tened by the release of the very unfortunate *Double Dynamite.*

"Unfortunate" is actually a mild word for *Double Dynamite,* because in
the first quarter of Frank Sinatra's film career, stretching from *Higher and
Higher* through *Meet Danny Wilson* (1951), *Double Dynamite* is the worst
film of all, worse even than *The Kissing Bandit.* It stands as a singular waste of
the talents of all involved, and the finished product offers proof of why the release of the film was delayed for nearly three years. The delay occurred at the
behest of RKO boss Howard Hughes, who surely not only recognized an awful film when he saw it, but also did not like Sinatra, since Hughes himself
maintained an ongoing interest in Ava Gardner.

Double Dynamite (the title seeming to be a rather obvious reference to
Jane Russell's well-publicized chest) was filmed at RKO in 1948, before *On*

the Town even began production. It's a film that could stand as exhibit A in charting the differences between RKO and MGM. It is cheap-looking, flatly photographed by the usually reliable Robert De Grasse, and directed in uninspired fashion by Irving Cummings (his last film as director), who had fared noticeably better before World War II with films at Fox starring Betty Grable and Shirley Temple.

The screenplay, such as it is, finds Frank cast as Johnny Dalton, a milquetoast bank teller with California Fidelity Bank. Johnny wants to marry fellow teller Mildred "Mibs" Goodhue (Jane Russell), but when his request for a raise is turned down, the conservative Johnny doesn't see how they can marry on his salary of $42.50 per week. Breaking up a back alley mugging, Johnny saves gambler Hot Horse Harris (Nestor Paiva), who insists on showing his gratitude by giving Johnny one thousand dollars, which the mobster then parlays into sixty thousand dollars. This winning streak occurs the same day that a shortage is discovered at the bank, and the predictable complications ensue. Eventually it is established that the bank shortage was caused by a faulty adding machine. Yep, that's the solution after eighty minutes of this gibberish. Johnny is cleared of stealing, and he and Mibs are free to marry.

Given that's all there is to the puny little story, the lingering question remains, Is there any fun to be had along the way? The answer is very little. Three songs by Jule Styne and Sammy Cahn are shoehorned in, but none prove to be of particular note. The first such number finds Johnny and favorite waiter Emile (Groucho Marx) so happy at Johnny's unexpected winnings that they sing "It's Only Money" (the original title of the film) as they nearly jog down the cheesy-looking studio set, complete with noticeably phony street footage projected behind them. Frank is here trying to keep pace with Groucho Marx's trademark loping walk, and he looks all the worse for the effort. In fact, Frank looks far worse here than in any other film he had made up to that point, appearing wan, older than his years, and completely worn out.

Aside from the rather sweet song "Kisses and Tears" in which Russell displays a nice voice, which would surface later both on film for *Gentlemen Prefer Blondes,* and on Broadway in the groundbreaking Stephen Sondheim musical *Company,* there's no fun to be had.

It is more than a stretch—indeed, nearly impossible—to accept the thirty-three-year-old Sinatra as a timid bank clerk who objects to gambling by whining, "I don't want any part of that." The persona of the naïve young man no longer works, a result of overexposure and Sinatra's age (not to mention the inevitable knowledge of his tempestuous behavior offscreen). Johnny's timidity, his defining characteristic, is a nonstarter. Frank Sinatra appears so dispirited by the action that when he tells the disbelieving Mibs that he didn't rob the bank, stating incredulously, "Do you think I'm a thief?!" he says so with absolutely no conviction, no passion, and, most damning of all, no interest whatsoever in her answer. For her part, Mibs's character is presented as being so naïve that she believes Emile's nonsensical talk that Johnny stole from the bank in order to marry her; this isn't naïveté on her part—it's stupidity. The utterly lackluster proceedings are even further hindered by unfortunate period dialogue along the way; when Emile states "I've got an open mind on this," Johnny replies, "That's white of you"—a line so startling in its offensive nature that it's surprising the then-outspoken-liberal Sinatra didn't object to it. Dialogue and acting alike are deserving of a big Bronx cheer.

The film ends with a car chase between Johnny, Mibs, and the police, leading to the only witty dialogue in the entire film. Says the police dispatcher in describing the "outlaws": "He wears elevator shoes, is anemic-looking, sporting an ill-fitting suit, and looks like Frank Sinatra." "She is five-seven, weight 135 pounds, which is [pause] *extremely* well distributed." Yes, it's an obvious joke, but after the paucity of humor in the previous 95 percent of the film, even a faint smile is a relief. All complications happily resolved (Johnny and Mibs will now, unbelievably, buy a ranch and grow oranges), the film ends with Frank, Jane, and Groucho singing a reprise of "It's Only Money." For Sinatra, it wasn't only money—it was the sight and sound of his film career slipping down the drain in the aftermath of a pallid, supposed farce, a third-rate farewell to his time at RKO. The film debuted to small audiences and poor notices, and justifiably so. It's an awful movie, and combined with a personal life now in a state of free fall, Frank Sinatra was in deep trouble.

That deep trouble soon turned into a bottomless pit, because for the first—and only—time in his professional life, Frank Sinatra now ignored his career. He had met Ava Gardner. The result was an affair and subsequent marriage so passionate, wild, mesmerizing, and self-destructive that it threatened to derail his entire career. The white picket fences on the MGM back lot would never be the same again. And neither would Frank Sinatra.

Ava and the Downfall

"All or Nothing at All," sung by Frank Sinatra
on the soundtrack
of *A Thousand and One Nights*

His voice and his woman, Ava Gardner, had quit him, in the early fifties, and sud-denly he was broke and he had no career. He would come to characterize this period with one sentence: "It was all Mondays."

—BILL ZEHME IN *THE WAY YOU WEAR YOUR HAT*

There isn't a building high enough for me to jump off of. —FRANK SINATRA

W HAT EXACTLY DOES one make of a relationship in which the couple's first date found them drinking and driving in the Palm Springs desert, shooting out streetlights and getting hauled into jail before the MGM publicist could be summoned to bail them out? Definitely not your standard first date, definitely not Andy Hardy time—and yet the romance only heated up from there. Frank and Ava may have first met in rather casual fashion when she was still married to Mickey Rooney, but the actual love affair took hold during early 1949, when Sinatra was thirty-four and Ava twenty-seven. In Ava's own words: "The blue eyes were inquisitive, the smile still bright and audacious, the whole face even friendly and more ex-pressive than I remembered. Oh, God, Frank Sinatra could be the sweetest most charming man in the world when he was in the mood."

Frank and Ava's liaison actually made a great deal of sense in many ways.

Both Frank and Ava were raised by silent fathers and go-getter mothers, both were uneasy about their lack of education, they shared highly passionate, hotheaded sexual natures, and most notably of all, each reacted suspiciously and resentfully when faced with authority in any form. Susceptible to loneliness and insomnia, and possessed of hair-trigger tempers, for all their genuine need for privacy, both Frank and Ava were also prone to the grand gesture, especially when drinking to excess. These were two highly strung artists who liked to suffer out loud, and usually at top volume. Just consider a fifteen-round doozy of a fight in Palm Springs, with Lana Turner, Ben Cole, and Ava's sister Bappie all bearing witness. It was a fight that escalated so rapidly and violently that neighbors called the cops, who, upon arrival, had to restrain Sinatra from trying to bodily throw his wife out of the house while she resisted by desperately grabbing on to the door. *Father Knows Best* it wasn't. Frank and Ava loved each other deeply, but they forged a relationship that seemed to vacillate between outright lust and unbridled anger. It was a match made in paradise and hell at the same time.

It's not just that fifty years later their romance has become the stuff of legend—the two passionate stars, each pathologically jealous, unable to live with or without the other. It's that even in the wild early days of their love affair, there was, Ava herself felt, "always an edge, a margin of unhappiness." After one tumultuous fight in 1950 while staying at New York's Hampshire House, Frank called Ava, announced "I've got nothing to live for anyway," and shot a gun as he said, "So long, baby, it's been fun." Ava rushed to his bedroom in the suite they were sharing, saw the smoke, and feared the worst—only to see him turn over with the gun and greet her with a casual hello. He had shot the gun into the pillow to make Ava come running after him. This is obsession—and acting of the highest order—and more than a little scary. Even if Mitch Miller, with whom Sinatra had a famously contentious relationship, labels the tale of an Ava-obsessed Frank rushing out of the recording studio in March 1951 after singing "I'm a Fool to Want You" "a bullshit story," it's still no wonder Frank sang that very song so brilliantly. In the terms of the song—he was. So was she. Said Nelson Riddle, "Ava taught him how to sing a torch song. She taught him the hard way."

The romance didn't just raise mere headlines back in 1949 and 1950; it quickly became legendary even while it was still unfolding. Indeed, so incendiary and voluminous was the press coverage of the Sinatra–Gardner liaison that the most fascinating anecdote about Sinatra's friendship with mobster Willie Moretti lies in the fact that Moretti saw fit to offer Sinatra marital advice at the time of his growing infatuation with Ava Gardner: "I am very much surprised what I have been reading in the newspapers between you and your darling wife. Remember you have a decent wife and children. You should be very happy. Regards to all." When mobsters are offering marital advice, it's safe to say that something out of the ordinary is happening with the romance in question. In any event, Moretti's telegram had no impact; as Betty Garrett sang to Frank in *Take Me Out to the Ball Game,* "It's fate, baby, it's fate." Suffice it to say, Sinatra seemed to make a better father than husband.

Sinatra and Ava were larger-than-life figures, capable of a passion to which most people only aspired or simply read about. Like characters in an opera, they had a relationship that existed entirely in capital letters, because both Frank and Ava were hyperbolic personalities. It's why they became a source of endless fascination, and why even they themselves thought about the relationship in larger-than-life terms. Witness Ava's words in her autobiography about the night they first made love: "Oh God, it was magic. We became lovers eternally."

Well, eternally turned out to be more like two years, because they separated one year after their marriage, remaining separated for four years until their divorce in 1957. Their passion and love never fully died, and they remained lifelong friends, sometime lovers, and ongoing antagonists. In a particularly revealing and heartfelt gesture, when Gardner experienced a few financial difficulties toward the end of her life, Sinatra paid fifty thousand dollars toward her medical expenses.

The pair's situation was made even more difficult owing to the fact that Frank was still married (even if separated), and as a result, both Frank and Ava were widely—and loudly—attacked in the press for carrying on an extramarital affair. In those less permissive times, the general public, particularly Roman Catholics, were outraged. Sinatra's evident devotion to his children, as well as his already numerous charitable fund-raisers, helped to mitigate the damage, but damage it was. Add in the public humiliation of "good wife" Nancy, Ava's sensual free-thinking public persona, and Sinatra's enemies in the right-wing press, and it all proved to be a recipe for disaster.

Ava Gardner did not present a warm and cuddly image to a public captivated by the affair. She was more than capable of giving as good as she got, matching Sinatra not only drink for drink, but with her equally possessive nature, temper tantrum for temper tantrum as well. As Ava herself related, "Unfortunately, we never had any trouble inventing other reasons to be at each other's throats." Ava was a first for Frank—a woman who was as unpredictable and quick to explode as Frank himself, and that's precisely why his infatuation grew into obsession; Ava did what she felt like doing, when she felt like doing it. She wouldn't kowtow to anyone, not even to Sinatra. Sinatra could never fully possess her, which meant that Ava could never be boring, and it was "boring" that registered as the biggest sin of all in Frank's personal and professional lives. Nancy Barbato Sinatra didn't bore Frank, but the domesticity of the marriage did. Frank's lifelong restlessness seemed fueled by the fight against the boredom of the ever-constricting familiar, the near horror of the routine. Frank Sinatra did not equate home and hearth with peace and comfort so much as an absence of the new, domesticity equaling a wan and colorless permanence. Permanent and domestic, Ava was not. She'd fly to Europe on a moment's whim and didn't care what anyone, Frank included, thought. The fights raged, the reconciliations found both professing eternal love, and all would be calm until Ava imagined Frank smiling at an attractive woman a little too warmly. Then—oaths were hurled, objects were thrown, and all hell broke loose. As Skitch Henderson, Sinatra's sometime bandleader, observed decades later, "it is a kind of legendary romance now, but I have to say the reality was even stronger."

If Gardner and Sinatra overwhelmed thirty feet high on the silver screen, their passion measured even higher. It couldn't last, of course, because in the words of the pop hit "Something's Gotta Give," "When an irresistible force such as you, meets an old immovable object like me . . . something's gotta give." And in their case, nothing did. Nothing ever would. As a result, there would be drunken brawls, a suicide attempt by Sinatra in the fall of 1951, and all the heaving passion that was not just the stuff of pop songs, but worthy of a grand opera composed by Verdi. How extreme were the emotions? Consider Ava's own words as she tells the story of a raging battle she and Frank had on a boat in Lake Tahoe shortly after their marriage. With both parties downing champagne in gulps, screams and threats ensued, at which point, Sinatra factotum Hank Sanicola, piloting the boat, ran it aground and, in the process, tore a hole in the hull. Ava's response? To stay on board as the boat sank. Sinatra's appeal to his new bride? " 'Get off that fucking boat while there's still time, you fucking fool,' he roared, shaking his fist in exasperation. . . . 'Go fuck yourself,' I replied, always the lady." Oh.

Indeed, Sinatra's third wife, Mia Farrow, came to write of Sinatra's unending passion for Gardner with uneasy and poignant words: "He looked so pained when he talked about her that it was a relief when he changed the subject." When Sinatra married Mia Farrow in 1966, he had his valet George Jacobs call Ava to tell her of the impending marriage before she read about it in the papers. It's a gesture entirely emblematic of Sinatra, both in his thinking of Ava's feelings and in his having valet George make the call rather than making it himself. As first wife Nancy pointed out, in his personal life, Sinatra always wanted to take the path of least resistance.

The fights with Ava, the subsequent divorce—it all lay in the future. For now, Frank was desperate to officially end his first marriage, but Nancy was holding on, convinced that her husband would see the error of his ways and return home. Finally, however, the last straw came with Frank's January 1950 Houston nightclub appearance, at which Ava showed up ringside. Sinatra ended up in a tussle with a photographer, and the resulting press coverage landed the lovebirds in newspapers all across America. It was all too much— as a properly brought up Italian girl, Nancy Barbato Sinatra did not appreciate her private life becoming a public spectacle; the locks were changed on the house and divorce papers were filed, ironically and perhaps intentionally, on Valentine's Day. Frank Sinatra now officially moved into Ava's house.

Obsessively involved with Ava, Sinatra ignored his career; years later, expounding on that time of turmoil, he said,

> I did it. I'm my own worst enemy. My singing went downhill and I went downhill with it, or vice versa—but nobody hit me in the throat or choked me with my necktie. It happened because I paid no attention to how I was singing. Instead, I wanted to sit back and enjoy my success and sign autographs and bank the heavy cash. Well, let me tell you, nobody who's successful sits back and enjoys it. I found that out the hard way.

The Frank Sinatra of 1950 faced a future with no record company, no agent, no movie studio contract, and a back-tax bill of nearly a hundred thousand dollars. The worst was yet to come, however, when he lost his voice

while attempting to sing "It All Depends on You" during a show at the Co-
pacabana on the night of April 26 (other reports peg the song, ironically, as
"Bali Ha'i"). In that one moment, Sinatra very likely thought his entire recording career, and possibly even his film career, might be over. At that point,
Frank's identity as an actor was still inextricably bound with his singing, and
now he couldn't sing a single note. Like so much in his life, it's tailor-made
for a moody noir film: a smoky club, 2:30 A.M., bourbon being poured on the
rocks, the camera moving in for a close-up of Frank—and then—nothing.
Dead silence except for the clink of ice cubes and the whir of the follow
spot. In Frank's own words: "I was never so panic stricken in my whole
life . . . about seventy people in the place—stunning, absolute silence. I
looked at them, and they looked at me. . . . Finally I whispered at the audience, 'Good night' and walked off the floor."

An interesting alternative view was provided by Frank's conductor for the
occasion, Skitch Henderson, who subsequently reported that the incident
"wasn't as tumultuous as it has been made out . . . I felt it was in part a manufactured trauma because of his mental state at the time." Whatever the va-
lidity of Henderson's assertion, Sinatra losing his voice just at the time his
career was already on the downswing made for a practical disaster. How
could the heavily in debt singer ever make money? In time, of course, the incident added layer upon layer to the Sinatra legend, and overlaid a near-
mythic show business archetype onto the Sinatra screen persona: the rise,
fall, and rise of Frank Sinatra.

For now, however, Sinatra's vocal cords had hemorrhaged, and while under
orders not to speak for a week, he flew to Spain, where Ava was making a movie,
and promptly embroiled himself in a raging argument with her about her affair
with a matador. It was such a difficult time in Sinatra's life that even while attempting to discuss it some years later, on his *Person to Person* CBS television
interview with Edward R. Murrow, he could only refer to it as a "dark period I
went through around 1951." It took fifteen years before Sinatra was able to
speak about that period with perspective—and even black humor—alluding to
it on the 1965 recording "A Man and His Music" as the time when "my voice
ran away from home and my records started selling like used Edsels."

Realizing that Sinatra was incapable of leaving Gardner, Nancy granted
him a divorce, which was finalized on November 1, 1951. The marriage had
degenerated into a battle about money and the terms of the settlement were

November 7, 1951: wedding day with Ava Gardner. Said Nelson Riddle: "Ava taught him how to sing a torch song."

steep: Nancy received a third of Frank's annual gross income up to $150,000 and 10 percent of all income above that sum. After twelve years of marriage, Sinatra was desperate for his freedom and the ability to marry Ava, and so acceded to the terms. Any guilt he felt wasn't over the divorce per se, but rather over the effect it would have on his three children. Divorce granted, six days later Ava and Frank were married in Pennsylvania, at the home of Manie Sacks's brother Lester, with Axel Stordahl serving as best man. In a particularly ironic touch, Sinatra arranger Dick Jones attempted to play "The Wedding March," but the living room piano was out of tune. Then again, so were Sinatra's finances. So dire was Frank's money situation that Ava had to pay for the honeymoon.

It's not that Sinatra had no career. He was still a name, but a tarnished one. One of the few jobs he landed at that time was a guest spot on a May 1950 Bob Hope television special, a job that formed Sinatra's lifelong gratitude toward Bob Hope and helps explain why he agreed to a silly cameo in Hope's last "Road" picture, 1962's *The Road to Hong Kong*. In fact, in his 1956

Person to Person interview with Edward R. Murrow, Sinatra himself pointed to the Hope special as the start of his comeback, an appearance that afforded him the chance to act in comic sketches as well as sock over "Come Rain or Come Shine" twelve years before his famous recording on the *Sinatra and Strings* LP. But one guest shot on a television special could not sustain Sinatra's long-term prospects. He needed a change, and fast. It came in 1953, with the history-making comeback in *From Here to Eternity,* but first came a fascinating role in Universal's *Meet Danny Wilson.*

Meet Danny Wilson represented Sinatra's first film under a newly signed three-year nonexclusive contract with Universal-International. It may be an up-and-down affair as a film, but it is leagues beyond the tired *Double Dynamite,* and brings several interesting changes to the Sinatra screen persona. Frank Sinatra was about to grow up on film—and fast.

What makes *Meet Danny Wilson* so interesting to view fifty-plus years after release are two factors: (1) for the first time, the "real" and "reel" Frank Sinatras intersect, and (2) the film represents the first comprehensive and decisive proof that Frank Sinatra had the makings of a dramatic actor. As such, it's an important precursor of what Sinatra was capable of onscreen, capabilities that were to be fully expressed in *From Here to Eternity.* With hindsight, it is easy to mark *Meet Danny Wilson* as the end of the first stage of Sinatra's feature film career, the second stage beginning nineteen months later, with the release of *Eternity.* At the time, however, *Meet Danny Wilson* registered as nothing so much as the Frank Sinatra story on film, albeit with a few minor changes.

Directed by Joseph Pevney, *Meet Danny Wilson* casts Sinatra as Danny, a down-on-his-luck singer complete with a chip on his shoulder and talent to burn. Sound familiar? In fact, the film, with story and screenplay by Don McGuire (costar of *Double Dynamite* and a Sinatra pal here doubling as associate producer) opens with Danny shoving a customer in a nightclub, starting a fight, and getting kicked out of the club. A peeved Danny growls, "I'm tired of being pushed around," to which best friend and piano player Mike (Alex Nicol) retorts, "Stop crowding people and you won't be." For the first time on film, here is the Frank Sinatra familiar to audiences from tabloid reports of his run-ins with the press. Sinatra looks haggard (so does the film itself), thinner than ever, but with an edge that is miles away from the rubes he played in *Anchors Aweigh* and *Higher and Higher.* Danny Wilson looks like he has been around the block a few too many times, just like Frank Sinatra himself.

Love interest Joy Carroll is introduced in the person of then Universal contract player Shelley Winters, and when Joy, Danny, and Mike become drunk, the men hit a police officer and end up in jail. It's not quite clear which is more unrealistic, Shelley's unconvincing drunk routine or the fact that while in jail, the boys end up in a cell next to musician Joey Thompson (Danny Welton), who plays harmonica while Frank sings "Lonesome Man Blues." And what do the other inmates do when Danny sings? Enthusiastically applaud, the way they always do in jail.

Hoodlum Nick Driscoll (a menacing and sepulchre-voiced Raymond Burr), who has more than a passing interest in Joy, springs Joy and the boys from jail. Driscoll auditions Danny for his club, where Joy is the vocalist, and hires him instantly. Anyone with half a brain would have, because Sinatra's audition song is absolutely terrific; launching into "She's Funny That Way," Danny Wilson not only displays a terrific, instantly memorable voice, but also exhibits a macho sex appeal that silences all the club workers, from cleaning lady to waiters. The very skinny Frank Sinatra is here singing with such intensity that his stardom nearly flies off the screen. It's Sinatra in full cry, and a welcome sight. In this meeting of Sinatra the man, Sinatra the actor, and Sinatra the singer, one can finally glimpse the extraordinary artist who was about to emerge. As his Capitol Records producer Dave Cavanaugh aptly commented, "Sinatra was like a lightning rod, particularly when he was in good voice. It discharged the hostile electricity." His singing enhanced by a fully fleshed-out screenplay, Frank Sinatra, film actor and movie star, was ready to spring forth in all his dark complexity.

There's just one problem when Driscoll hires Danny: He demands 50 percent of Danny's earnings, terms that the eager-to-get-ahead Danny forces his manager Mike to accept. It's Frank and Tommy Dorsey time all over again, and Driscoll is out for his pound of flesh, making that more than clear to Danny: "I don't worry—I have friends." Danny's reaction? A mocking gesture of holding his ear and smashing in his nose in order to indicate mob connections. Rumors may have abounded offscreen about Sinatra's supposed mob ties, but clearly Frank felt no compunction about playing with that image onscreen.

Danny is, of course, a smash hit on opening night, singing "That Old Black Magic." What else could he be with Sinatra singing "Old Black Magic" to a terrific arrangement (Joseph Gershenson) underpinned by a haunting solo oboe. Sinatra is here singing with real power, and for a movie audience, the line between actor and role has blurred. Are we watching Frank Sinatra in concert, or is that Danny Wilson onstage? "Old Black Magic" is a particularly interesting number in the film because both visually and vocally it's an all-in-one sampling of both the youthful balladeer and the older punchier swinger, the crooner from the Columbia Records years pointing the way to the fully mature vocalist who arrived on the scene at Capitol Records in 1953. Following "Old Black Magic" with "When You're Smiling," Sinatra's free-swinging arm gestures and confident legs-akimbo stance, present the first on-screen manifestation of the post-*Eternity,* Rat Pack, larger-than-life persona. He is confidence personified.

Which definitely cannot be said for leading lady Shelley Winters. She is here downright awkward, completely unconvincing in scenes requiring tenderness, and registering only when she plays tough; warning Driscoll to keep his distance, she snarls, "Don't get tough with me. I've two sharp nails and a flock of clippings . . . I don't need you." It's actually one of the few times in the film one believes Winters, because as a self-described "small-town girl with big-city notions," she fares better with a wisecrack than as the nice girl who can't return Danny's love. Winters's reported on-set disagreements with Sinatra show in their remarkable lack of chemistry, both actors delivering their performances with little regard for the other.

There are frequent references to Frank Sinatra in Danny's own self-description. Jiggling his shoulders he deadpans, "I'm not tough—just a little nervous." Sinatra really was all coiled energy, always on the prowl, and as a result, so much unceasing motion makes sense for the character of Danny. Danny is on his way to stardom, and a crisp montage of headlines from *Billboard, Newsweek, Colliers,* and *Life* details his rise to the top, culminating with his "in person" appearance at the Paramount Theater. It's all a duplication of Sinatra's own rise, right down to the police officer grousing about the screaming teenage female fans: "All this trouble for a freak with a frog in his throat."

In an interesting reflection of Sinatra's own oft-reported largesse—the insistence on picking up the check, the lavish gifts for friends and acquaintances—Danny is here presented as someone who thinks buying things is a sign of affection. For Danny and Sinatra alike, such gift-giving is a manifestation of power. (At one point in the film, Danny refers to himself as "the King.") There are even shots of Danny and Joy ringside at the fights, à la Frank and Ava Gardner. With all these levels of Sinatra's own life presented onscreen, why, then, doesn't the film register more strongly?

Well, for starters, Winters's performance remains an enormous impediment. Just as the love triangle between Danny, Joy, and Mike should be peaking, all interest deflates because of Winters's unconvincing acting. There isn't a shred of honest emotion in her flat delivery, a fact attributable to her being utterly miscast in the role, as well as her antipathy toward Sinatra. (Richard Havers, in his book *Sinatra,* describes the mutual dislike between Sinatra and Winters as so extreme that "on one notable take, Shelley got so cross that she punched Frank in the face.") Winters could be an effective actress, as she proved in the same year's *A Place in the Sun,* but she is completely at sea here. When, at Mike's behest, she surprises Danny at a studio party, a vision in white, she appears to be less a supposed bombshell who is also a talented pianist and pop singer, and more just a tough Brooklyn broad.

Making use of the fact that Sinatra himself was gaining a reputation for on-set impatience and a temperamental refusal to reshoot scenes, Danny Wilson is a rising movie star who is late and petulant on the set. Tempers flare even further when Danny discovers Joy and Mike locked in an embrace, and he turns on both friends, ordering them out. It's an effective display of dark behavior, at

Meet Danny Wilson (1952): a dark "reel" version of the "real" Frank Sinatra.

once self-pitying, bitter, and self-deluded, and one not previously seen from Frank Sinatra onscreen. After drunkenly disrupting a charity benefit, Danny ends up in a bar, head down, smoking a cigarette with a half-empty bottle beside him; Danny presents the audience with a Frank Sinatra they think they know, but he is a three-dimensional, fleshed-out human being, and when a bar patron puts on Danny's recording of "When You're Smiling," Sinatra's silent reaction of disgust with himself registers as a true harbinger of the acting heights he would subsequently scale.

Finally deciding to take matters into his own hands, Danny tells Joy that he is going to meet Driscoll himself at an empty ball field and, once and for all, settle their dispute: "Where am I going, Joy? I'm going to grow up." In a curious motif that occurred with regularity in Sinatra's early films, Danny has heretofore proved utterly ineffectual when involved in a fight. Truck drivers and Driscoll alike have laughed at the scrawny Danny's pathetic attempts to fight. Indeed, Sinatra's early films consistently present him as a wannabe "tough guy" who can't hurt anyone. In the lighter films, this was often presented with an easy joke about Sinatra's skinny physique. In the darker films, one begins to wonder if it's a not-so-veiled reference to Sinatra's offscreen reliance on an entourage of bodyguards who took care of business for Frank. Needless to say, after *From Here to Eternity,* this ineffectual milquetoast was rarely seen again, replaced by the tough leader of *Von Ryan's Express* or the hardened policeman of *The Detective.*

All of a sudden, Danny turns into a true tough guy, taking on Driscoll's henchman before shooting Driscoll himself. Quick as a flash, Mike and Joy marry, they travel with Danny to London, Danny sings "How Deep Is the Ocean?" the newlyweds embrace, and the movie ends. A film that has unrolled at an even tempo has wrapped things up in a decided hurry. Gunfights, marriage, transatlantic voyage, and singing—that's a lot of plot in five short minutes.

The film's parallels with Sinatra's own life became even stronger upon release, when Sinatra appeared in person at the Paramount Theater in New York City to hype the film. This time there were no sell-out crowds and no screaming fans, the film opening to very little interest on the part of the public. As *The New York Times* noted in its review of Sinatra's return to the Paramount: "But the sighs and screeches that greeted the crooner heretofore were somewhat subdued yesterday morning. . . . Perhaps it is the beginning of the end of an era. . . ." It was left to *The World Telegram and Sun* newspaper to most devastatingly sum up the turn in Sinatra's fortunes: "Gone on Frankie in '42; Gone in '52."

The film's mixed critical reception certainly did not help matters at the Paramount or anywhere else, with *Time* magazine harping on the overwhelming parallels to Sinatra himself: "Apart from romantic and melodramatic trimmings that it borrows elsewhere, the story cribs so freely from the career and personality of Frank Sinatra that fans may expect Ava Gardner to pop up in the last reel." However, in a review that pointed the way to better roles in the future, *Variety's* Brog wrote, "[The] title role is tailor-made for Sinatra and he plays it to the hilt with an off-hand charm . . . as for Sinatra, the actor, for the first time on the screen he seems completely at ease, and sure of himself and what he is doing."

The occasional positive review notwithstanding, the fact remained that Sinatra had just made his first film since *On the Town* two years earlier, and no one seemed to care. The film quickly disappeared from theaters, and Universal decided not to exercise its option for further Sinatra movies. Fired from MGM. Let go by Universal. His personal life in free fall. Frank Sinatra was nowhere at all, and had nowhere to go, which was the biggest sin of all in Hollywood. Actually, he had exactly one place to go—up. Which he did. Over and over again, for the next forty years, and to the surprise of every last person in Hollywood except Frank Sinatra himself.

The Comeback

"All the Way," sung by Frank Sinatra
in *The Joker Is Wild*

Don't despair. You have to scrape bottom to appreciate life and start living again.
—FRANK SINATRA

I showed those mothers . . . I was never finished!—FRANK SINATRA

FRANK SINATRA'S VERY NEXT FILM, *From Here to Eternity*, did more than merely boost him back up on top of the heap. With *Eternity*, Sinatra really hit the Hollywood trifecta: widespread acclaim, an Academy Award (as Best Supporting Actor), and a further cementing of the Sinatra legend. Frank had already transcended mere celebrity through the combination of superb singing, Hollywood motion pictures, offscreen brawls, and dalliances. With *From Here to Eternity*, he became a legend, not so much for the acting, acclaimed though it was, as for the comeback. Sinatra's resurgence from the depths of professional and personal despair to the heights of Oscar night became everybody's triumph, the comeback everyone who felt they were underappreciated desired. The groundwork for "My Way" had been laid.

According to Sinatra's own recounting, he became obsessed with playing the role of Angelo Maggio as soon as he finished reading James Jones's bestselling novel *From Here to Eternity*. (The title is taken from the Rudyard Kipling poem "Gentlemen Rankers," referring to British soldiers "out on the spree damned from here to eternity.") For its time, *Eternity* was a startling look at the peacetime army in Hawaii right before Pearl Harbor, a warts-and-all portrait that featured brutality, prostitution, less-than-noble commanding officers, and a doomed sad-sack private named Angelo Maggio: "For the first time in my life, I was reading something I really had to do. I just felt it—I just knew I could do it. I just couldn't get it out of my head." The part resonated with Sinatra because he not only knew men like Maggio while growing up in Hoboken—he saw *himself* in the character: "More than a book it was a portrait of people I knew, understood and could feel, and in it I saw myself as clearly as I see myself every morning when I shave. I was Maggio." Here was a chance to put Italian-American life onscreen in some complexity, a character who symbolized all the downtrodden "little guys" who never caught a break. Maggio was Sinatra's first unabashedly Italian-American character onscreen, and in the proud emphasis of his roots in this role, Sinatra really did pave the way for Al Pacino's, Robert De Niro's, and John Travolta's ascents to stardom some twenty years later. Times changed throughout the ensuing decades, but it was Frank Sinatra who led the way.

In hindsight, costar Burt Lancaster summed up the matter nicely with his perceptive comment that the performance worked so well because it contained so much of Sinatra himself:

> His fervor, his anger, his bitterness had something to do with the character of Maggio, but also with what he had gone through in the last number of years—a sense of defeat and the whole world crashing in on him, his marriage to Ava going to pieces—all of those things caused this ferment in him, and they all came out in that performance.

Lancaster saw firsthand how accurately Frank captured the essence of Maggio, but in 1953, Sinatra himself seemed to be the only one who felt he was right for the role. He had absolutely no reputation as a dramatic actor, and throughout Hollywood was viewed as a song-and-dance man, nothing more.

No one's first choice to play Maggio, Sinatra won the role only through a tenacious display of grit and determination. What he most assuredly did not do was win the role by means of the mob intimidating Columbia studio head Harry Cohn. That myth, which sprang into life with the publication of Mario

Puzo's novel *The Godfather,* evolved into accepted fact with Francis Ford Coppola's 1972 film version of the book. In both versions, a Sinatra-like singer and actor, Johnny Fontaine, covets a movie role, only to be turned down by the studio chief until the mob pays the mogul a little visit; when the mob's housecall results in the bloody, severed head of his beloved prize horse appearing on his bed, the studio chief grants Fontaine the part. Perhaps it was the larger-than-life image of the horse's head onscreen, or perhaps it was those eager to believe in Sinatra's mob connections—whatever the reason, even though throughout the years, production sources ranging from screenwriter Dan Taradash to director Fred Zinnemann have gone on record to state that such rumors were utterly false, the rumors persist to this day, so strong are both the Sinatra persona and the power of the *Godfather* film. (According to novelist Puzo, "The horse's head in the producer's bed was totally my imagination." As for Sinatra himself, when asked if he was "the *Godfather* singer," he tersely replied "No way.")

Sinatra, like Tony Bennett and Dean Martin, knew mobsters by virtue of the fact that the mob ran nearly all the top nightclubs in the 1940s and 1950s, but in Sinatra's case, it was as if he were proved guilty by association, the much-discussed photograph with Joe Fischetti in Havana raising its head yet again. Claiming that Sinatra won the *Eternity* role through mob connections ignores the pertinent question, Where was the mob in 1951 and 1952, when his career was at its all-time ebb? Surely the mob would not have waited for two years before stepping in to help Frank. Moreover, such a tale does the double disservice of dismissing Sinatra's talent—as if he could land a role only with mob help—and leads to the question of how the mob could make the storied career of Frank Sinatra yet seemingly not do the same for any other big-name entertainer in the twentieth century. If the mob really were that interested in Hollywood, it would have made stars out of many entertainers, all of them less talented than Sinatra. In the end, not surprisingly, there isn't even *one* other entertainment figure to whom commentators can point as having benefited from the mob on their way to superstardom.

The reality of how Sinatra won the role of Maggio is every bit as good a story as *The Godfather*'s version, because, like everything else of note in Sinatra's life at that time, it involved Ava Gardner. In his headlong pursuit of the role, Sinatra had taken to bombarding director Zinnemann and Columbia studio chief Harry Cohn with telegrams signed "Maggio," but it was Ava, a far bigger movie star than Sinatra at this time, who first broached the idea of Frank's casting to Cohn. Smartly floating the idea first through Cohn's wife, Joan, who proved more amenable to the proposal than Cohn himself, Ava in effect helped load the dice. According to Sinatra biographer and entertainment columnist Earl Wilson, Cohn's initial response to the idea of the seemingly washed-up song-and-dance man taking on the key dramatic role of Maggio was, "You must be out of your fuckin' mind. This is an actor's part, not a crooner's." (In Sinatra's version of the story, told to journalist Norton Mockridge in 1955, he relayed Cohn's words as, "Look Frank, that's an actor's part. You're a hoofer.")

In an anecdote that speaks volumes about Gardner's loyalty, passion, and nobody's fool persona, she proceeded to directly lobby Cohn in behalf of her husband. True to her lights, Ava did not sugarcoat her plea, studio head or not. Looking Cohn right in the eye, she bluntly informed him, "You know who's right for that part of Maggio, don't you? That sonofabitch of a husband of mine." So desperate was Sinatra for the role that he flew to Hollywood from Africa (with no work on tap, he was simply hanging around on set while Ava made *Mogambo* for director John Ford), filmed a ten-minute test, and then flew back to Africa to await word. Grueling as such a trip would be today, it was a true ordeal in 1952. Adding insult to injury, the cost of the flight came out of Sinatra's own pocket—or rather out of Ava's pocket. Broke at the time due to the huge back-tax bill he had run up, Frank charged the flight to Ava, as she later found out.

Complicating Frank's personal life even further, Ava had an abortion in November 1952, reasoning, in her own words, that the "sane, solid lifestyle" necessary for the raising of children would never be possible with Frank. Gardner underwent her abortion in England without consulting Sinatra, a situation made even worse by her getting a second abortion early in 1953. Some, including Sinatra himself, have disputed the story of a second abortion told by Ava in her autobiography, but others have confirmed her account. What confuses the matter even further is the suggestion by some that Sinatra was not the father of the child, who they claimed had been fathered by another member of the *Mogambo* cast or crew. With such tumultuous circumstances roiling the waters, it is no wonder that Sinatra suffered extreme emotional distress. In Ava's telling, the abortion left Sinatra "next to the bed with tears in his eyes."

It was in such emotionally trying circumstances that Sinatra awaited the verdict on his screen test. It had been a good one, with Frank filming two scenes for director Zinnemann, including an improvised bar scene (featuring the rolling of olives as gambling dice) that eventually found its way into the finished film. Still, Eli Wallach remained first choice for the role even as Sinatra, convinced that it took one scrappy little Italian to play another, continued inundating Zinnemann and producer Buddy Adler with the telegrams signed "Maggio." (It probably didn't hurt that Sinatra and Zinnemann had the same agent.) Finally, when Wallach refused to sign a standard seven-year studio contract and chose Tennessee Williams's *Camino Real* on Broadway over *From Here to Eternity,* Cohn called Sinatra in February 1953 to tell him that the role of Maggio was his. Sinatra's willingness to take the part for a paltry thousand dollars per week for the eight weeks of shooting cinched the deal (given this skimpy pay, no wonder Sinatra thenceforth insisted on a percentage of the gross when he regained his clout in Hollywood), but it was the right casting decision all the way around. Sinatra not only fit the role perfectly in ethnic terms, but his own physique—the skinny frame complete with nearly concave chest—ensured that audience sympathy would be Maggio's from the start.

Amidst all the justifiable hoopla over *Eternity*'s all-star cast, it is often forgotten that one of the key figures in the film's success was producer Buddy Adler. Adler proved invaluable for the simple reason that as a former member of the Signal Corps, he possessed military contacts that proved crucial in obtaining army approval of the film. In the early 1950s, *Eternity*'s largely negative portrayal of the army could have caused numerous problems for the filmmakers, the film's rather unflinching portrayal of army life being most unusual for that time. The advent of Senator Joe McCarthy's anti-Communist fervor had produced a pervasive fear of appearing "unpatriotic," and the U.S. Navy had, in fact, banned the film as "derogatory to a sister service." Adler's work in smoothing the way with military brass helped enormously during a long and difficult shoot, but even he could not win all the battles that cropped up. When, late in the film, Prewitt tries to sneak Maggio back to the base, Maggio drunkenly fights two military policemen, his skinny frame unequal to the task. Years after the film's release, however, Director Zinnemann related that the original plan called for Maggio to physically attack the policemen; so strong was the need of army approval fifty-plus years ago that Zinnemann had to bow to the army mandate that a seated Sinatra deliver only a verbal assault on the MPs. It's an unfortunate deletion that diminishes the impact of a pivotal scene.

Eternity's fully rounded portrait of the military was immeasurably aided by the understanding direction of four-time Oscar winner Fred Zinnemann. While the Austrian-born Zinnemann might at first have appeared an odd choice for that quintessentially American film, he had, in fact, already directed two solid films dealing with military life, *The Search* with Montgomery Clift, and *The Men* (Marlon Brando's film debut), as well as such memorable pieces of Americana as *High Noon* and *Member of the Wedding.* It was Sinatra, in his characterization of the scrappy Maggio, who most benefited from the fact that as the two previous military films made clear, Zinnemann inherently understood James Jones's underlying theme in *Eternity,* the battle to retain individuality in the face of an oftentimes cold and brutal military system.

In addition to Zinnemann's fine work, much credit for the film's success is owed to screenwriter Daniel Taradash, who effectively synthesizes the personal dramas of Jones's sprawling epic while at the same time casting them in bold relief against the looming backdrop of the Second World War. (Taradash's achievement becomes even clearer when contrasted with the unwieldy and diffuse screenplay by John Patrick and Arthur Sheekman for the five-years-later film adaptation of Jones's similarly epic-length novel *Some Came Running.*) In *Eternity,* Captain Dana Holmes (Philip Ober), the base commander, is desperate for a promotion, pulling strings to land bugler Robert E. Lee Prewitt (Montgomery Clift) in his company simply because Prewitt's prowess as a boxer will help win the regimental boxing matches, thereby ensuring Holmes's promotion. Holmes is stuck in a loveless marriage with nymphomaniacal wife Karen (Deborah Kerr), both spouses cheating repeatedly on the other. Rounding out the mix of leading characters is the scrappy, slight Private Angelo Maggio, a happy-go-lucky, not-terribly-bright recruit who leads with his fists and thinks afterwards.

It is the affair between Sergeant Milton Warden (Burt Lancaster) and Karen Holmes around which all the various plot strands coalesce, and Lancaster and Kerr, like all the actors involved, turn in first-rate performances throughout. Kerr and Lancaster make the mutual attraction absolutely clear from their first charged encounter, an attraction most famously on display in their clandestine meeting on the beach. Surf pouring over them as they lustily embrace in the sand, Kerr and Lancaster here enact one of the most iconic moments in screen history. Their surfside embrace, daring for its day, has been viewed, reviewed, and parodied so often that it is almost impossible to respond to it without a certain distance, yet it still carries a sizable erotic charge. Lancaster and Kerr make a good team here, her natural reserve ton-ing down his flashing teeth and bounding physicality, just as his passion helps to melt her coolness.

The second famous romance in the film, that between Prewitt and Con-gress Club hostess Lorene (Donna Reed), is nicely conveyed by both Clift and Reed, but what's most interesting about Prewitt's character is that he in effect carries on a second romance, one with Maggio. It is not a romance of hidden homosexual desire, but rather one between kindred spirits, one outsider be-friending another as they try to retain their sense of individuality in the midst of a military force that insists upon regimentation. Prewitt, still carrying the emotional scars from having caused a friend's blindness in a previous boxing match, not only refuses to box for the commander, but also has shut down emotionally. It is only when he and Maggio, drunk and feeling no pain, tumble into the Congress Club in their loud Hawaiian shirts that Prewitt comes alive, falling instantly in love with Lorene.

Clift, all hunched inward tension, convincingly portrays the noble yet tor-mented Prewitt, and it's also clear that the camaraderie Prewitt and Maggio display onscreen was helped by the close relationship that Clift and Sinatra forged offscreen. Drinking buddies they may have been, each tormented in his own way, but more important, it was Clift who helped coach Sinatra in his acting, the highly trained Method actor working through nuance and subtext with Sinatra, adding layers to a performance levels beyond any Frank had previously given. Said Sinatra in later years: "The way he pitched I couldn't help shining as a catcher."

You can see the lessons Sinatra absorbed from Clift in his very physicality; from this film forward, Sinatra often adopted trademark Clift mannerisms of hunched shoulders, clenched fists, and a wounded look of vulnerability. Sina-tra was here learning from the best, and it resulted in a fully fleshed-out char-acterization and a first-rate dramatic performance. Such detailed physical tics helped define the scrappy Maggio, and by the time of *Pal Joey,* four years later, Sinatra had developed a full arsenal of such small telling gestures: a raised eyebrow that could alternately convey skepticism or loneliness; a finger scratching the side of his nose to convey a studied display of casualness—they all helped Sinatra present recognizable human beings onscreen, compelling but flawed men far subtler than the one-note (if enjoyable) naïfs found in his early musicals.

*Consulting with costar Montgomery Clift and director Fred Zinnemann
on* From Here to Eternity *(1953).*

The influence of Clift on Sinatra the actor cannot be overstated. Such was his admiration for Clift that Sinatra not only rehearsed, but he also did it willingly. Sinatra explained,

> As a singer . . . I rehearse and plan exactly where I'm going. But as an actor, no, I can't do that. To me, acting is reacting. If you set it up right, you can almost go without knowing every line. . . . If I rehearse to death, I lose the spontaneity I think works for me. . . . With Montgomery, though, I had to be patient because I knew that if I watched this guy, I'd learn something. We had a mutual admiration thing going there.

Just as choreographer Bob Fosse utilized his own hunched shoulders and knocked knees in fashioning a trademark choreographic style, Sinatra here took on Clift's hunched posture, allowing it to emphasize his own vulnerable, frail physique. It's a physical approach that aided Sinatra immensely in conveying Maggio's "doomed gaiety." Maggio may have been a supporting role, but it made Frank Sinatra a top-drawer movie star. By blending small parts of Cagney's toughness with Bogart's jaded but vulnerable wiseguy, and overlaying the mix with his own distinctly Italian-American physicality—a lovable underdog with a chip on his shoulder—Sinatra arrived at an entirely original screen persona.

In his autobiography, director Fred Zinnemann discussed the interesting difficulty of blending Sinatra's acting with Clift's. Sinatra, in Zinnemann's view, was clearly best on his first or second take, losing spontaneity thereafter. Conversely, Clift layered in more detail on each successive take, his performance gaining in richness accordingly. Commented Zinnemann in a humorous aside: "With due respect it reminded me of the situation in one of my earliest films, *Eyes in the Night,* where a blind detective needed eight takes before he could remember his lines; his bored guide dog would run away and hide after the first take."

Director Zinnemann smartly emphasizes Sinatra's slight build to deepen the characterization—Maggio looks lost inside both his army uniform and the garish Hawaiian shirts he favors off base. He is not a physical match for any man, let alone the brutish Sergeant Fatso Judson (Ernest Borgnine) who has called him a wop. Sinatra here creates a surefire audience pleaser of a character: the put-upon common man, an essentially likeable everyday Joe who is his own worst enemy. In the continuing evolution of Frank Sinatra's screen persona, it's interesting to note how Frank's characterization of Maggio builds upon the characters he portrayed in his earliest films: Maggio is, for all his bravado, nearly as naïve and vulnerable as those earlier characters, a slight and appealing fellow who's out of his depth. Waiting on tables in the company mess, he's like an eager-to-please puppy, yet with enough of an edge to stand up to Fatso.

No wonder Sinatra felt desperate to play Maggio—the character is ingratiating, complex, a bit dim-witted, vulnerable, and ultimately doomed. It was a role that had Oscar written all over it.

Concurrent with Maggio's downfall, Prewitt and Sergeant Warden bond over their respective broken romances during a rather striking nighttime scene of drunken camaraderie. They have developed a healthy respect for each other—Prewitt for Warden's willingness to protect his men, Warden for Prewitt's unbreakable will and sense of self. No matter how many holes Prewitt has to pointlessly dig and refill, he still won't box. What's most noteworthy about this nighttime display of friendship, however, especially considering the repressed sexual atmosphere in 1953, is the scene's erotic subtext, with Warden putting his arm around the drunken, murmuring Prewitt and gently stroking his hair. It's a surprising scene that layers in an additional level of character development, the unexpectedly tender mood broken only by the stumbling arrival of Maggio. Bleeding, staggering, and barely able to hold himself up, Maggio has escaped from the stockade. Finally confessing that Fatso has brutalized him, and worried about what will happen if Prewitt himself ever falls under Fatso's control, Maggio whispers, "If they put you in the hole . . . just lay there, just lay there and be quiet Prew," and after an infinitesimal pause, he dies. It's a remarkably effective death scene from Sinatra, all the more affecting because it is underplayed.

This is all very far indeed from the world of *Step Lively* and *Higher and Higher,* and while Sinatra does appear to be too old for the role, it ultimately doesn't matter. He delivers the essence of Maggio in spades. (In an interesting side note, Burt Lancaster related that it was extremely cold outside at the time Maggio's death scene was filmed, with the actors being given brandy to warm up. As a result, Clift became drunk, barely able to stumble through the scene. In the end, his inebriated state may have added to Prewitt's tenderness toward Maggio. The only missing element is the scene's poignant original final line, which found Prewitt cautioning the soldiers who are placing the dead Maggio in the trunk: "See his head don't bump." It's a wonderfully evocative line, a pained tribute from one buddy to another. It has been reported that Clift was unable to say the line properly despite numerous takes, but according to Zinnemann, the moment was cut because of Cohn's decree that the film could not run even a fraction over two hours. Whatever the reason, it's a significant loss, a minuscule detail that spoke volumes.)

After Maggio's death, the finality of which is conveyed nicely through a shot of his bed, stripped bare of any trace of the man, the pace of the film accelerates noticeably. It's as if Maggio's death has turned the key: Fatso is knifed by Prewitt as revenge for Maggio's death, Prewitt is injured in their fight, and Holmes is told to resign for his cruelty in forcing Prewitt to box. As those personal dramas disintegrate into nothingness, Sunday church bells ring. It is December 7, 1941, and at 7:40 A.M. Japanese planes tear in on a bombing spree, American soldiers scattering like ants on the grounds. The army's somnolent state is broken at last. It's a different army, a different world, and not so coincidentally, a different movie. (The stock footage of the bombing is noticeably and jarringly different from Zinnemann's.)

Prewitt is killed trying to sneak back onto the base by soldiers who mistake him for the enemy. His fate and Clift's complex performance form a distorted mirror image of Sinatra's death scene as Maggio: Maggio is beaten to death trying to get out of the army, while Prewitt is shot while trying to get back in.

It's a remarkably bleak denouement to the film, with none of the characters achieving their dreams: Holmes is drummed out of the service; Maggio, Prewitt, and Fatso all have been killed, and none of them by the supposed "enemy." Instead, they have all found death at the hands of their fellow soldiers.

Eternity premiered in August of 1953 to overwhelmingly positive reviews. Both the film and supporting actor Sinatra received tumultuous praise, the *Los Angeles Herald Examiner* calling his performance "simply superb, comical, pitiful, childlishly brave, pathetically defiant." Mainstream publications lavished praise on Sinatra in a manner particularly gratifying to a man bent on proving himself a serious actor. In the simplest summation of all, *The New Yorker* pronounced, "As you can see, *From Here to Eternity* has a fairly yeasty content, and in the way of other gratifications, it reveals that Frank Sinatra, in the part of Mr. Clift's friend who winds up in the stockade, is a first-rate actor." Perhaps what meant most to Sinatra was the praise of director Zinnemann:

Maggio's death scene in Eternity.

"He was very, very good—all the time. No histrionics, no bad behavior . . . He played Maggio so spontaneously we almost never had to reshoot a scene."

The drumbeat for Sinatra's Best Supporting Actor Oscar began immediately upon the film's release. It wasn't just that he had delivered his best performance to date, in what proved to be the Oscar-winning Best Picture of the Year. It was that he had staged a triumphant comeback, and while Americans may love a Cinderella story, they love a juicy comeback even more. When Sinatra, in his Academy Award acceptance speech, said he was "deeply thrilled and very moved and I really don't know what to say. I'm terribly pleased," he wasn't acting. He was thrilled to be back on top, where he—and now a great many others—felt he belonged.

The success of *From Here to Eternity* ensured that Sinatra was taken much more seriously as an artist in every aspect of his career. A new contract for representation was negotiated with the William Morris Agency, and Capitol Records, at the insistence of Alan Livingston, signed Frank to a new recording contract. It was signed four months before the release of *Eternity,* but so low was the state of Sinatra's career that the contract was of a year's duration only, with options for another six years. Most incredibly of all, Sinatra had to bear the cost of the initial sessions himself. It was, however, those initial dates in 1953 that led to the first of the staggering 318 recordings made with arranger Nelson Riddle, the architect of the more mature driving sound that signified the full expression of Sinatra the recording artist. One listen to the ultimate Sinatra/Riddle collaboration from those initial sessions—"I've Got You under My Skin," all wailing brass and crisp full-bodied vocal attack—and one knows that Frank Sinatra was feeling his power. The arrangements are fuller, Sinatra is belting, and there's a swagger to his insistent delivery. Being the actor that he was, Sinatra could fully access the "I've Got the World on a String" emotions contained in the songs, and make them land with listeners right across the board. Gone are the flowing vocal lines, and in are the brass laden arrangements that so perfectly fit his slightly rougher voice. Even the titles of the albums, the insistently upbeat *Swing Easy!* and *A Swingin' Affair!* speak of a Sinatra back on top. Or, even more precisely, back in control.

This time of renewed recording success and extended concert dates in Vegas fed upon Frank's revived success in film, contributing to the public's growing perception of Sinatra as power personified: he was now the king of the hill, always at the center of the action, surrounded by a gang of hangers-on

Frank and Donna Reed with their Oscars for Eternity, *March 25, 1954.*

all eager to do his bidding. The public wanted in on the action as well, wanted to be included with Frank and his pals, but woe to those who thought they could belong without having earned the right. . . .

The Capitol releases introduced the idea of concept albums, entire albums organized around either Technicolor themes of elation (*A Swingin' Affair!*) or black-and-white urban angst (*In the Wee Small Hours*). Those albums were Sinatra's very own aural feature films, full-fledged productions with a meticulously laid-out flow of mood, conflict, and resolution, which he had first learned from Tommy Dorsey's carefully controlled playlists: "Above all, though, Tommy taught me discipline, self-discipline, total dedication to every detail of every musical effort. . . . I respect every record I make as if it's the last song I'll ever sing."

In control of his recording career, and now numbered among the major Hollywood players, Sinatra had, at virtually the same time, created major-league second careers as both film actor and recording artist, second acts richer and fuller in his maturity as both man and artist. With his switch from lightweight musicals to serious dramas onscreen, and the concurrent change in his recording career from the sweet billowing sounds of strings and flute with Axel Stordahl on Columbia Records to the heavier driving sound of

Nelson Riddle and Billy May on Capitol Records, Sinatra had pulled off a double comeback. Like the United States at the time, Frank was peaking, certain of his own right course of action, convinced the best was yet to come. In the years ahead, that state of affairs proved both beneficial and deleterious, but now, for star and country alike, the roll was just beginning.

The comeback was another early version of Sinatra doing things his way, yet doing them in a manner that resonated with everyone. The public knew that Sinatra had lived through exceedingly difficult times, both professionally and personally, not only surviving, but actually emerging in triumph. As Pete Hamill perceptively pointed out, even on the classic torch albums such as *Only the Lonely,* there was regret, but there was no self-pity. It wasn't just women who now anchored the Sinatra camp; men saw their own struggles mirrored in Sinatra. Frank had survived all the hard knocks life had dished out—including the self-inflicted wounds—and, the reasoning of the public now seemed to run, so could they.

The terrific performances in *From Here to Eternity* and the forthcoming *Suddenly* and *The Man with the Golden Arm* found their parallels on disc with the brilliantly boozy *Only the Lonely* and *Where Are You?* Sinatra was now singing about lost love and the bruises acquired in a hard-knock life with the authority of a master. In the star's own words, "I think I get an audience involved personally in a song because I'm involved. I can't help myself. I feel the loss (in the song) myself and I cry out the loneliness, the hurt and the pain." Note the words "I can't help myself." Sinatra couldn't help himself—it was as if singing a song or performing on film fed him, keeping the energy level up and the demons at bay. Like any true artist, he turned the personal into the universal. Audiences were fascinated by the dichotomy in Frank, both on-screen and on record. How, they wondered, could a man expose his vulnerability so beautifully as Maggio or on *In the Wee Small Hours*, exhibiting great tenderness in the process, yet at the same time engage in verbal and physical brawls with press and public alike? Well, as Gene di Novi so trenchantly observed, "Italians tend to break down into two kinds of people—Lucky Luciano or Michelangelo. Frank is an exception—he's both."

Sinatra's professional life was on the rebound big-time, but the tumult with Ava continued, reaching a nadir on November 18, 1953, when, alone in Jimmy Van Heusen's apartment in New York City, he cut his left wrist with a knife, saved only by Van Heusen's arrival at the apartment in time to have

Frank rushed to Mount Sinai. (Daughter Nancy has written of a previous suicide attempt in the summer of 1952, when the fights with Ava proved so painful that Frank inhaled gas from the kitchen stove in Manie Sacks's apartment.) The public was told that the hospitalization in November 1953 was due to nervous exhaustion and that he had endured a "domestic accident with a broken glass." Frank recovered—never again would his despair manifest itself in such fashion.

Daughter Tina, who writes about her father with great perspicacity, explained, decades later, "Dad's days with Ava were numbered. . . . To reinvent himself and revive his career, my father had to focus on his work. He couldn't do that and hold on to Ava, too. The stronger he got, the less responsible she felt for him." It's a particularly perceptive comment because it points up a recurring theme in the career of Sinatra, a quality he shares with his only female counterpart, Barbra Streisand. In any relationship involving either superstar, there was a triangle: Frank (or Barbra), love interest, career. Even in the throes of great passion, these two superstars who simply had to perform in order to express their feelings of loneliness and otherness, never lost sight of the work. It's as if by singing, all the complicated dramas and demons could be resolved—at least for those two hours. It's why they achieved so much in such brilliant fashion, why they could never stop, and why they exhausted themselves and those around them in the process.

Oscar in hand and brimming with confidence, Frank Sinatra proceeded to throw himself headfirst into his acting career, filming six major roles in 1954–55 alone. What made the level of activity even more impressive was the sheer variety of the parts he played in those six films: presidential assassin in *Suddenly,* pianist/composer in *Young at Heart,* doctor in *Not as a Stranger,* theatrical agent in *The Tender Trap,* lovable singing gangster in *Guys and Dolls,* and down-in-the-depths drug addict in *The Man with the Golden Arm.* It was a nearly unprecedented display of versatility in Hollywood annals; no other male movie star, not even Bing Crosby or James Cagney, has ever scored so convincingly and so consistently in such a short space of time while running the gamut in genres ranging from musical comedy to searing drama. This was sheer talent asserting itself all over the joint, and in this case, the joint was movie screens around the world.

As his all-important feature film follow-up to *Eternity,* Sinatra made a surprising choice: the black-and-white B movie *Suddenly,* an October 1954

United Artists release directed by Lewis Allen. First up, however, was the February 28, 1954, live NBC telecast of the classic Cole Porter musical comedy *Anything Goes,* costarring Bert Lahr and, recreating her original role from Broadway, Ethel Merman. Actually, costar is not exactly correct when it comes to Merman, because no one costars with Ethel. She's in a world of her own, barreling full-steam-ahead regardless of what her fellow actors are doing, leading Frank, amused expression on his face, to all but say "Well, I'll just stand back and watch Ethel do her thing—I'll chime in when I have a line." (Sinatra is similarly amused by the outrageous mugging antics of Lahr, grinning in disbelief as Lahr piles take upon take.) The end result is a nutty hour that provides pleasures of a decidedly unusual nature.

Adapted for television by Herbert Baker from the Broadway musical's original book by Guy Bolton and P. G. Wodehouse, this version of *Anything Goes* races breathlessly from song to song, the actors throwing out one or two lines of dialogue before launching into the next song. Ten songs, a shipboard romance, gangsters, mistaken identity, and a happy ending—all this in one hour including commercials. And that one hour even includes the opening of the show, where Merman appears as herself and introduces Frank and Bert before getting down to work.

Reappearing moments after the introductions, in a fur-trimmed gown and making her entrance perched on top of a luggage cart, Ethel yells out a line or two and then proceeds to belt out the title song. Eyes popping, her clarion voice loud enough to power the NBC generator all by itself, Merman is in a universe of her own making. There are some surprising aspects to Merman on film—who remembers that she had terrific legs?—but it's immediately apparent why she never became a film or television star; she was simply incapable of toning down her vocal or dramatic approach for the all-seeing camera. Charging her way through the title tune, her elbows fly in every direction and her body language underscores every word in the clever Porter lyrics. The trouble is, she's emphasizing every last syllable for a second balcony that doesn't exist in television. Merman was truly great onstage—the distance engendered by the proscenium arch helped the audience surrender to her. On film, all bets were off.

Merman is here playing nightclub singer and evangelist Reno Sweeney (there's no point in asking how she can be both), sailing to England in order to marry rich Sir Evelyn Oakleigh, even though her true love is one Harry

Dane, in the person of Frank Sinatra. Frank appears on the scene, begins to sing a tender "You Do Something to Me" directly to Merman, at which point Ethel does what Ethel Merman does best—she bellows the song in counterpoint right back at him. One can almost see the instant where Frank stops trying to act and just rolls along in Ethel's wake—of course, Ethel's turning of her head at the moment Sinatra's Harry is supposed to kiss her couldn't have helped matters much. It's not that Merman can't act at all; it's that she's rather purposefully unaware of the other actors, rarely if ever looking them in the eye, instead focusing solely on what she's supposed to say and do. The other actors are given nothing to play with or against as Merman plays directly to the audience—in this case, the camera itself.

Instead, while the audience tries to figure out exactly what is going on— and it's pretty damn hard to do so, given the extremely truncated nature of the presentation—one can enjoy the terrific Porter songs, some interpolated from other Porter shows, and all of them nicely orchestrated by Buddy Bregman and Nelson Riddle: "I Get a Kick Out of You," "Just One of Those Things" (from *Jubilee*), "All Through the Night," and "Blow, Gabriel, Blow" are all delivered in first-rate manner by Merman and Sinatra. Ethel even reprises her "Friendship" duet with Bert Lahr (from the fifteen-years-earlier show *Du Barry Was a Lady*) and survives Lahr (playing a gangster posing as a preacher) trying to break her up. The Merm doesn't flinch at Lahr's high jinks for a minute—one gets the feeling that a hurricane wouldn't stop her from hitting her marks, keeping time with her feet, and shoving a song at the audience. Ethel knows she's got business to tend to—like dueting with Frank on "You're the Top." By now, Frank has been reduced to playing straight man for Merman as he runs around the ship disguised as both a woman and a sailor, amusing himself with interpolated lyrics as he sings "You're the top— you're Crosby's salary" rather than the original "Garbo's salary."

Sinatra has exactly one moment when he is able to establish a flesh-and-blood character; thrown in the ship's jail, he sings "All Through the Night" in terrific voice, framed through the bars of the cell by director Fred Hamilton in one of the few moments Hamilton is not simply directing traffic. Finally allowed to catch its breath, the audience relaxes right along with Frank. It's a particularly welcome moment, coming as it does after Merman has let loose with the rafter-rattling "Blow, Gabriel, Blow"; ordering the "sinners" in that song to "clap your hands," Merman bawls out the guilty parties with such force that one expects her to belt them all if they don't comply. Problems all sorted out, the show ends with the audience exhausted, and Frank and Ethel about to embark on a highly unbelievable marriage. The cast takes a bow, Merman fills up the remaining time in the hour by yelling out another encore of the title tune, and bingo, show's over. Frank seems more wryly tolerant of Ethel's steamroller style than upset, probably figuring, *Hey—it's national television and Cole Porter. Fine with me if Ethel wants to run the show. I'm out of here and on to other shows.*

In fact, "on to other shows" would be putting it mildly, given the unceasing level of activity Sinatra was about to undertake in Hollywood. Frank now had no fewer than five feature films, most of them glossy multimillion-dollar extravaganzas, lined up back to back, but first up was the gritty, fascinating *Suddenly.* It was a film that marked the beginning of Sinatra's association with United Artists, a working relationship that would result in nine movies. *Suddenly* may look like a small film that was made as filler for a double bill, but it just so happened to star the then-hottest property in show business, and not so incidentally, turned out to be a terrific little film. The script attracted Sinatra because he found the depiction of a cold-blooded killer trying to assassinate the president for money to be "a challenge. I have never seen on the screen any character as consistently brutal as this man is." Coming hard on the heels of *From Here to Eternity, Suddenly*'s unremittingly dark aura wreaked havoc with Sinatra's wished-for career track of following a drama with a comedy (and then a musical), but fortunately Sinatra let the material, rather than a preordained plan, dictate the schedule.

The resulting film was tight and engrossing, and the exact opposite of *Eternity* in certain ways. It's small, not sprawling, registering as nearly stagebound in its use of one location, and Sinatra essays a completely unsympathetic character, rather than a crowd pleaser like Maggio. One thing, however, remained the same: It's a compelling film and features a terrific performance by Sinatra. Upon the film's release, *Newsweek* wrote a rave review, with special kudos reserved for Frank: "As simple and startling as a good scream . . . Sinatra becomes one of the most repellent killers in American screen history." More to the point, it marked the start of Sinatra's dramatic career on film as a leading man; there was no Burt Lancaster or Montgomery Clift in sight now. This was the Frank Sinatra show, pure and simple, a feature film that turned into a one-man showcase as soon as he appeared onscreen.

Suddenly does not constitute film noir per se; the setting is not the mean streets of the urban world, none of the action takes place at night, and the lighting does not particularly define the space, frame, or characters themselves. At the same time, however, it does share some characteristics of the film noir genre that flourished in the postwar years. The characters are alienated, trapped in a world where the old cultural certainties have vanished. The supposedly friendly and secure small town of Suddenly is invaded by a hired assassin. The heroine has lost her husband to the violence of war and is so unsure of herself and her place in this new world that she babies her young son as a means of protecting him. What the film also shares in common with the smaller noir pictures is an extremely lean running time (seventy-seven minutes) and a concern with money as the rotting obsession at the core of the story.

True to its B movie origins, *Suddenly* bolts out of the gate immediately. Richard Sale's script, which appears to have been inspired by President Eisenhower's train trips to Palm Springs, California, immediately establishes that Sheriff Tod Shaw (Sterling Hayden) is in love with Ellen Benson (Nancy Gates), mother of a young boy rather oddly named Pidge (Kim Charney). Ellen, still grieving for her husband killed in the war, considers his death to have been a horrific waste of life. Ellen and Pidge live with her father-in-law, Pete "Pop" Benson (James Gleason), a former Secret Service bodyguard for President Calvin Coolidge. Unlike daughter-in-law Ellen, Benson wears his patriotism front and center and condones certain types of violence: "Guns aren't necessarily bad. Depends on who uses them." Everything in this small somnolent town is about to change, however, because the president's train is passing through and the president will detrain in order to get into a car. The President of the United States is coming to town—and so is would-be presidential assassin John Baron (Sinatra).

Introducing himself as an FBI special agent, Baron ingratiates himself into the Benson household in a low-key fashion, telling the three occupants that he is making sure that their house on the hill is perfectly safe, because of rumors of an assassin wanting to fire on the president. Just one problem—Baron himself is the assassin, and within minutes of his arrival, he and his two henchmen Benny (Paul Frees) and Bart (Christopher Dark) have revealed their true colors. When Carney, a real FBI agent, shows up at the house, Baron kills the agent, wounds the sheriff, and casually mentions that he will "cut the throat"

of young Pidge if cooperation does not ensue. This Johnny Baron is one psycho killer, intending to take out the president himself with nary a second
thought. He's in it only for the money, and in his own words: "I have no idea
who's behind the assassination. I don't know and don't want to know." When
an incredulous Pops appeals to Johnny's patriotism—"But you're an American
citizen"—Johnny's cynical answer is, "At one minute after five, I'll be a very
rich American citizen."

Never once does Sinatra ask for audience sympathy. Bragging about his
record in World War II, taking credit for a Silver Star and the killing of
dozens of Germans, his eyes grow brighter, his manner ever more intense.
Johnny is on the verge of becoming unhinged, and to Sinatra's credit, one actually believes in this character, who easily could have slipped into caricature.
The slight figure is one unpleasant loser, and a man who casually, and with
great pleasure, utilizes the power derived from his gun. (He's also a man who
keeps his hat on indoors for nearly the entire brief running time—perhaps
because of Sinatra's sensitivity about his increasingly bald pate.) He may be
dwarfed by the physically imposing Sterling Hayden, but the slight Johnny, in
the figure of the alarmingly thin Sinatra, is one tough customer. He straight-
ens Sheriff Tod's fracture with his bare hands, actually enjoying the pain he is
causing, belts Pidge to the floor when the boy accuses him of stealing the Silver Star, and casually states that he would easily kill any of the Bensons—he
just doesn't like not being paid for it.

With his sinewy, tightly wound body, Sinatra's physicality reveals a man on
the edge; as M. A. Schmidt, the Hollywood correspondent for *The New York
Times,* reported after watching Sinatra during filming, "He tenses . . . but the
tension is caused by concentration, not by uncertainty. . . . When the action
was over, his whole body seemed to melt into relaxation." Like any first-class
actor, Sinatra conveys volumes of information through a subtle movement of
his eyes, precisely delineating his character's combination of psychosis and
overweening confidence. The smallest physical movements all speak to that
same psychosis, the sudden sharp hand gestures suggesting the barely suppressed violence of a seriously disturbed character.

The public's perception of Sinatra himself as a man of seemingly great
charm who could become enraged at a moment's notice helped to reinforce
the reaction to his acting herein; on a larger scale, Baron's barely suppressed
hysteria neatly dovetails with the neurotic 1950s underpinnings of the film

Playing a psycho killer in the first-rate thriller Suddenly *(1954).*

and the age of anxiety mid-'50s audiences were living through. In the wake of the atom bomb, nothing could be taken for granted, a jittery state of affairs which had led to the rise of film noir. *Suddenly* may not constitute film noir, but it's every bit as metaphorically dark as the classic noir films. Small-town California has been invaded by presidential assassins, and nothing's safe.

There is a tight claustrophobic look and feel to the film, which enhances its rather ruthless efficiency. Both the direction by Lewis Allen and the effective cinematography by Charles G. Clarke make this a grim black-and-white town that cannot escape the increasingly violent present. In 1954, when *Suddenly* was filmed, the threat of Communism was in the air and the Korean War had ended just one year previously: a sense of violence suffuses the film on every level. Whether it is an attempted assassination, pacifists resorting to the use of guns, or violence invading the safe sanctuary of home, there is no escaping the danger. Johnny's clipped dialogue refers to the lingering after-effects of the war: "I learned to kill in the war. Only I can do the job because

I have no feelings. . . . Feelings are a weakness that make you think of something besides yourself." It's as if Sinatra's Johnny is a Nazi transported to American citizenhood: "When you have a gun, you are a sort of god. . . . The first time I got my hands on a gun, I was a somebody."

Aside from a few obligatory shots of the town of Suddenly, and one gunfight between Johnny's henchman and the police, all of the film takes place within the confines of the Benson home. It's an oppressive atmosphere, which helps reinforce the feeling of being trapped—those living in Suddenly are captives, as is Johnny himself. In classic B movie fashion, backstory is sketched in with just a few declarative sentences: Baron speaks of his alcoholic father and unmarried mother—ergo the audience is supposed to believe that such crazy men are "raised that way." Johnny's psycho credits having been firmly established, the final forty-five minutes of the film unfold in real time, as lingering shots of the clock approaching 5 P.M. reinforce the president's impending doom. Having bolted a rifle to the table in order to shoot the president as soon as he leaves the train, Johnny spits out his chilling command to his accomplices: "Let's go to work." (Quentin Tarantino deliberately pays homage to those words before the robbery sequence in *Reservoir Dogs.*)

At the film's climax, Johnny's accomplice Bart is electrocuted after the Bensons ground the faultily wired television set; locked to his rifle, he cannot stop firing bullets before the president's 5 P.M. arrival. The train barrels through town right on schedule but doesn't stop. Face contorted by disappointment, Johnny wheels around from the rifle, screaming his frustration. He is shot first by the no-longer-pacifist Ellen and then by Sheriff Tod.

The ensuing image of Johnny lying dead on the floor is just one more eerie parallel to the nine-years-later shooting of President John F. Kennedy by Lee Harvey Oswald. Not only are the rifles employed in the shootings similar, but Johnny himself is killed, just as Jack Ruby killed Kennedy assassin Lee Harvey Oswald. In fact, according to Sinatra chronicler Daniel O'Brien,

Around 1970, Sinatra discovered that alleged solo Kennedy assassin Lee Harvey Oswald had watched the film just a few days before the Dallas slaying on 22 November 1963. Still shocked by the episode and slowly turning more politically conservative, Sinatra felt that such

inflammatory material should not be in the public domain and with-
drew *Suddenly* from circulation.

As a result, there were no further network television showings, and this
ban was not lifted until the late 1980s.

The assassin has been killed, but Ellen seems every bit as unsettled as she
was at film's start. Even if by necessity, she has now embraced the culture of
violence by shooting Johnny. There seems to be no escape from the blood-
shed that has been passed through three generations. With Johnny dead, the
plot's loose ends are tied up in world-record time, but in rather strange fashion at that. Consider the film's fade-out: a presidential assassination has been
foiled, Nancy has turned into a gun-slinging moll, there's a dead psycho on
the living room floor, and she has just one key question—

NANCY GATES: "Can I pick you up for church?"
SHERIFF TOD: "That'd be swell."

Fade-out.

To which the viewer can only respond, *Huh?* After all the catastrophic
events that have occurred, this is how it ends? It's a weirdly upbeat bit of dialogue with which to conclude a paranoid little thriller, but true to its roots,
the lingering shots of Suddenly at film's end make the town look as un-
friendly, depressed, and cold as ever.

The town of Suddenly may have looked depressed and cold, but Frank
Sinatra's film career was anything but. He had delivered a terrific performance, building on the dramatic chops displayed in *Eternity,* and further
erased any lingering thoughts of his being a mere song-and-dance man. He
may never again have played such an unrelievedly unpleasant character, the
unpleasantness being a key reason for the film's failure at the box office, but
he delivered the goods in spades. The ingratiating but ultimately lightweight
screen personality of *Higher and Higher,* one from whom such a complex
performance seemed impossible, had been completely exorcised. A true dramatic actor had emerged—Frank Sinatra was the real deal. *Cue* magazine
found that "*Suddenly* provides an excellent and welcome opportunity for
song-and-dance man Frank Sinatra to prove again that the dramatic talent
he suggested in *Meet Danny Wilson,* and which came to richer fruition in

From Here to Eternity is a solid and potentially richer talent than many suspected." It's a review to which the only possible response is, *No kidding.* One wonders what the heck took the critics so long to tumble. Was it the inferior vehicles? The inability of the critics to separate the overwhelming public persona from the actual onscreen work? Maybe it was a little of both, but whatever the reasons, all such doubts had now been eliminated.

In the space of one year, 1954, Frank Sinatra had won an Academy Award for a dramatic tour de force; delivered a sensational follow-up performance in *Suddenly;* been voted singer of the year by *Metronome* and top male singer by *Billboard;* hosted two radio series, *To Be Perfectly Frank* and *The Frank Sinatra Show;* etched the number-one single in the country with "Young at Heart"; propelled the Oscar-winning Styne/Cahn song "Three Coins in a Fountain" into the top ten of the charts; and placed two albums, *Songs for Young Lovers* and *Swing Easy,* into the top ten. Sinatra never stopped working, multitasking away, decades before the term was first invented. What was so fascinating about this mid-1950s period was twofold: first, that critical and popular success were joined hand in hand, a rare occurrence in any performer's life, and second, the fact that even more than wanting to work this often, Frank Sinatra *had* to work so insistently. Whether one worshipped Sinatra or loathed him, one couldn't ignore him. Barely forty years old, the star-turned-icon had become a show business legend.

The one-two punch of *Eternity* and *Suddenly* made it clear, in a way nothing else ever had, how much Sinatra's singing and acting reinforced each other. If Sinatra always thought of himself first as a singer, his much deeper approach to singing now reflected his onscreen dramatic abilities. In the masterly Capitol albums made with Nelson Riddle, Frank Sinatra now acted out his lyrics in a way no male pop vocalist had ever done before.

Bing Crosby was capable of enormous depth, and possessed a beautiful instrument, but he usually preferred to coast on his burnished sound and easy charm, his jazz roots lightly syncopating a majority of his cuts. For Bing, the illusion of ease was all. Sinatra, on the other hand, acted through his singing, wanting to let the entire world take his emotional temperature, whether deliriously happy or mired in anguish.

For all his macho bravado, Frank Sinatra was the first genuine male star who was not afraid to expose his vulnerability, and men identified with him, sensing a kindred spirit in his examination of the apprehension lying underneath the confident exterior. By combining the two extremes, he created a new kind of screen idol—an ethnic Mack the Knife had now hit town: warm, terse, overconfident, emotional, and above all, dangerous.

Frank Sinatra's time had come.

The Peak Years

"When You're Smiling (The Whole World Smiles with You),"
sung by Frank Sinatra in *Meet Danny Wilson*

He was a natural personality. No matter what he played, he was always Frank Sinatra, just as Clark Gable and Spencer Tracy were always themselves. His secret was complete concentration on what he was doing. There were no heights he couldn't reach, not much he couldn't do if he put his mind to it.

—GEORGE SIDNEY, DIRECTOR, *ANCHORS AWEIGH, PAL JOEY*

FRANK SINATRA WAS NOW DETERMINED to showcase his true versatility on film. And what better way to showcase that all-encompassing talent than by filming a musical drama, *Young at Heart*, one that allowed him to sing a half-dozen standards, emote all over the place, attempt suicide, and—oh, yes—romance America's sweetheart, Doris Day. The resulting film proved to be a fascinating mismatch.

When Sinatra and Day teamed for this musical remake of the John Garfield film *Four Daughters*, both superstars were heading into their peak years of the mid- to late 1950s, a period that saw their greatest work as both singers and actors. Doris Day was herein making the last film required under her seven-year Warner Bros. studio contract, and was soon to become not only the highest-paid female recording star in the business, but also deliver three near-consecutive performances that to this day stand unmatched as a display of (female) star-powered versatility: an indelible singing and acting tour de force in the searing musical drama *Love Me or Leave Me*, a superb dramatic turn in the Alfred Hitchcock thriller *The Man Who Knew Too Much,* and a rollicking first-class musical comedy performance in *The Pajama Game.* This pairing of Sinatra and Day should have registered as a triumph for both superstars. Instead, it's a curiously lumpy film, with both flashes of brilliance and lots of soupy exposition, all of it resulting in an overall audience wistfulness for "what could have been."

In an odd way, Day was more of a power on the film than Sinatra—or rather, she started out that way. It's not just that she received top billing, in the form of "Doris Day and Frank Sinatra in *Young at Heart,*" but also the fact that the film was produced by her husband, Martin Melcher. As detailed in numerous sources, primarily Day's autobiography, although Sinatra and Day continued their amicable and mutually admiring relationship (they had worked together in 1947 and '48 on Sinatra's radio show, *Your Hit Parade*), Sinatra took an extreme dislike to Melcher, ultimately refusing to work if Melcher was anywhere on the studio lot, let alone on the set. Wrote Day in her 1975 autobiography *Doris Day: Her Own Story,* "From the very beginning, Frank displayed an open hostility toward Marty. I remember one meeting that Frank attended during which he sat with a newspaper in front of his face, reading, for the entire time. I was the only person he talked to." In a fascinating several pages, Day, who always enjoyed the early-morning start to filmmaking, goes on to discuss Sinatra's lateness during production, including "some days when he missed his morning schedule altogether and didn't show until the afternoon." Day herself expressed mixed feelings over his behavior, understanding that there are days when an actor just doesn't feel up to the demands, yet also expressing her awareness of how many jobs on the set relied upon the star's prompt arrival, concluding her discussion with the flat statement, "I don't think Frank was concerned with what his absence meant to the other people on the picture."

Sinatra's on-set displeasure was not limited to Melcher, however. In yet another example of Frank's penchant for flexing his newly found movie star muscle, early on in the filming, he demanded that cinematographer Charles Lang (an Academy Award winner and eighteen-time Oscar nominee) be replaced. Warners Bros. acquiesced and replaced Lang with Ted McCord (who had very effectively filmed Day's moody, underrated *Young Man with a Horn*). According to Day, Lang was a painstaking craftsman who was "very fussy" about lighting. Sinatra, ever-restless actor that he was, refused to wait on set, prompting Day's observation that "the message was clear: it was either Lang or Sinatra. Of course Frank had no right to do what he did but when a picture is in production with all of its overhead in operation, there is no right and wrong; there is only that old devil, expediency."

As to the film itself, *Young at Heart* is, and plays like, a fancy 1950s soap opera dressed up with musical flourishes. The screenplay by Liam O'Brien borrows lavishly from the original *Four Daughters* script by Julius J. Epstein and Lenore Coffee, and centers around the three Tuttle sisters: Laurie (Doris Day), Fran (Dorothy Malone), and Amy (Elisabeth Fraser). (One of the original *Four Daughters* seems to have disappeared along the way to remake land, with the title also changed simply to take advantage of Sinatra's hit recording of "Young at Heart.") The sisters live in a surreally clean Connecticut suburb with their musician father (Robert Keith) and his sister Jessie (Ethel Barrymore). When composer Alex Burke (Gig Young) comes into the sisters' lives, enough romantic complications ensue for any four films: Alex loves Laurie; Amy and Fran both fall for Alex. Much heaving emotion follows, yet the sisters, all of whom play musical instruments, always seem to have time to knock out a sonata or two, led by Fran plucking away at her harp while Aunt Jessie watches the fights on television and clicks her needles contentedly in the background. Surreal, indeed.

It's Aunt Jessie who provides the one touch of grit in this overly sanitized world until exactly thirty-five minutes into the film, when Alex's musical arranger Barney Sloan arrives onscreen in the person of Frank Sinatra. In a star entrance befitting Sinatra's new onscreen status, he stands with his back to the front door, hat tilted backwards, slowly turning around to reveal a skinny physique and unsmiling face, complete with a cigarette dangling out of the corner of his mouth. Appearing to have aged drastically since the release of *Suddenly,* there are lines on top of lines in Sinatra's face now, and his Barney Sloan appears to have lived a hard-knock life, one far removed from the sweetness-and-light world of the Tuttle family. It's as if a touch of film noir has been injected into a musical "woman's film." (Well, why not—the same year's other Doris Day musical, *Love Me or Leave Me*, definitely contained noir elements.)

For the first time on film, Frank Sinatra appears older than his actual age (thirty-nine). One can only surmise that the tempestuous relationship with Ava Gardner and the hard living with booze and cigarettes have caught up with him, at least temporarily. His appearance is fascinating, a bit disturbing and utterly in keeping with the character. He may be outfitted with the WASPy name of Barney Sloan, but he comes across as nothing so much as the quintessential outsider, the ethnic, urban poor boy who has landed in the strange WASP world of the Tuttle family.

When Laurie and Barney first meet, the dialogue actually serves their characters well; since Barney has instantly made himself at home, settling in at the piano in the living room, Laurie, with just the right note of understatement murmurs, "My name is Laurie—I live here." Barney's reply? "You have a cigarette?" Barney's whiny sad-sack persona is immediately established with his lachrymose confession that "whoever gives out the breaks—lady luck—destiny—won't let me have a break." Citing everything from his orphaned childhood and the Depression to World War II in his self-pitying cry of "woe is me," Barney actually utters the words "Talking about my bad luck is the only fun I have." Bemoaning his fate, Barney grouses that he will probably be killed by lightning and "Pow! *D-e-d,* dead!"—the first onscreen example of the playful misspelling of words Sinatra would repeat in other films, most notably *Pal Joey.* Actor Sinatra is here improvising with words, just as the singing Sinatra occasionally displayed his improvisatory jazz leanings in a repetitive emphasizing of certain lyrics.

Laurie and Barney seem to have nothing in common, so of course they fall in love. They may not make much sense as a couple, but when two actors sing this beautifully, any audience is willing to forgive a great deal. Doris (the pianist in the family) plays and sings the beautiful ballad "Till My Love Comes to Me," only to be succeeded by Frank soloing on a sublime version of "Someone to Watch over Me" in a noisy bar where no one pays attention to him. In fact, Day's silent look at Sinatra as he sings this classic torch song, one usually associated with a female but here beautifully reinvented by a tough yet vulnerable male, shows such respect and indeed love for Barney/Frank, that this one glance conveys volumes about both characters and both stars. These two respect and admire each other, and the audience begins to wonder why the filmmakers don't just let the music take off and soar. The extremely brief wordless sequence is proof positive of Day's comments about Sinatra: "Despite Frank's sure and rather cocky exterior, I always felt there was a sad vulnerability about him. Perhaps that's why I always had understanding and compassion for what he did. . . . There were many lovely things about him that I admired." Given the personalities of the two stars, it is therefore not surprising that Laurie wants to take on Barney as a sort of home renovation project, "First your room, then you," and when he kisses her on the cheek, confessing he had planned it for a week, her crisp retort is, "That wasn't much for a week's planning."

That very exchange encapsulates the major problem with the film: Day is so straightforward, so forthright in her attack that you expect Laurie to tell Barney to snap out of it and get with the program. Although Day and Sinatra do share a common background as big band singers, vocalists whose artistic souls lay in their musical roots, she never sheds her hands-on-hips, head-on approach to life's problems, an attack worlds apart from Sinatra's moody methods. At times the two stars appear to be acting in separate movies. The only time they truly click onscreen is the scene where he yells at her, because their star personas inform the action. You know Sinatra is a volcano about to explode, and you know that Doris Day is a genuinely nice woman who can be hurt by someone treating her in such a manner. The audience can't help but feel that Laurie/Doris wouldn't give such a self-pitying whiner the time of day, just as Barney/Frank would be turned off by her relentless optimism.

As a result, it really is left to the musical moments to carry the film, and to a large extent they do. Day sounds terrific belting out "Ready, Willing, and Able," and is equally adept in a quiet beach scene singing "Hold Me in Your Arms," a vocal so totally relaxed and filled with emotion that one actually sees the movie that could have been.

Sinatra, for his part, hits a home run as he sings and plays "Just One of Those Things" in an empty bar. Nicely set up by director Douglas with an opening shot of someone mopping the barroom floor, the sequence continues as the camera closes in on Sinatra at the piano singing this classic Cole Porter song of heartache and regret. It's not just vocal ability that allows this one song to tell the audience everything they need to know about Barney and his unrequited love for Laurie; one look at Barney's silent reaction to the news that Laurie is going to marry Alex informs the situation every bit as much as the overripe dialogue that follows.

Laurie's marriage is supposed to take place in exactly one hour, and when she silently stands before Barney in the empty bar, Sinatra is able to put across the spoken words through sheer force of talent, confessing his love to Laurie as he passionately but quietly asks, "Why d'ya have to look so beautiful—looking like a convention of angels? . . . Why does the sunlight have to hit you just right?" In someone else's hands, such dialogue might induce derisive laughter, but in Sinatra's beautifully modulated delivery, it does the exact opposite, imbuing the situation and both characters with dignity and audience sympathy.

This entire sequence of Barney playing and singing "Just One of Those Things" is unequivocally the high point of the film. Sinatra and Day are both wonderfully understated, and Douglas has composed a beautifully lit shot. Day's light blue dress is the only bit of color in the dark and dingy bar as a desolate Barney, expressing such pain that he is barely able to articulate his words, never raises his voice above a near whisper. Like the leading man in a film noir, Barney is here a man without hope, one who feels hemmed in wherever he turns. In the midst of all the melodrama, the acting and singing are of such extraordinary richness that they redeem the entire film and then some.

It's also noteworthy that while Sinatra was given all the well-known standards to sing—songs by Porter, the Gershwins, and Johnny Mercer, complete with piano solos by André Previn, no less—Day sang only the new songs composed for the film, none of which, while competent, is especially inspired. (This may have been a result of husband Marty Melcher's well-known

Fascinating mismatched pairing with Doris Day in Young at Heart.
First-rate performance from Frank.

tendency to try to control all publishing rights to songs utilized in his wife's films, a feat much more readily accomplished with new songs by lesser known songwriters. Day herself theorized in her autobiography that an attempt by Melcher to control song rights may have been the trigger setting off Sinatra's antipathy toward him.)

Well, after that song, there's only one thing left for Laurie to do. She may be marrying Alex in one hour, but Barney really loves her, and what the heck, she has discovered sister Amy loves Alex, so she just elopes with Barney and sends a telegram informing all the waiting wedding guests that she's marrying someone else. It's all too much, way too much, but once again the musical sequences make it worthwhile. After Barney and Laurie marry, Barney is glimpsed playing and singing "One for My Baby" in a noisy bar where the patrons, incredibly enough, don't pay attention to him. It's a vocal so rich in characterization and shading, so evocative of the seen-it-all balladeer that when he reaches the phrase "You've got to listen to me, till it's all talked away," he invests the words with such tenderness and palpable vulnerability that it makes one overlook every last bit of Barney's self-pitying nonsense. His singing is so damn good in this portion of the film, so moving in delivering this cry of loneliness before a heedless crowd, that the viewer just wants the rest of the film to go away. Then again, one has the same reaction to Day's solo vocals; her acting may still be too bright here, especially in the early "happy family" high-spirited moments, but her singing, like his, is flawless. Ironically, it's their very individual brilliance that points up the problem with the film: their styles are so different, they actually can fully score only in their solos. It's no accident that the two screen icons share no duets, only briefly singing the final song of the film together before the credits roll. Each of these giant talents here exists in their own universe.

The remainder of the film really belongs to Sinatra. Barney is still worried that Laurie carries a torch for the now very successful Alex, and as Laurie sings "There's a Rising Moon," Sinatra's beautifully conveys all his conflicting emotions of jealousy, love, and insecurity in a remarkable series of silent reaction close-ups—the only smile he can manage is a tentative acknowledgment for Aunt Jessie. Hastily volunteering to take Alex to the train station, Barney receives a final blow when Alex hands him cash "for Laurie—use it any way that'll make her happy." Full of despair, Barney has reached the end of his rope—foot on the gas, he drives heedlessly into a blizzard, deliberately shutting off the car's windshield wipers. He's leaving it all up to the fates. It's an extraordinary piece of silent acting from Sinatra, the eyes full of pain and inarticulate rage.

And what happens next after that beautifully composed and acted sequence? The filmmakers dissipate all the carefully wrought tension by cutting to reaction shots of the family hearing about the accident. Barney is in desperate shape in the hospital, near death with a head wrapped in bandages, so it's a good thing that Laurie tenderly waits at his side to fulfill the role of any supportive wife—she lights a cigarette for him. Before his lifesaving operation. Laurie's not a dumb woman—what the hell is going on here?

It is interesting to note that while John Garfield was killed in *Four Daughters,* Sinatra refused to be killed in the remake. Day relates in her autobiography that she felt his decision to be an incorrect one, since "there was an inevitability about that character's death that would have given more dimension to Sinatra's performance. And enhanced the film." It's a mixed bag of a decision. On the one hand, the silly happy ending is completely unexpected, given all that has happened before. On the other hand, it's also true that audiences would, in theory, want their two stars to live happily ever after together. The decision may also have been due to the fact that after dying onscreen in both *From Here to Eternity* and *Suddenly,* Sinatra did not want to expire three times in a row on film, thereby losing audience interest. ("Ho hum, here comes another Sinatra death scene.") It may also have been a decision based on how he viewed his own onscreen persona, perhaps thinking to himself, *No movie star dies three times in a row on film.* Damned if you do, damned if you don't.

Barney survives the operation (the cigarette must have helped), and the film quickly cuts to springtime in the Tuttle living room, with Laurie and Barney's baby in Aunt Jessie's lap, as a freshly groomed and suited Barney sings and plays his finished song—"You, My Love." There must be something great in the water here in Happyville, Connecticut, because as soon as Barney received the news that he and Laurie were having a baby, he miraculously recovered. The strings swell up from nowhere, yet after all this emotional upheaval, the viewer is still strangely disengaged—disengaged, that is, until one fifteen-second sequence wherein Doris Day looks directly into Frank Sinatra's eyes with a glance so filled with emotion that it is downright erotic. There is a total connection—emotional and physical—but it's too little, too late, and the film ends as the camera pulls back for a shot of the strangely sanitized suburban street while Frank once again croons his hit recording of the title song over the closing credits. The song has no relation to the plot of the film, and after two hours of watching, viewers, still unsure why these two were ever attracted to each other, can be forgiven for now thinking, *They won't last one week together—especially with that damn harp in the living room.* Well, it didn't matter to audiences, because the film proved a major hit at the box office, a success that led to a bit of tantalizingly unfulfilled experimentation on the part of Sinatra—an animated film version of the Broadway musical *Finian's Rainbow.*

Undertaking an animated version of a classic Broadway musical constituted a risky endeavor on the part of all concerned, given the ambitious and satirical, if not fully successful, story of the piece. However, the musical did contain an extraordinary and much-loved score by E. Y. Harburg and Burton Lane, and the vocal talent assembled for the project was staggering: in addition to Sinatra and original Broadway star Ella Logan, the brilliant Ella Fitzgerald and Louis Armstrong had also signed on. Under the musical direction of Lyn Murray, the scoring and recording, which included four Sinatra solos, were fully executed. Unfortunately, the project then foundered after $300,000 had already been spent, because the necessary additional financing could not be raised. Such fund-raising difficulty may have arisen because of the film's politics; animated or not, the story, with its call for racial and economic equality, was considered radical at the time.

One of the more interesting rumors regarding the film's demise is that one of the key animators, Art Babbitt, had infuriated Walt Disney by working to unionize the Disney studio, a move that led to Disney himself trying to squelch *Finian's Rainbow.* A more likely reason is that when original director John Hubley refused to name names before the House Un-American Activities Committee, Chemical Bank, which was providing the funding, refused to continue bankrolling the film. The animated film was abandoned, with *Finian's Rainbow* eventually seeing the light of day as a 1968 live-action Francis Ford Coppola musical starring Fred Astaire and Petula Clark. The film would ultimately have worked better as an animated feature, the always-welcome presence of Fred Astaire notwithstanding. In the Sinatra filmography, *Finian's Rainbow* does not register as quite the full-scale loss that the soon-to-be-abandoned *Carousel* represented, but it's a major missed opportunity nonetheless. It certainly would have provided a fascinating window into the onscreen effectiveness of utilizing only Sinatra's voice, and judging from his completed vocal tracks, the musical results would have been sensational. Coupling Sinatra with the vocal genius of Ella Fitzgerald and Louis Armstrong (not to mention such terrific jazz musicians as Oscar Peterson and Red Norvo) was an inspired idea, but although the music and narration were both prerecorded, when money ran out, the film was never actually animated.

With *Finian's Rainbow* remaining uncompleted, Sinatra seemed to figure he'd repeat the box office success of *Young at Heart* by returning to the territory of soap opera in his very next film: the Stanley Kramer–directed adaptation of Morton Thompson's mammoth novel *Not as a Stranger*. It proved to be a odd choice of property, because viewing the resulting film today, one has a single overwhelming reaction: Why did Frank Sinatra bother to make this movie?

It's not his worst—there are several fruitier candidates for that honor. Rather, there is no discernible reason for the third-billed Sinatra to have taken on the role of Dr. Alfred Boone. Did he simply want to keep working continuously on A-list productions in order to build upon the success of *From Here to Eternity* and *Young at Heart*? Was it his well-known fear of being bored? Whatever the reason, Sinatra here took on a supporting role, playing a character who disappears for nearly the entire second half of the film. Granted, it was Stanley Kramer's first feature film as director (he had previously functioned as producer) but the end product is a rather stolid melodrama that plays to none of Sinatra's edgy strengths as an actor.

Instead, the black-and-white United Artists release concentrates on top-billed Olivia de Havilland (Swedish-American nurse Kristina Hedvigson) and stoic he-man Robert Mitchum (Dr. Luke Marsh). One knows right from the start where this film is headed because grim music (score by George Antheil) portentiously announces a serious treatment of the surgically gowned and masked medical figure glimpsed as the opening credits flash by. Well intentioned it might have been, but in an attempt to cover all thousand pages of the novel, the script by Edna and Edward Anhalt races from point to point and delivers no true insight. The end result? Eh.

The opening scenes of the film find Mitchum, Sinatra, and Lee Marvin portraying interns being taught autopsy procedures by crusty old professor Dr. Aarons (Broderick Crawford). First impression: Hippocrates must have been one of their classmates, because these are the oldest-looking interns imaginable. Second impression: Frank Sinatra is being purposely photographed in order to appear dwarfed by Marvin and Mitchum, thereby setting up the fact that he will be the character providing the comic relief.

Sinatra's Al Boone is depicted as a carefree yet ultimately sympathetic physician, his seemingly cynical exterior hiding an empathetic personality that helps make him a successful doctor. Of course, he has a ways to get there, because he's not exactly a diligent student; he's content to remember "seventy percent of the information—that's all that's expected"—not exactly a philosophy to inspire a patient's confidence. Mitchum's Luke Marsh, on the other hand, is brainy and a hard worker, but he exhibits little or no emotion. As his alcoholic father (Lon Chaney Jr.) says to him: "You won't make it; it's not enough to have a brain—you have to have a heart." It's a valid point, but the film undercuts its own premise in crucial ways: not trusting the audience, director Kramer and the screenwriting husband and wife Anhalts repeat this point over and over. Making matters worse, Mitchum's one-note performance gives absolutely no suggestion of contradictory, and therefore interesting, emotions roiling beneath the surface. The only change in Marsh's character comes in the last ten minutes of the film, a case of much too little happening way too late.

How will the perpetually poor Mitchum character finagle the additional money that will allow him to continue his studies? Enter Nurse Kristina (de Havilland) and her cartoonlike Swedish cohorts Oley (Harry Morgan) and Bruni (Virginia Christine). De Havilland, a beautiful and skilled actress, is here saddled with insurmountable handicaps: a set-in-glue old lady hairdo and a wardrobe that features a wedding-night negligee adorned with so many ribbons, shoulder pads, and geegaws that it's understandable when new husband Marsh drinks excessively on his own wedding night. It's all topped off by a Scandinavian accent not heard since the last Sonja Henie ice-skating extravaganza, her unfortunate accent matched only by Morgan's even more over-the-top attempt, which suggests Sweden as a suburb of the borscht belt.

Luke and Kristina begin to date, their first night out the occasion of an inside joke by the filmmakers. Having decided to go to the movies, they are seen exiting *The Barefoot Contessa,* which, according to the poster, stars Ava Gardner as the "world's most beautiful animal." Well, at least it wasn't Frank's Al Boone seen exiting that particular movie. Marsh decides to marry

Kristina for the money she has so diligently saved, setting the scene for the first genuinely involving confrontation of the film. When Marsh informs roommate Al of his plan, Boone snarls, "You're taking advantage of a poor squarehead who's afraid of being an old maid. . . . You're letting yourself be kept," whereupon the much larger Luke, on the verge of belting Al, slams him into the dresser.

It's an interesting confrontation because the supposedly cynical Al emerges as the fuller human being, upset with Marsh's utter lack of concern for Kristina. The success of the scene lies in the fact that for the first time in the film, characters are not drawn in the black-and-white simplicity with which Luke himself views the world. So interesting is the scene that the impact is not lessened even when it resorts to yet another ongoing Sinatra in-joke; referring to his own beanpole physique, Al yells in frustration, "Sometimes I wish I had seventy-five more pounds. I'd belt you one." (Mitchum once mused that Sinatra was the man he'd least like to fight because "every time I'd knock him down, he'd get right back up until one of us would have to get killed.") It's just that sense of scrappiness, the indomitable will trapped in a frail body that helped to fully inform Sinatra's portrayal of Maggio and makes audiences root him on.

Even more detrimental than the screenplay's paint-by-numbers two-dimensional characters, the dull look of the film turns off the viewer. First-time director Kramer here exhibits little visual flair, and his camera placement is perfunctory at best. The movie actually comes to life only when Sinatra is onscreen. When Al and Luke begin their practice on the ward, facing everything from violent patients to delivering babies in the back of ambulances, the pace of the movie improves noticeably—this is the stuff of human drama. Sinatra also has a nice moment when he quietly informs Marsh that his father has died. Back to the camera, Sinatra's body language and kind voice convey volumes about Al's basically caring character.

By way of contrast, when Marsh visits his now-deceased father's apartment, predictably enough, he smashes the remaining bottle of alcohol and cries, right on cue, to the accompaniment of a bombastic score. Mitchum's crying is filmed with the camera behind him, leaving the viewer suspicious that Mitchum could not or would not manage the tears. In his refusal to project any discernible emotion onscreen—his character neither laughs nor smiles once in the two hours and fifteen minutes—he gives off an air of nothing so much as "what a way to make a living." Mitchum could be remarkably effective in film noir, a sleepy-eyed seething volcano easily capable of summoning up that dark world of shadows, but he is never as fully alive onscreen as the jittery Sinatra.

When Marsh graduates from medical school and moves with Kristina to small-town country life in Greenville, not only does the film become a different movie entirely, but also, and most unfortunately for viewers, Sinatra's Al disappears for the next hour. Aside from the patient who swallows safety pins, the only three-dimensional and interesting person in the dull hick town is a rich divorcée who settles her sultry gaze on Luke.

The dimension may not exist in the writing—the screenwriters seem to equate divorcée with brazen hussy—but it sure registers in the playing of Gloria Grahame, a femme fatale who embodied insolence better than any other actress of her time. It's too bad that Grahame, so memorable in roles ranging from the "Girl Who Cain't Say No" in *Oklahoma!* to the tough broad whose face is splashed with hot coffee in *The Big Heat,* didn't reteam here with *It Happened in Brooklyn* costar Sinatra. Unfortunately, she is left to embody temptation for Dr. Luke.

One glance at each other when they first meet, and you know where this is heading, especially because this bored woman breeds horses. Quicker than you can say "1950s Freudian symbolism," they barely wait out the dance at their country club before shadows fitfully dance across the screen, and the stallions she breeds literally rear up onto their hind legs as Luke moves in for a smoldering embrace. Poor Kristina is still off canning her pickled herrings, and even the reemergence of Sinatra's Al thirty minutes before the end of the film won't help her.

De Havilland is forced to rush home and rip up baby garments she has hand-sewn, and as the music thunders up and down the scale, the hysteria abounds. Even an actress of de Havilland's skill can't survive such nonsense. This most competent of actresses ends up looking silly and more than a bit demented.

It's then up to Dr. Sinatra to set things straight. Waiting in his convertible outside the Marsh home, he bores in on old friend Luke with a succinct, "Don't you ever look at her? The time is now. See ya." And off Al drives. Sinatra's presence is always welcome in the film, injecting the one note of lightness amidst all of the heavy-footed emoting, but the image here is ridiculous; Frank is driving a convertible, appears to be happy as a clam, and as he cheerily leaves, one actually expects the soundtrack to begin playing "Come Fly with Me." As Frank drives off into the night, one realizes that he has not given a bad performance, just one that he could and did give with one hand tied behind his back. He is marking time, nothing more.

It's not an awful film—the actors involved are too good and the production values too strong, but it sure seems like a lot of Sturm und Drang over a kindergarten-level life lesson. Sinatra himself actually comes off the best of the three stars, his easygoing, appealing performance contrasting so favorably with Mitchum's glum stoicism that it led Jack Moffitt of *The Hollywood Reporter* to write, "Sinatra, who seems to become a better actor with each successive part, is simply terrific." Praise notwithstanding, it was time to leave the back-to-back landscapes of harp-playing sisters and Swedish meatballs and move onward to the promised land of classic musical comedy, and what should have been a slam dunk for Frank. The film turned out to be more like a wobbly free throw, but the fault sure wasn't his.

When Frank Sinatra agreed to star in the film adaptation of the smash Broadway musical *Guys and Dolls,* everyone involved had good reason for their high expectations; Frank Loesser's score for the show had been universally acclaimed as one of the greatest scores ever written for the stage, one without a single weak song. Even better, for once the book of a musical, here written by Jo Swerling and Abe Burrows, was clever, smart, and successful as both satire and romance. Produced by Samuel Goldwyn and directed by Joseph Mankiewicz, this big-budget musical boasted top-drawer talent from start to finish: with Sinatra, original Broadway star Vivian Blaine, a top-notch technical and creative team, choreography by Michael Kidd, and cinematography by the brilliant Harry Stradling, how could it miss? Well, there was just one tiny problem: Sinatra's costars were the top-billed—and decidedly nonmusical—Marlon Brando and Jean Simmons. Oh. Uh-oh.

Sinatra himself was upset at losing the lead romantic role of gambler Sky Masterson to Brando, but that's actually not the problem with the film, since even in the lesser role of comic gangster Nathan Detroit, Sinatra comes off the best of the four stars. He is the only one of the quartet who successfully negotiates the terrain between the lovably cartoonlike underworld of Damon Runyon and the grounded sentiment of the Save-A-Soul Mission House. The problem is that neither Brando or Simmons should have been in the film at all, a state of affairs made clear by one simple question: How good could a screen musical be if Marlon Brando sings as often as Frank Sinatra? Once again, Hollywood bungled a classic musical, insisting on casting box office stars instead of actors who could really sing. Interestingly, Goldwyn's first choice for the part of Sky Masterson, Gene Kelly, was a much better fit for the role, but MGM boss Nicholas Schenck refused to lend out Kelly. Similarly, Goldwyn first offered the part of Sister Sarah to Grace Kelly, but neither Kelly's schedule, nor that of second choice Deborah Kerr, allowed them to take on the role. As a result, Simmons, who had played opposite Brando in 1954's leaden Napoléon movie *Desirée,* was signed to reunite with him and make her Technicolor musical debut.

Mankiewicz, a true Hollywood giant, functioned as a triple threat talent: producer (*The Philadelphia Story*), screenwriter, and director, even managing the extraordinary feat of winning back-to-back Academy Awards as both screenwriter and director of *A Letter to Three Wives* and *All About Eve.* However, he had never before directed a musical, and it shows here. His staging is rather perfunctory, and his insistence on beefing up the script results in a film that oftentimes plays like a comedy/drama with songs attached, instead of the fully integrated classic American musical it is. Unlike William Wyler's highly successful direction of his one and only musical, 1968's *Funny Girl,* Mankiewicz's direction of *Guys and Dolls* reveals little inherent feel for the musical genre and, oddly enough, takes little advantage of the possibilities inherent in shooting a musical in CinemaScope. It's not that *Guys and Dolls* is without its pleasurable moments, because it has several of them. It's that the film as a whole registers as a prime example of "woulda, coulda, shoulda"— woulda been better with two different leads, coulda been sharper with a different approach, and shoulda been an all-time musical classic.

The film opens with a danced prologue establishing a highly stylized New York City, one with a cartoonlike assortment of gamblers, hard boiled dames, and lovable gangsters. In other words, it's fantasy time, which is fine, because *Guys and Dolls* is a musical fable. It's a nicely danced opening, Kidd's choreography aptly capturing the urban milieu, and at the end of the five-minute prologue, the film smoothly segues into rotund gangster Nicely-Nicely Johnson (a fine Stubby Kaye) beginning the famous "Fugue for Tinhorns" with his two fellow gamblers: "I got the horse right here—his name is Paul Revere." It's a great musical moment, but already something is off—big-time.

Original Broadway set designer, the estimable Oliver Smith, is here functioning as production designer, and he has opted for an extremely stylized Times Square set. The problem is that this is film, not theater, and film sets up expectations of a realistic setting. The backdrop settings are all two dimensional, a state of affairs especially jarring when real cars and buses drive around what are clearly soundstage sets. Right off the bat, the look of the film distances the audience from story and characters alike.

The stylized dialogue of the original play is retained, and works just fine—these are gangsters who speak without contractions: "I would dislike to take my business elsewhere." Such dialogue helps the audience accept the fable-like nature of the story, but the characters need to be saying these words in a different setting. When the audience is introduced to Save-A-Soul missionary Sergeant Sarah Brown, a young woman who is determined to save the corrupt citizens of Times Square, the dichotomy becomes all the more pronounced: Simmons, a beautiful and talented actress, is a fish at least halfway out of water here, sporting an accent that wavers in the Atlantic between Great Britain and New England. She looks a bit of a sylphlike Audrey Hepburn and certainly appears too frail to last even one night in the Times Square mission.

The next of the principal characters, Nathan Detroit (Sinatra) then enters the scene, and after the standard Sinatra in-joke (weighing himself and barely registering on the scale), he bemoans, in his pseudo-polished proper English, that he has no location for the crap game he runs. Lieutenant Brannigan (Robert Keith) is putting the heat on, and to make matters worse, Nathan has no anniversary present for his fiancée of no fewer than fourteen years, nightclub entertainer Miss Adelaide (Vivian Blaine). Nathan needs a thousand dollars—pronto—and sings of his desire to stage the "Oldest Established Permanent Floating Crap Game in New York." Sinatra may have wanted to play the romantic lead of Sky Masterson, but he is terrific in this character-establishing song, immediately lifting the audience into the territory of first-class musicals. The number is nicely staged by Kidd, with a chorus of gangsters in barber chairs, and Sinatra is here singing at his smoothest and most confident. It's immediately apparent to the audience who Nathan Detroit is, what motivates him—money—and what scares him—marriage. Miss Adelaide may want marriage, but Nathan wants one thousand dollars for the crap game, so when Sky Masterson accepts Nathan's wager that he can't successfully take strait-laced Sergeant Sarah to Havana for the evening, the game is on.

Guys and Dolls was not a particularly happy set: Sinatra, upset that he lost the role of Masterson to nonsinger Brando, was also still nursing a grudge that Brando had won the role of Terry Malloy in *On the Waterfront,* a role for which Sinatra had lobbied. (As a consolation prize, Sinatra was offered the supporting role of priest Father Barry, an offer subsequently withdrawn because Karl Malden had already accepted. Sinatra sued and settled out of court five years later.) To make matters worse, Brando's desire to continually rehearse wore on "one-take Charlie" Sinatra. Frank, fueled by instinct, not intellectual analysis, never did grow comfortable with cerebral actors and was not particularly circumspect in his critique of Brando's Method ways, referring to the estimable Brando as Mumbles. Or, as Sinatra pungently told director Mankiewicz, "Don't put me in the game, Coach, until Mumbles is through rehearsing." (Of course, Brando got his own back by proclaiming that when Sinatra dies, "The first thing he'll do will be find God and yell at him for making him bald.") In an amusing postscript to the backstage drama, in her book *My Father's Daughter,* Tina Sinatra recalls watching *Guys and Dolls* on television with her father one year before his death: "another time we laughed at *Guys and Dolls.* 'He still can't sing,' Dad would say, shaking his head at his costar Marlon Brando." Put two major stars with differing approaches toward acting in continued close proximity, factor in a history of clashing over roles, and you have a recipe for a mutual-aggravation society. Yet for all this backstage drama, their scenes together unfold in polished fashion, and the contrast between Brando's smoothly controlled Masterson and Sinatra's eager, nearly puppylike Detroit reads nicely onscreen. (Frank's clashes were not just limited to Brando. He may have greatly respected Frank Loesser's talent, but as Wilfrid Sheed humorously relates in *The House That George Built,* his excellent analysis of the golden age of the great American songbook, "Frank Sinatra . . . never forgave Loesser for telling him how to play Nathan Detroit. The nerve of some people.")

Given the structure of the screenplay, Sinatra probably came off better playing the role of Nathan Detroit than he would have as Masterson. He may not be particularly believable as a Jewish gangster, but the dialogue-heavy, visually static stretches when Sky attempts to lure Sarah to Havana slow down the film's tempo drastically. How could any actor overcome such a flat presentation? There are no musical numbers helping to explain character, just ten rather endless minutes of dialogue until Sarah and Sky finally sing the

Guys and Dolls *(1955). Brando's incessant rehearsing drove the ever-impatient Sinatra to distraction. The fact that Frank wanted Brando's role of Sky Masterson didn't help.*

classic Loesser song "I'll Know." Since neither Simmons or Brando sing particularly well, this beautiful number doesn't register at all. Sinatra was correct when he stated that he felt the casting of the film was wrong except for the original Broadway cast members (Vivian Blaine and Stubby Kaye) who had been retained for the film. Simmons unfortunately sings a half-tone flat during a fair portion of the song, and Brando, who does stay on pitch, delivers neither texture nor resonance in his singing. Brando's acting, of course, does convey the character, and he actually injects some believability into Sky—no small feat, given that he is playing a singing gangster who falls in love with a missionary. It's all for naught, however, because the point of a musical is that a character becomes so carried away with feeling that he can convey such heightened emotions only by bursting into song; it's the release of the song that carries the audience along with the actor. Instead, when Simmons floats into the beautiful Loesser song "If I Were a Bell," a number that should charm the audience, there's only tension: Will she hit the notes or not? The answer is half the time. Simmons is inherently charming and acts the role nicely enough. But what's the point of a musical when the leading lady can't sing?

Vivian Blaine's first number "Pet Me Poppa," where she dances with a dozen chorines in cat costumes at the Hot Box Nightclub, is a prime example of problem number two with the film: Frank Loesser wrote one of the greatest scores in Broadway history, but for unfathomable reasons, Goldwyn and Mankiewicz jettisoned a number of the songs and insisted that Loesser write new songs. "Pet Me Poppa" isn't a bad song, but it doesn't fit smoothly into the book the way all the numbers did in the Broadway show. Blaine is a talented musical performer, if a little cartoony compared with her three costars, but she can't overcome the ugly setting of the number, a backyard alley complete with cutout television antennas—it's one heckuva tacky setting for a bright brassy musical. Similarly, when Blaine delivers the hilarious "Adelaide's Lament," her comic ode to the perpetual cold she has nursed through a fourteen-year engagement, Loesser's beautiful marriage of music and words is undercut by the cramped ugly setting of Miss Adelaide's dressing room. What was a showstopper onstage registers as a ho-hum moment on film.

Fortunately Sinatra is on hand to help things along. Looking younger and healthier than he did in either *Suddenly* or *Not as a Stranger,* he is funny and fully delivers on his character's function as comic relief. This Nathan can find hope wherever (comically) possible: Miss Adelaide, eyes agleam in her ecstatic description of married life, gets no further than the phrase "in the second year," before a very anxious Nathan hopefully interjects, "Then we can get a divorce?!" Sinatra's occasional moments of appearing stiff, or maybe just uninterested in his character, are few and far between, and when he swings into the title song, joined by Stubby Kaye and Johnny Silver, he gives the film a zip utterly lacking in its many leaden sections. This jaunty singing gangster fits into the fable-like premise of the film—Sarah and Sky do not.

Even Sinatra, however, can't completely overcome the unfortunate choice of new songs shoehorned into the narrative. First the audience is told that Nathan will do anything to avoid marriage, but that is immediately followed by Sinatra singing a paean to the charms of "Adelaide." The song is fine and Frank sounds great, but not only does the new song contain no character or plot development, it also contradicts everything that has come before, leaving the audience nothing so much as confused. Does Nathan want to get married or not?

Finally the viewer arrives at the musical highlights of the film: "The Crapshooters Ballet" and "Luck Be a Lady." Nathan Detroit has finally found a safe place for the crap game, one far removed from the gaze of Lieutenant Brannigan: a sewer below the New York City street. Athletic, virile Michael Kidd choreography establishes the action without any words being required, full effectiveness undermined only by too many editing cuts. For once in the film, the stylized setting doesn't jar—it's a sewer where gangsters dance, so who expects realism? As Nathan Detroit crouches while dancers whirl by, the terrific choreography is immediately followed by Brando's launching into the anthemic "Luck Be a Lady."

One can only guess how difficult that must have been for Frank; both in his nightclub appearances and on record, Sinatra, buoyed by a brassy, swinging Billy May orchestration, delivered an electrifying all-stops-out attack on the song, complete with hand gestures and the pantomimed throwing of dice. In the space of four minutes on a stage, Sinatra delivered the goods and then some: it's a joy-filled ode to gambling and living life on the edge. On film, Brando very tentatively negotiates a gentle first line—"They call you lady luck"—and that's exactly where the entire song stays. Brando never sings out of tune, but there is no sense of tension and release, and that's what this classic Broadway belter is all about.

Even with Brando's lackluster singing, the song is so cannily crafted that the film is definitely on the upswing here, and the next musical moment is another highlight, the comic and touching duet of reconciliation between Nathan and Miss Adelaide, "Sue Me." It's a great tune with a witty lyric, delivered by the two real singers in the film. Even the dialogue is becoming funnier here, towering mob boss Big Jule proudly proclaiming at the prayer meeting that he is a "better man—thirty-three arrests and no convictions." When fellow gangster Nicely-Nicely (Stubby Kaye) steps to the fore and belts out "Sit Down You're Rockin' the Boat" in a soaring tenor voice, the film finally becomes the first-rate entertainment it should have been throughout. With Kaye's rotund physique, great voice, winning comic delivery, and surprisingly light movement, this jubilant acknowledgment that he has seen the light registers as the real thing. The exhilarating celebration, complete with a chorus of gangsters swaying in time to the music, becomes a great Hollywood musical moment.

As the film ends with the double weddings of Sarah and Sky and Nathan and Adelaide, it's clear that its last twenty-five minutes are a huge improvement on the preceding two hours, yet for all the intermittent charms of the film, one's overwhelming reaction is awareness of unrealized expectations. Indeed, a successful filming of *Guys and Dolls* may lie ahead, given the unceasingly remake-happy Hollywood of the twenty-first century, because critics were certainly disappointed by this 1955 version. Sinatra himself gained rather more critical approbation than his costars, *The Hollywood Reporter*'s Jack Moffitt accurately claiming that even in this musical fable, "[Sinatra] is always a man and never a buffoon," but the film was best summed up by *Time* magazine: "Faithful in detail, the picture is false to the original in its feeling."

Critical response notwithstanding, audiences made the film an enormous hit, and following *Young at Heart* and *Not as a Stranger,* the film registered as Sinatra's third box office winner in a row. Frank was proving his box office appeal repeatedly but needed another critically acclaimed film to build upon the dual successes of *From Here to Eternity* and *Suddenly.* Unanimous critical claim for Sinatra's dramatic abilities lay very near in the future, but first up was a comedy, *The Tender Trap.* In this first true cinematic version of his swinging bachelor persona, Frank landed himself a film that pleased audiences and critics alike at the time of its release, but fifty years later, the appropriate adjectives would seem to be "limp" and dated."

The Tender Trap represented Sinatra's first return to MGM in five years, and opened on November 17, 1955, a mere three days after the premiere of *Guys and Dolls.* The first-ever film to present Frank Sinatra as the leading man in a comedy, it even garnered some critical approval, with *The Hollywood Reporter* declaring the film "Colorful as a bright new lipstick and as merry as a sixth martini." Well, maybe six martinis is what is required to enjoy the film, because while it may have proved popular with audiences in the mid-'50s, it is, in fact, a pretty tired affair. Long stretches of the film are so tedious that, in Sinatra parlance, the film is *d-e-d,* dead, just like the fish—yes, fish—that his character of Charlie Reader carries around his apartment near the film's "climax."

Based upon a not-terribly-successful Broadway play of the same name by Max Shulman and Robert Paul Smith, and adapted for the screen by Julius Epstein, *The Tender Trap* tells the story of free-swinging New York theatrical agent Charlie Reader (Sinatra); his best friend, Joe McCall (David Wayne); and young ingenue Julie Gillis (Debbie Reynolds). Charlie is living the high life in NYC while Joe, feeling the need to spread his wings, has just left his wife, Ethel, after eleven years of marriage. And what exactly does the audience learn over the course of the ensuing, and very slow, two hours? Julie is an aspiring actress, but her real goal in life is to have a successful marriage; Joe disapproves of Charlie's hedonistic ways yet not so secretly envies them at the same time; Charlie and Julie fall in love despite themselves; and Joe returns to his wife. What's meant to be funny turns into a two-hour sermon, of curiosity value today simply for the window it provides into 1950s moralizing. The requisite light touch for such frothy goings-on is here wielded with all the finesse of a Mack truck.

Ironically, things get off to a sensational start, raising hopes for the rest of the film. Unfortunately the opening is one of only two first-rate sequences in the entire production—but what a terrific opener it is. As the screen slowly begins to gain light, the voice of Frank Sinatra is heard singing the bouncy Jimmy Van Heusen/Sammy Cahn title song. The camera picks up a very distant figure on the empty, sky blue CinemaScope screen, and as the jaunty tune continues, the figure of Frank Sinatra is glimpsed on the distant horizon, strolling casually toward the camera in perfect time with the song's syncopated beat. Hat at a rakish angle, here at last is the visual incarnation of the man who has the world on a string. As Sinatra exulted in an interview at the time: "Everything is ahead of me. Man, I'm on top of the world. I'm buoyant."

No wonder Sinatra sang these uptempo Van Heusen/Cahn songs so convincingly. Whether it was inviting the listener to "Come Fly with Me" or winking at "The Tender Trap," Frank was living large—and happily—for all the world to see. The latter is a great film song, its buoyant rhythm seeming to effortless propel Sinatra's onscreen figure forward. Never mind what it says about mid-1950s America that the very popular song equated love with a "trap," albeit a tender one. It's the swinging Sinatra persona just then being established on the seminal Nelson Riddle Capitol albums, come to life on film. Here at last is the Sinatra audiences are now expecting, a neat dovetailing of actor, persona, and role. *Ah,* the audience thinks as the song continues and Frank appears in focus and up close, *this is going to be great.*

It's not. Instead, once the song ends, the audience is thrust into a time capsule of 1950s high life, glimpsing Charlie in his swinging bachelor pad as he passionately kisses Poppy (Lola Albright), utilizing what the audience comes to realize is his favorite pickup line: "You are the softest girl." Charlie is interrupted by friend Joe, freshly arrived in New York and now in his headlong flight from the straitjacket of marriage, standing expectantly at Charlie's front door and waiting for his first martini. It's at this point that one of the interesting 1950s motifs of the film begins; throughout the entire film, Charlie, Joe, and everyone else in sight smoke and drink nonstop. Why have one martini when three will do just as nicely? How anyone functioned with that much booze in their systems is a mystery, but in 1955, such chain-smoking and imbibing of alcohol was presented as the height of New York sophistication. Even such ceaseless alcohol consumption, however, isn't quite so startling as Charlie's very casual yet apparently serious offer of Seconal or Benzedrine for anyone who wishes to partake. None of it is exactly on the American Medical Association's endorsed guide to healthy living.

The film's final major character is introduced when Julie Gillis (Debbie Reynolds) auditions for a new Broadway show and wins the job, right out of college. Never mind that Charlie's "classy" lady friend Sylvia Crewes (Celeste Holm), a violinist with the symphony orchestra who has nothing to do with Charlie's agency or putting together a Broadway show, attends the audition, complete with white gloves. What's much more startling is the fact that Julie is completely blasé about winning the job. In Julie's worldview, this Broadway stuff is nice, but "it's no substitute for marriage. A woman isn't really a woman at all until she's been married and had children—and why—because she's fulfilled—isn't that right."

Julie goes on to enumerate that she will have three children, live two years in New York City, and then move to the country. It's all planned out because "a person can't go through ad-libbing his way through life." This is such nonsense on so many levels that one waits—vainly—for Julie to discover that maybe starring in a Broadway show wouldn't be so bad, that a little spontaneity in life could be fun. But no—Julie remains a dogmatic, even irritating young woman throughout the film, and despite Reynolds's trademark perky delivery, she remains resolutely annoying. She never changes throughout the film; aside from falling in love with Charlie, she's entirely static, her worldview fixed at age twenty-one and a half, and a leading lady with no character growth is a leading lady of no real interest.

Julie doesn't even show up on the first day of rehearsal for her new Broadway show—and she's the star. Who can spare time for rehearsal when, like Julie, you're busy at a furniture display store, figuring out where the furniture should be placed after marriage to a fiancé who doesn't exist. This is foolishness of no interest to any audience.

What makes all this nonsense even worse is that director Charles Walters, who had previously directed the terrific musical *Easter Parade* and went on to direct first-rate movies such as *Billy Rose's Jumbo* and *Please Don't Eat the Daisies,* is completely at sea. Aside from the opening sequence, the film lies inert, with no use made of the wide-screen possibilities inherent with CinemaScope. Yes, the process was relatively new at the time and there were technical problems—distortion seemed to occur in many panning shots—but the film remains stubbornly earthbound, featuring endless dialogue about how Charlie should live his life. Characters remain seated for minutes on end, and the only action in view is the answering of Charlie's doorbell. It's all staged as if Walters plopped a camera in the fifth row of a theater and photographed whatever was on the stage, with no attempt to "open up" the proceedings and show the supposed glamour and excitement of Charlie's show business life in New York. One is even reduced to speculating why, even in crowd scenes, this movie presents a glamorous midcentury New York City populated by eight million inhabitants, not a one of whom is a member of a minority group. Maybe the filmmakers felt having a star whose last name ended in a vowel was "exotic" enough, but this sure is one white-bread version of New York City.

The audience's only consolation lies in the film's one other first-rate sequence, wherein Julie sings the title song in rehearsal for her Broadway show. Julie's too perky by half, displaying absolutely no understanding of the lyrics, so there's only one thing left to do: Julie's agent, Charlie, goes up on stage and shows her how the song should be sung. Well, it would never happen that way in real life, but no one in the audience gives a damn, because Frank Sinatra proceeds to "play" the piano and sing the title song, in the process telling the audience in three short minutes everything they need to know about love, marriage, and interdependence—in short, the whole damn shooting match. So secure and well thought out is Sinatra's phrasing as he sings the song at a slower tempo than the one employed in the film's opening sequence, that his sole song literally tells the audience more than they have learned in the preceding (and endless) first hour.

When Julie advises Charlie to "drop the girls . . . because I love you . . . even though you're too old, arrogant, selfish, and spoiled," it seems like such a terrible match that one wonders why he would ever fall for her. Indeed, the reverse is equally true: Why would she fall for Charlie? Sinatra can always be charming, and knowing the often-dazzling effect his efforts could have, here he doles out the charm as often as he changes suits and hats—which is to say, frequently. But his character is a selfish cad who loves 'em and leaves 'em, stringing along dozens of girls and never even returning their phone calls. When Charlie protests, "Marry? Well, who asked you?" Julie tartly replies that marriage means "a house, kids, and a life that makes some sense." In other words, this twenty-one-year-old fount of wisdom sagely informs us that unless you're married, your life makes no sense. At which point, Julie disappears from the movie for the next thirty minutes, until her reconciliation with Charlie. Must be because even she realizes how dopey her blinkered worldview really is.

It's all so misshapen that the film is really of interest only for what it tells the audience about 1950s America (or as Julie calls it, "the atomic age"). So buttoned up was the sexuality of the times that when Charlie and Julie are alone in her apartment (which she, of course, shares with her parents), they are actually aroused by watching Esther Williams in her rubberized bathing cap on television. The tension on display between the comforts/confines of domesticity and the swinging/empty bachelor lifestyle, reveals the two sides of the period. There was a morose underbelly to the bright-on-the-surface paeans to America prevalent in pop culture of the time, and with the two sides of Sinatra's own personality, the confident swinger and the vulnerable loner, he exemplified this paradox on film better than any other actor of the time. In the apt phrase of commentator T. H. Adamowski, there was a "willed nonchalance" to Frank's swinging demeanor, an exaggerated sexual drive that "points to a genuine crisis of male identity." (Of course, Sinatra's nonchalance was never so strongly willed as that of Bing Crosby. Crosby often gave the impression that he'd rather die than have you think any effort was involved.) In his recordings, Sinatra articulated those paradoxes; onscreen he personified them. As a result, it's safe to say that no other star could have followed *The Tender Trap* with *The Man with the Golden Arm*. It is those very contradictions that have allowed Sinatra to retain his iconic status not only throughout his lifetime, but also after his death. Just as there were two Elvis Presleys—the sneering, hip-swiveling country boy from the 1950s and the bloated, jumpsuited Vegas superstar of his later years, there were also two Frank Sinatras, and both proved equally interesting.

Career girl Sylvia Crewes presents the only character of real interest. She's holding down a good job, dresses well, and cracks wise with the best of them, but even she falls prey to the sermonizing: "Boys back home don't have what we want; we have our eye on something else—career, glamour, excitement. So we come here to New York—find excitement—do pretty well. Until one fine day we look around and we're thirty-three years old and don't have a man. And what's available? Drunks, married men, lunatics."

When Sylvia's quasi-beau Joe McCall, mindful of his own shaky marriage, observes, "There are worse things than not getting married," Sylvia ruefully responds, "Name three." This is dialogue the viewer expects from the simpering Julie, not from Sylvia. It's a sign of the times that at no point is there any discussion of combining marriage and career; it was simply one or the other. It's all a perfect illustration of a key discussion point put forth in Jeanine Basinger's seminal study *A Woman's View: How Hollywood Spoke to Women*—from the 1930s through the 1950s, a woman onscreen could rebel against the limited choices imposed upon her, could even go to the big city and establish a successful career, but she'd be punished for her freedom, and her success would prove empty without anyone to share it. In the end, the woman's only real choice remained marriage and a return to where she started.

Certainly the men are not immune from this bifurcated view either, a dichotomy exemplified by the strange character of Joe McCall. Joe's a married man having fun in New York while dating his best friend's girlfriend, yet he actually lectures pal Charlie on his evil ways, gloating when all of Charlie's girlfriends desert him: "It's retribution. It's payback for the girls you fondled and forgot, the phone calls you promised to return and didn't. You're a louse—one of the few indecent men I know." Charlie is no paragon of manhood, but coming from Joe, this supposedly moral voice is a joke. In fact, Joe actually confesses "I love you, Sylvia—marry me." When she points out the oh-so-slight problem that he is still married and that she doesn't love him, his basic reaction seems to be "Oh—okay. I guess I'll go home to nice sensible Midwestern Ethel now." It's as if the preceding two hours of the film never happened.

By the movie's end, all logic has flown out the window, with Charlie feeling obliged to marry Sylvia, throwing an engagement party to celebrate, and then running off to find Julie and declare his love for her. It's all so confusing and preposterous that when Julie tells Charlie, "You're a terrible, terrible man—I never want to see you again," she utters the line with absolutely no conviction. Debbie Reynolds probably had no idea what the hell was going on in the movie—seemingly no one did. Or maybe she realized how ludicrous the statement was, given the preceding two hours. One wonders what

Reynolds made of the silliness, given the fact that at the time of filming she was wrestling with the decision of whether or not to marry Eddie Fisher, in the process soliciting marital advice from Frank Sinatra (who might not be the first choice of marital wisdom for many). Reynolds later described Sinatra's explaining to her that being married to a singer could prove "very difficult . . . it's the singer's way of life . . . Please give this very deep and serious thought." Added Reynolds, "I didn't. I should have!"

Reynolds herself turns in an adequate performance, but it's not much more than that. A talented musical actress possessed of boundless energy, when undertaking nonmusical roles, she always fared better with those characters who brought out her tougher, bitchy qualities (*In & Out, Mother, What's the Matter with Helen?*). In *The Tender Trap*, she has nothing more than a cardboard mouthpiece to portray. It's not that she or any of the other actors are bad—they're not. It's that with the exception of Celeste Holm, whose character at least has some basis in reality, the performances, understandably enough, lack conviction.

Charlie and Julie are reunited at film's end, but by then it's impossible to care. Stuck with finding a love match for Sylvia, the screenwriters perfunctorily pair her off with Mr. Loughran (Tom Helmore), a man who has eyed her with interest in the elevator. Sad to say, this couple who don't even know each other appear to have more in common than do Charlie and Julie.

When the four principals end the movie by singing the title tune in a reprise of the movie's opening CinemaScope shot, the effect is totally diluted; it's the fifth version of the song heard in the film, and even this lightly swinging tune has now worn out its welcome. Stranger still, the principals then bow to the cameras. Aside from that theatrical device unfortunately reminding audiences that they have seen little more than a filmed play, these are not bows that seem particularly well earned. As for the fate of the characters—Joe appears headed back to Ethel, Sylvia is marrying a man who appears to live in the elevator, and just about the only certain result after two hours of these endless shenanigans is that Julie's nagging will result in Charlie upping his already prodigious intake of liquor. In a word—awful.

Sinatra followed up this exercise in treading water with the single biggest missed opportunity of his film career, beginning and then abandoning the role he was born to play, Billy Bigelow, the carnival barker/criminal leading man of Rodgers and Hammerstein's landmark Broadway musical, *Carousel*.

Bigelow's combination of macho exterior and tender sensitive interior dove-tailed perfectly with the Sinatra persona and Frank's acting and singing skills, and it would have provided Sinatra with a richly textured musical role that combines a first-rate book and a sensational score. Any performer is lucky if such a confluence happens even once in his or her career, and like Streisand's missed opportunity to play Madame Rose in *Gypsy* (she said she could only "hear Merman all over again") and Doris Day's botched deal to play Nellie For-bush in *South Pacific,* Sinatra's Billy Bigelow registers as the biggest "if only" of his entire film career.

In the case of Sinatra, the sense of frustration is greater, because he actu-ally started work on the film, rehearsing and prerecording songs from August 15 to 20, 1955, and even undergoing costume fittings. Frank desperately wanted to perform this role, telling costar Shirley Jones that so great was his interest that he "went back to that show five nights in a row." Signed for a fee of $150,000, Sinatra chucked the entire film when he arrived for location shooting in Boothbay, Maine, and learned that he would have to film certain scenes twice. The decree of double filming was due to Twentieth Century-Fox's decision to shoot the film in both conventional 35-millimeter Cinema-Scope, as well as the newly developed 55-millimeter CinemaScope, the latter to be utilized for reserved-seat "road show" engagements. One-take Sinatra balked, supposedly barked, "You're not getting two Sinatras for the price of one," and walked off the set. In Shirley Jones's recollection: "So, when he saw the two cameras, he said 'I signed to do one movie, not two' and back in the car he got, and back to the airport." Through the years, some have muttered that Sinatra was actually more concerned about whether he had the tools to successfully pull off the role, utilizing the two cameras dustup as an excuse. This scenario is shot down by *Carousel* producer Henry Ephron, who years later recalled Sinatra bluntly telling him at the time: "Well, forget it, kid. It's me or the camera. One of us has to go. Listen, Henry. You know me. You've heard me say it—it's been printed a thousand times—I've only got one good take in me."

Even more interestingly, Ephron went on to state that while prerecording songs for the film before leaving for the location shoot, Sinatra turned in a brilliant recording of "If I Loved You" but had difficulty with Billy Bigelow's "Soliloquy," the eight-minute rumination by Bigelow about what sort of boy his son will be. The song represents the ultimate challenge for singing actors, and whatever the reason for Sinatra's difficulties, whether the song was beyond his range or, more likely, that it was just a night when he was not in good voice, Frank stopped the session, telling Ephron, "Let's try it another time. I've had it for tonight." Sinatra never revisited the song for the film, and his completed recordings for the movie remain unreleased because of contractual difficulties. As a result, the listener must make do with a recording of "Soliloquy" made at Capitol six months earlier, and while that version is first-rate, the same song, in the context of the film, would have rated as an all-time great. Sinatra returned to the song throughout his career, and he performed it in concerts, but there were no further attempts made in the mid-1950s when he was in his vocal and dramatic prime.

Once Sinatra got the hell out of Dodge, or rather Boothbay Harbor, Maine, Fox sued Frank for a cool million; the suit was settled by Sinatra's agreeing to star in another, different film for Fox. Gordon MacRae took on the role of Billy Bigelow, turning in an acceptable performance, and singing beautifully, but without the passion, temperament, and excitement Sinatra would have brought along with him.

Experienced enough to access the deepest of emotions, chastened by life experiences, Sinatra could pour it out—and beautifully—whether onscreen or on a record. If any doubts existed about that ability—and there were now precious few—they were quickly dispelled by listening to the very next album he released at that time, the damn near perfect late-night torch song collection *In the Wee Small Hours*. Yes, the album was a top-ten-charting hit, but its real importance lies in the fact that for the first time ever, Frank was able to etch a full-bodied characterization on each and every cut and sustain a unified mood for the entire album. *Carousel* presented Sinatra with just such an opportunity on film, a chance to bring his extraordinary dramatic and singing abilities to what is possibly the greatest male role ever written for a musical, and due to his chronic impatience, he blew it. Big time.

Carousel was history, but Sinatra did then sing on film in the musical television version of Thornton Wilder's classic play *Our Town*. *Our Town,* in which he played the pivotal role of the Stage Manager, remained Frank's only dramatic part undertaken specifically for television until the 1977 filming of *Contract on Cherry Street*. It remains of great interest in the Sinatra oeuvre not only because it yielded the Emmy Award–winning hit song "Love and Marriage," but also because on the face of it, Frank Sinatra is the last person one expects to see playing the role of the all-knowing, paternalistic New England stage manager/narrator. Looking back on the television adaptation fifty years after its initial broadcast, one has two immediate reactions: first, what were the producers thinking by casting the anything-but-folksy Sinatra in the leading role of the avuncular stage manager, and second, network television was then a very different animal in its willingness to telecast an original musical adaptation of a great American play. It's a long way from Thornton Wilder to reality television, and it's downhill all the way.

Our Town was stocked with top-drawer collaborators, featuring orchestrations by Nelson Riddle, vocal direction by Norman Luboff, and a telecast slot in the prestigious "Producers' Showcase" on September 19, 1955. (One notes in passing that the associate director was the twenty-years-later famous novelist Dominick Dunne, who several decades in the future wrote of his clashes with, and strong dislike of, Sinatra). Written for television by David Shaw, and directed by Delbert Mann, the Jimmy Van Heusen/Sammy Cahn musicalization is professional throughout, worthy of plaudits for the smoothness of its live presentation, and ultimately proves to have been rather unnecessary for one very basic reason: Thornton Wilder's masterpiece is complete unto itself, filled with beautiful language, a universal message, and a surprisingly tough-minded subtext underneath the folksy trappings. This is a case where adding music does not enhance the piece—it only succeeds in bending it slightly out of shape.

Following Wilder's three-act structure, the television adaptation opens with Sinatra (who, the announcer intones over the end credits, has appeared "through the courtesy of Otto Preminger, the producer of *The Man with the Golden Arm*") strolling onscreen and whistling. Wearing his by-now-familiar snap-brim hat, Sinatra is a welcome presence, setting the scene for daily life in 1901 as he sings about "Our Town." He's in great voice, but it is immediately apparent that this is a major piece of miscasting: a pipe-smoking Frank Sinatra would never be content to while away his days in a very small New Hampshire town, and he certainly would never be found saying "by Jove." So strong is the Sinatra persona that hearing him utter those two words establishes an immediate disconnect between performer and material. Henry Fonda could and did believably portray the Stage Manager on Broadway, making such colloquial speech seem utterly authentic. Sinatra simply cannot. (Then again, no one would believe Henry Fonda playing *Pal Joey,* singing "The Lady Is a

Tramp.") Frank can say "ayah" and "evenin' " all he wants, but it's not believable. It's an act, and from a twenty-first-century perspective, strangely reminiscent of George W. Bush's concerted effort to drop his *g*'s and refer to Al-Qaeda as "those folks."

The main characters of the play are quickly introduced, beginning with Eva Marie Saint and Paul Newman essaying the roles of Emily Webb and George Gibbs, the teenage next-door neighbors who fall in love and marry. Both are first-rate actors, but she registers much more strongly than he. The then-thirty-year-old Newman stretches and then breaks all credulity as a teenager. By that point in his life, Newman reads as far too old and knowing onscreen, resulting in a performance that continually makes the viewer aware that he is ACTING in capital letters. (Newman was to fare much better fifty years later in his laconic portrayal of the Stage Manager in a Broadway revival of *Our Town.*)

The production is not without its pleasures, however, and certainly there is fun to be had along the way. The second song of the production finds Stage Manager Sinatra harmonizing with the town's newspaper editor and town doctor as they discuss the nature of the citizenry in some witty Sammy Cahn lyrics: "We're mostly Protestants, plus some Democrats, the rest are all suspect." What's funniest about the sequence is the grin Sinatra shoots on a particularly discordant harmonized note, as if to say, "Listen to these two try to sing—headlining in Vegas, they'll never be."

As George and Emily fall in love, however, the misshapen nature of the musical undertaking becomes apparent. It is Sinatra, as the observer, who sings the love ballad "The Impatient Years," but it's the lead characters of Emily and George who should now be expressing their heightened emotion in song. The producers have here bowed to the fact that Sinatra was the only bona fide singer in the cast, a cast in which acting ability took precedence over vocal talent. While all the actors are fine when not singing, particularly Ernest Truex as Dr. Gibbs and Peg Hillias as Mrs. Webb, it is apparent that this most American of plays simply doesn't need songs. By the time of the fourth and final song in Act I, a reprise of "Our Town," the music strikes us as nothing so much as a bit of an interruption.

Act II, titled "Love and Marriage," takes place three years later, the passage of time simply and movingly delineated in Wilder's language: "The sun has come up over one thousand times." When Mr. Webb speaks with George

Publicity shot for live television musicalization of Our Town *with Paul Newman and Eva Marie Saint. Frank's refusal to rehearse angered Newman.*

on the morning he is to marry Emily, he refers to the day-in, day-out nature of marriage with the mundane but all-revealing observation that time passes and "the white-haired woman by your side has eaten fifty thousand meals with you." It is particularly ironic that the now-classic song "Love and Marriage," with its lyrics extolling the fact that "Love and marriage . . . go together like a horse and carriage . . . ," is winningly delivered by Frank Sinatra. It's not just one's awareness of Sinatra's famous marital difficulties and his constant womanizing; it's that with Sinatra's impatience and low threshold for boredom, he'd never sit still to eat fifty thousand meals with the same woman.

Act II climaxes with the marriage of Emily and George, which means one even has the chance to hear Paul Newman and Eva Marie Saint sing. The verdict? Better than expected—just don't line up the recording contracts. Audiences today would never sit still long enough for even this streamlined (less than two hours) musical adaptation on television, one complete with sweetly singing townspeople, no less. Whatever the teleplay's shortcomings, in our unceasing haste and what is, ironically, our disregard of Wilder's clear-eyed gaze at the beauty of everyday life, the loss is ours.

It is *Our Town*'s third and final act, set in the summer of 1913, that delivers the play's tough message, one often obscured in audiences' hazy memories of what they regard as a "sweet play." Here, the material turns dark, with the entire act set in a cemetery. It's reminiscent of Frank Capra's *It's a Wonderful Life* because in both cases, audiences willfully remember the uplifting message, but choose to forget the discontent lying beneath the surface. Wilder, like Capra, recognizes that life is tough and full of unexpected sorrows: Emily has died in childbirth while still in her midtwenties. As she arrives to join others in the cemetery, she is heard to poignantly observe, "My, wasn't life awful— and wonderful." Director Mann shoots the sequence very nicely, composing the scene with the dead residents of the cemetery sitting in the foreground, those still living on earth placed in the background, all shadow and silhouette.

When Emily can't yet accept her death, she is granted the chance to revisit earth on any day she wishes. Choosing her eleventh birthday, Emily rewatches that seemingly innocent day, and at that point in the teleplay Sinatra sings the ballad "Look to Your Heart"; while he sounds terrific, it's unnecessary. Thornton Wilder's dialogue tells the story and delivers the message much more strongly all by itself.

Emily finds her return to earth wondrous but too painful to bear, and she bids good-bye to all the everyday objects she, and by extension everyone, takes for granted. "Good-bye to clocks ticking—and food—and coffee . . . Earth you're too wonderful for anyone to realize." It's fitting that it is in those final dramatic moments that Sinatra registers most strongly; it's as if his own sensitive, indeed poetic, nature fully comprehends his final dialogue with Emily as she returns to her place in the cemetery.

Given Eva Marie Saint's nuanced delivery, the queries take on an aching quality as she wonders, "Do any human beings ever realize life while they live it every, every minute?" In Sinatra's rueful, understated delivery, the answer lands beautifully: "No . . . Saints and poets maybe." One wonders if the miscast yet intermittently touching Sinatra fully appreciated the play's message regarding the beauty of everyday life, given the fact that he filmed this adaptation in the mid-1950s period, when he kept up an unparalleled frenetic schedule of recordings, movies, and concerts. Given his incessant work of the period, one doubts it, but it certainly would have proved most interesting to hear Sinatra's reactions to the material twenty-five years later as he grew increasingly reflective and became the one thing he never planned on—old.

Well, it wasn't *Carousel,* but Sinatra's next feature film, *The Man with the Golden Arm,* produced and directed by Otto Preminger, served his film career nearly as well as *Carousel* would have. A gritty black-and-white movie based on Nelson Algren's award-winning 1949 novel of the same name, *The Man with the Golden Arm* (United Artists, 1955) was, incredibly enough, Sinatra's fifth film release of the year. It's an amazing feat, one that looms very large in Sinatra's legacy as a film star and puts the lie to the knee-jerk claim that he was not a serious actor. All five films in 1955 were major releases: *Young at Heart, Not as a Stranger, Guys and Dolls, The Tender Trap,* and *The Man with the Golden Arm.* In addition, there were the aborted filming of *Carousel* and the major television production *Our Town.* Although other actors have made more than five films in a single year, Sinatra's roles were all leading men, and it is safe to say that from 1950 onward, no other actor in modern Hollywood history has ever starred in five major studio releases plus a major television film in one year. This is the work of a man serious about his craft, a man intent on stretching his range from dark musical (*Young at Heart*) to snappy musical comedy (*Guys and Dolls*) and on through to blistering drama (*The Man with the Golden Arm*). The range of Sinatra as an actor, the sheer level of his industry, remains extraordinary. The capper to this feat lies in the fact that *The Man with the Golden Arm* featured a terrific no-holds-barred Sinatra performance that built upon and expanded his performances in *From Here to Eternity* and *Suddenly,* in the process cementing his reputation as a dramatic actor of the highest order.

The backstory of how *The Man with the Golden Arm* came to be produced is nearly as interesting as the film itself, because it was John Garfield who originally bought the film rights to the novel and hired Lewis Meltzer to write the screenplay. Garfield, however, died before any filming could begin, leaving the lead role of Frankie Machine up for grabs. After losing the leads in *On the Waterfront* and *Guys and Dolls* to Marlon Brando, Sinatra (who is actually mentioned by name in the novel) here determinedly beat out Brando for the lead role, agreeing to undertake the part (for a salary of $100,000 plus 10 percent of the profits) without even reading a full script. (Costar Eleanor Parker was actually paid $25,000 more than Sinatra.)

If Brando proved the more inspired choice for *On the Waterfront,* it is nearly impossible to conceive of him improving on Sinatra's performance in *Golden Arm.* Sinatra's musicality helped to inform his portrayal of the drumming wannabe Frankie Machine in a way Brando could not have fully realized (Brando's drum playing not withstanding), and Sinatra's nearly palpable sense of otherness, of loneliness, likewise aided his impeccable performance.

Frank Sinatra possessed a bone-deep understanding of this "little man" determined to fight back and make something of himself. Like Maggio in *From Here to Eternity,* the street-smart Frankie Machine starts out thinking he's in control, only to find all his defenses stripped away, the macho facade revealed to hide the soul of a frightened boy. It takes a true artist to reveal these layers of character, and Frank Sinatra's portrayal of Frankie Machine, as of Bennett Marco in *The Manchurian Candidate*, is the most sustained piece of acting in his film career, rating right up there with the best performances of any A-list Hollywood star. It's a performance that succeeded in accomplishing what many thought impossible: Frank Sinatra the onscreen musical star had now been supplanted by Frank Sinatra, dramatic actor.

Sinatra so wanted the lead role of Frankie Machine that he actually agreed to rehearse many of the film's scenes, a far cry from his usual approach. In fact, according to Daniel O'Brien's *Frank Sinatra Film Guide,* "Sinatra arrived for work each day at 8 A.M. on the dot, rarely departing until the previous day's rushes had been screened nearly twelve hours later . . . Sinatra's energies entirely consumed by the *Golden Arm* production." According to director Preminger, Sinatra "was surprised to discover that he loved rehearsals. He could not get enough. When I wanted to quit, he would ask, 'Let's do it again, just once, please!' " Such dedication, however exaggerated in Preminger's recollection, may not have informed all of Frank's film career, but it paid off in spades here.

Hailed as groundbreaking for its mid-1950s depiction of drug addiction, *The Man with the Golden Arm* is indeed still harrowing in certain sequences, but what has been forgotten over the years is how even this powerful film was purposely toned down from the novel in order to appeal to a mass audience. While the drug addiction of Frankie Machine (Sinatra) is granted more prominence in the film than in Algren's novel, the novel is much darker in its depiction of the major characters: Frankie, not his wife, Zosch (Eleanor Parker), kills Louie the drug dealer. Zosch really is crippled as a result of Frankie's drunken car accident, and at the end of the novel there isn't even a remote suggestion of a happy ending. Molly (Kim Novak) becomes a prostitute, and Frankie hangs himself. Algren may have been rather famously upset with the "cleaning up" of his novel, but given the tenor of the times, it was not a surprising move on the part of director/producer Preminger, and the sordid, desperate quality of the characters' lives still rings through loud and clear.

Opening with the justifiably famous Saul Bass titles, all misshapen vertical and horizontal white lines that stagger across the screen in synchronicity with the score, the film immediately establishes the fact that the terrific jazz score by Elmer Bernstein will, for all intents and purposes, function as another character in the film. Suggesting jazz and blues in equal measure, occasionally even sounding like a bebop hot/sour version of "Harlem Nocturne," the music registers as terrific storytelling in and of itself. As to the plot of the film, the screenplay by Walter Newman, Lewis Meltzer, and Ben Hecht tells the story of ex-serviceman and hotshot card dealer Frankie Machine (Sinatra) who is returning to his Chicago neighborhood after serving six months for drug addiction.

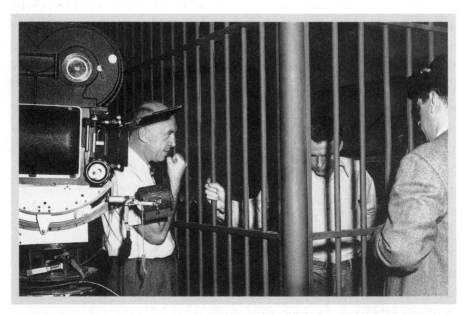

Preparing for the jailhouse scene in The Man with the Golden Arm *(1955) with director Otto Preminger. Contrary to expectation, the equally temperamental star and director got along well.*

The title of the film, in fact, refers not to Frankie's drug addiction, but rather to his extraordinary card-dealing ability, although it could also just as well reference his drumming ability. Machine is determined to go straight, wanting to land a job as a drummer. Trouble, however, looms on two fronts: Drug-pusher Louie (Darren McGavin) wants Frankie to function as dealer at his high-stakes illegal poker game. If it takes hooking Machine on heroin again in order to secure his participation, Louis sees no problem, silkily intoning, "The monkey never dies. When you kick him off, he just hides in a corner waiting his turn." This smooth customer in a suit and vest is trouble on all fronts, a fact made obvious in his very first scene as he casually torments a one-armed man who desperately wants a drink.

Despair also awaits Frankie on the home front. He has been languishing in prison for six months, yet can do nothing more than trudge up the three flights of tenement stairs to his apartment, so much does he dread his reunion with his crippled wife, Zosch (Eleanor Parker). With Zosch confined to a wheelchair and permanently disabled because of a car accident caused by Frankie, he continues to take care of her out of guilt, wearily putting up with this self-pitying whiner who smothers him both physically and emotionally. Completing a luckless love triangle is "good" girl Molly (Kim Novak), a first-floor tenant who loves Frankie but remains unable to break through his feelings of guilt over Zosch.

Thrown in jail because comic sidekick Sparrow (Arnold Stang) has stolen a suit for him, the emotionally fragile Frankie is totally unnerved when locked into a cell with a junkie. As the addict begins to scream and undergo withdrawal, Frankie bites his own arm, tears in his eyes as he watches the addict's agony. It is an utterly believable reaction in Sinatra's hands, and while he was justifiably praised for the later and more famous scene wherein Frankie undergoes withdrawal, that showy bit is easily matched by this earlier sequence, where he conveys layers of emotion and conflict utilizing only his eyes. It is Sinatra's inherent star quality, his own personality and dramatic instincts, that actually convey a certain sweetness and vulnerability in Machine, thereby ensuring the audience's interest in this oftentimes unpleasant character. Like all true movie stars, Sinatra keeps the audience riveted even when they dislike the character and want to look away.

Trapped by a return to his card-dealing past, hemmed in by Zosch and therefore unable to settle down with Molly, Frankie feels desperate. Restless, aimlessly shuffling cards, pacing around the dingy cramped apartment and desperate for a fix, he follows Louie across the street, and as the music begins to wail, Frankie hungrily waits for the heroin. As Louie lays out each piece of drug paraphernalia in orderly fashion, the music begins to overwhelm: needle (blast of brass), drug (blast), and finally tourniquet (blast). As Preminger brings the camera in for a close-up of Frankie's eyes, it is clear that Machine has taken his first step back into hell. Most startling of all, the jolt of bliss in Sinatra's eyes tells the audience the exact moment the heroin has begun coursing through his system. The monkey is back. (Mid-1950s taboos may not have allowed close-ups of the heroin being injected, but Sinatra's eyes convey the moment even more powerfully.)

At this juncture it becomes clear that the film plays much more success-fully inside the claustrophobic interior settings than on the city streets. The reason is simple: the supposedly grimy realistic Chicago streets look exactly like the prefabricated soundstage creations they are. It's a noticeable failing that undercuts any sense of the oppressive environment Frankie lives in, and hurts audience understanding of his difficult background (not to mention the fact that the city of Chicago appears to have a population of twelve; no won-der the film came in under budget—there's not an extra in sight for most of the film). Fortunately, the interior sets, which account for the bulk of the ac-tion, ring true throughout: grimy, sordid, and reeking of quiet desperation.

The relationship between Machine and Molly makes for an interesting and definitely unusual love match at the center of the film; it is only with Molly that Machine's wounded eyes display any warmth in place of their usual despair, a relationship whose effectiveness is heightened by Novak's own obvious vul-nerability. Novak, who was relatively inexperienced in terms of heavy dra-matic roles at the time of filming, is solid throughout, employing her soft voice to great effect. This woman has been so knocked around by life that she can no longer summon the energy to fully fight back. (At times, her voice is actu-ally reminiscent of Marilyn Monroe's breathy whisper.) In fact, Novak falters only when grand passion is finally called for vocally. When Molly tries to make Frankie face up to his problems, sarcastically asking him, "Why try to face your tough life like other people do?" the vocal attack just isn't there. This cry from the heart registers only as a plaintive plea, nothing more.

According to director Preminger, Sinatra was extremely understanding about Novak's inexperience: "She was terrified, and . . . sometimes we had to do even very short scenes as often as thirty-five times. Throughout the ordeal, Sinatra never complained and never made her feel that he was losing patience." Those who had expected fireworks between the volatile star and equally fiery director were also in for a shock, as Sinatra and Preminger bestowed nicknames of Ludvig (a friendly mispronunciation of Preminger's middle name) and Anatol upon each other, striking up a friendship as well as a solid working relationship.

Although Preminger publicly stated that Sinatra "has a chip on his shoulders all the time. He can be small in little things," the director came to admire Sinatra's talent greatly. Each man had respect for the other, knowing that together they had the chance to create a uniquely powerful film within the controlled and controlling studio atmosphere of the mid-1950s. In addition, although both men wanted to create a solid, challenging movie, they were also keeping their eye on the film's box office potential: *Golden Arm's* realistic depiction of drug addiction meant that it would never be granted the MPAA Production Code Seal of Approval, a fact Preminger actually liked, knowing that such a controversial refusal would hype press attention and hopefully pay off at the box office. (Ironically, the film received a Production Code Seal of Approval in June 1961, six years after it first opened.)

Undeniably effective the film is, but just as Frankie's repeated trips to Louie's apartment for a fix prove repetitious, so, too, does the film as a whole. Zosch's grasping character is shown over and over to be holding Frankie back, but no new information is imparted—she merely becomes a bore. Worse, just to make sure the audience doesn't miss the point, she is shown pasting clippings into her oversize scrapbook, which features, incredibly enough, oversize letters on the cover spelling out THE SCRAPBOOK OF MY ACCIDENT. Perhaps all the themes found in the film were so shocking in a mainstream 1950s Hollywood movie that the dangers of drug addiction had to be emphasized and reemphasized, but the repetition drags down the pace of the film and lessens its effectiveness.

So desperate is Machine for his next fix that he agrees to deal the big game, the point of which is to bluff the high-stakes gamblers out of their money. Hands shaking, his need for a fix accelerating along with the music, Frankie is caught cheating, smacked around by the gamblers, and left alone on the floor. Deserted by all except faithful sidekick Sparrow, Frankie races to his audition for a drumming job, but without any sleep—and still desperate for that fix—he is heading for doom. Hands shaking badly, crashing into the cymbals, dropping the drumsticks, and miscounting beats, Machine wordlessly stumbles out of the audition, his dream shattered. It's a harrowing sequence, beautifully handled by Sinatra in his dead-on rendering of a pathetic man, a never-was who's heading to oblivion.

When plot point number two of the film arrives—Louie surprises Zosch, finds her standing upright, and realizes that she has been lying for years—the film hits a rather large bump in the road because Zosch's character loses all credibility, and the film suffers.

Standing against the wall, eyebrows permanently arched, mouth open, Parker resembles nothing so much as Faye Dunaway on a rampage as Joan Crawford in *Mommie Dearest*. She undercuts nearly all the character establishment that has come before, her performance here tumbling into the territory of camp. Rushing after Louie, Zosch pushes him over the stairwell to his death, and she has no qualms about implicating Frankie in the death.

Machine may have run to Molly's new apartment desperate for money to secure a fix, but once he arrives, he decides to kick his habit cold turkey. There is no dialogue to explain his torment and misery, just physical action, and Sinatra delivers in full. He paces, gulps water out of a saucepan, clutches himself, and suffers shaking fits while wrapped in the fetal position. He is hunched over, literally rending his own garments, his frailty and agony conveyed by Preminger's smart decision to film Frankie from above, thereby isolating Machine in his solitary agony and emphasizing the no-way-out noirish theme of the material. Preminger shoots much of the film in smooth lengthy takes, the camera following Frankie as he prowls the room in his agony; it's a nicely realized blending of actor, director, and cinematographer, and oddly enough, the sequence is harmed slightly only by the fact that Bernstein's extraordinary score is here overwrought, the high volume pounding the action into the ground.

Desperate to escape and score another fix, Machine first threatens to kill Molly, and then begs her to kill him. Instead, she locks him in the closet, and when she lets him out, she tenderly swaddles him in blankets, rubbing his hands and lying on top of him in order to push some warmth into his frail, shivering body. The fifty years since the release of *The Man with the Golden Arm*'s then-revolutionary depiction of drug addiction have dissipated much of its shock value, but have taken away none of the power of

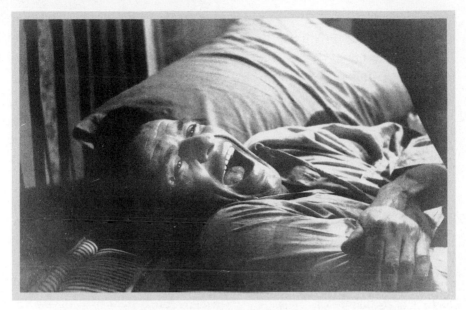

Harrowing withdrawal scene in Golden Arm. *Frank thought this should have been his Oscar-winning performance.*

Sinatra's own performance. This scene of withdrawal was, amazingly enough, filmed in a single take, an example of one-take Charlie at his best. (Perhaps Sinatra did not have the stomach for a second attempt; his brief study of a real-life addict before filming began had left him profoundly shaken. The "forty seconds" he spent watching the young addict trying to kick heroin was "the most frightening thing I've ever seen. I never want to see that again. Never.")

Sinatra may have the showiest role in the film, but in many ways he delivers the least melodramatic performance—he is in control throughout, no more so than in this withdrawal scene. Far from being the exercise in scenery-chewing it could have been, Sinatra's honest performance comes across as exactly the opposite. It is this sequence of withdrawal that undoubtedly ensured Sinatra's Academy Award nomination as Best Actor, and the loss of the Oscar to Ernest Borgnine for *Marty* hurt Sinatra. Years later he reflected, "I thought I won an Oscar for the wrong picture. . . . I did the finest work I ever did in my life on that film."

After suffering the agonies of withdrawal for three days, Frankie is now ready to turn himself in to the police and declare his innocence in the death of Louie. Going to his apartment to say good-bye to Zosch, Frankie so unsettles her with his declaration of independence that she jumps out of bed, as Frankie and the newly arrived police look on in horrified silence. It is clear that Zosch is responsible for the death of Louie, and she bolts out of the apartment, throwing herself over the side of the tenement and plunging four stories to her death. Fade-out on a silent Frankie walking away, Molly walking one step behind him as the camera moves in on a sign rather portentiously announcing NO RIGHT TURN.

Frankie Machine is walking into an uncertain future, but there was no uncertainty about what the role did for Sinatra's future: he was now firmly and indisputably ensconced on the very short list of top-flight dramatic actors in Hollywood.

Critical reaction to the film may have been somewhat mixed, but reaction to Sinatra's performance was universally positive. Summing up the most acclaimed performance of Frank's film career, Arthur Knight in *The Saturday Review* referred to Sinatra as the

> thin, unhandsome one-time crooner who has an incredible instinct for the look, the gesture, the shading of the voice that suggests tenderness, uncertainty, weakness, fatigue, despair. He brings to the character much that has not been written into the script, a shade of sweetness, a sense of edgy indestructibility that actually creates the appeal and intrinsic interest of the role . . . a truly virtuoso performance . . . he is an actor of rare ability.

And, for one of the very few times in Frank Sinatra's career, no dissenting opinions were voiced. *From Here to Eternity* and *Suddenly* had been equaled—and then some.

Following the triumph of *The Man with the Golden Arm,* and before starting a very strange trip to the Wild West with *Johnny Concho,* Frank agreed to film a brief cameo for the MGM musical *Meet Me in Las Vegas.* It's a hodge-podge of a film, which actually starts off on a humorous, musically appropriate note—rancher Dan Dailey has bad luck at the gambling tables unless he is touching ballerina Cyd Charisse—but the film quickly begins to lumber through endless cameo roles (Paul Henreid, Debbie Reynolds, Tony Martin) and comes to resemble nothing so much as a very large and expensive version of a 1956 television variety hour. There is some first-rate dancing by Charisse, but the film is overstuffed; Hollywood was feeling the pinch from television at the time, movie attendance was falling, and in an attempt to attract audiences, Hollywood producers fell into the trap of "bigger is better" thinking. The cameos might be of high caliber (Lena Horne) but they are clumsily inserted and stop the film dead in its tracks, making it play like a souped-up version of vaudeville.

Frank Sinatra's wordless (unbilled) cameo in the film occurs when Dailey and Charisse pass by a random slot machine and pull the lever for an unknown player, who is facing away from the camera. Bells ring, the jackpot is won, and the amazed slot machine player turns to face the camera—it's Frank Sinatra with a look of *Hey—whad'ya know* on his face. It's all wordless and flies by in less than a minute. Given such a brief appearance, the movie is really of glancing interest in the Sinatra canon for two reasons: (1) It registers as a giant plug for the Sands Hotel, the hotel that functioned as Sinatra's headquarters during his extended engagements in Vegas. (2) The cameo appearance of singer Frankie Laine and the contrast it provides with Sinatra.

Laine, an Italian-American vocalist (born Francesco Paolo Lo Veccio) with multiple hits like "Mule Train" to his credit, was actually outselling Sinatra on the singles charts at the time. However, Laine's three-minute appearance makes it clear why Sinatra became an enormous movie star and Laine never did. Sinatra instinctively knew how to scale down his performance for the all-encompassing camera; by minimizing his gestures, the impact was even greater. When Sinatra sang a song on film, he was not a singer, but rather an actor who used his voice to deliver a full-bodied characterization. Laine, by way of contrast, quasi-bellows his one song, and with his accompanying exaggerated gestures, seems to be giving a performance for a nonexistent second balcony—the Ethel Merman school of film acting. Sinatra, like fellow musical icons Fred Astaire and Gene Kelly, knew exactly how to calibrate his performance for the cameras.

Putting aside Sinatra's brief cameo in *Meet Me in Las Vegas,* exactly how did he follow up his unadulterated personal triumph in *The Man with the Golden Arm*? With one of the stranger efforts of his movie career, the little-seen Western *Johnny Concho.* An odd, compact little film which actually opened in the UK before the United States, it was the first film produced by one of Sinatra's own companies (Kent Productions). It made little impact with either critics or the public, but provides an interesting example of the variety of projects Sinatra was willing to explore at that point in his career. It's a fish-out-of-water version of Frank Sinatra, the second of his five Western films, following *The Kissing Bandit* and preceding *Sergeants 3, 4 for Texas,* and *Dirty Dingus Magee.* All five of the films were poorly received, with *Johnny Concho,* the least known of the group, proving the most interesting. The problem all five films shared? Frank Sinatra in the countryside ain't so great, especially if the countryside in question features the old-time American West.

Johnny Concho is an odd little mixed-up slice of a traditional Western, yet it does exert its own peculiar fascination. It is not a great film, but certainly better than its second-rate reputation would have it. A 1956 United Artists release, it was a Sinatra production all the way—screenplay by David Harmon and Sinatra's good friend Don McGuire (writer of *Meet Danny Wilson*), musical score by Nelson Riddle, associate produced by right-hand Sinatra factotum Hank Sanicola, and directed by McGuire. Frank Sinatra had always wanted to call the shots on his films, and now, for the first time, he could. As producer, all final decisions were his, and therefore the film's attributes and faults alike can be laid at exactly one door—Frank's.

What's most interesting about *Johnny Concho* is the extent to which it inverts all the standard action features of the Western film, the very films the young Sinatra grew up watching in the Hoboken movie palaces that fueled his imagination. There's an upside-down Alice in Wonderland quality to the film that makes sense in the post–World War II era; the old-fashioned values have vanished, nuclear bombs have become a reality, and the genre of the Western film, fluid in form, begins to tell new kinds of stories.

In the more standard Western, there are chases, gunfights, fistfights, and ofttimes a stampede. The strong silent cowboy knew right from wrong (as opposed to city folk whose effete Eastern ways could not be trusted) and generally took justice into his own hands in order to ensure that the correct natural order be reasserted. This Western hero would embark upon a quest for justice, although as film historian William K. Everson has pointed out, with the loosening of the Production Code the search for justice turned into a quest for vengeance, the ensuing acknowledgment of the darker human impulses serving to broaden and reinvigorate the Western film. Whether the motivating factor was vengeance or justice, over the years, the Western film morphed into its own myth, representing an idealized American past when Americans were God-fearing good neighbors who believed in an honest day's work for an honest day's wages. The darker aspects of that very Western life were conveniently forgotten: the horrible living conditions, the isolation, the dirt and filth, the cruelty toward Native Americans. In their place a romanticized past took hold, one acquiring an ever more rosy hue with the passing years.

As for the urban-dwelling Sinatra's attraction to such material, not only did the young Frank spend formative years watching cowboy heroes onscreen, but at such a young age, an age when all adults—let alone actors whose image looms forty feet high on movie screens—seem larger than life to children, the films had to have made, and *did* make, a strong impression on him. Those Westerns, much like the popular gangster films of Frank's youth, featured tough guys of unquestioned power who lived by their own lights, men who flouted the prevailing social code in order to achieve what they felt was justice. Sinatra, with his sense of otherness, unquestionably identified with the Western screen image of the solitary stranger in town.

Smart actor that he was, Sinatra clearly knew that he did not fit the physical mode of the traditional Western hero; far from being the strong silent man of the plains, Sinatra was a slight, Eastern-accented garrulous urbanite, but the sense of otherness connected star to genre and therefore Sinatra, in effect, inverted the genre to serve his purposes. Johnny Concho is a skinny scared, evil runt, living off his brother's fearsome reputation, even hiding behind the skirts of his woman until the ultimate showdown. For a star of Sinatra's stature, it's a fascinating risk to have taken in terms of screen image, and while it never really pays off, right down to the strange ending, it makes for interesting viewing all along the way.

Based on the story "The Man Who Owned the Town" by David P. Harmon, this black-and-white Western is set in the mean Arizona territory of 1875, a state of affairs made clear by the slithering menacing snake featured over the opening titles. The film opens with Johnny Concho (Sinatra)—the skinniest cowboy ever seen in the West, wild or not—walking down the center of small town Cripple Creek's main street. Full of bravado, acting like he owns the town, it's immediately clear that Johnny is disliked by every last person he passes. Turns out Johnny is tolerated only because everyone in town is scared of his brother Red, a ruthless killer whose "gun has a long shadow." In the pungent words of the sheriff, the townspeople regard Johnny as a "human tax assessment—like the new cesspool." Johnny "shoves people around" (though he is so slight of frame it doesn't look like he could shove anyone over fifty pounds), demanding saddles, blankets, and even a horse, all the while telling the owners to "put it on my bill," but never paying.

Johnny's skinny physique is matched by the truly bare-bones production that surrounds him. The film is so sparse (including the cleanest streets and sidewalks ever seen in the West) that for much of the time it looks and plays like a 1950s "golden age" television drama more than a feature film. In fact, the stark nature of the physical production reminds one of nothing else in the Sinatra film oeuvre so much as the stylized sets found in *Our Town*. It's no surprise, therefore, to learn that the story of *Johnny Concho* began filmed life as an episode of the *Studio One* television show.

Sinatra actually looks okay on a horse, but appears much more at ease in the poker game which is quickly organized at his demand. He's dressed up in his best Western finery, shuffling cards with dexterity, whiskey at hand—you can't picture Johnny out on the range, but he sure seems at home around the card table.

He cheats at cards, but because of his brother Red, remains unchallenged by the townspeople. Unchallenged, that is, until two strangers arrive in town, Tallman (an excellent, malevolent William Conrad) and his sidekick Walker

Skinniest cowboy in the West. The strange but interesting Johnny Concho.

(Christopher Dark). When Johnny tries to cheat Tallman at cards, Tallman laughs at him, casually announcing that he killed Red in a duel two days previously. Tallman has ensured that Johnny's days of a free ride are over and gives him one day "to draw or run." The cowardly Johnny most decidedly wants to run.

Everyone in town is scared of Tallman, and no one will fight back—no one, that is, except Johnny's love interest Mary Dark (Phyllis Kirk), who loves Johnny so much that she pulls a shotgun on Tallman when he tries to stop her from following Johnny. The intrepid Mary saddles up and tracks down Johnny, who, having discovered that no one in town is willing to take him in, is camping out in the wilderness. It's there in the wilderness that the film runs completely off track for the first time: Frank Sinatra does not look natural eating hardtack around an outdoor fire, and while neither would Concho himself, Johnny does have to appear to be a man of the West, which Sinatra simply does not pull off. When this Johnny Concho complains about the food, he sounds like nothing so much as the kid from Hoboken upset at the quality of the pasta being offered. More striking, it is impossible to understand why Mary is attracted to the cowardly Johnny. In Phyllis Kirk's interesting portrayal (supposedly, then-Sinatra-girlfriend Gloria Vanderbilt was originally cast in the role but was quickly let go when her lack of acting experience became evident), Mary is honest, devoted to her parents, bold, can ride and shoot—in short, she is everything Johnny is not. She even gives Johnny three hundred dollars to pay for their marriage and journey to California, yet Johnny refers to himself as a "dead mule who attracts jackals" and repays her generosity by stating "Congratulations—you just bought yourself a three-hundred-dollar rat." A match made in heaven it isn't.

All of this is underscored by the ponderous brass-heavy musical score by Nelson Riddle. Riddle would go on to score numerous Sinatra films such as *Ocean's Eleven* and *Robin and the 7 Hoods,* but what's most striking about his work within all these films, especially here on *Johnny Concho,* is that he is a competent but rarely inspired composer. His genius lay in his skills as an arranger, one able to showcase a singer's voice to maximum advantage by working in a variety of textures and orchestral combinations that were at once surprising yet somehow inevitable. His composing work, by way of comparison, while competent and seldom getting in the way of the film, rarely adds to the texture of a movie.

As the film unspools at a fairly quick pace toward its conclusion (like a true B Western, it runs a very tight eighty-five minutes), Johnny and Mary try to marry, but somehow it's only now that Mary exhibits the slightest doubt about Johnny. When she goes on to fervently tell Johnny, "I fell in love with you when you rode into town six years ago with your brother—what made you change?" the audience has a question of their own for her: "He's a loser who rode into town with his homicidal brother. What the heck did you ever see in him?" He's the same cowardly punk now as he was then. Johnny answers Mary that "a man gets scared when he's wrong—Red's courage was mine. . . . I'm dead, just ain't got the guts to lie down." It's an interesting, character-revealing answer, but Mary's a sharp cookie—didn't she understand that earlier? How is an audience supposed to believe any of this nonsense?

The exchange of dialogue also points up another of the film's main faults: this is a Western with a great deal of dialogue and very little action. Given the standards of *Johnny Concho,* it's difficult to figure out how the West was won—unless it was by talking everyone to death. In fact, so verbose is the film that when Tallman shoots the one townsman who dares to stand up to him, the surprise lies not in the shooting of the brave townsman, but rather in the fact that there's any physical action at all. If, as F. Scott Fitzgerald's dictum would have it, action equals character, there's certainly very little character revealed here.

When Johnny at long last screws up his courage and returns home, there is a terrific bit of acting by Sinatra as he rides into town during the night, eventually coming face-to-face with Tallman. In response to Tallman's sneering question "You lookin' for someone?" Johnny stares Tallman directly in the face for the first time, and murmurs a scared-sounding "Yes . . . I am." Sinatra manages to convincingly look and sound like a cowering weakling, yet at the same time convey the fact that Johnny is determined to force himself forward for the sake of the townspeople. Calling Tallman "scum like my brother," Johnny is now worthy of the town's respect and Mary's love. For the first time, he displays an actual conscience.

And yet, hard as it is to believe, the movie reserves its strangest little twitch for the end. The audience expects Johnny to finally shoot Tallman; after all, he has found courage, however tentative, and the audience waits, ready and eager for his redemption. But what actually happens? Tallman shoots Johnny, who collapses in the street as Mary rushes to help him. The townspeople, led by Mary's father (who has been the biggest coward of all), all let loose with their guns and shoot Tallman dead.

The payoff has been denied; Johnny has triumphed by words, not by action—it's the townspeople who shoot Tallman. It's a very strange denoue-ment in this most action-oriented of genres, one made all the stranger by Johnny and Mary walking down Main Street at film's end with arms wrapped around each other, the wounded Johnny now miraculously able to stop hold-ing his bullet wound mere seconds after being shot. As for Johnny's quest for self-knowledge and salvation—well, he does seem to have achieved an odd sort of redemption, but salvation does not exactly appear to be in the cards.

For all its peculiarities, *Johnny Concho* is not without interest, for the sim-ple reason that Frank has here added another layer in his evolution from song-and-dance man to serious dramatic actor. The public wasn't buying it, however, and when the film premiered at New York's Paramount Theater, even a singing appearance reuniting Sinatra with the combined bands of Jimmy and Tommy Dorsey could not noticeably boost the film's box office receipts. Critical reaction certainly didn't help matters, *The New York Times* suggest-ing bluntly that "Mr. Sinatra, the actor, might mention to the producer, who happens to be Mr. Sinatra, that he needs better writing and direction than he gets here."

Sinatra may have been riding high on the record charts at the time, with both *Songs for Swingin' Lovers* and *This Is Sinatra* registering as top-ten LPs during 1956, but the flop of *Johnny Concho,* his maiden producing venture, still hurt. It was time to regroup with a return to the much more congenial setting of the MGM musical, with an all-star remake of *The Philadelphia Story* titled *High Society.* It may not be one of the greatest musicals ever made, but it nonetheless rates as a very solid and entertaining effort, one that af-forded audiences the pleasures—and large they were—of seeing and hearing Bing Crosby duet with both Frank Sinatra and Louis Armstrong.

Sinatra, third-billed in alphabetical order after Bing Crosby and Grace Kelly, received a hefty fee of $250,000 for his participation in the John Patrick–scripted musicalization of Philip Barry's classic 1930s play. Detailing the marital comings and goings amongst the very rich, *High Society* transplants Barry's original story from Philadelphia's Main Line to the mansions of New-port, Rhode Island. Willful heiress Tracy Lord (Grace Kelly playing the role fa-mously originated by Katharine Hepburn) is about to marry safe, respectable

George Kittredge (John Lund), a stolid, reassuring contrast to her first husband, free spirit C. K. Dexter-Haven (Bing Crosby playing Cary Grant's original role). Tracy and Dexter still carry a torch for each other even if Tracy doesn't quite realize it yet, and when reporter Mike Connor (Sinatra in the James Stewart role) and photographer Liz Imbrie (Celeste Holm) show up to report on the wedding for *Spy* magazine, sparks begin to fly; Tracy enchants all three men, and it is only moments before the wedding is to take place that she realizes her true love for Dexter. One-two-three—there's a change of groom at the altar, and Tracy and Dexter are happily remarried. Well, as F. Scott Fitzgerald would say, the rich are different from you and me, right down to switching prospective spouses at the very last minute.

High Society reunited Sinatra with his *Tender Trap* costar Celeste Holm, as well as that film's director, Charles Walters, who also stages *High Society*'s musical numbers. It's a movie with three indisputable assets: Louis Armstrong, the terrific score by Cole Porter, and Frank Sinatra. When those three assets are allowed to drive the action, *High Society* soars to the top level of musicals. Without Sinatra and Armstrong onscreen, the film often treads water, just marking time until the musical stars swing into action. But when they do, especially when Crosby joins either man—well, as the score would have it, "they're sensational."

Opening with an aerial shot of the mansions of Newport, Rhode Island, the first sound heard in the film is the distinctive all-American voice of the great Satchmo, Louis Armstrong, singing "High Society Calypso." Satch and his band are on a chartered bus to Newport, arriving to play in the jazz festival and provide a little musical background for Tracy Lord's wedding festivities. Satchmo having arrived, Tracy herself, in the person of the extraordinarily beautiful Grace Kelly, bursts into the drawing room of the family mansion, loaded down with presents for her wedding the next day. It is left to her eleven-year-old sister Caroline (Lydia Reed) to make it clear that her pal Dexter is a much better choice as husband material than the stiff, boring George.

Well, what kind of chance does George really have if Dexter is friends with no less than Louis Armstrong? Moreover, while George would be more at home reciting stock market prices, Dexter can compose a song for Caroline on the spot, complete with Satchmo playing in the background and functioning as a one-man Greek chorus (his comment—a succinct "Right song, wrong girl"). Both Caroline and the audience are charmed, and although everyone knows where it's all heading by now, it doesn't matter; with stars like these, the audience is just happy to be along for the ride. Tracy may berate Dexter for being just a "jukebox hero" when he could have been a serious composer, but even a tin-eared hermit would tell her to get with the program after hearing "Little One." Crosby may not be making much of an attempt to play anything but the public's idea of Bing Crosby, but put him within shouting distance of a song, and he hits a home run every time at bat.

The press, in the form of Mike Connor and Liz Imbrie (Frank Sinatra and Celeste Holm), turn up twenty minutes into the film to cover the high-society wedding. Mike and Liz are welcome additions to the scene because, in contrast to the rather snobby Lord family (skirt-chasing Uncle Willie excepted), it is immediately established via their jaunty walks and even snappier patter, that the "real" American folk have now arrived on the scene. Eyeing the Lord mansion, Mike wisecracks, "I'm scared—I want to go home," to which Liz retorts, "This looks like the type of place where peace treaties are signed."

Grace Kelly, whose upcoming wedding to Prince Rainier of Monaco caused a speeding up of production on the film, not to mention her premature retirement from films, has a distinctly uphill climb throughout the first half of the film. She is not only competing with the ghost of Katharine Hepburn in her signature role, but she is also a nonsinging actress appearing in a musical film with the two most popular male singers of the time, both of whom are bona fide movie musical stars to boot. Her lack of musical chops is made evident by virtue of the fact that she sings only once, joining Crosby at the tail end of the "True Love" duet—any further vocals would simply have ruined the spirit of the film. She's game throughout, but saddled with most of the more ponderous dialogue, a state of affairs that results in Tracy seeming more like an East Coast snob who speaks in stereotypical lockjaw fashion than like a society girl whose brittle exterior barely masks her charms and zest for life (her "banked fires" in the words of Philip Barry's original play). As a result, there are occasional moments during the film when the audience simply wonders, Why are three men all interested in this snob?

Beautiful as she is, Kelly is also not helped by Walters in these sections, the director favoring flat long shots in dialogue-heavy scenes, as if trying to make sure the screen is filled for the VistaVision wide-screen filming process being utilized. Walters, known as a sensitive director of women (as with George Cukor, this phrase functioned as code for "gay director"), does well by the musical numbers in his dual functions as director and choreographer, but is better represented by other films, particularly his terrific handling of Doris Day in *Please Don't Eat the Daisies* and the underrated elegiac musical *Billy Rose's Jumbo*. In *High Society,* after the initial exposition, there's a long stretch without any musical numbers, and audience interest flags until Sinatra and Holm appear on the scene, inquiring of each other, "Who Wants to Be a Millionaire?" It may not be top-drawer Porter (although second-tier Porter is better than the best of most everyone else), but it sure is a lot of fun to see two renowned pros having a high old time of it. Good as it is, however, this song is immediately topped by the "True Love" sequence, featuring Dexter and Tracy.

When Dexter arrives to give his wedding present to Tracy—a model of their sailboat, the *True Love*—Walters employs a very nice cut between Tracy's launching of the toy sailboat in the pool and footage of Dexter and Tracy on the real boat. As Bing sings the beautiful Porter ballad "True Love" (Academy Award winner for Best Song) with concertina in hand, it's a picture-postcard idyllic moment. Who cares that waves and wind seem to have mysteriously disappeared, or even that Dexter, who seems to be an entire generation older than Tracy, seems somewhat disengaged, both physically and emotionally, from the woman who supposedly represents the great love of his life? This is Bing singing Cole Porter, and it's pretty terrific.

In a manner of speaking, the differences in Sinatra and Crosby singing on film can be appreciated in this very sequence; Crosby possesses an instrument of extraordinary beauty, a gorgeous baritone voice that effortlessly runs up and down the scales, but while Sinatra prefers to generate passion by singing directly to the object of his serenade, Crosby seems more at home gazing out to the horizon or singing to the camera. Physical proximity was not Crosby's strong point on film, and oddly enough, he and Kelly generated more heat as the unhappy husband and wife in *The Country Girl* than as this divorced, soon-to-be-rewed couple. Kelly, who later in life joked about her lack of singing ability, here joins in for some simple, effective closing harmony, and as the sequence cuts back to Tracy by the pool, the number circles back to its starting point, a three-act play complete unto itself.

The problem with the film is that the lighter-than-air feeling generated in such musical numbers rapidly disappears in the dialogue sequences, especially those with a strangely subpar Sidney Blackmer, who plays Tracy's father with an utter lack of vocal inflection. Fortunately, the film regains its stride when Mike and Tracy begin their mutual dance of seduction. First one does have to get past the eerily prescient sequence of Tracy ordering Mike into her sports car, whereupon she drives much too quickly on somewhat winding roads and tells Mike they are going to "the graveyard." Given Grace Kelly's own tragic death behind the wheel of her car on winding roads in Monaco, it's difficult to closely listen to the information being imparted, so disconcerting is the visual.

But—and it's a big "but"—this is followed by Sinatra singing another terrific Cole Porter song, "You're Sensational," directly to Tracy. It's a wonderful moment, and Walters stages the song beautifully, Sinatra singing verse and chorus in a two-shot (Sinatra and Kelly together in the frame) before then cutting between close-ups of the two stars. Mike is here making love to Tracy directly in song. So effective is Sinatra's singing, and so nicely conveyed is Kelly's wordless conflicted response, that the three-minute musical sequence not only serves to start the thawing of ice maiden Tracy, but it actually relaxes Kelly as an actress. She has been too tense in her attempt at conveying brittleness heretofore, never quite achieving the skillful balance of arrogance and charm that informed Katharine Hepburn's portrayal of Tracy in *The Philadelphia Story.* Her reactions to Frank's beautiful song—her understanding and delight—achieve what all the preceding words have not. Tracy is now worth the audience's rooting interest.

It's clear that Tracy belongs with the charming Dexter, and it's a weakness more evident here than in *The Philadelphia Story* that the priggish George, who is outraged when the tipsy Tracy suggests he "lie down with her," is a dolt. In John Lund's all too stolid performance, he is a straw man, unworthy of Tracy's love. He's not a creditable rival to Dexter, but Sinatra's Mike sure is. Sinatra is here in high charm mode, portraying an everyman working reporter with great ease; surveying the wealthy fancy-dress crowd at the rehearsal dinner dance, he captures all the fun and pretense in his smiling comment, "Quite a brawl." When Tracy becomes drunk on champagne, it's no wonder that she feels compelled to tell everyone at the dance that she's "sensational," so memorable is Sinatra's romantic rendering of the song.

That quiet moment is equaled and then topped by the two upbeat duets to follow: "Now You Has Jazz" sung by Bing and Louis Armstrong at the wedding-eve dinner dance, and Frank and Bing's duet on the clever and catchy

"Well, Did You Evah!" (originally written for the 1939 Broadway musical *Du Barry Was a Lady* and sung onstage by Betty Grable and *High Society* director Charles Walters).

"Now You Has Jazz" may be introduced with the flimsiest of pretexts— Dexter presenting his recently written song to friend Louis—but a great musical moment is achieved in the process. The two American icons, who clearly like and respect each other, let loose on a number that is sheer fun. Armstrong's impeccable trumpet playing and brilliantly versatile foghorn of a voice combine with Crosby's relaxed phrasing to lift the film, and the audience's interest, to an even higher plane. Crosby, whose musical roots lay in jazz and Dixieland, seems totally at ease.

Always known for his relaxed, casual style (he was known on the set as Nembutal, as opposed to the more manic Sinatra's moniker of Dexedrine), Crosby on film often gave one the sense that he was acting the role of a supremely mellow performer. Yes, he was relaxed, but he was also an actor, with a tightly coiled spring inside, a state of affairs attested to by the famously troubled relationship with his sons from his first marriage. Here, the sheer joy of singing and performing with his friend Satchmo unleashes his most expressive body language in the film—arms outstretched, fingers snapping, and entire body bouncing, he is a man at the top of his game.

Even better is the most fondly remembered sequence in the film, the "Well, Did You Evah!" musical number, which is beautifully staged by Walters and arranged in top-drawer fashion by Nelson Riddle and Conrad Salinger. When the dialogue between a drunk Mike and the imperturbable Dexter suggests that Tracy still may not understand how much Dexter loves her, the two men are off and running, gently swinging this engaging Porter "list" song:

What frills, what frocks!
What furs, what rocks!

Dancing first by themselves, then in tandem around the bar, where they help themselves to another round, the boys—and they are decidedly boys here—lift the song into the pantheon of great musical moments through the sheer force of their personalities. When Bing throws in his trademark word-

Sensational duet with Bing on Cole Porter's "Well, Did You Evah?" in High Society.

less crooning, all "ba ba boo," Sinatra cuts through with the smiling gibe: "Don't dig that kind of crooning, chum." Even better, Crosby then proceeds to one-up him with an ad-libbed, "You must be one of the newer fellows."

Frank and Bing are at their peak, making it appear that they're improvising the entire routine, just a couple of hail fellows well met breezing through the swellegant joint. The reality, of course, is far different. As so accurately deconstructed in Jeanine Basinger's trenchant study of *The Star Machine,* the two stars had to

sing, dance, hit their camera marks, respect the sophisticated Cole Porter lyrics, deliver scripted dialogue, stay within their characters, pretend to be slightly drunk, keep the beat of the orchestra playback, move around a specially designed library set with limited space while following a specific choreography that had to look improvised, and never forget that they were rivals for the audience's affection as Frank and Bing.

It's a tall order, and the boys fill it beautifully. This is not just the high point of the film; it's one of the great moments in the entire Sinatra film catalog. The sheer sense of fun these two pros have together, a palpable joy that, far from being an in-joke, spreads infectiously to the audience, is a delirious display of talent that leaves us grinning from ear to ear. Striding out of the library and into the ballroom to the beat of a Latin rhythm, the men turn right around and strut their way back into the library for another round of drinks. When they finish off the song, striding off in different directions as they joyously belt out the quintessential Porter lyric, "What a swellegant, elegant party this is," the apex of the film has been reached.

Because Crosby is coasting in the dialogue sequences, the audience is just as interested, if not more so, in watching Tracy with Mike. When Tracy escapes her own party, becoming even more drunk as she and Mike lounge on the patio, the erotic peak of the film is reached as they dance by the pool while Mike sings Porter's lilting rumba, "Mind If I Make Love to You?" The resolution of the plot hinges on fiancé George being reassured that Mike did no such thing, but the fact is, even though Tracy and Mike don't sleep together, he has made love to her through this song, and everyone in the audience knows it. Sinatra sounds at his best here, delivering a sexual charge as any true star does. Rarer still, he delivers it in song. Sinatra's vocal is actually much more seductive than the kissing he and Tracy engage in immediately following, and in his soft, intimate speaking voice, he seems to be such a good match for Tracy that the audience may find themselves thinking, *Never mind about George. Maybe Tracy should also dump Dexter for Mike.*

She doesn't, of course, awakening the next day with an excruciating hangover ("Do you like my dress? It's awfully heavy"), vastly relieved both to rid herself of George and to make up with her father. George is out, Dexter's in, and at fade-out, the marriage takes place to the strains of Louis Armstrong and his jazz quartet playing a swinging version of "Here Comes the Bride." Tracy has finally come to her senses—maybe because nobody but nobody could object to Satchmo playing the wedding march.

The film received a mixed critical reception, but proved popular with audiences, Sinatra's sixth hit out of his last seven movies (*Johnny Concho* being the only box office fizzle). Sinatra had reestablished his box office bona fides, claiming a spot as one of the top ten moneymaking stars of the year in the *Motion Picture Herald* poll. It therefore seemed only natural that Frank, along with every living actor and animal in Hollywood, would next indulge in a little "we're all in this together" Hollywood horseplay by filming a cameo in Mike Todd's Oscar-winning extravaganza, *Around the World in Eighty Days.*

Utilizing three screenwriters (James Poe, John Farrow, S. J. Perelman) and three directors (Michael Anderson, the uncredited John Farrow, and Sidney Smith for the documentary sequence), *Around the World* remains the cinematic vision of one man: producer Mike Todd. Employing hundreds of extras, and cameos by nearly fifty Hollywood stars from George Raft to Ronald Colman, Todd decided to dazzle the audience with his patented Todd-AO widescreen filming, the better to counteract the ever-growing influence of television. It was, in effect, a case of "Give 'em what they can't get on the small home screen." Not a bad philosophy, but also not a recipe for a great movie.

Filmed both on soundstages and in locations worldwide, *Around the World* is truly a mixed bag of a film, the end result playing not so much as a fluid, confident filming of the classic Jules Verne novel as much as a "this is Cinerama" wide-screen travelogue extravaganza with the Verne story tacked on. Employing the essential outline of the Verne novel, the screenplay centers upon English adventurer Phileas Fogg (David Niven) who makes a wager with his fellow gentlemen's club members that he can circle the entire world in eighty days. (The film is set in the late nineteenth century.) Bet accepted, Fogg and his manservant Passepartout (Mexican comedian Cantinflas) hurriedly pack, and the film is off running, training, paddling, and hot air ballooning around the globe.

It's a good premise but Niven's Fogg comes across as a particularly disagreeable snobby Englishman for most of the film, treating Passepartout in a condescending manner startling to modern sensibilities. In his quest to win the twenty-thousand-pound wager he has made with fellow club members, Fogg doesn't change one bit until the final scenes, making any audience sympathy for him questionable at best. Mostly the audience is reduced to spotting the stars: Noel Coward here, Peter Lorre and Buster Keaton there. None of the cameo-size roles require the slightest bit of acting, and the audience is left with a sense of stars larking about for the hell of it. Stretched to unreasonable length (prizes should be given to those who can sit through José Greco's endless dancing on a tabletop), the extended sequences cause the film to feel even longer than its three-hour running time.

When Fogg arrives in America for the final leg of his journey, he lands in a Western honky-tonk saloon presided over by Marlene Dietrich in a long blond wig, looking for all the world like she's thinking, *Oh, what the hell. Someone's got to be the madam here, and it might as well be me.* And someone else has to be the saloon's piano player, pounding out a brassy tune and making a helluva racket. The viewer is teased no fewer than three times with the back of the piano player's head before he turns around and, no—it's *not* the most famous of all 1950s pianists, Liberace. Cigarette dangling out of his mouth, blue eyes flashing and a slow small smile playing on his face, it's Francis Albert Sinatra making his presence known. No words, no further action; that's it for Frankie.

Sinatra is called upon to do neither more nor less than any of the other fifty guest stars, which leads to a consideration of the most interesting aspect of the film; this fitfully fun, occasionally leaden travelogue-cum–all-star extravaganza never could have won the Best Picture of the Year Academy Award (which it did in April 1957) if it had been made even five years later. As Bosley Crowther wrote in his *New York Times* review of the film "Mr. Todd . . . wasn't making a film that had a form. He was using the screen as a canvas on which to mount a giant variety show. . . ." When television invaded every American household, and technological improvement made it easy for audiences to sample global lifestyle without leaving their living rooms, the end of such globe-trotting festivities was in sight. Frank Sinatra was participating in one of the last all-star golden age Hollywood parties. As the studio system fractured and disintegrated, the last remnants of a sense of Hollywood community were also disappearing. Such community-wide participation would become nearly impossible in the future, and it is no accident that the early-twenty-first-century remake of *Around the World in Eighty Days,* starring global action icon Jackie Chan, was an enormous failure.

Cameo completed, Sinatra was on to new feature film territory. Unfortunately, the new territory meant a trip to old Spain with *The Pride and the Passion.* The ensuing production resulted in one of the unhappiest experiences of Sinatra's film career, and considering the turmoil he caused, it couldn't have been any better for producer/director Stanley Kramer.

A lavish MGM Technicolor epic, *The Pride and the Passion* was released in 1957, with Sinatra receiving second billing, after Cary Grant but ahead of Sophia Loren. It's a bloated self-important pic detailing the struggles of Spanish peasants to haul an enormous cannon across the countryside in order to defeat their French occupiers. Lavish in scope, the film proved a colossal undertaking, involving a budget of nearly $4 million, with a production crew of 400, and 9,400 extras, but the end product is, in a word, leaden.

The first warning sign for the film comes with the credits, announcing that the screenplay (based on the C. S. Forester novel *The Gun*) is by Edward and Edna Anhalt, with a musical score composed by George Antheil, the very same team responsible for the bloated *Not as a Stranger*. Unfortunately for the viewer, their contributions are not an improvement on that previous work. There's much heaving, a lot of angst, little pride—and no passion.

The object of all the strenuous effort is a cannon that is desired by the Spanish, the French, and even the English. The English are represented in the person of Anthony Trumbull (Cary Grant), an admiral who immediately butts head with Miguel (Sinatra), the leader of the Spanish peasants. Also along for the ride is lusty Spanish peasant Juana (Sophia Loren), Miguel's girlfriend, who falls in love with Trumbull. The screenplay occasionally tries to interest the viewer in the love triangle—and fails—but mostly the Anhalts are content to simply depict sequence after sequence of the cannon being dragged through mud, the muscles of the virtuous peasants heaving with the strain. It's an approach that leaves a mighty big problem: after the interesting initial low-angle camera shot of the giant cannon teetering along the edge of a cliff, the dramatic possibilities are pretty well exhausted. The cannon's big—end of story.

With no character development to speak of in the film, the viewer's interest is nil. It may have been the intention to show that the cannon is more important than the peasants, that it represents their ticket to freedom, but such an intent is better left for the history books or philosophy texts, because it certainly doesn't make for an engaging movie. Certainly, a large part of the fault lies with director Kramer. A noted Hollywood liberal, Kramer tackled the big ideas—nuclear bombs in *On the Beach,* racism in *The Defiant Ones,* not to mention the medical profession in *Not as a Stranger*—but he often seems more interested in the ideas themselves than in the characters he was presenting on-screen. Critic Pauline Kael, who particularly disliked Kramer's films, bluntly stated, "Stanley Kramer runs for office in the arts." Up to a certain point, Kael is correct—the characters in *The Pride and the Passion* resemble human "talking points" more than they do real people—but perhaps the most accurate assessment is that of Kramer's fellow director Norman Jewison, who simply stated: "Stanley was a better producer than he was a director."

The dreariness is made even worse by the film's total lack of humor. This is surely the glummest bunch of lusty peasants ever to grunt their way across the countryside. Worst of all, the overblown score assaults the viewer with incessant and strident martial airs. Director Kramer and composer Antheil inexplicably do not allow the viewers to discover anything for themselves, all but hitting the audience over the head with an approach that says, "This is an important moment because the instruments will now thunder." Suffice it to say, it's the sort of score that loudly plays "Rule, Britannia!" when Trumbull loses his hat and it is squashed underneath the cannon.

And what of the stars? None of them fare particularly well, with Sinatra coming off the worst. Cary Grant appears to have wandered in from another costume drama, never remotely suggesting that he is on Spanish soil, and this normally terrific actor is, in his squabbles with Miguel, reduced to a dyspeptic stick-in-the-mud. He is condescending toward the Spanish and all but states that he'd rather be back in a Mayfair drawing room. Of course, who can fully blame him, given the fact that at one point in the film, he is reduced to riding a donkey as windmills whirl in the background. "Gee," the filmmakers seem to be saying, "it's just like Cervantes's *Don Quixote,* and that was Spanish, too. Get it?" Ugh.

Sophia Loren, in her American film debut, appears markedly more Italian than Spanish, and one can't help idly contemplating the fact that evidently the Spain of 1810 featured numerous beauty parlors just out of sight of the camera, so perfect are her eyeliner, false eyelashes, and exquisitely shaped eyebrows. Foundation and lipstick flawless, Loren's Juana is one immaculately groomed nineteenth-century peasant. She exchanges fiery glances with Grant, but he appears nothing so much as bored (an odd reaction, considering that he proposed marriage to Loren during the filming of the movie). For its own entertainment, the audience might just as well spend its time wondering how Juana managed not only to wear extremely tight-fitting low-cut blouses during the grueling cross-country haul, but also to have a pair of wedgies handy, the better to dance a snappy flamenco in the town square.

Sinatra's performance is understated to the point that one very quickly begins to ask, Where is the passion that would cause this illiterate peasant to risk his life and lead thousands of his countrymen to fight for freedom? Sinatra's Miguel is so low-key that he appears more interested in making Juana a new pair of sandals than in fighting off foreign oppressors. Sinatra was capable of conveying great passion onscreen, and could have managed such an approach here but, together with director Kramer, appears to have eschewed any histrionics in his approach. So lacking is his performance in characterization, nuance, or audience interest, that it really does rank as the worst performance of his movie career. Nonsense like *Double Dynamite* never pretended to be anything other than the gibberish it was. *The Pride and the Passion,* however, seems to be attempting a self-important essay on the nobility of the peasants resisting foreign invaders. As to how well it achieves that goal, any native New Yorker would say in an accent matching Sinatra's New Jersey–cum-Madrid dialect, "Fuhgeddaboutit."

To make matters worse, Sinatra is here encumbered with a ridiculous wig—featuring bangs, no less. Never for an instant suggesting a peasant of the land, he exudes nothing so much as the air of a twentieth-century urban male, and an American to boot. This is one Spanish proletarian who'd be more at home in a Manhattan saloon than dragging a cannon across the countryside. In addition, Frank becomes trapped by the very structure of the epic film; in presenting a film of spectacle set in the past, filmmakers inevitably run up against an audience response of, *Oh, come on—they didn't really talk like that.* It's why the most successful epic films usually triumph through their pictorial aspects rather than by their often moralistic dialogue. Here, Sinatra suffers through the worst of both: he's competing with the cannon for space in the frame, and he's also saddled with ridiculous dialogue. Although it has been reported that Sinatra worked with his musician friend Victor Gomez to develop a convincing Spanish accent, the results are, to put it kindly, nowhere in evidence. Frank sounds like the Frito Bandito, asking "Chu vould like to see thees gun?" and worst of all, "Citizens of Delgado, I speet in your face." What the hell is going on? The answer's simple: nothing good—and it's no accident that Frank Sinatra did not attempt to change his speaking voice for another movie until the equally misbegotten *Dirty Dingus Magee,* thirteen years later.

Frank appears unhappy and ill at ease throughout, and his well-documented displeasure during filming registers onscreen. He may have started out with the best of intentions, happy with his $250,000 paycheck, but it sure doesn't show in the finished film. From the start, Frank was not in the best of moods on set, given the continuing problems with Ava; Gardner, who was living in Spain, became furious that Sinatra had arrived in Spain with young singer Peggy Connolly in tow, and Frank's displeasure with the Ava situation, coupled with his anger over delays on location, soon manifested itself in unprofessional behavior. Refusing to stay on location with the rest of the company, Sinatra insisted on staying at the Hilton in Madrid, a three-hour journey away from the location shooting, seemingly more concerned with his contractually required twenty-five dollars per day for tips and incidentals than with developing a coherent characterization.

Although he had guaranteed he'd be present for sixteen weeks of location shooting, Frank quit the location at the end of July 1956, with several weeks of shooting still remaining; after he flew back to the United States, his remaining scenes were filmed on a noticeably phony-looking soundstage. Sinatra's difficult behavior caused Kramer to throw up his hands in despair and simply work around, and not with, Frank. Sinatra wouldn't budge, and the film suffered as a

Sophia Loren, Frank, and Cary Grant, stuck dragging a cannon around Spain in the endless The Pride and the Passion *(1957).*

result. Just how difficult Sinatra proved for his director in that situation can be gauged by comments Kramer made when participating in a series of seminars at the American Film Institute in the 1970s. Asked "How do you handle difficult actors?" his blunt response was, "You don't. There is no resolution. Someone like Frank Sinatra had problems; he always did. . . . Once he said to me, in the middle of Europe, 'Hot or cold, Thursday I'm leaving.' I had seven weeks left to shoot. So he left. That's a problem. It was solved by two days' work back in a studio with potted palms." Unfortunately the solution didn't work—the soundstage scenes in question jar insistently, so phony do they look compared with the scenes shot on the Spanish locations.

The result of such actions, according to Daniel O'Brien: "The incident . . . reaffirmed his reputation as a difficult talent whose bad moods and lack of commitment did a lot more harm than merely upsetting his co-workers." That sort of behavior undoubtedly led to Kramer's barbed comment, "If Sinatra really wanted to work, prepare for a role, research it, he'd be the best in the world." Twenty-plus years after the film's release, Kramer clearly could not forget the difficulties Sinatra had caused; writing a tribute to Spencer Tracy, Kramer needled,

> Spencer Tracy liked Frank Sinatra. I guess it takes one impatient to know another. He would tell with great glee how Sinatra . . . made a company rebuild all its sets in California because he didn't want to go to Madrid. I didn't think it half so amusing as Tracy did, because it had also happened to me.

In point of fact, Frank's unreasonable behavior and the ensuing budget overruns would have been forgiven if the result was an artistic winner. It wasn't. Based on the onscreen evidence, it's impossible to even guess what reasons Sinatra could have had for making this film. The part is beyond his range—it's so poorly written that it is beyond anyone's range; certainly it must have become clear to Frank early on in filming that the stars were secondary to the Spanish countryside, with far more screen time devoted to panoramic shots of peasants hauling the cannon up hill and over dale than to such wacky elements as, say, character development. Elements that would have heightened audience interest—like the fact that the French invaders were hanging ten Spaniards every day—are not depicted. The audience is handed such potentially involving information via dialogue, yet nothing of the kind is shown onscreen, skimping on a visual element that would have aided comprehension of why the peasants were inflamed with passion.

Instead, the viewer suffers through several scenes of French General Jouvet, who, as played by Theodore Bikel, is remarkably un-Gallic but nonetheless pounds a map and chastises his subordinates for not catching the guerrillas. This isn't Spain in 1810—it's a group of talented actors posing stiffly in a ponderous period costume drama. When in doubt, Kramer resorts over and over to a wide-screen shot of columns of peasants marching along the horizon. *Ah,* the director and screenwriters seem to be telling us, *the nobility of the earthy peasant.*

What they're forgetting is that masses of peasants who are never personalized don't make for an interesting or involving story, epic background or not. The tragedy of one person explored in full, functioning as a metaphor for the suffering of thousands develops a lot more in the way of audience investment than do repeated shots of bedraggled men and women pushing an artillery piece. The damn cannon is shown so endlessly that the viewer begins to wonder if it had a particularly savvy agent who demanded his client receive more close-ups than Frank, Sophia, or Cary.

Sophia Loren heaves lustily, Cary Grant scowls, and a very bored Frank Sinatra speaks with a phony accent while the bangs of his wig never move an inch, no matter how grueling the physical action. So uninterested does Grant appear, and so uninvolving are his supposedly emotional onscreen confrontations with Sinatra, that the most noteworthy aspect of Grant's participation in the film actually comes from his up-close and rather succinct postfilming analysis of the Sinatra personality: "Frank fascinates the curious . . . hoping to discover those qualities responsible for the man's personal appeal. Well, I think I know the quality. It's truth. Simple truth. Without artifice."

When the stars actually do have dialogue, it unfortunately runs along the lines of Juana chastising the seemingly unfeeling Trumbull: "Captain, I have a feeling you'd like to act more like a man than a cold English piece of mutton." When Juana and Trumbull give in to their mutual passion, in true 1950s Hollywood style, it is all heavy breathing and heaving bosoms. As they passionately kiss, there is a "tasteful" fade-out to the heavens above, whereupon they are next glimpsed spotless and fully clothed, murmuring sweet nothings to each other on an artificial studio set that has absolutely nothing to do with the Spain of 1810 in the midst of the Peninsular War. Trumbull and Juana share no common interests and maintain different worldviews—the entire relationship strikes the viewer as ridiculous. One can't exactly picture Juana dancing the flamenco back in Mayfair.

Truth to tell, the only extended sequence of genuine visual interest occurs when the peasants are allowed to hide the cannon in a stupendous cathedral, while iconic depictions of Christ are wheeled around and about during the Holy Week festivities. It's not just the ironic juxtaposition of the cannon, simultaneously an instrument of destruction and liberation, being hidden within the holy building; it's the fact that Kramer and director of photography Franz Planer shoot the parade of icons from on high as well as on the ground, crosscutting between shots so that the viewer finally gains a simultaneous sense of both the physical and emotional stakes at hand.

Such interesting camera angles, however, cannot begin to make up for the lack of a compelling story. Perhaps out of desperation, the screenwriters take to wholesale pilfering from other, decidedly superior films. When at film's end Juana refuses to renounce Miguel for Trumbull—"Everything you mean to me, and it's so much, is not enough. I'm Spanish. I'm part of Avila"—the parallels to Ilsa at the end of *Casablanca* are noticeable. It's just that Ilsa sacrifices her love for Rick in order to help her husband continue his fight against the Nazis, whereas based on the preceding two hours, Juana appears to be renouncing her love for the good of . . . a cannon. Juana dies in Trumbull's arms, Miguel is slaughtered, and in a final bit of nonsense, Trumbull walks to the horizon and in noble profile motions for the peasants to follow him. This snobby Englishman has spent two hours disdaining the Spanish peasants, barely able to refrain from holding his nose when required to wear one of their jackets. Now he will lead them on their quest? All that's missing is a chorus of "The Impossible Dream." Instead, the overheated orchestra blares out a few final bars as a chorus of hundreds bellows out final notes of inspiration. Just awful.

The combined appeal of the three stars was enough to ensure that the film landed another box office hit for Sinatra, and it helped solidify his place in the list of top-ten box office stars. Critics, however, were not pleased, with Bosley Crowther in his incisive *New York Times* review finding "Not since . . . *The Ten Commandments* have we seen . . . such a casual disregard for plausibility. . . . Frank Sinatra as the Spanish leader is possessed of an evident inner fire that glows but fitfully on rare occasions. . . . Mr. Kramer has spread a mighty canvas, but it has virtually no human depth." In the end, Frank Sinatra himself delivered the final and most accurate verdict on *The Pride and the Passion.* Twelve years later, on his November 5, 1969, television special titled *Sinatra,* Frank included a humorous sequence wherein he made fun of his own worst movies. His three featured selections? *The Kissing Bandit, Johnny Concho,* and *The Pride and the Passion.* All three were "outdoor" films and all three were, to put it kindly, subpar. Sinatra even further singled out *The Pride and the Passion* for humorous self-ridicule on his 1973 television comeback special *Ol' Blue Eyes Is Back.* Frank knew. He usually did.

Between the release of the abysmal *The Pride and the Passion* and his next film, the flawed-but-worthy *The Joker Is Wild,* Ava was granted a divorce from Frank in Mexico City. The tempestuous love affair had burned itself out—not the love itself, but the love affair. Sinatra, like Gatsby—or more to the point, F. Scott Fitzgerald himself with his first love and lifelong muse, Ginevra King—seemed always in search of "the perfect hour," that rare time of completion when love feels passionate, eternal, and full of wonder. With Ava, perfect minutes abounded, and forever after, both Frank and Ava yearned for those quicksilver moments, convincing themselves that only the other had ever fully understood and fulfilled them, heart and soul. But a perfect hour? With the volatile temperaments that Frank and Ava possessed, a golden minute or two would always be the limit. A perfect hour could be found only onstage, where the emotional subtext found the audience granting Frank forgiveness for everything he couldn't forgive in himself.

Popular myth has it that Sinatra suffered more over Ava than the reverse, and it is likely true. When separated from Sinatra, Ava had no problem taking pleasure in the company of handsome matadors or costars such as Walter Chiari. At the same time, in the words of her friend Betty Sicre: "He was on her mind in some way just about every day of her life." Sinatra, on the other hand, seemed to burn with even greater passion when separated from Ava—the drama of it all fed his love, his rage, and his sadness. But as the reconciliations grew briefer and the dismay increased, even Sinatra bowed to the inevitable; the divorce became final on July 5, 1957.

After all the fights and reconciliations, the straw that broke the camel's back for Ava was the day Sinatra called her and announced on the phone that he was in bed with another woman. In Sinatra's view, if Ava was going to continually accuse him of adultery then he might just as well be guilty of such infidelity in reality. For Ava, this was, to use the title of one of Sinatra's brilliantly boozy albums, the point of no return. "It was a chilling moment. I was deeply hurt. I knew then that we had reached a crossroads. Not because we had fallen out of love, but because our love had so battered and bruised us that we couldn't stand it anymore."

Frank and Ava were to remain friends—and occasional adversaries—for the rest of Ava's life. Like Mia Farrow after her, she asked for no alimony, and according to Ava's longtime companion Mearene Jordan, Sinatra continued to phone Ava throughout the remainder of her life: "He was always calling her up; even when he was marrying Barbara, he called her several times and asked if she would come back."

In future years, Ava, who had always lived life as the ultimate realist, actually began to view her years with Frank through rose-colored glasses, smoothing away the rough edges until she found solace in her memories: "She had come to think of him as the one person in the world who understood her, who wanted nothing from her." In what may be the most startling image in the entire decades-long Sinatra/Gardner grand passion, restaurateur Claude Terrail described a scene in 1962 that found Ava playing Sinatra records and having a private conversation with him, answering his sung declarations of love with softly spoken words: "Yes, yes, I know. . . . No, don't say that. . . . You must forget." Powerful and ultimately more sad than any other aspect of the saga, if it were all just a movie, the fade-out would occur there, the key light on Ava fading to a pinspot and then total darkness as Sinatra's pain-filled murmurings fill the soundtrack. . . .

By the end of Ava's life, the battles, the angry words, and the vicious insults had all dissolved into a determinedly golden haze, but in 1957, she just wanted out. True to form, however, the reconciliations continued, and in 1963, the reunited lovers actually began planning a new life together, a thought that thrilled Dolly Sinatra. It had, after all, been Ava who effected Frank's reconciliation with his parents after two years of silence due to a dispute over money. It's certainly not a surprise that the equally earthy Ava and Dolly had taken an instant shine to each other:

I took one look at Dolly and saw where Frank got it all from: the blue eyes, the fair hair, the smile, the essential charm, cockiness and

determination. She took one look and hugged me like her own daughter. She always said I'd brought her son back to her.

(Just how simpatico they were is revealed by Dolly's "tender" words trying
to effect an earlier reconciliation: "You know you two kids love each other so
quit all this fuckin' shit for God's sake!")

Like Mia Farrow after her, Ava was happiest when alone with Sinatra; it
was the ever-present claque of hangers-on she could not face. In the words of
Mearene Jordan: "She loved him; she just didn't love some of the people that
he had to have with him." More specifically, what Ava hadn't counted on was
Frank's continuing friendship with Sam Giancana and others of questionable
background. Frank may have wanted—indeed, required—a placid acceptance of his friends, but with Ava, placid acceptance would never be in the
cards. Stated Giancana's longtime girlfriend, singer Phyllis McGuire, "Ava
didn't like those types of people at all. She hated the image. It wasn't just
Sam, either. Frank had others around him all the time and when Ava found
out . . . she really gave him hell." The fights started up in earnest, glasses were
thrown, liquor hurled in Sinatra's face, and when, in the aftermath of one passionate reconciliation, such an incident occurred in front of Giancana himself, the deep affront to Frank's Italian sense of pride and masculinity spelled
disaster. The reconciliation was over.

Continuing his affiliations with strong, no-nonsense women, it was during
this post-Ava time that Sinatra formed an intriguing liaison with Lauren Bacall. Sinatra, who had always greatly admired Bacall's husband, Humphrey
Bogart, for both his acting ability and his tough-guy persona, functioned as a
strong shoulder for Bacall after Bogart's death, and the friendship quickly
blossomed into a love affair. The affair culminated in an engagement that was
called off by Sinatra when word leaked to the press, and while Bacall was
devastated at the time, with the hindsight of years, she admitted that it would
have been a hopeless match, their two strong egos butting heads constantly.
Indeed, with the tough, no-nonsense practicality born of her years as Betty
Joan Perske of the Bronx, Bacall offered a perceptive insight into Sinatra's
character: "I'd say he is both terrified and fascinated by his own life, from
which he draws insufficient joy. He's kind of Don Quixote tilting at windmills, fighting people who don't want to fight."

His personal life in turmoil, Sinatra continued to work at a nonstop clip, relentlessly searching for the next great starring role. In that light, it's actually easy to understand what attracted him to the life story of comic Joe E. Lewis, *The Joker Is Wild*. It's a juicy show business saga in the traditional rise-fall-comeback mode, and as such provided Frank with plenty of opportunities to sing, tell jokes, and suffer both physical and mental anguish—the acting trifecta, as it were. The finished film proved a markedly uneven affair, but its first fifty minutes are consistently entertaining and deliver quite a jolt.

Having bought the rights to Art Cohn's book *The Joker Is Wild* while it was still in galleys, businessman Sinatra then forged an extraordinary deal with Cohn, Lewis himself, and Frank's director of choice, Charles Vidor: Partnering with the other three men, Sinatra sold the package to Paramount, with Frank himself collecting the biggest share of the deal: a fee of $120,000 plus 25 percent of the profits.

Given Sinatra's power and sense of control, it's no wonder he looks so thoroughly at ease as the film bolts out of the gate with a bracing display of confidence. Opening in Chicago during the Roaring '20s, the film quickly sketches in the fact that Joe E. Lewis (Sinatra) is a talented singer working in a dive run by mobsters. The smoky ambience of the club fits the period, and so do the songs—any movie that opens with Sinatra singing "At Sundown" and "I Cried for You" is definitely on the right track. What makes the start even more effective is a top-notch variation on the patented delayed Sinatra entrance, the camera here tracking into the Chicago speakeasy, the sound of his singing heard, but the first glimpse of Frank himself delayed until mid-song. (The terrific orchestrations for all songs in the film were the work of Nelson Riddle, with musical direction by Walter Scharf, who collaborated so memorably with Streisand on the film version of *Funny Girl*.) Throw in some funny dialogue—eyeing the legs of a chorus girl, Lewis croons "Whoo—what a contraption"—and the viewer has an immediate rooting interest in seeing Lewis succeed.

Conflict arises instantly when the club's owner, gangster Tim Coogan (Leonard Graves), forbids Lewis to accept the better offer he has received to sing at the high-class Valencia nightclub. Lewis refuses to be cowed, and even though pianist and sidekick Austin Mack (Eddie Albert) begs him not to cross the gangsters, it's off to the Valencia, where Lewis wows the crowd with "If I Could Be with You" and a terrific Van Heusen/Cahn song composed especially for the film, "All the Way." (Not surprisingly the song won the Academy Award as Best Song of the Year and spent longer on the *Billboard* charts than any other single in Sinatra's recording career.) When Coogan arrives ringside opening night (after sending a funereal wreath of black flowers), Lewis finds himself singing this most romantic of ballads with a murderous gangster staring at him. So slickly evil is Leonard Graves as Coogan, that when he shakes hands with the singing Lewis and refuses to let go of his hand, the tension is damn near palpable. Here are worthy adversaries—in short, everything *The Pride and the Passion* lacked.

Since Lewis refuses to leave the Valencia, Coogan and two cronies bide their time, and weeks later attack Lewis in his hotel room. Director Charles Vidor, who exhibited a similar first-rate understanding of the uneasy blend of show business and gangsters in the two-years-earlier *Love Me or Leave Me,* conveys this beating beautifully: the audience never sees Lewis being attacked. All we hear is the sound of the struggle behind the closed door. Finally, Lewis's bloodstained hand slowly slides out of the room, followed by a shot of his bloody face and ripped clothes. It's a nearly silent sequence, all the more effective for the understated approach utilized in the telling.

The viewer's next glimpse of Sinatra finds him lying in a hospital bed, swathed in bandages, pain etched upon his face. Groaning as he calls out for Austin, Sinatra is downright harrowing as he beats his head against the wall and croaks Austin's name; Coogan has not only beaten in Lewis's skull, he has also slashed his vocal cords. Lewis will never sing again.

Aside from some inconsistency in the period details (the men's clothes look more like those of the 1950s than the '20s and '30s), the film's storytelling registers as swift and sure, the high level of interest sustained as the damaged Lewis disappears to New York. Not wanting to be found by his friends, Lewis has landed in burlesque, working as a clown and drinking hard. Wildly nervous, devastated at losing his livelihood and very identity, Lewis begins to crack jokes about his lack of singing ability. It's a painful sight, especially with Lewis in the clown's outfit that he must wear for a humiliating burlesque bit, but the audience begins to laugh and the seed is planted for a new career.

In a beautifully realized sequence immediately after that benefit performance, Lewis avoids the celebrating partygoers, creeping backstage behind the cyclorama. It's an intriguing perspective, one from which Lewis, who feels like a ghost in show business, can glimpse the partygoers only as backlit shadows. (The atmospheric black-and-white photography is by Daniel L. Fapp, who would work again with Sinatra on *Kings Go Forth*.) When an unnamed singer, clearly based upon Bing Crosby, begins to sing "June in January," Lewis is joined behind the cyclorama by Letty Page (Jeanne Crain), a socialite on the benefit committee. As they quietly listen to the shadowy singer, Letty says to Joe, "He's wonderful, isn't he?" In Sinatra's beautifully calibrated one-word response of "yes," one hears sadness, acknowledgment of another's talent, and wistful jealousy, all at once. As Lewis and Letty quietly dance alone behind the cyclorama, the viewer is totally swept up in the world of the film: forty-five minutes in, nary a false note has been hit. It's almost too good to be true—and it is, but the wheels don't completely come off the train until later.

In the meantime, the audience can continue to enjoy Sinatra's first-rate performance, although the scenes with Crain are problematic. Crain could be an effective actress (*State Fair, A Letter to Three Wives*), but partially through the fault of the screenplay, she here reads as a 1950s debutante slumming in show business. In fact, it is when Letty begins to follow the increasingly successful Joe around the country that the movie hits its first large roadblock. In treating the audience to scene after scene of Lewis's stand-up routines, a sense of sameness creeps in, one that eventually engulfs the viewer. Every routine starts with Lewis uttering his signature line of "post time" as he raises a glass. Lewis drinks nonstop onstage, a tired gimmick that wears out its welcome even more quickly than anticipated because the routines are not particularly funny. Even more to the point, Sinatra is not a natural stand-up comedian. His bottled-up intensity does not readily translate to the role of a liquored-up comic at ease on stage. Dean Martin radiates that kind of relaxed, boozy charm naturally, but Sinatra's version of it has an almost nasty edge. He can barely get out the words, looking as if he is ready to jump out of his skin. Philip K. Scheuer, in his *Los Angeles Times* review of the film, actually pointed out this essential difference between Sinatra and Joe E. Lewis himself: "When Lewis, highball in hand, is reciting [the drunk monologues] his natural clown's grin takes the curse off their cynicism; from Sinatra the gags come out bitter and barbed." (For that matter, if Bing Crosby had played the role, the barely suppressed edge that always made him interesting to watch would have rendered the jokes mean-spirited.)

The Joker Is Wild, *Joe E. Lewis' life story. Terrific first hour.*

Unable to tell Letty that he loves her (says Lewis to Austin's wife, Cassie—"I can't tell her. It wouldn't get a laugh"), he loses her to another man. Sinatra is so sympathetic and vulnerable in this rueful admission to Cassie that he allows the audience to overlook Lewis's boorish behavior. We still want Lewis to triumph. He is increasingly bitter over losing Letty, but it's a bitterness made all the more interesting by Sinatra's hoarse singing of previously unheard lyrics to "All the Way." This Joe E. Lewis is drunk, vulnerable, and pretty damn interesting in Sinatra's warts-and-all portrayal.

The pace of the film has been slowing, especially when compared with the terrific first forty-five minutes, but only now does it turn downright tedious. Marrying chorus cutie Martha (Mitzi Gaynor), Joe embarks upon a new round of unhappiness and bitter behavior. Right off the bat, there's trouble in paradise with Martha up at the crack of dawn to make movies and Joe performing at all hours in nightclubs. Joe and Martha may have problems, but the movie has an even larger one: during its entire second half, Joe does not change at all. His jokes are all about excessive drinking and marriage. There is no jolt of self-recognition on Joe's part, and there is no variety to his behavior—no wonder Martha begins to drink as well.

One of the reasons Frank Sinatra became a movie star of the first rank is because audiences always felt sympathy for him, their interest in his persona encompassing a sympathy for the contradictions in his personality and behavior. Here the screenplay undoes him. Even Sinatra, with his infinite capacity for variation, cannot sustain audience investment when forced to strike the same one note over and over. He is admirably restrained in his playing of the drunk scenes, never resorting to scenery-chewing, but he isn't given any variety of moods to play. When Lewis is unhappy, he drinks. When he's nervous, he drinks. When his marriage bothers him, he drinks. To which the audience can only logically respond: When is he going to change? What will force him to become a different, more interesting person? Unfortunately, the answer isn't forthcoming until the final frames of the film, when it's all a case of too little, too late. It also doesn't help matters that all the nightclub scenes feature Lewis onstage with Austin in the background playing piano; the audience, of course, inevitably waits with great anticipation for a Sinatra vocal, but with Lewis's vocal cords slashed, the viewer receives nothing more than the occasional quick parody; it's historically accurate, but not what an audience most wants to see and hear.

At film's end, Joe strolls the foggy nighttime street alone, seeing the ghosts of his loved ones in store windows, until he finally confronts his own ghostly alter ego, who tells him the not-so-earth-shattering news that liquor does not solve problems. The audience has known that for the past ninety minutes, and it's the best the screenwriters can come up with to end the film? Joe's alter ego tells him, "You already have a pretty good life—you make other people laugh, how 'bout making me laugh," and the "real" Lewis replies, "I'll try—I'll really try," and bingo—the movie ends. We've watched him booze and self-destruct for two hours and now, he'll "try"? The scriptwriters might just as well have said, "We've run out of ideas, so we're going to end here." It's a sign of the film's biggest failing that in its last hour, the filmmakers have achieved the nearly impossible—they have made show business flat-out boring.

None of that is Sinatra's fault, because it is only his near-Herculean performance that almost makes the damn thing work. No other actor would have succeeded in making the second hour work either, and no one else would ever have clicked so memorably in the first half of the film. Director Vidor praised Sinatra as "the greatest natural actor I've ever worked with," high praise indeed from a director who guided James Cagney to one of his greatest performances in *Love Me or Leave Me*. Sinatra, with Vidor's help, achieved a terrific blending of actor, role, and persona, one best summed up by William Weaver in the *Motion Picture Herald:* "But sometime between the start of the picture, when he's all-Sinatra, and the end, when he's become all-Lewis, he gets a firm hand on the character he's re-creating and, at the same time, the audience he's creating it for. This is the essence of show-business." In those terms, Joe E. Lewis himself had it right when he told Sinatra, "You had more fun playing my life than I had living it."

Just as Sinatra in the recording studio would finish one song and bark "next tune," Sinatra the actor all but uttered the same words. *The Joker Is Wild* completed, *Pal Joey* waited in the wings, yet so insatiable was Sinatra's appetite for work (and interest in a large salary) that even with both his film and recording careers in high gear, he returned to television for a second series, this time on ABC. Debuting one week before the October 1957 premiere of *Pal Joey,* the series granted Sinatra an extraordinary deal in terms of financial reward and artistic freedom, but the results were the same as in his previous attempt: he and weekly television were not a good match, both in terms of his edgy personality and his still-staggering impatience.

Frank's deal with ABC television called for him to be paid $3 million up front plus a share of the profits, with ABC television buying stock in Sinatra's film production company, Kent Productions. The total package called for thirty-six half-hour shows with Sinatra receiving 60 percent of the residuals. They were not all to be musical episodes, but rather, in a nod to Sinatra's versatility, a blend of variety shows, dramas starring Sinatra, and dramas for which he would serve only as host. In the end, he performed in thirty-two shows. When all was said and done, however, the number of shows didn't matter, because Sinatra was not delivering strong ratings, and ABC canceled the series after twenty-six weeks.

Sinatra's smart-aleck personality didn't translate well on the home screen—it's a small screen, and his personality was too big. He could be a minimalist when required, but it wasn't his natural bent, and often it seemed as if the smaller screen could barely contain him. Making matters worse, he rushed through the series so hurriedly that the audience never received the feeling that he was, in effect, happy to make their acquaintance, glad to be hanging around their living room. Only at the end of each show, when Sinatra would sign off with the words, "Sleep warm," did any actual sense of comfort come through, and two words did not a successful television show make.

It's as if Sinatra's impatience with the medium, an impatience that at its worst translated as contempt, came through more clearly on the small screen than in any of his singing or movie roles. In the mid to late 1950s, Americans did not want television with an edge, and Sinatra was all edge. So impatient was he that at one point he tried to film eleven shows in a mere fifteen days, an impossible feat that also made for a drastic drop-off in quality. Sinatra observers may have continually commented on his film-set impatience, but in reality, that haste was a model of deliberation compared with his attitude on the two television series. Stated Mamie Manson, a performer on the second series: "It's not just that he didn't care about the acting or the ensemble. He wouldn't take the time to rehearse. He wouldn't even learn his lines. He just read them off the TelePrompTer—he was forty-two years old at the time, but he acted like a stupid teenager." Suffice it to say that Manson did not speak at the ceremonies for any of the lifetime achievement awards Sinatra received with great frequency in the 1980s and 1990s.

One reason families across America did not warm to Frank appearing in their living rooms every week—yet were happy to accept Dean Martin on his extraordinarily successful 1970s NBC series—is that while Sinatra's image worked against him, Martin's worked for him. Viewers were all too aware of Sinatra's tempestuous personal life, the two failed marriages, and the Sturm und Drang of life with Ava. Martin, on the other hand, may have presented the image of the amiable drunk, but audiences looked upon his long-standing marriage, the many children and sense of family he seemed to exude, and felt he was one of them. Martin's image was in large part just that—an image with little basis in reality—but viewers did not know that, nor did they seem to care. Sinatra, as always, came across as someone apart—someone who played only by his own self-made rules while exuding a disdain for the nine-to-five life in safe suburbia. The result was a second canceled television series. It was to be the last such attempt of Frank's career.

After the interesting biographical excursion of *The Joker Is Wild,* Sinatra filmed the last great musical of his career, the Rodgers and Hart classic *Pal Joey.* Adapted from the 1942 Broadway musical based upon John O'Hara's

New Yorker magazine stories of the same name, *Pal Joey,* with a screenplay by Dorothy Kingsley, retains a handful of songs from the original stage play and interpolates a number of other Rodgers and Hart standards such as "There's a Small Hotel" and "I Didn't Know What Time It Was." (Sinatra also recorded a knockout version of "Bewitched, Bothered and Bewildered" for the soundtrack, but within the film, it is sung, as it should be, by Rita Hayworth's Vera Simpson.) Unlike the meddling with the original score that hindered the effectiveness of *On the Town,* here, for the most part, the additions and deletions actually work. On the other hand, while the changes in the score might work, the decision to modify the ending does not, making for an uneven ride of a film. Nonetheless, the first two-thirds of the film is so consistently entertaining that it registers as a decided pleasure.

In the original Broadway version of *Pal Joey,* wiseguy hoofer and ladies' man Joey Evans was played by Gene Kelly. Although there was talk in the 1940s of reuniting *Cover Girl* stars Gene Kelly and Rita Hayworth for a film version of *Pal Joey,* the movie never came together, MGM's loan-out price for Kelly being too high. When a 1950s Broadway revival of the musical generated renewed interest in the property, new talk arose of a film version, one to be directed by Billy Wilder and starring Marlon Brando and, oddly enough, Mae West. Considering Brando's musical talents on display in *Guys and Dolls,* one can be thankful that he did not make the film, and it must have given Sinatra an added jolt of pleasure to land the lead rather than see another prime part go to Brando. (Of more interest than Mae West was the initial talk of casting Marlene Dietrich in the role of Vera Simpson.)

By the time filming finally began, it was Frank Sinatra front and center in the title role, and in acknowledgment of his star power, his production company, Essex Productions, negotiated a deal wherein Frank received a fee of $150,000 plus 25 percent of the film's net receipts. Frank may have gallantly suggested he receive second billing, between costars Rita Hayworth and Kim Novak, but there was no doubt who was the true power on the film set.

Wisely, the film version changed Joey from dancer to singer in order to suit Sinatra's talents, a switch that fortunately does nothing to harm the story: Joey's essential personality and inherent musicality remain intact. Laying out the story of the romantic triangle between Joey, rich society lady Vera Simpson (Rita Hayworth), and nice-girl chorus dancer Linda English (Kim Novak), the film makes it clear to the audience right off the bat that this is a musical with a difference, a musical with a leading man who is more antihero than hero. When a movie musical begins with (anti)hero Joey being "escorted" out of town by the police for having the mayor's underage daughter in his hotel room, there's definitely an unusual sort of musical journey lying ahead. Joey's insouciant take on the situation as he is about to be unceremoniously dumped on the next train out of town? "How did I know she was jailbait? She looked like she was thirty-five."

Complete with trench coat slung over his shoulder and snap-brim hat tilted at a rakish angle, Joey lands in San Francisco, on the hustle and looking for the main chance. It's a mark of how much Sinatra's onscreen persona had evolved by 1957 that just as the early "sailor suit" musicals believably presented him as a naïve small-town youngster, a mere thirteen years later he is firmly established as a jaded, seen-it-all hustler, a show business veteran with a penchant for the ladies and a winning if oftentimes disagreeable personality. In other words—a "swinger."

Pal Joey fit the Sinatra persona etched on disc with arranger Billy May on "Come Fly with Me." To the public, Frank was a man who could "pack up and fly away" at a moment's notice—on his time, on his terms. This was the Frank Sinatra who personified the USA in the 1950s: cocky, eye on the main chance, optimistic, and full of the sense of possibility. As Dean Martin humorously drawled to Frank: "It's your world. I'm just livin' in it." Frank Sinatra reigned as a movie star in the mid- and late 1950s because his image fit the times perfectly, his exuberance battling his anxiety, audiences never really sure how it would all end. America may have been sitting on top of the world, but such exuberance was tinged with uneasiness: Russia was also a superpower, had the atomic bomb, and didn't seem shy about rattling its sabers. Couple that vague unease with what could be the isolated and disconnected nature of the promised land of suburban living, and a new kind of screen figure embodying such complexities was ripe for success. In the Frank Sinatra of *Pal Joey,* that figure found its ultimate manifestation.

Sinatra put forth a physical and verbal nonchalance that appealed, but it was, of course, a willed nonchalance—in the darker moments, the effort showed, and audiences recognized themselves. Audiences were fascinated by the barely concealed anger because they understood that it was a manifestation of their own unease, albeit writ large in his figure onscreen. The character of Joey Evans encompassed all the multiple Frank Sinatra personalities: singer, swinger, rebel, idealist, cynical charmer, and vulnerable loner. It therefore makes sense that early on in the film, when Joey tells the club owner that he has plans, he announces in classic Sinatra speak, "I've got plans—Ring-A-Ding Plans." Frank Sinatra is probably the only star of the time who could have accomplished the difficult feat of planting an antihero front and center in a major Hollywood musical, yet he pulls it off with ease. It's as if the audience for *Pal Joey* feels it is seeing the "real" Frank Sinatra in both his onscreen and offscreen variations, yet at the same time, like any true movie star, he still maintains an air of mystery. He is such a mass of contradictions that the audience still wants to know more, trying to discern exactly what was going on behind those eyes.

The film of *Pal Joey* switches the locale of the original from New York City to San Francisco, and in the evocative cinematography of Harold Lipstein, San Francisco appears so ethereally beautiful that it nearly shimmers. One almost expects Tony Bennett to pop up singing "I Left My Heart in San Francisco." San Francisco itself may look glamorous, but the film quickly transplants Joey to his natural milieu—honky-tonk show business. Spotting the Barbary Coast nightclub where his old pal Ned Galvin (Bobby Sherwood) works as the pianist, Joey jumps up onstage in place of the club's missing emcee and proceeds to sing the classic Rodgers and Hart tune "I Didn't Know What Time It Was." Starting out as a ballad, the song segues into a gently swinging finger-snapping number. Will Joey get the job? Well, four measures of this singing, and the audience's reaction is one of wonder—not only wonder at how great Sinatra as Joey sounds, but also wonder that we're supposed to believe such a giant talent would be hanging around the fringes of show business in a second-class joint (kind of like watching Joel Grey and Liza Minnelli in *Cabaret*'s Kit Kat Klub flea trap).

Well, this is the nicest kind of audience disbelief, one helped by the fact that director Sidney and screenwriter Kingsley establish a realistic, somewhat seedy backstage atmosphere, complete with hard-boiled chorines who talk at the same time they're chomping down on celery, all the while exchanging barbs with Joey that are not in the least bit affectionate. Just like Joey, these dames have been around the block a few dozen times.

Tough guy Joey instantly casts his eye on chorus girl Linda (Kim Novak), but readily disregards her when he sees his main chance standing right before him in the person of rich society lady Mrs. Vera Simpson (Hayworth). (Ironically, Hayworth was actually three years younger than Sinatra but here played the "older woman.") Hired to entertain with the nightclub band at Mrs.

Simpson's society fund-raiser, Joey boldly sings, "There's a Small Hotel" directly to Vera, fixing her with a visibly erotic gaze. It's a terrific moment, not just a great song, but character-revealing as well: Joey is a hustler and Vera is annoyed . . . but attracted. Her annoyance only increases when Joey brashly announces that she will re-create her "Vera and the Vanishing Veils" show business number for the highest charity bidder. Vera, mortified that her past is being paraded before her disapproving high-society friends, then sings the witty "Zip," a cynical Lorenz Hart ode to what is really on a stripper's mind as she takes off her clothes. Doffing first one glove and then the other, Vera reveals her innermost thoughts. Witty they are, but they sure ain't sexual—

Zip! Toscanini leads the greatest of bands
Zip! Jergen's lotion does the trick for his hands

This song provides a last chance to see the beautiful Rita Hayworth in the final phase of her sex goddess years. (Hayworth's voice was dubbed by Jo Ann Greer.) Still ravishing, and with a terrific figure, Hayworth moves with a liquid grace that reveals why it has long been rumored that she was Fred Astaire's favorite dance partner. She is beautiful, sexy, and communicates an innocent delight in the freedom that dancing grants her. It is in no way apparent that this was her first film in three years (and the last under her contract with Columbia Pictures). The number as staged by Hermes Pan also serves as a very nice homage to Hayworth's immortal "Put the Blame on Mame" number from *Gilda,* an eleven-years-earlier number that also featured a mock yet highly erotic striptease in which only her gloves were shed. All that's missing from the *Gilda* tribute are Hayworth's long, flowing auburn tresses—Vera, an uptight society lady masking her show business past, is, for the present time, all upswept, self-contained respectability.

Screenwriter Kingsley has retained some cynical, snappy lines from the original and also written some new ones of her own, in the process fashioning that rarest of all species: an adult musical. When Joey protests to Charlie the piano player that Linda (Charlie's putative girlfriend) is "not his type," Charlie wearily replies, "They're all your type, Joey."

The film's effectiveness is also greatly aided by a smart structure that places all the early musical numbers in a performance setting, whether in a nightclub or at Vera's society fund-raiser. Given the cynical nature of the leading characters, such a move ensures maximum credibility; the audience neither expects nor wants these world-weary adults to sing "moon-June" declarations of love directly to each other.

As the movie progresses, a growing disparity between the performances of Novak and Sinatra unfortunately begins to take hold. Novak, a beautiful woman who proved effective in carefully tailored roles, delivers a problematic performance; she is not a natural singer or dancer (her voice was dubbed by Trudy Erwin), and with her whispery voice, startlingly reminiscent of Marilyn Monroe's, she's a near cipher upon whom Joey and the movie audience can project their own fantasies. Surely a chorus girl like Linda would be a little tougher around the edges.

As it is, the filmmakers resort to having Joey buy a cute little terrier named Snuffy in order to solicit sympathy. Columbia may have been sanitizing the character of Joey by devoting so much screen time to the pooch, but Sinatra never stoops to begging for audience approval of the "gee, Joey's not really such a bad guy" school. He's always got his eye on the horizon for his next opportunity, coming across as a very cool customer who thinks nothing of shoving Snuffy into Linda's arms with a muttered, "Take him for a walk," as soon as the rich Vera arrives at the club. Only Sinatra's charm—the vulnerability an audience always sensed in him, no matter how rotten the character—enables Joey to generate any audience sympathy.

The dance of attraction/rejection continuing between Vera and Joey, Vera deliberately walks out of the club, and when she returns days later, swathed in a floor-length orange dress and matching fur, the result is the single greatest musical sequence to be found in any Frank Sinatra film. Singing "The Lady Is a Tramp" directly to Vera, Sinatra/Joey is so charming, so effortless as he glides through the film like the full-fledged movie star he is, that audience capitulation is total and complete.

The setting is classic Sinatra, the nightclub deserted by all but Vera, Joey and the band. Joey starts to play the bright red onstage piano, smoking a cigarette he nonchalantly rubs out and knocks off the stage while crooning the opening lyrics. Managing the not-so-easy trick of kicking the piano to the back of the stage without missing a single beat of the song, Sinatra is in great voice, resting on top of an extraordinary Nelson Riddle arrangement, and biting into the terrific Lorenz Hart lyrics with, in Derek Jewell's apt phrase, an "insolent caress."

Like any true artist, Sinatra delivers the unexpected, putting across what is usually an uptempo finger-snapper with true lyrical depth, making love to Vera through the song. With the band in the lower right-hand corner of the screen, the onstage light in the upper portion of the screen throws a near halo over Frank's image, and given the way he sings here, that's not much of an overstatement on the part of Sidney and cinematographer Lipstein. The song keeps gathering momentum, layer upon layer, image upon image, until Vera is totally seduced, right along with the audience. Best of all, when Sinatra reaches the penultimate lines—"She's broke and it's oke"—he leaves out the rhyme, joyfully swinging "She's broke" and then expressing the nonforthcoming rhyme with an insouciant yet joy-filled shrug of his shoulders that tells you Joey has it all under control. It's a startling, original moment—all thought out yet seemingly casual, a piece of business so brilliant that the audience, caught up in the headlong rush of the moment, all but wants to yell out the missing three words themselves. The audience is in the palm of his hands because he has made them come to him—at his withholding, they are all the more eager, just like Vera herself. Forget the rest of the film and Sinatra's great performance—for

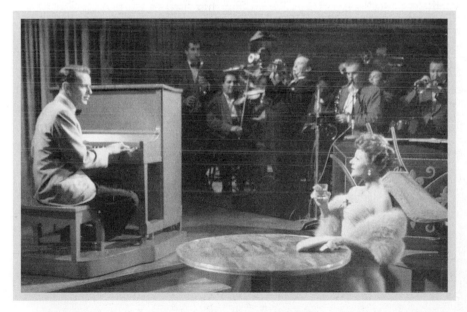

Singing "The Lady Is a Tramp" to Rita Hayworth in Pal Joey *(1957)—Sinatra's finest moment on film.*

this sequence alone, he fully deserved his Golden Globe Award as Best Actor in a Comedy or Musical.

Hayworth is also superb here, her initial affront at the title words melting as she realizes that Joey is telling her that far from being a tramp, she is in fact a classy lady. Song finished, Joey bows to Vera and the band. All is dead quiet until the tension is released in the best possible way for a musical: Joey and Vera dance together on the deserted stage, the band softly playing in the background. Joey, an expression of "What'd you expect—of course I got her" playing across his face, breaks away from Vera, who glances his way and in an all-knowing voice purrs, "Come now, beauty." Whew—a gigolo and a man-hungry widowed society dame—this is all a far cry from Mickey and Judy putting on a show in the barn. The band plays Vera and Joey out the door, with Joey's self-aware and self-mocking leg-kick behind him on the final note putting a perfect button on the number. Sinatra here reaches the high point of his movie musical appearances, the perfectly sung and staged sequence leaving the audience downright exhilarated. Just as happened with the "New York, New York" opener of *On the Town,* one is left with a feeling of utter and complete satisfaction—and the knowledge that it doesn't get better than this.

Referring to the fact that Vera's husband died two years previously, and euphemistically telling her that "two years is a long time between drinks," Joey is promptly rewarded with a full-throttle smack across the face, at which point they embrace—but it's an embrace with a difference. Instead of a nonsensical cut to the immaculately clad lovers murmuring sweet nothings on a hill, as happened with Cary Grant and Sophia Loren in *The Pride and the Passion,* here we cut to a very happy, negligee-clad Vera lounging in bed. Her hair falling loosely to her shoulders, Gilda is back—older, a bit more tired-looking, but still pretty damn sensational. As Vera begins to sing "Bewitched, Bothered and Bewildered" (given the sanitized version of the lyrics utilized herein, it's a song most people forget is a tribute to Joey's prowess in the bedroom: "horizontally speaking, he's at his very best"), she arches her back and sits up, her luxurious mane swinging easily around her in a deliberate echo of Gilda's first entrance in that 1946 film. The song makes perfect sense in terms of both plot and character, but with Vera singing the song around her apartment and in the shower, it also represents the first song not delivered in a show business setting, and as such, jars a little.

Increasingly drawn to Linda, Joey gives her the solo on the "My Funny Valentine" number in the nightclub show, a musical sequence that at once demonstrates the strengths and weaknesses of Novak. Saddled with the silly press nickname of "the lavender girl," Novak, forced to wear purple throughout the film, is photographed singing the tender song while perched in a tacky-looking purple-trimmed heart. Dubbed voice or not, it is obvious that Novak is not in any way, shape, or form inherently musical, and she displays a curious lack of passion. Refusing to perform the nightclub's striptease routine, Novak cries out "I won't do it"—yet there is neither conviction nor anguish in her voice. She might as well be reciting the grocery list. At the same time, however, Novak is extremely appealing in her abundant vulnerability, ensuring an audience sympathy that is heightened by the oftentimes startling beauty revealed in her close-ups. When all is said and done, Novak was much better served by roles such as that in *Vertigo*, where audiences could project their own emotions and subtext onto her mystery-woman facade.

That quibble aside, it's only in the final section of the movie that *Pal Joey* noticeably droops. The musical sequences are uninspired, and the sense of cynical enjoyment dissipates. The film turns to mush as soon as Joey realizes his love for Linda, because the audience is not fully prepared for it. Only now, near the end of the film, do Linda and Joey engage in "getting to know you" dialogue, wherein she reveals her background and her ambitions. It's too little, too late. Placed earlier in the film, it would have helped the audience understand why these two were so attracted to each other. As it stands, they seem a rather mismatched pair, Joey seemingly attracted to Linda only because she's a "mouse" (in Joey's rather condescending term) who happens to be "stacked" (in her own words). Joey treats Linda horribly, dumping her repeatedly as soon as Vera crooks her rich little finger. By this point, the show business setting has disappeared along with the musical numbers, the dialogue is no longer biting, and the audience is reduced to hearing second-rate Sinatra-isms like "One false move, and I'll be out on my Francis."

In the end, Joey, alone in his darkened nightclub that will now be shuttered before ever opening, plunks away in disconsolate fashion at the piano, leading into the by-now-overused movie musical device of a dream ballet ("What Do I Care for a Dame?") that spells out the leading characters' romantic dilemma. Such a dream ballet may have broken new ground when seen on Broadway in *Oklahoma!* but after *Lady in the Dark*, *Oklahoma!* and

Carousel, audience reaction changed from a sense of discovery to a feeling of "ho hum." It doesn't help matters that after the faces of the two leading ladies bob around onscreen in a disconcerting manner reminiscent of Busby Berkeley at his most surrealistic, there is a very perfunctory dance with the three leads that appears to have been severely truncated in the editing room. Nothing is explained, no insight is gained, and at ballet's end, the only audience reaction is one of bafflement.

Joey's dilemma resolved (evidently he got more out of the ballet than does the audience), he strolls out of the empty nightclub, trench coat slung over his shoulder, hat firmly back in place, and bids a fond farewell to his Thunderbird convertible. He is prepared to wend his way alone into a new future in Sacramento, a move that injects a new level of disbelief into the proceedings—he'd trade San Francisco for that show business hot spot of Sacramento? The problem is that in the most ludicrous touch of all, as Vera and Linda sit in the backseat of Vera's car watching Joey, Vera graciously gives Linda a smile of approval to chase after Joey, and after some feeble protests from Joey, he and Linda stroll off into the sunset, the Golden Gate Bridge looming overhead. It's a silly, sappy ending to what had been a tough, tart movie for the first two-thirds of its running time. More to the point, it also rates as a complete subversion of the stage play's much more fitting ending wherein Joey loses both Linda and Vera. It's as if the movie didn't have the courage of its convictions, undercutting the entire setup and much of the plot for the sake of a nod to 1950s morality. It's an unfortunate end, but the ride up until then was a doozy. Said *Look* magazine, in a very accurate summation,

> the story has a "happy ending." But its bite remains. . . . Frank Sinatra plays Joey with all the brass the role demands. He has a gleam in his eye and a chip on his shoulder. . . . He tosses off both dames and songs with equal artistry, and almost singlehandedly makes *Pal Joey* a wonderfully entertaining movie.

The release of *Pal Joey* ranked as Sinatra's third major film of the year, and if *The Pride and the Passion* rated as a stinker, *The Joker Is Wild* and *Pal Joey* were eminently watchable, at times compulsively so. Two out of three is a much higher batting average than most stars achieve in Hollywood, a feat that becomes even more impressive in light of the fact that in these same years of

1956 and 1957, Sinatra was releasing one truly great album after another: *Close to You, A Swingin' Affair!* and the soundtracks to *High Society* and *Pal Joey,* all of which really were sensational from start to finish.

As recording artist, Frank Sinatra had made a complete transition from callow boy singer to mature artist. He was no longer recording catchy singles, instead releasing albums organized around thematic emotional concepts. As Sinatra aged, so, too, had his audience; they were now adults with families and wanted to listen to someone they felt understood the joys and problems of being alive, of being an American in the second half of the twentieth century. It was a role Sinatra came to fill in spectacular fashion, and the unequaled run of recording success may be the reason Sinatra's film work has so often been unfairly denigrated. During the decades of the 1940s and 1950s, and well into the 1960s, nearly every Sinatra LP was a masterpiece of one sort of another, whether uptempo, torch song, or swingin' affairs. Track after track, the brilliant concept albums redefined the nature of the pop vocal art. By way of contrast, Sinatra made many good films during that time period, but not every one was a home run—some were simply base hits, and some, like *The Pride and the Passion,* were ignominious strikeouts. Even on the rare occasions that he basically struck out as a vocalist—*Watertown, A Man Alone,* and *The Future* discs in the *Trilogy* set come to mind—scorn was never heaped upon those efforts in quite the same fashion as with the subpar films.

In actuality, a fairly persuasive argument can be made that the late-career Sinatra worked at a higher level as a film actor than as a singer. Films like *Contract on Cherry Street* and *The First Deadly Sin* were variable in quality, but Sinatra was first-rate throughout, particularly in the latter. It is actually easier and more satisfying to watch those last films of Sinatra, wherein he exhibited all the craft he had acquired during his four decades in Hollywood, than it is to listen to the sometimes tattered voice displayed on *Duets* and *Duets II* or even the earlier *The Main Event.* Even with all the stinkers in Sinatra's film career, a dozen first-rate films out of his forty-four starring roles actually represents a high percentage amongst Hollywood stars.

Sinatra had no problems recording up to thirty takes of a song, because he was in total control, not just of the material, but also of the process. Work in the recording studio stopped, started, rewound, and took shape at his command and his only. On film, conversely, other artists fulfilled various creative roles; Sinatra was neither the director nor generally the producer, neither editor nor cameraman. He did not have total control of the finished product—no actor does—and as a result, he had a great many misses and near misses on-screen, as do all movie stars. A mixed track record is inevitable given the inherent nature of both Hollywood and the filmmaking process, and when placed in that context, one senses that Sinatra was ofttimes unfairly criticized, the criticism filtered through a reaction to his huge personality as much as to the work itself. No one can justify a film like *4 for Texas,* but by the same token, a reflexive dismissal that Sinatra "slummed" in his later films causes an unfair denigration of the style and authority he brought to *Tony Rome,* and the terrific acting he displayed in *The First Deadly Sin.*

It's also worth noting that an unhappy Sinatra could occasionally slam his way through a recording session in the same spectacularly impatient manner with which he treated subpar films. Forced to record a final album at Capitol, Sinatra reunited with Axel Stordahl for *Point of No Return.* Barely bothering with retakes, Frank's approach to the session was the antithesis of his usual painstaking approach and reflected nothing so much as an attitude of "let's get this over with—and now." Said trombonist Milt Bernhart:

> After an hour he was through with six numbers, and he said good-bye and was out the door—and he did that two nights in a row. We got no more than one or, tops, two takes on everything. On several, Cavanaugh came out of the booth and said, "Frank, we had a little trouble with the bass on that last take" but by that time Frank had torn up the sheet. "I'm sorry," was the way he put it. "Next number."

Between the recordings and the highly successful films, Frank Sinatra was on top of the show business world, a state of affairs that encouraged him, like any true artist, to take chances on different types of material. It's a type of risk-taking, or rather image-bending, that led to his next film *Kings Go Forth,* a strange misshapen movie that nonetheless shows that his interests and instincts were in the right place. It's just the film's screenplay that wasn't up to snuff.

Sinatra appears to have been attracted to *Kings Go Forth* in part because of the literary pedigree of the novel. In fact, the theatrical trailer for the film depicts Sinatra in a book-lined study with copies of *From Here to Eternity* and *The Man with the Golden Arm,* the filmmakers clearly trying to position *Kings Go Forth* as following in those literary footsteps. In addition, the film's stand against racial prejudice must also have appealed to Sinatra's well-known liberal instincts, and in that regard, it makes perfect sense that *Kings Go Forth* reunited him with Frank Ross, who had produced 1945's tract against religious prejudice *The House I Live In*.

Kings Go Forth represents Sinatra's first true venture into war movies, a genre he was to visit with increasing frequency throughout the remainder of his film career. In *Anchors Aweigh* and *On the Town,* he may have played a sailor in the Second World War, but his character is on leave; the war hovers in the background, but no combat sequences are depicted onscreen. Similarly, *It Happened in Brooklyn* begins as the war ends, and in *From Here to Eternity,* nearly the entire film takes place right before Pearl Harbor and America's entry into the war. With *Kings Go Forth* and *Never So Few,* however, Sinatra was visiting the genre in a more combat-oriented fashion. These were combat films with a difference, however, because by the time Sinatra began his exploration of the World War II combat film in earnest, enough time had passed since the end of the war that the very questions asked by the war films had begun to change.

What's most striking about *Kings Go Forth* is that it spends as much time on the romance between Sinatra's character and Natalie Wood's as it does on the combat mission his character undertakes. Thirteen years had passed since the end of World War II, and Americans now questioned more, wondering if the Korean War (no one's idea of a "good war") really would keep them safe at home. Because Sinatra's inherent nature, as well as his public persona, exuded the air of someone who questioned authority in all its forms, he became a surrogate for an increasingly restive audience. If one of the characteristics of the war film is that a mission must be undertaken by a collection of various ethnic types—Italian, Irish, and Jewish (kind of like a wartime version of the ballplayers in *Take Me Out to the Ball Game*)—then the collection of men must include not only both an innocent youngster and a veteran family man, but also a cynic who functions as a stand-in for the movie audience. With Sinatra, the cynic landed front and center as the leading character. His often dark persona fit the mood of the times, and personified a postwar world that was suffused with violence, beginning and ending with the ultimate violence of the atomic bomb.

Directed by Delmer Daves (director of the original *3:10 to Yuma* and co-scriptwriter of the Irene Dunne/Charles Boyer classic *Love Affair*) in capable if rarely inspired fashion, *Kings Go Forth* ultimately registers as an uneasy mix of World War II combat picture, doomed love triangle, and indictment of racial prejudice. It's too much by half to blend into one coherent film, but for all its failings, the film does hold the viewer's interest and contains a first-rate performance by Sinatra.

One of the particularly interesting aspects of Frank's performance lies in the fact that his "unofficial" acting coach on the film was one of his favorite actors, Boris Karloff. Frank Sinatra and Boris Karloff—who knew? Yet, in terms of influences upon Sinatra, Karloff actually makes perfect sense. Along with the gangster and Western films Sinatra lapped up in his youth, horror films provided another source of pleasure. More than gangsters, more than Western heroes, it was the monsters who proved to be the ultimate misunderstood loners, appealing to outsiders of all stripes. Given the fact that Sinatra had always been a fan of Karloff's performance as *Frankenstein,* it's not so surprising to learn that when Karloff found himself in the south of France at the same time Sinatra and company flew in for location work, the informal coaching arrangement began.

Karloff's most interesting piece of advice to Sinatra was to tell Frank, "You must learn to act with your *voice* as well as your face." Oh. It's not exactly like Sinatra didn't perform the hell out of a saloon song by acting out the lyrics with his voice, but evidently in Karloff's view, this had not translated into his film work. In fact, Sinatra does deliver a full-bodied and full-voiced performance in *Kings Go Forth,* so maybe Karloff was on to something here.

Of course, Sinatra's admiration for Karloff may also have been a result of the fact that Karloff's acting philosophy remained strikingly similar to that of another of Sinatra's acting heroes, Spencer Tracy. In Karloff's words: "Say your lines. Hit your mark. Get out." Now those were words that summed up Sinatra's approach to filmmaking—hell, his approach to life in general—perfectly.

Sporadically narrated by Sinatra, who plays Lieutenant Sam Loggins of the American Seventh Army, the black-and-white film takes place in the south of France in 1944, shortly after Paris has been liberated. Loggins is a tough native New Yorker, a combat-hardened GI who takes an instant dislike to pretty-boy newcomer Corporal Britt Harris (Tony Curtis). Britt, who is to serve as the company's new radio operator, is a rich college-educated boy from New Jersey. Or, as Sam bluntly asserts, "I don't trust him—he was born

Kings Go Forth *(1958)— three films in one. Just read the ad copy.*

rich and handsome and I was born poor and not handsome." These two butt heads from the moment they meet, and their conflict is all the more interesting for the sardonic manner in which it is occasionally handled: when Harris disobeys Loggins's order not to venture into a heavily mined apple orchard in order to try to save fellow soldiers, Loggins does not, as expected, launch into a screaming tirade. Rather, he casually inquires of Harris: "Got a razor? Good—then use it to cut off your stripes."

An entirely different side of Loggins is revealed when he is granted a twenty-four-hour leave to Nice, where he promptly falls in love with Monique Blair (a young and very beautiful Natalie Wood). Monique, an American by birth who has lived her entire life in France, instantly captivates Loggins, and Sinatra does a beautiful job of conveying his character's uncertainty around such a young innocent girl. This Sam Loggins is a far cry from the combat-hardened lieutenant who barks orders at his men. Nothing would make Loggins happier than simply sharing a meal with Monique, but he finds himself incapable of expressing that desire. He is, in fact, so hesitant in declaring his affections that his character resembles nothing so much as the naïve rubes Frank portrayed in the early musicals. Sinatra is here integrating two different aspects of his film persona, and doing so beautifully, a measure of how much his dramatic skills had grown in the fifteen years since his feature film debut.

So far, so good, but after Loggins meets Monique's mother (a too-young Leora Dana decked out in a set-in-concrete gray old-lady wig), he kisses Monique for the first time and declares, "I could have hit a home run for the Giants and climbed an Alp"—dialogue that may exist in the mind of screenwriters but would never be uttered by a living, breathing soul, let alone a war veteran. It's all so overblown that one nearly expects Frank to start belting out "Secret Love."

Loggins may love Monique, but she is hiding a big secret from him: "My father was a great man. He was also a Negro." At that bombshell—well, it was 1958—Loggins closes his eyes in dismay, and Monique runs out of the room. Loggins is so unsettled by the news of the man's racial background that he can't bring himself even to look at the man's photograph. All this information is conveyed in a lengthy monologue delivered by Monique's mother, wherein Sinatra remains silent, sitting motionless on the armrest of the living room couch. This most volatile of actors here achieves a moving affect by doing nothing at all, drawing the audience into his pain and lack of understanding.

By the standards of 1958, this disclosure would have been a very big deal, and there is some nice dialogue to underscore the point. When Loggins, fully realizing his love for Monique, returns to her house in order to apologize, her mother says, "You're a good man, Sam," and Sinatra, in a very nice bit of understatement, ruefully admits, "I'm a little better than I was a week ago." Tough and tender—the ideal Sinatra film persona, the one audiences most admired. So, what is really wrong here?

Well, for starters, there is nothing about Natalie Wood that even remotely suggests she is half African-American. Perhaps it was her dark hair and eyes that caused her casting as an African-American here and as a young Puerto Rican three years later in *West Side Story,* but it doesn't work and never feels authentic. (In order to secure Wood's participation, Warner Bros., Wood's home studio, received seventy-five thousand dollars for her ten weeks of work, and a further promise that Sinatra would make a future film at Warners, a film that turned out to be *Ocean's Eleven*.) An African-American actress in the role would have given the film an interesting and authentic complexity, as well as many more layers of character development. Truth be told, African-American or not, any actress would have had a difficult time portraying this young woman. Monique is presented as so sweet and unsoiled that she appears never to have had a doubt or angry moment in her entire life. What the audience is missing here is the yearning, self-doubt, and anger that would surely have informed the character of a young biracial woman in 1958, especially one who never really knew her father and was raised in a foreign country.

Most damaging of all, when the film spins off into the love triangle of Monique, Sam, and Britt, it begins to flounder badly. Harris is a smooth-talking pretty boy, a user who instantly sets his sights on Monique, more for the conquest than out of any genuine love. It makes the audience not just annoyed with Britt, whose shallowness is overdone by Curtis's overly facile performance, but more than a little annoyed with Monique for not seeing through him in the slightest.

The love triangle registers in off-kilter fashion, most notably because Tony Curtis is the protagonist and it is Sinatra who has the passive role. Sam represents the moral center of the film, and even though Curtis has the showier role, Sinatra's superior acting range throws off the balance of the film. It is only when Sam finally decks Britt for his callous treatment of Monique that Sam turns into the film's man of action and the Sinatra of most interest to the viewer; unfortunately it's too late in the game for audience capitulation.

When Britt complains to Sam that he knows he's rich, talented, and handsome but possesses no character—"I just figure out what I have to say to get what I want"—it's all a little too pat and once again a little too late in the film. Fortunately, Sinatra's silent reaction of disgust laced with anger and hurt over losing Monique goes a long way toward audience acceptance of such baldly stated assertions. This greatest of singers, who communicated volumes by the inflections he chose in his vocals, now was capable of conveying just as much information merely by a glance or fleeting facial expression.

The antagonistic relationship is carried through right to the end of the movie, when Britt is shot by the fleeing German soldiers. Cradling the dying Britt in his arms, Sam first says "Thinking of Monique? Too late now," and then modulates this bitterness to consolingly croon, "You'll be all right"—whereupon Britt dies. It's an interestingly ambiguous note on which to end the film, but wait—just when it seems impossible, there's more!

In a coda right out of a television soap opera, the film now cuts to a reha-bilitation hospital, where, Sam's voiceover narration informs us, he has spent the past seven months after losing his right arm. (Sinatra's missing arm is actu-ally very convincing.) Determined to find Monique one last time, Sam, now a captain, finds her running a school for orphans out of her former home. Her mother has died, but not before telling Monique, "Everyone in life has a burden—it's not the burden that's important—it's how you carry it." True enough, but for such an important character, she has disappeared with little explanation or attention, a failing that greatly lessens the film's emotional cli-max. Here one day, dead the next. Oh.

As the film fades out, the orphans sing a song in honor of Sam, and the camera pulls back, Sam alone at one end of the room, Monique and the chil-dren standing at the other. A little ambiguity may be good with such complex material, but after nearly two hours with these characters, the audience would like some indication of their future (or lack thereof). Instead, the or-phans warble, and bingo—the movie ends.

Such herky-jerky storytelling came in for criticism from the major review-ers, the *Los Angeles Mirror-News* finding that "the movie *Kings Go Forth* doesn't come close to having the guts of the book by Joe David Brown and the result is a film which is all surface and little depth. . . ." However, even if the screenplay does in Curtis and Woods, Sinatra still manages to survive and nearly triumph. As the *New York Daily News* critic Wanda Hale succinctly put it, Sinatra "may not be the best actor in the world, but there is none more interesting to watch." Which is, when you think about it, a very good way to have survived a soap opera.

Before Sinatra followed up this portrayal of an active World War II soldier by playing a returning WWII vet in 1958's *Some Came Running* (the first of a new three-movie deal with MGM), he did take time to film a brief appear-ance in a British-made short film titled *Invitation to Monte Carlo*. Filmed in July 1958 when he gave a concert in Monte Carlo to raise money for the United Nations Refugee Fund, Frank undertook the role as a favor to an old friend, and the new Princess of Monaco, Grace Kelly. He appears in one scene of the forty-six-minute film, and, like Princess Grace and Prince Rainier, played himself. Written, produced, and directed by Euan Lloyd, there is a very slight story line about British orphan Lindy, who is chosen to give a pres-ent to Princess Caroline, the firstborn child of Prince Rainier and Princess

Grace. And what might that present be? A kitten called Tosca. Needless to say, this featurette about Lindy's trip from London to Monte Carlo is not exactly a searing examination of the human condition, existing only as a Technicolor invitation for tourists to come spend money in beautiful Monte Carlo.

Sinatra was to film a similar travelogue in 1962, a twenty-two-minute film called *Sinatra in Israel,* which was made during his concert tour of Israel. A longtime supporter of the Jewish state, Sinatra agreed to appear in the film singing "In the Still of the Night" and "Without a Song," and he narrated the movie as well. More noteworthy than the film is the fact that his eight-day stint in Israel from May 2 through May 10 (part of a tour of Europe and Asia) found Sinatra overseeing the start of construction on the Frank Sinatra International Youth Center (for Arab and Jewish Children). As Sinatra himself nicely phrased it, the tour was intended as a means by which "underprivileged children" could be helped by "an overprivileged adult."

Whether the charity in question was local to California, or halfway around the world like the International Youth Center, Sinatra's commitment to helping others remains unparalleled in Hollywood history. Sinatra historian Rick Rossi, who has studied Sinatra's career from its 1935 beginning with the Hoboken Four through to the end of his life, concluded that "a year never went by when he didn't do at least a dozen or more charity events. It was mentioned at the public celebration of his eightieth birthday that he had raised over one billion dollars for charities during his lifetime." Like everything else about Sinatra, the contradictions inherent in his behavior remain decidedly larger than life: on the one hand, dozens of documented examples of boorish behavior, an intermittent but decided lack of courtesy toward fellow actors, violent bouts of temper—and on the other, $1 billion raised for charity.

Favor for Princess Grace dispatched, Frank was back in the United States to film *Some Came Running,* a lush CinemaScope adaptation of James Jones's hefty best seller of the same name. Directed by Vincente Minnelli, the resulting movie is a strange mix of styles: part soap opera, part melodrama, part social commentary, and part mess. Yet it's a film that is, in its own peculiar way, fascinating, and it represented Frank's first onscreen pairing not only with Dean Martin, but also with sole female "Clan" member Shirley MacLaine. Indeed, it was this first-time teaming of the three performers, coupled with the location-shooting antics complete with visits from reputed organized crime figures, that began the legend of the Rat Pack/Clan. Martin actually turns in the best performance of the trio, but it was MacLaine who was to walk off with the critical plaudits—thanks to Sinatra.

With John Patrick and Arnold Sheekman adapting Jones's sprawling book (in his autobiography, director Minnelli talks of never meeting Jones, who was totally uninvolved with the film), *Some Came Running* tries to be all things to all people, and ends up being not much to anyone. It's not that it's awful, but rather that the compression of events that worked so well in the cinematic adaptation of Jones's *From Here to Eternity* doesn't work so well here; the stakes aren't so high, and director Minnelli attenuates the events to the breaking point. Minnelli, an extraordinary director and a brilliant visual artist responsible for some of the greatest musicals ever made—*Meet Me in St. Louis, The Bandwagon,* and *Gigi*—doesn't always help his own cause, shooting the majority of the film in medium shot. Was he trying to comment on the distance between the main characters? That answer is unknown, but what is clear is that this decision slights the connections between characters, thereby undercutting the audience's interest.

What the viewer will be presented with throughout is evident in the opening set piece: returning World War II vet David Hirsh (Sinatra) is taking the bus back to his hometown of Parkman, Indiana, after a sixteen-year absence, bitter and clearly still angry about the small-town hypocrisy of that place. In a nice character-defining touch, it is made clear that Dave is one tough and cynical customer, because even on this empty bus, the drunken Hirsh keeps his bankroll in his underwear. Trusting and warm he ain't.

Dave has come back to Parkman more from a lack of anything else to do than from an overwhelming wish to see his family. There is such a lack of familial affection that Dave does not even know that his long-absent father died "four or five years ago," and the gossiping busybodies in the town know of Dave's return before he even thinks of telling his older brother Frank (Arthur Kennedy) that he is back. Why the familial disconnect? Turns out that Dave is carrying a massive chip on his shoulder from a childhood during which Frank, a successful Babbitt of a jeweler, placed parentless Dave in an orphanage rather than allowing him to live with Frank and his wife, Agnes (Leora Dana). Well, with that bitterness in the foreground, no wonder Elmer Bernstein's score is unceasingly bombastic right from the opening frames of the film. The music thunders in a minor key—all is not happy in post–World War II

Middle America. The dialogue and filming will make that point repeatedly, but Bernstein, presumably with Minnelli's approval, underscores the viewpoint loudly just to make sure no one within five blocks of the movie theater misses it.

Still dressed in his army uniform three years after the war has ended, Dave is accompanied by dim-witted, good-natured floozy Ginny Moorehead (MacLaine). He dumps Ginny as soon as they drunkenly stumble off the bus, handing her fifty dollars and telling her to get lost. Not exactly a knight of the Round Table is our Dave. He is, however, a writer with two books behind him. You know he's a "serious" writer because Minnelli pointedly films close-ups of Hirsh pulling well-worn books by F. Scott Fitzgerald, Faulkner, and Wolfe out of his bag. There aren't many professions less congenial to carrying a film than writing, and it says a great deal about Frank Sinatra's skill as a film actor that he manages to hold the viewer's interest for over two hours while portraying a man immersed in that most sedentary of professions.

Screenwriters Patrick and Sheckman do plunk down the occasional nugget of biting dialogue; says Hirsh to the inattentive hotel clerk—"I could have robbed the joint," to which the bored clerk replies, "Only if you wanted stamps." The problem with the screenplay, however, is that it is overstuffed, perhaps an inevitable failing given the 1,200-page novel from which it is adapted. Love, hate, violence, sexuality—it's all there, spread over so many characters that it is ultimately not so much moving as wearying for the viewer trying to keep up with the many subplots.

Sinatra does deliver a naturalistic performance throughout, establishing a believability that unfortunately is not matched by Arthur Kennedy as his brother Frank. Kennedy, generally a fine actor, here bellows all his words at high-decibel level, rendering it impossible to believe that he and Sinatra are brothers and proving exhausting in the bargain. It's already clear that the character is a close-minded bigot more interested in his own standing than in helping his brother, but Kennedy and Minnelli repeatedly highlight this trait with Kennedy's unceasingly loud performance. No wonder Dave stayed away for sixteen years.

The smorgasbord of acting styles on display serves only to heighten audience confusion. Leora Dana (from *Kings Go Forth*) is on hand as Agnes, Frank's wife, delivering her interpretation of a small-town bigot in capital letters, as if to say, *Look at me acting—I'm not like this woman.* Martha Hyer as putative love interest Gwen French similarly overdoes her interpretation of the intellectual teacher who believes in Hirsh's writing ability, telegraphing her intent to gradually thaw from her very first scene onward. It's a mishmash of acting styles, which means it is up to MacLaine and Dean Martin, who plays hard-drinking gambler Bama Dillert, to generate interest from viewers. Fortunately, both actors come through—with Martin particularly impressive in this, his first and best of nine onscreen pairings with Sinatra.

For her part, MacLaine portrays Ginny as the kind of sad-sack girl, desperate for love and clinging to the next available man, who paints her fingernails while sitting at the bar waiting for Prince Charming to arrive. She is all clanging jewelry, tatty fur, and overeagerness. Martin's Bama Dillert, by way of contrast, is a laid-back "seen it all" gambler, always wearing his hat for good luck, even while shaving. Nothing can ruffle his feathers or change his humorously laconic delivery. Eyeing the disheveled, hungover Hirsh, Bama casually drawls, "Man, you sure don't look pretty this morning." It's a smooth deliberate characterization that dovetails nicely with what came to be viewed as the "real" Dean Martin, the ultracool hipster known as Dino.

Indeed, Martin himself often seemed to move beyond laid-back and into a world of simply not caring, one divorced from feeling. As Shirley MacLaine pointedly wrote in her autobiography *My Lucky Stars,* "the Italians . . . had a more apt word for it, menefreghista, which means 'one who does not give a fuck.' Dean Martin was basically a menefreghista." It was an attitude that would only increase with the passage of time, as if Martin, from the mid-1960s on, didn't care—or, more accurately, didn't give a fuck—about his singing, his acting, his movies, or, for that matter, the whole damn country. Sinatra may have acted like he didn't care about certain films, but with Frank there was always the sense that he didn't want people to know how much he cared underneath the facade, that the pretext of not caring shielded him from true criticism. Martin just *didn't* care, rendering him a strangely unknowable man, in many ways cut off from feeling. As second wife Jeanne stated, "He *cannot* communicate. . . . He's one of the rare human beings who's not comfortable with communicating. He's just not interested. . . . He can literally do nothing. All he needs is a television set and a Western. . . . He was always content in a void."

Here guided by a first-rate director, Martin turns in a terrific performance, revealing a talent not really evident in most of his nineteen previous lightweight films. One look at a sample title—*Ten Thousand Bedrooms*—tells you that Martin had not exactly been delving into the Shakespearean canon. At this point in his career, however, Martin still cared, here taking the time and effort to explore the range first demonstrated in his superior turn opposite Marlon Brando and Montgomery Clift in the film adaptation of Irwin Shaw's *The Young Lions.* Ironically, according to Martin and (Jerry) Lewis biographer Arthur Marx, that breakout role was at one point to be offered to Sinatra. Given Sinatra's personal military history, and the related press coverage, one wonders what his reaction would have been to that meaty role of a Broadway singer who is scared of combat in World War II.

Bringing his own background as a card dealer to the role of Bama, Martin conveys a sense of hidden danger, an exceedingly calm exterior masking the tough interior. Martin is facile in an amusing but never self-centered manner, and even lays the foundation for one of his enduring hit records. As Dave and Bama rake in the chips after a particularly successful run of gambling, Hirsh turns to Bama, grin plastered on his face, and exults, "Ain't that a kick in the head." The phrase obviously stuck in Sinatra's mind, because two years later, favored songwriters Jimmy Van Heusen and Sammy Cahn were commissioned to write a song with that very title for *Ocean's Eleven,* the resulting cock-of-the-walk tune garnering Dino a hit record.

In point of fact, Sinatra had exerted his clout with the studio to insist on the casting of Martin. He had also pushed for relative unknown MacLaine over both Shelley Winters and Marilyn Monroe after spotting her on the *Dinah Shore* television show. In Sinatra's words: "the cuteness, the strength, the humor—everything we wanted in Ginny—was wrapped up in that one package."

MacLaine's waifish humor served the character of Ginny well, but what's not humorous is the outrageously sexist and racist dialogue, redolent of America in the mid-1950s. Casting a glance at the sad duo of Ginny and her sidekick Rosalie (Carmen Phillips in a wince-inducing cutout peekaboo dress) after a night of carousing, Bama offers a brutally matter-of-fact assessment: "I don't know what it is about these pigs, but they always look better at night." It's all offensive, and only partially redeemed by Bama's sarcastically humorous retort when informed that it's Ginny's birthday. Drinking and playing cards, he barely looks up before cynically muttering, "I've got a cake in the oven."

Such bigotry is presented in all-too-offhand a fashion, although one senses that at least the characters are behaving true to their natures. By way of contrast, what's not believable is the secondary love story of Dave and school-teacher Gwen French (Martha Hyer). Hirsh meets Gwen, instantly falls in love, stops drinking, buys new clothes, and as soon as she expresses approval of the short story he has written, they passionately kiss. He has undergone a complete personality change in exactly twenty-four hours, and she has melted from ice maiden teacher to sensuous woman in the same ridiculously short space of time. In case the audience is unsure of her transformation, Hirsh un-pins her hair, and bingo—Gwen adopts a wild-eyed look more appropriate to a horror movie (she does seem to flinch every time he touches her) as they fervently embrace.

In many ways, the contradictions inherent in this scene are emblematic of the film as a whole. Minnelli starts the action in shadow, moving the actors to-ward the darker part of the room, their kiss seen in silhouette before the se-duction ends in darkness. It's a nice concept, beautifully staged, but it doesn't much matter, because the characters simply don't make sense. To wit: the prim and proper English teacher kisses Dave wildly but then seems to once again change her mind, angrily protesting, "I'm not one of your barroom tarts," be-fore kicking him out of her home. Not only is Hirsh confused as to her real feelings, but so too, is the audience. Yesterday's pent-up virgin, today's schizo-phrenic. And, for that matter, why the hell is Dave so attracted to her? That one might take Dr. Freud himself to puzzle out. Strangely enough—or maybe not, given the motion picture Academy's love of wild-eyed histrionics—Hyer's very uneven performance snagged her an Academy Award nomination as Best Supporting Actress. (Shelley Winters claimed the Oscar that year for *The Di-ary of Anne Frank*.)

Maybe the mutual attraction rests in the fact that Dave himself could use some mood stabilizers—he veers wildly from clean-cut well-spoken writer to disheveled gambler and world-class drinker. He appears to be sensitive, but in a bit of dime-store philosophizing, his lack of self-worth is presented as the cause of his hyperemotional behavior. Lacking sufficient motivation, this ex-planation mostly registers as a glop of sappy moralizing served up to cover the heaving dramatics. Jones's underlying point—that people want to be loved more than they want to love—wears rather thin over the two-plus-hour running time. At the most lugubrious moments, churlish instincts make one just want to tell the characters to listen to Nat King Cole's "Nature Boy" and

call it a day. It's only three minutes long and plunks down the same message—
"the greatest thing you'll ever learn is just to love and be loved in return." As it
is, Dave's behavior plunges between such wild extremes that at times he seems
like two entirely different men trapped in the same body, which does not exactly provide a recipe for coherent characterization.

What with the parallel love story of Gwen having sold Dave's short story
to *The Atlantic* (that's some clout for an unknown teacher of high school English in Middle America), a fact that causes her to fall in love with him yet
again, it all begins to play like a Douglas Sirk melodrama. The problem is that
Minnelli does not seem notably captivated by examining the underside of
small-town morality in the same masterly fashion that Sirk managed. Minnelli
does not seem taken by the film's very setting. He is interested in the lush, the
musical, and the melodramatic, as evidenced by his brilliant look at Hollywood in 1952's *The Bad and the Beautiful*.

The characters in small-town Parkman, Indiana, do not seem to engage his
total interest, because the universe of Vincente Minnelli at his finest represents
nothing so much as the triumph of the imaginary over the real, and Parkman,
Indiana, is reality personified. Yes, craftsman that he is, Minnelli (in conjunction
with Sinatra's soon-to-be-favorite director of photography, William H. Daniels)
makes fine use of CinemaScope, filling the space beautifully with his fluid
lengthy camera takes and presenting the conflicting characters and forces with
the increased depth that confident handling of CinemaScope affords. However,
his sensibility is worlds away from that of his leading men, and it therefore comes
as no surprise to read MacLaine's revelation that neither of her costars ever felt
totally comfortable with the director, terming him "too precious."

For his part, Minnelli, a man of pronounced reticence, did comment in his
autobiography about the "towering rages" of which Sinatra was capable,
while at the same time discussing Frank's fierce gift for friendship. Smart man
that he was, Minnelli goes on to perceptively state, "Of course, he's prone to
tell friends how he'll help them rather than ask how he can help. But I suppose that's the prerogative of any leader of the clan." In other words, you
couldn't help Frank more than he helped you, because in the Sinatra worldview, he should be, and always would be, the paterfamilias dispensing aid. It
was, in short, a very Italian male attitude, circa mid-twentieth-century America. Stripped down to its most elemental, it represented a means of expressing friendship best summed up in his statement to Shirley MacLaine, "Oh, I

just wish someone would try to hurt you so I could kill them for you." Clearly, Sinatra was not one for Hallmark cards.

Sinatra's antipathy toward the Minnelli style came to a head when Minnelli painstakingly set up the camera for the climactic carnival sequence, only to state that the Ferris wheel, which was the focus of the sequence, had to be moved three inches. Of course, the making of such a demand after hours spent waiting for the complicated technical setup to be completed infuriated a man of Sinatra's limited patience, but Minnelli regarded the request as a practical one and, as related in his autobiography, had a different distance in mind than chroniclers of the tale would have it: "The camera wouldn't pick [the Ferris wheel] up in the long shots unless it was moved six feet." Point taken, but why not move the camera itself? What Minnelli doesn't go on to detail is that when he ordered the Ferris wheel moved, Sinatra bailed out and flew back to Los Angeles, Dean Martin in tow. He did not return for several days, until producer Sol Siegel reassured him that there would be no further instances of such directorial obsession.

Press reports at the time abounded with stories of Sinatra's dissatisfaction with small-town life in Madison, Indiana, dissatisfaction that manifested itself in tearing a telephone out of the wall and terming Madison a dump comparable to Los Angeles' skid row. According to Minnelli himself, Sinatra and Martin's manager became embroiled in a "shoving match" with an elderly hotel clerk in Madison—over an order of hamburgers. It was incidents like those that led even the strongest Sinatra defenders to deem some of his actions unforgivable, textbook examples of power run amok. The violent displays of temper often seemed to start when Sinatra sensed weakness on the part of others, as if the sight of such weakness infuriated him, perhaps because it reminded him of weaknesses within himself.

Simpatico or not, Minnelli drew a first-rate performance from Sinatra, and the on-set strains never manifest themselves onscreen. What helped Minnelli coax that excellent performance from Frank was the fact that he quickly learned the wisdom of catering to Sinatra's preference for one quick take. In order to capture the desired impact on film, Minnelli rehearsed the other actors with Sinatra's stand-in, limiting Frank's participation to a final rehearsal and the actual filming. Minnelli may have irritated Sinatra with his painstaking craftsmanship, but the director had no quarrels with Sinatra's performance: "He gave me everything I wanted." Shirley MacLaine posits that she and Dean Martin actually thrived under Minnelli's direction because he trusted the actors' own instincts, providing little in the way of concrete instruction. Conversely, in MacLaine's view, Sinatra disliked Minnelli's style of working because "the freedom of choice exposed him too much."

There is some truth to the assertion, yet it is offset by the fact that Minnelli, like Otto Preminger, favored the shooting of scenes in one continuous take, a style that actually helped the instinctive Sinatra approach. Indeed, Minnelli seems to fit in the middle of the directorial continuum ranging from strong-willed decisive men such as Fred Zinnemann (*From Here to Eternity*) and John Frankenheimer (*The Manchurian Candidate*), under whose guidance Sinatra gave his greatest dramatic performances, to, at the other end of the spectrum, directors like Sidney J. Furie (*The Naked Runner*) with whom Sinatra clashed repeatedly.

Going out of his way to keep Sinatra happy, Minnelli changed the Los Angeles studio shooting hours from the typical early-morning start to the Sinatra-centric hours of noon to 8 P.M. In Frank's view, it all made sense: "Performers work better in the afternoon and the girls look better. They don't run out of gas at five like they usually do." Well, who knows. But what Minnelli and producer Sol Siegel realized was that Sinatra held the power on the picture, and they quickly adjusted to please the star. It was all a long way from the days of Louis B. Mayer booting Frank off the MGM lot.

As to MacLaine's career-breakout performance as Ginny, the verdict is mixed. MacLaine is certainly an actress capable of great pathos, but in her determination to show that Ginny gives too much affection (while Dave and Bama grant none at all), it's all laid on a little thick. Less would have been more here, especially because her accent wanders all over the map from Chicago to the Deep South; it's as if MacLaine is auditioning for the title role in *Sweet Charity,* but she wouldn't film that musical story of a dance hall "hostess" with a heart of gold for another ten years. MacLaine's more-is-more approach works better in the physical schtick sections of the film, but while Ginnie is indeed touching, she often comes across more as a simpleton than as a naïve but well-intentioned young woman. Over the years, MacLaine did evolve into a first-rate dramatic actress, but while the part of Ginny netted her the first Academy Award nomination of her career, her work became infinitely more textured and layered in the later films *Terms of Endearment, The Turning Point,* and *Postcards from the Edge.*

Martin carries off the acting honors here, appearing effortless in his ability to draw a fully realized character. Hospitalized after a knife fight, Bama, sitting up in bed with his hat on, flirts with nuns in full habit, and the effect is charming, not smarmy. Flirting with nuns? Dino makes it work. Similarly, Bama refuses to stop his drinking after receiving a diagnosis of diabetes, yet Martin's performance makes that decision appear utterly consistent with Bama's character and not the action of a thickheaded dolt. It's therefore no surprise to see the look of concern and love Hirsh shoots Bama upon hearing the diagnosis of diabetes. The look speaks volumes about Frank Sinatra and Dean Martin as friends and actors, as well as about their respective public personas. The concern and caring is masked under layers of joking, but as Sinatra said upon Martin's death, "He was my brother. Not through blood but through choice. Our friendship traveled down many roads over the years and there will always be a special place in my heart and soul for Dean."

Even more than Dave and Bama, it is Ginny around whom the final third of the film revolves. She's a memorable character in MacLaine's performance, precisely because there is no limit to the abuse she will tolerate in her desperate quest for affection. When she plaintively pleads, "Dave—be in love with me," the naked vulnerability and the palpable neediness put the audience on her side in a way all the calculated and supposedly heartwarming displays of vulgarity never could. Gone is the sloppy eating of the hamburger, the garish dress and speech. Instead, MacLaine's innate ability induces a feeling of protectiveness in an audience. The less schtick employed, the better MacLaine comes off. It's a welcome sign, pointing the way to a command of her craft that would grow throughout the years.

In an odd way, Dave is suited for Ginny, even knowing that he doesn't love her. Because Sinatra was a male film star unafraid to express his vulnerability, the audience is ready to forgive him his terrible treatment of Ginny as soon as he softly tells her, "I'm sorry if I hurt you." Blue eyes blazing with sincerity, this most naturalistic of actors manages the neat trick of playing a heel who still can engage audience sympathy—David Hirsh is, in other words, the nonmusical Joey Evans.

Dave doesn't really love Ginny and never will, which makes the manner in which he looks away from her at the end of their pitiful marriage ceremony all the sadder and more affecting. The casual brutality of it all would and does affect even the most hard-hearted of viewers. It's a singularly beautiful moment wrought by Sinatra, MacLaine, and Minnelli, one that reinforces the viewer's realization that what's most interesting about Sinatra's performance in the film is that he presents a much more compelling figure when he is playing the cynical boozing loser rather than the cleaned-up Goody Two-shoes who favors cardigan sweaters. Anger comes naturally to Sinatra—he is never more believable than when he yells at his sanctimonious brother to "get the hell out of here." It's a startling anger that he hurls at his pathetic new wife as well, and, perhaps most notably of all, at himself. Audiences knew that character and star alike were men of ungovernable passions, and even when at his most disagreeable on screen, Frank Sinatra, like any true star, kept audiences riveted by the endless contradictions.

At film's end, Ginny's jealous Chicago "boyfriend" Raymond (Steve Peck) tracks Ginny and Dave through the flashing carnival rides and crowds celebrating Parkman's centenary in a minutes-long, largely dialogue-free sequence reminiscent of Hitchcock's work in *Strangers on a Train.* Yes, as Bernstein's score thunders along, one may wish that Minnelli had employed more cross-cutting to focus in on the principals, but it is this very sequence that illustrates Minnelli's masterly use of CinemaScope. Far from echoing the flat visual style Charles Walters employed in the static *Tender Trap,* Minnelli utilizes the entire frame to enhance the impression of depth, the characters blending in and out of the flashy surroundings and thereby increasing audience suspense about how and when they will cross paths with the murderous Raymond.

When the characters do collide, the film includes one inspired final touch: after Raymond fires at Dave, and it is unclear to the viewer whether Dave is still alive, Ginny rushes to save him, only to be mistakenly killed by her ex-boyfriend. The death is unexpected—the most vulnerable and nicest of the characters is the only one to be killed—and in a first-rate piece of screen acting, Sinatra, in tight close-up, silently registers all Dave's conflicting emotions: horror, regret, sadness, guilt, and maybe just a little relief.

For all the talk that Sinatra's refusal to perform more than one take made him a selfish actor, it is worth remembering that it was Frank himself who insisted that Ginny die, knowing her death would heighten audience sympathy for MacLaine and ensure her an Academy Award nomination. Right on both counts. What makes it all a bit more complicated is the fact that this gesture emanated from the same contradictory and concurrent impulses informing so much of his work. In the case of *Some Came Running,* Sinatra, impatient with the lengthy shooting schedule that kept falling further and further behind due to Minnelli's time-consuming methods, ripped twenty pages out of the script and refused to film the scenes contained therein. As detailed in MacLaine's autobiography, Sinatra's insistence that Ginny be killed was not only an inspired idea about audience involvement, but also an unspoken (and it was always unspoken) Sinatra apology from MacLaine, the deleted pages having contained flashy acting opportunities for her. Sinatra's show business instincts were, as usual, right on the money. Jones's novel, as well as the original film script, ended with the murder of Hirsh, but his essentially unlikeable character would have made it impossible for audiences to respond to that death with the same degree of emotion they exhibited for the pathetic but sympathetic Ginny.

Life magazine termed the movie "an unforgettable vignette of American life," but enough critical brickbats were thrown at the film to disqualify it from status as a real triumph. In a particularly negative review, *Time* magazine wrote,

> Yet as bromide follows bromide the spectator slowly comes to a drugged realization that the script is not making fun of anybody's beliefs, but simply stating its own. After that, there is nothing to hang around for except . . . the spectacle of Director Vincente Minnelli's talents dissolving in the general mess of the story, like sunlight in a slag heap.

It's a particularly nasty and rather over-the-top assessment that didn't stop audience members from turning the film into a box office hit.

With another hit film to his credit, no fewer than three LPs topping the charts and an ever-growing schedule of concert dates in Vegas, the question for the peripatetic Sinatra became, What next? Well, what turned up was *A Hole in the Head* and another director of legend, Frank Capra. Tempers flared and the collaboration resulted in a decidedly up-and-down film, but it's one very much worth watching as the only collaboration between two very different Italian-American film industry giants.

A Hole in the Head was Capra's return to A-list Hollywood filmmaking after an eight-year absence spent mostly working in television (his last film having been 1951's *Here Comes the Groom*). In fact, *A Hole in the Head* represented Capra's penultimate feature, with only 1961's *A Pocketful of Miracles* to follow. In a sign of how much the balance of power had shifted in

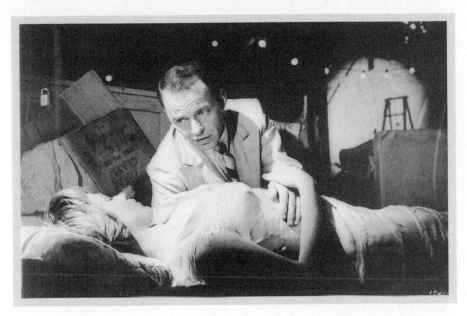

Fine work in Some Came Running *(1958). It was Frank's idea to have Shirley MacLaine killed in the movie: "She'll get nominated for an Oscar." She did.*

Hollywood, it was Sinatra, not star director Capra, whose participation guaranteed that the film would be made. To that end, a deal was structured wherein SinCap Productions, as the joint Sinatra/Capra enterprise was termed, would grant star and director equal vote on all matters, a far cry from the studio-dominated ways of Capra's glory years.

Not only did Capra have to team up with Sinatra in order to get the film made, but with a fifty-fifty vote on all co-venture matters, a third party would be employed to settle any disputes, that arbiter being Abe Lastfogel, head of the William Morris Agency. As to the ultimate ownership of the film, Sinatra granted Capra one-third ownership and his own production company retained two-thirds. That was, for Capra, a brave and disconcerting new world. In his autobiography, *The Name Above the Title,* Capra quotes his friend Bert Allenberg as telling him, "It's not the Hollywood we used to know. It's not a director's business, but an actor's business now. They pick their own stories and their own directors. So if you're thinking of making pictures again, you're gonna have to shack up with a star, or the banks won't lend you a quarter."

Capra genuinely wanted to work with Sinatra, but he also knew that Sinatra's clout made for a delicate balancing act between star and director. Even the estimable Capra could not compete with a one-man conglomerate who reigned as movie star and top-ten box office attraction, film producer, Grammy-winning vocalist (for 1959's Album of the Year *Come Dance with Me*), soon-to-be political power, and all-around cultural icon. If Capra wanted to continue making films—and he did—he had no choice: either come to terms with the rules of the new Hollywood or forever give up the idea of directing A-list Hollywood films. Capra came to terms.

Capra was rusty after eight years away from feature films, and it showed in both his handling of the admittedly thin material and his somewhat uneven use of the CinemaScope filming process. He was, however, a very smart man and unquestionably one of the all-time great Hollywood directors (*Meet John Doe, You Can't Take It with You, It Happened One Night, It's a Wonderful Life*). In fact, in his autobiography, Capra delivers what may be the most knowing assessment of Sinatra the film actor that was ever recorded by one of his coworkers. First acknowledging him to be a world-class singer, Capra goes on to note that when giving live performances,

> The excitement of moving and reaching the hearts of live audiences with his lyrical virtuosity makes his blood run hot. He has total command of his performances. . . . Sinatra is also a great actor, but he cannot bewitch an audience of dispassionate cameramen, soundmen, script girls who have seen it all before. If directors keep him busy, he maintains an easy truce, for having started something Sinatra's next goal is to finish it—but fast. He bores easily; can't sit still or be alone; must be where the action is.

Capra's right: faced with lesser material, where further rehearsal might have helped both the director and his fellow actors, Sinatra lost interest, and often ran over the material. Frank simply could not tolerate any prolonged period of inactivity. This impetuous behavior was not arbitrary, but rather seemed to be embedded in his DNA. It was as if Frank Sinatra could not help himself. Whatever demons he was battling, be they marital problems or the specter of loneliness that had haunted him from childhood, the demons could return much more readily in the "hurry up and wait" atmosphere of a film set than in the recording studio. In Frank's own words: "once you're on that record singing, it's you and you alone. . . . With a film it's never like

A Hole in the Head *(1959).*
Frank's one collaboration
with the great Frank Capra.

that, there are producers and scriptwriters, and hundreds of men in offices and the thing is taken right out of your hands. With a record, you're *it.*"

Based on the mildly successful Broadway play of the same title by the movie's screenwriter Arnold Schulman, *A Hole in the Head* opens on a terrific note: a dolphin leaps out of the water in perfect unison with an upsweep of billowing strings, and as the camera pans up to a blimp pulling the title credits across the sky, Frank Sinatra begins to sing the beautiful Jimmy Van Heusen/Sammy Cahn ballad "All My Tomorrows." It's a sensational start, the best title sequence in Sinatra's entire filmography, and it raises viewers' hopes for the rest of the movie. After all, this film received the plush MGM treatment: Edith Head costumes, Nelson Riddle music, and William Daniels cinematography. (Capra credited favored Sinatra cameraman Daniels, "one of the fastest and best of Hollywood's top cameramen," for helping to bring the film in under schedule at a low cost of $1,800,000.) In addition to such top-drawer collaborators behind the scenes, Sinatra was here paired with a supporting cast that featured the sensational Edward G. Robinson and

Thelma Ritter. First class all the way, indeed. The problem is that the film never quite delivers on that promise.

Sinatra's character, Tony Manetta, age forty-one and a widower with an eleven-year-old son, Ally (Eddie Hodges), runs a Miami Beach hotel called the Garden of Eden, barely staying one step ahead of his creditors. Tony, it turns out, is more of a child than Ally. He is seemingly a "dese, dem, dose" kind of guy, his speech pattern occasionally verging on *Guys and Dolls* territory, and a loving if very unorthodox father; when he returns from a date at 4 A.M., he plays cards with his son and tests his knowledge of boxing trivia. Tony is supposed to be charming, and in Sinatra's hands, he is—up to a point. He is full of grand schemes, and his business ideas are good ones, remarkably prescient for 1959. He envisions "buying up real estate in South Beach" and building a Disneyland in Florida.

But how charming is the audience supposed to find Tony when he takes "free bird" girlfriend Shirl (Carolyn Jones) to the beach instead of going to the airport to pick up his brother and sister-in-law? Mario and Sophie (Robinson and Ritter) have flown to Miami on a moment's notice because Tony, needing their money in order to save the hotel, has tried to rouse their sympathy by telling them that Ally is sick. That isn't charming—it's boorish. In a sequence redeemed only by Sinatra's acting during the telephone call, he alternately shoos his son out of the room, stalls for time, and stammers out the nonsense about Ally's stomach problems. Tony is not, to say the least, a truthful man, but Sinatra presents the character in a very honest, human fashion, thereby ensuring that the audience will go along for the ride, albeit grudgingly.

The problems become worse when Mario and Sophie arrive in Florida, because they are set up to be cardboard figures of respectability. Mario is a tightwad who wears a three-piece suit throughout his entire stay in tropical Miami, and the movie comes to a grinding halt while the three adults discuss Tony's dire financial situation and Mario calls Tony "a bum" fifteen times in a row. Tony may be irresponsible, but endless cries of "you bum" turn the audience completely against Mario. It's a very curious decision for a skilled director of comedy like Capra to repeat that annoying bit of dialogue endlessly, a repetitive motif also utilized with the running gag of Mario sitting in a noisy spring-laden chair; after Mario unsuccessfully attempts to sit in the chair four times in a row, the payoff of having Tony use the chair without a problem just doesn't land, given the protracted setup. Yes, Capra and Daniels do a nice job

of utilizing the CinemaScope format to divide the screen into sections, showing the warmhearted (and ever-appealing) Ritter in the middle of the screen
as she referees the fight between her husband and brother-in-law, but the two
men are so irritatingly presented that any visual appeal is largely negated.

Strangest of all, Robinson, who played an Italian gangster to great effect
in the classic *Little Caesar*, plays Mario with a full arsenal of stereotypical Jewish inflections and gestures, all shrugged shoulders and incredulous questions. He is ill served by Capra or, perhaps more accurately, is ill served by the
leaden screenplay. (Oddly enough, in its original Broadway incarnation, *A
Hole in the Head* possessed a distinctly Jewish flavor.) As a result, it's just too
damn hard to believe that the Manetta brothers are actually siblings.

In Capra's autobiography, he details the problems he encountered with his
two stars, Sinatra refusing to take part in the extensive rehearsals Robinson
wanted, not only because of boredom, but also because of his belief that his
first take was always his best. Sinatra would not budge on the matter, simply
telling Robinson, "I don't believe in exhausting myself before the take. On
the other hand, I read the script fifty times before I ever go to work. So you
can't say I'm unprepared."

Unlike Sinatra, Robinson grew better and better with each rehearsal.
Capra's solution was a crafty one, based on his belief that Sinatra was a per
former first, and actor second. Capra's right, insofar as he draws that distinc-
tion, but there is a further step involved; Sinatra was always acting when he
sang, particularly on the ballads, and in that regard actually functioned first
and last as an actor, the acting just often happened to come in the form of a
song. Given those layers of complication, Capra instructed Sinatra's fellow
cast members that there would be few rehearsals, encouraging costars Keenan
Wynn and Joi Lansing to ad-lib and jump on each other's lines. Such an approach wouldn't work with many actors, but it did with Sinatra because it
kept him on his toes and interested, and an interested Sinatra delivered. In
the end, Capra came to feel that he and Sinatra achieved a genuine rapport,
"mostly unspoken. We liked, respected, and admired each other and never
said anything about it."

Capra's directorial approach results in a mixed bag, some sequences working beautifully, others meandering to no discernible effect. At the start of the
film, there's a terrific bit of classic Capra-esque physical comedy as Tony carries
the free spirit bongo-playing Shirl up the stairs of the hotel after their date.

Given the fact that Shirl is nearly the same size as Tony, he resorts to hitching himself up the stairs backwards on his rear, with Shirl plopped in his lap. When he reaches the top, he lands on a footstool and falls backwards, tumbling head over heels, entwined with Shirl. It's a funny bit because setup, execution, and payoff have all been handled swiftly and in perfect lockstep. On the other hand, although Capra's framing and sense of color are intact, he is unable to overcome the all-too-apparent stage origins of the piece when Tony first meets proposed love match Mrs. Rogers (Eleanor Parker). The proscenium arch is all but visible as the four adults statically sit on the chairs and couch, Sophie, Tony, and Mario arguing interminably while Mrs. Rogers looks on, bewildered. As the scene wanders to its conclusion with no payoff in sight, more than ever one misses the signature expert pacing from the Frank Capra of yore.

Capable and attractive as Eleanor Parker is, Mrs. Rogers appears to be much older than Tony in dress and demeanor, someone the free-spirited Tony would never consider a true soul mate. It's son Ally who does the real falling for Mrs. Rogers, a very funny expression of pure bliss appearing on his face when he first meets her. The film perks up noticeably whenever Ally appears onscreen, young actor Eddie Hodges achieving a genuine rapport with Sinatra. Frank always worked well with children on film, his gentle quality coming to the fore as their innocence relaxed him. Lovingly calling his son a "nag," Sinatra's Tony Manetta hugs and kisses the eleven-year-old, sounding more like a child than Ally himself as he spins beachside tales of buying a new refrigerator and "cooking spinach, just like a normal family." It's a lifestyle Tony will never be able to deliver, but that sweet heart-to-heart talk with Ally leads into the terrific Cahn/Van Heusen song "High Hopes," which Sinatra and Hodges deliver together.

An infectious blend of music and clever lyrics ("Just what makes that little ole ant think he'll move that rubber tree plant"), the song's presented in perfect understated fashion by Capra, the grand master back in top form. Only after Frank begins to sing a capella does the music rise very gently underneath, Ally joining in with a bungled version of the lyrics that makes the song all the more charming. Warbling their way through this ode to unfettered optimism, Sinatra and Hodges radiate real father-and-son kinship before ending the song as gently as it began—a capella. Whoever made the decision to present the song in unadorned fashion rather than in a full-blown orchestrated version—whether Frank's decision alone or one arrived at in conjunction

Tony Manetta and son Ally (Eddie Hodges) during the scene of the Oscar-winning "High Hopes" duet in A Hole in the Head.

with Capra and Riddle—the choice was a great one. It's an utterly winning moment, the best in the entire film, and the song proves more than worthy of its Academy Award as Best Song of the Year.

Mrs. Rogers's first name is finally revealed to be Eloise (with Sinatra's expression making it clear he'd probably prefer to call her Mrs.), and her subsequent date with Tony allows the film to finally quiet down. Back at her apartment after the date, there is no yelling, and the characters reveal their basic needs, allowing audience sympathy and interest to finally take hold. Eloise discloses the loss of her son and husband, and the loneliness she endures as a result—"worst of all, nobody needs me." Tony unexpectedly discusses his late wife, describing her as a short fun-loving woman who was also very religious, quietly stating, "I wish I were religious." He's not, but he has a yearning for a sense of belonging, and the audience begins to root for the two unexpectedly lonely people to connect. The scene works because it's exactly what much of the rest of the film is not—low-key, three-dimensional, and full of humanity. Fine actors that they are, Sinatra and Parker here invest the characters with inherent dignity and believability. Capra directs them both most sympathetically, capped by the quirky but enjoyable added twist of having Sinatra impersonate Sigmund Freud as he analzyes Eloise's loneliness in a gently mocking but essentially caring manner. What could easily have become cloying instead reads as humorous.

What makes this mass of contradictions all the more frustrating is that three-quarters of the way through the movie there is a terrific sequence at the racetrack when the audience is introduced to Tony's old pal, entrepreneur Jerry Marks (Keenan Wynn, from *Johnny Concho*), a fast-taking promoter with scads of money and no taste. Tony sells his car in order to fund a trip to the racetrack with Marks and his shrewish blond girlfriend Dorine (Joi Lansing). Capra and cameraman William Daniels here film a terrific series of race sequences (evidently the scene was written by Capra's oft-collaborator Myles Connolly, but Schulman retained sole credit), the darkened track lit only by the oval railing of light around the race course, as the noise of the race drowns out the conversation Tony and Jerry are having about investing in a Florida Disneyland. It's a smartly executed sequence by an old pro at the top of his game, audience interest heightened precisely because the viewer cannot hear what is being said.

When dealing with artists of Sinatra and Capra's caliber, one waits for a particular moment of insight and emotion that makes the entire enterprise worthwhile, and together, director and star deliver just such a gem toward the end of the film. When Tony slumps into the hotel after gambling away all his money, only to be greeted by all his friends with the "congratulations—you saved the hotel" party that Ally has organized, the expression on Sinatra's face speaks more about Tony's mix of hurt and self-loathing than could any ten pages of dialogue. However, just as happens throughout the film, a beautiful moment is undercut by what follows: Tony has gambled away his son's future, but all of a sudden, Mario tells Tony, "You're not a bum—nobody in the family's a bum." It's a statement totally at odds with his previous endlessly repeated characterization, and also with the fact that Tony is, for the first time, completely worthy of the label "bum." Instead, in a misguided attempt to save Ally by sending him away with Mario and Sophie, Tony is deliberately cruel to Ally, yelling, "I don't need you. I don't want you around any more," and slapping his son across the face. At which point, Mario embraces Tony. Go figure.

Naturally enough, the audience next sees Ally running down the highway to embrace his father as they fall into the surf. They then walk off into the sunset along with Eloise. (One can only hope she ditched the high heels when she went in the water.)

In other words, Tony has gambled away the money that would have saved the hotel, is still full of grand schemes with no practical plan to ensure their success, spends all his money on his own suits, will presumably be bailed out once again by his brother, and appears to be marrying a widow with whom he has been out on one date. By now, thanks mostly to Capra and Sinatra, audiences care enough about the characters to want this happy ending—it's just that somehow one wishes the journey to that destination had been undertaken in different fashion.

Newsweek probably delivered the most accurate assessment of the film, claiming that the film possessed "a soap-opera plot, if there ever was one. . . . Sinatra manages to arouse sympathy without employing sentimentality; Robinson . . . almost steals the show from Sinatra. Not quite, of course. No one these days ever completely steals the show from Sinatra." No kidding.

As to director Capra, his return to feature films was nicely summed up by Philip K. Scheuer in *The Los Angeles Times,* who found that while "he has not performed any major miracle with *A Hole in the Head,* he has at least dressed up a so-so stage comedy with laughs, human interest, a shot of sex, and even a suspicion of a tear toward the close." Capra's participation in this film shows exactly how much the rules were changing in Hollywood. He had retained enough of the old magic to bring the audience along on the sometimes bumpy ride; indeed, without Capra at the helm, *A Hole in the Head* would have turned into *The Tender Trap.* He was still such a superb craftsman, so full of humanity, that individual sequences in the film, particularly those featuring Sinatra and movie son Eddie Hodges, work very well. However, Capra was competing against his own exalted reputation and high standards, and registers as an older man having a tough go of it keeping up with the times. He does keep up, but it's a struggle. This name-above-the-title director, who had always functioned as the true auteur of his films long before the term became fashionable, had to cede power and even methods of filming to Sinatra.

The fact that Sinatra and Capra eventually came to a good working relationship makes it all the more unfortunate that they never reteamed on their much-talked-about project, the life story of Jimmy Durante. Focusing on Durante and his two trusted sidekicks, the film would have starred Sinatra and featured Bing Crosby and Dean Martin, all of them eager to salute a performer they and director Capra greatly admired. As detailed in Capra's autobiography, the production fell apart because in the new Hollywood, such a film involved making complicated deals with three major legally incorpo-rated Hollywood stars, each of whom came complete with a lawyer, agent, and accountant who had to sign off on every contractual detail. Not so sur-prisingly, it was Capra himself who pulled the plug on his participation. He had made an uneasy peace with the new Hollywood, but it didn't mean he had to like it.

After working with two legendary directors in Minnelli and Capra, Sinatra next collaborated with solid professional John Sturges on the MGM release *Never So Few*. Sturges, director of the first-class *Bad Day at Black Rock, Gun-fight at the O.K. Corral,* and *The Great Escape,* here turned in an uneven job. Produced by Sinatra's own Canterbury Productions, *Never So Few* is a mish-mash of a movie. Trying on various hats as war movie, romance, exploration of moral ambiguity, and tract on the psychological fitness of leaders in wartime, it fully succeeds as none.

The Millard Kaufman screenplay, based on the novel by Tom T. Chamales, centers around the Overseas Special Services combat operations in North Burma, where a thousand Kachins, under British and American leadership, held off forty thousand Japanese soldiers. There are top-notch technical credits along the way, with an appropriate score by Hugo Friehofer and evocative loca-tion cinematography by William Daniels. Filmed fourteen years after the end of the war, that very distance from the war allows the filmmakers to present a more nuanced view of the conflict and helps the viewer react to different ideas, rather than concentrating solely on the issue of a soldier's survival. The hitch is those ideas never fully tie together, because both screenwriter Kaufman and director Sturges fare better with the action sequences than with the love story.

Never So Few is not without its singular pleasures, but unfortunately, both Frank and the movie stumble right off the bat with his first appearance: sport-ing a ridiculous goatee, Sinatra, playing Captain Tom Reynolds, does not look like any commander ever seen in World War II. It's not an insignificant point, because Sinatra, with his lived-in face, is ideally cast as a combat-hardened veteran, cynical yet idealistic beneath the tough-guy exterior. Frank Sinatra with a growth of stubble absolutely looks the part of such a com-mander. A ridiculous goatee, on the other hand, simply reminds the audience that they are watching superstar Frank Sinatra play a soldier. The goatee looks like an affectation left over from a late night in Vegas.

Silly goatee aside, when Sinatra begins to speak, he is thoroughly believable and it is that very sense of authenticity that helps the audience to accept what film historian Jeanine Basinger posits as the basic questions any war film is asking: What is worth dying for? What makes a "good" person? What constitutes a "good" and righteous cause? Those issues would become particularly prominent in Sinatra's self-directed 1965 film, *None But the Brave,* but even in *Never So Few* it's clear that the questions Americans asked themselves were growing increasingly complicated. Is it always good to be an American? Are there times outside of combat when it can be morally acceptable to kill? American audiences needed and wanted to have those questions asked, and they are part of Sturges's film—it's just that the answers aren't always forthcoming in a coherent fashion.

The bifurcated nature of *Never So Few* is made plain early on with the very first combat sequences. Just as the audience settles in for an examination of wartime issues framed against the backdrop of intense combat, all traces of the war disappear, and—bingo!—Carla Vesari arrives on the scene in the figure of Gina Lollobrigida. A Japanese soldier, she ain't. Clearly the powers that be at MGM hoped to sell the movie on the basis of the Sinatra/Lollobrigida pairing, as evidenced by the trailer for the film: Bold letters fill the screen, proclaiming SOONER OR LATER THIS HAD TO HAPPEN—SINATRA MEETS LOLLO-BRIDGIDA as flames envelop the screen. Mamma mia—was subtlety verboten at MGM? Evidently the executives felt that all Italians were so hot blooded that having not one but two famous Italians would, of course, ignite the screen. After sitting through the film, viewers were bound to have a message for the executives—"guess again." Oddly enough, just as proved to be the case with Sinatra and Sophia Loren in *The Pride and the Passion,* no sparks fly between the stars. It may simply be the case that Sinatra was, famously, Italian-American, not simply Italian. He reads 100 percent American onscreen. Make that 100 percent urban American, because it stretches all boundaries of the audience's credulity to hear Sinatra refer to himself as a Midwesterner who worked in his father's Indiana hardware store. This not-so–Middle American is instantly smitten with Carla, telling her, "You're on the green side of twenty-five and put together like a Christmas package," but Carla (not surprisingly) finds Reynolds juvenile, and audiences sensibly enough found Lollobrigida and Sinatra to be a wet firecracker of a team.

What actually proves to be of greater interest is the introduction of Steve McQueen in the role of Corporal Bill Ringa, a piece of casting instigated by

Sinatra himself. McQueen wasn't yet the actor he would become, but in purely physical terms he made an even more believable combat soldier than did Sinatra. It may have been early in his career, but McQueen already possessed a commanding screen presence, a fact Sinatra recognized at once. What makes his participation even more noteworthy is the fact that the part of Ringa was originally intended for Sammy Davis Jr., not an actor who was exactly fighting for the same roles as McQueen. Sinatra wanted to make a point of including an African-American soldier in the film and lined up the role for his friend Sammy. All bets were off, however, after Davis gave an interview in February 1959 to radio reporter Jack Eigen and stated, "Talent is not an excuse for bad manners. I love Frank, but there are many things he does that there are no excuses for. . . . It does not give you the right to step on people and treat them rotten." When word of both this unguarded statement and Davis's further claim that he was now America's number-one singer reached Sinatra, Sammy was, to put it mildly, disinvited from participating in the film. Gone was his seventy-five-thousand-dollar paycheck and so, too (temporarily), was his friendship with Sinatra. (In one of his autobiographies, *Hollywood in a Suitcase,* Davis offers a different scenario, claiming that Sinatra pulled him out of the film because they differed over interpretation of the character. It's an explanation that doesn't hold much water.) Exit Sammy, enter McQueen.

The casting of Steve McQueen proved a felicitous choice in many ways, starting with the fact that from the standpoint of historical accuracy, there weren't any African-American infantrymen fighting in Burma. The pairing of Sinatra and McQueen is in many ways the most interesting relationship in the film, two screen icons who patented differing varieties of cool staking out their territory in friendly rivalry. Unlike Reynolds and Carla, Reynolds and Ringa strike sparks immediately, with Reynolds watching Corporal Ringa take out two MPs, and subsequently learning that this particular kind of renaissance man even makes his own gin. "Ever seen combat?" asks Reynolds. Ringa's laconic reply: "New York City mostly—Hell's Kitchen and Williamsburg." Supported by Sinatra, who bluntly told Sturges to "give the kid closeups," McQueen registers strongly throughout, a big first step in his career, which led to his working again with Sturges on *The Magnificent Seven.*

Just as the Ringa–Reynolds relationship heats up, the movie abruptly switches gears yet again, reverting to a soap opera romance starring Frank and Gina. All of a sudden Captain Reynolds and his pal Danny (Richard Johnson) are off on holiday for two weeks (they seem to spend as much time on holiday as they do in combat), with Reynolds arranging to vacation in exactly the same spot where Carla lives with her wealthy paramour, Nikko (Paul Henreid).

It's a romance mostly couched in terms redolent of the late 1950s; when Carla and Reynolds playfully talk of their imaginary married life together, he tells her, "Your place, woman, is at the stove," and his idea of a marriage proposal is, "Tell Nikko I'll keep you barefoot and pregnant and on the edge of town." Yet even there Sinatra manages to salvage the clichéd dialogue with his simple confession of love: "Carla—I'm falling in love with you, I think." Sinatra lowers his voice confidentially, and in that one line manages to suggest not only a masculine sexy war veteran, but one who is vulnerable as well. It's a one-line delivery that sums up exactly why women found Sinatra so attractive over the course of a six-decade performing career: In his macho mode, they wanted to sleep with him. In his vulnerable guise, they wanted to mother him.

There is a problem with the romance, however, and it's a big one: Lollobrigida's performance. She is a beautiful woman with a sexy, knowing presence, but she delivers her lines in a heavily accented Italian version of English that simply becomes monotonous after ten minutes of screen time. She actually seems bored, barely expressing a flicker of emotion, let alone the supposed passion she feels for Sinatra's Captain Reynolds. Add in a wardrobe that does absolutely nothing to suggest the 1940s World War II time frame of the film (she appears to be modeling late-1950s designer fashions), and the romance begins to derail the film.

One of the expected developments in a World War II film is that the lovers will be torn apart by the war, but Reynolds and Carla's incessant meeting and parting does nothing so much as grate on the audience. There is no sense of surprise in her constant reappearance, and even less in their perfunctory fighting. It may be the fault of the original novel, or the problem may lie with Kaufman's script, but even Dame Judi Dench would not have been able to do anything with Carla's line, "I kiss you and the bells ring wildly in my temples." No wonder Lollobrigida comes off as nothing much more than a very attractive decoration—granted, one who always appears with quite a bit of décolletage. The camp dialogue seems more at home in a Maria Montez movie.

Along the way there are some beautiful panoramic scenes of the jungle setting (location lensing having taken place in Burma, Ceylon, and Thailand), but the scenes set in the wartime jungle encampments jarringly scream "soundstage." Just when the viewer is drawn in by an interesting plot twist or a nicely judged bit of dialogue ("The movies have got it all wrong—a cigarette tastes lousy when you're wounded"), the phony soundstage setting hauls the viewer back to the realization that he or she is just watching a movie. In fact, the most interesting scene in the second half of the film finds an injured Reynolds in the hospital with wounded Kachins, yelling at the captain to serve food they'll like—"red peppers and monkey entrails"—instead of chicken soup and salads.

It's an effective scene precisely because the setting does appear realistic, the dialogue neatly upends the viewing expectations of the Western audience, and Sinatra gets a chance to let loose with his anger. An angry Sinatra onscreen is always a Sinatra worth watching, one possessing a (dangerous) sense of freedom in action and speech.

One of the interesting characteristics of war films made after the hostilities ended is the increasingly prominent role minorities played in the diverse ethnic mix of soldiers; it was no longer only Irish, Italians, and Jews who formed the combat unit, but also Native Americans, African-Americans, and in this case, Kachins. (Sinatra's own *None But the Brave* took that multicultural evolution one step further by presenting a sympathetic portrayal of the Japanese enemy.) The earlier manifestation of the combat unit fit Americans' view of themselves as a melting pot nation. The diverse combat unit served up the lesson that in wartime, we put aside our individual differences—the collective dream of America is presented as bigger and better than all of us. Beginning with the late 1950s, however, the collective dream began to sour, reflecting the anxiety of a postwar era defined by the existence of the atom bomb. The nature of the questions being asked by war films, and the collective reassurance underlying the response, began to change greatly as a result. In that light, films such as *Never So Few* may not prove to be particularly successful, but the questions they raise always prove to be of note.

Reflecting the increased cynicism of the time, the film introduces a nice element of moral ambiguity by asking, At what point does national loyalty stop and personal loyalties take over? Or, as one of the war-weary officers views the situation: "The longer the war goes on, the smaller my loyalties get." As evident in the dialogue between Reynolds and his superiors, the boundaries are no longer clear—

COLONEL PARKSON: Doesn't it strike you, Tom, that your actions were, to say the least, unprecedented?
REYNOLDS (IN A QUICK RETORT): And doesn't it strike you that we're fighting an unprecedented kind of war?

It's all food for thought, but by the time this dialogue occurs, also a case of too little, too late. We are two hours into the movie, and when General Chiang Kai-shek announces that he wants Reynolds exonerated, Reynolds is quickly reunited with Carla—and the movie abruptly ends. It leaves the audience with a great many unanswered questions: Will Reynolds resume command? What the heck did I just watch? Was it a combat film or a soap opera? How come Reynolds seems to spend more time on leave than fighting? What happened to the monkey he carried on his back around base camp? Was that a ham-fisted representation of the emotional baggage Reynolds carries with him, or a reference to Sinatra's drug-addicted character in *The Man with the Golden Arm*? And how did Gina find all those Western-style high heels in the middle of wartime? And—well, never mind. There are no clear-cut answers to any of those questions, leaving the viewer with the feeling that the entire film plays like a slightly inferior version of *Kings Go Forth*. It's all a little cuckoo, a little interesting, and a lot confusing. Too herky-jerky in execution to satisfy audiences, the inconsistency of execution in *Kings Go Forth* was reflected in the indifferent response from critics and audiences alike.

As for Frank himself, he was now on to bigger and better things, severing his relationship with Capitol Records in order to start his own label, called Reprise. The move granted him unprecedented clout in the recording industry. Couple the creation of his own record label with the A-list Hollywood films he regularly turned out, as well as the most financially rewarding contracts in the world for concert appearances, and Frank Sinatra had finally arrived exactly where he wanted to be. He was, in the words of magazine profiler Richard Gehman, "Not merely an entertainer and a personality, but an immensely powerful force—a law unto himself." He could do whatever the hell he wanted, and if his next film, *Can-Can,* wasn't exactly at the top of his wish list, it did represent a relatively painless way to fulfill his need to make settlement with Twentieth Century-Fox for having walked off *Carousel* five years earlier. *Can-Can* wasn't a great career move on his part, but it did prove a lucrative one, with Frank receiving a fee of $200,000 plus 25 percent of the gross

Then–Soviet Premier Nikita Khrushchev and his wife on the set of Can-Can *(1960).*
Their visit was more noteworthy than the film.

profits for his participation. It was all for naught, however, because the on-set visit by then–Soviet premier, the bellicose Nikita Khrushchev, proved more interesting than anything ultimately seen onscreen.

In the beginning, hopes actually ran high for *Can-Can.* After all, it represented Sinatra's first musical since *Pal Joey* three years earlier, and the production team boasted musical royalty: a score by Cole Porter, based on his 1953 Broadway hit of the same name, choreography by Astaire/Rogers stalwart Hermes Pan, and music arranged and conducted by Nelson Riddle. The resulting film, however, was anything but classic. It's not without interest, and it does feature one "as good as it gets" musical moment with Sinatra, but there's an awful lot of dreck to slog through in order to arrive at that moment.

Produced by Jack Cummings (*It Happened in Brooklyn*) in conjunction with Sinatra's own Suffolk Productions, *Can-Can* was directed by Walter Lang, who had done well by *The King and I,* and less so with *There's No Business Like Show Business.* After some sharp opening credits filmed against a period-appropriate background of Lautrec-like paintings, the movie begins with attorney François Durnais (Sinatra) singing about the joys of "Montmartre" in 1890s Paris along with costar Maurice Chevalier (magistrate Paul

Barriere). It's a pleasant-enough opening, and Chevalier had already proved his musical film heft with starring appearances in two classics of the genre: *Love Me Tonight* and *Gigi*. Sinatra and Chevalier sound good together, but as they stroll into the Bal de Paradis nightclub run by Simone Pistache (Shirley MacLaine), the first problem with the film is already glaringly evident: paired with Maurice Chevalier, that quintessential resident of Paris, Frank Sinatra is making no attempt at playing a Frenchman. There is not even the slightest effort made to utilize French-accented English akin to Chevalier's. Maybe Sinatra was scared of accents after his critically reviled Spanish accent in *The Pride and the Passion,* but to hear Sinatra's Hoboken-meets-Hollywood patois next to Chevalier's Gallic-inflected English is to immediately be hauled out of the fairy-tale rendition of 1890s Paris and back to twentieth-century America.

This problem is compounded by Shirley MacLaine's similar refusal to attempt the slightest French inflection. Supposedly it was MacLaine who talked Sinatra out of attempting a French accent, but she should have paid closer attention to her own efforts, because she plays a bohemian Parisian nightclub owner in so broadly American a fashion that her name might as well be Betty Sue Anderson of Smalltown, USA. Sinatra had insisted on MacLaine's casting, a demand that required Fox to buy out her Columbia Pictures contract for *Who Was That Lady?* It was an unfortunate choice, because MacLaine's broad and unappealing performance ruins the very fabric of the film.

When Simone's nightclub is raided for allowing a "lewd and lascivious" performance of the scandalous can-can dance, one does at least receive the pleasure of watching the first-rate title number led by the terrific Juliet Prowse. In fact, Prowse does a very nice job of acting and dancing herein, and also delivers the film's single best line when she warns Sinatra's character: "I don't like to gossip, François, but I think Simone is going to shoot you." The public performance of the can-can results in all parties ending up in court before conservative judge Philipe Forrestier (Louis Jourdan), who sits alongside chief magistrate Barriere (Chevalier). Good luck to any audience member who can even concentrate on those plot developments, however, because all the viewer's powers need to be utilized in order to solve the mystery of the disappearing accents. How can one believe that the very French Jourdan and Chevalier live in the same country as Yankee Doodle Sinatra and Apple Pie MacLaine? Unfortunately, because Sinatra and MacLaine share the most screen time, the wrong country wins the battle of the accents.

As for Frank himself, to paraphrase the words of the famous *Chorus Line* song "Dance 10, Looks 3," he receives marks of "Song 10, Acting 3." When first launching into the classic Porter song "C'est Magnifique," he sings in such a rich warm voice that one doesn't really give a damn that he does not resemble a Frenchman in any way, shape, or form. Well, one doesn't give a damn, that is, until near the song's end, when he inserts "Ring a ding ding ding" into the Cole Porter lyric. Porter himself must have blanched at such a liberty being taken with his precisely calibrated lyric, because it's an insertion that destroys the very flow of the song. Porter was not present during filming, and undoubtedly director Walter Lang did not dare tell Sinatra to stick with the lyric as written. With this one ad-lib, the viewer loses all belief that Sinatra is a Frenchman, or will even attempt the characterization of a French lawyer. "Ring a ding ding" makes it impossible to accept Chevalier's French accent next to Sinatra's Americanese, which could, in fact, have happened in a well-crafted movie. Alas, this one phrase instantly yanks the viewer out of Paris and back to Las Vegas. The concept of *Can-Can* as a coherent piece has vanished. Now the viewer simply watches the Frank Sinatra show. It's interesting, but it's just a show, not a performance.

It may just be one ring-a-ding-ding, but it is a significant moment in Sinatra's film career, because after appearing in forty films, it's the first time Frank doesn't bother to try. As the king of show business in 1960, Sinatra had, by that time, firmly passed from stardom into the land of legend. And with the interpolation of "ring a ding ding" he is, in effect, saying, "Hey, I'm Frank Sinatra—I'll coast along here on my charm. I don't need to act and work at a genuine characterization." He's taking his pleasure and winking at the audience. Such an attitude can be charming in a nightclub, but on film it's disconcerting at best, and deadly at worst.

Sinatra still had some terrific film performances in front of him (*The Manchurian Candidate, Von Ryan's Express*), but laziness would now be exhibited with increasing frequency. It was the start of personality acting as opposed to acting on film as a craft, and anyone doubting the shift need only take a look at *Marriage on the Rocks, Assault on a Queen,* and *Dirty Dingus Magee.* The key point to remember is that it wasn't a result of Sinatra's not caring about his movies. Rather, as his persona cast a larger and larger shadow over the landscape of American pop culture, his demeanor on set changed from impatient to short-tempered. If Frank felt one take was enough, then everybody else needed to see it that way as well. It was Sinatra's way or the highway.

For the purposes of the *Can-Can* film, director Lang broadly altered Porter's Broadway score, eliminating hefty portions and freely substituting other Porter numbers that were never intended for use in *Can-Can*. It's all too symbolic of this sloppy approach that "I Love Paris," the score's best-known song, is barely heard, registering only during the main title sequence and then again when sung by a chorus at the very end of the film. Even stranger, Ira Gershwin and Sammy Cahn supplied new lyrics to "It's All Right with Me" when Porter refused Sinatra's demand for new lyrics. Gershwin and Cahn rewriting Porter? It's as if Rembrandt painted over da Vinci—wrong on about twelve levels at once.

When Simone is prosecuted for the public indecency of the can-can dance, defense attorney François arrives in court sporting a rakishly tilted Cavanaugh hat. It has absolutely nothing to do with the wardrobe of a Parisian lawyer in 1890, and the disconnect is made worse when a very French prison guard interacts with the very American Sinatra and MacLaine. Sinatra is not even trying; his performance is all thumbs in his waistcoat, as if he prepared for playing a lawyer by looking at political cartoons. The slipshod work is a very long way from the meticulous preparation found in *From Here to Eternity* and *The Man with the Golden Arm*. Even in song, Sinatra is atypically disconcerting at times, employing offensive gestures such as raising his eyes to form narrow slits while singing the lyric "In old Japan, all the Japs do it" from the song "Let's Do It (Let's Fall in Love)."

Bad as Sinatra is, however, MacLaine comes off even worse, delivering an unendingly shrill performance that finds her shrieking when she pretends to have been dishonored by Judge Philipe, shrill when arguing with François about marriage, and downright grating at film's end, when François finally agrees to marry her. In reality, it is Louis Jourdan who emerges best of all, with a characterization that makes you truly believe that the straitlaced judge could slowly melt into a recognizable human being because of his love for Simone. Delivering his songs in agreeable speech-song, Jourdan's versions of "Live and Let Love" (a duet with Chevalier) and "You Do Something to Me," actually help the viewer to understand his character.

Very occasionally, there is a funny line of dialogue or bit of business. When Simone reviews her accounts and finds that a certain Toulouse-Lautrec has once again paid off his tab with a sketch, she angrily mutters, "I want the money—not this," whereupon she proceeds to tear up an original Lautrec sketch. Such moments are few and far between, but there is one number in the film that is so beautifully staged and sung that it actually makes sitting through the rest of the film bearable: to watch Frank Sinatra sing "It's All Right with Me" directly to Juliet Prowse is to witness a great moment in movie musical history.

Viewing such a gem in the midst of a musical mess is what makes the sequence even more noteworthy, a startling example of how great Sinatra really could be on film when all the elements lined up properly. Disconsolate at being rejected by Simone, François pours himself a drink in the empty club, and when Claudine (Prowse) wanders in, Sinatra begins to sing "It's All Right with Me" directly to her, accompanied only by a solo piano. As he's fixing Prowse with an unwavering gaze from those steely blue eyes, the erotic charge between the two actors is nearly palpable. At that point in time, Sinatra and Prowse were genuinely in love, subsequently becoming engaged, and the heat between them shows up onscreen.

Lighting a cigarette midsong, continuing to sing in his still-smooth voice that had now acquired an effective layer of grit, Sinatra then delivers the crowning touch; arriving at the song's midpoint, he unexpectedly twists the phrasing of the lines "It's the wrong game, with the wrong chips," investing the slightly altered notes with extra emotion. It's a seamless choice that only a great singer could pull off, and as the song flows toward its climax, Sinatra kisses Prowse and quickly walks toward the exit as the camera pulls back.

It's a beautiful sequence, and one to be savored.

Unfortunately, the remainder of the film quickly intrudes. The audience even has to suffer through a very peculiar ballet before arriving at film's end, one in which the "Adam and Eve"–themed dance finds Simone herself flying in on giant butterfly wings. . . . There is sexy dancing from Juliet Prowse as the snake with the apple, but even so, there are some very odd and discordant period notes sounded. If this is a ballet in 1890s Paris, why is the snake's entrance emphasized by the sound of bongos? Well, that's no stranger than the fact that after Adam and Eve bite the apple, the choreography abruptly changes to the style of jazz master Jack Cole, the orchestration begins to sound like the theme to *Peter Gunn,* and the whole strange enterprise ends with a blast of stripper music.

This wacked-out number is followed by the sight and sound of Louis Jourdan wearing his hat à la Frank Sinatra, singing "It's All Right with Me," complete with the "ring a ding ding" lyric. It's a game effort, but he ends up sounding like no one so much as Cary Grant. The court case over, the ribald can-can number is finally performed full-out—the audience heretofore has only been teased by snippets—and it's a fun, galvanizing number, but it's not enough (not to mention that if any dance should be banned, it's the violent and bizarrely degrading "Apache Dance"). After watching Shirley MacLaine's Simone gravitate toward Louis Jourdan's Philipe for the second hour of the film, the audience is then more than a bit dumbfounded when she reverses course and chooses François after he finally asks her to marry him. In other words, forget logic—the stars have to end up together. Exit Prowse; so long, Jourdan; the happy ending exists only for MacLaine and Sinatra. Given how modern and American sounding these two intrepid Parisians are, one can only imagine that they will head off to the Sands Hotel in Vegas for their honeymoon.

It's no wonder the film is best remembered today for the international headlines it generated when then–Soviet Premier Nikita Khrushchev visited Twentieth Century-Fox for a lavish luncheon attended by dozens of Hollywood's big names. The luncheon was followed by a live presentation of musical highlights from *Can-Can,* for which Sinatra acted as master of ceremonies. Now there's one definite culture clash: Francis S. and Nikita K. It's not too surprising to learn that Khrushchev, then presiding over a dour film culture that seemed to specialize in epics extolling the latest wheat harvest, was promptly scandalized by the skirt-flashing, high-kicking can-can number. Nikita may have professed shock, terming the dance "lascivious, disgusting and immoral," but at least he saw the only snappy number in the whole lopsided confection. Hopefully it gave him something to talk about at the next politburo meeting, because it undoubtedly made a much bigger impression on him than it did on discerning American audiences who rejected the whole bloated enterprise.

Putting honorary Rat Packer Nikita K. aside, *Can Can* marked Sinatra's second film experience with MacLaine, following *Some Came Running.* MacLaine cameos in *Ocean's Eleven* and *Cannonball Run II* were to follow, as well as a joint concert tour with Sinatra in 1992. With a history of shared films covering the nearly three decades from *Some Came Running* (1958) to

Cannonball Run II (1984), MacLaine retained a unique position from which to evaluate Sinatra the actor. Writing in her Hollywood memoir titled *My Lucky Stars,* Shirley may have earned Sinatra's enmity for her candid observations about his concert tour behavior in 1992, but she did deliver a compelling critique of Frank's acting technique:

> His potential is fantastic. . . . The thing is, I wish he would work harder at what he's doing. He won't polish. He feels polishing might make him stagnant. He doesn't even like to rehearse. . . . If he shows anybody he's working hard and it doesn't come off, he's got no excuse. If he's not working hard . . . he can then say to himself at least, "Well, I wasn't working up to my peak." I do think he works at singing. But at acting, the way he goes, he always knows that people will say, "My goodness, think of what that man could do if he *really* worked. . . ."

The observation contains more than a kernel of truth—the insistence on no rehearsal and one take really did insulate him against criticism regarding lack of ability. It's a viewpoint shared by brilliant director/writer Billy Wilder, who bluntly stated,

> I think this: if, instead of involving himself in all those enterprises, nineteen television shows and records by the ton and four movies all at once and producing things and political things and all those broads— this talent on film would be stupendous. That would be the only word. Stupendous.

Indeed, such a comment makes one wonder all the more about what could have been if Wilder's approved casting of Sinatra, Tony Curtis, and Marilyn Monroe had actually occurred for *Some Like It Hot*. The macho Sinatra in drag would have been a very funny sight—as is the similar notion that in the late 1980s the seventy-plus Sinatra expressed interest in starring as a gay nightclub owner in an American remake of *La Cage aux Folles*. (The film was eventually made in 1996, directed by Mike Nichols with Robin Williams in the role Sinatra would have played.)

Sinatra liked the script for *Some Like It Hot*—who wouldn't?—but chose to make *A Hole in the Head* instead. It's a measure of Sinatra's stature as an actor that he was choosing between Wilder and Capra, two of the greatest directors in Hollywood history. As to Wilder's pointed comments about Frank the actor, they contain some truth, yet just as with MacLaine's book, give short shrift to the fact that he was an instinctive actor who really did usually perform at his best on a first take. As director George Sidney summed it up: "His first take is better than most people's tenth. He always went for the best and took risks."

Part of the reason for that one-take approach to acting may also have been the fact that Sinatra never did study acting; if he had for even one year, or pursued acting in school, he may have embraced the rehearsal process instead of developing what was at best a fitful willingness to rehearse on such first-rate films as *Anchors Aweigh, From Here to Eternity,* and *The Man with the Golden Arm.* What should be borne in mind, however, is that on all three of those films, Sinatra had something to prove and, with his will of iron, would go to any lengths to prove it: On *Anchors Aweigh,* he needed to serve notice as a film actor and prove himself a genuine musical star, one worthy of costarring with the great Gene Kelly. On *Eternity,* he wanted to establish his bona fides as a dramatic actor who could and would sustain an entire, and heavily dramatic, nonmusical performance. With *Golden Arm,* he was determined to prove that he was capable of carrying a serious film on his shoulders, that the supporting turn in *Eternity,* far from being a fluke, could be repeated and even improved upon. Sinatra proved his point with all three films, and once he had succeeded in doing so, he no longer needed to prove it with every single film. If the project excited Frank, as *The Manchurian Candidate* did, he went the distance. If not, his reasoning seemed to run, *What the hell do I have to prove to anyone?*

As for the idea of studying acting in school, it would have been a nonstarter at any point in Sinatra's life. He was a very intelligent man with street smarts, but one who had no patience with school. Coming of age in the midst of the Great Depression, the focus was on earning money, not on studying art, and if parents Dolly and Marty scoffed at the idea of their only child spending his life as a singer, one can only imagine the epithets Dolly would have unleashed upon hearing that her teenage son had decided to become an actor.

With the choice to film Capra's *A Hole in the Head* instead of *Some Like It Hot,* Sinatra lost one of a few chances at starring in a film with his friend Marilyn Monroe. The onscreen pairing of the two legends certainly would have guaranteed audience interest, and several of the proposed films were actually solid ideas, the most notable being musical remakes of *Born Yesterday* and *A Tree Grows in Brooklyn.* As it was, the closest the two ever came to actually starring together was in *Pink Tights,* a remake of the Betty Grable film *Coney Island.* When a disgruntled and troubled Monroe did not show up for the start of filming in December 1953, the film was abandoned and the best chance for a Sinatra/Monroe film disappeared.

As for Frank himself, the ring-a-ding-dings interpolated into *Can-Can* served one function—they paved the way for Sinatra's first—and best—feature film venture into Rat Pack territory, the iconic original version of *Ocean's Eleven.* Audiences around the world had been reading about Sinatra and his Clan kicking up their heels in Vegas, a living, breathing case of arrested development centered around booze, women, and gambling—every adolescent's fantasy life. For the middle-class American public fascinated by those larger-than-life exertions, there would now be two ways to fully share in the fun: in person at the Sands Hotel, or onscreen in *Ocean's Eleven*. JFK was running for president, the "Greatest Generation" was now in charge, and the older generation (exemplified by President Eisenhower) was ceding its place center stage. It was time for the Frank Sinatra show.

In his dual roles as movie star and singer, Sinatra came to represent the epicenter of American culture, because in 1960, a cultural consensus still proved possible. The concurrent belief in unfettered growth and a happy lifestyle in the suburbs all centered around a national confidence that, as an American, one was living in the greatest country in the world. As Sinatra commentator Charles Granata has pointed out, Frank Sinatra's style—on- and offstage— spoke to the emerging and powerful post–World War II middle class. It's as if Sinatra, like the United States itself, could be overbearing yet maintain an unwavering belief in the strength of that vision as the world's "good guy"— flawed but essentially decent. It took Sinatra growing old, and a United States battered by Vietnam and Watergate for erosion in those beliefs to occur. In 1960, however, life was ring-a-ding-ding 24-7. Everyone wanted in on the act, and in those last years before the deluge of the late 1960s social upheavals, Frank Sinatra succeeded in nothing less than altering the American consciousness, in effect asserting his will on the entire damn country. Not to mention having one helluva good time in the process. Now, that's life.

The Rat Pack

"Style," sung by Frank Sinatra,
Dean Martin, and Bing Crosby in *Robin and the 7 Hoods*

The Rat Pack depended for its vitality on what Gore Vidal has called the "great national nap" of the 1950s—at times Frank and "the Clan" seemed the only people awake after 10 P.M." —T. H. ADAMOWSKI

If I had to choose between making records and making pictures I make pictures too, you know— at my age you gotta diversify, have more than one string to your bow . . . I just changed my mind—I'm not gonna choose between records and pictures.
—FRANK SINATRA ON *A MAN AND HIS MUSIC*, NOVEMBER 1965

IN THE SINATRA FILM OEUVRE, *Ocean's Eleven* occupies a top-tier position—not because of quality, which it possesses in fits and starts, but because of how it changed, indeed solidified, the public's perception of him as an all-encompassing package of entertainer, swinger, political power player, and movie star. *Ocean's Eleven* presents the Frank of Rat Pack legend—on top of his game and on top of the world in Vegas, the city that was really his "kind of town" much more than Chicago ever could be. (Sinatra referred to his coterie of friends as The Summit, but the term that resonated with the public was Rat Pack, Lauren Bacall's choice description of husband Humphrey Bogart's circle of friends and fellow partiers, which had included Sinatra.) There's just one hitch with *Ocean's Eleven*—the mythology of the Rat Pack has obscured the true nature of the film; it's the Sinatra film everyone thinks they know, but that very few do.

The confluence of mobsters, politics, Hollywood, and Vegas—it all fit the tenor of the times, so it made a perfect kind of sense that *Ocean's Eleven* began life through the efforts of Peter Lawford. Having heard the concept of a group of ex-servicemen simultaneously robbing five Vegas casinos from aspiring director Gilbert Kay, Lawford bought the rights to the idea for ten thousand dollars. (In all-too-typical Hollywood fashion, the film grants Kay absolutely no credit.) Lawford, who had recently been granted a decent-size role in *Never So Few,* was now back in Sinatra's favor, evidently due in no small part to Sinatra's awareness that Lawford's brother-in-law might just prove to be the next President of the United States.

Indeed, at a time when celebrity involvement in politics was rare, volumes of press coverage ensued when then-presidential-candidate Kennedy turned up in Vegas on February 7, 1960, in order to see the nightly Summit onstage at the Sands. It's not just that Kennedy was enamored of the larger-than-life Hollywood glamour Sinatra personified: Kennedy was determined to use the Hollywood connection in order to help his campaign. New times called for new techniques, and just as FDR utilized the radio for his fireside chats, JFK would employ television and the celebrity age to serve his purposes.

Since it was Lawford who brought the original idea for *Ocean's Eleven* to Frank's attention, producer Sinatra approved a fifty-thousand-dollar salary for Lawford's acting in the film, and also granted him a profit-share amounting to one-sixth of the profits. It all made for a nice payday, although substantially smaller than the one-third profit Lawford had originally requested. Regardless of the percentage, it was a bonanza for Lawford, his original ten-thousand-dollar investment eventually turning into $500,000.

After Lawford presented the idea for the film to Frank, Sinatra brought the property to Warner Bros., to whom he owed another film (because of Natalie Wood's participation in *Kings Go Forth*). Jack Warner bought the script, granted Sinatra control over the casting, and together with Frank settled on Lewis Milestone (most famous for *All Quiet on the Western Front*) as director. This was one production that found Sinatra happy throughout filming, beginning with the fact that director Milestone, like Sinatra, preferred a noon-until-seven shooting day. Milestone, a solid director of staunch liberal sensibility who had rather famously run afoul of the House Un-American Activities Committee, certainly knew exactly who held the power on the set. It was star and producer Sinatra who stood right next to him behind the camera whenever his presence was not required for the scene being shot. Happy for the work he may have been, but Milestone didn't appreciate Sinatra's all-encompassing power upsetting the director's autonomy, later bluntly characterizing the filming in the following fashion: "When Frank wasn't actually acting himself, he would say 'Get him to do this' or 'make sure he does that.' Ask me which was my least favorite film that I ever made and it has to be *Ocean's Eleven.*"

Milestone may have felt frustrated, but Frank himself was having—well— a ring-a-ding-ding time. At ease in Vegas, loving the nightly shenanigans onstage with his costars, Frank Sinatra was, atypically, a happy actor throughout production. Frank looked upon the film, in essence, as a very well-paid vacation. He did not invest any of his artistry or passion in it, but rather viewed it as a means to make money and have fun with his friends. As he said two years after the film's release, "Of course they're not great movies, no one could claim that . . . but every movie I've made through my own company has made money." Point taken—after all, Frank himself was acutely aware of the bottom-line nature of the film business from his years under contract with RKO and MGM. If anyone understood why it's called show business, not show art, it was Frank Sinatra. He wanted to continue making movies, and box office success ensured his continued viability. (Even with his own record company, Sinatra was keenly aware of sales figures, to the point of chasing after the young record-buying audience with ill-advised mid- and late-1960s attempts to record contemporary material.)

With *Ocean's Eleven,* Frank and Company ushered in a new era of screen cool. Cool dictated that you didn't get mad, you got even, which is exactly what Danny Ocean and his pals proposed to do. They were determined to get even with the casinos and inject some sorely needed excitement into their postwar lives, which had been disappointing in their blandness and rigidity. In effect, the American dream had proved to be hollow, so the boys would invent their own American dream. No wonder the film resonated with audiences and continues to do so decades later. Onstage and onscreen, Frank Sinatra and friends were living out the fantasies of all middle-aged men who felt trapped in marriage, suburbia, and playing by the rules. They were men who wanted their freedom back. News reports of the Vegas fun Frank and the Rat Pack were

The Rat Pack at its height: Frank, Dean Martin, and Peter Lawford strolling in Vegas during the filming of Ocean's Eleven *(1960).*

having in January and February of 1960 succeeded both in heightening nationwide awareness of the film and in making Vegas the destination for early-1960s Americans seeking a little—or a lot of—fun away from their ofttimes stultifying hometowns. Frank was doing it his way, and many Americans wanted to follow his lead. It's a state of mind borne out by Frank Sinatra Jr.'s observation that the Sands turned down eighteen thousand requests for seats in the eight-hundred-seat Copa Room. Everyone wanted in because in the nicely turned phrase of James Wolcott, "The Rat Pack is the Mount Rushmore of men having fun."

The Mount Rushmore of fun it was, but it also stands as the Mount Rushmore of grown men who continued to act like adolescents—Peter Pan role models for the mid-twentieth-century American male. Or, as Nancy Sinatra Jr. said from the perspective of 1965: "When you have a Daddy you kind of want him to be a Daddy all the time. And sometimes when he's with his friends, they carry on like a bunch of kids." Just take a look at footage of Frank, Dean, and Sammy cutting up onstage in Vegas during the filming of

Ocean's Eleven: pratfalls, drinking, endless ribbing of each other—standard behavior . . . for fifteen-year-old boys. The biggest stars in the world were indulging in any and every possible behavior in order to avoid the worst of all possible insults in the world of an adolescent male: "This is boring." Indeed, when those very words were uttered by forty-eight-year-old Frank Sinatra on the helicopter flight from Vegas to location shooting of *Sergeants 3*, Dean Martin's solution was to buy two .22-caliber rifles, the better for the boys to shoot out of the helicopter the next day while flying over the desert. Oh . . .

It's all a style of prolonged adolescence that caused legendary singer Rosemary Clooney to remark that when she observed movie star nephew George and his pals playing basketball and "hanging out" together, it reminded her of nothing so much as Sinatra and his cronies, the two Rat Packs separated by forty years but joined in a mutual refusal to grow up.

For all his adolescent carrying on, however, Sinatra was a devoted, if largely absent, father, one adored by his children, particularly his two daughters. When Tina Sinatra was undergoing a period of adolescent rebellion, chafing at what she considered her mother's overly restrictive rules, and angry at her father's continued absence from her life, she began analysis. Sinatra actually attended several of the therapy sessions himself, an undertaking daunting even to a full-time hands-on parent. Knowing he would be in line for severe criticism, Frank still "gave himself fully to our discussions and readily accepted a parent's responsibility for whatever our relationship lacked—for all the times I needed him and he was not there. His sorrow was deep and genuine, and freely expressed," said Tina. Out of the difficult sessions came a renewed bond between father and daughter, and a bit of classic parental advice, couched in vintage Sinatra speak: "Don't be a pain in the ass to your mother."

Tina herself and sister Nancy may not have been much in evidence during the filming of *Ocean's Eleven*, but Frank Jr. was present during the location shoot, and he was therefore a firsthand witness to the endless shenanigans, typified by his forty-five-year-old father happily surviving on three to four hours of sleep per night.

The lack of sleep is actually revealing of Sinatra the man for reasons that range far beyond his insomnia. It was as if with all the friends, the partying, and the constant work, Frank continued a desperate race to outrun a loneliness that never fully left him. Frank himself stated: "I'm for anything that gets you

through the night, be it prayer, tranquilizers, or a bottle of Jack Daniel's."
Sinatra was not, contrary to popular belief, in psychic pain much of the
time—this really was a man who enjoyed his life. But he was a man who possessed fear—not fear of others, but fear of loneliness and disillusionment. It
seemed to be fear of being alone with his own thoughts that drove Sinatra
ever onward at a relentless, nearly reckless pace. It's not surprising that Sinatra was nearly alone amongst golden age Hollywood stars in his refusal to
write an autobiography or cooperate with an outside biographer. Reveal his
most private thoughts? Face them by himself? No way. The idea of an autobiography written with the help of Pete Hamill never went past the discussion
stage, nor did the talk of a biography written, with Sinatra's cooperation, by
veteran New York City journalist Sid Zion. Express himself in his art, both on
disc and onscreen? Sure. On the written page? Never could happen.

So the frantic pace continued. The nightly high jinks onstage at the Sands
Hotel may have appeared to be spontaneous and entirely ad-libbed, but in
point of fact, Joey Bishop actually wrote most of the "ad-libbed" jokes ahead
of time. What's most arresting about footage from those shows is the revelation that Sinatra wasn't quite so good as Dean when it came to the "improvisation." With his immaculate throwaway delivery. Dean made it all look
effortless. For Sinatra, one can see more effort involved, just as one senses
Sammy Davis Jr.'s near desperation to please. Dean was the master of such
entertainment because he just didn't care, but there was no mistaking the fact
that it was still Sinatra who ran the show.

And it was some crazy show that Frank ran. Consider Daniel O'Brien's detailed chronology:

> The Summit members often did two shows a night, their 5 A.M. finish
> leaving them precious little time for sleep before getting back to work
> on the film the next day . . . it appeared to suit Sinatra perfectly well.
> Awaking mid-morning, the star took care of his various business inter-
> ests while relaxing in the Sands' steam room, filming not beginning un-
> til noon. After the day's shoot, he returned to the steam room around
> 7 P.M. grabbing a bite to eat before the first show.

Fun it may have been, but there was also the sense of a command performance to all the late-night carousing. Only Joey Bishop seemed to escape the

endless partying—presumably because he had "ad-libs" to write. In the epic run of nonstop work, Sinatra appeared to have finally found the perfect combination of filming and singing to fit his endless nervous energy. Staying up all night further appealed because such behavior broke the rules, and represented the exact opposite of the stereotypical nine-to-five suburban existence he could not even understand, much less live. It therefore makes a curious kind of sense that Sinatra played a suburban father only once on film, in the execrable *Marriage on the Rocks*: that role didn't fit him in life or onscreen.

It wasn't just Frank who ran at a frantic pace. For all his contemporaries, there was a decided sense that after surviving a global near-apocalypse, they were anxious to make up for lost time, plunging themselves headlong into a return to school, jobs, and family life. Underlying the hectic pace was a sense that key years had been irretrievably lost, that life could end in a moment and better be grabbed hold of instantaneously. As a result, part of that anxious behavior manifested itself in the heavy drinking and smoking that ran rampant at the time. Why not have fun, they seemed to ask, when we could all die tomorrow? Unlike those men, however, for Sinatra the carousing never really stopped, and when he died at age eighty-two, it seemed miraculous that his body had withstood as much punishment from drink and late nights as it had.

Because of the mythology of the offscreen behavior, audiences, in the parlance of 1960, remember the film as a "gasser." In the collective memory, *Ocean's Eleven* lives on as a fun-filled caper featuring Frank and the boys cutting up, having a great time, and robbing casinos in the process. In reality, the only accurate part of that memory is the fact that Danny Ocean and his friends rob casinos. So strong is the aura the film has acquired over the years that no one really remembers the truth: *Ocean's Eleven* is a surprisingly sober film. Top-billed Sinatra does not smile once during the entire two-plus hours. It is a businesslike caper, not a free-wheeling boys night out, and for all intents and purposes, only Sammy Davis Jr. smiles or appears to be having fun during the movie.

Shooting out of the gate with vibrant Saul Bass titles that spell out the credits in Vegas-inspired lightbulbs, the film underscores each star's name with a different arrangement of the Cahn/Van Heusen song "Eee-O-Eleven." (Similarly, during the actual casino heist, Riddle's score plays "Auld Lang Syne" in a different key for each of the five casinos being robbed on New

Year's Eve.) The plot is set in motion when Beverly Hills–based Danny Ocean (Sinatra) recruits ten of his old army pals to simultaneously rob five Vegas casinos on New Year's Eve. Yes, the heist is about money, but the reason underlying the caper seems to be an attempt to recapture the excitement of wartime, or as Danny says, "Why waste all those cute little tricks that the army taught us, just because it's sorta peaceful now?" It's unfortunate that the idea of postwar letdown experienced by many veterans was not explored in more detail, as it certainly would have granted extra texture to the characterizations and a greater sense of urgency to the plotting.

Instead, the first full hour of the film lays out the recruitment of the men for the job while sketching in their varied talents and backgrounds: Peter Lawford plays spoiled rich mama's boy Jimmy Foster, a man desperate to prove himself. Sammy Davis Jr.'s Josh Howard is a strange amalgamation of wartime medal winner, garbage truck driver, and unsuccessful professional baseball player. Joey Bishop is on hand as ex-boxer Mushy O'Connor, a profession that appears far-fetched in the extreme, given Bishop's milquetoast demeanor and gait. There is even comic relief provided by the fractured English of "idea man" Spyros Acebos, played by Akim Tamiroff. Tamiroff certainly appears to be funny, but listening to his line readings is akin to attending a session of the United Nations General Assembly without benefit of a translator. For all the casual viewer can actually comprehend of his speech, he might be explaining Einstein's theory of relativity, but Einstein's theory is more easily digested than Tamiroff's accent.

As the momentum gathers in this first hour of the film, the most startling aspect for today's viewer is the fact that the film functions as a near-perfect time capsule of the early 1960s. It's not just a case of eyeballing the glitzy Vegas surroundings at the height of the Rat Pack era. It's watching Danny, clad in a trademark Sinatra orange sweater, come into the room where Foster is receiving a massage and casually tell the two women present, "Okay, girls— time for your nap—beat it." A statement like that would simply be hooted off the screen today. Even more striking: all the characters drink and smoke nonstop throughout the film. It's almost a template: enter a room, walk over to the bar, mix a drink, and light a cigarette. Result? Instant sophistication.

Another surprise lies in the fact that it is only when Dean Martin enters the scene (as Sam Harmon) that a musical element is introduced. Singing the Cahn/Van Heusen "Ain't That a Kick in the Head" while exuding effortless authority, Dino induces one overwhelming reaction in the audience: How could a guy this cool, so good-looking, and possessed of such a great voice ever be stuck in a lounge? He would be in the main showroom—pronto.

Sammy Davis Jr. provides additional musical texture, singing another top-notch Cahn/Van Heusen song, "Eee-O-Eleven," a bluesy lament first heard in the rather unusual musical setting of a garage filled with garbage trucks! Like Dino, Sammy sounds great, but listening to both men sing leads one to wonder, When's Frank going to sing? The surprising answer: never.

Audiences think they remember the Frank of *Ocean's Eleven* singing in Vegas casinos, but in fact, the closest to a Sinatra vocal occurs when Nelson Riddle's score accentuates a discreet scene of a stripper with a horns-wailing version of "The Tender Trap." There's also some brief background music for the Vegas scenes featuring an instrumental version of the Sinatra standard "Learnin' the Blues," but that's it. It all registers as a lost opportunity because Frank was here at the height of his vocal powers. Okay, maybe Danny Ocean wasn't a singing kind of guy, but Sammy sings, and it's not like there are a lot of singing garbagemen running around Vegas.

Rather than sing, Danny hatches the plan for the heist. True to the ensemble nature of the piece, Sinatra doesn't garner any more screen time than any of the other actors. Female presence in the film is nearly nonexistent, except for Angie Dickinson as Ocean's estranged wife, Beatrice. Fed up with a married life that centers around gambling, Beatrice wryly tells her erstwhile mate, "Danny, you're the only husband in the world who would proposition his own wife . . . the only thing you love, Danny, is danger." Problem is, after that interesting confrontation, Angie basically disappears from the film, taking her intriguing and unexplained backstory with her. She exudes cool authority and actually would have made great sense as a part of the heist—the movie suffers from her absence. Dickinson seems utterly comfortable with Sinatra—perhaps the result of her ongoing ten-year casual yet loving affair with him. She holds her own with Frank—no easy task—and exudes her own brand of star power. (In Sinatra's witty tribute to Dickinson, who refused to tell tales out of school regarding her relationship with President Kennedy: "How wonderful it is to meet a lady who's a gentleman.") Angie or not, no woman would have been given much to do, because anyone wanting to know exactly what the sexual attitudes of 1960 America and the Rat Pack were need look no further than this screenplay. Dean Martin's Sam Harmon casually states that he'd like to repeal the Fourteenth and Twentieth Amendments and "turn women into slaves." In other words, it's the men—and only the men—who should have the power that flows from money.

The Hollywood/Vegas/Washington D.C. synergy so symbolic of the times even made its way from offscreen to on, with Peter Lawford's character of Jimmy Foster claiming, "I think I'll buy me some votes and go into politics." It's a rather startling line, given the Kennedy money that helped ensure voter turnout for JFK in the West Virgina primary. In the politically oriented section of the film, Sam calls Jimmy "our latest senator" and Ocean himself offers the idea that he work as an ambassador. In one fell swoop, this inside humor has referenced Sinatra, Sam Giancana, Senator and soon-to-be President Kennedy, and his father, Joseph P. Kennedy (the former and controversial ambassador to England). It doesn't get more "insider" than that.

Whatever the real-life parallels, up to that point, the film has rather methodically sketched in each of the characters but exuded little sense of danger. Because five casinos are being robbed, the film actually suffers from the repetition of laying out the same preparations for the heist five times in a row. Milestone makes little use of the wide screen, the sense of danger and excitement in Vegas reduced to repeated shots of the hotel marquees. With constant crosscutting among the eleven men, and the lack of any clearly delineated dialogue telling us who and what these characters are, the film leaves the viewer somewhat confused. Until all of the men are gathered together (which occurs twice in the entire film), it's anybody's guess exactly who they are or what the hell they are up to.

However, when the eleven men do meet to plan the robbery, the pace instantly accelerates. Gathering around a pool table, all objections pushed aside, they set hands one on top of another to express solidarity in their plan to "liberate" millions of dollars from five casinos. The Riddle score picks up tempo, and with an immediate jump cut to the neon-lit Vegas skyline, the brass-heavy score tells the viewer, "Now the action starts." Which it does.

As the men go to work learning the layouts of the five casinos they plan to rob, the American audience of 1960, not yet fully familiar with Vegas, is treated to an entertaining travelogue of sorts: glittering marquees for the casinos are featured (particularly that of the Sinatra hangout, the Sands), slot machines jingle merrily in the background, and each hotel features a chorus line of scantily clad women strongly reminiscent of the Hot Box Girls in *Guys and*

Planning the casino heists in Ocean's Eleven. *One of only two scenes in the entire film when the whole gang is together.*

Dolls. There's a sense of lightness to the film now, thanks to both the caper and Vegas itself. In those far-off days, the charm of Vegas lay in the newness of the adult playground, the still-prevalent small-town feel so unlike the forced gaiety of big-city Vegas today.

Blowing the electrical towers outside of town enables the boys to enter into the vaults, steal the money, and walk away undiscovered in the ensuing blackout. Finally, the audience develops a rooting interest in the gang. With their constant repartee and the fun gimmick of glow-in-the-dark footprints that point the way through the blackout to the vault, Danny Ocean's gang represents wish fulfillment of the highest order for every would-be (or never-was) hipster. It's a kick to watch the boys, especially when they toss the bags of stolen money into a garbage truck (driven by Sammy Davis Jr.) that is then unloaded at the landfill outside of town. In the midst of garbage and filth, the gang finds themselves instant millionaires.

When Jimmy's soon-to-be stepfather Duke Santos (Cesar Romero) figures out who pulled the heist, he wants 50 percent of the take as payment for not spilling the beans. The boys try to outsmart him by hiding the money in Anthony Bergdorf's (Richard Conte) casket. In a terrific final plot twist,

Bergdorf is cremated and the entire take literally goes up in smoke. While the original ending of the film found all eleven men dying when their plane crashed—after all, in those far-off Production Code days, the boys would not be allowed to successfully steal $5 million—it was director Milestone who came up with the crematorium twist. As Sinatra recounted the story during a years-later appearance on Johnny Carson's *Tonight Show,* "Milestone said, 'I saw that happen once' . . . because while the rabbi was doing all the prayers, they could hear this noise—the crematorium."

The movie ends with the entire gang walking up a rather drab sidewalk away from the strip—in a self-referential nod, they walk right past the marquee of the Sands Hotel, which features the names of Sinatra, Martin, Davis, Lawford, and Bishop—as Sammy reprises "Eee-O-Eleven" in voiceover (a scene to which Quentin Tarantino pays homage in *Reservoir Dogs*). Interestingly, it is Davis who receives the lion's share of camera time in the closing sequence, but he, like all the gang, heads glumly into an uncertain future. Fade-out on a downbeat note so unlike the boozy camaraderie that audiences think they remember.

It's the mythology of the Rat Pack to which audiences in the new millennium most relate, but at the time of the film's original August 1960 release, the mixed critical response seemed to focus most heavily on the fact that Ocean's gang, the film's "heroes," were, in fact, common criminals. In a sign of how greatly the Hollywood landscape has changed in the ensuing forty-eight years, this film without either sex or violence still earned an admonition from the *Los Angeles Herald Examiner* that it was "something you should keep your children away from."

Sinatra, dismissive of the critics' censorious tone, took a rather pragmatic ring-a-ding-ding approach to the entire enterprise: "We're not setting out to make *Hamlet.* The idea is to hang out together, find fun with the broads and have a great time. We gotta make pictures that people enjoy seeing." The best characterization of the movie was to be found in the *Variety* review by Tube, who wrote, "Laboring under the handicaps of a contrived script, an uncertain approach and personalities in essence playing themselves, the Lewis Milestone production never quite makes its point, but romps along merrily unconcerned that it doesn't. . . . *Ocean's Eleven* figures to be a money maker despite itself." *Variety* was right on the money; Sinatra may have waltzed through the film playing a version of himself, but audiences lapped it up, a fact that helped Sinatra land the number-six spot on the annual list of top-ten box office attractions.

The highly popular George Clooney–led 2001 remake of *Ocean's Eleven* retains the original's aversion to hard-core violence and sex, but actually lands as a crisper, wittier, and more exciting version of the story than the original. The less said about Clooney's and director Steven Soderbergh's self-congratulatory 2005 sequel, *Ocean's Twelve,* the better, although the Clooney team regained much of its capital with the second sequel, 2007's *Ocean's Thirteen*. It was the last installment of the franchise that featured the most direct homage to Sinatra, the background score utilizing first "Strangers in the Night" and then at film's climax, Frank's own recording of "This Town." Just how strongly did Frank's ultracool demeanor continue to resonate nearly one half century after the original film? Consider the fact that in *Ocean's Thirteen,* the act of having shaken Sinatra's hand is utilized as proof of character.

Clooney and his pack—and make no mistake, Clooney held the center of his clan, just as did Sinatra—still carried a bit of post-modern self-reflexive irony with them, but beyond that, all of the neo-swingers responded to Sinatra because they knew the real deal when they saw it: a superb musician and actor who lived his life with an unself-conscious sense of style to which they aspired. (Never mind the various *Ocean's Eleven* remakes. What, one wonders, would Frank have thought of a film like 1996's hipster homage *Swingers?*) The more complicated the territory between men and women grew, the more Frank's un-fettered and self-confident approach appealed, chauvinism be damned.

The personal contract with Frank that qualified as proof of character in *Ocean's Thirteen* certainly must have sufficed back in 1960 as well, because it was Frank's word that made possible an arm's-length transaction between Joseph P. Kennedy, on behalf of his son, the presidential candidate John F. Kennedy, and Chicago mob boss Sam Giancana. It's not just that Sinatra exercised a power previously unknown in the entertainment world, one that allowed him virtually unlimited access to the most powerful politicos in the nation. It's that the 1960 presidential primaries represented the most note-worthy and fully substantiated of all the stories regarding Sinatra and organized crime. It's an American morality tale complete unto itself—fascinating, disturbing, and even frightening in equal measure. What made the Sinatra–Giancana–Kennedy entanglement resonate all the more was the fact that it was in early 1960, after Kennedy had begun his run for the presidency, that

Sinatra introduced Giancana to Judith Campbell, who was already Kennedy's paramour. Just like that, the soon-to-be President of the United States and the head of the Chicago crime syndicate were sleeping with the same woman. It all represented a confluence of money, bad judgment, and most of all, power, and only served to heighten Giancana's wrath about Bobby Kennedy's fight against organized crime.

The Sinatra-assisted Kennedy–Giancana political liaison occurred when the ever-pragmatic and ruthless Joseph Kennedy Sr. asked for Sinatra's help in securing votes for JFK in the West Virginia primary. At the request of Joe Sr., Sinatra asked Chicago mob boss Giancana for help in delivering 120,000 West Virginia primary votes to Kennedy. The votes were, in fact, delivered after Frank told Giancana that the favor—"muscling support in an anti-Catholic, union organized region"—was a "personal" one, and not to expect repayment from the Kennedys. The votes were secured, and in quick succession, Kennedy won the West Virginia primary, the Democratic nomination, and the extremely close November election against Richard Nixon. It all represents an extraordinary convergence of political power, entertainment heavyweights, and organized crime that came to light and raised eyebrows and concerns only years after the fact, so different was the role of the press in 1960. If Barbra Streisand represents Sinatra's only rival in Hollywood history for the blending of political power with heft on both film sets and in recording studios, it is, to say the least, nigh onto impossible in the new millennium, for both personal and press reasons, to imagine Streisand introducing her close political friends Bill and Hillary Clinton to the Russian mob bosses now ensconced in her native Brooklyn.

Back in 1961, however, what Giancana and Sinatra did not anticipate was that Attorney General Bobby Kennedy would begin a systematic war against organized crime. Giancana may not have expected any repayment for the favor he granted, but crime boss or not, he did not expect to be attacked. The furious Giancana wanted revenge. Relating the incident decades later, Tina Sinatra records that a shaken Frank asked himself, " 'What have I done?' . . . He'd gone to Giancana out of friendship for Jack Kennedy and expected nothing back. What he did not expect was to be set up like a blindsided innocent, like a fool to take the fall." Contrary to what popular imagination would hold, Giancana, although furious with Sinatra and the Kennedys, did not attempt to kill anyone involved. As a rather startling sidelight, however,

July 10, 1960 Democratic National Convention in Los Angeles. Frank and friend, soon-to-be President John F. Kennedy.

an FBI wiretap detailed a mobster associate of Giancana's floating the idea of killing Sinatra as revenge for Bobby Kennedy's actions, only to have the idea dismissed by Giancana. Instead, what Giancana did extract from Sinatra—and pals Dean Martin and Sammy Davis Jr.—was a "settling of the debt" by having the trio perform for free in November 1962 at the organized crime–owned Villa Venice nightclub in Illinois.

Mobsters, presidential politics and mistresses, recordings, the filming of *Ocean's Eleven*—the 24-7 level of activity still wasn't enough for Frank, who, along with Dino, Sammy, Peter Lawford, and Joey Bishop, squeezed in a cameo role in George Sidney's *Pepe* while still filming *Ocean's Eleven*. Released in December 1960, a scant four months after *Ocean's Eleven, Pepe* is a labored, ofttimes strenuously unfunny, attempt to capitalize on the popularity of Mexican comedian Cantinflas after his star turn in *Around the World in Eighty Days*. The effort isn't much good, and it arrived four years too late to benefit from *Around the World in Eighty Days,* but it's not completely lacking in interest in terms of the Sinatra filmography.

With a three-plus-hour running time, which feels more like three weeks, it's another of those "let's put every Hollywood star we can find into the movie" epics so popular at the time. Such a more-is-more philosophy usually ensues when the film at hand is a weakly scripted affair, and *Pepe* is the proof of the pudding: three hours and two dozen star cameos later, the film remains what it was at the start: a condescending "comedy" about the love affair between an "ethnic" male and his horse. That's right—Pepe spends the entire film trying to be reunited with the horse (Don Juan) he very strangely refers to as his son. Truth to tell, the horse acts with more conviction than most of the stars involved.

The plot finds peasant horse wrangler Pepe (Cantinflas) trotting off to Hollywood in search of his horse, all the while charming dozens of stars playing themselves—Zsa Zsa Gabor, Janet Leigh, Tony Curtis, Bing Crosby, and even Jack Lemmon in his *Some Like It Hot* drag. Along the way, he falls in love with Suzie Murphy (an unconvincing Shirley Jones playing a tough girl with a heart of gold), wins $250,000 to help her producer fiancé Ted Holt (Dan Dailey) film his comeback movie, and is dumped by Suzie. At the fade-out, Pepe merrily accepts the loss of his love (not to mention the diamond ring he gave her) to Holt, and dances off into the sunset with his horse.

After watching the limp proceedings, one is struck by how emblematic *Pepe* is of 1960 Hollywood's attitude toward Hispanics. When, at film's end, Suzie chooses a life with Holt, the all but explicitly stated assumption is, "Of course she'll go off with Holt. He's white, not a simple Mexican." Pepe is presented as an endearing simpleton who is downright hilarious because of his garbled English. When Greer Garson admonishes Pepe at the beginning of the film because he has deceived her, she speaks to him as if to a nursery school student. Never mind that he is a grown man, albeit one who appears to be in love with a horse. It all, most uncomfortably, smacks of white man's burden. Interestingly, Kim Novak's cameo as herself near the film's end is the one exception. Helping Pepe pick out an engagement ring for Suzie, Novak is not only beautiful, but vulnerable, warm, and instantly appealing to boot. Playing herself, she is the nicest person in the film, treating Pepe as a fellow human being and not an object of comedy. With a surprisingly relaxed and welcome screen presence, she is light-years away from the tentative performance she offered when previously directed by George Sidney in *Pal Joey*.

As for Sinatra's participation, he pops up, naturally enough, in Vegas. Presented as one of the owners of the Sands, he first appears onscreen giving gambling money to women, the action staged in front of a prominent photo of himself hung on the wall. After speaking briefly with Pepe, he returns only after Pepe's winnings top out at $250,006, which happens to be just enough to finance Holt's $250,000 film and give casino owner Sinatra a six-dollar tip.

What's interesting about that appearance is that it is the one feature film appearance where Sinatra plays himself at the height of his career. In this three-minute cameo, he is appealing, looking fit and handsome in his offbeat manner—somehow even Pepe seems mesmerized by the blue eyes. Watching the brief appearance is the best example extant of the "reel" Frank Sinatra playing the "real" Frank Sinatra, both merging into the one Frank Sinatra who owned the world while everyone else just lived in it.

Sinatra may have been at his peak, but neither he nor the dozens of other stars recruited for *Pepe* could prevent the film's flop at the box office. The fact that Sinatra was selected by the Film Exhibitors of America as the year's number-six-rated box office attraction had everything to do with *Ocean's Eleven* and nothing at all to do with the lumbering *Pepe*. Audiences in 1960 America were now too sophisticated to accept the spectacle of dozens of stars playing themselves as reason enough to go to the movies, especially when the film in question was as leaden as this beached whale. Television poured hours of daily entertainment directly into the living rooms of homes across America free of charge, and with the face of entertainment changing drastically as a result of that revolution, Hollywood needed to come up with something better than this dopey mess to tempt viewers out of their homes.

After the message-free *Ocean's Eleven*, Sinatra was eager to tackle a serious film and make his directorial debut as well. The film in question, also to be produced by Frank, was to star Steve McQueen in the title role of *Private Slovik*, a World War II GI who became the only U.S. soldier since the Civil War executed for desertion. Gearing up for the first stages of production, Sinatra confidently hired the formerly blacklisted writer Albert Maltz (screenwriter for *The House I Live In*) to adapt the underlying source novel by William Bradford Huie. At that point, however, the entire project unraveled with ever-increasing speed, not because of star or writer demands, but because of the political climate of the time.

The blacklist may have been over, but the announcement that Sinatra was going to hire Maltz brought a firestorm of criticism down on Frank's head. Sinatra was hiring a man who had refused to cooperate with the House Un-American Activities Committee in 1947, one who subsequently served one year in jail for contempt of Congress before moving to Mexico (where he churned out screenplays under pseudonyms). Senator Joseph McCarthy may no longer have held office, but the cold war was still in full swing, and with the Communistic Soviet Union perceived as the number-one threat to United States security, conservative elements in the country rose up in protest against Sinatra. Adding another level of scrutiny to the mix, Sinatra pal John F. Kennedy was running for president at the time the film was announced: by now Sinatra was so firmly entwined with Kennedy in the public's mind that Cardinal Spellman of New York went so far as to tell Joseph Kennedy Sr. that having the controversial Maltz writing about such a politically sensitive topic could cost JFK the election. In other words, by hiring one screenwriter, Sinatra was now confronting the Catholic Church, the Kennedy family, the blacklist, and presidential politics. All that was missing was the mob—a shortcoming soon rectified by the West Virginia primaries.

Smelling fresh blood in their ongoing battle with the then-still-liberal Sinatra, the conservative Hearst-led press went to work. There were insinuations that because back when he was a war general, President Eisenhower had ordered Slovik's execution, Sinatra was bashing Eisenhower and his vice-president, the soon-to-be Kennedy opponent Richard Nixon. As the press scrutiny continued, producer/director Sinatra took the unusual step of placing ads in *Daily Variety* and *The Hollywood Reporter* on March 28, 1960, nearly one year before the planned start of shooting.

> Since I will produce and direct the picture I am concerned that the screenplay reflects the true pro-American values of the story. . . . Under our Bill of Rights I was taught that no one may prescribe what shall be orthodox in politics, religion or other matters of opinion. . . . As the producer of the film I and I alone will be responsible for it. I accept that responsibility. I ask only that judgment be deferred until the picture is seen.

Going on to specifically address his ties to JFK, Sinatra bluntly stated, "I do not ask the advice of Senator Kennedy on whom I should hire. Senator Kennedy does not ask me how he should vote in the Senate. . . . I repeat: In my role as a picture maker, I have—in my opinion—hired the best man to do the job." Far from quelling the storm, the ads only increased pressure in the press: so raw was the fear of Communism that the *New York Mirror* termed Maltz "an unrepentant enemy of the country" and the *Los Angeles Examiner* dubbed the film a vehicle for Communist propaganda.

According to daughter Tina's autobiography, Sinatra had withstood the pressure up to that time, telling both Bobby Kennedy and Joseph Kennedy Sr. that contrary to their demand, he would not fire Maltz, regardless of how it would affect his place in the presidential campaign. With his unrivaled sense of power, entitlement, and stubbornness, Sinatra thought he could ride out the storm, but the combination of the Kennedys and the right-wing press did him in. In daughter Tina's telling of the story, the tipping point came when a grade school classmate asked her if she were a Communist like her father. Sinatra folded his tent in April of 1960, announcing,

> In view of the reaction of my family, my friends and the American public, I have instructed my attorneys to make a settlement with Mr. Maltz. I had thought that the major consideration was whether or not the resulting script would be in the best interests of the United States. . . . But the American public has indicated it feels the morality of hiring Albert Maltz is the more crucial matter and I will accept this majority opinion.

Frank canceled the film but paid Maltz his full fee of seventy-five thousand dollars. Sinatra may have been the most powerful man in Hollywood between his acting and recording careers, but when politics entered the scene, even he faced limits on the clout he could exercise.

Private Slovik represents a tantalizing what-if in the Sinatra filmography, a missed opportunity whose import ranks only below that of *Carousel* and *Dirty Harry*. Given Sinatra's still strong liberal political beliefs and the McCarthy-esque gauntlet he experienced in trying to make the film, one can only wonder at the texture he would have brought to his directional debut. As it was, *The Execution of Private Slovik* did not make it to the screen until 1970, and then in a first-rate television movie starring Martin Sheen. By 1970 the blacklist lay twenty years in the past, and with the divisive Vietnam War raging, the political controversy generated in 1960 proved a nonissue. *The Execution of Private Slovik* unspooled as a first-class television movie, but it was just that—a television movie. With its larger-than-life themes of bravery, cowardice, and wartime, the story of Private Slovik was a natural for the big screen. If only.

The cancellation of the film for political reasons proved all the more ironic, considering Sinatra's late-middle-age conservatism, a conversion that resulted in his serving as a courier for the CIA and the State Department. With a private plane that allowed him to slip in and out of countries "carrying papers and people alike," Sinatra told daughter Tina, "It's no big deal. I'm never in any danger. But you cannot tell anybody about it." Which Tina didn't until the publication of her autobiography two years after her father's death.

With *Private Slovik* canceled, Frank spent most of 1961 in the recording studio. He released no fewer than six albums recorded during that one year. In the present day and age, which finds artists taking years to complete a single compact disc, it is downright staggering to think of Sinatra recording six albums, five of which landed in the top ten: *Sinatra's Swingin' Session, All the Way, Ring a Ding Ding, Come Swing with Me, Sinatra Swings*. Over the course of seventeen sessions, Sinatra cut no fewer than seventy-one songs with five different arrangers.

These top-drawer recordings kept Frank in the public eye in a year that found him in the unusual (for him) position of releasing only one film, *The Devil at 4 O'Clock*. For Frank Sinatra, the attraction of *The Devil at 4 O'Clock* lay in the fact that it provided him with the chance to work with his acting idol, Spencer Tracy. So deep was Sinatra's respect for Tracy that he ceded top billing to his friend, the opening credits of the Columbia Pictures release reading SPENCER TRACY AND FRANK SINATRA. That respect carries through into the film itself, because the movie is really Tracy's: he not only garners the most screen time (the *Variety* review of the film even referred to Frank's work as "first-class but minor"), but it is also his character, Catholic priest Father Doonan, who drives the action of the film.

For his part, Tracy acknowledged Sinatra's status as the power behind the film, noting, "Nobody had his power. *The Devil at 4 O'Clock* was a Sinatra picture. Sinatra was the star. Although we worked very differently, he knew what he wanted. Some people said there would be fireworks, but there wasn't." The difference in styles seems to have been mostly about Sinatra using his off time from the picture to campaign throughout the film's shooting locale of the Hawaiian islands for then-presidential-candidate John F. Kennedy, as well as his propensity for staying up partying throughout much of the night. What the two stars shared, however, was a dislike of repeated takes, and by most accounts, the two legends, under the watchful on-set eye of Katharine Hepburn, got along well. As for the film itself, Tracy turns in his customary professional performance, as does Sinatra, but as directed by the veteran Mervyn LeRoy, the film is a rather perfunctory affair. (LeRoy, who had directed two terrific Warner Bros. crime films, *Little Caesar* and *I Am a Fugitive from a Chain Gang,* had, of course, previously directed Sinatra in *The House I Live In.*) In fact, while the trailers for the film boldly proclaimed "In the tradition of *The Guns of Navarone* and *The Bridge on the River Kwai,*" it's a claim to which the only logical response is: *not exactly . . .*

The plot of the film finds three prisoners (Sinatra, Grégoire Aslan, and Bernie Hamilton) on their way to prison in Tahiti. The pilot (Jean-Pierre Aumont) taking them there must first stop off at the French island of Talua to drop off fellow passenger Father Joseph Perreau (Kerwin Mathews), a young priest set to replace the veteran Father Matthew Doonan (Tracy). Problem is, there's a volcano about to erupt on the island and Father Doonan wants to rescue the leprous children to whom he ministers. In the language of the film's trailer: "Father Doonan, the man who thinks he has lost everything. Three criminals—men who have nothing to lose." Throw in a stew of prejudiced islanders, a disease of the week (leprosy), the Catholic Church and disillusioned priests, three convicts, a reformed prostitute, and a blind leading lady—well, it all ends up as a case of plopping everything into the oven turning the heat up high, and hoping that a soufflé will rise. It doesn't—but the film is not without its moments.

The audience's first glimpse of Harry (Sinatra) is, in patented and effective Sinatra fashion, a slow reveal. He is lying on the floor of the cargo plane, hat over his face, scratching himself with hands chained to those of his fellow prisoners. He is belligerent and cynical, dismissively calling young Father Perreau "white collar." Sinatra is, in fact, a rather believable convict. This solid start is heightened by the first glimpse of Tracy's Father Doonan, the older priest introduced by a nearly silent sequence in which he awakens, looks with self-loathing in the mirror, and begins his day by drinking. With his craggy, lived-in face, Tracy is able to transmit all this information with nary a word—the audience knows this is not a standard-issue priest.

It is Father Doonan who actually saves the three convicts from being buried in a closed pit by the sadistic governor of Talua, but far from being grateful, Harry is more belligerent than ever. In the best dialogue of the film, Harry and Father Doonan exchange verbal darts:

> FATHER DOONAN: Where you from, tough guy? You spit your *t*'s—
> that'd be Jersey.
> I come from just across the river—Hell's Kitchen. We used to eat
> punks like you.
> HARRY: Maybe that's when you had your teeth. . . .

This is great tough dialogue, setting up very high expectations in the audience. Unfortunately, those expectations are rarely fulfilled, but the audience interest is, for the most part, maintained.

Viewers are next introduced to the matron, the proverbial tough broad with the heart of gold who runs the leprosy hospital along with her beautiful young ward, the blind Camille (Barbara Luna). Harry puts the moves on the young and beautiful Camille, his sexual drive seemingly running in tandem with a dawning self-awareness, wooing Camille by saying, "I've been a bum most of my life." The problem is that only after moving in to kiss Camille does Harry realize she can't see. Sinatra carries the moment off well, looking stricken and upset with himself, but the audience is jolted out of the moment in simple storytelling terms: You mean it *really* took him ten minutes and an up-close and personal moment before he realized she was blind?

When Sinatra does kiss Camille, Father Doonan is so furious at the transgression that he tries to strangle Harry and damn near succeeds. This burned-out, nearly alcoholic priest is a far cry from Tracy's much-loved portrayal of Father Flanagan in 1938's *Boys Town,* but with his extraordinary naturalistic acting abilities, he is equally adept at the idealistic and the cynical. Tracy's performance is also notably more believable than an out-of-his-depth Kerwin Mathews as idealistic young Father Perreau. Perhaps the filmmakers realized how inexperienced Mathews read onscreen, because Father Perreau basically disappears from the film once he breaks his leg in an earthquake. You see, there's this earthquake, and the earthquake happens because the volcano has exploded, and the erupting volcano will cause the island to sink, and the children will be killed and . . .

Protracted discussions about the islanders turning on Father Doonan for helping the lepers move Sinatra offscreen for rather lengthy stretches at a time. The convicts return to the foreground only after the volcano explodes for the first time, and Harry convinces his fellow prisoners to parachute onto the hospital grounds along with Father Doonan in order to save the children. Oddly enough, it is during this action-packed final third of the movie, when the children are saved, that the film founders. After a tough, interesting start, Harry now turns into a marshmallow, all of a sudden caring about little children and, most inexplicably, marrying Camille—offscreen. Not only does the event ring false—Father Doonan has very quickly moved from strangling Harry because of one kiss to happily marrying the couple—but in the next shot after the marriage, the now flawlessly groomed couple embraces tenderly. This is a not-insignificant point: how is the audience supposed to believe in the action, a desperate attempt to escape molten lava, when the bride and groom in question appear to have just stepped out of a beauty salon?

The other major problem at this point in the film is that while the location photography on Maui by cinematographer Joseph Biroc (here lensing the first of his five films with Sinatra) is gorgeous, with sweeping panoramas of the ocean, beach, and jungle, the escape from the exploding volcano takes place on noticeably phony interior sets that in no way realistically resemble a path through the jungle. The flowing lava and splitting boulders resemble nothing so much as papier-mâché rocks left over from a particularly low-budget early episode of *Flash Gordon.*

Determined not to abandon Father Doonan and Charlie, Harry returns to await a certain death with both men. When the hospital matron sadly informs him that by doing so he'll miss the schooner and his only means of escape from the island, Sinatra deftly underplays his quick retort: "Lady, I missed the boat a long time ago." Charlie and Father Doonan are trapped on the far side of a gorge with no way out, and in the midst of what could register as an utterly hokey situation, the gently smiling Tracy, his voice full of compassion, makes the audience believe in the priest whose faith has been restored by convicts. One wonders what playing the scene was like for Tracy, a famously guilt-ridden Catholic in real life, tortured over both his long-term liaison with Katharine Hepburn and his son's deafness (and, according to William Mann's exhaustive study of Hepburn titled *Kate,* tortured over his own homosexual leanings). Whatever his personal feelings, Tracy delivers beautifully in that sequence as he says a prayer over the dying Charlie's body. Having returned right before Charlie dies, Harry quietly watches this scene, finally saying to Father Doonan as they prepare to die, "It's just you and me, Pops—New Jersey and New York." Yes, there's a heavenly choir that mysteriously begins to sing in the background, and Harry's rather abrupt shift to martyrdom does test audience patience, but as Father Doonan offers a prayer of contrition and the heretofore-nonbelieving Harry makes the sign of the cross, it is all curiously moving.

For such a lengthy—indeed, overly long—film, the nonstop plot developments feel rushed, with Sinatra's character never fully scoring as the heartwarming cad-turned-hero that he should have been. (Sinatra may always have been impatient on his film sets, but he was now in the midst of making some very long films—*Some Came Running, Never So Few, Can-Can, Ocean's Eleven,* and *The Devil at 4 O'Clock* all ran over two hours.) Sinatra is fine throughout, but *The Devil at 4 O'Clock,* occasionally moving yet curiously truncated, ultimately registers as Spencer Tracy's show. Well, the priests nearly always get the good lines, what with the tortured consciences and temporary losses of faith that are staples of religious films. One thing was for sure, however—there wouldn't be a priest in sight for Sinatra's next movie, a nutty Western outing for the Rat Pack titled *Sergeants 3.*

Sinatra had so enjoyed making *Ocean's Eleven* that he quickly developed a plan to make a series of five movies over five years with his Rat Pack buddies. To that end, eighteen months after the release of *Ocean's Eleven,* he reunited with Dean, Sammy, and Peter Lawford for *Sergeants 3,* an updating of the Rudyard Kipling poem, "Gunga Din," which had previously been captured on film in a classic 1939 RKO film, as well as in a 1951 MGM remake titled *Soldiers Three.* Transposing the original setting from India to the American West of 1873 is actually a pretty good idea for a film, but the resulting movie could not make up its mind what it was mean to be: Serious Western? Buddy movie? Rat Pack hipster epic? As a result, while there are some enjoyable individual sequences in the film, in overall terms it's a mess.

With Sinatra's Essex Productions producing in conjunction with Dean Martin's Claude Productions, Howard Koch Jr. served as executive producer, the first of his six collaborations with Sinatra. Technical credits are first-rate throughout, with the John Sturges–directed movie filmed on location in Bryce Canyon National Park. In fact, the cinematography of Winton C. Hoch is far and away the outstanding element of the film, the wide-open Western vistas lending a starkly beautiful credibility to the story. Hoch, who won three Academy Awards (*Joan of Arc, She Wore a Yellow Ribbon,* and *The Quiet Man*) as well as a fourth Oscar for technical achievement, understood the Western landscape of the United States in a way few if any other cinematographers have. Indeed, the most highly acclaimed of John Ford's Westerns all featured cinematography by Hoch, and even in a knockabout production like *Sergeants 3,* his screen compositions are often dazzling. With Bryce Canyon National Park standing in for Ford's beloved Monument Valley, Hoch achieves the same visual results, layering texture and a deliberate color scheme onto the ofttimes pedestrian (and downright silly) story. The red dirt of the ground that the horses' hooves stir up is a variation of the blood spilled by soldier and Native American "red man." alike, just as the panoramic vistas of the blue skies complement the blue army uniforms, and are occasionally augmented by startling close-ups of Sinatra's blue eyes. It all forms a remarkable achievement by Hoch, but it still can't overcome the film's number-one problem—the story. It's the characters placed within the landscape and environment that lend surroundings meaning, but Hoch is forced to utilize his talents in order to frame nitwits. What may have seemed acceptable on the page in W. R. Burnett's screenplay plays flaccidly onscreen and often registers as downright juvenile in execution. It's all a very long way from Burnett's acclaimed screenplays for *Scarface* and *The Asphalt Jungle.*

The three sergeants of the title (Sinatra, Martin, Lawford) are actually introduced after the audience first meets Jonah (Sammy Davis Jr.), a freed slave (the equivalent of the native water-bearer in *Gunga Din*) who is seen playing a bugle and tap-dancing on top of a bar. A full-scale brawl quickly ensues and right off the bat, the movie takes a very wrong turn. The film had started out with beautiful shots of the Western scenery, accurately establishing time and place, and even the score by longtime Sinatra arranger Billy May had eschewed his normal swinging brass-heavy sound for a rather subdued and appropriate string-laden sound. But when the barroom fight starts up, the music switches to melodies and orchestration more appropriate for a Warner Bros. Looney Tunes cartoon, and reality flies right out the door. Combine the inappropriate score with visual jokes that are endlessly repeated until the originally amusing idea is beaten into the ground, and you have a rather inert start to what is supposed to be a lighthearted romp.

John Sturges, a thorough professional who had recently directed *The Magnificent Seven* to acclaim, had actually staged the opening Indian attack on the town of Telegraph Bend in realistic fashion, a stylistic decision that led to hopes for a well-grounded film. However, in staging this saloon fight between the mountain men and the sergeants three, one has the feeling that Sinatra (and cronies) informed director Sturges that the fight would be played for laughs and that was the end of the discussion. It's all attenuated to the point of lost audience interest and after ineptly staged contretemps, viewers resignedly settle in for a "Rat Pack has fun in the Wild West" type of farce. Which is exactly what doesn't happen.

Instead, as punishment for the destructive barroom brawl, the colonel in charge of the cavalry sends the three sergeants to Telegraph Bend to investigate why the telegraph lines are dead. As the men ride into town, Sturges sets the scene very nicely in a nearly silent sequence, the seemingly deserted town eerie in its loneliness, May's score striking an ominous and appropriate note to increase the tension. When the Native Americans ambush the investigating army men, Sturges stages the sequence in fine fashion, employing a minimum of dialogue and a maximum of action.

So it is that after the first three sequences of the film, Sturges is batting two out of three—not a bad average. It's therefore all the more frustrating that the movie now runs into an insurmountable problem—the acting by the stars. Peter Lawford is here cast yet again in another variation of his spoiled rich boy character; he fulfills the limited requirements of his role in acceptable fashion, although his vaguely Etonian accent jars, to say the least. Sammy coasts on his personality, "acting" up a storm, nearly begging for audience sympathy and undermining his credibility as a result. His natural acting talent simply appears to be subsumed by his place in the Rat Pack pecking order. Lawford and Davis certainly wouldn't win any awards here, but the real problems lie with the film's two best actors, Frank and Dean. Both men are acting by the numbers, Sinatra dutifully fulfilling his role as the leader of the men, Dean establishing his persona as the more laid-back sidekick. They're not trying very hard, and as a result, the audience doesn't care very much.

Even as one tries to take Frank and Dean seriously as army men in the Wild West, they blow up the entire enterprise in a winking, "look at us having fun" aside. To wit, in the middle of a rather nicely staged life-and-death fight between Frank, Dean, and the Native Americans, Sinatra's Sergeant Mike is dragged underneath a speeding runaway wagon (a stunt Sinatra performed himself). As Frank grimly hauls himself up the side of the runaway wagon, Dean's Sergeant Chip (not exactly a name associated with the Old West) cuts him a sideway glance and mutters, "Would you stop clowning around and get up here?" The filmmakers have blown it: they can't have it both ways—either it's a real Western, or else it's a spoof, but by trying to be both, it ends up being neither.

The audience is still—barely—hanging on for the ride, but with the introduction of numerous additional plot elements, viewers begin to simply tune out. In short succession, there is a tiresome poker game between Sergeant Chip and a blacksmith, the joke being that instead of money, they play with hatchets and tools. Sammy appears to fall in love with his mule, much like Cantinflas and his horse in *Pepe*—was it a rule that any nonwhite male wasn't allowed a fully developed adult character? Such sloppy writing and execution rank as a waste of the talents of everyone involved, yet worse was to come.

How much worse? Well, for starters, after Chip becomes drunk, fights with Mike, and ends up in jail, Jonah frees him by having his beloved mule literally knock down the jail by the force of his hooves. That's up there on the believability scale with Amelia (Ruta Lee), the prissy citified fiancée of Sergeant Larry Barrett (Peter Lawford), agreeing to ride out into the wilds with him when he oh-so-romantically asks her, "Would you mind being alone with thirty-six men?" and she answers, "Why, no, Larry—not if you're there." There are rampaging Native Americans around, the soldiers in question are not exactly the cream of society, but she blithely agrees without a single quibble, an answer that makes her appear to be more than a little simple. Why is Amelia even in the movie? There's absolutely no discernible reason except that Ruta Lee is here filling the one female role required as part of each Rat Pack movie. It doesn't work, because she's a stick figure, her role nowhere near as interesting as Angie Dickinson's abbreviated turn as Sinatra's estranged wife in *Ocean's Eleven*. Lee did, however, provide very trenchant insight into Sinatra's infamous one-take technique:

> He'd come in at eleven, but he'd say, "I'm giving you all the time in the
> world to set up the shot. I'll come in and do a walk-through. I don't

want to hear after I've done a walk-through that there's a shadow here, that the sound isn't right there. Take all the time in the world, but when I walk in, I want it perfect."

By film's end, the audience finally gives up, done in by a climax set in a noticeably phony-looking cave and a ridiculously superhuman Sammy, who survives a stabbing and a close-range shooting with enough strength left over to haul himself up a sheer rockface and blow a bugle with such force that he successfully warns the approaching army soldiers who are still miles away. Even a witty nod to the ending of *Ocean's Eleven* does not make up for the mess the audience has endured for nearly two hours. Neither a full-fledged comic Western nor a serious examination of the genre, *Sergeants 3* represents nothing more than slapdash writing that gave Frank and the boys a chance to fool around and get paid a lot of money.

For 112 minutes, Frank, Dean, Sammy, and Peter have all been in on the joke, but the audience feels left out and more than a tad resentful. Reviewing the film in *The Hollywood Citizen-News,* Hazel Flynn cynically observed, "Somewhere east of Suez the ghost of Rudyard Kipling must be whirling like a dervish in its grave . . . it's more din than Gunga, believe me, starting with a barroom brawl and ending with a howling massacre." *Variety* put it more bluntly: "His Cub Scout troupe are pioneering in a new art form: the 4 million dollar home movie." The film garnered bad notices aplenty, but actually performed more than respectably at the box office. What no one knew at the time, however, was that the film functioned as the last of the full-fledged Rat Pack movies because Lawford, soon to fall out of favor once again, did not appear in the subsequent Rat Pack extravaganzas, *4 for Texas* and *Robin and the 7 Hoods.*

The reason for Lawford's fall from grace, unsurprisingly, stemmed from yet another intersection of presidential politics and Hollywood, complete with myriad attendant complications. The contretemps that so hurt Lawford's standing in Sinatra's circle began with President Kennedy's cancellation of his March 1962 weekend stay at Sinatra's Palm Springs compound, and only accelerated when Lawford was delegated by the Kennedys to deliver the news to Frank. Sinatra's subsequent reaction to the news represented, for all intents and purposes, a case of shooting the messenger.

As to the event causing Lawford's exile, two markedly different theories have been floated to explain the president's cancellation: The first, which has passed into legend in Sinatra-land, holds that Attorney General Robert Kennedy, uneasy over Sinatra's supposed ties to the Mafia, insisted the president cancel his visit for the sake of propriety. A second, more "official" explanation, held that the layout of Sinatra's home was literally too open for purposes of assuring adequate security, with the Secret Service insisting that the visit be canceled for reasons of safety.

In her autobiography *Mafia Princess,* Sam Giancana's daughter Antoinette cites a December 11, 1961, letter from FBI director J. Edgar Hoover to Attorney General Robert Kennedy that certainly seems to point to the former theory; in fact, the memo seems to constitute a de facto start to the subsequent troubles between Sinatra and the Kennedys. In this letter regarding gambling activities in Las Vegas, Hoover details that the FBI had received information that Giancana had asked "(name deleted)" to act as a go-between on his behalf with Robert Kennedy. According to FBI agent William Roemer, it is Frank's name that is here blanked out. The memo goes on to state that the "overtures" were to be made through Joseph Kennedy Sr., and that "(name deleted)" rejected the suggestion. As Giancana posits, such a memo has to have made Robert Kennedy realize that the FBI knew of the rather byzantine Giancana–Sinatra–Kennedy connections, which makes the events regarding the canceled presidential visit to the Palm Springs compound more readily comprehensible. A mere ten days after the memo, the FBI taped a conversation between Giancana and associate John Roselli in which Roselli denigrated Sinatra's Kennedy connection with a muttered "You know Pierre Salinger [press secretary] and those guys. . . . They don't want him. They treat [him] like they treat a whore."

Whichever the reason for the change of venue, President Kennedy kept his plans for a weekend visit to California, but stayed at the supposedly more security-friendly home of Bing Crosby. Sinatra was none too pleased over the switch to Crosby's home, and it wasn't just because of the ever-present friendly rivalry between Crosby and Sinatra. It's that Crosby was a well-known Republican to boot, a fact that surely exacerbated Sinatra's feeling of being stigmatized.

Frank, hurt and angry at the change of plans, turned on Lawford in his role as Kennedy factotum, and as a result, the proposed roles in both *4 for Texas* and *Robin and the 7 Hoods* quickly disappeared. As legend would have it, upon hearing the news, Sinatra's explosive temper got the better of him and he took a jackhammer to the would-be presidential helicopter landing pad he had installed. It's an exciting story, one even depicted in the HBO television film *The Rat Pack,* but as with so much about Sinatra, it happens to be false. Wrote daughter Tina: "He didn't tear any walls down or take a jackhammer to the helipad, as the yellow journalists would have it."

Kennedy's withdrawal hurt Sinatra's pride and his sense of both position and power—but true to form, he recovered by burying himself in work. With his next major film effort, the brilliant *Manchurian Candidate,* Frank reached a new career peak, but first up was a brief cameo in the last—and possibly least—of the Bob Hope/Bing Crosby "Road" pictures, *The Road to Hong Kong.* Reportedly agreeing to the brief appearance as a favor to Crosby (in addition to his continuing gratitude to Hope for the guest-starring television spot when his fortunes were at an all-time low twelve years earlier), Sinatra's cameo—as an extraterrestrial, yet—comes at the end of the film, in a very brief appearance with fellow space traveler Dean Martin. In actuality, the real interest of the film lies in what it reveals about Sinatra's only true contemporary rival as singer, actor, and all-media phenomenon, Bing Crosby.

Road to Hong Kong, the seventh and final "Road" movie, was filmed ten years after the penultimate entry in the series, *The Road to Bali.* A black-and-white UA release shot at Shepperton studios in London (the only one of the "Road" films produced outside of Hollywood), the film gets off to a terrific start, with a first-rate Sammy Cahn/Jimmy Van Heusen song, "Teamwork," sung and danced in top-notch fashion by Crosby and Hope. When combined with some nifty Maurice Binder–designed titles featuring chopsticks picking names out of soup bowls, the viewer understandably enough concludes that Bing and Bob haven't missed a step. It's true that the boys are still in great shape, but the screenwriters sure have missed a step or ten, because after that opening, it's all downhill. Quickly.

The dated, early-1960s origin of the film is immediately apparent in the opening dialogue (by screenwriters Norman Panama and Melvin Frank), which finds the announcer intoning "This is Hong Kong—sprawling dragon nestled in the soft underbelly of China." It's dialogue straight out of 1932—all that's missing is a dragon lady spewing venom and girls being sold into "white slavery." It's all unfortunately revealing of the then-prevalent American attitude of condescension toward all things Asian, further evidenced by the voiceover narration detailing "sports car racing" in Asia, a statement accompanied by footage of a very slow water buffalo plodding through rice paddies.

With Crosby and Hope quickly introduced as Harry Turner and Chester Babcock respectively, the self-referential nature of the film becomes immediately apparent: Edward Chester Babcock is the birth name of Jimmy Van Heusen, composer, ladies' man, bon vivant, and reported role model for Sinatra the swinging man about town. Right off the bat, Bing turns to Bob and states, "Don't blame me—it's a plot point," the constant breaking of the fourth wall informing this film as it had all the "Road" pictures. The difference this time around lies in the fact that Joan Collins is on hand as the love interest instead of "Road" series regular Dorothy Lamour. Collins, outfitted in a crazy bouffant hairdo crowned by a wiglet plopped on top, does not even attempt to hide her boredom with the proceedings at hand, delivering her lines and strolling through the action with a distracted air of condescension, as if to say, *I'll agree to stay, but only if I really must.* Well, the audience is at least granted the hilarious sight of Joan in a full-length evening gown leading Bing and Bob out of evil Robert Morley's subterranean lair by exclaiming, "We can escape by submarine—I can handle it." Which leads the audience to wonder, *How? By cleaning the windshield of the submarine with your wiglet?*

The contrast between Collins and Lamour is made perfectly clear when Lamour emerges near film's end, playing herself in a stage show as she vainly tries to hide the boys from the villains. Of course, the talented and ever-appealing Lamour knows it's all ridiculous, but she enters into the spirit of silliness with zest and genuine musical ability, the film's energy level rising several notches during her one sequence.

Yes, Crosby and Hope do detonate some solid wisecracks along the way. When Hope, in patented cowardly fashion, whines to Bing that he's afraid of the sharks primed to eat them, Bing reassures Bob that the sharks don't eat people. Bob's rejoinder, "What about actors?" is met with Crosby's snappy retort, "We're safe." It's a funny line, self-referential in the best way, and an interesting example of one of the few times in the film that Bing delivers his lines with zest. Crosby could be a first-class actor in films such as *The Country Girl,* and was an enormous movie star with a far-ranging talent that matched his wide box office appeal. He could carry a film himself, or mesh easily with a variety of partners ranging from Fred Astaire to Ann-Margret.

But, just as in *High Society,* he is so intent on appearing relaxed and nonchalant that he shortchanges himself, Hope, and the audience. He has carried the non-chalance beautifully displayed in the previous "Road" pictures to the breaking point. It's as if Crosby never wanted the effort to show, and perhaps out of fear that he would be mocked if he exerted himself and the results were not first class, he protected himself by displaying a detached sense that all but says, *See I'm not taking any of this too seriously—you can't blame me or criticize me.* It's a formula that Burt Reynolds aped much less successfully in the 1970s when he was at the height of his popularity, and it reveals a decided contrast between Sinatra and his onetime idol Crosby.

Sinatra could and would barrel through material he didn't care about, making out-of-scale demands that could hinder his performance and those of his costars, but when he cared about the material, Sinatra communicated the depth of his commitment to the audience, bringing them along for the ride. There is nothing even remotely distanced about his terrific performances in *From Here to Eternity, The Man with the Golden Arm, Pal Joey,* and *The Manchurian Candidate*; he never holds the audience at a distance as Crosby did, and Sinatra's films, as well as his legacy as a movie star, loom much larger with the passing years than do Crosby's. Sinatra was a hot performer, and Crosby a very cool customer. It's why Sinatra as a rule registered better on film and Crosby better on television. Crosby's remove, like that of Perry Como, worked well on the small screen, whereas Sinatra, in his weekly 1950s series, seemed ready to jump through the screen. Sinatra on television was at his finest in his terrific variety specials, such as *The Man and His Music.* With the concert setting at hand, the energy and music pouring out of Frank seemed natural and proper. In the end, Crosby's cool, so reassuring in his early film roles, came to inhibit his full development as a film actor, legendary though that film career was.

By the end of the film, mad scientist Morley has managed to launch Hope, Crosby, and Collins into outer space, where they end up on the planet Pluto-nius. Rocket ship having landed, it's time for a little song and dance, and just as the boys launch into a reprise of "Teamwork," the song is interrupted when Joan spots two fellow space travelers: Frank Sinatra and Dean Martin. Kissing first Dean and then Frank, Joan happily snuggles up to the new duo, leading Hope and Crosby to exclaim, "The Italians have landed. . . . That's the grape and the twig isn't it?" It's as if Hope and Crosby are passing the torch for buddy movies to the new generation. Just as Hope and Crosby made their seven "Road" films together, Dean and Frank were now in the midst of their nine joint film appearances, a run that began with the flawed but worthy *Some Came Running,* continued through the entertaining *Ocean's Eleven,* and ended with the abysmal *Cannonball Run II.* If Crosby and Hope were all song-and-dance energy, the love-starved Hope always losing the girl to the smooth Crosby, the passing years had dictated that America's new favorite team revolved around Frank's king-of-the-hill routine contrasted with the boozy laid-back cool of Dino. The America amused by the knowing shenanigans of Crosby and Hope as they broke the fourth wall to let the audience in on the fun had evolved into the JFK era of "Ring a Ding Ding" swingers and the adult playground antics of Las Vegas. As America changed, so, too, did its favorite movie stars.

Frank and Dean together with Bob and Bing presented audiences with an interesting "summit" of spectacular talent slumming and having a grand time of it, but audiences had an entirely different reaction to Sinatra's next film, John Frankenheimer's brilliant 1962 classic, *The Manchurian Candidate.* This all-time great, which, along with *The Man with the Golden Arm,* featured the best, most fully realized and sustained acting of Sinatra's career, served to remind audiences all over again what a terrific actor Frank Sinatra could be when given the right material. Making the film while in the midst of recording his masterly concept LPs, Sinatra is so good that his terrific performance registers as a feat akin to Marlon Brando having followed up his beautiful performance in *On the Waterfront* by recording *Only the Lonely. The Manchurian Candidate* serves as a welcome reminder that no other male performer ever delivered so consistently as both actor and singer. Indeed, *The Manchurian Candidate* is such a superb film that it makes one forgive Sinatra every last *Kissing Bandit* and *Sergeants 3.* The artist once again reigned supreme.

After numerous false starts and stops that mainly centered on Hollywood concerns over the political content of the material, *The Manchurian Candidate* finally began production after Sinatra met with President John Kennedy in Hyannisport, Massachusetts, and obtained presidential support for the film. Kennedy, a fan of Richard Condon's original 1959 novel, did not object in the slightest to the political content, even making a phone call to United Artists president Arthur Krim to allay UA concerns. On the DVD reissue of the film, Sinatra relates that Kennedy thought the book would make a fine film, and had one specific query: Who was going to play the role of the evil mother?

The film itself is very much a product of its time, an era when, before total disillusionment set in with the Vietnam War, Americans were more paranoid than cynical, afraid of the Russians and in some ways afraid of and for themselves. At the same time, the key to the film's brilliance lies in the fact that it investigates issues as relevant in the day and age of the war in Iraq as they were in 1962: Is all behavior acceptable in "defense" of freedom? What exactly constitutes genuine patriotism? Does the far right cloak its machinations under claims of national security? The resulting film never hammers the audience over the head with answers, preferring that viewers draw their own conclusions. As a result, the film's impact is all the more devastating.

The Manchurian Candidate is that rarest of films, one wherein the entire team of creative personnel functioned at the top of their game: director John Frankenheimer, screenwriter George Axelrod, and director of photography Lionel Lindon not only turned in career best efforts, but they were matched every step of the way by their all-star cast—Sinatra, Laurence Harvey, and Angela Lansbury. Harvey, a fine actor who alternated between terrific performances in fine films like *Room at the Top* and silly melodramas like *Walk on the Wild Side,* displayed a welcome and unsuspected depth. Lansbury, a mere thirty-seven at the time of filming, had already fallen prey to the Hollywood typecasting mind-set, playing mother to both Elvis Presley in *Blue Hawaii* and Warren Beatty in Frankenheimer's *All Fall Down. The Manchurian Candidate* provided her with the role of a far different sort of mother, and she responded with the single best performance of her six-decade film career, further proof of her extraordinary versatility.

It's worth noting that Sinatra originally wanted Lucille Ball to play the role of Evelyn, an idea that makes a great deal of sense. As Ball aged, she grew into an increasingly hardened performer, losing all traces of the vulnerability that so informed her brilliant multiyear run on television's *I Love Lucy.* The resulting quality of toughness would have suited the role of Evelyn very well, although it is anyone's guess whether or not Ball would have felt comfortable delving into the dark recesses of Evelyn's warped character. Fortunately, after Frankenheimer had Sinatra watch Lansbury's performance in *All Fall Down,* Sinatra agreed on Lansbury, a decision that proved absolutely essential to the film's jittery effectiveness. (In a curious turnabout, Lansbury was denied the opportunity to re-create her showstopping signature role as *Mame* when that Broadway musical smash was filmed, the plum role going instead to the decidedly non-musical Lucille Ball.) Lansbury was rightly nominated for an Academy Award for her performance in *The Manchurian Candidate,* and although after winning the Golden Globe Award she lost the Oscar to Margaret Rutherford in *The V.I.P.s,* she, like Sinatra, justifiably regarded the film as a career high point.

Director Frankenheimer's first feature, *The Young Stranger* (1957) had displayed a youthful talent, but he fully hit his stride in 1962 with the remarkable one-two-three punch of *All Fall Down, Birdman of Alcatraz,* and *The Manchurian Candidate.* He ran a remarkably smooth set, filming taking a mere thirty-nine days. Handling Sinatra just as had Vincente Minnelli and George Sidney, Frankenheimer would rehearse other cast members in advance, bringing in Sinatra for only one pre-shoot run-through before the actual filming of a scene. Keeping the need for retakes to a minimum, Frankenheimer thereby ensured Sinatra's continued goodwill.

Shot in evocative black-and-white (cinematographer Lionel Lindon had previously worked with Frankenheimer on *All Fall Down* and won an Academy Award for his work on *Around the World in Eighty Days*), that stylistic choice displays and comments upon cold war jitters, suffusing the film with paranoia. Indeed, the seemingly handheld camera work exacerbates the nervous, jangling mood of a film set during the Korean War, a conflict that had made America question itself in an unprecedented fashion. Korea was not, to use Studs Terkel's loaded phrase, a "good war," a fact made clear in the very first scene, when Raymond Shaw (Laurence Harvey) and Bennett Marco (Sinatra) are betrayed by their Korean interpreter (Henry Silva), taken prisoner, and flown off in helicopters to an unknown destination. It is only after the opening ambush that the film credits run, all of them flashing onscreen against a background of the Queen of Diamonds playing card that will figure so prominently in the film. It's a terrific opening—ratcheting up the mystery while leaving the audience asking the many questions necessary to sustain any suspense film: What happens next? Why are Shaw, the humorless enforcer of rules, and Bennett, the cynical bystander, thrown together? Who are these people? What happened after the soldiers were captured?

Plenty happened, as it turns out, but for now the leading cast of characters is completed with the introduction of Shaw's mother, Evelyn (Angela Lansbury); she's an overbearing woman who pushes her way into the political rally where Shaw receives the Medal of Honor, a photographer in tow in order to garner publicity for her politico second husband, Senator John Iselin (the excellent James Gregory). Dismissing Shaw's new employer, journalist Herbert Gans, with a withering, "He's a Communist," Evelyn is a woman with whom one does not trifle, and also a woman no one likes—a state of affairs made clear by her own son's disdain. (The subsequent scene of the Iselins on their private aircraft utilized Sinatra's own plane.)

With the reintroduction of Sinatra as Major Bennett Marco of Army Intelligence in Washington, D.C., Axelrod's savvy screenplay lifts off to a sustained level of psychological suspense from which it never lets down. Bennett is plagued by terrifying nightmares, and in Sinatra's sweat-stained restless sleep, the terror is nearly palpable. In the depiction of these nightmares, Frankenheimer, Axelrod, and production designer Richard Sylbert, aided by the superb cast, deliver the film's most memorable sequence: Bennett's horror of a surreal garden party attended by his fellow soldiers. As a slightly overbearing garden club member lectures the assembled GIs on the care and cultivation of hydrangeas, Frankenheimer has the camera move in a circular pan around the assembled crowd, until it arrives back at its starting point. This time, however, there is no sign of a benign garden club, but rather, walls filled with pictures of Communist leaders Stalin and Mao. Only now does it become clear that the nightmare is a flashback to brainwashing in Manchuria. The juxtaposition of the brainwashing with the lily-white setting of a garden club is not only an inspired choice, but also one that is heightened by the ensuing action: Lieutenant Shaw is forced to strangle a fellow soldier, the murderous action accompanied by genteel harpsichord music. Action completed, Shaw blankly addresses his captor Dr. Yen Lo (Khigh Dhiegh) as "Ma'am," at which point Bennett wakes up, Sinatra's terrified face and scream filling the screen. Suspense, political commentary, great acting—and the film is only twenty minutes old.

Editor Ferris Webster's Oscar-nominated work is particularly adept in the garden party sequence, merging seamlessly with Frankenheimer's 360-degree pan to suggest the interplay between what the soldiers actually experienced—brainwashing by Soviet and Chinese officers—and what they were brainwashed to believe they experienced—a lecture by a Mrs. Henry Whittaker on "Fun with Hydrangeas." Frankenheimer stated that the scene came directly from Condon's original novel and that "we filmed this scene with about six different combinations . . . and we put the whole thing together in the editing room. . . . Now, by editing together all these unique combinations, the way we shot the scene . . . it takes on a very surrealistic quality." The garden club sequence is repeated later in the film in order to show African-American Corporal Melvin (James Edwards) experiencing the same nightmares as did Bennett, that second brainwashing sequence, according to Frankenheimer, having been "edited . . . at random with no thought to continuity whatsoever. Just to make it weird." Weird it is, not to mention extraordinarily effective.

The terror of the sequence is nicely contrasted with the introduction of a second plotline, that of Evelyn's machinations in behalf of her husband's rise to political power. In a beautifully filmed scene, Senator Iselin insists during Senate hearings that there are 207 Communists working in the Defense Department, a bombshell pronouncement delivered with stentorian authority—except it is Evelyn pulling all the strings here, feeding this surefire headline-grabber to her incompetent husband. It is Evelyn who makes sure there is a full contingent of television and print reporters present to trumpet word of the sensational developments, and to spread the news of her husband's name. Frankenheimer composes that scene beautifully, beginning with his capturing Lansbury's profile in the foreground of the screen as she nods the go-ahead to her husband. As the senator bellows his accusations, the entire scene is simultaneously shown on a television monitor placed in the foreground of the screen; in this one sequence, the filmmakers have managed to comment on the Red Scare tactics of Senator Joseph McCarthy, the then-real Communist threat represented by both the Soviet Union and the Chinese, and most notably of all, the overbearing presence of a television-dominated media, which in its hunger for a soundbite, has forever distorted the political give and take at the foundation of American democracy. It's a very ambitious agenda, but Frankenheimer et al deliver on every count.

As the action deftly switches gears back to another brainwashing sequence, Lieutenant Shaw is further instructed to murder a second fellow soldier, which he does by means of pointing a gun in the direction of the camera, the bullet flying through the soldier's skull, blood splattering onto the photo of Stalin (whose crimes of mass slaughter were finally being made public at the time of filming by then–Soviet Premier Nikita Khrushchev). Audacious and startling in design and impact, the sequence's blend of the technical with emotional storytelling is downright extraordinary.

In their very different ways, both Shaw and Bennett manifest what one character calls the "uniquely American qualities of guilt and fear," and it is at that point, as Bennett falls apart after being fired from his job in army public relations, that Sinatra delivers a set piece that is arguably the single best he ever committed to film. As the nightmares continue to haunt him, unable to explain how and why it is all happening, Bennett, a captive to his own nerves and paranoia, is consigned to an indefinite sick leave. Sitting on a train speeding through the Maryland countryside, an increasingly unhinged and desperate Bennett is so nerve-ridden that he cannot manage the simple act of lighting a cigarette. Lurching out of his seat and running out of the compartment, he is all the while observed by Rosie Chaney (Janet Leigh), who follows him out of the car and onto the platform between compartments.

Sinatra's sweat-drenched face filling the screen, he attempts to carry on a normal conversation with Rosie. Trying to answer her questions, speaking in a halting fashion and on the point of nervous exhaustion, Sinatra is letter perfect. It is a beautifully controlled performance, never faltering in tone, mannerism, or behavior. Delivering layers of shadings to his portrayal, he creates a fully realized character in the space of that one sequence. It may not be so flashy as the withdrawal sequence in *The Man with the Golden Arm,* but it is, if anything, even more fully realized. This terrific scene was completed in a single take, undoubtedly increasing Sinatra's appreciation of Frankenheimer's directorial skills. Said the director, "This is the kind of scene that could have taken three days if it didn't go well." It did go well and was completed in precisely three hours.

Sinatra and Leigh make an effective team, even managing to overcome the fact that their romance doesn't really lead anywhere. Rosie is a mystery woman who appears midway through the film and exists mostly to bail Marco out of jail after his fight with Chunjin, the traitorous interpreter from the film's opening scene. Of course, gold medals are in line for any audience member who can fully explain the conversation between Bennett and Rosie, what with Rosie referring to herself as a Chinese worker who "lay the railroad tracks" and Bennett asking the very all-American-looking Rosie if she is Arabic. It's all perplexing and leaves unanswered questions, but it's also fitting for a film dealing with paranoia, brainwashing, and the unanswered questions of a nihilistic modern life.

When the film cuts back to the Iselins' grasp for political power, Evelyn, alternately full of fake sympathy for and disgusted by her husband's ineptitude, tells him with outright contempt, "You're good at a great many things, but thinking isn't one of them." Just like the real-life Senator Joseph McCarthy, Senator Johnny cannot quite remember the exact number of Communists he is supposed to have uncovered. It's Evelyn, in a wonderfully cynical moment, who spies the label on the ketchup bottle with which Johnny is crudely smothering his dinner, and seizes upon Heinz's fifty-seven varieties of ketchup as the key: there will now be fifty-seven Communists in the Department of Defense. It's a number even Johnny can remember. The number of Communists in the 1950s was constantly changed by McCarthy, so why not fake the number in the film by taking the total from a condiment bottle? It's witty comment upon so much of the absurdity in political life and the attendant susceptibility of the American public, one that would be downright hilarious if it weren't so frightening in its long-range implications. It's sequences like that one that make *The Manchurian Candidate* land as powerfully in the new millennium as it did in 1962—the more things change, the more they stay the same.

Then-startling martial arts fight in the brilliant Manchurian Candidate *(1942), Frank's finest film.*

Spying Raymond's Medal of Honor, Bennett begins to fit the pieces of the puzzle together. Sinatra smartly downplays the moment—there is no literal or figurative shout of "Eureka!" but rather, a soft note of wonder as he begins to grasp what has happened. Slowly Shaw and Bennett begin to bond, and the reasons for Shaw's intense dislike of his own mother begin to emerge. It was Evelyn herself who destroyed her son's romance with Jocelyn Jordan (Leslie Parrish), fiercely dismissing Jocelyn, the daughter of liberal Senator Thomas Jordan as a "Communist tart." Insisting that Shaw sign the letter she has drafted denouncing Jocelyn as a Communist, Lansbury is spectacular, employing the forceful whisper that all but smothers Raymond, making it plain how such a weak-willed character had no choice but to follow her wishes. Lansbury's well-groomed attractive facade makes the poison she whispers seem all the more evil, suggesting layers of venom by the insistently intimate tone she adopts.

Like Lansbury, Harvey is terrific throughout in what is in many ways the film's most difficult role. Playing a remarkably unsympathetic character whose horrible mother and brainwashing have led him to commit heinous acts, he still manages to depict a man who slowly changes into a recognizable human being, one for whom the audience can develop sympathy and a rooting interest. Harvey has the decidedly difficult task of making the brainwashing and robotic behavior believable, and he does so admirably. In fact, the 1988 interview that accompanies the film on DVD found Sinatra praising Harvey and talking of having considered the role of Shaw but feeling that he could not make it work. (The only time Harvey falters is when his brainwashed state leads him to mistakenly hire the traitorous interpreter Chunjin as his valet. It's not just the disconcerting appearance of the noticeably Caucasian Henry Silva as the supposedly Asian valet Chunjin; it's that Harvey's natural British accent slips through in this sequence, punctuated by his pronunciation of the word "valet" as the very British-sounding "valette." It's a jarring but fleeting moment.)

In order to further her plans, Evelyn has decided that she wants her son to marry Jocelyn, the very "Communist tart" she had maligned two years earlier. Organizing a costume party to which she has invited the Jordans, Evelyn dresses as Little Bo Peep, with Johnny costumed as Abraham Lincoln. It is to Axelrod's credit that the Abraham Lincoln motif, which here is depicted in its most literal manifestation, has been carried out so seamlessly throughout the film. Whether Frankenheimer is filming a scene that begins with Iselin's image reflected in a picture of Lincoln, or allowing his camera to linger over Iselin's ludicrous Lincoln-esque costume at this costume party, he is following Axelrod's cleverly fleshed-out conceit stressing the contrast between a great president and a moronic yet dangerous aspirant to the office. It is a comment that never seems forced, because it is inserted with subtlety and is every bit as valid nearly fifty years after filming as it was when first shot. *Just take a look at what we have wrought,* say Axelrod and Frankenheimer. *We have all created a United States government now dominated by the Iselins of the world rather than the Lincolns, a world of politics dominated by soundbites pandering to the electorate's worst instincts, rather than thoughtful speeches.* Strong though the filmmakers' feelings may be, all is depicted without comment, the images thereby speaking all the more powerfully by themselves.

When Evelyn asks her son, "Raymond, why don't you pass the time by playing a little solitaire," the full extent of her evil is revealed—it is Evelyn who is behind the use of her own son as a brainwashed assassin. Bennett, with the assistance of an army psychiatrist, has figured out the use of the Queen of Diamonds as the control mechanism (in a nice touch of irony, Sinatra had the Queen of Diamonds imprinted on the bottom of his own swimming pool), but Evelyn is a step ahead: she shows Raymond the Queen of Diamonds so that he will comply with her plan to kill his soon-to-be father-in-law, Senator Jordan. As the pajama-clad senator gathers a midnight snack, the robotically approaching Raymond mechanically announces that he is going to kill the senator, whereupon he fires a bullet directly into the senator's chest, the bullet flying through the milk carton clutched to his torso, wholesome (mother's) milk flying everywhere like blood. Frankenheimer and Lindon cannily utilize stark lighting that emphasizes the emotional and physical remove of the characters, a stylistic decision that makes the ensuing coup de grâce even more startling. Carrying out the brainwashing suggestion that he shoot anyone who discovers him at the site of a killing, Raymond calmly murders the one person who has wandered into the scene of the crime—his own fiancée.

This assassination may be the most shocking event in the film but it is not the climax. Showing Raymond the Queen of Diamonds from a pack of playing cards, Bennett fans the cards out to reveal a full flush of Queens of Diamonds—telling Raymond, "It's over—the links are busted." Harvey is superb here, confessing his sins as his face twitches, never telegraphing the emotional distress but rather showing it in understated fashion. He is hesitant in his recall, sweating through the distress. It's a tough characterization to pull off without making the audience laugh, and Harvey succeeds admirably. Frankenheimer himself told an instructive story about the scene being filmed in one nigh-perfect take, discovering afterwards that Sinatra was out of focus, only his uniformed medals reading clearly onscreen. Sinatra agreed to refilm the scene, but after ten takes, Frankenheimer realized that none of the subsequent takes matched the power of Frank's first attempt. As a result, Frankenheimer utilized the first take, lack of focus and all. Upon release, critics actually granted the director kudos for supposedly presenting this sequence from the brainwashed Shaw's distorted point of view.

This is more than an amusing anecdote about lucky accidents in filming. Its importance lies in the fact that a first-rate director like Frankenheimer is flat-out stating one of the central truths about Sinatra the film actor: "It's important to know that Frank Sinatra was a man who really was better on the first take. It wasn't a question of the fact that he would only do one take, as rumor has it sometimes. He was just *better* on the first take." His most definitive scenes etched on film—the train and deprogramming sequences in *The Manchurian Candidate* and the withdrawal scene in *The Man with the Golden Arm*—all were achieved on the first take. Similarly, given the collaborative nature of film-making, it makes sense that Sinatra's very best performances were always achieved under the guidance of first-rank directors: John Frankenheimer, Otto Preminger, and in the case of *From Here to Eternity,* Fred Zinnemann. Yes, the absolute need for input from many sources on the film set only increased Sinatra's impatience, but like any good actor, he needed to collaborate with a fellow artist of the top rank in order to fully explore his own protean talent. When the team clicked, the end result was terrific. With lesser material, or when Sinatra bullied his way through, the resulting film was, oftentimes, a mess.

Here, however, the results were not only terrific from start to finish, but actually increased in effectiveness sequence by sequence, until genuine suspense permeates the entire film. When Evelyn calls her son, telling him "it's time," the full extent of her perfidy is revealed. Calmly informing Raymond that he must shoot the presidential nominee in the head, Lansbury underplays beautifully. She announces the heinous task with an emphasis that is all the more involving because of what she leaves out. She does not scream her life's ambition, but rather emphasizes it in a hushed delivery. It is only when she details the specifics of the plan, seeing the fruits of her fanatical dreams about to blossom, that her energy and volume increase:

> You are to shoot the presidential nominee through the head. And Johnny will rise gallantly to his feet and lift Ben Arthur's body in his arms. . . . I shall force someone to take the body away from him, and Johnny, facing the microphones and camera, blood all over him, fighting off anyone who tries to help him, defending America even if it means his own death, rallying a nation of television viewers into hysteria to sweep us into the White House with powers that will make martial law seem like anarchy.

It's not just the full sweep of Evelyn's mania that disturbs. It's the filmmakers' eerily prescient take on the power of television to distort presidential politics away from the issues. Evelyn's twisted vision centers around stagecraft, not substance: falling bodies and blood-smeared heroes all send a message of a fanatical determination to get "them." Forty-five years after the film was made, the message resonates even more strongly, a stark reminder of how the events of 9/11 were twisted in the run-up to war in Iraq.

Leaning ever closer to Raymond, insisting that she didn't know the Russians would make him the assassin, she goes on to insist that she now wants revenge against the Russians: "I served them, I fought for them, and they paid me back by taking your soul away from you . . . and when I take power, they will be pulled down and ground into dirt for what they did to you—and what they did in so contemptuously underestimating me." Whispering those words with a maternal fierceness, Lansbury kisses Harvey on the forehead, on the cheek, and then in a still-unsettling Oedipal display, directly on the mouth. She covers the gesture by slightly cupping her hand over their mouths so that the audience is never completely sure exactly what has happened. (The gesture was Frankenheimer's suggestion, according to Lansbury's illuminating interview on the DVD reissue of the film.) Evelyn now feels free to fiercely emphasize the words "when I take power." It's not when "we" take power and certainly not when "Johnny" takes power, but rather "I." Lansbury's characterization is all the more chilling for her refusal to scream the word "I." In her delivery, less is more—much more.

As Frankenheimer's unceasing close-up on the scene continues, Lansbury delivers such a finely calibrated depiction of evil, political fanaticism, and deranged motherhood that she succeeds in completely unsettling the audience. It's so beautifully realized that even Meryl Streep's portrayal of the mother in the 2004 remake can't compare in effectiveness to Lansbury's depiction of maternal evil. In her matronly clothing and lacquered upswept hairdo, Lansbury effortlessly convinces the audience that she is portraying Laurence Harvey's mother, even though the two actors were separated by only three years in age. There is no use of old-age makeup or jowls; instead, in her own words, "it all had to do with the way I carried myself—my demeanor." As to her own take on the film, and its place in her extraordinary sixty-year career, Lansbury stated in 2007, "This is the film I want to be remembered for." That she will be.

As Bennett frantically races to stop Raymond from assassinating the presidential nominee, Frankenheimer, with the help of editor Ferris Webster, propels the action forward with successive rapid cuts between the cheering crowd and Marco's desperate race to stop Raymond at the Madison Square Garden rally. Such cuts not only quicken the pace of the film, but they also serve as an interesting forerunner of the MTV-type editing that forever changed the pace of filmmaking in the 1980s. (Indeed Webster's quick cutting technique, along with the then very new overlapping style of dialogue, is so cannily employed that it helps to overcome the few plot inconsistencies in the film.)

Marco is not in time to stop Raymond, who shoots not the candidate, but both Senator Iselin and his own mother, all the while wearing his Congressional Medal of Honor. Ultimately rejecting the phony medal around his neck, Shaw turns the gun on himself. This ending represents one all-important change from Condon's novel; rather than have Marco order Shaw to assassinate his mother and stepfather, Marco here thinks he has successfully deprogrammed Shaw: "They can't touch you anymore. You're free." As a result, when Shaw does, in fact, assassinate his mother and stepfather, it is Shaw's decision, and his alone, a fact that makes the assassination all the more chilling and his film-ending suicide an eerily logical conclusion.

It's a bleak and utterly uncompromising ending to the film, leading to a fade-out where Frankenheimer's camera closes in on Sinatra's face as Major Marco delivers a "tribute" to Raymond Shaw, with the ironic final words of the film: "Made to commit acts too unspeakable to be cited here, by an enemy that had captured his mind and his soul. He freed himself at last—and in the end heroically and unhesitatingly gave his life to save his country." In a concluding image every bit as fitting and memorable as Brando's final whisper of "the horror . . . the horror" in *Apocalypse Now,* an entirely dismayed Marco utters at the last an exhausted, "Hell . . . Hell," standing before a rain-splattered window as thunder—or is it a gunshot?—crashes in the background.

Response to the film from major critics was highly favorable, with the majority downright effusive in their praise. The overall consensus was neatly summed up in Anby's review in *Variety:* "Every once in a rare while a film comes along that 'works' in all departments, with story, production and performance so well blended that the end effect is one of nearly complete satisfaction. Such is *The Manchurian Candidate.*" As for Sinatra himself, the prevailing response was captured by *The New Yorker,* which raved, "The acting is all of a high order, and Sinatra, in his usual uncanny fashion, is simply terrific."

Twenty-five years later, Sinatra may have simply stated, "We just set out to do Dick Condon's book," but all involved certainly accomplished much more than that. In the process of creating a taut top-notch thriller that spoke to cold war paranoia, the threat of Communism, and media intrusion into presidential politics, the filmmakers succeeded in creating a disturbing, compelling look at the state of modern America. As Angela Lansbury herself later said, "I thought this might be something extraordinary—and it was." Acknowledging that she "knew Frank wasn't the easiest person for John to work with," Lansbury added, "He knew what a tremendous opportunity it was." Artful as ever, Sinatra rose to the challenge beautifully and himself put it accurately: "I remember a wonderful enthusiasm on the part of everyone involved in the film. . . . It was a wonderful, wonderful experience—it only happens once in a performer's life." Following his own acting mantra to listen intently and react spontaneously, Sinatra is completely convincing in delineating all the different aspects of Marco's character—Korean War GI, brainwashing victim, and army loner alike. By turns cynical and resentful, yet never quite extinguishing the last flickers of his patriotic hope, Sinatra's Bennett Marco stands as a perfectly wrought example of the disillusioned modern American male in post–World War II twentieth-century America.

So powerful is *The Manchurian Candidate* that in the forty-five years since the film's initial release, parallels to the assassination of President John F. Kennedy still unavoidably spring to audience minds. Popular myth has it that

The Manchurian Candidate disappeared from all public view following JFK's assassination because the similarities between the film and events in Dallas, Texas, proved too painful for Sinatra. There is truth in this reading, and it certainly plays into the mythology of both Sinatra and JFK, but the additional theory, one publicly acknowledged by Frank, makes even more sense: the usually very sharp businessman Sinatra actually did not know that he owned the film. Sinatra, who bought up the rights to the film in 1972, actually forgot he controlled those rights, a fact that delayed the film's rerelease until 1986. "I didn't know we owned the rights. Whoever was working for me apparently made a pretty good deal." When the film came back into circulation with that successful rerelease in theaters, it garnered a fresh set of rave reviews, a brand-new audience, and further acclaim as a masterpiece ahead of its time.

After the total triumph of *The Manchurian Candidate,* Frank next tossed in a lighthearted cameo in director John Huston's 1963 film *The List of Adrian Messenger.* This is certainly the best of the numerous films to which Sinatra contributed cameos, and more to the point, the myriad star cameo appearances contained therein carry none of the self-congratulatory air that mars those in films such as *Around the World in Eighty Days.*

Interestingly enough, the opening credits of the film list the various guest stars (Robert Mitchum, Tony Curtis, Burt Lancaster, Frank Sinatra) first, ahead of the nominal stars of the film—George C. Scott and Kirk Douglas. In reality, however, the true star of the film is makeup artist Bud Westmore (with assistance from John Chambers, David Grayson, and Nick Marcellino), who created the elaborate disguises for all the actors. Without his first-rate work, the entire charade would have fallen apart, with audiences easily guessing the identity of the star in question. Even forty years later, Westmore's work stands out, only Kirk Douglas's identity easily discernible (which was the filmmakers' intention).

It is evident fairly early on that George Brougham (Douglas) is the villain of the piece, but this film is not so much a whodunit as a whydunit. The fun lies in following retired British intelligence agent and friend of the aristocracy Anthony Gethryn (George C. Scott) as he puzzles out why his friend, well-known writer Adrian Messenger (John Merivale), gave him a list of twelve names right before boarding a flight that explodes in midair. After it turns out that nearly all the names on the list have died in suspicious "accidents," the question of who is behind the deaths and—more to the point—why, is what underlies Gethryn's quest to solve the puzzle.

Beginning with the extraordinary first six minutes of the film, wherein not one word of dialogue is spoken, Huston is in terrific form throughout. Appropriately enough for any film of suspense, the emphasis is on the visual, the forbidding atmosphere heightened through the use of fog, acute camera angles, and insistent crosscutting between shots of Brougham in various disguises (vicar, shuffling old man in a waterside dive) and his latest method of murder (elevator plunging without a safety cord, a bomb stuffed into a suitcase). What makes the guest-star gimmick work is the fact that Huston takes great pains to make sure his superstar bit players disguise not only their faces, but their voices and body language as well. Sinatra, in fact, is totally unrecognizable in his role as a gypsy, sporting an earring, battered hat, thick eyebrows, curly hair, and a gap in his teeth. Fog swirls about him as he intones, "I want to see the young lord," the famous Sinatra voice totally unrecognizable. He seems evil, but ultimately proves benign, delivering a horse to the marquis's young heir Derek (played by director Huston's son Tony) before drifting away into the fog.

In fact, Sinatra is unrecognizable for the simple reason that it has been widely reported that he, like his fellow cameo actors, didn't actually film his sequence, instead appearing only in the film-ending credit roll wherein the guest stars rip off their face masks to reveal their identities. According to Jan Merlin, Dave Willock, an actor with a facial structure remarkably similar to Sinatra's, filmed the horse-trading sequence; it's a terrific doubling, because the two men really do appear to be one and the same, right down to height and overall physical appearance. When, during the end credits, the cameo identities are revealed, Sinatra tears off his mask, grins at the camera—not a self-satisfied grin, but that of an actor who has had some fun—and walks into the sunset seventy-five thousand dollars richer. Nice work if you can get it.

What was most noteworthy about Sinatra's film oeuvre by 1963 was how many top directors he had worked with: Stanley Donen, Gene Kelly, Frank Capra, Lewis Milestone, Charles Vidor, Otto Preminger, Fred Zinnemann, Vincente Minnelli, John Frankenheimer, and now John Huston. In fact, although Sinatra was to film thirteen more movies and three cameo roles after *Adrian Messenger,* Huston was the last top-tier director he worked with.

Very few other actors had worked so consistently with so many top directors, and certainly no other musical stars had been afforded the opportunity. It says everything about Sinatra's talent, and the best directors' acknowledgment thereof (not to mention Sinatra's power and box office standing) that he worked with so many extraordinary directors, and almost always in nonmusical roles.

Frank followed up the enjoyable *Adrian Messenger* with a rather formulaic comedy, Neil Simon's *Come Blow Your Horn*. Released only one month after *Adrian Messenger,* it is not so bad a film as its reputation would lead one to believe, but neither does it make any real use of Sinatra's talents. It's best understood as the third in his trio of swinging bachelor comedies, and while not so good as *A Hole in the Head,* it is still a decided improvement upon *The Tender Trap.*

Sinatra was now at the height of his swinging-singles persona, as the inside humor of the somewhat smarmy trailer for the film shows. Appearing as himself, Frank speaks with a series of moviegoers who are presented as having seen and loved the movie. First up is a surgeon who found the film so funny that he laughs uncontrollably while hard at work, and botches an operation just thinking about the film. Next up is a mother-to-be who has found the film uproarious. Smirks Sinatra to the camera, "Take it from me—all you mothers are going to enjoy *Come Blow Your Horn.*" The audience sees a pregnant woman, but Frank's smirk tells us that when he says "mothers," he's leaving off an additional seven letters. Even worse, when a ditsy woman talks about how she and her parakeet (that's right, parakeet) both loved the movie, he grins and says, "If your bird needs cheering up, take him to see *Come Blow Your Horn.*" In Sinatra parlance, a bird referred to a man's penis. It's just the sort of humor that led to the flop of his television series and characterized the Rat Pack films at their worst—all but shouting to the audience, *Who cares if you like the film? You may not be hip enough to appreciate all the inside humor, but we don't care—we had a good time.* The capper to a decidedly unfunny parade of testimonials comes when a husband and wife disagree over whether the film is funny, and when the wife says no, the husband hauls off and smacks her across the face. Says a grinning Frank, "If you don't want to laugh, *Come Blow Your Horn* is a slap in the face." That isn't funny—it's just dumb.

As to the film itself, *Come Blow Your Horn* feels and plays exactly like what it was—the very first of Neil Simon's smash-hit Broadway comedies. Here produced by Tandem Productions (Bud Yorkin and Normal Lear) and Sinatra's Essex Productions, it's a boulevard confection that satisfied Broadway audiences in the early 1960s with its semiautobiographical tale of two brothers and their attempts to escape their domineering father. Throw in a put-upon Jewish mother (Molly Picon) plus some atmospheric shots of New York City at its most glamorous, and the stage is set for a lighthearted romp. And in that phrase lies the problem—the *stage* is set, with all its attendant artificiality.

After some effective opening credits featuring the now-familiar images of a grinning Frank Sinatra sporting a rakishly tilted fedora and a coat slung over his shoulder, *Come Blow Your Horn* never really escapes its stage setting. The proscenium arch oftentimes feels present in a way that the successful filmings of such Simon comedies as *The Odd Couple* and *Biloxi Blues* managed to avoid. The first half of the film in particular isn't bad, but bits of business that would have worked onstage are telegraphed when displayed in close-up on screen. The film is loaded with top-notch talent—William Daniels served as director of photography, Nelson Riddle wrote the music and Norman Lear the screenplay—but the resulting film feels misshapen, beginning with the casting itself.

It's not just that the source material has a particularly Jewish flavor to it; it's that Lee J. Cobb and Molly Picon, as the parents of brothers Buddy (Tony Bill) and Alan (Sinatra) Baker, are so quintessentially Jewish in their inflections and gestures that it comes as something of a shock to be told that the decidedly non-Yiddish-inflected Sinatra is their son. It's the exact same problem that undermined *A Hole in the Head,* right down to another father figure endlessly calling Sinatra a bum, but *A Hole in the Head* did have the saving grace of direction by Frank Capra. In this picture, Sinatra appears to have wandered in from another family entirely, as does the overeager Tony Bill (who does, however, bear a startling resemblance to the youthful Frank Sinatra Jr.).

Opening at the Baker family home in Yonkers, the film quickly establishes its early-1960s time period, with overly protective, self-martyring Molly Picon muttering, "Khrushchev should have such a backache." Younger son Buddy is sneaking away from the family home and his father's stultifying artificial-fruit business in order to make his way to his swinging bachelor brother's glamorous apartment in New York City. Sinatra, first glimpsed in trademark orange (ski parka) ten minutes into the movie, looks great—in peak condition, actually—but he appears more like Buddy's father than like his brother. The age gap proves so noticeable that the screenplay takes great pains to explain that Alan is eighteen years older than Buddy, and one groovy guy to boot. Various characters unfortunately spew "hip" dialogue—Sinatra dubs a situation "crazy" while ditsy girlfriend Peggy John (Jill St. John) states, "This apartment—every time I see it, it just sends me." The finishing touches are added when Alan puts on a Frank Sinatra record (the Reprise label purposely visible) and Buddy, in his bid for sophistication, sports that ultimate symbol of swinging bachelorhood, an orange alpaca cardigan. "Crazy," indeed.

Audiences do find some interest inherent in watching Alan trying to escape his father's domineering ways, and one is mildly given to rooting him on. The reason this does not register as more consistent fun lies in the performances. Cobb, a brilliant actor in the right role—the original Willy Loman in *Death of a Salesman*—overdoes the father's heavy-handed methods, literally screaming his way through the film. Cobb wears an audience down instead of making it chuckle, and his methods are as ill-conceived as Tony Bill's goofily overeager performance. *Come Blow Your Horn* represented Bill's first major film role, and it shows. Overdoing the naïve rube persona by half, he all but says "golly gee whiz" with his every utterance. Compare Bill's performance here with Sinatra's own similar characters in *Higher and Higher* and *Anchors Aweigh,* and you see the difference between a midlevel actor and a skilled one with star presence. Bill did act in two further films with Sinatra, *None But the Brave* and *Marriage on the Rocks,* but his acting career never really took off, and he fared much better as director of a little gem of a movie, *My Bodyguard.*

The plot of *Come Blow Your Horn* turns around Sinatra's difficulties in choosing among the three women in his life: nice girl Connie (Barbara Rush), airhead Peggy (Jill St. John), and voluptuous siren Mrs. Eckman (Phyllis McGuire). From the get-go, it's no contest at all, which makes the entire plot play in rather perfunctory fashion. Jill St. John's character is a dimwit, and Mrs. Eckman (no first name provided, which gives one an idea of the depth of characterization) turns out to be married. By the process of elimination, that leaves only Connie, and while Barbara Rush isn't given much of a character (no last name here either), she does underplay nicely. It's a cardboard setup, but in the early going, there is pep to the action, and the audience receives a sense of Alan's joie de vivre—no wonder he seldom shows up for work at his father's wax-fruit factory.

When Buddy asks older brother Alan, "What am I supposed to do?" and Alan answers, "Grow up—take a bite out of the real fruit of life," the movie speeds into Sinatra's rendition of the title song (written by Sammy Cahn and Jimmy Van Heusen). It's a fun moment with Sinatra singing the catchy tune while striding down a busy Manhattan boulevard, buying his younger brother new clothes and all the while hopping in and out of cabs stalled in traffic. This one musical interlude provides an interesting convergence of character requirements with Sinatra's swinging real-life persona, and it's a great moment, gleefully showcasing the charms of a man who could sing "The Best Is Yet to Come" and make an entire nation not only believe in those sentiments, but want to join in the fun as well.

Finishing the song in the middle of bumper-to-bumper Manhattan traffic, Frank has provided the audience with such a terrific few minutes that one doesn't even care that if he tried the cab-hopping routine in real life, a New York City cabbie would have told him to get the hell out of the way—or run him over. In that brief sequence, Sinatra delivers like any real star: he makes you think of possibilities, about the excitement of life at its best, especially in the glamorous Oz-like setting of Manhattan. Good thing the sequence works so beautifully, because Frank was willing to shoot it only once. In an anecdote that speaks volumes about Sinatra's on-set impatience, director Yorkin detailed Frank's growing frustration as William Daniels painstakingly lit the Madison Avenue location. When the fidgety Sinatra finally received the go-ahead, an earpiece feeding him the music to which he would lip-synch, he strode down the street, "walked the block, stepped off the curb, flagged the first taxi that came along—and was gone for the day. We didn't know whether we had it or not. We had one crack and that was it." Whew—that's pressure on a director—big-time. Well, in Sinatra's view, it wasn't just that the first take was his best—performing more than one take was "like singing a song twice for the same audience." In other words, *it ain't gonna happen.*

Unfortunately nothing else in the film measures up to that sequence, and it's straight downhill from there. Alan induces Buddy to impersonate McIntosh, a supposed Hollywood producer, in order to keep Peggy occupied while he romances his other women; this all helps turn the heretofore mildly enjoyable film into a cartoon, wherein Peggy's sexual encounter with Buddy is symbolized by a loud explosion from the Western film on television as their feet—in close-up—fall limply to the side.

The caricatures continue with the arrival of Mrs. Eckman's husband, the towering and bull-like Dan Blocker, who proceeds to punch Alan in the face and destroy a waxed-fruit sampler right in front of father Harry. Alan has been romancing Mrs. Eckman because she controls the Neiman Marcus waxed-fruit account. (See, it sounds dopey even in outline.) Given the film's markedly casual attitude toward Alan's romancing of a married woman, the audience is left scratching its head at just what the heck his character is all about. Gee, one wonders, maybe Alan shouldn't have taken up with a married woman, especially since there are two other attractive women readily available, but any such logical query is stomped underfoot right along with the wax-fruit display. The screenplay by Norman Lear is so casual in execution that once Mr. Eckman beats up Alan, both Eckmans simply disappear from the film. It's all so lackadaisical that even at that climactic moment, Phyllis McGuire's Mrs. Eckman is deprived of a first name—she's just Mrs. Eckman. (McGuire, lead singer of the then-very-popular singing McGuire Sisters, was a onetime girlfriend of Sinatra's, and the subject of much conjecture through the years due to her long-term liaison with Sam Giancana. She was a genuinely pretty and talented woman, but the film does her no favors, pushing her front and center complete with lacquered appearance and camera angles that make her appear Amazonian in stature.)

Completing the Sinatra in-crowd aspect of the film was an uncredited cameo by Dean Martin as a drunken panhandler. Martin's appearance doesn't serve the plot and just reads as an example of the boys cutting up onscreen, a silly in-joke that leaves the audience out in the cold. Martin's appearance also destroys any remaining credibility in the film, with Dino addressing the camera directly with a whiny, "Why didn't I tell him the truth?" Well, the audience asks, who the hell are you, and why are you showing up now?

With the passage of three months, Buddy and Alan begin to reverse roles, with Buddy becoming the swinger and Alan morphing into a stay-at-home conformist. Alan doesn't like the man Buddy has become: "I won't have my kid brother carrying on like this—like a bum." The heavy-handed echo of Lee J. Cobb calling his two sons bums is worth noting for exactly one reason. It helps to reinforce the film's prevailing message, and that of most Hollywood films at the time: If you defy the prevailing norms and don't settle down with one "good" woman, in this case Barbara Rush, then you are doomed to unhappiness and life as a no-goodnik. It's a philosophy remarkably at odds with the first half of the movie, because all the sense of fun in the film, all the excitement, comes from Alan's carefree existence and glamorous New York lifestyle. According to the screenplay, however, in the end, you can take only a small bite out of life; you better blow your horn only in a very muted manner, or else you, too, will end up a bum. It's a worldview that would disappear almost completely from Hollywood studio films in five years' time, when the social upheavals of the 1960s ensured that audiences would no longer settle for such spoon-fed bromides.

The entire movie washes over the audience, making absolutely no impact. Sinatra is fine, but he can play this role with one hand tied behind his back, and although the critical response was rather mixed, Bosley Crowther in *The New York Times* weighed in with a pan that found the film induced "a feeling of vapid boredom," with Sinatra himself appearing "so indifferent and coolly self-satisfied that he moves and talks in the manner of a well greased mechanical man." Ouch. Many other critics liked both film and star, however, and even the *Los Angeles Times* found that "Frankie tries harder this time not just to do his usual walk-through, and in general succeeds." The film proved popular with audiences, and for his troubles, Frank received a Golden Globe Award nomination as Best Actor in a Comedy or Musical. Go figure.

Frank's next offering, the self-indulgent and sophomoric *4 for Texas* wouldn't deliver nominations to Frank or anyone else involved. This grade-Z Western felt doubly disappointing following so closely upon Frank's extraordinary performance in *The Manchurian Candidate*. The larger problem lay in the fact that even bigger wastes of his talent were to come. Quickly.

Representing Sinatra's third release of 1963, *4 for Texas* continued the Rat Pack movie gimmick of including a number in the title—there's no real point to it, but motif established, the trick continued even longer with the forthcoming *Robin and the 7 Hoods*. Released on Christmas Day of 1963, *4 for Texas* was not much of a present for the holiday season, but remains worth examining because of the insight it gives into how much fun the Rat Pack movies could have been if more care had been exercised by all involved. The first twenty minutes of the film are so thoroughly enjoyable and so successfully executed on all counts that an audience member becomes downright irritated with the subpar remainder of the film and at the waste of first-class talent it represents.

4 for Texas is very much a Robert Aldrich film, Aldrich here functioning as director, producer, and coauthor of the screenplay (with Teddi Sherman). A topnotch director of action movies (*The Dirty Dozen*), noir (the sensational *Kiss Me Deadly*), and even gothic horror films (*What Ever Happened to Baby Jane?*), Aldrich recruited Ernest Laszlo (who had helmed *Kiss Me Deadly*) as director of photography, only to replace Laszlo with favored Sinatra lenser Joseph Biroc when Laszlo's time-consuming setups proved anathema to both Aldrich and Sinatra. Well, this time around, Laszlo didn't need to painstakingly stylize his lighting. He wasn't lighting a film where the characters were losing their moral bearings as they did in noir. He was lighting a film where the nitwits onscreen possessed no bearings at all. Considering the finished product, Laszlo was the lucky one.

All hands involved must have started out with the best of intentions, however, because the movie opens in so rousing and entertaining a slam-bang fashion that the viewer has to ask himself, Why couldn't the rest of the film be that good? The very first shot features a close-up of the menacing-looking Charles Bronson (playing the homicidal Matson), with Dean Martin (Joe Jarrett) narrating the action as the screen opens up to a panoramic view of the Western landscape. Matson ambushes Jarrett's stagecoach as Jarrett attempts to defend the coach from inside the vehicle, at the same time his buddy Zack Thomas (Sinatra) fires at Matson's gang from his position on top of the coach. It is only when the stagecoach crashes in spectacular fashion that the opening credits flash onscreen, by which time, the viewer is hooked. It's a terrific opener, which only gets better once Zack escapes the wreckage and nonchalantly helps himself to the hundred thousand dollars being carried on the stagecoach. Helps himself, that is, until his friend Jarrett pulls a gun on him and demands the money.

Sinatra and Martin are great together here—there is no clowning, yet they are effortlessly charming. Even the dialogue is utterly appropriate, with Jarrett laconically describing another stagecoach passenger's fate with a simple, "He took dead." The two stars then engage in a first-rate battle of wits, with Jarrett holding a gun on Thomas while demanding the money. Thomas's response is an ever-widening grin—and in Sinatra's hands, or rather face, it's a full-fledged star's grin—a response that serves only to heighten audience involvement. For once, the question, What the hell is going on here? is being asked out of curiosity, not annoyance.

As Jarrett rides away, Thomas, discovering a rifle right near the money, takes his own sweet time exacting revenge. Slowly walking to pick up the rifle, leisurely setting himself in place, he then casually shoots the rapidly retreating Jarrett. Jarrett's horse buckles beneath him, leaving Jarrett with two choices: return and hand over the money—or be killed. It's a great opening because surprise is layered upon surprise. Even here Jarrett startles by pulling a pistol from his hat and retaking the money. The actors seem to be having a great time, and even the obligatory in-joke doesn't grate. (In a nod to daughter Nancy's top-of-the-charts single, Sinatra looks at Jarrett's feet and exclaims, "They tell me those boots ain't built for walkin'.") The byplay between Sinatra and Martin appears to reference and represent a more overtly comic version of Aldrich's own *Vera Cruz,* with its Burt Lancaster–Gary Cooper film-opening stand-off, but it doesn't matter. It's a shot of adrenaline right out of the gate, with credit due to all involved.

And that's about it for the good news, because the very next sequence finds Jarrett returning to an orphanage that looks like nothing so much as Tara in *Gone with the Wind.* Who knew orphanages in the American West of the 1870s resembled five-star hotels? Turns out Jarrett was raised in the orphanage, and became a lawyer (!) before he "drifted to the wrong side of the law." Five-star orphanage or not, whenever the film ventures indoors, it completely unravels. Plop Zack inside with girlfriend Elya (a zaftig and remarkably bored-looking Anita Ekberg), and the film starts to play like nothing so much as an episode of the television Western *The Wild Wild West,* a takeoff on James Bond films set in the nineteenth century. The slavishly devoted Elya, aided and abetted by her French maid and manicurist Fifi (who appears to have attended the same French high school as Frank did in *Can-Can*), barely manages to shave Zack in between her constant changing of clothes. Between the nail filing and shaving, all of a sudden Zack Thomas appears to be a twentieth-century metrosexual instead of the convincing outdoorsman of the film's beginning.

There's no consistency in tone, and in the confusing screenplay, it's hard to tell if Zack and Jarrett are good or bad. With the tone careening wildly between all-out action, slapstick humor, and love story, the audience isn't hooked, just bored. Aldrich presumably intended all this as a Western spoof, but the spoof doesn't work, and the Western vitality quickly seeps out of the film.

Just as Zack has a blond, well-endowed girlfriend (Ekberg), so, too, does Jarrett acquire a bosomy blond girlfriend (Maxine, played by a remarkably beautiful Ursula Andress). After the care established in the film's opening sequence, all of a sudden Dean Martin is in a smoking jacket, kissing Max like

Four for Texas. *The worst of the Rat Pack films. Anita Ekberg, Frank, Dean Martin,
and Ursula Andress in nineteenth-century Texas by way of 1963 Las Vegas.*

it's the prequel to a Matt Helm film, and she's ironing his shirts—right after
trying to shoot him with her rifle. It makes about as much sense as the fact
that in the middle of nineteenth-century Galveston, Texas, all the women appear to speak with either Swiss or Swedish accents (or in Fifi's case, a French-
flavored version of Jersey-ese). Once one hears Maxine utter the words, "A
man as a partner I don't understand, but as a master—him I know how to
handle," one can only wonder, Where are we? Texas in 1873? Las Vegas in
1963? Ancient Rome? (The sexist atmosphere only becomes worse when Jarrett's idea of a compliment appears to be telling Maxine, "You've got
brains—you're just like a man.")

It's all so ineptly staged that the most interesting question soon becomes
which of the two women—Andress or Ekberg—can show more cleavage, and
it's a fight to the finish. Jane Russell herself had nothing on these two in *The
Outlaw*—except for the fact that Russell had an intriguing sense of humor
about herself that nicely complemented her surprisingly versatile range. It has
absolutely nothing to do with Galveston in the nineteenth century, but it's the
one and only feature likely to hold audience interest. (The sexiest part of the
film actually came with the trailer, when Andress, in disheveled cowgirl attire,

rises from a bed and says, "Howdy, partner—call me Tex," in a downright erotic fashion never remotely equaled in the film itself.)

The film has now become so discombobulated that it doesn't even surprise the audience to see the Sinatra favorite, the Three Stooges, show up dockside as the renovations to *La Maison Rouge,* riverboat-cum-gambling-hall, are being finished. The Stooges smack each other, are belted themselves by Ellen Corby, and serve only to jolt the audience into yet another universe, that of lamebrain physical comedy. There is enough blame for all to share in this spectacular waste of talent, but certainly Aldrich bears the lion's share of responsibility in his multiple roles as director, producer, and co-screenwriter. He must have known what an unfocused mess the film was turning into, and reports of his difficulties with Sinatra certainly couldn't have helped matters during filming. (So intense were the arguments that executive producer Howard Koch actually spoke of them at Aldrich's memorial service—reports of such conflicts not normally constituting standard fare for eulogies.)

The film represents such a mishmash of styles that after the Three Stooges cut loose, the only thing missing is a Broadway-style production number, which is exactly what one expects from the bird's-eye shot of the riverboat waiters right before *La Maison Rouge* opens. Since Maxine is dolled up in a sparkling red dress, surrounded by waiters, and the boat itself contains a centrally located large staircase ringed by musicians, it all looks so reminiscent of a certain Broadway musical that one expects Ursula to let loose with a Swiss-accented rendition of "Hello, Dolly!" She might as well have, because as the guests promenade down the staircase just like Dolly herself, television personality Arthur Godfrey appears in period clothes, only to be followed by a close-up of a quizzical-looking Dino saying in voiceover, "That's right—Arthur Godfrey." *What's* right? Are these guys as clueless as they appear? After all the nonsense, the film climaxes with a full-scale brawl, pitting Zack and Jarrett against Matson. Hundreds of men fight each other, but somehow no one besides Matson has a gun. What the hell kind of Wild West is this?

At film's fade-out, Zack and Jarrett marry Elya and Maxine, and a wedding tableau is presented with both women modeling wedding-day outfits that appear to be taken from a Dior fashion show of 1963. It's all crazy and nonrealistic in a slipshod kind of way, a visual sloppiness matched perfectly by Dino's silly final voiceover: "If it don't work out, Zack and me, we can always light out—and, oh yeah—this is the end." And not a moment too soon. The film was cut by nearly ten minutes after its premiere, but such editing could not help—it was so sloppy that it performed the extraordinary feat of making *Sergeants 3* look successful by comparison. Sadly, the film puts the lie to Sinatra's statement in his *Playboy* magazine interview that "you can be the most artistically perfect performer in the world, but an audience is like a broad—if you're indifferent, endsville. That goes for any kind of human contact: a politician on television, an actor in the movies. . . ." Sinatra himself is the personification of indifference here, and the critics quickly informed an in-agreement public that the movie was not worth anyone's time—star's, critic's, or audience's. In a rather revealing *Time* magazine review, it was referred to as

> one of those pictures that are known in Hollywood as Clanbakes . . . Unfortunately they are not much fun to see. . . . What's mainly wrong with *Texas,* though, is what's wrong with all Clan pictures: the attitude of the people on the screen. They constitute an in-group and they seem bored with the outside world. Sometimes, perish the thought, they even are obviously bored with each other. . . . They appear less concerned to entertain the public than to indulge their private fantasies. Maybe they ought to call their next picture 30.

Harsh—and unfortunately quite accurate.

Shortly after the release of *4 for Texas,* Frank sold Reprise Records to Warner Bros, remaining with the label as a recording artist while concurrently signing a three-picture deal with Warner Bros. Films. The evolution of Sinatra's recording career was now complete: starting with RCA Records, he had segued to Columbia, moved to Capitol for his unsurpassed series of concept albums in the 1950s, and started his own Reprise label. Having built the label into a recording industry powerhouse, he finally sold the company for an estimated price of $80 million. The significance of the sale lies in the fact that it afforded Sinatra, in the words of daughter Nancy, "big money, real security for the rest of his life."

To put it in the parlance of his native Hoboken, Frank finally possessed genuine "fuck you" money. Not only had he reaped millions from the sale of his record company, but his new three-picture deal guaranteed him $250,000 per film plus 15 percent of the gross, figures making him amongst the highest paid, if not the highest paid, of actors in Hollywood. *4 for Texas* already completed, the upcoming *Robin and the 7 Hoods* concluded Sinatra's old deal with Warners, with the new three-film contract set to begin with the self-directed *None But the Brave*. Sinatra's position at Warners was now so strong that "it was thought for a while that he might take over as head of the studio when Jack Warner retired." That executive position never came to pass, and wisely so, for Sinatra would never have had the patience to run a major Hollywood studio and deal with all the attendant problems, large and small, let alone do so while concentrating on his own film and recording careers.

Instead of running a studio, Sinatra diversified his portfolio, establishing enterprises ranging from music publishing companies and ownership of radio stations to extensive real estate investments, most notably a partial owner's stake in both the Sands Hotel and the Cal-Neva Lodge. By 1965, the list of business enterprises also included his film production companies of Artanis Productions (Sinatra spelled backwards) and Park Lake Enterprises, the Cal Jet Airway charter plane business, and Titanium Metal, a business providing parts for planes and missiles. Sinatra took an active part in overseeing his business empire, and although by necessity employed lieutenants to carry out the day-to-day work of running the businesses, the final word was always his, with Frank himself signing off on all major decisions.

It was the Cal-Neva hotel ownership that now caused extensive negative press coverage for Sinatra and ratcheted up the rumors of mob connections to an unprecedented degree. In order to reopen the summer vacation spot of Cal-Neva, a Lake Tahoe hotel that featured entertainment and gambling along with outdoor sports, Frank had begun a partnership with Sanford Waterman and his own right-hand man Hank Sanicola (at the same time he also increased his share in the Las Vegas Sands Hotel to 9 percent). Having established himself as a major player in the worlds of hotel and casino ownership, Frank quickly found that position turning into an albatross around his neck when the Nevada State Gaming Board learned that Sam Giancana had been seen at Cal-Neva with Phyllis McGuire. (A Nevada State Gaming Control Board document, filed in 1963, stated, "Giancana sojourned at the Cal-Neva Lodge at various times between July 17 and July 28, 1963, with the knowledge and consent of the licensee [Sinatra].") With strict gaming commission laws forbidding any fraternization with known or suspected underworld figures, Sinatra soon found himself summoned to a hearing, a request that put his gambling license on the line. (As things turned sour for Sinatra, press reports surfaced that Sinatra had called Control Board Chairman Edward A. Olsen and utilized what Olsen, in his eight-page complaint against Sinatra, characterized as "'vile, intemperate, base and indecent' language in an attempt to bribe him.") When Jack Warner learned of the hearing, he asked longtime Sinatra attorney Mickey Rudin to have Frank attend the hearing, Warner himself being concerned that Frank's new deal to make three films and maintain office space on the lot could suffer from adverse publicity regarding organized crime.

Sinatra, who admitted seeing Giancana at Cal-Neva, maintained that Giancana had not been invited; an opposite viewpoint was put forth by Antoinette Giancana in her 1984 autobiography, wherein she relates that her father had in fact told her that he and Frank "had an interest in the casino together." (Although Frank was to publicly state that he had only known Giancana since early 1960, Antoinette denies that claim, citing a friendship that stretched back years earlier.) Antoinette has no supporting evidence for such claims—it is just her recall of events—but she does repeatedly cite social meetings between Sinatra and Giancana that occurred over more than a decade.

Rather than face the avalanche of innuendo and negative press that would have resulted from such a hearing, Sinatra turned in his license. According to daughter Nancy, an additional reason for his sale of ownership lay in the fact that Frank "would not allow his self interests to hurt John Kennedy." Nancy may have been her father's biggest cheerleader, but she was so tuned in to his psyche that her further analysis of the Cal-Neva problem rather perceptively sheds light on Sinatra's persona from that time forward:

> In my mind he never recovered from not being able to fight to save Cal-Neva—and his reputation. . . . In burying his desire to make this a fight to the finish . . . he buried a lot of anger. . . . Suddenly a new element was forced into his core—one with which he had great difficulty . . . it encouraged him to carry a grudge. It made him defensive . . . from this point on, general statements were made—Frank Sinatra versus the American press—instead of small separate disputes with individuals.

Finally, in 1965, Sinatra addressed the organized-crime rumors head-on in a rare extended television interview for CBS News. There was no discussion of the 1960 presidential campaign, the West Virginia primary activities not yet having come to light. Instead, having allowed a CBS crew to follow him over a period of six months, both in performance and on the road with family and friends, Sinatra then sat down with Walter Cronkite and, holding his temper in check, spoke about the mob rumors in a rather circuitous manner: "Then came the ridiculous accusations and statements that I was consorting with mobsters and gangsters, and that added fire to it after a while, and I just kept resenting it all the time, but I just couldn't stop it. . . ." Sinatra went on to discuss the controversy over his ownership of the Cal-Neva lodge:

The fact that I used to be involved was a legitimate business reason . . . Finally there was so much work to be done in my own natural vocation— pictures, singing, recording—that I just dropped all of the fringes of businesses. But I do meet all kinds of people in the world because of the natural habitat from day to day in theatrical work. . . . There's really not much to be said about that and I think the less said the better. There is no answer. . . . When I say no, it's no. But for some reason it keeps persisting, you see, and consequently I just said, I just refuse to discuss it because it can't make a dent anywhere.

Seemingly the last recorded instance of Sinatra's thoughts on mobsters in general, and Giancana in particular, came in a discussion he had with daughter Tina in the early 1990s. Proving the aptness of her autobiography's title— *My Father's Daughter*—Tina bluntly asked Frank how he could befriend a known murderer like Giancana. Frank's response in its entirety: "I never reacted beyond how he treated me. I wasn't unaware of what he was, and I didn't bring him to your first Communion, but he was always decent to me."

Nancy Jr.'s analysis that the Cal-Neva controversy caused Frank to bury his anger and reflexively nurse a grudge is remarkably consistent with Sinatra's loner mentality: he may have been the biggest star in the world, but he could never outrun the defensive posturing born of life in Hoboken. It's a chip-on-the-shoulder attitude that influenced his choice of film roles and the decision to basically retire from films after *Dirty Dingus Magee* received scathing reviews in 1970. Sinatra felt hurt and defensive after *Magee's* abysmal reception, and even after ending his short-lived 1971 retirement, took on only two further starring roles during the remaining twenty-five years of his life: the first a 1977 television movie titled *Contract on Cherry Street* and the second his final feature film, *The First Deadly Sin* (1980). After suffering critical abuse and nursing a grudge, it's as if Sinatra's attitude toward his film career and the critics evolved into a defensive stand of "Who needs this?" Well, Frank did, and so did the audience, but neither side fully understood that equation at the time.

Such virtual retirement lay one decade in the future, however. For now, Frank was to return onscreen six months after the release of *4 for Texas,* with an intermittently rewarding Rat Pack extravaganza, *Robin and the 7 Hoods*. When Sinatra, at the urging of studio head Jack Warner, decided to return to the land of movie musicals, it was in that increasingly rare species, the original movie musical. Representing Sinatra's final movie musical, *Robin and the 7 Hoods* did afford audiences the chance to at long last once again watch Frank cut loose onscreen musically. As farewells go, it wasn't half bad.

Sinatra originally intended to produce *Robin and the 7 Hoods* with his old musical pal Gene Kelly. This plan called for *Robin* to be followed by a second film in which Kelly would star with Sinatra, and a third that Kelly would direct. Sinatra himself was to act in all three films. Unfortunately for all involved, Kelly's participation in *Robin* and the subsequent films fell by the wayside, with Sinatra's old reluctance to rehearse undermining the pre-production work Kelly rightly knew was essential to achieving a successful musical. Gene and Frank's roles had reversed mightily since *On the Town,* and no matter how it was dressed up, Kelly was now, in effect, an employee of Sinatra's. Gene Kelly was an extraordinarily talented movie musical auteur—a singer, dancer, actor, director, and choreographer who revolutionized the genre. He would have demanded great effort from Sinatra, knowing how much his former costar was capable of delivering when inspired and tested. Even without Kelly's participation, *Robin and the 7 Hoods* still proves enjoyable, but it's not the film that it could have been. In Kelly's own words:

> [Frank] kept telling Howard Koch . . . that he'd be arriving the next
> day, then the day after that and so on, until I decided the tension and

the waiting wasn't doing any of us any good, and I told Jack Warner I was quitting. . . . I really loved [Frank] and that was the reason I was walking out because it was my intention to remain friendly with him, and if I stayed on, as a kind of paid laborer, our relationship would be over.

Kelly or not, what of the film itself? By no means a classic of the genre, it still entertains in fine fashion, and when looked at in the context of Sinatra's entire screen career, inspires one rather startling reaction on the viewer's part. By the time of its release in 1964, so thoroughly had Sinatra remade his screen image into that of a dramatic actor, that it is actually something of a shock to see him in a musical again. It's a testament to his all-encompassing talent that viewers had become more familiar, and more at ease, with Sinatra the dramatic actor than with the crooning sailor of *Anchors Aweigh*. That is one long journey onscreen, utterly remarkable in and of itself.

For all the talk of Sinatra and his gangland associations, *Robin and the 7 Hoods* casts Sinatra as a mobster for the first and only time in his film career. Significantly, he is here portraying a comic mobster, as if Frank himself is winking at all the rumors of Mafia involvement. Of equal interest along those lines is the fact that seven years later, when Paramount bought the film rights to Mario Puzo's novel *The Godfather*, Otto Preminger was slated to direct, and, it has been noted, had Sinatra in mind for the title role. *The Godfather* certainly would have made an interesting reunion for *The Man with the Golden Arm* director/star team, but Sinatra declined to participate. Preminger went so far as to state that he would excise the uncomfortably familiar character of Johnny Fontaine, the singing star whose Hollywood stardom is assured when his mob friends deposit a horse's head in the studio chief's bed, but Sinatra would not be budged. The part, of course, was famously played by Marlon Brando in his Oscar-winning comeback, the film ultimately directed by Francis Ford Coppola. And on the Sinatra/Brando rivalry went, into yet another decade. . . .

Frank Sinatra playing Don Corleone is a fascinating idea, but in hindsight the decision was the correct one: how could audiences ever have effectively separated actor from character, factoring in Sinatra's real-life persona and reputed connections, while simultaneously dealing with the Johnny Fontaine character and the parallels to Frank's own career? Sinatra's participation would have turned the film into a figurative hall of mirrors shootout, and all involved were better off without his participation. Adding complexity to the tale is the fact that when *The Godfather: Part III* was filmed in 1990, Coppola approached Sinatra about playing older mafioso Don Altobello, in what proved to be a supporting but substantial role. Frank, who was keenly aware of the Academy Award Best Film–winning credentials of the first two *Godfathers*, is said to have liked the script, but disliked the lengthy shooting schedule and declined. (According to a 1996 profile of Barbara Sinatra by Douglas Thompson, it was Barbara herself who talked Frank out of taking on the role, which if true, certainly points to Barbara's extreme sensitivity about her husband's image.) And who did play the part? Eli Wallach, Frank's rival for the role of Maggio in *From Here to Eternity.* Considering that *Part III* was not up to the standards of the first two *Godfather* films, it proved a wise decision on Frank's part.

As to *Robin and the 7 Hoods* (which was produced by Sinatra's own Park Lake Enterprises), the film served to once again team Sinatra with the men who had by now evolved into his most frequent film collaborators: director of photography and associate producer William H. Daniels, executive producer Howard W. Koch, musical director Nelson Riddle, and composer and lyricist James Van Heusen and Sammy Cahn. Frank might not have taken over the running of Warner Bros. studio, but by virtue of his status, he had now assembled what was, in effect, a traveling Sinatra film studio, working with talented collaborators who set up shop wherever the boss landed. On *Robin and the 7 Hoods,* Sinatra was also reunited with director Gordon Douglas, who had elicited a fine performance from him in 1954's *Young at Heart.* Douglas here does a more-than-credible job with the musical genre, and meshed so well with Sinatra that he went on to direct the star in his late-1960s trio of detective films: *The Detective, Tony Rome,* and *Lady in Cement.*

In the agreeably cartoonlike screenplay by David R. Schwartz, which updates the Robin Hood legend to Chicago in the 1920s, Sinatra plays gang leader Robbo, a hoodlum vying for control of Chicago with rival mobster Guy Gisborne (a young Peter Falk). Sinatra appears to be having a good time onscreen, perhaps feeling lightened by the return to his musical roots. After some flashy opening titles, with machine gun bullets spelling out all the names, the film opens with the birthday celebration—and subsequent shooting death—of mob boss Big Jim (Edward G. Robinson); given the musical comedy version of gangland put forth throughout, it makes sense that Big Jim's is the only murder depicted onscreen in the entire film.

When Robbo lands back in town after Big Jim's death, top priority on his agenda is an inquiry into the murder of Big Jim. The man responsible? Guy Gisborne, of course—but in musical-comedy land, Gisborne's first order of business is not a shootout, but, that's right . . . a song. And it's not just any song, but rather, one memorably rendered in "you have to hear it to believe it" fashion by Peter Falk. Falk is a bad singer of such staggering proportions— off pitch, tone deaf, and lacking even the most elementary phrasing—that one listens to the number in a grinning state of disbelief. He's like a forty-five-years-early version of a failed *American Idol* contestant. He is, however, such an effective foil to Sinatra throughout the film that with his one musical number out of the way, the movie takes off into an extended series of set pieces that rarely fail to amuse. Besides, in the musical department, the film happens to boast some mildly talented singers and actors by the names of Frank, Dean, Sammy, and one Harry Lillis Crosby, aka Der Bingle. It doesn't get any better than that in the talent department, and when the boys are given some solid tunes, as they are here, the result is an audience-pleasing, exuberant, musical free-for-all.

In the silly world of singing mobsters, the first scene post-funeral features a humorous graveside service for Big Jim, complete with a bugler who blows the racetrack "call to post" instead of the expected "Taps." Always sticklers for decorum, the gangsters insist on a twenty-one-gun salute—it just happens to feature twenty-one mobsters holding their handguns in the air and simultaneously firing bullets.

According to Frank Sinatra Jr.'s audio commentary on the DVD version of the film, the graveyard scene was shot in an actual Los Angeles cemetery on November 21, 1963, the day before President Kennedy was assassinated; other accounts place the filming on November 14. In Frank Jr.'s telling, Sinatra wandered off between takes in order to smoke a cigarette. Leaning against a tombstone, he took note of the name inscribed thereon: JOHN F. KENNEDY, 1873–1940. It's an eerie coincidence that Sinatra never forgot, just as, according to his son, he remained forever haunted by Robbo's line to Gisborne: "You come over like George Washington, and I'll send you back like Abraham Lincoln." While all the United States underwent a period of prolonged mourning for President Kennedy, Sinatra felt heightened grief, given his long-standing friendship with JFK, fight over the stay in Palm Springs or not. After the assassination, Sinatra shut down production on the film for three days, and when filming resumed, what had started out as a high-spirited set quickly changed; in Sinatra Jr.'s words, "The spell had kind of been broken."

The mood darkened even further when the then-nineteen-year-old Frank Jr. was kidnapped at gunpoint in Lake Tahoe on December 8, 1963. Held captive for five days, he was eventually released by the rather amateurish kidnappers during a ransom exchange of $240,000. The kidnappers were caught within two days, but during the ordeal, Frank once again shut down production. In Bing Crosby's understated words: "Then there were a lot of delays. And our coordination fell apart."

Bing and Frank may have unavoidably felt the darkening mood on set, but the difficulties never bleed through onscreen. Instead, the film actually zips along nicely as Robbo's associates (the equivalent of Robin Hood's gang of merry men) are introduced. Sammy Davis Jr. pops up as Robbo's sidekick and enforcer Will—a visual gag that works simply because Sammy is one of the few actors who could succeed in making the still-slim Sinatra appear hefty of physique. Next up is new associate Little John (Dean Martin), who casually introduces himself to Robbo while hustling him at pool. What makes that sequence so terrific is Martin's gentle crooning of the lullaby "Any Man Who Loves His Mother" as he sinks every ball on the table. Nudging Robbo aside as he lines up shot after shot without missing a beat—or a song lyric—he calmly relieves Robbo of thirty-two thousand dollars. (Technical adviser for the pool sequences was none other than Milton Berle.) Drawling "when your opponent is left holding all the aces, only one thing left to do—kick over the table," Martin's ultracool demeanor contrasts so nicely with Sinatra's unending energy that even Robbo, incredulous that he has been outhustled by a lullaby-singing sharpie, knows his only solution is to team up with that very hustler.

Robbo and Gisborne engage in a battle for territory, but Robbo and Little John have one secret weapon—Will the dancing mobster. Yep, he's a tap-dancing gangster who jumps up on the bar and shoots out hundreds of bottles with a machine gun, all the while singing and hoofing to the song "Bang Bang." In an acrobatic display wherein he leaps, slides, and generally lights up the screen, Davis is in a world of his own and gives full evidence of his performing genius. This number actually constitutes the most violent part of the movie, guns blazing, audio turned up full blast, bottles smashing—who knew a musical number could be so violent? In many ways, it plays like a forty-years-early version of the "Nowadays/Hot Honey Rag" finale to *Chicago,* wherein murderesses Velma Kelly (Catherine Zeta-Jones) and Roxie Hart (Renée Zellweger) sing, dance, and shoot out a screen full of lights with their machine guns. As always seemed to happen with Davis on film, he relaxes in the musical number, confident of his extraordinary musical skills. In nonmusical moments, however, even in a lighthearted romp like *Robin and the 7 Hoods,* he tries too hard, desperate to ingratiate himself with the audience, his well-known devotion to Sinatra making him seem like an eager puppy trying to curry favor. Dean Martin, on the other hand, may have been Sinatra's close pal and buddy, but even as regards Frank's approval, Dean always gave off the air of simply not giving a damn.

The relationships amongst Frank, Dean, and Sammy were inevitably spilling over into film portrayals like these. When looking back at footage of the Rat Pack clowning on stage in Vegas from the vantage point of the twenty-first century, there is an uncomfortable racial element to the proceedings, with Sinatra casually calling Sammy by the name Smokey, and Martin picking up Davis and calling him a "trophy from the NAACP." Yes, it was all scripted ahead of time, but why exactly did Davis put up with that treatment? Well, for starters, Sinatra gave Davis a break when no one else did, insisting that Sammy's nightclub act (a trio with his father and uncle) be put on the same bill with him, and demanding a 400 percent salary increase for them; in typical Sinatra fashion, all was accomplished without telling Sammy or anyone else. Sinatra also stood by as Sammy's best man when he married blond Swede May Britt, a marriage so controversial at the time that Sammy received hate mail. It's further true that Davis never forgot the fact that Frank arranged medical care for him after he lost his eye in an auto accident, but perhaps more than any other reason, Sammy's devotion to Frank stemmed from the simple fact of age. Sammy consistently looked up to the ten-years-older Sinatra as the big brother he never had. Both men were only children who shared a desperate need to perform, connecting with the audience and thereby warding off loneliness. Best of buddies they were, and yet Sammy could be, and was, the brunt of tasteless racial gibes, and after incurring the Chairman's displeasure, he found himself doomed to exile before prostrating himself for readmittance to the inner circle. Complex, joy-filled, and sad all at the same time, their relationship made for a three-act play in and of itself.

Once Sammy's barroom brawl of a musical number is dispatched, the movie next introduces Marian Stevens (Barbara Rush), a mystery lady in white who places a flower on Big Jim's grave and is subsequently revealed to be his daughter. (To the film's detriment, Robbo and company appear to simply accept Marian's statement at face value, and although she initially insists that she wants revenge for her father's death, that important detail is quickly ignored altogether, with the result that Marian registers only as a money-hungry, amoral woman.) After Marian's failed attempt to seduce him over a dinner in her lavish apartment, Robbo storms out. But wait—shouldn't there be a song here? A nice ballad of love gone wrong? Well, yes, but as Frank Sinatra Jr. points out in his interesting DVD commentary, it is exactly at that point that producer Sinatra made a decision to speed up the film by deleting a planned musical number—a bad choice on Sinatra's part because he cut the top-drawer lightly swinging Cahn/Van Heusen ballad "I Like to Lead While I Dance." The song would not only have afforded audiences a chance to hear another Sinatra solo, but also further explained his character. The clever original plan called for it to be featured each time Marian gave dinner to a man she was trying to snare in her quest for cash and revenge. What could have been a very interesting multilayered song ended up excised completely; according to lyricist Cahn, it was cut not because of time constraints, but simply because Sinatra couldn't be bothered to learn the proper lip-synching for the proposed three different versions.

It's a major missed opportunity, but fortunately at this point Bing Crosby comes along, making a very welcome appearance as the fastidiously dressed, five-dollar-word-spouting wannabe hood Allen A. Dale. Bing's arrival really just proves a ready-made excuse for the boys to sing and dance together, and when Robbo and John decide that Allen's hopelessly out-of-style clothes have to go, they begin to sing "Style," while Crosby quick-changes from one hopeless outfit into another. When he finally emerges dressed in a tuxedo and boater that put Robbo and Little John to shame, Frank and Dean join him in their own tuxes, singing a three-part roundelay reminiscent of the opening "Fugue for Tinhorns" in *Guys and Dolls.* To watch Sinatra, Crosby, and Martin sing and cakewalk in such insouciant fashion, all three utterly relaxed and in great voice, is to experience a great movie-musical moment, one worth watching repeatedly.

Performing the first-rate "Style" with Bing and Dean in Robin and the 7 Hoods *(1964).*

No one knows what's happening in the plot, there is no sense that the three men are even playing characters, and it doesn't matter one damn bit. The audience is simply watching Frank, Dean, and Bing in top form, and that's plenty good enough. Sinatra appears to be having an absolute ball—and with good reason. He is performing a clever song with his onetime idol (Crosby) and his best film pal (Martin). This was Frank's kind of film, and it shows.

Crosby is in top form, sounding terrific and charming the audience with his eccentric but effective dance style. The joy Frank Sinatra Jr. says Crosby felt at once again making a full-scale musical registers on film. Perhaps the friendly rivalry between Bing and Frank caused each man to try harder; it's remarkably cheering to see them both dig a little deeper.

Marian, now wanting all the money for herself, seduces Little John with another of her candlelit dinners, and when, momentarily frustrated by his indifference, she sighs, "We're on two different tracks," Dean casually replies, "Just keep talking, honey—we'll arrive at a junction." To watch Dean Martin in those moments is to realize that he was, in his own unique way, postmodern in his approach. He knew the lines were corny and laden with double entendre, but rather than either show his dismay or knowingly wink at the audience, he lightly throws the line away as if to say, *Well, it may not be art, but it's a helluva good way to make a living. Hope you're entertained along the way.* Martin never took any of it too seriously, in marked contrast to Sinatra, and while not so significant an artist as Sinatra, he remained a unique and first-rate star in his own right. Having proved that he could act in *The Young Lions* and *Some Came Running,* he never really bothered again, with the exception of *Rio Bravo*—but, both he and the audiences seemed to rationalize, who the hell cared? It was still a fun ride.

Freed from jail (the presiding judge is played by Sinatra's longtime personal lawyer, Milton "Mickey" Rudin), Robbo now leads the cheering crowd in a salute to their home city, belting out "My Kind of Town" to the assembled throng. Who cares that the men's clothes bear little resemblance to the actual style of the 1920s? Or that the courthouse steps, like most of the interior sets, look suspiciously clean and devoid of all character or period detail? That the sets look so flimsy that a gentle breeze would blow them over? That the color palette is strangely muted? This is a great, great song, sung by Frank at the peak of his powers. The finger-snapping beat perfectly suited to the Rat Pack–era Sinatra, the song custom-tailored with a terrific Nelson Riddle arrangement, Sinatra lets loose and soars. Those crowds are right to cheer—he's a star in top-notch form, and the song soon became a staple of Sinatra concerts. (Strangely enough, the song lost the Academy Award to "Chim Chim Cher-ee" from *Mary Poppins,* one of the lesser songs in that film's generally terrific original score by the Sherman Brothers.)

It is only near the end of the movie, after "My Kind of Town," that the musical noticeably sags. Plot developments abound in too plentiful a fashion, and it's hard to keep track of what is happening. All of a sudden, Robbo, Little John, and Will are ringing bells for charity dressed in Santa outfits, while Marian alights from a limo with Allen A. Dale. None of this is logical in the slightest, but the audience does get to watch the Santa-clad trio belt out a chorus of "Don't Be a Do-Badder" as the film ends. It's a great musical moment even if it arrives out of nowhere, and it leaves the viewer with a satisfied feeling; the last fifteen minutes of the film may have been rushed and subpar, but it has been a fun ride up until then, and provides a gratifying end to Sinatra's movie-musical career.

Released on June 27, 1964, the film received generally encouraging reviews. James Powers, critic for *The Hollywood Reporter,* and an ofttimes spot-on Sinatra film critic, held that *"Robin and the 7 Hoods* is the latest out-ing for the Group—Frank Sinatra, Dean Martin and friends . . . [it] is better than its predecessors because there are not so many inside jokes, because there is more story and with it, new jokes, and because the stars work harder." Right on all counts.

Robin and the 7 Hoods also marked the true end of the Rat Pack movies—gone was the dream of a group movie made every year. Sinatra reteamed with Dean Martin in the subpar 1965 *Marriage on the Rocks,* and after Dean and Sammy appeared in the surprisingly successful *Cannonball Run,* Frank and Shirley MacLaine filmed cameos in the abysmal 1984 sequel, *Cannon-ball Run II.* That was it for group efforts, however. Instead, Sammy Davis went on to successfully conquer Broadway in the musical *Golden Boy,* and Dean Martin achieved huge popularity as the star of the long-running NBC television variety series *The Dean Martin Show.* Sinatra continued to churn out eleven more films, some first-rate, some utterly pedestrian, as well as record a series of extraordinary albums for his own Reprise label. All three men achieved further great success, but never again was the team to be in ac-tion. It was just as well; times were changing, and Rat Pack capers were los-ing both their surprise and their entertainment factor. By 1965, the Rat Pack was becoming a nostalgia act, even, in the words of T. H. Adamowski, "to its members."

If 1964 found Sinatra with two top-ten LPs—including, aptly enough, *Days of Wine and Roses, Moon River and Other Academy Award Winners—* 1965 was to prove even more of a banner year, with Frank scoring a top-ten album in *Sinatra '65,* and Grammy wins for *September of My Years* as Album of the Year and "It Was a Very Good Year" as Best Pop Solo Performance. That extraordinary run was capped with an Emmy Award for *Sinatra: A Man and His Music* as well as a Peabody Award for Distinguished Achievement in Video Programming. Sinatra the actor and Sinatra the singer meshed beauti-fully in those projects; indeed, watching Frank record "It Was a Very Good Year" on the CBS News video *Sinatra: Off the Record* is to see him etch a vi-sual as well as vocal portrait. On the phrase "small-town girls and soft sum-mer nights," he hunches his shoulders and closes his eyes, as if the memory of those far-off days is both wonderful and a bit painful. Frank was right: he had always been acting when he sang. More to the point, Frank Sinatra had now evolved both on screen and on record, from bobby-soxer idol to exemplar of the middle-aged disenchanted American male. (His take on "Days of Wine and Roses" sums up twenty years of regrets and missed opportunities in three minutes.)

Sinatra was still sexy to women; his female audience had aged right along with him, and he remained a touchstone to their youth. With men, on the other hand, the audience grew exponentially over the years because Frank was able to convey, better than any other actor or singer on the scene, the feeling that, in Donald Clarke's phrase, the greatest loneliness lies in disillusionment. It wasn't just that Sinatra and his male contemporaries did not understand rock music, let alone how it could so quickly come to dominate the cultural landscape. It was that the Vietnam War was heating up by the day, race riots coursed through inner-city America, and citizens of all stripes were growing increasingly mistrustful of government. The very fabric of American society was changing, much to the mutual displeasure of Sinatra and his audience. Witness Frank's statement about New York City: "When I first came across that river, this was the greatest city in the whole goddamned world. It was like a big beautiful lady. It's like a busted-down hooker now."

Sinatra did not give up, would not give up, and neither did his audience. Which is exactly why it made a curious kind of sense that just as the Vietnam War escalated, Frank Sinatra made his directorial debut with the strongly antiwar film *None But the Brave.*

It is a hit-or-miss affair but holds a prominent place in the Sinatra filmography for the simple reason that it's the single feature film Sinatra himself directed. Gordon Douglas may have supplied an uncredited assist with the directing chores, but there is no mistaking the Sinatra stamp on the film— *None But the Brave* is Frank's film from top to bottom.

Sinatra had spoken of directing as far back as a 1955 interview with Joe Hyams, wherein he put forth an extraordinary and altogether characteristic rationale for assuming the mantle of director. Asked what made him think he could be a director, he simply replied, "The same thing that made me think I could be a singer and an actor." Oh. No use staying up late at night worrying about Frank's self-confidence. As the film eventually revealed, Sinatra was actually a pretty good director, so it's too bad he didn't follow up with other self-directed efforts, à la Streisand. With his inherent understanding of the musical genre, he would definitely have made an interesting director of musicals, but then again, he most assuredly did not have the patience required for that most painstaking of film genres. A World War II combat film represented more familiar territory for the fledgling director, and the resulting movie, if not entirely successful, certainly proved to be a fascinating effort.

As the trailer for the film makes clear, far from being a "rah-rah" movie about the glories of patriotic war, Sinatra, still a highly visible liberal at that stage of his life, was aiming for nothing less than an examination of the futility of war. It's an effective preview of the film because it's straight from the heart—no insider humor like the smarmy trailer for *Come Blow Your Horn* here. Instead, director/star Sinatra addresses the camera and says, "You're supposed to hate the enemy—works pretty good when the enemy's a faceless stranger on the battlefield. What happens when he has a name and a familiar face? When he's somebody you know and respect. Can you still pull the trigger? Now that's something very few can answer—none but the brave." (The title comes from the John Dryden poem "Alexander's Feast": "None but the brave deserves the fair.") It's a pretty effective summing up of the film's message, and while not all those high-minded questions are successfully answered, the parts where the film does work are effective enough to carry the rest of the movie, as well as the audience, right along with it.

Director Sinatra in action on None But the Brave *(1965).*

The film gets off to an unexpected start with the onscreen title first appearing in Japanese letters—even the Warner Bros. logo initially floats onscreen in Eastern letters. This effective bilingual approach is reflected in the fact that the screenplay was written by the binational team of American John Twist and Japanese Katsuya Susaki (from a story by Kikumaru Okuda). What's most interesting about the opening sequences is that the Japanese soldiers speak in their native language with subtitles appearing onscreen. It was a rather daring move for a mainstream Hollywood film in 1965, and one that anticipated Clint Eastwood's *Letters from Iwo Jima* by four decades. Indeed, in the opening stretches of the film, there are numerous sequences where the Japanese soldiers, who are stranded without communication capabilities on an isolated Pacific island, speak with no English translation provided; the action serves to convey the meaning to the audience. When the Japanese soldiers dance on the beach, the momentary relief from their privations is complete in and of itself, no translation required.

Even more impressive is Sinatra's decision to present the Japanese as well-rounded individuals. Rather than the stereotypical Hollywood depiction of the "Japs" as bucktoothed, nearsighted savages, the soldiers are given defining personalities that round them into recognizable human beings. The Japanese combat unit contains men from all walks of life: a happy-go-lucky fisherman, a Buddhist priest, a man who's a complete failure at all military matters—in other words, real people. These soldiers fight not because they are blood-thirsty savages, but because they must uphold the honor of their country.

The Americans enter the scene literally and figuratively when their aircraft crash-lands on the island after a dogfight with two Japanese planes. The American unit, led by Captain Dennis Bourke (Clint Walker), includes Chief Pharmacist Mate Francis Maloney (Sinatra), a character who, in the hands of Sinatra, proves to be hands-down the most convincing soldier of the lot. A hard-drinking medic, he improvises solutions with the limited tools at his disposal: a dislocated shoulder is put back in place by using a baseball! Sinatra always succeeded as soldier or detective on film because the audience expectations fit such characters perfectly. Both onscreen and off, his knocked-about face and whiskeyed, knowing voice smoothly fit the archetype of a cynical yet vulnerable loner. With his stubble and ever-present bottle of booze, Sinatra is the only one of the American soldiers who looks battered, as if he has actually lived through combat. The uniforms of the other soldiers are too clean by half, but Sinatra's world-weary take on the role reads as the real thing. When the gung-ho Lieutenant Blair (Nancy Sinatra Jr.'s then-husband Tommy Sands) spits out the epithet "dirty Jap," Maloney's cynical retort is a disgusted "Dirty Jap, Lieutenant? They invented the bathtub." Sinatra is a hero for the post–World War II combat film: tough, practical, resilient, and disillusioned.

It wasn't just Sands who benefited from Sinatra's continued practice of affirmative nepotism. His cousin's son, Ray Sinatra, was cast in a minor role, and crony Brad Dexter claimed the role of the overbearing and insubordinate Sergeant Bleeker. Dexter wasn't much of an actor, turning in a performance that is broad and one-note, but his presence on the Kauai location literally saved Sinatra's life when Frank was pulled into an undertow while himself attempting to rescue his swimming partner, producer Howard Koch's wife, Ruth. Never one to actually say thank you, Sinatra expressed his gratitude by granting Dexter an executive position with Sinatra Enterprises, a move that blew up in the faces of all parties involved during the two-years-later filming of *The Naked Runner.*

When both the Japanese and the Americans are stranded without any communication, a temporary truce is called, both sides now totally isolated. Japanese fish are exchanged for American cigarettes, and the Japanese commander, sensing Captain Bourke's "lonely detachment from others," doesn't shoot his American counterpart when the opportunity presents itself: "In the loneliness of command, we are brothers."

Sinatra and company are using the familiar trappings of a war story to explore the new ideologies that resonated with audiences twenty years removed from the Second World War. The theme of good-hearted men being shoved around as pawns by powers that be who have completely forgotten them is worked to good advantage yet not overdone, the inherent contradiction of "friendly" enemies appealing to the curious of all stripes.

Nearly one hour into the film, Sinatra himself has garnered very little in the way of actual screen time. However, he now comes to the fore in the single best sequence of the film, wherein a deal is struck between the Japanese commander and Captain Bourke: if Corpsman Maloney will tend to a Japanese soldier with a severely injured leg, the Americans will be given access to water, dried fish, and potatoes. Corpsman Maloney's silent reaction as he goes to treat the Japanese is a finely wrought bit of acting by Sinatra—he is at once

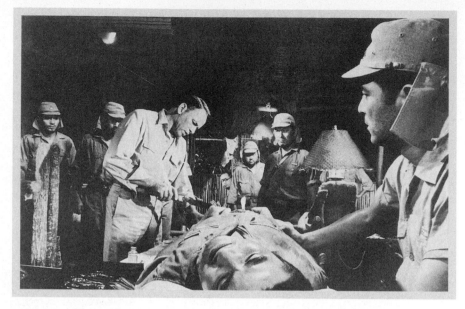

The terrific operating sequence in None But the Brave, *Frank's only feature-film directorial credit.*

inquisitive, jaded, and scared. Confessing, "I'm a Band-Aid man—not a surgeon," he must amputate an enemy soldier's leg without any proper equipment, forced to perform surgery with only a sword that has been sterilized in whiskey and set on fire.

As a Buddhist priest chants in the background, Sinatra stages the sequence in sure, fluid fashion. Camera silently panning the Japanese soldiers who are watching the operation, there is little dialogue in either language, the only sounds those of the jungle. As the insects, birds, and animals eerily call back and forth, the visibly sweating Maloney crosses himself with a knife and prays: "Don't just look down on me—help me." The capper to the sequence occurs when, just as the operation is set to begin, the camera pans away to the jungle and the only sound heard is that of the wounded Japanese soldier screaming in pain. It's a scream that carries all the way to the American camp, unsettling the nerves of soldiers on both sides. Directed, acted, and designed in utterly believable fashion, the entire sequence represents a first-rate piece of filmmaking, one remarkably assured for a neophyte director.

Unfortunately, the remainder of the film is simply not up to the standards set by that rather harrowing scene of an improvised operation. Clint Walker, whose enormous physique does indeed convey a sense of command, is stolid, nothing more, possessing none of the vocal resources necessary to fully develop his character. Tony Bill, as radio operator Keller, visibly overacts just as he did in *Come Blow Your Horn,* never once remotely suggesting a skilled combat veteran. Although Tommy Sands as the overly gung-ho Lieutenant Blair bore the brunt of criticism in the press, he, in fact, turns in a much more interesting performance than does Bill. (Of course, Sands's performance, which is variable throughout, is not aided by dialogue that finds him saying, "I'll be a son of a buck." Somehow, one doubts very strongly that the phrase "son of a buck" was uttered very often by combat veterans in the middle of the Second World War.)

Further problems occur when scenes exploring the temporary truce are played on phony-looking sets: the much-sought-after water hole is so artificial-looking that one expects to see the set decorator puffing on a cigarette in the background. If wartime combat films are all about gritty reality, a sanitized Kmart-decorated water hole jolts the viewer out of the film's world and right back to an awareness of watching a movie. It's a curious weakness in a film whose panoramic shots of the Kauai landscape (the cinematography chores handled by *Pal Joey* lenser Harold Lipstein) do indeed suggest an isolated wartime island.

Most damaging of all, however, the screenplay simply falls apart with a flashback revealing Captain Bourne's backstory. It's an unnecessary "this is what makes him tick" sequence, one that purportedly explains the commander's relentless nature (and truth to tell, he really doesn't appear to be all that relentless in Walker's monotonous vocal performance). Anxious to underscore Bourne's motivation, Sinatra makes a fledgling director's mistake of repeating the same information in both visual flashback and dialogue. The audience disconnect is made even worse by the noticeably fake outdoor patio setting where Bourne quarrels with girlfriend Laurie, as well as by Laurie's wardrobe, which is more suggestive of a mid-1960s visit to the Las Vegas Sands Hotel than the Pacific theater of war.

When the flashback is over, so is the truce—the Americans now have a working radio. Contact reestablished with the outside world, the fighting inevitably must resume. The battle rages, many Americans are killed, but all the Japanese lose their lives. The film ends with a very nice touch from director Sinatra: Purposely leaving the tattered Japanese flag waving in the palm tree as a tribute to the courage of the enemy, Maloney must literally step over all the dead bodies, Japanese and American alike, on his way to the safety of the ship. As the film's final credit has it: "Nobody ever wins." Yes, the words are too literal, but in a film that has been so conscientious about presenting the Japanese viewpoint, it strikes the viewer as permissible. In fact, in a way it's symbolic of director Sinatra's film as a whole. It's a little heavy-handed but it's also an effective piece of craftsmanship.

Sinatra deserves credit for forcefully delivering an antiwar picture, one that played on screens across America even before the antiwar fervor of the Vietnam era fully took hold. He has very deliberately crafted a film bereft of a stereotypically glorious finale complete with all-American heroics. Instead of order being wrought out of chaos, the reverse has happened. To make matters more disturbing, the ensuing chaos is moral in nature. Having lived through World War II, the Korean conflict, and now the escalating war in Vietnam, Sinatra is reflecting the very questions asked by the American public: Why are we fighting yet again? Why are we "over there"? In asking the bottom-line question, Will we ever learn? Sinatra presents a rather unflinching look at the waste of war. Stumbles and all, *None But the Brave* is a worthy film, and it's too bad Sinatra didn't continue to test his talent with further directorial efforts. (He had previously directed a Christmas television special in which he starred with Bing Crosby, but never again a feature film.) It's a particular loss given Frank's self-revealing comment, "Directing's my favorite medium. It keeps me busier and I like that." A busy Sinatra on a film set meant a Sinatra who was more attentive to the material at hand, with less chance to grow bored and hurt the film. Good intentions and desire existed, but continued directorial efforts were not to be.

As evidenced by this major directorial effort, and contrary to popular belief, Sinatra was still taking his film career very seriously as he turned fifty. In an April 1966 interview with Peter Bart, Sinatra detailed the many evenings he spent reading scripts and novels in a hunt for possible feature-film material: "I'm well aware of the shortcomings of some of my recent pictures. I guess the trouble has been that at the time I did these pictures nothing better seemed to be available. It all boils down to material." In other words, the ever-restless Frank preferred filming second-rate material to not working at all. It is fortunate, then, that when Sinatra read the novel *Von Ryan's Express,* he knew he had found a first-rate story, one ripe for filming. When informed that he had been outbid for the film rights by Twentieth Century-Fox, he simply

On his wedding day with third wife Mia Farrow, July 19, 1966.
Short-lived marriage, lifelong friends.

called the studio directly and offered his services as star. A deal was struck, which certainly proved to be a smart move by all parties involved, because *Von Ryan's Express* turned out to be a fast-paced, enjoyably tough combat film.

With its mix of soundstage interior sequences and evocative location photography in Spain and Italy, *Von Ryan's Express* was emblematic of changing times in film production. Many more movies were now filmed on location, the days of shooting entirely on soundstages quickly fading. The soundstage sections of *Von Ryan's Express* may be far less jarring than those found in *None But the Brave* and *Never So Few,* but they are actually best remembered as the setting for Sinatra's initial encounters with Mia Farrow, who was then filming her enormously popular television series *Peyton Place* on the Fox lot. Once the romance became public, the tabloids were provided with months' worth of front-page headlines, the blaring coverage insistently focusing on the thirty-year age difference between the two. It all proved irresistible to newspaper and magazine readers around the world in those pre-Internet days, Farrow's ethereal flower-child persona laid out in stark relief against Sinatra's tough-guy come-on.

Sinatra and Farrow were, of course, wildly mismatched in many ways. Not only did they have to surmount a three-decade age difference (Farrow herself chronicled how she greeted Frank's talk of "the band days with Tommy" with the question "Who's Tommy?") but their political differences over events such as the Vietnam War ultimately proved too large a gap to bridge. At the same time, however, what is easily forgotten is how much the couple actually had in common. Both experienced an ofttimes debilitating sense of loneliness with an attendant yearning for closeness, and both held a decidedly wary view of Hollywood—he from decades of experience, she from growing up the daughter of a famous director (John Farrow) and actress (Maureen O'Sullivan). Even with their age gap, when alone they shared a genuine companionship. For all her youth, Farrow was a perceptive observer of human nature and understood what made Sinatra tick: "Although the armies of his heart and mind did frequent battle and left him isolated and restless, in matters of conscience and of human hope, they were one." No, the problem actually began whenever Sinatra reverted to "Frank the Vegas swinger" mode and surrounded himself with cronies. That was a world so foreign to Farrow that she felt an outsider in her own marriage.

For all their good intentions, Frank and Mia found it impossible to sustain the relationship, but they remained friends until Sinatra's death. In actuality, the most startling comment of all about the relationship came from no less an authority than Ava Gardner, whose romantic history included not only the legendary romance with Sinatra, but also a fling with Farrow's director father, John. Writing in her autobiography *What Falls Away,* Farrow records that she and Ava "got along so well together that once, in a jumble of warm emotions, she declared that I was the child she and Frank never had." Oh. Whoa.

As to *Von Ryan's Express* itself, all the technical elements are first-rate, from the rousing score by Jerry Goldsmith (who went on to provide a similarly excellent score for *The Detective*) to the crystalline location photography by William H. Daniels. (Goldsmith's score, which heightens the film's suspense without ever turning bombastic, sounds strangely familiar to latter-day ears due to the fact that certain musical themes appear to have been utilized in the hit sitcom *Hogan's Heroes*.) With a crisp and suspenseful script by Wendell Mayes and Joseph Landon, based on a novel by David Westheimer, *Von Ryan's Express* built upon a solid foundation, scoring as an example of Hollywood studio filmmaking at its most professional.

Even with all these solid elements in place, however, it is still remarkable that the film turned out as well as it did, for one simple reason: with overt friction between Sinatra and director/executive producer Mark Robson, a smooth collaboration proved an elusive commodity. The strong-willed Robson, who had fashioned a solid career beginning with his RKO films (*Seventh Victim*) lensed for producer Val Lewton, clashed with Sinatra regarding Frank's desire to film as quickly as possible with the bare minimum number of retakes. Robson, a thorough professional who knew he had a first-rate script on his hands, balked at Sinatra's intransigence, but it's not too difficult to guess who carried the day. Robson may have been the executive producer, but it was Sinatra who held the ultimate power—along with a percentage of the gross box office receipts (and a salary of $250,000). When all was said and done, Hollywood was always about the bottom line, and it was Sinatra's star power that had fast-tracked the film and pushed it into the public consciousness. Robson knew Sinatra held the final say and as a result, their quarrels were shot through with real animosity. In the words of Sinatra chronicler Nigel Havers, "Robson was the only director that Frank actively ever disliked, which must have meant he really disliked him, because he had been uncooperative, difficult and downright rude on other sets." Maybe the clash wasn't such a bad thing, because out of the creative animus came a first-class film, Sinatra's best since *The Manchurian Candidate.*

Getting off to a literally explosive start, the film opens in 1943 with Sinatra, playing U.S. Army Air Corps pilot Colonel Joseph L. Ryan, crashing his plane in Italy, just before the Allied landing in Sicily. Taken to a POW camp, Ryan immediately clashes with the ranking British officer Major Eric Fincham (Trevor Howard) over everything from tactics for escape to the pill supply for the malaria-ridden prisoners. What makes *Von Ryan's Express* the best of Sinatra's war films is not just the fact that with his natural sense of authority he makes a believable high-ranking pilot. It's that his very American demeanor contrasts so well with the stiff-upper-lip Fincham. When Fincham disdainfully watches Ryan demonstrate how he intends to strangle the German railroad guards, he sarcastically bellows, "Learn that from the cowboy films, did you?" (In fact, the scene of Fincham and Ryan strangling the German guards on top of the train is terrific—exciting and suspenseful in equal measure.) Howard may shout too much by half in his blustery performance, but he's a good foil for the improvising American. (As pointed out by author

Daniel O'Brien, Howard actually enjoyed the shoot, Sinatra's hurry-it-up behavior and all: "Having weathered Marlon Brando's tantrums during the tortuously drawn-out production of *Mutiny on the Bounty,* he found Sinatra largely affable by comparison.")

Suspense sequences work just as well as the flat-out action sections of the film, with a particularly terrific ten-minute segment that features Sinatra's silent and highly effective reaction when Gestapo officers follow him back to the train. The Gestapo, who think Ryan is German and want his American watch, ask him in the German he does not understand what he wants in return. In a remarkably staged sequence, Sinatra's Ryan plays it utterly cool, never deigning to answer the Gestapo officer directly, displaying remarkable sangfroid as he shakes his head to turn down all the Gestapo's overtures until he mutely agrees to barter the watch for cigarettes. Watching Sinatra's eyes in this sequence as he speaks nary a word of dialogue enables the viewer to see how much he has grown as an actor; he wordlessly conveys all the necessary information about the obvious fear Ryan masks under a silent facade of contempt for the Gestapo officer. It's purely visual storytelling, an expertly written sequence brought fully to life by skillful direction and a terrific performance by star Sinatra.

First-class action film, Von Ryan's Express.

As the Allied prisoners try to escape on the train—and by now the train has become the main character in the movie—they are bombarded by three Messerschmitts in a beautifully staged aerial sequence. The entire escape comes down to a climactic battle on foot between the Germans and Allies, hundreds of feet in the air on railroad tracks leading into Switzerland. As the temporarily stranded train finally begins to move again, Fincham jumps on-board while Ryan desperately chases the train on foot in order to haul himself to safety. Reaching for the train's last car, Ryan lunges—and is shot in the back by the Germans. His dead body sprawled on the track, Ryan is left there as the train pulls away, bringing his fellow prisoners to freedom in Switzer-land. It's not the ending audiences expected, but it's the right one, the impact heightened by Robson's smart decision to film Ryan's death from the vantage point of the train's caboose, thereby leaving Ryan's solitary body receding into the distance as the train pulls away. It's an ending notably different from that found in the novel, wherein Ryan successfully escapes into Switzerland with his fellow prisoners, and it was Sinatra himself who insisted on the downbeat ending—the last time he was to die on film. With his impeccable dramatic instincts, Sinatra knew that ending the film with his death would bring an extra layer of emotion to the story, and thereby make it resonate more fully with the audience.

It's remarkably cheering to see Sinatra back in top form and portraying a new kind of hero, a recognizably flawed human being who makes mistakes in judgment and alienates fellow soldiers but ultimately saves others through his own death. *Von Ryan's Express* may not have the texture or strongly antiwar viewpoint of the more ambitious *None But the Brave,* but it's a more fully in-tegrated film and ranks at the top of the many World War II films in which Sinatra starred. Audiences and critics alike responded favorably, and for the last time in Sinatra's movie career (the compilation film *That's Entertainment!* excepted), the positive critical response was near unanimous. Aside from the increasingly standard pan from Bosley Crowther, most critics cheered Sinatra's turn, a situation nicely summed up by the *Hollywood Citizen-News,* which found that "as the steely-eyed, curt American officer who takes command as an unpopular chief, Frank Sinatra underplays his role neatly and purposefully . . . this is Sinatra at his best as an actor . . ."

Von Ryan's Express showed that the fifty-year-old Sinatra had lost none of his power onscreen. Young and trim enough to still lead the charge in action films, yet experienced enough to now deliver a full-blooded characterization in whatever the genre, Sinatra was back on top. Which is why, given the solid popular and critical response to *Von Ryan's Express,* it's all the more difficult to fathom Sinatra's follow-up film. Yes, Frank oftentimes spoke of enjoying comedy, and with his impeccable timing, proved himself adept in comedic roles— but why oh why did he ever think a film should be made of such grade-Z material as *Marriage on the Rocks*, not to mention the inept *Assault on a Queen* and *The Naked Runner*. For absolutely no discernible reason, Frank Sinatra was about to suffer from a serious lapse in judgment. For anyone less talented than Frank, their film career would soon have been *d-e-d* dead. For Frank—well, he was Frank Fucking Sinatra, wasn't he? He'd make what he wanted, when he wanted. He'd survive. And he did.

Barely.

A Waste of Talent

"It's Only Money,"
sung by Frank Sinatra with Groucho Marx
in *Double Dynamite*

He has an insatiable desire to live every moment to its fullest because, I guess, he feels that right around the corner is extinction.

—BRAD DEXTER, ACTOR AND ONETIME VICE-PRESIDENT
OF SINATRA ENTERPRISES

RELEASED A MERE THREE MONTHS AFTER *Von Ryan's Express, Marriage on the Rocks* represents major talent slumming its way through junk. Sinatra made few films that rate lower on the quality scale than this tired farce, material so weak that it leaves audiences scratching their heads and thinking, *Why did anyone bother?*

Produced by Sinatra Enterprises in conjunction with William Daniels, the film represented the first of two lackluster back-to-back Sinatra movies helmed by Jack Donohue. Truth to tell, bad as the direction is, the film's failures are not just Donohue's; blame must be shared with the Brand X original story and screenplay by Cy Howard, which is so witless that it even managed the not-insubstantial feat of insulting an entire country. Specifically, when Sinatra's character of Dan Edwards tells wife Val (Deborah Kerr) that it's not just the water to avoid in Mexico, but rather, "The secret is not to come to this place at all," so offended were certain sensibilities in Mexico that Sinatra eventually enlisted well-known attorney Louis Nizer to negotiate his clearance back into the country. Needless to say, it was a while before Frank was singing "South of the Border" again.

Of course, what can be expected from a film featuring cartoon characters who never develop into recognizable human beings, instead changing only to fit the requirements of the screenplay. It's a level of characterization evident from the very opening credits, which feature stick figures and announce a special appearance by the then-very-popular and decidedly nonactor talent, Trini López.

The screenplay, such as it is, features Frank as ad executive Dan Edwards, a man too busy with his career to pay attention to his wife, Valerie (Deborah Kerr). Dan thinks he has a fulfilling life, only to be told by Valerie that she is bored and wants a divorce. Rounding out the complications is best friend Ernie Brewer (Dean Martin), a carefree bachelor Valerie rejected in favor of Dan eighteen years previously.

Okay, there have been worse premises for films. So, one asks, how bad can it really be? Answer: worse than you think. How about the fact that when Val tells her lawyer she wants a divorce, he treats her like a ten-year-old, telling her not to do it, but instead to buy a black negligee called Viva la Derriere in order to reignite Dan's interest. Dan's the guilty party here, but according to the screenplay's logic, a skimpy negligee should solve the problem that he works too much and can't even remember his own anniversary. Daughter Tracy (Nancy Sinatra) wants to move out of the house and into a "pad" with her go-go pal Lisa (Davey Davison), and Valerie's mother, Jeannie MacPherson (Hermione Baddeley), rounds out the household by marching around the house playing the bagpipes. That's right, the bagpipes. Indoors. In suburbia.

Unfortunately, the bagpipes get all the laughs here. Nancy Sinatra, a major pop recording star of the time ("These Boots Are Made for Walkin'"), simply did not possess the acting chops to make her role register in any meaningful way. She may have inherited a certain odd sort of vocal talent from her father but seemingly got very few of his acting genes, as her spoken delivery is without inflection. In defense of Nancy, she did have three strikes against her before filming even began: she had no training as an actress, she had to play opposite her father, a "one-take Charlie" Academy Award winner with over forty films to his credit, and she was then in the midst of marital difficulties with her husband at the time, Tommy Sands. How much of a chance would any actress have when saddled with a film that presents her teenage character flouncing out of the house in full teen rebellion while wearing a prim dress accessorized with white gloves. That, sad to say, was Hollywood's idea of youth culture in the mid-1960s. It all plays like a bad episode of *The Brady Bunch,* one so ineptly constructed that it's often hard to fully understand what's happening. Even the usually reliable Nelson Riddle fails here, delivering a noisy score that indicates Dan's anger by banging bass drums loudly.

The very anniversary upon which the plot is supposed to hinge is presented in desultory fashion; Dan puts on a black tie for a trip to the Café A-GoGo, and when Val charges onto the dance floor to "boogie" with Ernie, they manage to look nothing so much as ridiculous. (Even worse is the later and highly unfortunate sight of a go-go dancing Sinatra flailing his arms in a silly 1960s dance requiring no skill or style—a long trip in reverse from the first-rate dancing he had displayed in *Anchors Aweigh* and *Take Me Out to the Ball Game.*) There is an in-joke featuring Frank and Dean as unable to clap in time to the music, but it's all a lot of nonsense simply designed to show Dan as so preoccupied with his next day's work that he bolts his own anniversary celebration to go home, leaving Ernie and Val free to visit Ernie's groovy bachelor pad together. That is not how people behave in real life. It's only how they act in second-rate "reel" life in order to twist the plot in a new direction.

The film jerks the viewer back and forth in so many directions that it is impossible to care about any of the characters, and when Dan and Val decide to take a second honeymoon in Mexico, the film dissolves into an utter mess, with Cesar Romero delivering an exhausting performance as a Mexican divorce lawyer who doubles as hotel manager and doctor. Along the way, Sinatra greatly overdoes his depiction of Dan feeling sick, in the process delivering an encyclopedia's worth of groans, grunts, and whines. It's all so dull that the audience is reduced to vaguely wondering whether Joi Lansing's performance as sexpot Lola is worse than Anita Ekberg's in *4 for Texas.* The answer: it's actually a tie. Neither can act, and they both display as much cleavage as humanly possible in a Hollywood film circa 1965. Lansing is more monotonous in delivery, if that's possible, but Ekberg's accent rendered her incomprehensible. Dead heat.

As for the two leads, Sinatra actually comes off better than Kerr in the film, but that's not saying a great deal. He appears to try—a little—and doesn't shamble through the film to the same degree as he did in the ersatz Westerns with the Rat Pack. He even essays a few genuinely funny moments, such as when he wags his head from side to side in exact rhythm with his mother-in-law's endless—and very loud—litany of complaints, but those thirty seconds are about it in the acting department. For her part, Kerr, a genuinely fine actress, is here completely miscast. An actress of inherent dignity and reserve, she is ill-equipped to handle the role of a vaguely dissatisfied wife who wants to snap her husband to attention. It's the sort of role the highly energetic Doris Day was perfecting in her sex comedies of this time, injecting zip and outrage into the most outlandish scenarios. By way of contrast, Kerr, who sounds remarkably similar to Audrey Hepburn, can't help but display an inherent refinement and reserve. She is much better showcased in films like *The King and I* (and her first film with Sinatra, *From Here to Eternity*), where she is able to suggest layers of passion buried beneath a seemingly proper exterior. She does not hear the rhythm of her comic lines, emphasizing the wrong beats and generally behaving as if she'd rather be in an English garden reading Jane Austen. Well, who can blame her?

Due to plot exigencies, Dan can't stick around in Mexico to get remarried to Val after they're accidentally divorced; instead, best pal Ernie flies to Mexico, where the elaborately scheduled remarriage proceeds with fireworks and musicians. According to this screenplay, no one can simply stop the nonsense and say, "Wrong man—he's not her husband." Instead, a minister performs the ceremony, Ernie faints at the idea of now being married, and Val simply proceeds in married life with Ernie in order to make husband Dan jealous. This is utter nonsense; there is nowhere, except in this grade-Z Hollywood movie, where a wife would behave in such a ridiculous fashion and have both her husband and "fake" spouse amiably go along with the plan. Ernie moves in with Val, Dan takes over Ernie's bachelor pad, and daughter Tracy's young friend Lisa puts the moves on dear old dad. (This occasions one of the very few good quips in the film, when Val snaps at Lisa that she'll buy them a wedding present: "A crib for you and an oxygen tent for Dan.")

There is a witless attempt to spice things up when Ernie moves into Dan's home, though dumb as this move is, it does afford the viewer a chance to analyze the performance of Dean Martin as Ernie. By that date, Martin had basically given up attempting to forge a true characterization. Instead, he coasts by on his extraordinary charm, giving the audience a big-screen version of what they assumed Dino to be in real life—a "chick magnet" who was always ready with a quip, several drinks, and a refusal to get ruffled, no matter what

Wasting his talent in the abysmal Marriage on the Rocks, *with Dean Martin (1965). Mother-in-law Hermionne Baddeley plays the bagpipes. And this was one of the better scenes.*

the outlandish circumstances. That charm can sometimes redeem the worst of situations, and does provide a genuinely funny moment when he interviews prospective secretaries in their bikinis.

Similarly, when Dean and Frank subsequently place their arms on each other's shoulders, the secretary casts one sidelong glance at this Rat Pack–esque moment and snaps at Dean, "Why don't you let the little one lead?" It's the amiable look of befuddlement on Dean's face that makes the gag work, but the Dean Martin who essayed memorable characters in *The Young Lions* and *Some Came Running* had vanished by now; even his climactic punch line to Dave—"You can't force me to stay married to your wife"—falls flat. Given that the entire situation setting up the line is singularly unfunny, it's not Dean's fault that the line thuds. Dino isn't bad—he's too talented to be truly awful. Rather, it was clear that he didn't really feel like trying anymore, waltzing through the lackluster material without any conceivable effort, seemingly happy simply to score a nice paycheck.

On the flip side, it's exactly that sort of nonchalant performance that came to inform the persona serving him so well on his hugely successful NBC television series, *The Dean Martin Show*. The relaxed charm that refused to take anything seriously may have hurt his film legacy enormously, but on the small screen it ingratiated him into living rooms all across America. It's an amiability that Sinatra was incapable of displaying for extended periods of time. Like most major male stars, Frank carried an edge, and in the early to mid-1960s, suburban fathers on film rarely carried an edge. It's therefore no accident that *Marriage on the Rocks* served as the only film in Sinatra's extensive film catalog wherein he played a married suburban father with two children, the so-called average American male. There was nothing average about Frank Sinatra, and that's why he excelled at playing outsiders. Frank wanted his emotions and lifestyle front and center. Not for him the sort of quiet madness found in the suburban nighttimes.

By film's end, it's as if the screenwriters have looked at each other and said, *We need to wrap this up because none of it makes sense anymore.* Dan gives flowers to Val; she tells him she's pregnant from their one night together in Mexico, whereupon he says "Okay, we'll get married." Out the front door they walk, presumably to tell eighteen-year-old Tracy she's going to have to start babysitting again. If she had any sense, she'd have left town long ago, along with the film's audience. The Rat Pack revels that had carried Frank and Dean through eight films together had completely run out of steam, interesting neither the audience nor the stars themselves. Only their leaden turns in *Cannonball Run II* lay ahead; their occasionally first-rate and always-interesting screen partnership had here sadly come to a desultory end.

Warner Bros.' advertising for the film had trumpeted "the story of the tired husband, the bored wife, the happy bachelor with the mad pad and the big switch that began with that go-go girl in a cage!" After viewing the finished film, one can only reason that if Warner Bros. had taken out all the words in the ad copy with the exception of "tired" and "bored," they could have written their own review of the movie. As for Frank's performance, it's best summed up in *The New Yorker*'s blunt review: "Mr. Sinatra is his usual uncannily confident self—in one scene he doesn't even bother to stop chewing gum—but the picture betrays him at every turn."

Frank's schedule at the time remained so packed with films and recordings that he appeared to give the lie to James Brown's claim of being the hardest working man in show business. That title would appear to be Sinatra's—the man never stopped. In 1965 and 1966 alone, he appeared in six feature films (four in starring roles, two in cameos), directed one of the films, produced three, and even managed a two-and-a-half-minute appearance complete with narration, for the trailer soliciting funds in behalf of the Will Rogers Hospital and Teaching Institute in upstate New York.

In that relentless quest to keep busy, Sinatra also produced the inaugural gala for (Democrat) Governor Pat Brown of California, tucked in a marriage to Mia Farrow, gave numerous concerts, oversaw his far-flung business investments, recorded the *September of My Years* LP, appeared on the CBS Reports television documentary *Sinatra: An American Original* (hosted by Walter Cronkite), and recorded the double LP *Sinatra: A Man and His Music* (Grammy Award for Album of the Year). Further adding to the incredible tally was the November 1965 recording of *Moonlight Sinatra*, followed by the number-one best-selling single and LP *Strangers in the Night*. (This single not only gave Frank his biggest hit single in years, but it also won him the Grammy Award for the highly coveted Record of the Year.) Of course, just to make sure he wouldn't be bored, Frank also squeezed in a live recording of *Sinatra at the Sands* with Count Basie and Quincy Jones, as well as the persona-defining hit single "That's Life." It's an astonishing output, with every one of the recordings, and the parallel television specials, of the highest quality. The film work remained much more variable in quality, with *None But the Brave* and *Von Ryan's Express* registering as first-class work, *Marriage on the Rocks* qualifying as a waste of time, and, in a class all by itself, his next film, *The Oscar.* There's no question that *The Oscar* is a classic film—it's just that it's a classic of camp.

The Oscar, for which Frank contributed a film-closing cameo playing himself, was the first of his three film releases in 1966. Riddled with show business clichés and inadvertently hilarious lines, the Russell Rouse–directed film plays like the forerunner—and male version—of 1967's *Valley of the Dolls.* Based on the novel of the same name by Richard Sale, with screenplay written by Harlan Ellison, Clarence Greene and director Rouse, *The Oscar* chronicles the rise and fall of Hollywood star and all-around no-goodnik Frankie Fane (Stephen Boyd). Narrated by Fane's pal and gofer Hymie Kelly (Tony Bennett), the film is told in flashback, describing Fane's rise from burlesque barker to gigolo to Hollywood movie star and heel.

The film exerts its own peculiar kind of fascination with its over-the-top dialogue (Sample: "Frankie's on the biggest narcotic of all—success") and ridiculous period details (Hymie, leading the swinging life in Hollywood with pal Frankie, wears an assortment of multicolored cardigan sweaters). So absurd is the screenplay that Frankie's soon-to-be wife, the costume sketch artist Kay Bergdahl (Elke Sommer) arrives in Hollywood and somehow on her sketch artist's salary is able to live in a beautiful, fully furnished Beverly Hills mansion.

Boyd, an ever-tense actor who could score when working with top-notch directors (William Wyler's *Ben-Hur* and Charles Walter's *Billy Rose's Jumbo*), here delivers an unremittingly shrill and manic performance. This is not a human being, but a cartoon figure who is evil personified. Or, as the screenplay so delicately puts it: "It's that seed of rot inside of you . . . When you lie down with pigs, you come up smelling like garbage." Couple such purple dialogue with melodramatic music by Percy Faith, and you have one big camp fest.

Along the way, one can marvel at how Elke Sommer's blond bouffant doesn't move an inch during a convertible ride, that she depicts her anguish by literally biting her fingers, and most of all, at the fact that here is a movie where the always-larger-than-life Milton Berle (as Frankie's agent Kappy Kapstetter) actually delivers the film's most subtle performance.

There is exactly one line of dialogue that does ring true, and sums up the false sentiment so often rampant in Hollywood. Says Frankie about deliberately leaking news of his long-ago arrest in order to generate sympathy for his Oscar bid: "I can't rig the votes, but I can rig the emotions of the voters." It's a remarkably clear-eyed look at the Hollywood machine, and sums up a year's worth of Hollywood spinmeisters' work. But the film itself sure doesn't make any claims upon the emotions of its viewers, the audience long since having tuned out, or settled into laughing at—not with—the film.

So it is that in the film's final sequence, Merle Oberon, playing herself, comes onstage to announce the Academy Award for Best Actor. The nominees' names are read off, and when Oberon announces the winner as "Frank . . . ," Frankie Fane leaps to his feet—only to hear her complete the winner's name with the surname of Sinatra. At which point, Frank Sinatra leans over to kiss daughter Nancy, bounds up onstage to accept the Oscar, and tells the audience, "Thank you very much," as the Sinatra standard "All the Way" plays. The audience follows Frankie Fane's misbegotten gesture and joins in a standing ovation for Sinatra. The film then mercifully fades out, but not before Stephen Boyd delivers one last bit of overwrought histrionics, clapping so hard in a mixture of despair and self-loathing that he genuinely appears to be having a convulsion. The entire fiasco was pungently summed up by Richard Schickel in *Life* magazine, who simply noted, "But this is that true movie rarity—a picture that attains a perfection of ineptitude quite beyond the power of words to describe. You have to see it to disbelieve it."

Sinatra looks great playing himself—vibrant and youthful and much younger than his then-fifty years—but the real note of interest to Sinatra observers is that *The Oscar* represents the one and only starring role on film for Tony Bennett. Bennett, a brilliant vocalist who was hailed by Sinatra as his favorite singer, wrote in his autobiography that he had repeatedly been offered film roles, turning them all down because he was only asked to play gangsters. Whatever the pluses and minuses of those proposed vehicles, they had to have contained material superior to this, because far from turning Bennett into the newest star in town, *The Oscar* most notably served to make clear why the Tony Bennett of 1965 did not register as strongly on film as did Sinatra. Bennett may have been granted a solo screen credit reading, AND INTRODUCING TONY BENNETT AS HYMIE KELLY, but the film proved a total nonstarter for Bennett's screen career.

For a man who appears so comfortable onstage singing, Bennett looks mighty uncomfortable on film, hunched over throughout and radiating a sense of vague unease to the viewer. Sinatra, even in his earliest film appearances, conveyed superb body language: stiff backed, striding with confidence, always the star. Bennett appears vaguely embarrassed to be a part of the movie, and who can blame him? The makeup and clothes do him no favors, and as photographed by Joseph Ruttenberg, none of his intelligence, warmth, or onstage charisma is conveyed. Sinatra's sculpted face always photographed well, the planes catching the light in interesting and odd ways—no such care is here granted Bennett. He delivers the ridiculous narrative dialogue as well as anyone could, and his slightly husky voice is capable of conveying shadings and meanings, but Sir Laurence Olivier himself could not have overcome the vacuity of this screenplay. It may be that Bennett was not ready to act on film at that point; never so tortured as Sinatra, he also never carried the Sinatra-esque aura of intrigue. With the second, and highly successful, phase of his recording career beginning in the early 1980s, Bennett appeared more relaxed onstage, fully in command of his craft, and able to convey the meaning of his beautifully chosen classic popular songs in a soulful manner that had deepened noticeably since his salad days. Seemingly much more comfortable in his own skin, Bennett, like Rosemary Clooney, matured enormously as an artist, and in his sixties and seventies became an interpretive artist of the very highest rank. It's an interpretive ability that should have carried over onto film, but in strictly acting terms, it had not yet fully evolved by the mid-1960s.

Camp histrionics of *The Oscar* out of the way, one month later, Frank popped up onscreen in another cameo, this time in *Cast a Giant Shadow.* This story about the founding of Israel in 1948 is a much more substantial piece than *The Oscar,* but as frequently happened with Sinatra's cameo appearances, the reasons for Frank's participation are a lot more interesting than the film itself.

Sinatra, a lifelong sympathizer with Jewish causes, had very much enjoyed his 1962 concerts in Israel, and felt a personal attachment to the Frank Sinatra International Youth Center that he had opened at that time. When the opportunity came about for Sinatra to film his cameo in *Cast a Giant Shadow,* he insisted on shooting in Israel, and not in the previously suggested locale of Rome. After his three days of filming in June of 1965, Sinatra donated his entire fifty-thousand-dollar fee to the Youth Center. His participation in the film represented a labor of love on his part, the material's exploration of international brotherhood one Sinatra had been exploring on film in one form or another since the Academy Award–winning *The House I Live In.*

Written and directed by Melville Shavelson, the film stars Kirk Douglas as Mickey Marcus, an American Jew instrumental in the founding of Israel. For all the crowd scenes of struggling peasants, the film is basically a one-man show, which Douglas dominates to intermittent effect. Douglas, an unremittingly earnest actor capable of exhausting an audience, here portrays an American soldier with a desire to help Jewish survivors of the Holocaust establish the state of Israel. He's a man who can't resist the action, or as wife Emma Marcus (Angie Dickinson) says to him: "You're more excited by war than by me." Which makes him either extremely dedicated—or a little crazy.

Trying to fight the Arabs as well as elude the British military personnel still on the scene, Marcus hatches a campaign of deception that, in the screenplay's oh-so-subtle words, "has got to be the biggest deception since the invention of falsies." Oh, so that's how the state of Israel was born. Along the way, there are impressive battle scenes, dopey dialogue, and encounters with guest stars John Wayne (whose Batjac production company produced the film for United

Artists) and Yul Brynner. Eventually Mickey realizes he should renounce lusty peasant Magda (Senta Berger) and go back home to wife Emma, only to be shot by a nervous sentry right before he departs. The last casualty before the truce is declared, Marcus dies while Israel lives. *Oy vey.*

The founding of Israel is certainly a worthy and compelling story for the screen, but dialogue about falsies and Marcus realizing he belongs with a wife in whom he has shown little interest does not exactly have the ring of historical truth to it. And where does Frank Sinatra fit into the proceedings? A little over an hour into the film, he shows up as Spence, a pilot and mercenary of sorts, who is referred to as the Pride of Passaic. Wearing a bomber jacket that makes him look as if he's still about to board *Von Ryan's Express,* Sinatra at age fifty-one looks youthful and far more vibrant than he had fifteen years earlier as the bedraggled title character in *Meet Danny Wilson.*

Frank's brief appearance most notably finds him readying for takeoff before dropping bombs on the Arab enemy. There's just one problem for the intrepid Spence: he has not been given any bombs, the fledgling Israeli army possessing little in the way of ammunition. Instead, he is told to drop seltzer bottles from his ancient-looking propeller plane because they will "scream on the way down." Retorts Sinatra in one of the film's few truly funny lines, "Great—that'll make two of us."

When Spence's plane is attacked, his gun jams, he is reduced to the futile gesture of squirting seltzer at the approaching enemy plane, and it's no surprise to see his plane crashing in the next frames. Sinatra looks fine throughout his brief appearance, he's a believable pilot, and it all unrolls smoothly until the squirting of the seltzer.

The squirting may have happened in real life, but dropping seltzer bottles on film simply looks like another childish prank by Sinatra and his buddies, a problematic intersection of actor and persona actually pinpointed by director Shavelson: "It might have been better with an unknown playing it. People might have believed it more. All of those things really happened. But having real movie stars in it made people think it was all phony and *nothing* was true, as if the war itself never happened." It's an astute assessment and symptomatic of what can happen with a star of Sinatra's magnitude, one whose outsize talent is matched by his outsize personality.

Sinatra's heart was in the right place, the film was an honorable but botched attempt to address issues regarding the Middle East, and it's a far more worthy use of Frank's time and talents than the meaningless cameos found in *The Oscar* and *Pepe*. Yet, in the end, it doesn't hang together, because Sinatra is simply too big a personality for so small a role. Damned if you do, and damned if you don't. Or, as the reviews would have it, "Frank Sinatra, looking all of 28 years old, lights up the screen as a soldier of fortune flier but" . . . "*Cast a Giant Shadow* is an embarrassing movie." . . . "another exercise in movie biography [that] may be filed as a case of mistaken identity: any resemblance to persons living or dead is sacrificed to make elbowroom for Hero Kirk Douglas." . . .

Cameos completed, it was back to starring roles with *Assault on a Queen,* a film that continued his affiliation with Paramount Pictures following *Come Blow Your Horn* and the college musical *For Those Who Think Young.* The latter film, produced by Sinatra Enterprises, did not star Frank, instead featuring Nancy Sinatra in a nearly unwatchable mess that plods along as one very long plug for Pepsi-Cola. The plot—which is much too strong a word for the on-screen shenanigans—focuses on surfing college students who seem to spend all their time watching "comedian" Woody Woodbury whenever they're not racing off to surf in the extremely placid ocean. Nancy plays opposite Bob Denver, while other unfortunate actors dragged along for the ride include Ellen McRae (soon to find fame as Ellen Burstyn) and Paul Lynde. Billed as the "swingin'est young people's picture of the year!" it proved to be anything but.

Many Sinatra commentators reserve particular scorn for *Assault on a Queen,* but the truth is, it's not that bad—it's just perfunctory in its low-budget kind of way. The harsh treatment of the pic seems to stem from a sense of Sinatra wasting his prodigious acting talents on such caper films, but while the movie didn't even remotely test his talents, it's not offensive, and certainly rates as an improvement on the first Sinatra/Donohue collaboration, *Marriage on the Rocks.*

Based on the novel by Jack Finney (author of the cult time-travel novel *Time and Again*), *Assault on a Queen* was produced by William Goetz, who along with wife Edie (L. B. Mayer's daughter) was particularly close to Sinatra at this time. Talent abounded behind the scenes, with William Daniels returning as director of photography, a screenplay by Rod Serling of *Twilight Zone* fame, and a score composed by the great Duke Ellington. So, with all that talent on board, what actually resulted? Short answer: a standard caper film, one that plays like a smaller, less interesting, nautical version of *Ocean's Eleven.*

The plot concerns a motley gang of six: three World War II veterans, a beautiful woman, an ex-drunk, and a grifter of no discernible morals. Together, the ad hoc gang raises a German submarine scuttled during the Second World War and, using just the sub and a dummy torpedo, attempts to rob the *Queen Mary*. It's a fantastical conceit—which is exactly the problem with the film. It's just too fantastic to buy, even after suspending an inordinate amount of disbelief.

After a (literally) jazzy title sequence in which a pencil intriguingly marks the location of treasure on a sea chart, the film opens with the death of a deep-sea diver who has been on a treasure-hunting expedition put together by Vic Rossiter (Anthony Franciosa) and his rich girlfriend Rosa Lucchesi (Virna Lisi). Right off the bat, Rossiter's utter lack of concern for the dead man paints him as the villain of the piece; Rossiter approaches charter fisherman and former submarine commander Mark Brittain (Sinatra) and his sidekick, Bahamian native Linc Langley (Errol John), to resume the hunt for treasure. The search proves futile, but Brittain's dives reveal a German U-boat buried at sea, at which point, the plan to rob the *Queen Mary* is instigated.

Sinatra looks the part of the cynical World War II vet—unshaven, hard-drinking, card-playing, and chain-smoking. In Brittain's own words, "I live my life as I see fit—and I have a ball." Not exactly a stretch for Frank himself to understand those words, nor for the audience to accept his saying them. There is even some nice crisp dialogue establishing his seen-it-all toughness. After Brittain knocks the dockmaster into the water for demanding his monthly docking fee, Linc worriedly asks him, "Can he swim?" The terse reply: "We'll check the morning papers." Signing on for the job, Mark is immediately attracted to Rosa, a mutual interest that even leads to some nicely judged repartee; when Rosa explains that she won't steal from the poor, a bemused Brittain murmurs, "How do you like this? A blond Italian Robin Hood."

Ironically, it is only when Brittain gets the sub to float and the conspirators put it into a shed for refurbishment that the film, yes, starts to sink. For starters, if the sub had really been underwater for twenty years, it's laughable to presume that it would be in as good condition as is here presented. The gang merely applies a little elbow grease, all but burst into "Whistle While You Work," and presto—it's operational. Couple this with the noticeably phony-looking shots of the sub running underneath the water, and the premise becomes unhinged. The cheap-looking miniatures harm the film far more than the obvious use of a double for Sinatra's underwater diving. No one expects to see Frank himself swimming in scuba gear underneath the ocean, but they do expect to believe they are watching an actual sub, not a model left over from *Voyage to the Bottom of the Sea.*

Surprisingly, Virna Lisi's character of Rosa is actually granted same depth. When bad guy Rossiter casually refers to "owning" Rosa, she instantly retorts "No one owns me." She's a woman with guts. Granted, in the big midnight bathing sequence, Lisi does get stuck wearing a feathered bathing cap that looks suitable for Big Bird on *Sesame Street,* but she actually does a credible job here. There is a toughness about her that enables her to register more strongly with Sinatra than did either Gina Lollabrigida (*Never So Few*) or Sophia Loren (*The Pride and the Passion*). Lisi herself (or the film's publicist) had some remarkably perceptive things to say about Sinatra, the man and the icon.

> To me he was always a symbol of what I wanted the American male to be. Not what I thought he was, of course, but what I wanted him to be—magnetic, animal, sensuous. That is Sinatra and it happens in his voice when he sings and in his acting when he makes love. Yes, I guess you would say I enjoyed working with him.

For his part, Frank returned the compliment, even deftly adding in a refutation of the perennial Mafia rumors: "If they'd had Virna in the Mafia, I'd never have torn up my membership card."

Even given the occasional witty line, the dialogue is still an up-and-down affair; Errol John (Linc), whose British accent appears to come and go with the breeze, is saddled with clunky exposition, but it's Sinatra who is saddled with the single worst line in the movie: referring to his passion for Rosa, he actually is forced to utter the words, "She's so deep in my gut, we breathe together." It's a tribute to Sinatra's inherent believability that the audience doesn't laugh out loud at such purple dialogue.

Donohue and Serling obviously did not trust their audience's intelligence very much, because although it is clear that Brittain's cynicism masks a big heart, the audience is still hit over the head with that fact; Linc must solemnly inform all concerned that "I think amongst this whole motley crew, Mark has the most substance." If only they had trusted the abilities of their actors, the film would have improved noticeably—witness Sinatra's silent shrug of wonderment to Linc when the sub is found to actually operate underwater. That small gesture says more about the improbability and surprise of the caper than does all the leaden exposition with which the actors are saddled. Similarly, Sinatra's wordless reaction to seeing Rosa the morning after they have slept together says everything about their relationship. Viewers can supply their own dialogue here because when Brittain spies Rosa, Sinatra grins his movie star grin, winks at her, and in that one brief silent sequence once again tells the audience what the characters are feeling and why he became a movie star: blue eyes flashing, a devil-may-care grin on his face, he is like all true stars, heady with the promise of sex yet equally appealing to men and women, albeit for different reasons.

The gang succeeds in stealing jewelry and bullion from the *Queen Mary*, but are forced to leave the too heavy stolen loot in the raft, along with Rossiter. By now, Rossiter's dead and so is the movie. The blatantly miniature submarine shots once again dissipate all tension; they're pulling off a million-dollar robbery, and the submarine looks like it's a child's toy floating in a bathtub. Moreno is shot dead, and the film ends with Brittain, Rosa, and Linc alive in an inflatable raft. Brittain's final wisecrack to Linc? "Start paddling—South America is that way." Just as in *Ocean's Eleven*, the caper has been pulled off, but the criminals end up with nothing.

It all makes for a rather nice ending to a decidedly up-and-down affair, and while Sinatra's not bad in the film, neither does he stand out. Given the uneven nature of the screenplay, he's just marking time, swanning his way through the film by playing not the film's character, but rather, Frank Sinatra the movie star. He deserved better and could do better. Frank clearly knew the script wasn't great, but with his need to keep working, appears to have figured "what the hell." It all amounted, at best, to running in place. By working for the sake of work, he appeased his restless nature but shortchanged his own talent.

Maybe Frank was just too damn preoccupied with his personal life and couldn't fully concentrate on the work, because eight days before the July 1966 release of the film, he and Mia Farrow were married. Neither the marriage nor the film fared well, although at least Sinatra and Farrow remained friends for the rest of his life. The film, on the other hand, sank with barely a trace and came in for a noteworthy pan from the *Monthly Film Bulletin*: "Just about as enthralling as plastic boats in the bath." That was the verdict of the general public as well, because the mild box office returns meant that Sinatra had now suffered through two box office disasters in a row, a streak that only lengthened with his next film, 1967's *The Naked Runner.*

The Naked Runner rates as one of the true "might have beens" of Sinatra's film career. Portions of it work extremely well, and the seeds of a superior film can be glimpsed from time to time. When all is said and done, however, Sinatra and the movie are done in by director Sidney J. Furie, screenwriters Francis Clifford and Stanley Mann, and cinematographer Otto Heller.

The Naked Runner came to Sinatra through Brad Dexter, who was now ensconced as executive vice-president in charge of motion picture production at Sinatra Enterprises. Initially, it was William Goldman's first-rate script for *Harper* that Dexter had brought to Sinatra's attention, but when the deal for *Harper* fell through, Dexter then pushed *The Naked Runner* to his boss. Based on the novel of the same name by Francis Clifford, the screenplay by Stanley Mann follows the recruitment of American World War II veteran Sam Laker (Sinatra) as the would-be assassin of freed political prisoner Rudolph Feisen. Fearing Feisen's return to Moscow with top-secret information—and unable to utilize normal operatives who would be recognized by East German intelligence—British intelligence officer Martin Slattery (Peter Vaughan) recruits his old war buddy Sam Laker. A former sharpshooter who has remained in England for twenty years postwar, Laker has no interest in such an endeavor and so must be tricked into undertaking the assassination of Feisen. It's a strong premise for a thriller—the audience knows Sinatra will succumb. The question is how he will do so.

The slow but certain capitulation of Laker due to guilt over abandoning agent Karen Gisevius (Nadia Gray) during World War II, the grim echoes of the cold war—it is all set up in nice fashion, beginning with Sinatra's very appearance. Rounder of face, but still trim of torso, Sinatra looks lived-in, but never haggard. Furie favors startling close-ups of Sinatra's blue eyes, but it's never just star-gazing time. In Sinatra's nonverbal acting, one can recognize the conflicting emotions Laker feels. A widower with a twelve-year-old son, Patrick (Michael Newport), he is loath to upset the careful life he has created, but haunted by guilt, he agrees to deliver a message to an agent in Leipzig.

The fish has been baited and is now reeled in—when Sam leaves Patrick alone in the Leipzig hotel lobby, Patrick is kidnapped by orders of British intelligence in order to coerce Sam's participation in the assassination attempt. Sam is made to believe that his son has been kidnapped by East German secret police officer Colonel Hartmann (Derren Nesbitt), but the supposedly Communist operative is, in fact, a British agent in disguise. In a particularly harrowing sequence, Laker is marched into a forest, where Colonel Hartmann pulls a pistol on him; Sinatra, his face drenched in perspiration, looks exactly like a man who senses his imminent death, and when Hartmann lowers the pistol and cynically states, "Not today, Mr. Laker," Laker vomits. There is a quick cut to Sinatra back in a sterile room, his face immersed in a bowl of water in order to combat the nausea and the horror of his near death. It's a very effective sequence that not only delineates how he could be reeled in for such a plan, but also effectively conveys Laker's utter fear—for his son and for his own life.

Best of all is a first-rate sequence wherein Laker deliberately misses the bull's-eye target Hartmann insists he shoot. Hartmann's response? He simply—and silently— places Patrick's German–English phrasebook in front of Laker, a signal that he has kidnapped Laker's son. An angry and frightened Laker mutters "you bastard" and rapidly fires off five perfect shots into the bull's-eye, a sign that he will now sign on as assassin. With just two words and five perfect shots, the viewer is told everything he or she needs to know about the character, his love for his son, and the lengths to which the British government will go in order to ensure his cooperation. Sam Laker cannot outrun his past.

So far, so good, which is why it is all the more disappointing when the film begins to fall apart with great alacrity. For starters, and most notably, Furie's screen compositions, which fascinate at the beginning, become familiar and then downright irritating when repeated endlessly. Faces are distorted when shot through patterned glass, nearby buildings are reflected upon the actors' faces, ensuring that the audience is never granted the opportunity to look at the actor's face head-on. Furie repeatedly shoots from low angles for no discernible reason other than to draw attention to his artistry. The incessant alternating of close-ups with wide-screen panoramas doesn't further the story, confuses the viewer, and exists only for its own sake—it's show-off filmmaking. Making matters worse is the fact that the film is very dimly lit throughout. It's a deliberate choice by Furie and director of photography Otto Heller (*The Ipcress File*), but what starts out as an effective comment on the drab atmosphere of the cold war soon becomes wearing. The film is relentlessly dark and grainy, ultimately saddled with the look of a severely underbudgeted British television program.

It's not just the cinematography that irritates. For some odd reason, Furie and screenwriters Clifford and Mann insist on having the characters verbalize exactly what has already been shown onscreen. After the hatching of plots and shadowy counterplots, not to mention all the footage of spying, the characters still must announce, "You're hooking him into an espionage scheme and lying to him every step of the way." Uh, no kidding. It's as if Clifford and Furie don't trust the audience to analyze the sequences themselves. Strangely enough, the filmmakers seem to have forgotten that theirs is a visual medium, making the film a dialogue-heavy piece of theater. Bad decision all around.

The one point of interest is Sinatra himself and his depiction of a man slowly edging to the brink. After being detained by the police, he is rattled to the core and, shades of *Suddenly,* ready to become an assassin. It's worth noting that Sinatra's roles as crook, soldier, assassin, and detective found him playing men who carried guns in no fewer than twenty-two of his films. As Bosley Crowther said in his *New York Times* review of *The Naked Runner,* "It is curious how Frank Sinatra repeatedly gets himself involved in films about fellows who do violent things with guns—gangsters, soldiers, or assassins. He seems immensely attracted to stories in which he as the leading character is called upon to kill." In other words: surburban dad, no; gun-toting tough guy, yes.

When Laker receives (falsified) word that his son has died, Furie elects to shoot only Sinatra's slackening hand as a sign of the anguish he feels. It's a nicely understated touch, and it therefore comes as a bit of a shock when the film reaches its climactic assassination attempt and, once again, Furie showily frames Laker between the stalks of a flower. Such blatantly arty shots inevitably dilute the suspense by calling attention to themselves, rather than serving the story. Alfred Hitchcock's meticulous visual construction always lay in service to the plot, but here the exact opposite holds true.

Running through the tunnel at full speed, pumping bullet after bullet into a car which then explodes, Laker thinks he has killed German operative Hartmann, but he has, in fact, killed the intended target, the Communist spy who is returning to Moscow. All of a sudden, Laker finds out that both Hartmann and his son are still alive, learns that he was set up by British intelligence, is now confronted with the unexpected appearance of Hartmann (the man he thinks he has just killed), and learns that he has now assassinated a very important cold war operative. That's a lot for one man to take on board, and how does the film treat the numerous revelations? Laker's minder simply states, "C'mon, Sam—get in the car," and the film ends.

Any thinking viewer can only ask, *Where's the son?* Given the fact that Laker participated in the assassination plot only because he thought his son Patrick had been killed, aren't we even going to see father and son reunited? Why the long setup and the abbreviated payoff? Do the director and screenwriter know the film doesn't really make sense? After a deliberate and fairly clever setup, the film has rushed through an extremely hasty wrap-up, left the audience dangling with many unanswered questions, and generally exuded an overall air of the filmmakers wanting to get the damn thing over with.

Commentators have cited Sinatra's new and quickly fraught marriage to Mia Farrow as a compelling reason for the film's difficulties, and in fact, Sinatra had stopped production on the film shortly after shooting began, in order to marry Farrow in Las Vegas. (So determined was he to avoid press coverage of the actual wedding that he did not tell his own daughters of the ceremony, nor did he allow Farrow to tell her mother.) When the press did learn about the marriage, the resulting coverage was worldwide, but marital problems soon gave the press even more to write about.

In fact, when Edie and Bill Goetz threw a party for the bride and groom, the difficulties waiting down the road already lay in plain view. This was a whole new kind of generation gap in Hollywood. Aside from Mia's brother Patrick and his wife, as well as her sister Prudence, the remainder of the guest list was Hollywood royalty, all of whom were at least Sinatra's age, if not older: George Cukor, Katharine Hepburn, Spencer Tracy, Edward G. Robinson, Ruth and Garson Kanin. For proto-hippie Mia Farrow, it was a different world: surrounded by people her parents' age, none of her peers invited, and finding herself the same age as her husband's children. This, she must have thought, is going to prove very difficult. Which it did. But—tabloid-ready marriage or not, the Frank–Mia personal drama can't be taken as the only reason for the slapdash nature of the film and its poor reception.

The resulting debacle was really due to a combination of many factors in addition to the ill-conceived marriage. For starters, there were well-documented fits of temper, Sinatra refusing to travel to any locations by car rather than by helicopter. Not to be left out of the general unpleasantness, director Furie himself also displayed piques of temper. Sinatra, always unhappy on location shoots at the best of times, not only disliked being in London, but felt at sea in the "swinging London" of the 1960s. Carnaby Street and the rock revolution were a long way from the elegant London of Sinatra's black-tie past. In the words of his longtime valet George Jacobs, "Mr. S. hated London for being taken over by the Carnaby Street Mod atmosphere so much that he basically dumped the picture, went back to LA and let the producers worry about putting together what footage they had." The hurry-up-and-wait atmosphere of an overseas film shoot? Always a bad idea with the younger Frank, it proved to be a recipe for disaster with the fifty-year-old version.

In the further recounting of Brad Dexter, Sinatra even returned to California during shooting in order to campaign at a rally for California governor Edmund Brown (whose opponent was Frank's soon-to-be close friend Ronald Reagan). Once back in California, Frank dispatched attorney Mickey Rudin to inform Dexter that he would not return to Copenhagen, and would instead film his remaining scenes in Los Angeles on a soundstage. Dexter and Furie then decided to finish the film without Sinatra, utilizing a double where absolutely necessary. For his troubles, Dexter was fired from Sinatra Enterprises.

One can understand why Sinatra was initially attracted to the source material, but whatever disappointment he felt in the ultimate outcome must be weighed against the fact that he basically bagged the film before it was even finished. After the interesting and rather successful one-two punch of *None But the Brave* and *Von Ryan's Express,* the utterly indifferent response to *The Naked Runner* marked Sinatra's third flop in a row after the flaccid *Marriage on the Rocks* and *Assault on a Queen.* The fact that it was the best of the three flops must have provided scant consolation indeed, especially given the negative reviews it received upon its release in July of 1967, most famously Pauline Kael's scathing putdown in *The New Republic* that "*The Naked Runner* might be a good movie to read by if there were light in the theater." It was actually Charles Champlin in the *Los Angeles Times* who summed up Sinatra's acting turn best:

Of Sinatra, it must be said that even in this undemonstrative rendition of undistinguished material, he commands the screen. Given the plot there must have been a temptation to shout, moan and chew the scenery. He put the temptation down, way down, and understates the histrionics. The result is a sense of power held in check, of power wasted.

"Waste" is exactly the right word, and Sinatra found himself in an odd position, where his acting ability was being wasted on second-rate screenplays at the same time that his vocal legacy was burnished with an extraordinary series of masterly concept albums. Early 1967 found the fifty-one-year-old Frank at the peak of his autumnal powers as he recorded one of his unquestioned vocal masterpieces, *Francis Albert Sinatra and Antonio Carolos Jobim.* That beautiful album consists of an extraordinarily effective blend of bossa nova and lightly swinging jazz vocals, and succeeds in creating an unbroken mood of romance and regret. With songs delivered in murmured vocal lines that suggested a lifetime's worth of love and loss, the album justifiably received Grammy nominations as Album of the Year and Best Male Vocal Performance.

Why was the disconnect between the recording studio and the film set so much more pronounced at this time than in the previous twenty-five years of Sinatra's film career? That really constitutes the key question to ask regarding his work of the era, because after his extraordinary run with many first-class films right up through *Von Ryan's Express,* the bottom had fallen out with the trio of *Marriage on the Rocks, Assault on a Queen,* and *The Naked Runner.* People forgave Frank a great deal, but three subpar outings in a row seemed to break the loyalty of even his most devoted movie fans. The productions looked cheap, Sinatra sleepwalking through certain sections of the movies with a decidedly unconcerned air, and the finished pictures registered as so slapdash that audiences began to ask themselves, *Why should I care if he doesn't?* Frank was filming when he should not have been, working not out of passion for the material but for the money and, what is more noteworthy, out of his insatiable need to stay busy. Ironically, it was that very need to stay busy that bothered Frank on the film set now more than ever. The intensive concentrated work of the recording studio found Frank "on" all the time, singing, performing (Sinatra preferred to record in front of a live studio audience), and in effect both producing and directing the sessions. It's not just that filming, by way of contrast, proceeded in one- or two-minute bits that required time-consuming elaborate setups. It's the fact that while the young

Frank put up with those impediments in order to prove himself as an actor, the older Frank, having proved himself many times over on film, and now increasingly wealthy and powerful, ceased to find the process worth his effort. There were more films to follow, and some contained moments of inspiration, but increasingly Sinatra appeared to ask himself, *Who needs this?*

It therefore seems fitting that Frank recorded "My Way" at this stage of his life. He certainly did everything his way by that point, and if he famously held a love-hate relationship with the song, fans took to it wholeheartedly, responding to the inflated self-heroic lyrics "I took the blows . . . and did it my way" as if Sinatra were singing of his very own life. Great artist and actor that Sinatra was, in later years he took to singing the song in a less bombastic manner, undercutting the grandiosity with a reflective approach that still scored, the socko orchestrations supplying the rush the audience craved.

"My Way" or not, Frank felt the need for a change of pace, and determined to give films one more try, he next ventured into the territory of the detective film, beginning with 1967's *Tony Rome.* For the most part, the results were decidedly worthwhile. Yes, *Tony Rome*'s debt to Raymond Chandler (*The Big Sleep*; *Farewell, My Lovely*) is noticeable, but it all works, and at times even feels fresh, because the persona of a private investigator fit Frank Sinatra perfectly. Given the ensuing intersection of persona, actor, and character, it's understandable that from 1967 through 1980, Sinatra played a detective in five of his last six starring vehicles (the only exception being his turn as a dumb outlaw in the extraordinarily dopey Western *Dirty Dingus Magee*). Audiences expect detectives to resemble their idealized version of Frank Sinatra: the man in question has been around the block more than once, is bruised, tough, cynical yet still possesses a small private reservoir of hope. Tough with men, wary with women, the chivalrous knight who has seen it all but still fights the daily fight—it all fit Frank Sinatra like one of his custom-made suits. For the first time in quite a while, critics and audiences alike responded, and Frank had himself a final, sustained, and fully satisfying rush of movie star popularity. The fire still burned.

Knight-Errant

"Someone to Watch over Me,"
sung by Frank Sinatra in *Young at Heart*

I believe in complete honesty, no cheating, in all my work. —FRANK SINATRA

I N THE LATE-CAREER SERIES of detective films Sinatra began shooting in 1967, he developed an onscreen image that most closely fit the public's perception of Frank Sinatra the man. From *Tony Rome, The Detective,* and *Lady in Cement* through to *Contract on Cherry Street, The First Deadly Sin,* and a guest appearance on *Magnum, P.I.* he morphed into everyone's rose-colored version of the offscreen Frank Sinatra. A hero with more than a touch of the loser about him, in all these films he portrays a character who refuses to play by the rules of society. As a result, he bungles promotions and loses money and power, yet maintains his personal honor. The hardened outer shell hides the grizzled yet still vulnerable idealist, with nary a trace of sentimentality—women are won and lost, and at the end, the knight-errant always stands alone, bloodied but unbowed. So persuasively did Sinatra embody the role, both to the audience and to himself, that those rugged investigators finally became the film persona most closely identified with Frank Sinatra. Even more than the sailor-suited-musical boy next door or the intense dramatic actor involved in assassination plots, the onscreen Frank Sinatra lives on in popular imagination as this solitary urban soldier. He epitomizes the ultimate paternalistic figure—it's a brutal world and no one escapes unscathed, but father knows best. Trying to make the world safer for those who are, in effect, his children, he is the knight-errant attempting to right society's wrongs. That the attempt fails as often as it succeeds only serves to underscore the detective's valiant, ofttimes heroic effort.

With those roles, Sinatra may have developed into the ultimate paterfamilias onscreen, yet the dearth of roles in which he played an actual father is no accident, and in some ways that was reflected in his own life. A devoted but frequently absent father, one who later in life acknowledged that he had often been unavailable when needed by his own children, Frank could never have developed a career based on a comforting feeling of family and togetherness for the basic reason that his art, whether on disc or on film, was solitary by nature. His subject was almost always that of loneliness and, even more specifically, a particularly American form of loneliness that informed so much of the post–Second World War suburban landscape. If the men and women in a midcentury suburban America at the height of its powers were compulsive joiners of clubs, sports leagues, and charitable organizations, they still experienced a disconcerting solitude, a solitude Frank both sang about and personified onscreen. At the same time, the offscreen corollary held true as well: Sinatra, the happiest of men when surrounded by the tumult of a friendly entourage, remained at heart a markedly solitary figure.

It is therefore all the more ironic that with Sinatra's great wealth of actual living experience and the concomitant overlay of his huge personality onto his roles, the public finally came to accept—indeed, demand—that he function as an all-knowing parent in his art. It's the final and ultimate manifestation of his song "That's Life"; the lyric tells us he has tried on many different life roles and he knows just one thing: "Each time I find myself flat on my face—I pick myself up and get back in the race." It's what parents tell children—"get up, get back on the horse, and participate in the journey of life—there is no other choice." Which is exactly what Frank Sinatra, half father figure, half perpetual adolescent, did over and over, onscreen and off.

The archetype of the paternalistic loner can be seen clearly in the very first of the detective films, the November 1967 release *Tony Rome*. Made for Twentieth Century-Fox and based on the novel of the same name by Marvin H. Albert, the film reunited Sinatra with his *Robin and the 7 Hoods* director Gordon Douglas, as well as favored cinematographer Joseph Biroc. With a score by musical compadre Billy May, and a title tune sung by daughter Nancy, Sinatra was in familiar territory and it shows onscreen: He's relaxed and in command. (The title song does feature a rather strange lyric, given that Nancy is singing about her father: "Mothers, lock your daughters in—it's too late to talk to them. Tony Rome will get 'em if you don't watch out.")

Oddly enough, for all the verisimilitude Sinatra brings to the role, when the film opens with shots of Rome on board his houseboat, one's immediate reaction is that the nattily dressed Rome appears too neat for a private detective. Tony sports a yellow mock turtleneck, pressed trousers, and a nautical cap. Isn't that all wrong? Shouldn't he be hungover, bleary-eyed, and grizzled around the edges? It's when Rome changes into the more formal attire he sports for the bulk of the film—all dark suits and fedoras—that he looks the picture of a private detective, one whose clothes now successfully convey the noirish aspects of his work.

The tongue-in-cheek opening—which jump-cuts from the close-up of a woman's derriere that Tony is ogling to a boxer's butt—tells the viewer that the film possesses a sense of humor, and that even while Tony solves a murder, the film will not exactly be delving into a philosophical examination of the meaning of life. Instead, the plot finds Rome called upon by his fink of an ex-partner Ralph Turpin (Robert J. Wilke) to help rescue the wealthy and very drunk young Diana Kosterman Pires (Sue Lyon), who is passed out on a hotel bed (the ex-partner being the hotel detective). Nothing seems to faze Rome. Eyeing the rotund hotel owner who clearly would like to forget about paying Rome the second half of his fee, Rome barks at his ex-partner, "Tell chubby here it wouldn't be healthy if he forgets the other hundred dollars." (Of course, in an unfortunate time capsule moment, the dialogue also features the following comment about Tony: "Someone will squeeze something out of Tony the day Georgia elects a colored governor.") Rome, so confident an operator that he has bookies call him at police headquarters, dislikes his partner but owes him for saving his life. Ergo, Tony arrives to rescue young Diana and deliver her to the home of her wealthy father, developer Rudy Kosterman (the appropriately belligerent Simon Oakland).

Even, or make that especially, when meeting "dames," the wisecracks never leave Tony, the atmospheric repartee not only establishing character and situation, but also landing plenty of laughs along the way. Even better is Rome's imperturbable facade; returning to his own boat, he is greeted by a pistol shoved in his face. His response to the thugs is simply a nonchalant "How are ya?" He is chloroformed for his troubles—even saying "when" to the thugs in order to indicate that they have applied enough chloroform to make him pass out. His boat is subsequently trashed, but nothing stops Tony, which is just the way audiences like their private eyes: in trouble yet ultimately still in control. As such, like a real private eye and a true movie star, Sinatra always radiates the illusion of ease.

After Rome discovers the dead body of erstwhile partner Turpin underneath his desk—a fact that barely causes him to interrupt his conversation—the rather byzantine plot picks up steam nicely. Clearly, Diana Kosterman and the entire Kosterman family spell trouble; Diana is a sexually suggestive troubled young drunk, father Rudy is a rich bully used to getting his way, and stepmother Rita is rather enigmatic and protective of her past. (Rowlands, who is terrific even in such an abbreviated role, occasions one of Rome's best lines. When she offers him a bribe so that he won't tell her husband certain information, Rome replies: "First Diana hires me. Then your husband hires me. Now you wanna hire me. If you had a bigger family, I could retire.")

Rome may be intermittently dealing with Rita and her stepdaughter Diana, but it's Ann Archer, in the person of Jill St. John, who hovers in the background throughout. St. John is a rather limited actress with some understanding of how to deliver the lines, but lacking the vocal equipment to shade the meanings. (At

Booze, broads, and brawls. Here with Jill St. John in the entertaining Tony Rome *(1967).*

the time of filming in 1967, St. John was rumored to be a real-life paramour of Sinatra's.) Here she scores a bit better than usual, thanks to her above-average dialogue. Spelling out her view of Miami to Tony, she sourly observes, "Miami Beach—twenty miles of sand looking for a city. Twenty miles of pure jerks." She makes sense with Rome—matching him drink for drink, no matter what time of day or night—and it's she who spills the beans about Rome's father, a cop who ultimately committed suicide after refusing to co-operate with a corrupt politician. In other words, it turns out Rome comes by his solitary-knight routine genetically.

Director Douglas, who favors cleanly composed two-shots of Rome (in the foreground) screen left and Archer (in the background) screen right, here stages a "getting to know you" scene very nicely, with Rome and Archer lying on the floor side by side, facing the camera. When Rome obtains the information he desires from Archer, he simply gets up and steps over her. He is one tough character, treating men and women alike with equal disdain, and Douglas keeps the film speeding along nicely, utilizing tracking shots to set a pace appropriate for a restless private detective always on the prowl. It's a streamlined style that not only fits the film, but especially suited the frenetic star, because far from changing Sinatra, time had only underlined his impatience. Said producer Aaron Rosenberg: "He's a restless actor. We get everything lighted up before he arrives and do it immediately. We seldom have to take more than two takes, never more than four." It's a style of acting that makes one wish Sinatra had worked with Clint Eastwood, a superb and extremely economical director famous for a minimal number of takes. Excellent though Don Siegel's *Dirty Harry* was, what, one wonders, would *Dirty Harry* have been like if Sinatra had starred in the film under Eastwood's direction?

In fact, *Tony Rome* only truly stumbles once, in an unnecessary double entendre–laden sequence wherein Rome's services are sought by an older woman whose cat is missing. It's all too smarmy by half, with the woman telling Rome, "You could at least meet my pussy," and Rome responding, "No—try the Burns Agency—they specialize in pussies that won't smile." It's not just the crude nature of a heretofore-solid screenplay; it's that the scene adds nothing to the film and stops it dead in its tracks before the detecting can resume again.

The sequence is quickly forgotten, however, in light of the first-rate action scene that immediately follows; with the denouement hinging on a cache of missing jewelry, Rome tracks the jewelry store owner to his home, where he is ambushed by a thug of a bodyguard and finds himself confronted with a dead body floating in the bathtub. Rome throws himself into the action, heaving a vase directly into his attacker's face, leaping and rolling onto the floor and shooting both men. For all his vulnerability, Frank Sinatra could play rough guy with the best of them—at one point Rome exacts revenge on a brutish night-club owner by smashing his hands in a drawer—his sense of danger and barely hidden anger making him a tough guy to savor even at age fifty-one. Through-out his career, Sinatra performed his own stunts whenever possible, executing the ofttimes rough-and-tumble physical action with considerable skill and en-thusiasm so anxious was he to prove himself physically as well as emotionally onscreen. (The then-startling martial arts fight in *The Manchurian Candidate* left Sinatra with a permanently damaged finger.) These genuinely tough physi-cal qualities were another reason men and women alike responded to Sinatra. Frank Sinatra could be rough and tumble with the best of them, both onscreen and off; Robert Mitchum had it right—Sinatra was the type of man who'd keep on fighting until death was the only alternative.

In a sign of the film's surprising depth, there's a very nicely textured scene where Rome has a lunch date with Ann Archer, and on the way to their table, Rome asks Archer to pay for a tie being sold outdoors by a down-on-his-luck ex-fighter (played by real-life champ Rocky Graziano). Rome may have a wise-crack for Archer's skimpy outfit ("What's the matter—couldn't you afford a whole dress?"), but he's out of cash and has no problem asking her to pay. The dockside restaurant is presided over by Sal (played by longtime Sinatra associ-ate Michael Romanoff), who gives Rome a prime table while simultaneously handing him cash winnings from his latest bet; police station or waterside restaurant, Rome's gambling winnings find him anywhere. The point of the se-quence is that Rome takes the money, pays back Ann Archer for the cost of the tie, and hands the rest of the cash to prizefighter Packy, so that Packy can bury Rome's ex-partner Turpin. Rome detested Turpin, but in his code of ethics, everyone deserves a proper burial. The accumulation of details in those scenes, the insight they bring to Rome's personality, is what marks *Tony Rome* as land-ing several cuts above the average detective film.

It's a consistency of style carried through right to film's end. When Rome holds one of the killers at gunpoint, the murderer desperately pleads with Rome, "You're being ridiculous," to which Rome ripostes in letter-perfect succinct fashion: "Maybe, but the gun ain't." End of discussion. That is exactly how audiences want their private detectives to speak—cynically humorous, unfazed by anything thrown in their paths, and able to make a little order out of the overwhelming chaos of daily life. As fantasy figures go, Frank Sinatra's Tony Rome rates pretty damn high.

In truth, the surfeit of plot elements does become a bit confusing, what with bigamy, murder, blackmail, double-crossing partners, and jewelry theft. It's easy to lose sight of exactly what the central mystery is and precisely who has murdered whom and for what reason, but that doesn't really matter. In the end, *Tony Rome* scores as an interesting and entertaining updating of classic 1940s private-eye-film noir, and as Murf stated in his *Variety* review of the film "By fadeout, few will particularly care about the mystery angle. . . . Credit Sinatra's excellent style, and the production elements, for pulling it off." If the ending feels unnecessarily rushed, it still doesn't spoil the overall impression of an entertaining film.

Critical reception to the film was mixed, although it delivered solidly at the box office. Longtime *New York Times* film critic Bosley Crowther completely missed the boat here, writing, "It is provoking . . . to see this acute and awesome figure turning up time and again in strangely tricky and trashy motion pictures that add nothing to the social edification and encouragement of man." Evidently Bosley didn't think that a detective flick counted unless it contained a bona fide Aristotelian dialogue, but the reason his review is worthy of further consideration is because of his continued and even odder analysis: Crowther wrote on to recall praising Sinatra for his first-rate work in *Suddenly,* a review that caused Sinatra to write Crowther a letter reading in part, "glad to have you on my team." Crowther's fourteen-years-later interpretation of the exchange? "That did it. I've had misgivings about Mr. Sinatra ever since." Crowther is here resorting to an unfortunate tactic employed by many: reviewing Sinatra's personality and his own reaction thereto, rather than responding to the work itself. More typical of the reaction to *Tony Rome,* Hollis Alpert in *The Saturday Review* stated, "Frank Sinatra has been a talent in search of a role ever since *The Manchurian Candidate,* and at last . . . he has found himself one . . . *Tony Rome* is lively and entertaining, and for this we must thank both the capable Mr. Sinatra and the persistent ghost of Mr. Bogart."

Many of the critics seemed to harp on Sinatra's supposed homage to his close friend Humphrey Bogart, all such critics choosing to place Sinatra at the feet of Bogart. Playing into those assessments was Sinatra's well-known regard for Bogie as both actor and friend, as well as his own near marriage to Bogart's widow, Lauren Bacall. Forgotten in the rush to infer that Sinatra was copying Bogart was the fact that any major star portraying a private eye on film is following in the footsteps of Bogart. Beginning with his turn as Sam Spade in *The Maltese Falcon* and continuing through his legendary teaming with Bacall in *The Big Sleep,* Humphrey Bogart not only set the standard but also created the archetype. Sinatra was not undertaking a mere homage, however; his Tony Rome is battered but breezy, ofttimes ready with a quip, and jauntier than Bogart's private eyes. Sinatra's Rome is equal parts detective and swinging ladies' man, his entire characterization overlaid with a patina of show business "ring a ding ding" that ultimately registers as a less dour variation on Bogie's brilliant characterizations.

What's interesting about Sinatra's onscreen transformation into cynical urban detective is that it underlines just how often Sinatra reinvented himself onscreen, doing so with a dizzying frequency that in its own way foreshadowed the unceasing reinvention the Italian-American Madonna has undertaken in her recording and MTV careers. Madonna, of course, does not possess anywhere near the requisite acting chops to carry off such a transformation onscreen in feature films. Having revealed all in her videos and books, there is simply no mystery left for onscreen portrayals, a state of affairs underscored by the lack of vocal coloring when she speaks. By way of contrast, Sinatra, with his genuine acting ability and continuous air of surprise, had succeeded in positioning himself onscreen first as sweet singing crooner, then musical comedy sailor, followed by dramatic actor (*Eternity*), Rat Pack swinger (*Ocean's Eleven*), and finally weary detective.

In the midst of Sinatra's successful run of detective films, there was a tantalizing rumor floated that he might star opposite Barbra Streisand in the film version of her Broadway success *Funny Girl.* Sinatra was also mentioned as the possible male lead opposite Streisand in Vincente Minnelli's film version of *On a Clear Day You Can See Forever. Clear Day* was a bad idea from the start for Frank, given the one-dimensional nature of the male lead and Sinatra's antipathy toward Minnelli's directing methods. The *Funny Girl* idea is certainly the more interesting notion, given the all-media superstar status of the two icons and the healthy respect each maintained for the other. (Streisand kept the telegram of praise Sinatra sent her in the 1960s when she was beginning her rise to superstardom, going so far as to enlarge it and post it for inspiration in the recording studio when she recorded her half of the "I've Got a Crush on You" duet with Frank for his *Duets* album.) Sinatra's participation in *Funny Girl* would have necessitated a restructuring of the material in order to beef up both the dramatic and the musical aspects of the leading male role, and would certainly have given Streisand pause, as it would have radically altered a vehicle that is first, last, and always the key to the Streisand legend. The idea of Sinatra as costar never got off the ground, however, given producer Ray Stark's opposition to the idea.

At any rate, it was certainly a more intriguing notion than another proposed pairing at the same time, that of Frank starring opposite another screen legend, Elizabeth Taylor, in the film version of Frank Gilroy's Broadway flop *The Only Game in Town*. In point of fact, both Sinatra and Taylor had signed on for the film, which was postponed after one of Taylor's many illnesses. When Sinatra's schedule didn't accommodate the delay, the part went to Warren Beatty. *The Only Game in Town* plods onscreen as a particularly lugubrious tale of gamblers in Las Vegas, and looking at Sinatra's bad track record with films based on Broadway flops (*The Tender Trap*), it's fortunate that he didn't try to redeem that notably sour and uninvolving story. In the end, the resulting film proved a resounding flop at the box office.

Frank's follow-up to *Tony Rome*, the 1968 Fox film *The Detective*, was based on former policeman Roderick Thorp's best-selling novel of the same name. The film did have a rather checkered preproduction history, not only because the rights were first held by not-yet-superstar producer Robert Evans, but even more so because Mia Farrow, then Mrs. Frank Sinatra, was originally cast in the role of Norma MacIver. What makes Farrow's near participation in the film particularly interesting is not just her marital status, but the fact that her involvement ended because of her starring role in Roman Polanski's *Rosemary's Baby*. Originally scheduled to end filming only days before *The Detective* was to commence shooting, director Polanski's film immediately fell behind schedule. When Farrow did not acquiesce to Sinatra's demand that she leave the Polanski film, she was dropped from *The Detective*; in daughter Tina's words, Frank "had an obligation to the studio . . . and felt professionally embarrassed in front of his crew." It wasn't just Sinatra the star who was embarrassed, it was Sinatra the old-school Italian-American, to whom respect was of paramount importance. It was the end of Frank and

Mia's one proposed screen teaming, and the end of a marriage that, although loving, had been fraught throughout its brief existence.

Underneath her waifish exterior, Mia Farrow possessed great ambition, and her career antennae were right on the money; the role of Rosemary made her film career, earning her rave reviews upon the film's release, and while the role of Norma in *The Detective* would have provided a very interesting look at Mr. and Mrs. Sinatra acting together onscreen, the role itself was nowhere near so rich as that of Rosemary. (Jacqueline Bisset eventually played the part, in rather perfunctory fashion.) As Farrow herself has related, while still filming *Rosemary's Baby* in November of 1967, she was met on set by Sinatra's attorney Mickey Rudin, who held an official application for divorce in his hand—Rudin's appearance constituted the first-ever hint of divorce. Farrow remembers signing each page without reading it: "If Frank wanted a divorce, then the marriage was over. I told Mickey Rudin that I would do whatever they wanted. I would have no need for any legal counsel myself." As had been the pattern with Ava Gardner, Sinatra and Mia continued to speak on the phone, even spending time together in Palm Springs, but the marriage was over.

With the hindsight of thirty years, Farrow later wrote: "I had come to Frank Sinatra as an impossibly immature teenager. . . . I loved him truly. But this is also true: it was a little bit like an adoption that I had somehow messed up and it was awful when I was returned to the void." The marriage was seemingly doomed regardless. As Sinatra himself stated before the nuptials even took place, "I don't know, maybe we'll only have a couple of years together. She's so young. But we have to try." Even after the divorce, their friendship remained secure, seemingly cemented by Farrow's response to the question of what she wanted as her divorce settlement: "Just your respect and friendship." A Mexican divorce was finalized in August of 1968, but Farrow and Sinatra remained friendly to the day Frank died. Mia herself told director/actor Peter Bogdanovich, with whom she was acting in a film shortly before Sinatra died, that she "had been speaking with him or his two daughters nearly every day," and her ties to Sinatra remained strong enough thirty years after the divorce for her to attend his funeral, reportedly at the request of Nancy Jr. Given Farrow's renown as a pioneer in multicultural adoptions, it seems fitting that she chose to name her adopted Vietnamese daughter Frankie Minh, in honor of Sinatra.

It was shortly after Frank and Mia's divorce that Farrow's immediate predecessor, Ava Gardner, returned to the scene. Summoned to Florida with reports that Frank was deathly ill with pneumonia, Ava arrived to find the illness not nearly so bad as advertised; there were fights, her old disapproval of the hangers-on reared its head, and she flew out of town quickly. It was, however, a turning point, because their relationship now entered its final phase; they resumed their routine of late-night phone calls and, as in the old days, indulged in the reaching-out across years and oceans. Now, however, "There was . . . no return to the sexual relations they had—prior to his remarriage—enjoyed, intermittently but intensely, in many of the years since their own formal separation and divorce."

Indeed, for the rest of her life, when Ava felt well enough to travel, she took full advantage of Sinatra's generous invitation for her to use his various apartments and houses. It was only when Sinatra married Barbara Marx, ex-showgirl and former wife of Zeppo Marx, in July 1976, that the Frank-and-Ava connection began to slowly but surely wither away, reportedly at the insistence of the new Mrs. Sinatra. After Ava suffered a stroke in 1986, Sinatra called her, and while she could not speak with clarity, she listened as Frank reportedly told her, "I love you, baby. It stinks getting old." When Ava died in January of 1990, Frank's publicists released a statement simply saying, "Ava was a great lady and her loss is very painful." Privately, as daughter Tina wrote, Frank went into his room, sitting alone through the night, barely able to speak above a whisper.

As to *The Detective*, with or without Farrow it's a viable film, with Sinatra admirably trying to stretch the boundaries of the genre. The end result veers between moments of fascination and gratuitously violent plot twists, but stands as evidence that nearly thirty years into Sinatra's feature film career, he was still trying to expand his horizons as an actor.

Teaming once again with producer Aaron Rosenberg and director Gordon Douglas, Sinatra is here portraying a police detective, not a private investigator, and it is clear right from the start that it's going to be one tough-minded film, containing little of the leavening humor found in *Tony Rome*. To the strains of the bluesy jazzlike score by Jerry Goldsmith, Sinatra's Sergeant Joe Leland takes control of an investigation into the violent murder of Teddy Leikman, the son of a highly successful New York City businessman. Just how dark is the subject matter? Leikman's penis has been cut off, his skull smashed in, and his fingers snapped off. In other words, it's not *Anchors Aweigh.*

Looking heavier than in the past, Sinatra etches a portrait of a veteran cop who knows his way around a crime scene and has clearly seen it all. This hardened veteran is one tough customer who is anything but easily rattled. The look of loneliness—indeed, wonder—that informed many of Sinatra's films from the 1940s and 1950s, has been replaced by a glare that speaks to the character's toughness and cynicism. Sinatra prepared meticulously for the role of Sergeant Leland, a sure sign that he cared about the material and realized it presented him with strong possibilities as an artist: "I used to chat with [veteran cop Johnny Broderick] about little idiosyncrasies that they have. . . . And I tried to put in all those little things that he told me about. . . . I want you to believe that I am thinking that I am the cop. . . . You're playing a cop with a badge, and the authority. I was always trying to keep a little tenderness in it somewhere. . . ."

This is one police sergeant who is not at all bothered by the homosexuality of the victim, a rather startling frame of mind for a major Hollywood film in 1968 starring an actor of Sinatra's stature. There were, needless to say, many stars of Sinatra's standing who ran scared of even the mention of homosexuality in 1968. Sinatra, to his credit, is portraying a character who replies to the examining doctor's disgusted query of "They don't disturb you?" with a simple headshake in the negative, followed by the statement, "I've got my own bag." Sinatra may have been turning more conservative in his political beliefs, morphing from outspoken liberal to Ronald Reagan supporter, but his sense of social liberalism remained intact thirty years after his outspoken support of FDR. Similarly it can be no accident that with acting opportunities for minorities still extremely limited, social liberal Sinatra once again had an African-American friend and coworker by his side in the film (Al Freeman Jr. as ambitious young detective Robbie Loughlin), just as he did in *Ocean's Eleven, Robin and the 7 Hoods,* and *Assault on a Queen.* Sinatra never forgot the segregated Southern hotels from his days on the road with Harry James and Tommy Dorsey, and in whatever way possible, he still wanted to send a message.

Sergeant Joe Leland may be a member of the police department, but he's still in many ways a solitary knight, instantly running afoul of a powerful councilman who threatens to corrupt his murder investigation. Leland is driven by a sense of ethics that seems sadly antiquated in the modern age, causing his captain (Horace McMahon) to wearily mutter, "I know—nothing matters to you but your dignity." He remains a man of mystery, the initial introduction of wife Karen (Lee Remick) revealing that there is a strain in their relationship, but the viewer not yet told why. As the film flashes back to Joe and Karen's initial meeting, Douglas's camera closes in on Sinatra's hardened blue eyes, and the viewer is drawn in—we think we know what is going on behind those eyes, but we can never entirely be sure. What memories are crowding Leland's tenuous peace of mind? Like all good actors, Sinatra makes the viewer come to him, never telegraphing and never pandering.

Instead, the film teases by doling out the key information in selective blocks. The viewer is shown Joe and Karen's first meeting on campus at Columbia University and in Remick's portrayal, Karen is alternately warm and distant, but always alluring. Remick, a first-rate actress who had scored with both *Anatomy of a Murder* and especially *Days of Wine and Roses,* knew her way around complicated wife roles. With her inherent warmth, she makes a good foil for Sinatra, and when she flat-out asks him, "Why are you trying to be so tough?" he immediately blurts out, "I *am* tough." He's right—it's part of his appeal, just as is his willingness to always speak his mind. Attending the theater with sociologist Karen and her intellectual friends, forced to listen to their high-minded discussion of drama, he munches on a hot dog before barking, "You and your friends give me a pain in the ass." Again—he's right. They're pretentious pseudointellectuals, with Karen the only one in the bunch worth a damn. When Karen tells Joe, "If I don't marry you, I'm crazy," Sinatra's ensuing enormously appealing wide-eyed grin makes him appear to be all of eighteen years old, one of the few moments of warmth and humor in an increasingly dark film.

Surprisingly humane given the late-'60s setting of the film, the somewhat sympathetic treatment of gay men continues in unexpected fashion during the interrogation of the murder victim's roommate, Felix Tesla (Tony Musante). Ordering the cops who have been badgering the silent Tesla out of the room, Leland takes the opposite tack, softly talking to Tesla, purposely taking his hand in his own. It's a nice piece of acting, certainly different from anything else Sinatra put on film. Given his aggressively macho persona, it's the last action one expects from him, but then again, any actor so secure in himself wouldn't be bothered by the display of affection. Of course, it all has a purpose, because it is only after this display of pseudotenderness, a near seduction, that Leland, growing louder and louder, eventually wrings a confession of murder out of Tesla. It's an unexpected and interesting way of arriving at a confession, but Musante, generally a fine actor, overdoes the hysteria by half. He has moved from silence to hysterics in seconds, with no stop along the way, and none of it seems organic. One is always conscious of an actor giving a performance, and it represents the first misstep in a heretofore fine film. Douglas simply didn't guide Musante properly, failing to rein in the scenery-chewing in what is already a showy role.

Unfortunately, there is worse to come with the second flashback in the film. Karen confesses her adultery to Joe, but it all becomes much more overwrought when Joe subsequently follows her as she leaves a nightclub with another man, and learns that she is a nymphomaniac. Karen tritely confesses to Joe, "You're the only one who ever made me feel like a woman," by which point, all that's missing is Aretha Franklin singing "Natural Woman." It's not that Sinatra and Remick aren't good here; in fact, neither one falters even when the dialogue rings false. The problem actually is that with the newfound freedom of late 1960s cinema, the filmmakers appear to be reveling in sensationalism for its own sake; by signaling their willingness to tackle heretofore taboo topics, all involved are telegraphing their serious cinematic intentions. Unfortunately, just because the subject is serious doesn't mean that the film is automatically a good one.

When Joe is finally made lieutenant, the first bit of action after the congratulatory party is that he—and the audience—must watch Tesla being electrocuted for the murder of his boyfriend, Leikman. It's a disturbing scene made all the more memorable by Douglas's decision to position the camera above Tesla, looking down as he walks to the electric chair. Less felicitous is Douglas's decision to place images of Tesla's electrocuted body on either side of Leland's face; it's overkill—the point has already been made, and it's surprisingly showy coming from a nonflashy professional like Douglas. When that is immediately followed by a scene wherein a man is killed in a fall from the roof of a racetrack, audiences can be forgiven for thinking, *Enough already.* The film is only slightly more than halfway through, and thus far there has been a severed penis, a crushed skull, amputated fingers, nymphomania, death by electrocution, and murder. Throw in weapons of mass destruction, and the list would really be complete.

After all the sordid details, it's with a sense of relief that the viewer is introduced to Norma MacIver (a young and beautiful, although rather green, Jacqueline Bisset). Of course, Norma's not exactly happy-go-lucky herself, arriving on the scene because it was her husband, Colin (William Windom), who fell from the racetrack roof. Flashbacks reveal Colin in an all-pink gay bar (which makes a viewer think the film wasn't so forward thinking after all). As the song "Laura" is played in the background on the electric organ, one can only hazard a guess that somehow composer David Raskin probably did not have that particular orchestration in mind when composing the song. Colin makes eye contact with a younger man (Leikman), goes home with him, and is so disgusted at his own behavior that he kills the younger man—the victim seen at the beginning of the film. It's all played in rather hysterical fashion, but then again, in the late 1960s, most gay men were still deep in the closet. Colin confesses, "I felt more guilty about being a homosexual than murderer," which probably was a fairly accurate reflection of American society up to that point.

The film adopts a rather schizophrenic viewpoint on the issue; on the one hand, Leland displays sympathy toward homosexuals, treating them with respect, but of the three main gay characters in the film, one is a murderer, another is hysterical and falsely confesses to murder, and the third, a thoroughly unpleasant man, is killed. It's a motif that runs throughout all of Sinatra's late-1960s detective films; as a rule, the Sinatra character does not personally find the gay men repellent, but the gay men are presented as "bad" men, either killers or hysterical queens, while the women are depicted as oversexed and somehow not worthy of the hero's love.

Given the fact that Colin, not Tesla, murdered Leikman, Leland now realizes that he forced a false confession out of Tesla, unjustifiably causing Tesla's death by electrocution. It's an interesting twist on Leland's character because, contrary to the audience's false assumption, he is shown to be far from a flawless solitary fighter. He turns in his badge with a simple "I was a good cop. There are things I want to fight for and I can't fight for them when I'm here." Unsure whether he'll go back to wife Karen, Joe says good night to Norma, leaving her side to drive off into the night. Alone. It's all admirably intentioned in theme and scope, but the film has undercut its own effectiveness by trying to be all things to all people. What started out as a promising adult love story mixed in with gritty realistic police detective work has been turned into an overly grim and unnecessarily violent mush, throwing every possible crime into the stew in order to prove the serious intentions of all involved. Sinatra is first-rate throughout, never once begging for audience sympathy or coming across as less than believable, but he is done in by the film's self-consciously tough screenplay. Valiant try all around, but although it performed well at the box office, there was a general feeling that the film bogged down in its own aspirations—indeed, pretensions. Sinatra was still scoring personally as a detective, but the next time out, it would be back to the safe, more congenial territory of Tony Rome, in Sinatra's first R-rated film, *Lady in Cement.*

The return to the character of Tony Rome found Sinatra, in effect, slipping into a specially tailored set of clothes. If there was nothing new to the look, it hardly mattered. It was a sleek fit, with the star battling mayhem, cracking wise, and solving murders all around Miami. Private eye Tony Rome enabled Frank to project all the qualities the public associated with him at his finest, perhaps even tapping into Sinatra's own idealized self-image. In this second film, Rome is still insouciant, courageous, ready with a quip, possessor of a more-than-healthy libido, and for all his cynicism, still feels the need to right at least a few of society's wrongs. Underneath all the cynicism beats the heart of an aging idealist.

Wisely, Sinatra retained the original *Tony Rome* team of producer Aaron Rosenberg and director of photography Joseph Biroc, all in service of a wise-cracking script by Marvin H. Albert (with Jack Guss) based on Albert's own novel. In fact, only one technical element in the film is less than first-rate, and that is the downright grating score by Hugh Montenegro. Right from the start, with a Bacharach-lite late-1960s sound and wordless vocal filling the screen over the title sequences, the score captures none of the moody flavor that Jerry Goldsmith brought to *The Detective,* instead signaling in highly inappropriate fashion a jokey, cartoonlike commentary on the proceedings. Time after time in the film, the audience is hooked, only to have the score telegraph a goofy musical joke at the climactic moment.

Nicely lensed by Biroc, the film captures the sun-soaked atmosphere of Miami, the water, sand, and palm trees lending verisimilitude to the plot. In Sinatra's performance, Tony Rome is at ease in such lush surroundings; it's a key component in the film because if the audience is to trust the private detective and go along on his ride, then they must have the feeling that he is in control of the situation, no matter how dangerous the circumstances. Beginning with the very opening sequence of Rome playing cards on his houseboat with police lieutenant pal Dave Santini (Richard Conte), Sinatra is in charge, exuding star authority and oceans of seen-it-all humor.

Diving overboard to search for the purportedly gold-laden shipwreck in the area, Tony comes across a rather more unexpected sight—while fending off sharks by kicking them in their heads (no wimp here), Rome spies a beautiful naked blond woman whose feet are, indeed, encased in cement. Hair floating in the sea, the dead woman represents a startling underwater version of Botticelli's Venus. Given the unending level of press attention paid to Sinatra's supposed mob connections, it's interesting to note that Tony Rome has no problem commenting on mob protocol, disdainfully stating, "Dumping people in cement. That went out with violin cases."

After Rome receives a phone message—no name, just an address—he investigates the address, only to be manhandled upon arrival by the truly gargantuan Waldo Gronsky, adeptly played by Dan Blocker. His character clearly inspired by the archetypal giant Moose Malloy in Raymond Chandler's *Farewell, My Lovely*, Blocker turns in a terrific performance, mixing menace with humor so that what emerges is a full-fledged and quite fascinating character, a worthy foil for Rome. Emphasizing low camera angles, director Douglas underscores the fact that Rome is no physical match for Gronsky, a humorous mismatch with which Sinatra plays along. Looking down on Rome, who is prone on the floor, Gronsky plucks him up before unceremoniously dumping him on the bar, as if Rome were no more than a rag doll; intrigued and only half-trusting of Gronsky, Rome signs on to help him, a mission that next leads him to the pool of one Kit Forrest.

Unfortunately, it's a location that lands the film in trouble for the simple reason that Kit is played by Raquel Welch. Welch is certainly beautiful, and her Venus-like initial entrance, rising out of her pool in a skintight skimpy bikini, showcases her sensational body. But, at that point in her career, Welch simply could not act. She flashes a lot of white teeth and enough hair for any three women, but she doesn't display a shred of acting ability. Her first line to Rome is a taut zinger, "Should I scream rape now or wait and phone in a complaint?" yet she delivers the line as if reciting her grocery order. She appears to be incapable of supplying any color to her line readings, and the film suffers markedly as a result. Kit does occasion some funny wisecracks from Rome—"You'd look good in a paper napkin, but that won't get me any answers"—but Welch's lack of mystery in a role that is supposed to be the essence of dangerous charm harms the film greatly. In a part that calls out for the insolence and smoldering heat of the young Lauren Bacall, Welch can't deliver. Instead of the audience being intrigued by the femme fatale's air of mystery, we are more likely to wonder if she spends all day teasing her hair.

The real pleasure of the film comes in the ofttimes very funny bits of dialogue that perfectly fit the intriguing cast of characters. When Kit's protector, the diminutive "reformed" hood Al Munger (an effective Martin Gabel) advises his dumb blond girlfriend to keep quiet and read a book, her response is to shriek "For a whole hour?" At the other end of the spectrum, Rome visits his undercover cop friend Rubin, nicely played by comedian Pat Henry, who is now in drag while attempting to solve a run of crimes that has victimized prostitutes. Rome carries on a full conversation with his cross-dressing crony, and exchanges information about his own case, at which point, conversation concluded, Rome wordlessly adjusts his friend's fake breasts and departs. Unexpected, character-revealing, and humorous all at the same time.

Vignettes such as those lend a sense of ironic fun to the proceedings utterly lacking in the relentlessly grim *The Detective.* No matter that the stakes involve murder—when Rome surprises the elusive Gronsky with a gun, only to have both of them instantly ambushed by a pair of murderous thugs, Rome's riposte to the first assailant's snarled query, "Who are you?" is to spit out, "I'm a registered nurse." A major brawl ensues, which features the first instance of the mountainous Gronsky thumping the head—indeed, entire body—of his would-be attacker against a car. Rome's pithy take on Gronsky? "You're a menace to urban renewal." The wisecracks land perfectly because, with his impeccable musical timing, Sinatra hears the lines internally, in effect rhythmically shooting the line out at precisely the most effective beat.

It's evident Sinatra is having fun with the private eye flicks—his pleasure transmits itself to the audience and is light-years away from the labored efforts of *Assault on a Queen* and *The Naked Runner.* Fifty-two years old at the time of filming, he looks great, is still trim even if a bit heavier, and appears capable of handling whatever is thrown his way. When he tangles with a gay dance director and his beefy butch boyfriend, Rome wins the day because he's not afraid to move quickly and fight dirty. First punching out the choreographer, he then smashes a billiard ball in the face of the football player boyfriend. It's tough, fast, interesting, and most important of all, believable.

At times, director Douglas even displays a particularly welcome and heretofore unsuspected light touch—when the wealthy, heavily boozing Kit plays craps with men in the back of a mortuary, Rome rests atop a soon-to-be-utilized casket. In reality, however, these very sequences with Raquel Welch prevent the film from rising above its status as a pleasant diversion into the realm of top-notch suspense entertainment. Rome and Kit engage in a love-hate relationship, her verbal dart, "You smoke too much," delivered in counterpoint to his "You drink too much," but Welch can't punch out the words with the authority that would allow them to land. Granted, the audience is afforded a chuckle when Rome tells Kit, "Maybe you're the kind of dame collects hoods—I used to know a broad collected bullfighters." Fifteen years after his divorce from Ava Gardner, Sinatra still carried the torch. But the allusion to Ava lays out the difference between the two actresses in bold relief: Gardner could have handled the role with style and ease, but when Welch tries to snarl, "You're a bastard, Mr. Rome," she is out of her league.

Ava, with her earthy glamour and come-hither look, seemed like she never gave a damn, not caring whether the man stuck around or not, thereby intriguing all the more. Welch, like Jill St. John, plays at those attitudes, trying them on like new dresses but never understanding how to make the goods fit. It's a significant lack in these films because the myth of the private detective or lonely urban knight demands a fully realized woman, villainous or not, to round out his quest. Here the woman in question acts like she won't join the crusade because the effort would muss her hair.

When, at film's end, the filmmakers inform us that Gronsky is the killer, it's a revelation that leads to the very logical query, If that's the case, why did Gronsky hire Rome in the first place? To draw attention to his own crime? Why does Rome treat Gronsky the murderer in such casual fashion?

It's pretty damn hard to understand why the filmmakers lavished time and attention on the first three-quarters of the film, only to wrap up the final act as quickly as possible. Sinatra's great, the first 75 percent of the film is fun, but all one can wonder is if Frank told the filmmakers, "I'll give you only three more days of shooting time," causing them to rush toward the finish line. The film's still entertaining and worth a viewing to see Frank in full star mode, but the sloppy ending harms the film's overall effectiveness.

The movie scored fairly well at the box office, and the mixed critical reception never veered into the overly harsh personal attacks with which critics sometimes greeted Sinatra movies. If the recently hired *New York Times* critic

Vincent Canby found it to be "consistently crude," *The Hollywood Reporter* conversely wrote that the film had "fun at its own expense rather than relying wholly on leering bad taste," judging the script "fresher . . . with lighter hands playing than on *Tony Rome.*" As for Sinatra himself, most critics agreed with Charles Champlin in the *Los Angeles Times*: "He projects the ex-cop turned private shamus with a time tested fictional blend of insouciance, cynicism, battered but surviving idealism, wisecrackery, courage, libido, thirst and all the more interesting hungers. He clearly enjoys the role and it is this evident pleasure which carbonates the thin material with lively amusement."

While searching for the right property for his return to the big screen after *Lady in Cement,* Sinatra hit the newspaper headlines again, but this time on the political front: erstwhile Democrat Sinatra would now back Ronald Reagan in his bid to be reelected governor of California. Why the support for the conservative Reagan? Because, in Sinatra's own words, Sinatra shared the "same desires as the Governor for the welfare of the state of America," going on to praise the governor's "guts and fortitude." That was all a long way from supporting accused Communist screenwriter Albert Maltz, but thereafter, from Reagan's presidential campaigns through to Sinatra's application for a Nevada gaming license, Frank's friendship with and support for Ronald Reagan—a man he had openly criticized in the 1950s—remained rock solid. Sinatra would go on to produce Reagan's first presidential inaugural gala— the outsider from Hoboken was now officially and forever one of "them," welcome at the very epicenter of American power. The bond between star and politician may not have lasted with the Democratic Kennedy administration, but Frank Sinatra had now made it into the highest echelons of the conservative Republican party.

Indeed, in February 1981, when Sinatra successfully applied for a gaming license in Nevada, a letter of support from President Ronald Reagan formed part of his application. The letter may have been written before Reagan's actual inauguration, but writing through his attorney, the President of the United States was now on record vouching that Frank Sinatra was "an honorable person—completely honest and loyal." Sweet salve indeed for the insult of Kennedy's last-minute refusal to stay at Sinatra's Palm Springs compound, yet even in that 1981 hearing, the twenty-years-earlier alleged tie to Giancana was not forgotten. Stated Sinatra yet again during the application process: "I never invited Mr. Giancana to Cal-Neva. I never hosted him and I never saw

Erstwhile liberal, now a conservative Republican: Frank at Governor Reagan's inaugural gala, 1971. Left to right: Sinatra, Governor Reagan, Vicki Carr, Nancy Reagan, John Wayne, Dean Martin, Jack Benny, Jimmy Stewart.

him at Cal-Neva." Well, the combination of President-elect Reagan's letter of support and Sinatra's own testimony must have worked, because the commission, voting 4–1 to grant Sinatra a "key employee license," praised him for his charitable works and, according to newspaper accounts, further "chastised the news media for repeating what it said were unfounded rumors of organized crime connections."

Although it was to be two years before Sinatra's next film release, acting remained much on his mind, both in a constant search for appropriate material and in how he approached his still-flourishing recording career. Speaking about his decision to record an album of Rod McKeuen songs titled *A Man Alone* (1969), Frank explained, "Real singing is acting. I sang well because I felt the lyrics here [pointing to his head], here [pointing to his heart], and here [pointing to his gut]." With an instinctive actor such as Sinatra, that approach makes sense, yet it also leaves one to wonder what part of his anatomy he was thinking with when he decided to film the abysmal *Dirty Dingus Magee*.

One can only imagine that the farcical Western was designed to bring a few laughs to Sinatra after the January 24, 1969, death of his father from heart disease. The solitary Marty did not possess the firecracker personality of mother Dolly, but he loved Frank, and his influence on his son was profound. As Nancy Jr. wrote about *Magee* and Marty's death: "When his father died, something snapped . . . he needed this silliness after Grandpa died."

So distraught were Frank and his mother over Marty's death that one year later, Frank moved Dolly to Palm Springs, where they lived in very close proximity to each other, loving and squabbling right up until the day Dolly tragically died in a plane crash. The desire to bury his grief about Marty's death in lighthearted work is certainly an understandable reaction on Frank's part, but *Dirty Dingus Magee* proved the wrong vehicle with which to do so. To put it charitably, the film stinks—and that really is being charitable.

Released in November 1970, *Dirty Dingus Magee* was produced and directed by Burt Kennedy, and required the services of three screenwriters—Tom Waldman, Frank Waldman and Joseph Heller (yes, that Joseph Heller)—to craft a script from David Markson's novel *The Ballad of Dingus Magee*. (Perhaps the warning signs about what lay ahead should have begun with the fact that the highly regarded Markson structured his book around the exploits of a nineteen-year-old Dingus Magee. Sinatra was fifty-four at the time of filming.)

Strangely enough, given Sinatra's intelligence and general discernment about scripts when not in a Rat Pack frame of mind, he gave up his $1 million film fee, taking instead a larger percentage of the box office gross. It was a rare bad business decision. Perhaps he was simply blinded by his love of the Western genre, stating at the time of filming, "As a person, I look pretty bad, but as for the part, I think it's one of the best-looking I've ever had." Well, even a performing genius can be dead wrong on occasion. And he was.

Sinatra certainly understood the principles of comedy very well, correctly analyzing that

> the old time comedians like Chaplin, Keaton, and Laurel and Hardy . . . epitomized a lot of situations in which the ordinary fellow was always pushed around . . . and when one of those comedians threw a pie in the villain's face . . . there probably wasn't a single person in the theater who didn't visualize himself doing the same thing to a mean boss or somebody else who had been pushing him around for a long time . . . laughter is an emotional release, just like tears. In fact, laughter is dry tears.

Sinatra's right, all the way down the line, but there were neither tears nor laughter to be had here—just an excruciating sense of boredom.

Burt Kennedy's direction of the film did not help matters much, a state of affairs doubly surprising, given the success of his two-years-earlier comic Western *Support Your Local Sheriff,* as well as the interesting if not entirely successful allegorical *Welcome to Hard Times.* The problems with *Magee,* however, really begin and end with the script; structured as both a farce and a satire of Western film clichés, the film does not work as either. Yes, two years prior to this film, the Waldmans had scripted the Blake Edwards comedy *The Party,* a similar mix of slapstick and double entendres, but that uneven film did contain some genuinely funny moments, employing a farcical tone that in *Magee* eluded all concerned. In an odd way, *Dirty Dingus Magee* appears to be trying for the same brand of lunacy Mel Brooks's *Blazing Saddles* found four years later, but it never fully commits to the satire. As a result, the film simply registers as uneven, and the critics treated it as a serious (albeit awful) Western. A more consistent tone in approach would have allowed critics to respond as they did to *Blazing Saddles*—"it's all a joke and let's have some fun." Instead, the audience is faced with the sight of Frank Sinatra in faded red long johns making "bim-bam" in the bushes with a blatantly Caucasian actress (Michele Carey) who is portraying the Native American Anna Hot Water in extraordinarily unrealistic fashion. How unrealistic? Well, Anna sports a light tan minidress and knee-high boots that she appears to have stolen from Nancy Sinatra's "These Boots Are Made for Walkin'." Of course, Anna's surname is no worse than that of her fellow Native American, an amply endowed woman who is called—what else?—Two Moons. (The film actually is an equal-opportunity offender, what with an Asian prostitute who speaks pidgin English telling George Kennedy's Hoke, "If you no come, Miss Belle say she kick you in honorable ass.")

Director Kennedy tries to help matters by harking back to classic Sinatra films with a delayed reveal on the star's first entrance; Dingus (or in this case, an obvious double for Sinatra) is shown riding a bucking bronco. He is eventually tossed off the horse, and as the camera closes in, the audience first sees Dingus, flat on the ground, with his back to the camera. Slowly he turns to reveal the famous blue eyes, and the audience has one instantaneous reaction: *What the hell is that bad toupee he's wearing?* It would take thirty-seven years and Tom Hanks's silly hairstyle in *The Da Vinci Code* before a major male star's hair would make him look this ridiculous again. Bad hair and all, Dingus turns out to be a lovable scoundrel, a thief always looking for a quick score as he ambles about the countryside of Yerkey's Hole, New Mexico, in the 1880s. Spying his old friend Hoke Birdsill (George Kennedy), Dingus proceeds to rob Hoke while Hoke is urinating against a wall. That's right, while he's peeing . . . Which, come to think of it, is one of the classier sequences, given the fact that the very next scene depicts soldiers fleeing the bordello run by Belle Knops (Anne Jackson) as one of the prostitutes chases after a soldier and thrusts a rooster at him while yelling, "You forgot your cock!" Not exactly Ernst Lubitsch territory.

It's not that the idea of a Western spoof was a bad one—1965's Oscar-winning *Cat Ballou* had shown that the time was ripe for a Western satire, if lovingly executed. Here, unfortunately, the jokes are all obvious and ofttimes crude. Sinatra, affecting a hybrid Southern/Western accent—"pretty" comes out "purdy," and "fine-looking" becomes "fahn-lookin"—isn't completely awful; it's just that the material is so thin that normal standards regarding acting can't even apply. He appears wryly amused by the goings-on, but not in the "we're in on the joke, and you're not" manner that so harmed the Rat Pack Westerns. Instead, confronted by such a weak screenplay, he simply wanders amiably from one comic tussle with Hoke to another.

Just as bad as the script is the downright annoying score by Jeff Alexander (complete with a grating title tune written by Mack David and sung by those well-known country western legends, the Mike Curb Congregation). Echoing the filmmaker's lack of trust in audience intelligence, Alexander repeatedly employs a tuba for comic effect and beats every scene into the ground with musical punctuation; when Dingus punches Hoke for what is approximately the three hundredth time, Alexander still finds it necessary to punctuate the moment with the sound of a bell akin to that which sounds the rounds at a prizefight, in the process all but shouting, *See, Hoke and Dingus are fighting, so I'll remind you of a prizefight.* Then again, maybe Alexander and director Kennedy realized early on that they simply had nothing to work with. Either way, Alexander, who did much better work on *The Tender Trap,* has here written a score that noticeably detracts from the film. (There is an additional music credit for Billy Strange, so perhaps the blame should be spread around.)

The film does possess one singular asset—the beautiful cinematography by Harry Stradling Jr. (*Funny Girl*), which captures the wide-open spaces of the Western plains in evocative fashion. Framing beautiful vistas dominated by the bright blue sky, Stradling gives the audience a sense of the West's vast unsettled territories; it is actually Stradling who finds the key to commenting on the Western genre, capturing images ranging from the silhouette of a single house against the horizon to a solitary horseman riding down an empty main street at a deliberate clip. The fact that in this case the solitary horseman is the rather inept villain John Wesley Hardin (Jack Elam) allows this to be one sequence where the spoof works well. Even that joke is eventually ruined, however, by protracted shots of Hardin being literally run over by both the U.S. Army Cavalry and Native Americans (not to mention the fact that what are supposed to be hordes of soldiers and Indians appear to barely top a dozen in number, leading one to guess that the budget was really stretched tight by this point in filming.)

The plot, which feels extraordinarily attenuated even at a mere ninety-one minutes, finds Dingus and Hoke locked in a running battle of theft and countertheft, constantly trying to one-up each other in pursuit of riches. Belle, the town madam, makes first Hoke, and then Dingus, sheriff (don't even attempt to sort out the inane logic of how the town madam has that power), and in trying to put across such thin material, none of the actors, save John Dehner as Brigadier General George, manage to strike the right note. For his part, Dehner finds just the right amount of self-parody as a fatuous army commander who is so inept that he practices yelling "Charge!" Genuinely funny in his self-deluded bluster, Dehner is the one performer who takes the farce absolutely seriously, an iron-clad necessity for sustaining the tone of believable illogic that will keep all the plot machinations afloat. Given that Burt Kennedy did not elicit a similarly fine performance from any other actor, one suspects that Dehner arrived at his solid level of performance by himself.

Maybe Frank had the right idea by sporting a wry smile at all times, but by film's end, he's the only one in the theater still smiling. There isn't one genuine human being in the entire misbegotten screenplay, and while it's true that the film is styled as a farce, the audience still must care about the characters, an impossible task, given the circumstances.

The climactic gunfight between the townsmen and villainous Jack Elam is so poorly staged that all an audience member can contemplate is how Jack Elam's six-shooter magically seems to hold five hundred bullets, thereby making it all the easier to hold off hordes of rifle-toting adversaries. Finally, at

*Making "bim-bam" in his
long johns in the awful* Dirty
Dingus Magee *(1970). Short-
lived retirement followed
soon thereafter.*

film's end, director Kennedy treats the audience to a lingering shot of a dog urinating. In other words, this film began with Hoke urinating and ends with a dog urinating, bookended actions that form a pretty accurate critique of the entire movie.

For once, the critics' harsh assessments were right on the mark, with Kevin Thomas of the *Los Angeles Times* proclaiming the film "disgusting" and Arthur Knight in *The Saturday Review* noting that Sinatra "seems ineffably bored and totally uncommitted as well he might be." It was all best summed up by Roger Greenspun in *The New York Times,* who found it "a dreadful parody Western . . . seeing the film is rather like hearing an interminable traveling-salesman story repeated by somebody who has been told all the elements but doesn't himself get the point." Bingo.

Always one to look forward, not back, Sinatra had planned to follow up *Dingus* with a film that ranks just below *Carousel* on the list of "if only" film projects—*Dirty Harry*. Sinatra, with his seen-it-all demeanor that so smoothly fit the urban cop persona, was, at age fifty-five, ripe for that tale of an older cop chasing after a vicious killer in modern-day California. (The film was to have been directed by Irving Kershner, a solid professional whose credits include *The Empire Strikes Back, Robocop,* and *Never Say Never Again.*) Sinatra certainly understood such a character, and it's a near certainty that he would have scored a big box office hit after the disappointment of *Dingus.* Unfortunately, due to a condition called Dupuytren's contracture, one that made it extremely painful even to hold a microphone, Frank had to undergo surgery on his hand and dropped out of the film. He was replaced by Clint Eastwood in what proved to be a career-defining role for Eastwood.

Dirty Harry represents a major missed opportunity in the Sinatra filmography, similar to the five-years-earlier proposal that he star in *Harper,* a taut suspense film that almost assuredly would have provided Sinatra with approbation by critics and audience alike. As it was, less than a year after *Dingus* flopped in theaters, Sinatra proclaimed his desire to retire from show business. Giving a star-studded farewell concert (Barbra Streisand was the opening act), Sinatra, brilliant showman that he was, whispered the final words to his classic torch song "Angel Eyes"—" 'Scuse me—while I disappear"—and vanished into the dark. It was a brilliantly staged exit, and Frank's retirement triggered an avalanche of awards, most noticeably the Jean Hersholt Humanitarian Award at the 1971 Academy Awards (in recognition of the millions he had raised for charity) and the 1972 Screen Actors Guild Award, given for "the highest level of career achievement."

Of course, during this retirement, Sinatra couldn't give up the spotlight completely, demonstrating that he was as volatile as ever in his public proclamations. The newest controversy arose after Joseph Barboza, an admitted killer of twenty-seven people, claimed that Sinatra held interests in two hotels as a front for Raymond Patriarca, the alleged Mafia boss of New England. Patriarca himself testified that he had never had any business dealings with Sinatra and had "never met the gentleman in my life," but Barboza's allegations generated enormous press, prompting Frank's testimony before a committee of the House of Representatives. In an appearance *The New York Times* characterized as "alternately bellicose and bored," Sinatra spat out his response to Barboza's claims: "This bum went running off at the mouth and I resent it. I won't have it. I'm not a second-class citizen. All I'm asking is for somebody to be fair about it." It may have been a House Committee, but Frank Sinatra wasn't measuring his words for anyone, and five days later, he returned to the subject in his own op-ed piece titled "We Might Call This the Politics of Fantasy." Published in *The New York Times* on July 24, 1972, Sinatra's column addressed the ongoing allegations about his ties to organized crime and the Congressional testimony he was forced to give: "There is a form of bigotry abroad in this land which allows otherwise decent people, including many liberals, to believe the most scurrilous tales if they are connected to an Italian-American name. They seem to need the lurid fantasy; they want to believe that if an entertainer is introduced to someone in a club, they become intimate friends forever." It was the Sam Giancana story all over again, one seemingly fated never to end.

Congressional testimony aside, Sinatra's mercurial nature began to overwhelm the supposed benefits of his retirement. Maybe it was the awards, maybe it was the realization that he was still only fifty-eight years old, but given his restless temperament, it was no surprise that he soon un-retired. How much golf could such an unsettled man actually play? Out went the golf clubs, and in came the concert dates, the comeback officially beginning with the 1973 television special and recording *Ol' Blue Eyes Is Back.* Most fittingly, the terrific one-hour show featured only one guest—Gene Kelly. Film clips were screened from *Anchors Aweigh, Take Me Out to the Ball Game,* and *On the Town,* but great as the clips were, the highlight of the hour occurred when the two icons joined forces on "We Can't Do That Anymore." Mock complaining that they could no longer sing and dance with their past skills, the pleasant discovery for audiences lay in realizing that, in fact, they could do just that: not with the same verve and not with the same bounce, but with every bit as much style.

The two old friends—and legends—appear so delighted with each other that it is startling to read the account of the show's writer, Broadway legend Fred Ebb, that he saw Frank "be extremely cruel to Gene Kelly." Going on to discuss Sinatra's initial wish that the sole guest be comedian Redd Foxx, Ebb details how he explained to Frank, " 'I'm more at home with musical personalities, and I would very much like the guest to be Gene Kelly.' Frank allowed that to happen, but he was not happy about it at any time, and I honestly don't know why." Oddest of all, on the night of taping, Ebb recounts how Frank called him over ("Frank was not ungracious with me, though he would snap his fingers to call me too") and stated that he wasn't going to record the number. When Ebb asked why, Sinatra replied, "I've turned on it. I don't like it and I don't want to do a number like that with Gene." Fortunately, when a recording engineer, who was unaware of the brewing controversy, asked Kelly if he was ready, Gene walked onto the floor and Sinatra did sing along with him. It's a good thing the recording engineer was oblivious, because the ensuing number proved sensational.

Such was the undiminished power of Sinatra that the newly coined nickname Ol' Blue Eyes instantly caught on with the public. Fresh out of retirement, Frank Sinatra had invented yet another persona for himself, one so memorable that when, a mere two years later, Bette Midler titled her television special *Ol' Red Hair Is Back,* everyone got the joke. It's a sobriquet that remained with Sinatra for the rest of his life, culminating in a tribute on the night of his death that found the Empire State Building, that ultimate symbol of New York City, bathed in blue light as a salute.

Sinatra now began to pay tribute to his own peers and idols, hosting the 1974 American Film Institute's televised lifetime achievement award to James Cagney (and in the process related how Cagney called Sinatra's "you dirty rat" impersonation the "worst he'd ever heard"). He returned the very next year to host the AFI's salute to Orson Welles, and in that same year of 1975, himself received the Cecil B. DeMille Golden Globe Award for lifetime achievement. The awards continued to proliferate, but at age sixty, Frank and his film career seemed to temporarily center on a nostalgic look back, a tribute to what he had already accomplished. It's a state of affairs that Frank, with his insatiable need to perform, must have found simultaneously pleasing and frustrating.

In his quest for quality scripts, even Frank Sinatra, with all his power and influence, faced two huge obstacles: very few scripts were written with leading roles for sixty-year-old men, and huge changes had forever altered the Hollywood landscape. The era of the studio system was over, the major studios were selling off their back lots, and glamorous nightclubs like Ciro's and Trocadero had fallen out of favor and closed. Movie stars were no longer glamorous be-gowned and black-tied idols. Indeed, it ofttimes seemed like a competition, however phony, as to which star could most strongly show that they, too, were "just folks." Gritty low-budget films like *Easy Rider* were all the rage. It was a world of filmmaking as foreign to Sinatra's acting sensibility as rock and roll was to his musical one. As Hollywood declined, so, too, did Frank's interest in film acting. Without the umbrella of the studio system and its attendant roster of salaried employees, Hollywood grew ever more cost conscious, and the sense of fun inherent in the process disappeared. He would have liked to find challenging material, but he no longer felt a compulsion to churn out one feature film after another. The movie business had changed forever, and so had he.

It therefore made a perfect kind of sense that when Sinatra came back to the big screen, it was to appear as himself in MGM's surprise hit tribute to its own movie musicals, *That's Entertainment!* Produced by Jack Haley Jr. and shot on the MGM studio lot, this salute to the brilliant MGM musicals of yesteryear featured classic clips supplemented with introductory narration by MGM stars ranging from Elizabeth Taylor to Gene Kelly. The film's astonishing box office success and cultural impact resulted from two factors: The first was the fact that in that pre–home video era, audiences were afforded the thrill of rediscovery, a chance to once again view favorite film clips that had heretofore been available only on the late, late show. Second, *That's Entertainment!* was a brilliantly entertaining tribute to a vanished musical era, the wealth of riches hitting audiences with tremendous force because of the depth and range of talent on display. As a result, there was a cultural resonance to the film, one that made it seem only fitting that it opened and closed with Frank Sinatra, a genuine MGM musical star, and the most successful all-around talent to emerge from the fabled studio.

The chance to revisit such stylish and brilliantly executed musical memories charmed critics and audiences alike, but amidst all the hoopla, one important fact was obscured: by cannibalizing past treasures, *That's Entertainment!* was really announcing the fact that the original movie musical was dead. At the time, no one quite realized *That's Entertainment!* was functioning as a eulogy. It's as if the audiences were tourists gazing at a war memorial—impressive, moving, and a salute to all that had been irretrievably lost.

Released in 1974 with the tagline "Boy, do we need it now," *That's Entertainment!* was the last film to be shot on the already-crumbling MGM back lot, the still-standing sets bulldozed shortly thereafter in order to make room for a real estate development. Originally aimed as a television salute to the fiftieth anniversary of MGM, writer/producer/director Jack Haley Jr. soon realized that with such a treasure trove of material, a full theatrical release was warranted. The decision was a smart and lucrative one, because *That's Entertainment!* proved to be the right film at the right time; for an increasingly disillusioned American public, it fulfilled the need to hark back to a simpler time, one long before the double scourges of Vietnam and Watergate caused Americans to doubt themselves and the place of their country in the world.

The fact that Frank Sinatra opened and closed the film functioned as a tacit acknowledgment that he was, in fact, the star amongst stars. He may not have been the biggest box office attraction of all, but with his combination of movies, recordings, concerts, and television appearances, he was the biggest entertainment star in the land, and no one, but no one, cast a longer shadow. He had not only emerged as the single biggest all-media star in post–World War II America, but his participation in the film proved doubly interesting because of his particularly clear-eyed view of his time at MGM. He had generally enjoyed his tenure at the studio, but his very demeanor on camera spoke of his refusal to look back. Sinatra was acknowledging his storied past, but that proved to be no bath in nostalgia for Francis Albert. Like his mother, Dolly, his eyes were still fixed on the horizon ahead.

After credits that list the star narrators in alphabetical order, Sinatra's is the first voice audiences hear. Describing how, with *Hollywood Revue of 1929,* MGM produced the first "all-talking, all-singing, all-dancing film ever" (in actuality, that honor would seem to be held by the nine-months-earlier *Broadway Melody*), he strolls out of the front door of the MGM studios, and one's first reaction is to Sinatra's changed appearance. Four years earlier, in the ill-begotten *Dirty Dingus Magee,* he was still slim and full of energy. Here, four years and one short-lived retirement later, he is noticeably heavier and sporting a badly styled toupee. The *Dirty Dingus Magee* toupee was just a silly choice for a dopey film, but Frank Sinatra's own hairpiece and the forward-combed bangs certainly did him no favors either. And yet. Speaking in that distinctly New Jersey accent of his, he matter-of-factly states, "It's been quite some time since I first came to this place. And MGM certainly isn't the same studio, and Hollywood is not the same town. But the films that were made here are still around. Musicals may not tell us where our heads were at, but they certainly tell us where our hearts were at."

Not for Frank the misty-eyed revelations of Elizabeth Taylor, the film's second narrator. Sinatra sets just the right tone, letting the clips speak for themselves and throwing in a bit of humor with his reference to the chorus line in *Hollywood Revue of 1929* as a group of "slightly overweight chorus girls." Segueing through increasingly elaborate numbers in the evolution of the musical film, the highlight of Sinatra's host segment is the brilliant Fred Astaire and Eleanor Powell tap routine to Cole Porter's "Begin the Beguine," a number so stylishly executed that it jump-starts the film to heights from which it never falls for the rest of the two-plus-hours' running time. As Sinatra states in a thoroughly deserved tribute to all the giant talents preserved in these stylish MGM musicals: "You can wait around and hope, but you'll never see the likes of this again." In his own hosting segment, the only clip displayed of Sinatra himself is his grin-inducing duet with Jimmy Durante on "The Song's Gotta Come from the Heart" from *It Happened in Brooklyn*. Even removed from the context of the film, the genuine affection between the Schnoz and the Voice shines through. It's a great number and leads to Sinatra's reflection: "The work was hard, but it was great fun." The endless rehearsals under the tutelage of drill sergeant Gene Kelly ("that brute" in Sinatra's fond recall through the years) may have proved to be more than Sinatra had bargained for, but he was justifiably proud of the results. Finishing up his own segment, Sinatra introduces second host Elizabeth Taylor, whose strangely emotional segment includes the snappy fun-filled title number to *Take Me Out to the Ball Game*.

During the remainder of the film, Sinatra features in two other film clips, the first being the brilliant "New York, New York" number from *On the Town*. Introduced by Fred Astaire, the number, even in the midst of a treasure trove of riches, once again registers in bold relief: This is as good as it gets. End of discussion. The second outstanding Sinatra clip is the joyous "Well, Did You Evah!" duet from *High Society,* a clip introduced, naturally enough, during Bing Crosby's hosting segment.

Just as Sinatra ended his Edward R. Murrow CBS television interview in 1956 by playing not one of his own records, but Bing Crosby's recording of "Where the Blue of the Night Meets the Gold of the Day," here Bing slyly returns the favor. In trademark Crosby fashion, Bing lists off all the *High Society* stars, and at the end casually adds, "Oh yes, there's another featured performer in there—what was his name—a brash newcomer—Frank, uh, Frank—a clever kid—he had a lot to offer," and with that the rollicking duet unfurls. It's such a witty and fun-filled number that, like the best routines included herein, one wants the clip just to keep going. And going. Then again, that's the whole point of the film—leave them wanting more. As critic Nora

Sayre wrote in *The New York Times,* "This isn't nostalgia, it's history." And entertainment.

Even amongst this cavalcade of stars, three talents leap out as the best of the best: the sublime Fred Astaire; Gene Kelly, whose astonishing athleticism shines throughout; and the magnificent Judy Garland, with her unequaled blend of beautiful singing, sense of fun, and vulnerability. Sinatra's best clips stack up pretty damn well next to those of the three giants, and when one throws in his dramatic films and the ceaseless flow of vocal masterpiece albums, the overall body of work registers as rather staggering. Sinatra may, understandably enough, land a tad less strongly in this film than do Astaire, Kelly, and Garland (so did every other star involved), but in the two-years-later sequel called—what else?—*That's Entertainment II,* it is Sinatra who registers most strongly of all.

That's Entertainment! was so successful that it took the edge off Sinatra's following subpar LP and accompanying television special, *The Main Event.* Neither version of *The Main Event* did him any favors, but with the all-media synergy of film, television, and album, the nearly sixty-year-old Sinatra remained constantly in the news. The old controversies still trailed him, and a 1974 dustup with the press in Australia garnered worldwide attention. Railing at the journalists with vintage epithets, Sinatra let loose: "They are bums and parasites who have never done an honest day's work. Most of them are a bunch of fags anyway." As for the female journalists, he found them to be "buck-and-a-half hookers." Leave it to Frank to take on an entire continent. No wonder Bacall likened him to Don Quixote tilting at windmills. After Sinatra's comments were widely reported in the press, stagehands at his Australian concert venues stopped work and maintenance workers refused to refuel his jet unless an apology was proffered. His apology, one for which the word "grudging" might have been invented, eventually saw the light of day, and Sinatra's plane finally took off. He was about to enter his seventh decade of life, and he couldn't stop stirring up controversy—or stop working.

It may have been growing increasingly difficult to find a suitable film role, but in an interesting refusal, Frank turned down the lead role in *Death Wish,* the part making a major star out of his *Never So Few* costar Charles Bronson. Perhaps Sinatra was particularly sensitive about the public possibly mixing up his increasingly conservative public persona with the revenge motif of the film. (Unlike the movie, the original novel centered around a Jewish leading character and contained a much less overt vigilante element than did the subsequent film.) Even turning down roles, however, Sinatra still relished his connection to the Hollywood community, and the next year of 1975 found him co-hosting the Academy Awards for the third time. On Hollywood's biggest night of the year, Frank Sinatra very purposefully was reminding the entire film community that he was one Academy Award–winning star very much alive and kicking, and most assuredly interested in remaining a working actor.

In the meantime, and until a suitable starring role could be found, while the concert tours and charity fund-raisers continued unabated, Frank married for the fourth and final time on July 11, 1976. Marriage to new wife Barbara Marx shaped up as a very different sort of partnership. Barbara was not an actress, and unlike Ava Gardner and Mia Farrow, she did not have career ambitions of her own. With Barbara, Sinatra had found himself a wife who could and would devote herself completely to his needs, adjusting herself to the requisite late nights while still providing the constancy he seemed to desire. For her part, Barbara had now married the biggest and most famous star of her generation, and she seemed to enjoy all the power and prestige that accrued to her as a result. She was clearly no pushover, and Sinatra allies commented on the fact that Barbara came to assume increasing power in the marriage, especially as Sinatra grew older and more frail. Devoting herself to raising $2.5 million in order to establish the Barbara Sinatra Children's Center for sexually abused children, she naturally enough traded on her husband's name and connections, but emerged as a powerful fund-raiser in her own right. Barbara Sinatra was, if nothing else, remarkably clear-eyed about her husband, and after the center opened in November of 1986, forthrightly stated that she wouldn't allow him to visit the center "because my husband's from a totally different school. My husband wants to break their legs. He wants to round up all the men and break their legs. . . . So he's not allowed in here, you know."

Those who picture Barbara Sinatra as a creampuff who simperingly devoted herself to her husband had it all wrong; she was strong-willed and could give as good as she got. It's just that, unlike the white-hot battles with Ava, arguments with Barbara found Frank dealing with a partner whose anger could turn cold, all speech and emotion withheld after the battle was joined. Said Barbara's good friend Dinah Shore about the marriage: "Because of the way they are, they explode every once in a while at each other. And then when they come back together their relationship is that much better."

This was destined to be the longest-lasting of Frank's marriages, enduring for nearly twenty-two years until his death in 1998.

What's most interesting about that final marriage is the reversion to his roots. Barbara, like first wife Nancy, was utterly devoted to Sinatra. This liaison, however, carried an additional layer of subtext, at least in the view of daughter Tina: "But with his last try, with Barbara, Frank finally got it right. He finally married his mother." Tina's pointed parallel to her grandmother Dolly is a fascinating one. Both Barbara and Dolly possessed limited education, but by sheer force of will had made positions for themselves in the world, especially through their familial connection to Frank Sinatra. Tina, in fact, delivers an evenhanded assessment of her grandmother, recalling her as warm and fun, yet also—and here Tina's intended parallel to Barbara is unmistakably laid out—as a "self-serving, rough and ready woman who perpetually had her hand out. She used her son like a courtesan, and he'd give her the world; she just wanted more."

Indeed, the entire second half of Tina's autobiography reads like nothing so much as *Stepmommie Dearest,* as Tina catalogs a litany of grasping and controlling behavior on Barbara's part, behavior she feels hurt her father enormously, as the relationship between husband and wife devolved, according to Tina, into an endless series of negotiations aimed at Barbara acquiring more and more money. (Although Barbara Sinatra had a six-figure annual allowance, at her prodding, Sinatra eventually agreed to rescind his prenuptial agreement and thereby allow her to garner 50 percent of all his income earned during the marriage.)

Frank continued working, money continued to flow, and in May 1976, the inevitable sequel titled *That's Entertainment II* opened across the country. Frank filmed no new sequences for the film, yet there he was in theaters nationwide once again. In effect, Frank, handily enough, was taking a curtain call without even having to work. This time around, it was Frank who registered as the biggest star of all, even with the then-seventy-six-year-old Fred Astaire and sixty-three-year-old Gene Kelly acting as hosts throughout the film. This sequel took a slightly different approach to the ransacking of the MGM vaults than did its predecessor, including classic comedy scenes ranging from the Marx Brothers to Tracy and Hepburn, along with the brilliant musical numbers. After a particularly clever series of opening titles, credits that feature everything from different seasons of the year to collapsing dominoes, the film settles down into a succession of vintage clips linked by the singing and dancing narration from Astaire and Kelly. The two great dancers are nearly done in by a particularly cheap- and unattractive-looking set consisting of garish blue and pink geometric objects. But with talent like theirs, one simply forgets the ugly surroundings and enjoys the beautiful sight of the two geniuses still gliding around the screen with nary a hint of effort. These new introductory sequences, directed by Kelly himself, complete with snappy musical arrangements by Nelson Riddle, showcase the still-in-shape duo and their ever-graceful hoofing. Astaire in particular is pretty damn terrific—how the hell could anyone at age seventy-six still exude such style and generate such smooth lines? Then again, he's a genius—and genius has its privileges.

There are some revelations in the film, notably the humorous and eye-popping Bobby Van dance number that finds him literally hopping all over town in *Small Town Girl,* but it's the classic Sinatra moments that really stand out. The first is the terrific title song sequence from *The Tender Trap,* a segment so elegantly staged and sung that it reminds the viewer once again that they should have released the title sequence alone and scrapped the rest of the film. With Gene Kelly narrating, vintage footage of Sinatramania at the Paramount Theater in December of 1942 is screened, with the particularly apt script by Leonard Gershe sharply pointing out, "When he walked out onto the stage, it was not merely the birth of a star but the creation of a legend." Over an audio of Sinatra singing "I'll Walk Alone," the narration continues, "It was inevitable that Sinatra hysteria would lead him to Hollywood and equally inevitable that producer Arthur Freed would choose him to sing Kern and Hammerstein's classic 'Ol' Man River.' " Well, the latter is certainly a debatable assertion, given the variance between a song expressly written for an African-American and Sinatra's Italian-American roots. If it was inevitable for anyone, it should have been for Paul Robeson, but as Kelly rightly states over footage of Sinatra singing "I Fall in Love Too Easily" from *Anchors Aweigh,* "There's something about a Sinatra ballad that makes it automatically unforgettable."

This is not just standard-issue Hollywood hyperbole. Gene Kelly, one of the unquestioned masters of the movie musical, knows of what he speaks, because as Sinatra demonstrated in one musical after another, even in second-rate offerings like *It Happened in Brooklyn,* such ballads did indeed prove unforgettable. Sinatra is the only star represented in *That's Entertainment II* who receives a full-fledged montage of his greatest moments, first warbling "I Believe" from *It Happened in Brooklyn* and "You're Sensational" from *High Society,* followed in quick succession by rapid-fire clips from *The Kissing Bandit, Take Me Out to the Ball Game, Anchors Aweigh, The Tender Trap, Meet Me in Las Vegas,* and even the nonmusical MGM offerings *Never So Few* and *Some Came Running.* All these clips unfurl to the audio accompaniment of "Ol' Man River" from *Till the Clouds Roll By,* and while it is indeed an otherworldly experience to view a clip of Frank and Gina Lollabrigida in *Never So Few* while "Ol' Man River" keeps rolling along, the entire montage still delivers.

Of course, the overall film did not score nearly so strongly as had the first *That's Entertainment!* but how could it? Most of the classic clips had been utilized the first time out, and the inclusion of a large number of comedy clips diffuses the impact of the musical numbers. Nonetheless, it's great to see Astaire, Kelly, and the vintage Sinatra once again, and the reception was still strong enough that eighteen years later, MGM released a third helping, titled, not very surprisingly, *That's Entertainment III.*

That was definitely the last—and least—of the three installments, and a curiously uninspired compilation at best. Written, produced, and directed by Bud Friedgen and Michael J. Sheridan, the format is similar to the first two pictures: a lineup of big-name MGM stars introduce segments of classic clips. It's just that this time around, although some of the hosts—Mickey Rooney and Debbie Reynolds—are the same, the clips aren't all that classic. It's a measure of how haphazard the selection was that the creators actually saw fit to include the utterly forgettable Ricardo Montalban/Ann Miller flamenco-style "Dance of Fury" from the much-maligned *The Kissing Bandit.* It's a mediocre dance from a grade-Z movie, and with a little more ingenuity, surely the creators could have chosen better. As it is, Sinatra is represented very briefly, with a portion of the title song from *On the Town,* a fleeting clip of the "She Begged Me" dance with Gene Kelly in *Anchors Aweigh,* and a still from *Till the Clouds Roll By* as the end credits roll.

After Frank's 1974 newly filmed appearance in *That's Entertainment!* another three years passed before he appeared on camera again. In the interim, tantalizing rumors of a possible return to the world of original movie musicals began to make the rounds, because Frank had expressed a keen interest in the Stanley Donen–directed Lerner-and-Lowe musical version of *The Little Prince.*

Sinatra liked the score, and upon learning of his interest, Frank Yablans, then president of Paramount Pictures, had leaned on Donen to utilize Sinatra in the lead role of the pilot. Donen, battle-scarred from working with Frank on *Anchors Aweigh* and *Take Me Out to the Ball Game,* felt strongly that the ever-impatient Sinatra, especially nearing age sixty, would never stand (or sit still) for the required location shooting in Tunisia: "In two days he will not want to work. He'll kill the movie. Frank Sinatra is *not* doing this picture." Donen carried the day, and Richard Kiley ultimately played the pilot. (As it turned out, the film was a flop, both artistically and commercially, most notable for Bob Fosse's last onscreen dancing appearance—as a snake clad in black from head to toe.)

Frank may not have returned to the screen with *The Little Prince,* but he was once again in the news, and for exactly the reason he didn't want: rumors of Mafia involvement. Continuing his frantic rate of concert dates, Frank had appeared at the Westchester (New York) Premiere Theatre in 1976 and had his picture taken backstage with Carlo Gambino and Jimmy Fratianno. Given the notoriety of both men, a brand-new round of headlines regarding Frank's mob connections hit newspapers and radio. Lost in the hubbub of what such a picture supposedly told the general public was one salient fact: yes, Sinatra posed for the picture, but it was the alleged hoodlums who had far more to gain from the photo than Frank himself. It was Sinatra who was world famous, so any photograph with Frank proved to be a trophy for those surrounding a smiling star.

In the end, Sinatra himself addressed the controversy head-on by stating,

Did I know those guys? Sure I knew some of those guys. I spent a lot of time working in saloons. . . . They paid you and the checks didn't bounce . . . if Francis of Assisi was a singer and worked in saloons, he would've met the same guys. That doesn't make him part of something. They said hello, you said hello. They came backstage. They thanked you. You offered them a drink. That was it.

Mob rumors and all, Frank continued his heavy schedule of concerts, the live performances filling the void left by the lack of movie roles. His absence from the screen since filming the narrative sequences for *That's Entertainment!* was about to change, however, and not because of finding an ideal script. Rather, his return to filmmaking sadly grew out of his mother's death in a January 6, 1977, plane crash while she was en route from Palm Springs to Las Vegas in order to see her son perform. Dolly Sinatra had adored her son, an affection Frank returned, but she also famously and openly fought with him throughout his life. Tough-talking Dolly had functioned both as Frank's harshest critic and his biggest supporter, a relationship best summed up in very perceptive fashion by daughter Nancy:

> They'd fought through his childhood and continued to do so until her dying day. But I believe that to counter her steel will he'd developed his own. To prove her wrong when she belittled his choice of career . . . Their friction first had shaped him; that, I think, had remained to the end a litmus test of the grit in his bones. It helped keep him at the top of his game.

Frank felt the loss of his mother keenly, dealing with his grief in the way he knew best—through work—once again attempting to outrun his loneliness by means of ceaseless activity. As a tribute to his mother, Sinatra now developed a television film based on one of her favorite books, *Contract on Cherry Street*. By doing so, Frank purposely broke his career-long vow of never filming a movie for television.

In reality, while the desire to honor his mother provided the main reason for making the film, it was not the only impetus. Three years out of retirement, Sinatra still wanted—indeed, needed—to perform onscreen. Speaking of his desire to work on a "real cop story," Sinatra told an interviewer from *TV Guide*: "I saw Duke recently and he said 'What have you read, little fella?' And I said, 'Nothing. What you have you read, big fella?' We agreed there was not much around in the way of exciting scripts." Two giants of the movie business, nearly two hundred feature film credits between the two of them, and they both still wanted to perform, both needed to act. That naked desire plus a boatload of talent is what helps to separate the legends from the stars. Sinatra and Wayne were international icons, and they couldn't stop. All that hunger and all that passion translated onscreen. Big-time. Couple that hunger with the grief Sinatra felt over the death of his mother, and the decision was made to begin filming *Contract on Cherry Street* for NBC television.

The film itself, based on the novel by Philip Rosenberg, plays exactly like what it is: a glossy television movie, elevated above the usual such fare only by the presence of Frank Sinatra. Filmed during the summer of 1977, it aired on November 19, 1977, and drew acceptable ratings. Directed by William A. Graham, with a screenplay by Edward Anhalt (*The Pride and the Passion*), the movie cast Sinatra as Inspector Frank Hovannes, a New York City cop and all-around stand-up guy who helps to run the organized crime unit. Investigating the reach of organized crime into the annual $170 million business of stealing cars and selling parts, Hovannes and his fellow cops slide down the slippery slope of attempting to stop rival crime gangs by resorting to violence themselves. Ultimately, the entire investigation end up in multiple deaths and despair.

More than anything else, the film conveys the late-1970s feeling of society unraveling, of a New York City so impossible to control that citizens and police alike take the law into their own hands. In some ways, the most interesting part of the telefilm is the insight it gives into the changing mores of the late 1970s; talking in bed with his supportive but emotionally neglected wife, Emily (a strangely placid Verna Bloom), Hovannes indulges in his own take on the blossoming feminist movement: "Man is a different kind of equal. Man goes out and kills the bear. I do my thing for us. You do your thing for me." Such an attitude was already going the way of the dinosaur, and while the filmmakers may have been trying to make the point of how baffling a Frank Hovannes found the new world order, the end result is a film that plays like a law-and-order politician's essay on why society no longer works. As Hovannes says, "every time we try to hit something, it's protected." It's a sentiment Ronald Reagan himself would have endorsed, and one here even shared by the mobsters; when the heads of two rival crime families sit down to business, at the country club yet, the aging Italian mob boss tells Jewish mobster Baruch Waldman (Sinatra's frequent costar Martin Gabel), "The trouble in our business is not between one family and another. It is between the old and the young in the same family. The world belongs to the young." For mobster and cop alike, in this brave new world it seems there just ain't no respect.

This is a dark look at the urban world of the late 1970s, but there are some funny one-liners doled out along the way, most of the humor coming from skinny, strung-out stool pigeon Fran Marks (a terrific Steve Inwood); afraid that the Manzero mobsters will see him talking on the bus with Hovannes's fellow cop Lou Savage (Michael Nouri), Marks whines that the tinted glass won't protect him: "Italians can see through anything. . . . When Manzero gets ahold of me, my legs will be in Bed-Stuy and they'll be playing stickball with my head in the South Bronx." Such sardonic one-liners are few and far between, however, and the movie turns from dark to pitch black when a chop-shop bust goes awry and the evil Otis Washington (a first-rate Johnny Barnes) kills good cop Ernie Weinberg (Martin Balsam). One look at the rage in Sinatra's face after this murder tells the audience what will happen next—picking up a shotgun, Hovannes blasts Washington into oblivion, the movie then nicely sliding into the next scene of Weinberg's graveside service, a small ring of mourners dwarfed by the encroaching skyscrapers of the city. Sinatra, who looks trimmer and somehow hungrier than he did in the *That's Entertainment!* footage shot three years earlier, here hits top gear, wordlessly conveying the desperation of a man who has lost both his partner and his faith in the system. Cleaning out Weinberg's desk, silently handling his friend's gun, handcuffs, and badge, Sinatra makes all these little gestures count, even his smallest movement echoing throughout the empty station house. Playing the slot machine that stands sentry in the squad room and winning for the first time, Hovannes shakes his head at the futility of it all. Sixty-two years old and the very model of the seen-it-all twentieth-century American male, Frank Sinatra could distill urban angst better than anyone else on the planet.

It's that feeling of despair, of society going to hell in a handbasket, that leads Hovannes and his fellow cops Savage and Polito (a fine Harry Guardino), to take the law into their own hands. Murdering gang boss Manzero themselves, they play the Manzero and Weinberg families against each other, but by killing Manzero, Hovannes has charted his own downward path. Unfortunately, just when the film should begin heating up with its tale of renegade cops, Sinatra disappears for lengthy stretches and the film begins to sag noticeably. Rather than rising organically from the action, emotions seem to be shoveled in according to the demands of the plot, and the net result is a film that looks and plays like a made-for-television movie, not a feature film that happened to be made for television. It's no wonder that plans to release the film in theaters overseas were shelved.

Sucked into an unending cycle of violence by his actions, Hovannes shoots first Polito and then two murderous thugs, whereupon one of the dying gang members kills Hovannes himself. A fellow cop finally arrives, but it is too late to save Hovannes, who dies alone on the street. Once again, Frank Sinatra has died onscreen, and as the camera pulls back to focus on the sign reading

In Contract on Cherry Street
*(1977) as world-weary New
York City cop Frank
Hovannes, Sinatra's one
starring role in a dramatic
television film.*

CHERRY STREET, it picks up a second sign hanging immediately below: ONE
WAY. The "message" of the signs, is, like the film itself, a little too heavy-
handed. Taken as a whole, the telefilm is simply attenuated; in a reflection of
the times, the era of President Jimmy Carter's proclaimed "national malaise,"
the entire film is a downer, with no emotional catharsis in sight. On the plus
side of the ledger, it has served the purpose of showing that after a seven-year
acting lay-off, Frank Sinatra hasn't lost a bit of his touch, but the critics were
not impressed by the film itself. Judith Crist was particularly acerbic in her
criticism, branding the film a "10th rate Kojak. . . . Why Sinatra chose this
brew of murder and mayhem for his TV-movie debut is the only intriguing aspect." More typical criticism was voiced by John J. O'Connor in *The New
York Times,* who wrote "From Mr. Sinatra on down, there are a number of
quite good performances wasted in this curious exercise. . . . The birdbrained
plot of *Contract on Cherry Street* proves fatal to all concerned." Much more of
such doom and gloom lay ahead, because in Sinatra's next—and last—feature
film, *The First Deadly Sin,* he is trapped in an unremittingly gloomy scenario

that makes *Contract on Cherry Street* seem like the comedic *Married to the Mob* by comparison. It's all exceedingly grim, with one large saving grace: Sinatra turns in a sensational performance, one that provided him with a terrific swan song to the starring roles of his feature film career.

That movie, however, lay three years in the future. For now, interesting rumors of additional feature film projects floated by, rumors that lead any casual observer to rue the missed opportunities contained therein. The most notable of all of those whispers occurred two years after *Contract on Cherry Street,* when novelist Richard Condon (*The Manchurian Candidate*) raised the possibility of a screen reunion with Sinatra in the film version of his presidential assassination novel *Winter Kills.* The script by William Richert met with Sinatra's approval, but he turned down what would have been a fascinating role—that of a Joseph Kennedy–like figure—because the then-nearly-sixty-five-year-old Sinatra felt the character was too old for him. Instead, the role went to director John Huston, who garnered rave reviews for his performance.

With no film on the horizon, recordings and live performances occupied the bulk of Frank's time. He filmed a television special celebrating *Sinatra: The First Forty Years,* recorded the *Trilogy* LP, which garnered six Grammy nominations, and received the coveted Trustees Award from the Grammy Awards. Narration was provided for a documentary film in behalf of the World Mercy Fund, and most notably of all, he gave a concert before the then largest paying live audience for a solo recording artist in history, a crowd of 175,000 in Rio de Janeiro.

By 1980, Sinatra's voice had coarsened, losing much of its power and flexibility, but audiences didn't care. They—and particularly his contemporaries of the World War II generation—just wanted to be in the same room with him. Seeing Frank alive and kicking and definitely not out to pasture reminded his fans that neither were they. Older, wrinkled, heavier—sure but the game was still on. Or as Frank would have it, "You gotta love livin', baby, 'cause dyin's a pain in the ass."

Sinatra's voice had provided the soundtrack for people's lives, and by this time, his evolution in many ways mirrored the changing nature of America itself: from youthful crooner full of promise and high spirits to the disillusioned postwar balladeer who had seen and survived the worst life could offer, from Rat Pack swinger through to retirement, creative rebirth, and finally increasingly dogmatic elder statesman, Frank Sinatra, in all his excesses and vulnerability, spelled "America" to citizens worldwide.

Sinatra's voice may have been an iffy proposition day to day, but when he finally hit the big screen again, in 1980's *The First Deadly Sin,* his resulting performance proved extraordinarily rich, featuring layer upon layer of characterization. In the negative reaction to that very dark film, everyone lost sight of one central fact: sixty-five-year-old Frank Sinatra was acting better than ever, more economically, with greater nuance, and a fuller commitment to the material. *The First Deadly Sin* may have been a mediocre film, but for Sinatra personally, it made for one terrific farewell.

Based on Lawrence Sanders's best-selling novel of the same name, *The First Deadly Sin* represented Sinatra's first starring role in a feature film since *Dirty Dingus Magee* ten years earlier; for an actor who had appeared in no fewer than five major feature films in 1955 alone, the prolonged period of inactivity was significant in and of itself. It was as if Sinatra now, more than ever, simply found the search for a good script too much trouble for an increasingly questionable payoff. So—why even attempt to return?

The answer: because with his ambition banked but not extinguished, Sinatra, like any true artist, wanted to prove that he still could play the game, that he still mattered. It's precisely the spirit that makes *The First Deadly Sin* so curious to contemplate today, because twenty-five-plus years after its release, when it is mentioned at all, it is referred to simply as Sinatra's last starring role in a feature film. Such shorthand misses the point. It may be his last starring role, but it is also a helluva good performance, one that puts to use all the craft he had absorbed in his forty years in Hollywood. As a valedictory performance, it's one of the all-time greats.

With a taut screenplay by Mann Rubin, photography by Jack Priestly (*Contract on Cherry Street*), and music by favored Sinatra arranger Gordon Jenkins, the film was directed by Brian G. Hutton (director of the thoroughly professional if somewhat uninspired *Where Eagles Dare*). Filmed on location in Manhattan in the spring of 1980, *The First Deadly Sin* reflected the beaten-down New York of that era, a city personified by the battered-by-life star of the film. Opening on gritty rain-slicked streets, the film quickly establishes its tough veneer, crosscutting between a psychopathic killer on the loose and graphic close-ups of intestinal surgery. As the killer strikes his latest victim, the film cuts to an incision being made on an operating room table. The blood spurts in the hospital just as the victim dies in the shadow of the ironically named Mount Pleasant Church. Yes, the intention to contrast the taking and saving of life is more than a little obvious, but it's not overly intrusive, and it does grab the audience's attention instantly.

The first close-ups of Sinatra, who portrays police sergeant Edward X. Delaney, reveal an aging star. He looks completely different here from in the three-years-earlier *Contract on Cherry Street.* No longer slim—indeed, somewhat overweight—Sinatra's puffy face and thick black glasses speak of a man who has lived a tough life. It's the first time that the onscreen Sinatra has appeared—well, there's no other word for it—old.

It is only in scenes with wife Barbara (Faye Dunaway) that Sergeant Delaney's tough exterior eases. Visiting Barbara in the hospital (it's Barbara who was being operated on in the film's opening sequence), offering the daily chatter and loving gestures that have helped make up a successful marriage, Delaney softens. When he smiles, Delaney—and Frank Sinatra—appears fifteen years younger. As Barbara continues to slip away, Delaney answers her whispered cry of "I'm trying," with a kiss of her hand and a choked sob of, "Oh, please God." Desperate for a cure, Delaney even goes to church, and one has the sense that Edward Delaney is a man who has not attended church in years. Hand in hand with Delaney's return to church is a viewer's sense that such a scene must have resonated for Sinatra himself; never a regular churchgoer, Sinatra reportedly began to attend the Catholic Church of his youth with more frequency after marriage to Barbara. Sixty-four years old at the time of filming, Sinatra was—however hesitantly—facing his own mortality for the first time.

Sinatra's scenes with Dunaway are among the most extraordinary of his long film career. Dunaway is fine here, managing the not-so-easy feat of giving an entire performance while supine in a hospital bed, but it is Sinatra who most thoroughly impresses, speaking in a hushed but loving voice, tenderly spinning tales of how husband and wife will move into their dream house just as soon as she gets better. When Delaney buys her a copy of one of the Honey Bunch books she so revered as a child, books whose "everything turns out right" stories are so far removed from her disease-ridden present, he gives the books to her with such tenderness that it's difficult to remain unmoved. Most impressive of all is the effect achieved when Sinatra reads from the book; his voice rarely rising above a murmur, he manages to soothe and comfort his wife with the merest inflection, allowing her to finally relax in her agony. Sinatra was, of course, famously the master of nonpareil phrasing when singing, but watching him with Dunaway, and listening to him read as he expresses his love for her through the simple words of a children's book, is a master acting class on its own.

The First Deadly Sin is really two films in one: the story of Delaney's marriage to a dying wife he loves greatly, and his tracking of the psychopathic killer Daniel Blank (David Dukes) who slays random strangers with a clawlike rock-climbing hammer. In fact with director Hutton constantly crosscutting between the two stories, the one—and rather large—serious shortcoming in the suspense of the film occurs because of the decision to show Blank's face in the film's opening sequence of murder; there is no suspense as to who has done the killing, simply a question of whether Delaney can stop him before he strikes again. Dukes, a solid actor who successfully played a wide range of starring roles on Broadway before his untimely death, is creepily convincing here, but he, and the film, would have gained from a more detailed buildup to the revelation of his actual identity.

One of the more rewarding, if disturbing, aspects to the film lies in the fact that it eschews bromides and easy answers. Barbara is dying, and Doctor Bernardi (George Coe) appears, in Delaney's eyes, oblivious of her suffering. Pinning Bernardi against a wall, Delaney gets louder and angrier, shaking him and accusing him of indifference. Sinatra is quite startling here, and it's not just because it's the first time in Sinatra's feature film career that the audience is hearing constant profanity issuing from his mouth: addressing the doctor, Delaney laces his conversation with "bullshit" and "goddamned." It's because the film does not make it entirely clear that the doctor really is indifferent. Yes, he's seemingly less caring than the rumpled coroner (a first-rate James Whitmore) who goes out of his way to help Delaney, but Bernardi also appears to be a doctor who is doing the best he can, a man, like most in modern life, who simply does not have the answers others would like. It's a nice moment in the film's portrayal of Delaney, pointing up the fact that Delaney is fully confident and in charge while solving gruesome murders on the streets, but helpless to control, or even understand, what is happening to his own wife. The disconnect between the personal and professional seeps through the life of this aging man as it does for so many, leaving fear, rage, and confusion in its wake.

The audience is left with a sense of sadness—indeed, depression—over his fate, an overall mood not helped by the lack of any humor and the exceedingly dark look of the film. The darkness reads here both literally and figuratively: Sinatra is clad throughout in dark suits, overcoat, and hat, the lighting all shadows with nary a scene in clear sunshine. Metaphorically speaking, the darkness proves even more extensive, the weeks-away-from-retirement Delaney simply stating that in this tough environment, "nothing's safe."

In the film's most remarkable sequence Delaney follows Blank in and out of scaffold-enshrouded buildings, with nary a word of dialogue spoken. Accompanied by Gordon Jenkins's highly effective string-heavy score, one that emits an entirely appropriate sense of eeriness and forthcoming doom, director Hutton utilizes tracking shots reminiscent of Hitchcock's, specifically the silent twelve-minute sequence at the climax of 1956's *The Man Who Knew Too Much*. Delaney, standing stock-still in the dim, rainy shadows, faces down Blank, forcing him to retreat on a run back to his own apartment. That sequence remains a highlight for the simple reason that it is one of the few times during the nearly-two-hours' running time that suspense is injected into the proceedings, the audience hooked by the question of if and how Delaney will catch Blank. It's a welcome shot of adrenaline for a film that unfortunately is long on gloomy atmosphere and short on genuine suspense.

After such a successful chase, Blank's unraveling is more than a little anticlimactic, as he mumbles half-finished phrases referring to a tortured childhood that found him forced to wear a collar and strip naked in a dark cellar. Dukes is such a solid actor that he convincingly portrays a psychopath, even one who crazily rationalizes his murders with mumbo-jumbo that the hammer allows him to "enter into another person—they're part of my life and I love them and they love me." Unfortunately, it's all too perfunctory a denouement, one that plays like a surreal blend of the song-and-dance nervous breakdown at the end of *Gypsy* and Roxie Hart's lament in *Chicago* that "the audience loves me and I love them and they love me for loving them and that's because none of us got enough love in our childhood." After a buildup of nearly two hours, Blank's psychobabble explanation seems oddly abbreviated, causing audiences to react with the feeling that such an explanation does not justify sitting through two hours of gore and an unrelentingly depressing atmosphere. The rather startling climax of the film is reached when Blank calls the police to report Delaney's breaking and entering, and Delaney, aware that he has broken all rules of evidence, shoots Blank in the head, killing him on the spot.

Just like Hovannes in *Contract on Cherry Street,* Delaney has taken the law into his own hands (it also serves as yet another indication of how believable Sinatra would have been as *Dirty Harry*) and immediately upon killing Blank, returns to the police station to turn in his badge. In a nicely biting bit of dialogue, the desk sergeant informs Delaney of a killing on West Eighty-third Street—does he want to investigate? It's the very murder Delaney has just committed, but his laconic response is "No. I just turned in my badge." Referring to Delaney's retirement, the sergeant exclaims, "You really did it—congratulations . . . won't be the same here without you." Whereupon Frank Sinatra the actor perfectly sums up Francis Delaney's exhausted worldview with his beautifully calibrated weary response: "It's always the same, Sergeant."

The nighttime New York City landscape dominated by a shot of the Empire State Building, the film concludes with a voiceover of Delaney reading to Barbara from the Honey Bunch book as she dies. With his tough but extraordinarily tender voice, Frank Sinatra's Delaney continues to read aloud from the book even after she dies, holding her hand to his face, finally

Beautiful performance as an NYPD detective in his last starring feature,
the extremely dark The First Deadly Sin *(1980).*

breaking down as he reads aloud of Honey Bunch's last visit to her garden in the woods, a garden that will "flourish and grant new life." The camera, which has been held in close-up on Sinatra's weather-beaten face, now pulls back as the film fades to black. It's an extraordinary moment because in that last starring role, the final scene has achieved the exact emotional blend that so brilliantly informed Sinatra's singing: this most masculine and tough of men has allowed his vulnerable side to break through, expressing the mass of contradictions inherent in the life of any human being. The last scene of the last starring role in Frank Sinatra's film career also happens to be among his very best.

It may be the unsparing and bleak nature of the film's denouement that sealed its failure at the box office. As proves true for Delancy himself, there is no release here for the audience. The psychopathic Blank remains just that to audiences—a blank—and the film ends with Delaney, now a murderer, bereft of both wife and job. Not exactly a recipe for audience pleasure.

This film is, in its own way, even harder for an audience to swallow than *The Detective,* for the simple reason that it rings truer, and audiences for glossy Hollywood movies were and are not used to accepting their pills without sugar coating. Critics were rather peremptory in their dismissal of the film, simply noting Sinatra's return to the world of feature-filmmaking after a decade-long absence: Cart, in *Variety,* did at least find the film "the first one in some time . . . that he appears to have taken with complete seriousness . . . he's serious, direct and not at all the wise guy, amounting to a decent perf. . . ." Well, it's a lot more than a decent performance, and while, with the passage of time, the film itself may not look much better than it did originally, Sinatra's performance does. Nuanced, complex, and extremely moving in its portrayal of one aging man's vulnerability, his work therein is really of the highest rank, right up there with his turns in *From Here to Eternity, Suddenly,* and *The Manchurian Candidate.* In fact, in strictly emotional terms, it is the most involving of all because Frank Sinatra has etched a warts-and all portrayal of a weary everyman whose humanity resonates across the widest-possible spectrum. Sinatra the actor has here surpassed Sinatra the singer. By 1980, his voice was an iffy proposition, its emotional force intact but the sound quality wildly variable. By way of contrast, Sinatra the actor was better than ever.

Great as he was, however, audiences rejected the film, a reception that surely heightened Sinatra's disenchantment with the world of filmmaking. He continued to search for another property, but the rules of Hollywood had changed. Slam-bang action pictures ruled at multiplexes, the easiest financing available only for sketchy films replete with cartoonlike levels of violence aimed at the target audience of teenage boys. Smaller character-driven adult-oriented movies were now just that—smaller. There was no turning back.

Sinatra may have been through with starring roles on the big screen, but he sure as hell was not about to retire, not by a long shot. In 1981, proud Republican Sinatra produced and directed the inaugural gala for newly elected President Ronald Reagan. While he no longer released multiple LPs and films each year, as had happened in the salad days of the 1950s and '60s, he still maintained a full schedule of concerts supplemented by one multimedia venture each year. The first of these, in 1982, found Frank starring in his first cable television special, *Sinatra: Concert for the Americas,* filmed in the Dominican Republic. At the same time, a rumor surfaced that Frank was interested in the starring role of low-rent lawyer Frank Galvin in *The Verdict,* but he lost that plum part to Paul Newman. It was therefore sweet consolation when, one year later, Frank received the Kennedy Center Honor for Lifetime Achievement in the performing arts.

The *Concert for the Americas* and the Kennedy Center Honors were both prestigious and dignified affairs, which is what made it so difficult to watch Sinatra's final big-screen appearance, a cameo role playing himself in the June 1984 film *Cannonball Run II.* This Burt Reynolds version of the Rat Pack films, featuring "performances" by Dean (his last feature film), Sammy, and Shirley MacLaine, represented the last onscreen gathering of the old gang, Sinatra's participation requiring only that he fly to Tucson and supposedly work for a grand total of four hours. Frank's cameo actually came about at the request of Sammy Davis Jr., who was, like Dean Martin, already contracted for the film. (In producer Albert Ruddy's version of the proceedings, Sinatra asked Dean Martin to include him in the film, a modern-day attempt to recapture the fun of the Summit/Rat Pack movies from the 1960s.) This may be the closest the old gang ever came to making another Rat Pack movie, and it's too bad they didn't leave well enough alone, because it is, in a word, horrible—stupefying in its unpleasant mix of equal parts cynicism and self-congratulation.

Sinatra himself actually looks great, but he is here stuck in a film of such surpassing stupidity that it qualifies as the single worst movie of his career. The lion's share of the blame must be laid at the feet of Hal Needham, stunt man–turned–writer/director, but there is certainly plenty of blame to spread around. What's most disconcerting about it is how so many first-rank talents could sink to that level: producer Albert Ruddy had fallen from producing the first *Godfather* film to overseeing a movie about a cross-country car race that's won by an auto-driving orangutan. Even more ridiculous is the fact that this idiotic film, stuffed with dozens of star cameos (if you consider Susan Anton and football's Joe Theisman to be stars), actually represented Shirley MacLaine's follow-up to her Oscar-winning turn in *Terms of Endearment*. At the time MacLaine was sitting on top of the entertainment world with her pick of offers, and she actually chose a car chase film that required her to dress in either a full nun's habit or hot pants and stiletto heels.

It's an inane confection that finds J. J. McClure (Burt Reynolds, sporting tinted aviator glasses and the worst toupee seen onscreen since Sinatra's in *Dirty Dingus Magee*) trying to win the $1 million prize for a cross-country car race sponsored by an Arab prince (Jamie Farr) and his father (Ricardo Montalban, whose accent suggests that Arabia lies next to Mexico). With an atrocious script, laughable acting, and an apparent budget of $1.25, the entire level of believability is summed up by the fact that Dom DeLuise is here presented as Marilu Henner's love interest. It's all so sloppily and perfunctorily executed that when a man is punched out and soars through the air (it's the sort of movie where he can't just fall, but must fly through the air, cartoon-style), the wires holding him up are completely visible.

And where does Frank Sinatra fit into the lunacy? Well, it's not saying much to acknowledge that he comes off the best of anyone involved, but he does. Unlike pals Sammy and Dean, who are supposed to play actual characters, Sinatra only has to play himself, which he does not only well, but with a sense of humor sorely lacking in the rest of the film. After Sammy and Dean state, "We have royalty in this country," J.J. and his fellow supplicants are led in by Jilly Rizzo to ask favors of Frank, who is seated behind his desk Godfather-style. Tanned and still commanding onscreen, Sinatra displays a nicely tuned sense of self-parody that allows him to tell the fawning J.J. "You may call me Frank." It's a statement that thrills J.J. until Frank adds, "Not yet. I'll let you know when you can." Asked by J.J. how he should be addressed in the meantime, Sinatra's quick retort is "Call me Sir." It's all delivered crisply and with the same awareness of his own iconic status that allowed him over the years to playfully introduce "My Way" in concert as "The National Anthem."

Cameo playing himself in his last feature film, Cannonball Run II *(1984). Left to right: Burt Reynolds, Dean Martin, Shirley MacLaine, Sammy Davis Jr., Sinatra.*

According to director Hal Needham's commentary on the DVD release of the original *Cannonball Run,* Sinatra showed up early for the filming of this scene and left before any of the other actors arrived. A close examination of the scene would seem to bear this out; when Sinatra is supposedly interacting with the other characters, the camera shows his (double's) back—it's only the other actors who directly face the camera. Sinatra later turns up for a brief scene halfway through the race, whereupon he joins the cannonball rally himself. (Never mind that he has not bothered to drive in the earlier part of the movie—it's the kind of film utterly lacking in even elementary logic.) The best that can be said about Sinatra's participation is that he donated his entire salary to charity.

So it was that Sinatra ended his big-screen career as the one bright spot in a truly awful film, one so inane that Warners did not release the film in the United States until six months after it came out in Japan. Yet in a curious kind of way, it made sense that Sinatra finished his nondocumentary feature-film career exactly as he had begun it: playing himself. In *Higher and Higher,* Sinatra made Marcy McGuire faint merely by stating, "Hello, I'm Frank Sinatra," and forty-one years later, he caused grown men to fawn and quake in his presence.

Frank continued giving concerts, often to benefit selected charities, keeping up a pace both surprising and admirable for a seventy-year-old. If the need for constant work had not changed, neither had the quick temper that could so often explode in the casual hurling of insults. Such episodes felt shocking in and of themselves, but especially so when delivered by someone so well-known as a champion of the underdog.

Consider one such episode at the end of 1983, when Frank and Dean, joined by Barbara Sinatra and Mort Viner, walked into an Atlantic City casino and began fooling with cards that the female Korean dealer had already fanned out on the gaming table. Frank blithely asked the dealer to ignore the rules and deal by hand instead of the eight-deck shoe. When the rather intimidated woman hesitated, Sinatra snapped, "If you don't want to do it, go back to China." The casual brutality of it—the fact that Sinatra snapped out the insult as soon as he didn't get his way—it all spoke of a then-sixty-eight-year-old man who could still act like a petulant adolescent.

Just as the concert dates continued to proliferate, so, too, did the awards, which ranged from the 1985 Presidential Medal of Freedom, the nation's highest civilian honor, to a citation of which Sinatra was particularly proud, the 1987 NAACP Lifetime Achievement Award. Somewhere along the way, even the baby boomers—who had once derided Sinatra as an outdated symbol of the sexist white establishment—began to come around. Yes, it all contained an element of the winking condescension found in any appreciation of pop culture in the irony-laden years at the end of the twentieth century; at the same time, however, with the reevaluation of the great American songbook jump-started by the surprising success of the Linda Ronstadt/Nelson Riddle collaboration "What's New," Sinatra's work was now being reassessed, his status as the foremost interpreter of popular standards confirmed. Far from being the sentimental and passé objects baby boomers had initially considered them to be, the beautifully wrought ballads gained stature from reexamination, the inherent honesty in Sinatra's work making plain just how startling and original it was.

At the same time, the upcoming theatrical reissue of Frank's greatest film, *The Manchurian Candidate,* refocused attention on his screen legacy, a fact that may have provided the final impetus for him to take on a dramatic television appearance as the guest star of the February 25, 1987, episode of *Magnum, P.I.* Through the years, Sinatra had put in singing appearances on a number of television variety shows ranging from *Texaco Star Theatre* (1953) and *The Jimmy Durante Show* (1956) to *The Dean Martin Show* (1965) and *Rowan and Martin's Laugh-In* (1969). He had appeared as himself in non-musical series as well, essaying star turns that ran the gamut from an unbilled cameo on *Burke's Law* (1963) to a stint as a host of *The Dick Powell Show* (1963). Such scattered appearances even included a turn on the silly but briefly popular *Soupy Sales Show* (1965), a more noteworthy appearance as the mystery guest on *What's My Line?* (1966), and actually continued right through to the late-career cameo on *Who's the Boss* (1989). As for non-cameo dramatic turns on television, however, his series acting was limited to this one episode in the seventh season of *Magnum, P.I.*, a turn made even more inter-esting by virtue of the fact that as a longtime fan of that highly successful tele-vision series, it was Sinatra himself who proposed the guest appearance to star and producer Tom Selleck. Billed with the careful wording "And special guest star Frank Sinatra as Detective Sergeant Michael Doheny," Sinatra turned in a performance that shows he had lost none of his acting chops. Daughter Tina Sinatra wrote in her autobiography that the *Magnum* appear-ance followed Frank's hospitalization for diverticulitis, a hospitalization that revealed a man "helpless and frail," but none of the illness shows onscreen. He looks fresh, relatively trim, and—most of all—vital. Performing some of his own stunts, Frank utilized the guest-starring role as a smart reminder to a very large segment of the American public that Frank Sinatra was still very much on this scene.

Titled "Laura," the *Magnum* episode finds Sinatra's Sergeant Doheny re-tiring from the New York City police department right before his grade school granddaughter is savagely raped and killed. Tracking the two killers to Hawaii, Doheny joins forces with private detective Magnum but hides his family connection to the girl. When called on his lie, Doheny, in Sinatra's wonderfully understated delivery, ruefully states, "There's truth and there's truth."

It's as if Doheny is the latest incarnation of Edward Delaney of *The First Deadly Sin*. He is, once again, a solitary avenger, a decent man neglected by the system who feels it necessary to take justice into his own hands. As such, Sinatra's initial set piece is the barroom brawl where he first meets Magnum, a nicely staged fight that includes a Sinatra on-set improvisation wherein he pours water on the head of a thug he has just beaten. For a one-hour dramatic television series, the episode, directed by Alan J. Levi, contains some very nice touches, especially in a dialogue-free extended montage that has Magnum following Doheny as the latter tracks the killers. With only the blaring rock song "Get Me Out of Here" heard on the soundtrack, the sequence climaxes in the unexpected spectacle of Doheny smashing the head of an uncooperative witness into the plate-glass window of a Chinese restaurant. Following the killer (Geiger) to a rooftop, Doheny snarls, "She was my granddaughter, you slimy bastard," before pummeling the criminal until he falls to his death on the concrete below.

What's interesting about Sinatra's surprisingly vigorous performance here at age seventy-one is the contrast with the series' star. Selleck, a strapping, buffed six-footer, is an amiable television star but contains none of the edge Sinatra inherently carries with him; there is never a hint of danger about Magnum, and older or not, Doheny is far more the man of heft and power than is Magnum. The contrast between the two actors is the difference between a movie star and a successful television actor. Selleck, his rather high-pitched voice oddly incongruous with his massive physique, plays against type nicely and always manages to inject a touch of wry self-deprecation, but he is not a compelling screen presence. There is a reason his stardom never managed the jump to feature films. The small box of television suits him just right. Sinatra, on the other hand, remained a movie star of the first rank for four decades. The gravitas that he always carried with him even in his silliest vehicles simply eludes Selleck, who registers as a personable television actor—nothing more, nothing less. (According to Selleck, Sinatra's one-take methods had clearly not changed a jot in the decade since his last dramatic television appearance: "Working with him is real interesting, because Frank has the patience of a saloon singer—and, in his defense, he's ready on the first take. . . . And he had a tendency to want to do one take and say, 'That's it, let's move on.' And he was always good, but somebody else might not have been.")

At episode's end, when the police lieutenant overseeing the case asks, "What happened here?" Magnum, after a momentary pause, simply states, "Geiger had a knife." Doheny is mute, and a range of emotions plays across his features, from satisfaction at revenge to a palpable self-loathing as he departs the scene with a weary silent walk. In the episode's final moments, Sinatra, dressed all in black, visits his granddaughter's grave. Kissing the floral lei he has brought with him as a gesture of remembrance, he drapes it on her headstone, quietly intoning, "I got him, honey. I got him," in an anguished—indeed, touching—tone. Bending syllables, a rough catch in his voice, Sinatra manages to be both forceful and touching in the space of one forty-seven-minute (plus commercials) episode of a network television series. Impressive.

One year later, in 1988, a highly publicized Rat Pack Reunion Tour with Sinatra, Dean Martin, and Sammy Davis Jr. hit the road for performance dates in fifteen-thousand-seat arenas, settings that proved quite a change from the intimate atmosphere at the Sands Hotel nearly four decades earlier. It was a vain attempt to recapture the magic of the past, with Sinatra in variable voice throughout and an increasingly befuddled and uninterested Dean Martin dropping out of the tour early on. Martin's premature departure caused a rift between Sinatra and Martin that would last through seven long years of silence until Dean's death in 1995.

Rat Pack Reunion Tour completed, Sinatra agreed to participate in the 1990 film salute to Quincy Jones, *Listen Up: The Lives of Quincy Jones,* as a means of paying tribute to the arranger and composer with whom he had enjoyed a nearly forty-year working relationship. Sinatra's participation in the film is minimal—he appears for no more than ninety seconds—but his agreement to be filmed speaks to the mutual esteem each held for the other. Smart man and brilliant musician that he is, Jones understood Sinatra's enormous talent as soon as they crossed paths decades earlier: "He was an incredible actor and to him every song was a role. This man could turn a two-bar song into a three-act play." The brilliant work Jones and Sinatra did together at the Sands in the 1960s, preserved both on the original 1966 album *Sinatra at the Sands* and on the 2006 four-CD boxed set titled *Sinatra: Vegas,* stands as proof positive of the power and emotional heft great popular music can deliver.

How happy was Jones with that 1966 gig at the Sands? First, consider all his brilliant accomplishments as composer, musician, arranger, and producer, and then note his response to the *Vanity Fair* Proust questionnaire and the specific query, "When and how were you happiest in your life?" The answer: "Conducting Frank Sinatra and the Count Basie Band, age 31." In the notes to the *Sinatra: Vegas* retrospective, Jones elaborates: "Having arranged and conducted the live album from the Sands was one of the greatest musical experiences of my life. . . . It was not just talent. It was education and hard work. Frank was hip, street, straight up, and straight ahead—a monster musician with big-band roots." How did Sinatra himself feel about that same gig? He simply called it "Possibly the most exciting engagement of my professional life. Quincy in those days was the conductor—kept the orchestra together. We did things that were jumping." No wonder Sinatra wanted to participate in *Listen Up*—this was some mutual-admiration society Quincy and Francis Albert had going. Which leads to the question, How's the documentary itself? Answer: it's an interesting albeit somewhat unsatisfying homage to the multi-talented Jones, but one that is all the better for Sinatra's tribute to his old friend. (In a film stuffed with snippets of interviews ranging across a veritable who's who of the twentieth-century American music world, interviews featuring everyone from Ella Fitzgerald, Ray Charles, and Dizzy Gillespie to Ice-T and Flavor Flav, Sinatra, is, along with Barbra Streisand, one of the very few white artists interviewed.)

Directed by Ellen Weissbrod, the film follows Jones on a return visit to the run-down Chicago neighborhood where he grew up, and while Jones's story is a fascinating one, Weissbrod undercuts her own material with a surfeit of jiggly handheld camera shots, and incessant jump-cuts that shortchange both the music and the words of the music legends interviewed. Jones's life holds inherent interest for any viewer, and there are noticeable parallels with Sinatra's own life, especially in the fact that this well-known "ladies' man" (in the words of his own children) has spent his life endlessly driven to express the music that seemed to burst out of him. A workaholic who came to realize (at least partially) the need for balance between the professional and the personal only late in life after surviving two aneurisms, Jones has been driven by the tumult of his childhood, just as Sinatra was by the loneliness of his own upbringing.

Discussing Jones's working method of "constantly running side by side with me through an orchestration," Sinatra is glimpsed in footage from the 1965 Newport Jazz Festival, singing "Fly Me to the Moon" with the Basie Orchestra. Summing up his love of performing with Count Basie and Jones, Frank declares, "Quincy had a key to the Count Basie Orchestra more than any other orchestrator." It's a relaxed Sinatra on camera, one who discusses his professional colleague in an analytical, appreciative, yet totally unemotional manner. This onscreen thank-you to his great friend constituted Frank's penultimate appearance of any sort on film; only a final brief cameo playing himself in the 1995 television movie *Young at Heart* would follow.

In fact, even with daughter Tina heading up a constant search for suitable film material, these last appearances of Frank's all found him playing himself. Whether in *Cannonball Run II, Listen Up,* or the television film *Young at Heart,* it's as if Sinatra's iconic status meant that no role could any longer contain his enormous personality. In playing himself, Frank Sinatra was playing his biggest role of all, that of the ever-restless second-generation son of immigrants, whose astonishing talent and overwhelming need for recognition could never—and would never—be sated. Ever searching and always insisting upon his say, Frank Sinatra could conceive of only one exit strategy—a fight to the finish.

That's Life

"Ever Homeward,"
sung by Frank Sinatra in *The Miracle of the Bells*

*I never studied, you know. I never went to any of the schools or anything like that. . . .
I thought that acting is playacting like we did when we were kids. But . . . suddenly
you're grown-up and it's for real.*
— FRANK SINATRA IN AN INTERVIEW WITH LARRY KING

*Later on in Frank's life he told me he believed he had lived before and would live
again.* —SHIRLEY MACLAINE

WHAT MUST IT HAVE BEEN like to continue playing the role of Frank Sinatra at age seventy-five? How could anyone fully live up to that overwhelming legend? Did people really leave concerts satisfied just to have seen Frank in person, or was there a noticeable subtext of *Sinatra's no longer Sinatra—I want him to stop now while my memories are intact.* What if the man in question didn't want to stop?

Being Frank Sinatra was always a difficult business, but never more so than now, when the inner circle of trusted friends grew ever smaller. In that regard, 1990 proved a particularly difficult year, as three of the people he loved and held closest to him died in quick succession: Ava Gardner on January 25; Sammy Davis Jr. on May 16; and finally pal, confidant, and ofttimes role model Jimmy Van Heusen six weeks later on July 2.

The core group of intimates was shrinking, but Frank bulled ahead, almost

Still singing, still looking for that last great film role.

as if saying to himself, *If I stop, I'll cease to exist.* So he didn't stop, and he kept up an astonishing schedule of concerts that would have taxed the energy of a man half his seventy-five years. Sinatra gave sixty-five concerts in 1990, seventy-three in 1991, and eighty-four in 1992, hopping the globe to seventeen different countries as far away as Australia and Japan. (Contrast this with Barbra Streisand's first-ever European tour in 2007 at age sixty-five, a tour that consisted of fewer than twenty-five concerts.) Connecting with a live audience, feeding off the energy, Frank felt alive and the old belligerence still kicked in, age seventy-five or not.

Consider Sinatra's comments in a September 1990 concert at the Garden State Arts Center in New Jersey. Not for Frank the measured tones of the avuncular elder statesman. Instead, blasting away at Irish singer Sinéad O'Connor's refusal to perform at that very same venue if the national anthem was played, Frank let loose: "This must be one stupid broad. . . . I'd kick her ass if she were a guy . . . she must beat her kids to stay in shape. . . ." Such concert monologues in effect functioned as live op-ed pieces, the stream-of-consciousness controversial opinions also finding their way into print, with letters to editors making it clear that after an entire adult lifetime spent in the public arena, Frank Sinatra couldn't, and didn't want to, stay out of the public eye. He relished his status, appreciated his privileged position, and never forgot the lean years of the early 1950s.

Referring to the then-well-publicized woes of the "reluctant" pop star George Michael, Sinatra's letter to the *Los Angeles Times* made it clear that he had no time for the so-called tragedy of fame: "The tragedy of fame is when no one shows up and you're singing to the cleaning ladies in some empty joint that hasn't seen a paying customer since St. Swithin's Day."

Frank may not have been acting in films himself, but he still relished the connection to the film community, and even made an appearance to present the humanitarian award to Leo Jaffe at the American Cinema Awards in January of 1991. A reevaluation of his screen legacy was beginning to take hold, one that culminated in a ten-film retrospective at the School of the Arts Institute in Chicago. Far more than just screening *From Here to Eternity* and *The Man with the Golden Arm,* the salute ranged across the full spectrum, from musicals to drama. With Sinatra no longer acting on film, the ameliorative effect of time had kicked in, and prestigious cultural institutions like the School of the Arts Institute—as well as the general public—correctly felt the time was ripe for a reevaluation. At long last, Sinatra's lifestyle was no longer being reviewed, just his artistry, and the Chicago salute was followed by a career achievement award at the Palm Springs International Film Festival.

Realizing that finding screen material of substance suitable for a seventy-five-year-old man would only continue to grow in difficulty, Frank at long last gave his blessing to daughter Tina's long-gestating project of the television miniseries biography, *Sinatra.* The four-hour film, with a then-record miniseries budget of $18.5 million, covers the years of Frank's life from childhood to 1974, attempting to place the full scope of Frank's achievements within the cultural landscape of mid-twentieth-century America. Starring Philip Casnoff as Sinatra, the miniseries generally lands as a first-class production, and for a family-produced affair, surprisingly and gratifyingly does not skate over Sinatra's multiple marriages or even the Sam Giancana–JFK liaison with the West Virginia primary in 1960.

That *Sinatra* saw the light of day at all was due to the perseverance of executive producer Tina, who had labored on the film for close to a decade before production began. Originally Tina had broached the idea that Frank write his autobiography, but he declined by stating, "I could fill volumes but the biggest part of my life would be missing. My music, my songs." A more unguarded response to the idea of an autobiography had actually come decades earlier in a 1962 interview with *New York Daily News* columnist Marilyn Beck, when Sinatra told the veteran journalist that an autobiography "will never happen because I'm not proud of too many things I've done." As an alternative to an autobiography, Tina's suggestion of a miniseries about her father's life met with his clipped response: "Good idea. You do it."

Filming commenced in February of 1992, with the finished movie airing in November of the same year. It's a solid effort that ultimately won the Golden Globe for Best Television Miniseries, and received a total of nine Emmy nominations (winning for Best Director, James Sadwith; and Best Costume Design, Shelley Komarov). Philip Casnoff, a solid actor and veteran of both television and Broadway musicals, strikes all the right poses as Sinatra, convincingly etching Sinatra's mannerisms and gestures. He looks enough like Frank that the visual never jars, but he inevitably suffers by comparison with the real Sinatra. He simply doesn't possess the star quality, the charisma of Frank himself, but then again, no one in the role would. Casnoff does come off better than Marcia Gay Harden, who delivers a not-particularly-believable Ava Gardner, but the best one here is a tough-talking Olympia Dukakis as Dolly. It's a nicely produced film, written by William Mastrosimone, and one complete with extensive period detail. Smartly, the film utilizes the original Sinatra recordings rather than forcing Casnoff to attempt the impossible task of trying to live up to the original recordings on his own.

Oddly enough, the film does not really pay a great deal of attention to Sinatra the singer, and the fabled Capitol recording sessions never seem to be shown. The focus instead lands squarely on his films and live performances, a decision that presents a rather lopsided depiction of the all-around artist. That said, the script is fairly truthful, covering the supposed mob connections, the temperamental outbursts, and even the compulsive womanizing. Liberties are certainly taken from time to time in order to present a more sanitized version of Sinatra's life, but all in all, it is a cut above the average television miniseries, and when all was said and done, served to burnish the Sinatra legend rather nicely. Sadly, in Tina's recounting, she's not sure her father ever saw the completed film, due to what Tina perceived as interference from Barbara: "Dad should have watched *Sinatra* in a safe, supportive environment. Had he watched it with my mother, I believe that he would have enjoyed every frame."

In the same year of the miniseries' telecast, Frank suffered another blow when Jilly Rizzo was killed on May 6. The only remaining member of the entourage was the now-estranged Dean Martin, who died on Christmas Day 1995. With Jilly's death, Frank Sinatra's intimate circle had shrunk to a fraction of its former size. If, in 1974, he had remarked to journalist Pete Hamill, "I go to too many goddamned funerals these days," eighteen years later, he was now fully face-to-face with his own mortality. No matter how frantically he worked to keep the loneliness at bay, maintaining a grueling schedule when his voice was in tatters and his stamina shrinking daily, he could not outrun either time or the abuse to which he had subjected his own body via cigarettes and booze. What, one wonders, did Sinatra think of in his last few concerts when he virtually declaimed the famous opening words to "My Way": "And now the end is near and as I face the final curtain." Only now, in his late seventies, did those words truly make sense in terms of Sinatra's own life. Did he consider his own fading health and looming death, or did he not think about the words at all, coasting along on the music until receiving a thunderous ovation at song's conclusion? Did the ovation even matter now?

What did matter to Frank was one last triumph, and he received it with the 1993 release of the *Duets* concept CD. Recording once again at the Capitol studios, Frank cut thirteen new versions of classic Sinatra tunes, tracks that were then intercut with separately recorded versions of the same songs by some of the biggest recording stars of the 1990s. The irony underlying the entire project lay in the fact that none of the other artists ever recorded face-to-face with Sinatra. With his voice in such iffy condition by that time, Frank simply chose to etch his half of the duets in isolation, his fellow artists recording their contributions at a later date.

With Sinatra's voice in poor shape and his partners, for the most part, ill-suited to his style of pop singing, the result was uneven. Aretha Franklin and Anita Baker do not sing out of the same tradition as Sinatra, and in the end, only Natalie Cole, Tony Bennett, and Barbra Streisand registered as appropriate partners. (Streisand comes off best of the bunch on her duet to "I've Got a Crush on You," which makes sense given her status as the last of the great Tin Pan Alley songbirds.) *Duets* may not constitute a standout Sinatra disc, but it did, ironically, rise to the top of the Billboard charts upon its October 1993 release. It went on to become Frank's best-selling album ever, and a fourteen-song follow-up, *Duets II,* released the next year, although of lesser quality, also sold in large numbers.

One final major award was to come Frank's way, the coveted Grammy Legend Award for lifetime achievement. The March 1, 1994, live telecast of the Grammys found Sinatra delivering a rather rambling acceptance speech (which daughter Tina attributed to problems in stabilizing his various medications), the speech cut off midstream by the show's producer. Interrupting Sinatra in the middle of his comments was an extraordinarily embarrassing moment, symbolic of the changing culture—this was, after all, Frank Sinatra, the king of the recording industry. The appearance did, however, yield one startlingly accurate observation from U2's Bono (a partner on *Duets*), who presented Frank with the award. Referring to Frank as the original rock star, Bono claimed, and rightly so, that "Rock and roll people love Sinatra because he's got what we want—swagger and attitude—he was the big bang of pop." Before rock and roll existed, Sinatra's rebellious "fuck you all" attitude represented the very attitude that would come to dominate rock and roll. The difference lay in the fact that in Sinatra's case, the attitude was manifested while singing standards in black tie while backed by a forty-piece orchestra. The rebellion lay within the artist, not the external trappings.

On February 25, 1995, Frank gave his last-ever public concert at the Palm Desert Marriott Ballroom, an event followed a mere two weeks later by the nationwide airing of his last-ever appearance on film, a cameo playing himself in daughter Tina's television movie titled *Young at Heart.* The role is very brief, with Frank appearing at the door of Sinatra-obsessed widow Rose Garaventi (Olympia Dukakis), who has used his music throughout the years to help her through tough spots in her life. (Dukakis's character is named Rose Garaventi as a tribute to Frank's maternal grandmother, who had saved his life at birth.) When at film's end, Rose opens a restaurant on the location of her late husband Joe's club (which had been burned down by a mobster), Frank himself appears at the restaurant. The film presents Sinatra as a near-mythic figure, one who by virtue of his very appearance amongst mortals—in this case, Dukakis's Garaventi—instantly makes them better. Lourdes comes to New Jersey.

When Rose asks Sinatra why he has come, he simply answers, "Joe sent me." In other words, the audience is asked to accept the fact that Frank Sinatra is such an all-powerful and pervasive presence that he can commune with the dead. It's as if the skinny boy from Hoboken who was so determined to leave his hometown has now returned to that very same town as a spiritual figure.

Frank had started his career in order to escape the stifling confines of family life in Hoboken, and was now working for the last time on film as a willing employee of his very own daughter, in a movie actually set in Hoboken. Producer Tina did, in fact, relate a smile-inducing anecdote in writing about her father's arrival on the set: by the time shooting commenced in 1994, Frank's health was failing and she was concerned about his ability to shoot his one scene. As a result, she hired a private jet to fly him from New York to location shooting in Toronto, but paid him scale for his cameo! Private jet or not, producer Tina actually transported her father from the airport to the set in a minibus, leading to Frank's quip, "I started my career on the bus, and I guess I'm ending it the same way."

In a fascinating anecdote about Frank the actor, Tina wrote of her father's one day of filming:

> Dad seemed a foot taller than I'd seen him in years. He was a man at home in this environment; he took command. We were so well prepared that the whole thing was over in forty minutes—it went by almost too fast. . . . Later that night, the director of photography told me that when he took his mark, Dad could tell that he wasn't quite in the right spot. Before the camera operator could make an adjustment, Dad inched into his key light. He knew precisely where he was supposed to be; his instincts were still intact.

When the film was broadcast on the night of March 12, 1995, audiences saw a Frank Sinatra who was appreciably heavier, even jowly, voice and body thickened with age—and it didn't matter one bit. Frank Sinatra gave a glance with his still-blazing eyes, and his star presence burst forth one last time.

There was a final public appearance when Frank suffered through an ABC television eightieth-birthday salute taped in November of that same year, appearing distinctly uncomfortable with the proceedings. Tina summed up the misbegotten appearance with the blunt statement, "I could tell that he hated almost every minute of it." Retirement was inevitable, if never formally announced, and Sinatra began spending more and more time at home. Trips to the hospital occurred with increasing frequency, and after the televised celebration of the 1995 birthday, public sightings of Frank became nearly nonexistent. When the Congressional Gold Medal of Honor was bestowed upon him on December 15, 1997, his eighty-second birthday, he watched the ceremonies on C-SPAN at home, his failing health making it impossible for him to attend in person. (At the May 13, 2008, unveiling of the Frank Sinatra postage stamp in New York City, Frank Jr. related that after watching the proceedings on television, a frail, tearful Sinatra pulled himself erect and forcefully stated, "And I'd do it all again, too." Ah, the lion in winter.) Five months later, on May 14, 1998, Frank Sinatra died of a heart attack at Cedars-Sinai Hospital emergency room.

The news of Sinatra's death resulted in front-page headlines around the world, as well as extended television coverage on cable and network stations alike. As the tributes poured in from around the world, extensive press reports of friction between wife Barbara and Frank's children surfaced, reports that centered on Barbara the gatekeeper having kept the children away from their father, as well as alleged tiffs over money. (Barbara eventually received the real estate holdings, while the three Sinatra children divided the music catalog.)

In the end, however, all the squabbling was forgotten in the avalanche of press coverage that ensued. It wasn't just that the widely acknowledged "greatest pop vocalist of all time" had passed away. It wasn't even that one of the last links to the golden age of Hollywood was gone. It was the fact that underlying all the thousands of articles was an acknowledgment that an entire way of life, one peculiarly American in nature, had ended. The Greatest Generation was irrevocably fading away along with their leading cultural figure. No, not all members of that generation were symbolized by, or even liked, Sinatra. But while Sinatra was still a vital, indelible presence, so, too, were they. His endurance had resonated with fans of his own generation because for an entire generation who had grown to feel increasingly unappreciated, especially in the 1960s and 1970s—their hard work and sacrifices, their patriotism, dismissed and shoved aside—Sinatra served as a potent reminder that they still were alive and that they mattered. With Sinatra on the scene, this Greatest Generation had not yet been rendered invisible, and as a result of that cultural resonance, the coverage of his death assumed an increasingly elegiac air.

Yes, baby boomers had reversed course and finally acknowledged the World War II generation, embracing Tom Brokaw's *The Greatest Generation* and Steven Spielberg's *Saving Private Ryan* with what Frank Rich of *The New York Times* dubbed a "fetishistic" zeal. At the same time, however, during all the years before the World War II monument was built in Washington, D.C., and a cultural reappraisal occurred, it was Frank Sinatra who had willfully stood tall as one of the few remaining vital symbols of an entire generation's cultural way of life.

At the end of the millennium, America had become an extraordinarily cynical country. Even in the rediscovery of a great singer like Tony Bennett there was a trace of condescension involved, as if the boomers were still a bit scared of admitting how such artists could cut through all the layers of self-protective irony and touch the heart directly. Baby boomers in particular seemed scared of genuine emotion, gingerly approaching the shores of adulthood as a foreign country, one best greeted by youthful dress and attitudes that mirrored those of their own children. By way of contrast to this generation often bent on presenting themselves as their children's best friends, Sinatra's presence was a particularly adult one, from dress and attitude down to music and movie roles.

Sinatra's relentless quest for unfettered personal freedom exemplified "the American Century," one in which the seemingly endless horizons promised a no-limits freedom, curtailed only by a man's own frailties, both personal and psychic. As such, Sinatra's life began and remained a fight to the finish: a fight against prejudice, expectations, and limitations imposed by others, a fight against loneliness and mortality. In this light, it makes perfect sense that Sinatra's last words to wife Barbara were, "I'm losing." The official cause of death— heart attack—was true enough, but the real cause was the inevitable collapse of the body after a lifetime of drinking and smoking, of late nights and little sleep, a collapse that was seemingly the only limitation Sinatra could never outrun, the only fight he could not continue.

At the time of Sinatra's death, then-president Bill Clinton stated, "His music and movies will ensure that Ol' Blue Eyes is never forgotten," but it was the more effusive tribute of director Martin Scorsese that pegged it most accurately: "He was an idol of mine and millions. A great Italian-American, a great American—and a great *actor* by the way—great, great actor just alone in films like *Some Came Running* and *The Man with the Golden Arm* and *From*

Here to Eternity. . . . There will never be another him. You know, he's the idol. He was the original."

Like all great original artists, Frank Sinatra, movie star, ultimately existed sui generis: ironic and battered, honest, tough, yet capable of great tenderness, he created an entirely new type of film hero—the disillusioned, saddened, yet tentatively hopeful American male of the World War II generation, one who hung on to his last flickering hopes with a grimly beautiful tenacity, battling until the very end. "I'm losing" indeed.

True artist that he was, Sinatra produced the exceptional in order to create an out-of-the-ordinary reaction in his audience—and in himself. Alone in the spotlight or in the frame, Sinatra removed the audience from their everyday existence, providing a pocket of understanding and empathy in the midst of life's chaos. Uplifted and enlightened, the audience could then return to its "normal" life—star and audience soothed alike.

In person or on record, Frank could and did console, but on film, the tone was tougher; there would be no sweet romances and certainly no hymns to the joys of suburbia so central to the American dream in the postwar era. Instead, at his best, Sinatra onscreen, like the man himself, exuded a blend of unshakable self-assurance mixed with occasionally naked vulnerability. The audience was always aware of a barely leashed temper. Sometimes it simmered underneath the surface, sometimes it exploded in verbal and physical pyrotechnics, but whether unchecked or leashed, the temper gave Sinatra a star's air of authority and mystery. A question always existed with Sinatra—he was impossible to fully pin down and therefore always remained in part unknowable. Just as the best storytelling leaves an audience asking what will happen next, Sinatra at his best onscreen left audiences wondering, *What will he do next?* His trademark cocky attitude mixed with a rueful acknowledgment that life is not completely controllable by anyone, Sinatra's screen persona exuded a sense of irony that dovetailed beautifully with an increasingly ironic post–World War II American society.

As Katharine Hepburn said of herself, "Whatever *it* is, I've got it." So, too, did Frank Sinatra the film actor, over an incredible fifty-four-year run of full-length motion pictures ranging from 1941 through 1995. The greatest male pop singer in the history of America, he had evolved from a pleasant lightweight performer on film to the most versatile male presence in movies, equally at home in a first-class musical such as *On the Town* or in the heaviest of dramas, like *The Man with the Golden Arm*. In his seventy-one film appearances, Frank Sinatra crafted a body of work unparalleled in American film history in its versatility. No other actor in Hollywood history had ever ranged so widely and so believably over such a long period of time. He may have made quite a few movies of little or not discernible merit, but as director George Sidney flatly declared: "There were no heights he couldn't reach."

Sinatra himself summed up the film career by stating: "I made some pretty good pictures . . . and I tried a few things that turned out to be mistakes." Frank's own words constitute a remarkable bit of understatement, for both good and bad. To find that a few things "turned out to be mistakes" does, in fact, downplay: *Dirty Dingus Magee, The Pride and the Passion,* and *Double Dynamite* are horrible movies —or in the words of Sinatra's own well-turned quip, having to watch *The Kissing Bandit* is akin to a "sadistic form of torture." Yet Sinatra's choice of words is instructive here— he "tried"—that he did, over and over. *The Pride and the Passion* is terrible by any measure, but Sinatra tried a foreign accent, even receiving coaching to help achieve the desired effect. He attempted to make a satirical Western with *Dirty Dingus Magee*—it just fell totally flat. Insisting on one take did not mean that Sinatra did not try—it was simply how he worked best. It was only when he truly *didn't* try—on *The Naked Runner* or a half-baked Rat Pack picture like *4 for Texas,* that he did his own screen legacy a complete disservice, in the process cheating both himself and his audience.

Similarly, calling *Anchors Aweigh, On the Town, From Here to Eternity, Suddenly, The Man with the Golden Arm, Pal Joey,* or *The Manchurian Candidate* "pretty good" undercuts those achievement by half. They are fascinating films, featuring musical and dramatic performances that not only impress with their breadth and depth, but also surprise with an intense and passionate originality. Boy next door, sad-sack GI, presidential assassin, drug addict, charming heel, or army intelligence officer—in Frank Sinatra's hands, the sweep of those decidedly American characters sprang to life in all their flawed humanity.

Ranging across the full scope of modern American life, etching indelible portraits that brought him acclaim, success, and an unassailable position as an international screen icon and one of the last legendary movie stars of the twentieth century, Frank Sinatra, through sheer force of talent, succeeded in carving out a singular position in film history. Actor and idol. Personality and artist.

Then. Now. Always.

Career Scorecard

YEAR	WORK	GRADE	COMMENT
1935	*Major Bowes Amateur Theater of the Air*	D	Just that—amateur time
1941	*Las Vegas Nights*	C	FS as himself in true antique—1 song
1942	*Ship Ahoy*	C	FS as himself; nutty—2 songs
1943	*Reveille with Beverly*	C	FS as himself; wacky—1 song
1943	*Higher and Higher*	B	FS as himself; his real debut
1944	*The Road to Victory*	B	FS as himself; 1 song
1944	*Step Lively*	C	First actual role; learning
1945	*The All-Star Bond Rally*	B	FS as himself; 1 song
1945	*Anchors Aweigh*	A	Great musical; great Frank
1945	*The House I Live In* Winner: Honorary Academy Award, shared with Frank Ross, Mervyn LeRoy, Albert Maltz, Earl Robinson, Lewis Allan	A	FS as himself; heartfelt short film
1946	*Till the Clouds Roll By*	C	The infamous "Ol' Man River"

YEAR	WORK	GRADE	COMMENT
1947	*It Happened in Brooklyn*	C	Cheap-looking; nice teaming with Jimmy Durante
1948	*The Miracle of the Bells*	C	Frank as priest; not great but oddly affecting
1948	*The Kissing Bandit*	D	Frank's review: "Please don't let my granddaughters watch it."
1948	*Lucky Strike Salesman's Movie 48-A*	C	Short film—true oddity
1949	*Take Me Out to the Ball Game*	A	Great fun; singing and hoofing up a storm
1949	*On the Town*	A	Groundbreaking; a musical peak
1951	*Double Dynamite*	D	Tired and dumb
1952	*Meet Danny Wilson*	B	Flawed but fascinating meeting of "real" and "reel" Frank
1953	*From Here to Eternity* Academy Award: Best Actor in a Supporting Role Golden Globe Award: Best Supporting Actor	A	The comeback; terrific film and first-class Frank
1954	*Anything Goes*	C	Wacky live television musical pairing of Frank and Ethel Merman as lovebirds
1954	*Suddenly*	A	Tough, taut suspense
1955	*Young at Heart*	B	Interesting mismatch with Doris Day; excellent Frank
1955	*Not as a Stranger* BAFTA Film Award nomination: Best Foreign Actor	C	Medical soap opera
1955	*Our Town*	B	Miscast Frank but smooth musicalization for television
1955	*Guys and Dolls*	C	Should have been better
1955	*The Tender Trap*	D	Annoying nonsense
1955	*The Man with the Golden Arm* Academy Award nomination: Best Actor in a Leading Role	B	Uneven film; brilliant Frank

YEAR	WORK	GRADE	COMMENT
	BAFTA Film Award nomination: Best Foreign Actor New York Film Critics nomination: Best Actor		
1956	*Meet Me in Las Vegas*	C	Minuscule cameo
1956	*Johnny Concho*	C	Interesting Western misfire
1956	*High Society*	B	Breezy fun; great Frank
1956	*Around the World in Eighty Days* Quigley Top 10 Money Makers Poll: #10	B	Overstuffed; wordless cameo
1957	*The Pride and the Passion*	D	Turgid; endless
1957	*The Joker Is Wild*	B	Solid Frank; brilliant first half then drops off noticeably
1957	*Pal Joey* Golden Globe Award: Best Motion Picture Actor Musical or Comedy Golden Laurel Award: Top Male Musical Performance Quigley Top 10 Money Makers Poll: #5	A	Iconic Sinatra. Career peak: "The Lady Is a Tramp"
1958	*Kings Go Forth*	C	Mixed up but interesting
1958	*Some Came Running* Golden Laurel Award: Top Male Dramatic Performance Golden Laurel Award nomination: Top Male Star of Year Quigley Top 10 Money Makers Poll: #10	B	Overbaked but good Frank (and great Dean)
1959	*A Hole in the Head*	B	Uneven but worthy teaming with Frank Capra
1959	*Invitation to Monte Carlo*	C	Cameo in travelogue
1959	*Never So Few* Quigley Top 10 Money Makers Poll: #7 Golden Laurel Award nomination: Top Male Star of the Year	C	Frank's okay, but the movie's overstuffed
1960	*Can-Can* Golden Laurel Award: Top Male Musical Performance Golden Laurel Award nomination: Top Male Star of the Year Quigley Top 10 Money Makers Poll: #8	C	Subpar but redeemed by "It's All Right with Me"

YEAR	WORK	GRADE	COMMENT
1960	*Ocean's Eleven*	B	Best of the Rat Pack flicks
1960	*Pepe*	D	Cameo in bloated "comic" epic
1961	*The Devil at 4 O'Clock* Golden Laurel Award nomination: Top Action Performance Golden Laurel Award Nomination: Top Male Star of the Year	C	The one screen pairing with idol Spencer Tracy; should have been better
1962	*Sergeants 3*	C	Lesser Rat Pack movie
1962	*The Road to Hong Kong*	C	Cameo in last "Road" picture
1962	*The Manchurian Candidate* Golden Laurel Award nomination: Top Action Performance Golden Laurel Award nomination: Top Male Star of the Year	A	Brilliant Frank; brilliant film
1962	*Sinatra in Israel*	B	Short film—2 songs
1963	*The List of Adrian Messenger*	B	Cameo in fine John Huston film
1963	*Come Blow Your Horn* Golden Globe Award nomination: Best Motion Picture Actor Musical or Comedy Golden Laurel Award nomination: Top Male Star of the Year	B	Pleasant and forgettable
1964	*4 for Texas*	D	Least of the Rat Pack films—get the boys back to Vegas
1964	*Robin and the 7 Hoods* Golden Laurel Award nomination: Top Male Star of the Year	B	Last musical of Frank's film career; solid fun
1965	*None But the Brave*	B	Flawed but worthy; Frank's sole outing as director
1965	*Von Ryan's Express* Golden Laurel Award nomination: Top Action Performance	A	First-class WWII movie
1965	*Marriage on the Rocks*	D	Awful
1966	*The Oscar*	D	Brief cameo as himself in campy Hollywood pic
1966	*Cast a Giant Shadow*	C	Cameo as pilot; somewhere in there is a good film

YEAR	WORK	GRADE	COMMENT
1966	*Assault on a Queen* Golden Laurel Award nomination: Top Male Star of the Year	C	*Ocean's Eleven* at sea; leaky vessel
1967	*The Naked Runner*	C	Starts out well; turns into a mess
1967	*Tony Rome* Golden Laurel Award nomination: Top Male Star of the Year	B	First and best of the private eye flicks; Frank in his element
1968	*The Detective*	B	Tough but overly ambitious
1968	*Lady in Cement*	B	*Tony Rome,* Part II—fine Frank
1970	*Dirty Dingus Magee*	D	Terrible; the less said, the better
1971	Academy Award: Jean Hersholt Humanitarian Award Golden Globe Award: Cecil B. DeMille Award for Lifetime Achievement		
1973	Screen Actors Guild Award: Life Achievement Award		
1974	*That's Entertainment!*	A	Frank as one of the hosts for a brilliant musical compilation
1977	*Contract on Cherry Street* Golden Apple Award: Male Star of the Year	C	Frank's only starring television movie; he's better than the film
1980	*The First Deadly Sin*	B	Bleak, not entirely successful, but Frank's better than ever; his last starring role
1984	*Cannonball Run II*	F	FS brief cameo as himself; worst film of his career
1987	*Magnum, P.I.*	B	Nice guest-starring role on popular television series
1990	*Listen Up: The Lives of Quincy Jones*	C	Very brief appearance as himself in tribute to good friend Quincy
1992	American Cinema Awards: Lifetime Achievement Award Desert Palm Lifetime Achievement Award—Desert Palm International Film Festival		
1995	*Young at Heart*	B	Surprisingly touching TV movie; FS ends as he began, playing himself

Filmography

Major Bowes Amateur Theater of the Air

Biograph Productions/Distributed by RKO
Released October 1935
Producer/Director: John H. Auer
Directors of Photography: Larry Williams, Tommy Hogan
Short Films: *The Night Club* (Sinatra cast as waiter), *The Big Minstrel Act* (Sinatra cast as blackfaced member of chorus)

Las Vegas Nights

Paramount Pictures, Inc.
Released March 1941
Producer: William LeBaron
Director: Ralph Murphy
Screenplay: Harry Clork, Ernest Pagano, Eddie Welch
Original Story: Ernest Pagano
Director of Photography: William C. Mellor
Staging of Musical Numbers: LeRoy Prinz
Musical Arrangements: Axel Stordahl
Cast: Phil Regan (Bill Stevens), Bert Wheeler (Stu Grant), Tommy Dorsey (Himself), Constance Moore (Norma Jennings), Virginia Dale (Patsy Lynch), Frank Sinatra (as himself, vocalist with Tommy Dorsey Band)
Sinatra Solo: "I'll Never Smile Again"

Ship Ahoy

Metro-Goldwyn-Mayer Inc.
Released May 1942
Producer: Jack Cummings
Director: Edward N. Buzzell
Screenplay: Harry Clork, Irving Brecher, Harry Kurnitz
Directors of Photography: Robert H. Planck, Leonard Smith, Clyde DeVinna
Musical Arrangements: Léo Arnaud, George Bassman, Sy Oliver, Conrad Salinger, George E. Stoll, Axel Stordahl

Cast: Eleanor Powell (Tallulah Winters), Red Skelton (Merton K. Kibble), Bert Lahr (Skip Owens), Virginia O'Brien (Fran Evans), Tommy Dorsey (Himself), Frank Sinatra (as himself, vocalist with Tommy Dorsey Band)
Sinatra Solos: "The Last Call for Love," "Poor You"

Reveille with Beverly

Columbia Pictures Corporation
Released February 1943
Producer: Sam White
Director: Charles Barton
Screenplay: Albert Duffy, Howard J. Green, Jack Henley
Director of Photography: Philip Tannura
Cast: Ann Miller (Beverly Ross), William Wright (Barry Lang), Franklin Pangborn (Vernon Lewis), Dick Purcell (Andy Adams); Count Basie, the Mills Brothers, Duke Ellington, Ella Mae Morse, Freddie Slack, Frank Sinatra (as themselves)
Sinatra Solo: "Night and Day"

Higher and Higher

RKO Radio Pictures
Released December 1943
Producer/Director: Tim Whelan
Screenplay: Jay Dratler, Ralph Spence (additional dialogue by William Bowers, Howard Harris); based on the play by Josh Logan and Ralph Spence
Director of Photography: Robert De Grasse
Musical Arrangements: Gene Rose
Musical Arrangements for Frank Sinatra: Axel Stordahl
Cast: Michèle Morgan (Millie Pico), Jack Haley (Mike O'Brien), Frank Sinatra (Himself), Leon Errol (Cyrus Drake), Marcy McGuire (Mickey), Mary Wickes (Sandy Brooks), Mel Tormé (Marty)
Score: Jimmy McHugh (music), Harold Adamson (lyrics); "Disgustingly Rich" from original Broadway play, Richard Rodgers (music), Lorenz Hart (lyrics)
Sinatra Songs: "I Couldn't Sleep a Wink Last Night," "The Music Stopped," "You're on Your Own," "A Lovely Way to Spend an Evening," "I Saw You First"

The Road to Victory (The Shining Future)—short film

Warner Bros. Pictures
Released May 1944
U.S. Treasury Dept. War Activities Committee "Release #98"
Producers: Gordon Hollingshead, Arnold Albert
Director: LeRoy Prinz
Screenplay: James Bloodworth
Musical Director: Leo Forbstein
Cast: Jack Carson, Bing Crosby, Cary Grant, Dennis Morgan, Frank Sinatra (as themselves)
Sinatra Solo: "(There'll Be A) Hot Time in the Old Town of Berlin" (arranged by Axel Stordahl)

Step Lively

RKO Radio Pictures
Released June 1944
Producer: Robert Fellows
Director: Tim Whelan
Screenplay: Warren Duff, Peter Milne (based on the play *Room Service* by Allen Boretz and John Murray)
Director of Photography: Robert De Grasse

Score: Jule Styne (music), Sammy Cahn (lyrics)
Musical Arrangements: Axel Stordahl
Orchestrations: Glen Rose
Cast: Frank Sinatra (Glenn Russell), George Murphy (Gordon Miller), Adolphe Menjou (Wagner), Gloria DeHaven (Christine Marlowe), Walter Slezak (Joe Gribble), Eugene Pallette (Simon Jenkins), Anne Jeffreys (Miss Abbott)
Sinatra Songs: "Come Out, Come Out, Wherever You Are," "As Long as There's Music," "Where Does Love Begin?" "Some Other Time"

The All-Star Bond Rally—short film

Twentieth Century-Fox Film Corporation
Released May 1945
U.S. Treasury Dept. War Activities Committee "Release #120"
Producer: Fanchon
Director: Michael Audley
Screenplay: Don Quinn
Orchestrations: Arthur Morton, Herbert Taylor, Herbert Spencer, Gene Rose, Maurice De Packh
Orchestrations for Frank Sinatra: Axel Stordahl
Cast: Bing Crosby, Linda Darnell, Betty Grable, Bob Hope, Harry James and His Orchestra, Fibber McGee and Molly, Frank Sinatra (as themselves)
Sinatra Solo: "Saturday Night (Is the Loneliest Night in the Week)"

Anchors Aweigh

Metro-Goldwyn-Mayer Inc.
Released July 1945
Producer: Joe Pasternak
Director: George Sidney
Screenplay: Isobel Lennart
Original Story: Natalie Marcin
Directors of Photography: Charles P. Boyle, Robert H. Planck
Origing Songs: Jule Styne, Sammy Cahn
Choreographer: Gene Kelly
Assistant Choreographer: Stanley Donen
Orchestrations: Axel Stordahl
Musical Director: George Stoll
Cast: Frank Sinatra (Clarence Doolittle), Kathryn Grayson (Susan Abbott), Gene Kelly (Joseph Brady), José Iturbi (Himself), Dean Stockwell (Donald Martin), Pamela Britton (Girl from Brooklyn)
Sinatra Songs: "We Hate to Leave," "The Cradle Song (Brahms' Lullaby)," "I Begged Her," "If You Knew Susie Like I Know Susie," "What Makes the Sunset?" "The Charm of You," "I Fall in Love Too Easily"

The House I Live In

RKO Radio Pictures
Released September 1945
Producer: Frank Ross
Director: Mervyn LeRoy
Screenplay: Albert Maltz
Original Concept: Frank Sinatra
Musical Director/Arranger: Axel Stordahl
Sinatra Solos: "If You Are But a Dream," "The House I Live In (That's America to Me)"

Special Christmas Trailer—short film

Metro-Goldwyn-Mayer Inc.
Released December 1945
Director: Harry Loud
Musical Directors: Nathaniel Shilkret, Axel Stordahl
Sinatra Solo: "Silent Night"

Till the Clouds Roll By

Metro-Goldwyn-Mayer Inc.
Released November 1946
Producer: Arthur Freed
Directors: Richard Whorf, George Sidney, Vincente Minnelli
Screenplay: Myles Connolly, Jean Holloway
Original Story: Guy Bolton
Story Adaptation: George Wells
Directors of Photography: George J. Folsey, Harry Stradling Sr.
Music: Jerome Kern
Director of Musical Numbers: Robert Alton
Orchestrations: Conrad Salinger
Cast: Robert Walker (Jerome Kern), Van Heflin (James I. Hessler), June Allyson (Specialty), Judy Garland (Marilyn Miller), Lena Horne (Julie in *Show Boat*), Van Johnson (Bandleader), Cyd Charisse (Dance Specialty), Angela Lansbury (Specialty), Frank Sinatra (Finale Soloist)
Sinatra Solo: "Ol' Man River"

It Happened in Brooklyn

Metro-Goldwyn-Mayer Inc.
Released March 1947
Producer: Jack Cummings
Director: Richard Whorf
Screenplay: Isobel Lennart
Original Story: J. P. McGowan
Original Songs: Jule Styne, Sammy Cahn
Director of Photography: Robert H. Planck
Choreographer: Jack Donohue
Musical Supervisor/Director: Johnny Green
Musical Arrangements: Axel Stordahl
Piano Solos: André Previn
Cast: Frank Sinatra (Danny Miller), Kathryn Grayson (Anne Fielding), Peter Lawford (Jamie Shellgrove), Jimmy Durante (Nick Lombardi), Gloria Grahame (Nurse)
Sinatra Songs: "Whose Baby Are You?" "The Brooklyn Bridge," "Invention #1," "I Believe," "Time After Time," "The Song's Gotta Come from the Heart," "La Ci Darem la Mano," "It's the Same Old Dream"

The Miracle of the Bells

Jesse Larkey Productions/RKO Radio Pictures
Released March 1948
Producers: Jesse L. Lasky, Walter MacEwen
Director: Irving Pichel
Screenplay: Ben Hecht, Quentin Reynolds, DeWitt Bodeen (based on the novel by Russell Janney)
Director of Photography: Robert De Grasse

Cast: Fred MacMurray (William Dunnigan), Alida Valli (Olga Treskovna), Frank Sinatra (Father Paul), Lee J. Cobb (Marcus Harris), Harold Vermilyea (Nick Orloff), Charles Meredith (Father J. Spinsky)
Sinatra Song: "Ever Homeward" (by Jule Styne and Sammy Cahn)

The Kissing Bandit

Metro-Goldwyn-Mayer Inc.
Released November 1948
Producer: Joe Pasternak
Director: László Benedek
Screenplay: John Briard Harding, Isobel Lennart
Director of Photography: Robert Surtees
Choreographer: Stanley Donen
Score: Earl K. Brent, Nacio Herb Brown, Edward Heyman
Cast: Frank Sinatra (Ricardo), Kathryn Grayson (Teresa), J. Carrol Naish (Chico), Mildred Natwick (Isabella), Mikhail Rasumny (Don José), Sono Osato (Bianca); Ricardo Montalban, Cyd Charisse, Ann Miller (Specialty Dancers)
Sinatra Songs: "If I Steal a Kiss," "Senorita," "Siesta," "What's Wrong with Me?"

Lucky Strike Salesman's Movie 48-A—short film

Producer: American Tobacco Co.
Released 1948
Musical Conductor/Arranger: Axel Stordahl
Cast: Frank Sinatra (Himself)
Sinatra Song: "Embraceable You"

Take Me Out to the Ball Game

Metro-Goldwyn-Mayer Inc.
Released April 1949
Producer: Arthur Freed
Director: Busby Berkeley
Screenplay: Harry Tugend, George Wells, Harry Crane
Original Story: Gene Kelly, Stanley Donen
Director of Photography: George J. Folsey
Score: Roger Edens (music); Adolph Green, Betty Comden (lyrics)
Choreographers: Stanley Donen, Gene Kelly
Cast: Frank Sinatra (Dennis Ryan), Esther Williams (K. C. Higgins), Gene Kelly (Eddie O'Brien), Betty Garrett (Shirley Delwyn), Jules Munshin (Nat Goldberg)
Sinatra Songs: "Take Me Out to the Ball Game," "Yes, Indeedy," "O'Brien to Ryan to Goldberg," "The Right Girl for Me," "It's Fate, Baby, It's Fate," "Strictly U.S.A."

On the Town

Metro-Goldwyn-Mayer Inc.
Released December 1949
Producer: Arthur Freed
Directors: Stanley Donen, Gene Kelly
Screenplay: Adolph Green, Betty Comden (based on their Broadway play)
Director of Photography: Harold Rosson
Score: Leonard Bernstein, Roger Edens (music); Adolph Green, Betty Comden (lyrics)
Orchestrations: Conrad Salinger
Musical Supervisor and Conductor: Lennie Hayton

Cast: Gene Kelly (Gabey), Frank Sinatra (Chip), Betty Garrett (Brunhilde Esterhazy), Ann Miller (Claire Huddesen), Jules Munshin (Ozzie), Vera-Ellen (Ivy Smith), Alice Pearce (Lucy Shmeeler)
Sinatra Songs: "New York, New York," "Come Up to My Place," "You're Awful," "Count on Me," "Pearl of the Persian Sea," "On the Town"

Double Dynamite

RKO Radio Pictures
Released December 1951
Producers: Irwin Allen, Irving Cummings Jr.
Director: Irving Cummings
Screenplay: Melville Shavelson
Original Story: Harry Crane, Mannie Manheim, Leo Rosten
Director of Photography: Robert De Grasse
Original Songs: Jule Styne, Sammy Cahn
Cast: Jane Russell (Mildred "Mibs" Goodhue), Groucho Marx (Emile J. Keck), Frank Sinatra (Johnny Dalton), Don McGuire (Bob Pulsifer Jr.), Nestor Paiva (Hot Horse Harris)
Sinatra Songs: "It's Only Money," "Kisses and Tears"

Meet Danny Wilson

Universal-International Pictures Inc.
Released 1952
Producer: Leonard Goldstein
Director: Joseph Pevney
Screenplay: Don McGuire
Director of Photography: Maury Gertsman
Musical Arranger/Conductor: Joseph Gershenson
Cast: Frank Sinatra (Danny Wilson), Shelley Winters (Joy Carroll), Alex Nicol (Mike Ryan), Raymond Burr (Nick Driscoll), Vaughn Taylor (T. W. Hatcher)
Sinatra Songs: "All of Me," "How Deep Is the Ocean?" "You're a Sweetheart," "She's Funny That Way," "A Good Man Is Hard to Find," "Lonesome Man Blues," "That Old Black Magic," "I've Got a Crush on You," "When You're Smiling (The Whole World Smiles with You)"

From Here to Eternity

Columbia Pictures Corporation
Released August 1953
Producer: Buddy Adler
Director: Fred Zinnemann
Screenplay: Daniel Taradash (based on the novel by James Jones)
Directors of Photography: Floyd Crosby, Burnett Guffey
Cast: Burt Lancaster (First Sergeant Milton Warden), Montgomery Clift (Private Robert E. Lee Prewitt), Deborah Kerr (Karen Holmes), Donna Reed (Alma "Lorene" Burke), Frank Sinatra (Private Angelo Maggio), Ernest Borgnine (Staff Sergeant James "Fatso" Judson), Philip Ober (Captain Dana Holmes)

Suddenly

Libra/United Artists
Released October 1954
Producer: Robert Bassler
Director: Lewis Allen
Screenplay: Richard Sale
Director of Photography: Charles G. Clarke

Cast: Frank Sinatra (John Baron), Sterling Hayden (Sheriff Tod Shaw), James Gleason (Pop Benson), Nancy Gates (Ellen Benson), Kim Charney (Pidge Benson), Willis Bouchey (Dan Carney), Christopher Dark (Bart Wheeler)

Young at Heart

Arwin/Warner Bros. Pictures
Released January 1955
Producer: Henry Blanke
Director: Gordon Douglas
Screenplay: Liam O'Brien (adapted from the original screenplay by Lenore J. Coffee, Julius J. Epstein; based on the story *Sister Act* by Fannie Hurst)
Director of Photography: Ted McCord
Musical Director/Arranger/Conductor: Ray Heindorf
Piano Solos: André Previn
Cast: Doris Day (Laurie Tuttle), Frank Sinatra (Barney Sloan), Gig Young (Alex Burke), Ethel Barrymore (Aunt Jessie), Dorothy Malone (Fran Tuttle), Robert Keith (Gregory Tuttle), Elisabeth Fraser (Amy Tuttle), Alan Hale Jr. (Robert Neary)
Sinatra Songs: "Young at Heart," "Someone to Watch over Me," "Just One of Those Things," "One for My Baby (And One More for the Road)," "You, My Love"

Not as a Stranger

Stanley Kramer Picture Corp/United Artists
Released July 1955
Producer/Director: Stanley Kramer
Screenplay: Edna Anhalt, Edward Anhalt (based on the novel by Morton Thompson)
Director of Photography: Franz Planer
Cast: Olivia de Havilland (Kristina Hedvigson), Robert Mitchum (Lucas Marsh), Frank Sinatra (Alfred Boone), Gloria Grahame (Harriet Lang), Charles Bickford (Dr. Dave Runkleman), Broderick Crawford (Dr. Aarons), Lon Chaney Jr. (Job Marsh), Harry Morgan (Oley), Virginia Christine (Bruni)

Our Town

NBC Television—Live Broadcast "Producers' Showcase"
Aired September 19, 1955
Director: Delbert Mann
Screenplay: David Shaw (based on the play by Thornton Wilder)
Score: James Van Heusen, Sammy Cahn
Orchestrations: Nelson Riddle
Vocal Direction: Norman Luboff
Cast: Frank Sinatra (Stage Manager), Paul Newman (George Gibbs), Eva Marie Saint (Emily Webb), Ernest Truex (Dr. Gibbs), Peg Hillias (Mrs. Webb)

Guys and Dolls

Goldwyn/Metro-Goldwyn-Mayer Inc.
Released November 1955
Producer: Samuel Goldwyn
Director: Joseph L. Mankiewicz
Screenplay: Joseph L. Mankiewicz, Ben Hecht (based on the Broadway play by Abe Burrows and Jo Swerling; original story by Damon Runyon and Abe Burrows)
Director of Photography: Harry Stradling Sr.
Score: music and lyrics by Frank Loesser
Orchestrations: Alexander Courage, Skip Martin, Nelson Riddle, Albert Sendrey

Choreography: Michael Kidd
Cast: Marlon Brando (Sky Masterson), Jean Simmons (Sarah Brown), Frank Sinatra (Nathan Detroit), Vivian Blaine (Miss Adelaide), Stubby Kaye (Nicely-Nicely Johnson), Johnny Silver (Benny South-street), B. S. Pully (Big Jule)
Sinatra Songs: "The Oldest Established (Permanent Floating Crap Game in New York)," "Guys and Dolls," "Adelaide," "Sue Me"

The Tender Trap

Metro-Goldwyn-Mayer Inc.
Released November 1955
Producer: Lawrence Weingarten
Director: Charles Walters
Screenplay: Julius J. Epstein (based on the Broadway play by Max Shulman and Robert Paul Smith)
Director of Photography: Paul C. Vogel
Title Song: Jimmy Van Heusen (music), Sammy Cahn (lyrics)
Cast: Frank Sinatra (Charlie Reader), Debbie Reynolds (Julie Gillis), David Wayne (Joe McCall), Celeste Holm (Sylvia Crewes), Lola Albright (Poppy Masters), Carolyn Jones (Helen)
Sinatra Song: "(Love Is) The Tender Trap"

The Man with the Golden Arm

Carlyle/United Artists
Released December 1955
Producer/Director: Otto Preminger
Screenplay: Walter Newman, Lewis Meltzer, Ben Hecht (based on the novel by Nelson Algren)
Director of Photography: Sam Leavitt
Musical Score: Elmer Bernstein
Titles: Saul Bass
Cast: Frank Sinatra (Frankie Machine), Eleanor Parker (Zosch Machine), Kim Novak (Molly), Arnold Stang (Sparrow), Darren McGavin (Louie), Robert Strauss (Schwiefka)

Meet Me in Las Vegas—cameo appearance

Metro-Goldwyn-Mayer Inc.
Released February 1956
Producer: Joe Pasternak
Director: Roy Rowland
Screenplay: Isobel Lennart
Director of Photography: Robert J. Bronner
Cast: Dan Dailey (Chuck Rodwell), Cyd Charisse (Maria Corvier), Agnes Moorehead (Miss Hattie), Jim Backus (Tom Culdane), Lili Darvas (Sari Hatvani), Lena Horne (Herself), Frankie Laine (Himself), Frank Sinatra (cameo)

Johnny Concho

Kent Productions/United Artists
Released July 1956
Producer: Frank Sinatra
Director: Don McGuire
Screenplay: Don McGuire David P. Harmon (based on the original story "The Man Who Owned the Town" by David P. Harmon)
Director of Photography: William C. Mellor
Original Score: Nelson Riddle
Titles: Saul Bass
Cast: Frank Sinatra (Johnny Concho), Keenan Wynn (Barney Clark), William Conrad (Tallman), Phyllis Kirk (Mary Dark), Christopher Dark (Walker)

High Society

Metro-Goldwyn-Mayer Inc.
Released July 1956
Producer: Sol C. Siegel
Director: Charles Walters
Screenplay: John Patrick (based on the play *The Philadelphia Story* by Philip Barry)
Director of Photography: Paul Vogel
Songs: Cole Porter
Orchestrations: Nelson Riddle, Conrad Salinger
Cast: Bing Crosby (C. K. Dexter-Haven), Grace Kelly (Tracy Lord), Frank Sinatra (Mike Connor), Celeste Holm (Liz Imbrie), Louis Armstrong (Himself), John Lund (George Kittredge), Sidney Blackmer (Seth Lord), Louis Calhern (Uncle Willie)
Sinatra Songs: "Who Wants to Be a Millionaire?" "You're Sensational," "Well, Did You Evah!" "Mind If I Make Love to You?"

Around the World in Eighty Days—cameo appearance

Michael Todd Productions/United Artists
Released October 1956
Producer: Mike Todd
Director: Michael Anderson, Sidney Smith (documentary sequence)
Screenplay: James Poe, John Farrow, S. J. Perelman (based on the novel by Jules Verne)
Director of Photography: Lionel Lindon
Cast: David Niven (Phileas Fogg), Cantinflas (Passepartout), Shirley MacLaine (Princess Aouda), Robert Newton (Inspector Fix), Noel Coward (Hesketh-Baggott), Robert Morley (Ralph); cameos by Ronald Colman, Peter Lorre, George Raft, Red Skelton, Marlene Dietrich, Buster Keaton, Beatrice Lillie, John Mills, Ava Gardner, Frank Sinatra (piano player)

The Pride and the Passion

Stanley Kramer Productions/United Artists
Released June 1957
Producer/Director: Stanley Kramer
Screenplay: Edna Anhalt, Edward Anhalt, Earl Felton (based on the novel *The Gun,* by C. S. Forester)
Director of Photography: Franz Planer
Musical Score: George Antheil
Cast: Cary Grant (Anthony), Frank Sinatra (Miguel), Sophia Loren (Juana), Theodore Bikel (General Jouvet), John Wengraf (Sermaine)

The Joker Is Wild

AMBL Productions/Paramount Pictures, Inc.
Released October 1957
Producer: Samuel J. Briskin
Director: Charles Vidor
Screenplay: Oscar Saul (based on the book *The Life of Joe E. Lewis,* by Art Cohn)
Director of Photography: Daniel L. Fapp
Original Songs: James Van Heusen (music); Sammy Cahn (lyrics)
Orchestrations: Jack Hayes, Nelson Riddle, Leo Shuken
Musical Director: Walter Scharf
Cast: Frank Sinatra (Joe E. Lewis), Mitzi Gaynor (Martha Stewart), Jeanne Crain (Letty Page), Eddie Albert (Austin Mack), Beverly Garland (Cassie Mack), Jackie Coogan (Swifty Morgan)
Sinatra Songs: "All the Way," "I Cried for You," "If I Could Be with You (One Hour Tonight)," "At Sundown," "Out of Nowhere"/"Swingin' on a Star," "Naturally"/"Ah, So Pure"/"Naturally," "Chicago (That Toddlin' Town)"

Pal Joey

Essex-Sidney/Columbia Pictures Corporation
Released October 1957
Producer: Fred Kohlmar
Director: George Sidney
Screenplay: Dorothy Kingsley (based on the play by John O'Hara)
Songs: Richard Rodgers, Lorenz Hart
Director of Photography: Harold Lipstein
Orchestrator: Arthur Morton
Choreographer: Hermes Pan
Cast: Rita Hayworth (Vera Simpson), Frank Sinatra (Joey Evans), Kim Novak (Linda English), Barbara Nichols (Gladys), Bobby Sherwood (Ned Galvin), Hank Henry (Mike Miggins)
Sinatra Songs: "I Didn't Know What Time It Was," "There's a Small Hotel," "I Could Write a Book," "The Lady Is a Tramp," "What Do I Care for a Dame?," "Bewitched, Bothered and Bewildered" (soundtrack only)

Kings Go Forth

Ross-ETON/United Artists
Released June 1958
Producer: Frank Ross
Director: Delmer Daves
Screenplay: Merle Miller (based on the novel by Joe David Brown)
Director of Photography: Daniel L. Fapp
Musical Score: Elmer Bernstein
Cast: Frank Sinatra (First Lieutenant Sam Loggins), Tony Curtis (Corporal Britt Harris), Natalie Wood (Monique Blair), Leora Dana (Mrs. Blair), Karl Swenson (Lieutenant Colonel Loggins), Pete Candoli (Musician), Red Norvo (Musician)

Some Came Running

Metro-Goldwyn-Mayer Inc.
Released December 1958
Producer: Sol C. Siegel
Director: Vincente Minnelli
Screenplay: John Patrick, Arthur Sheekman (based on the novel by James Jones)
Director of Photography: William H. Daniels
Musical Score: Elmer Bernstein
Cast: Frank Sinatra (Dave Hirsh), Dean Martin (Bama Dillert), Shirley MacLaine (Ginny Moorehead), Martha Hyer (Gwen French), Arthur Kennedy (Frank Hirsh), Nancy Gates (Edith Barclay), Leora Dana (Agnes Hirsh), Betty Lou Keim (Dawn Hirsh)

A Hole in the Head

Sin Cap/United Artists
Released July 1959
Producer/Director: Frank Capra
Executive Producer: Frank Sinatra
Screenplay: Arnold Schulman (based on his Broadway play)
Director of Photography: William H. Daniels
Score: Nelson Riddle
Songs: Jimmy Van Heusen, Sammy Cahn
Cast: Frank Sinatra (Tony Manetta), Edward G. Robinson (Mario Manetta), Thelma Ritter (Sophie Manetta), Eleanor Parker (Eloise Rogers), Carolyn Jones (Shirl), Keenan Wynn (Jerry Marks), Eddie Hodges (Ally Manetta), Joi Lansing (Dorine)
Sinatra Songs: "All My Tomorrows," "High Hopes"

Invitation to Monte Carlo—short film—cameo appearance

Valiant Films/Richmond Productions
Released 1959
Producer/Director: Euan Lloyd
Screenplay: Euan Lloyd, Jack Davies
Cinematography: Tony Braun, John Wilcox, Egil S. Woxholt
Cast: Germaine Damar (Jacqueline), Gilda Emmanuelli (Linda), Katharine Page (Matron); cameo appearances by Prince Rainier of Monaco, Princess Grace of Monaco, Frank Sinatra (as themselves)

Never So Few

Canterbury/Metro-Goldwyn-Mayer Inc.
Released December 1959
Producer: Edmund Grainger
Director: John Sturges
Screenplay: Millard Kaufman (based on the novel by Tom T. Chamales)
Director of Photography: William H. Daniels
Cast: Frank Sinatra (Tom Reynolds), Gina Lollobrigida (Carla Vesari), Peter Lawford (Captain Grey Travis), Steve McQueen (Bill Ringa), Richard Johnson (Captain Danny De Mortimer), Paul Henreid (Nikko Regas), Brian Donlevy (General Sloan), Charles Bronson (Sergeant John Danforth), Dean Jones (Sergeant Jim Norby)

Can-Can

Suffolk-Cummings/Twentieth Century-Fox Film Corporation
Released March 1960
Producer: Jack Cummings
Director: Walter Lang
Screenplay: Dorothy Kingsley, Charles Lederer (based on the Broadway play by Abe Burrows)
Director of Photography: William H. Daniels
Musical Score: Nelson Riddle
Songs: Cole Porter
Choreographer: Hermes Pan
Cast: Frank Sinatra (François Durnais), Shirley MacLaine (Simone Pistache), Maurice Chevalier (Paul Barriere), Louis Jourdan (Philipe Forrestier), Juliet Prowse (Claudine)
Sinatra Songs: "Can-Can/Montmartre," "I Love Paris," "C'est Magnifique," "Let's Do It (Let's Fall in Love)," "It's All Right with Me"

Ocean's Eleven

Dorchester/Warner Bros. Pictures
Released August 1960
Producer/Director: Lewis Milestone
Screenplay: Harry Brown, Charles Lederer
Original Story: George Clayton Johnson, Jack Golden Russell
Director of Photography: William H. Daniels
Musical Score: Nelson Riddle
Original Songs: Sammy Cahn, Jimmy Van Heusen
Cast: Frank Sinatra (Danny Ocean), Dean Martin (Sam Harmon), Sammy Davis Jr. (Josh Howard), Peter Lawford (Jimmy Foster), Angie Dickinson (Beatrice Ocean), Richard Conte (Anthony Bergdorf), Cesar Romero (Duke Santos), Joey Bishop (Mushy O'Connors), Akim Tamiroff (Spyros Acebos), Henry Silva (Roger Corneal), Patrice Wymore (Adele Ekstrom), Ilka Chase (Mrs. Restes); uncredited cameo by Shirley MacLaine

Pepe—cameo appearance

G.S.-Posa International Films/Columbia Pictures Corporation
Released December 1960
Producer/Director: George Sidney
Screenplay: Claude Binyon, Dorothy Kingsley
Original Story: Sonya Levien, Leonard Spigelgass
Director of Photography: Joseph MacDonald
Cast: Cantinflas (Pepe), Dan Dailey (Ted Holt), Shirley Jones (Suzie Murphy); cameo appearances by
Bing Crosby, Tony Curtis, Sammy Davis Jr., Jimmy Durante, Zsa Zsa Gabor, Greer Garson, Peter
Lawford, Janet Leigh, Jack Lemmon, Dean Martin, Kim Novak, Edward G. Robinson, Frank Sinatra

The Devil at 4 O'Clock

Le Roy/Kohlmar/Columbia Pictures Corporation
Released October 1961
Producers: Mervyn LeRoy, Fred Kohlmar
Director: Mervyn LeRoy
Screenplay: Liam O'Brien
Director of Photography: Joseph F. Biroc
Cast: Spencer Tracy (Father Doonan), Frank Sinatra (Harry), Kerwin Mathews (Father Joseph Per-
reau), Jean-Pierre Aumont (Jacques), Grégoire Aslan (Marcel), Alexander Scourby (The Governor),
Barbara Luna (Camille), Martin Brandt (Doctor Wexler), Bernie Hamilton (Charlie)

Sergeants 3

Essex-Claude/United Artists
Released February 1962
Producer: Howard W. Koch
Director: John Sturges
Screenplay: W. R. Burnett
Director of Photography: Winton C. Hoch
Cast: Frank Sinatra (Sergeant Mike Merry), Dean Martin (Sergeant Chip Deal), Sammy Davis Jr.
(Jonah Williams), Peter Lawford (Sergeant Larry Barrett), Joey Bishop (Sergeant-Major Roger
Boswell), Henry Silva (Mountain Hawk), Ruta Lee (Amelia Parent)

The Road to Hong Kong—cameo appearance

Melnor Films Production/United Artists
Released April 1962
Producer: Melvin Frank
Director: Norman Panama
Screenplay: Melvin Frank, Norman Panama
Director of Photography: Jack Hildyard
Songs: Jimmy Van Heusen, Sammy Cahn
Cast: Bing Crosby (Harry Turner), Bob Hope (Chester Babcock), Joan Collins (Diane), Robert Morley
(The Leader), Dorothy Lamour (Herself); cameo appearances by David Niven, Peter Sellers, Zsa
Zsa Gabor, Dean Martin (outer space traveler), Frank Sinatra (outer space traveler)

The Manchurian Candidate

MC Production/United Artists
Released October 1962
Producers: George Axelrod, John Frankenheimer
Director: John Frankenheimer

Screenplay: George Axelrod (based on the novel by Richard Conden)
Director of Photography: Lionel Lindon
Cast: Frank Sinatra (Bennett Marco), Laurence Harvey (Raymond Shaw), Janet Leigh (Rose Chaney), Angela Lansbury (Evelyn Iselin), Henry Silva (Chunjin), James Gregory (Senator John Iselin), Leslie Parrish (Jocelyn Jordan), John McGiver (Senator Thomas Jordan), Khigh Dhiegh (Yen Lo)

Sinatra in Israel—short film (documentary)

Released 1962
Produced By: Israeli Federation of Histadruth
Narration: Frank Sinatra
Sinatra Songs: "In the Still of the Night," "Without a Song"

The List of Adrian Messenger—cameo appearance

Joel Productions/Universal-International Pictures Inc.
Released May 1963
Producer: Edward Lewis
Director: John Huston
Screenplay: Anthony Veiller (based on the novel by Philip MacDonald)
Director of Photography: Joseph MacDonald
Cast: Kirk Douglas (George Brougham), George C. Scott (Anthony Gethryn), Dana Wynter (Lady Jocelyn Bruttenholm), Clive Brook (Marquis of Gleneyre), John Merivale (Adrian Messenger), Tony Huston (Derek); cameo appearances by Robert Mitchum (Jim Slattery), Frank Sinatra (Gypsy), Burt Lancaster (Woman)

Come Blow Your Horn

Essex-Tandem/Paramount Pictures, Inc.
Released June 1963
Producers: Norman Lear, Bud Yorkin
Director: Bud Yorkin
Screenplay: Norman Lear (based on the Broadway play by Neil Simon)
Director of Photography: William H. Daniels
Songs: Jimmy Van Heusen, Sammy Cahn
Score: Nelson Riddle
Cast: Frank Sinatra (Alan Baker), Lee J. Cobb (Harry R. Baker), Molly Picon (Sophie Baker), Barbara Rush (Connie), Jill St. John (Peggy John), Tony Bill (Buddy Baker), Dan Blocker (Mr. Eckman), Phyllis McGuire (Mrs. Eckman)
Sinatra Song: "Come Blow Your Horn"

4 for Texas

SAM Company/Warner Bros. Pictures
Released December 1963
Producer/Director: Robert Aldrich
Screenplay: Robert Aldrich, Teddi Sherman
Director of Photography: Ernest Laszlo
Musical Score: Nelson Riddle
Cast: Frank Sinatra (Zack Thomas), Dean Martin (Joe Jarrett), Anita Ekberg (Elya Carlson), Ursula Andress (Maxine Richter), Charles Bronson (Matson), Victor Buono (Harvey Burden), Nick Dennis (Angel), Richard Jaeckel (Pete Mancini), Ellen Corby (Widow)

Robin and the 7 Hoods

Claude-Essex/Warner Bros. Pictures
Released June 1964
Producer: Frank Sinatra
Director: Gordon Douglas
Screenplay: David R. Schwartz
Director of Photography: William H. Daniels
Score: Nelson Riddle
Original Songs: Jimmy Van Heusen, Sammy Cahn
Cast: Frank Sinatra (Robbo), Dean Martin (Little John), Sammy Davis Jr. (Will), Bing Crosby (Allen A. Dale), Peter Falk (Guy Gisborne), Barbara Rush (Marian Stevens), Victor Buono (Sheriff Alvin Potts), Robert Foulk (Sheriff Glick)
Sinatra Songs: "My Kind of Town (Chicago Is)," "Mister Booze," "Style," "Don't Be a Do-Badder"

None But the Brave

Tokyo Eiga Co. Limited/Toho Film/Artanis/Warner Bros. Pictures
Released February 1965
Producer/Director: Frank Sinatra
Producer Japan: Kikumaru Okuda
Screenplay: John Twist, Katsuya Susaki
Original Story: Kikumaru Okuda
Director of Photography: Harold Lipstein
Cast: Frank Sinatra (Chief Pharmacist Mate Francis Maloney), Clint Walker (Captain Dennis Bourke), Tommy Sands (Second Lieutenant Blair), Brad Dexter (Sergeant Bleeker), Tony Bill (Air Crewman Keller), Tatsuya Mihashi (Lieutenant Kuroki), Takeshi Katô (Sergeant Tamura)

Von Ryan's Express

P-R Productions/Twentieth Century-Fox Film Corporation
Released June 1965
Producer: Saul David
Director: Mark Robson
Screenplay: Wendell Mayes, Joseph Landon (based on the novel by David Westheimer)
Director of Photography: William H. Daniels
Musical Score: Jerry Goldsmith
Cast: Frank Sinatra (Colonel Joseph Ryan), Trevor Howard (Major Eric Fincham), Raffaella Carrà (Gabriella), Brad Dexter (Sergeant Bostick), Sergio Fantoni (Captain Oriani), Edward Mulhare (Captain Costanzo), Wolfgang Preiss (Major Von Klemment), James Brolin (Private Ames), Adolfo Celi (Battaglia)

Marriage on the Rocks

A-C/Sinatra Enterprises/Warner Bros. Pictures
Released September 1965
Producer: William H. Daniels
Director: Jack Donohue
Screenplay and Original Story: Cy Howard
Musical Score: Nelson Riddle
Cast: Frank Sinatra (Dan Edwards), Deborah Kerr (Valerie Edwards), Dean Martin (Ernie Brewer), Cesar Romero (Miguel Santos), Hermione Baddeley (Jeannie MacPherson), Tony Bill (Jim Blake), Nancy Sinatra (Tracy Edwards), Joi Lansing (Lola), Trini López (Himself)

Will Rogers Hospital Trailer—short film

Released 1965
Trailer soliciting contributions for the Will Rogers Memorial Fund. Sinatra appears and narrates.

The Oscar—cameo appearance

Greene-Rouse Productions/Paramount Pictures, Inc.
Released February 1966
Producer: Clarence Greene
Director: Russell Rouse
Screenplay: Harlan Ellison, Clarence Greene, Russell Rouse (based on the novel by Richard Sale)
Director of Photography: Joseph Ruttenberg
Musical Score: Percy Faith
Cast: Stephen Boyd (Frankie Fane), Elke Sommer (Kay Bergdahl), Milton Berle (Kappy Kapstetter), Eleanor Parker (Sophie Cantaro), Joseph Cotten (Kenneth Regan), Jill St. John (Laurel Scott), Edie Adams (Trina Yale), Ernest Borgnine (Barney Yale), Tony Bennett (Hymie Kelly); Bob Hope, Hedda Hopper, Merle Oberon, Frank Sinatra, Nancy Sinatra (as themselves)

Cast a Giant Shadow—cameo apperance

Batjac-Lleuroc-Mirisch Productions/United Artists
Released March 1966
Producer/Director: Melville Shavelson
Screenplay: Melville Shavelson (based on the book by Ted Berkman)
Director of Photography: Aldo Tonti
Cast: Kirk Douglas (Colonel Mickey Marcus), Senta Berger (Magda Simon), Angie Dickinson (Emma Marcus), John Wayne (General Mike Randolph), Yul Brynner (Asher Gonen), Topol (Abou Ibn Kader), Frank Sinatra (Vince Talmadge)

Assault on a Queen

Seven Arts—Sinatra Enterprises
Released June 1966
Producer: William Goetz
Director: Jack Donohue
Screenplay: Rod Serling (based on the novel by Jack Finney)
Director of Photography: William H. Daniels
Musical Score: Duke Ellington
Cast: Frank Sinatra (Mark Brittain), Virna Lisi (Rosa Lucchesi), Anthony Franciosa (Vic Rossiter), Val Avery (Trench), Richard Conte (Tony Moreno), Errol John (Linc Langley), Alf Kjellin (Eric Lauff-nauer)

The Naked Runner

Sinatra Enterprises/Artanis/Warner Bros. Pictures
Released July 1967
Producer: Brad Dexter
Director: Sidney J. Furie
Screenplay: Stanley Mann (based on the novel by Francis Clifford)
Director of Photography: Otto Heller
Cast: Frank Sinatra (Sam Laker), Peter Vaughan (Slattery), Derren Nesbitt (Colonel Hartmann), Nadia Gray (Karen), Edward Fox (Ritchie Jackson), Michael Newport (Patrick Laker)

Tony Rome

Arcola-Millfield/Twentieth Century-Fox Film Corporation
Released November 1967
Producer: Aaron Rosenberg
Director: Gordon Douglas
Screenplay: Richard L. Breen (based on the novel by Marvin H. Albert)
Director of Photography: Joseph F. Biroc
Musical Score: Billy May
Title Song: Lee Hazlewood (sung by Nancy Sinatra)
Cast: Frank Sinatra (Tony Rome), Jill St. John (Ann Archer), Richard Conte (Lieutenant Dave Santini), Gena Rowlands (Rita Kosterman), Simon Oakland (Rudy Kosterman), Lloyd Bochner (Vic Rood), Robert J. Wilke (Ralph Turpin)

The Detective

Arcola-Millfield/Twentieth Century-Fox Film Corporation
Released May 1968
Producer: Aaron Rosenberg
Director: Gordon Douglas
Screenplay: Abby Mann (based on the novel by Roderick Thorp)
Director of Photography: Joseph F. Biroc
Musical Score: Jerry Goldsmith
Cast: Frank Sinatra (Sergeant Joe Leland), Lee Remick (Karen Leland), Ralph Meeker (Lieutenant Curran), Jacqueline Bisset (Norma MacIver), William Windom (Colin MacIver), Tony Musante (Felix Tesla), Al Freeman Jr. (Robbie Loughlin), Robert Duvall (Nestor), Pat Henry (Mercidis), Sugar Ray Robinson (Kelly)

Lady in Cement

Arcola-Millfield/Twentieth Century-Fox Film Corporation
Released October 1968
Producer: Aaron Rosenberg
Director: Gordon Douglas
Screenplay: Marvin H. Albert, Jack Guss (based on the novel by Marvin H. Albert)
Director of Photography: Joseph F. Biroc
Musical Score: Hugh Montenegro
Cast: Frank Sinatra (Tony Rome), Raquel Welch (Kit Forrest), Richard Conte (Lieutenant Dave Santini), Martin Gabel (Al Munger), Lainie Kazan (Maria Baretto), Dan Blocker (Waldo Gronsky)

Dirty Dingus Magee

Metro-Goldwyn-Mayer Inc.
Released November 1970
Producer/Director: Burt Kennedy
Screenplay: Tom Waldman, Frank Waldman, Joseph Heller (based on the novel *The Ballad of Dingus Magee* by David Markson)
Director of Photography: Harry Stradling Jr.
Musical Score: Jeff Alexander, Billy Strange
Cast: Frank Sinatra (Dingus Magee), George Kennedy (Hoke Birdsill), Anne Jackson (Belle Knops), Lois Nettleton (Prudence Frost), Jack Elam (John Wesley Hardin), Michele Carey (Anna Hot Water), John Dehner (Brigadier General George)

That's Entertainment!

Metro-Goldwyn-Mayer Inc.
Released April 1974
Producer/Director: Jack Haley Jr.
Screenplay: Jack Haley Jr.
Directors of Photography: Allan Green, Ennio Guarnieri, Ernest Laszlo, Russell Metty, Gene
  Polito
Cast: Fred Astaire, Bing Crosby, Gene Kelly, Peter Lawford, Liza Minnelli, Donald O'Connor,
  Debbie Reynolds, Mickey Rooney, Frank Sinatra, James Stewart, Elizabeth Taylor (Hosts/
  Narrators)

Contract on Cherry Street

Artanis/Columbia Television/NBC Television
Aired November 1977
Producer: Hugh Benson
Director: William A. Graham
Teleplay: Edward Anhalt (based on the novel by Philip Rosenberg)
Director of Photography: Jack Priestley
Cast: Frank Sinatra (Deputy Inspector Frank Hovannes), Martin Balsam (Captain Ernie Weinberg),
  Verna Bloom (Emily Hovannes), Martin Gabel (Baruch Waldman), Harry Guardino (Ron Polito),
  Michael Nouri (Lou Savage), Henry Silva (Roberto Obregon), Steve Inwood (Fran Marks), Johnny
  Barnes (Otis Washington)

The First Deadly Sin

Artanis-Cinema 7/First Deadly Sin Company/Filmways Production
Released October 1980
Producers: George Pappas, Mark Shanker
Director: Brian G. Hutton
Screenplay: Mann Rubin (based on the novel by Lawrence Sanders)
Director of Photography: Jack Priestley
Cast: Frank Sinatra (Edward Delaney), Faye Dunaway (Barbara Delaney), David Dukes
  (Daniel Blank), Brenda Vaccaro (Monica Gilbert), Martin Gabel (Christopher Langley), An-
  thony Zerbe (Captain Broughton), James Whitmore (Dr. Sanford Ferguson), George Coe (Dr.
  Bernardi)

Cannonball Run II—cameo appearance

Warner Bros. Pictures
Released June 1984
Producer: Albert S. Ruddy
Director: Hal Needham
Screenplay: Harvey Miller, Hal Needham, Albert S. Ruddy
Director of Photography: Nick McLean
Cast: Burt Reynolds (J. J. McClure), Dom DeLuise (Victor Prinzim/Captain Chaos), Dean Martin
  (Jamie Blake), Sammy Davis Jr. (Fenderbaum), Shirley MacLaine (Veronica), Marilu Henner
  (Betty), Jamie Farr (The Sheik), Frank Sinatra (Himself)

Magnum, P.I.—guest star

CBS Television
Aired February 1987
Producers: Chris Abbott, Chas. Floyd Johnson, Tom Selleck
Director: Alan J. Levi

Teleplay: "Laura" by Chris Abbott, Donald Bellisario, Glen A. Larson
Cast: Tom Selleck (Magnum), John Hillerman (Higgins), Roger E. Mosley (T. C. Calvin), Larry Manetti (Rick Wright), Joe Santos (Police Lieutenant Nolan Page), Frank Sinatra (Detective Sergeant Michael Doheny)

Listen Up: The Lives of Quincy Jones—cameo appearance

Curt Productions/Warner Bros. Pictures
Released October 1990
Producer: Courtney Sale Ross
Director: Ellen Weissbrod
Screenplay: Ellen Weissbrod
Cinematographer: Stephen Kazmierski
Cast: Ray Charles, Miles Davis, Billy Eckstine, Ella Fitzgerald, Flavor Flav, Dizzy Gillespie, Michael Jackson, Barbra Streisand, Frank Sinatra (as themselves)

Young at Heart—cameo appearance

TS Productions/CBS Television
Aired March 1995
Executive Producer: Tina Sinatra
Director: Allan Arkush
Teleplay: Judith Paige Mitchell
Cinematographer: Alar Kivilo
Cast: Philip Bosco (Patsy), Richard Cox (Marco), Olympia Dukakis (Rose Garaventi), Joe Penny (Mike), Louis Zorich (Joe Garaventi), Tony Longo (Vinnie), Frank Sinatra (Himself)

Notes

March 25, 1954

1 "deeply thrilled and very moved" Frank Sinatra, acceptance speech, 26th Annual Academy Awards, RKO Pantages Theatre, Hollywood, CA, March 25, 1954.
"and I'd just like to say" ibid.

2 "greatest comeback in theatre history" *Variety*, March 1954, as cited in Daniel O'Brien, *The Frank Sinatra Film Guide* (London: Butler & Tanner, 1998), p. 66.
"I couldn't even share" Nancy Sinatra, *Frank Sinatra: An American Legend* (Santa Monica, CA: General Publishing Group, 1995) p. 18.
"a whole new kind of thing" Frank Sinatra, acceptance speech, 26th Annual Academy Awards, RKO Pantages Theatre, Hollywood, CA, March 25, 1954

3 "I made some pretty good pictures" Nancy Sinatra, *Frank Sinatra: An American Legend*, p. 329.

Well, Did You Evah (Care)?

4 "Frank Sinatra is beyond talent" Will Friedwald, *Sinatra! The Song Is You* (New York: Scribner, 1995), p. 497.
"The trouble with me" Frank Sinatra as quoted in Robin Douglas-Home, *Look Magazine*, December 14, 1965.

5 "His passion for his films" Michael Feinstein, "You're Sensational" in *Liner Notes, Frank Sinatra: The Hollywood Years 1940–1964*, p. 7.
"As I listened to Sinatra" Michael Feinstein, *Nice Work If You Can Get It: My Life in Rhythm and Rhyme* (New York: Hyperion, 1995), p. 288.
"Obviously winning the Academy Award" Frank Sinatra on *The Tonight Show,* hosted by Johnny Carson, NBC Television, as quoted in Scott Allen Nollen, *The Cinema of Sinatra* (Baltimore: Luminary Press, 2003), p. 299.

6 "Although movies were a crapshoot" George Jacobs with William Stadiem, *Mr. S: My Life with Frank Sinatra* (New York: HarperCollins, 2003), p. 67.
"I do believe that singing on one-nighters" Frank Sinatra as quoted in *Liner Notes, Frank Sinatra: The Hollywood Years 1940–1964*, "Sinatra! The Visual Factor" by Will Friedwald (Bristol Productions Limited Partnership under exclusive license to Reprise Records, 2002), p. 86.
"He has the most amazing sense of timing" Chris Ingham, *The Rough Guide to Frank Sinatra* (New York: Penguin Group, 2005), p. 292.
"I went around to all the different sets" Frank Sinatra in *Liner Notes, Frank Sinatra: The Hollywood Years 1940–1964*, p. 86.

"I always try to remember three things" Arnold Shaw, *Sinatra: The Entertainer* (New York: Delilah Books, 1982), p. 38.

7   "I have my own technique" Frank Sinatra to Betty Voigt, *Newsweek,* July 1959.

8   "Sinatra's first take is better" J. Randy Taraborelli, *Sinatra: Behind the Legend* (New York: Citadel Press/Kensington Publishing Corp., 1997), p. 204.

"My Way," music by Claude François and Jacques Revaux, French lyrics by Claude François and Gilles Thibaut, English lyrics by Paul Anka.

"That's Life" by Dean Kay, Kelly Gordon.

"I've been up and down in my life" Nancy Sinatra, *Frank Sinatra: An American Legend,* p. 115.

9   "They have it all wrong" Mia Farrow, *What Falls Away* (New York: Doubleday, 1997), p. 99.

"Raised a Catholic" Tina Sinatra, *My Father's Daughter* (New York: Simon & Schuster, 2000), p. 160.

"There is heartbreak" Frank Capra, *The Name Above the Title* (New York: Macmillan, 1971), p. 463.

10 "In time of course" John Lahr, *Sinatra: The Artist and the Man* (New York: Random House, 1997), p. 3.

"The greatest loneliness is in disillusion" Donald Clarke, *All or Nothing at All: A Life of Frank Sinatra* (London: Macmillan, 1997), preface, p. xii.

11 "A Sinatra film never reached down" Pete Hamill, *Why Sinatra Matters* (New York: Little, Brown, 1998), p. 178.

Hoboken

12 "In Hoboken when I was a kid" Gene Ringgold and Clifford McCarty, *The Films of Frank Sinatra* (Secaucus, NJ: Carol Publishing Group, 1971,1993), p. 3.

"If England's future wars" Souvenir Program, *Frank Sinatra Concert Tour 1976.*

"Sinatra told the truth" Bill Zehme, *Newsweek,* May 25, 1998.

13 "follow the path of least resistance" Tina Sinatra, *My Father's Daughter,* p. 168.

15 "I loved him but" Pete Hamill, *Why Sinatra Matters,* p. 71.

"He could do no wrong" Tina Sinatra, *My Father's Daughter,* p. 14.

"In that he was" ibid.

"One thing about Dolly" Pete Hamill, *Why Sinatra Matters,* p. 61.

16 "the stillness, attention and unequivocal adoration" John Lahr, *Sinatra: The Artist and the Man,* p. 102.

"They fly in his plane" John Bryson quoting a Sinatra intimate in Nancy Sinatra, *Frank Sinatra: My Father* (New York: Doubleday, 1985), p. 193.

"very lonely for" Nancy Sinatra, *Frank Sinatra: An American Legend,* p. 18.

17 "being an eighteen karat manic-depressive" Frank Sinatra with Joe Hyams, *Playboy,* February 1963.

18 "He's St. Francis of Assisi" Douglas Thompson, "Frank's Lucky Lady," *London Sunday Express.*

"If what you do is honest" Scott Allen Nollen, *The Cinema of Sinatra,* p. 19.

19 "the first time in [his] life" Pete Hamill, *Why Sinatra Matters,* p. 105.

"The radio was like a religion" ibid., p. 53.

20 "She was a pisser" Shirley MacLaine, *My Lucky Stars* (New York: Bantam Books, 1995), p. 85.

"He was so unsure of the larger world" Tina Sinatra, *My Father's Daughter,* p. 64.

21 "Attending A. J. Demarest High School" Richard Havers, *Sinatra* (New York: DK Publishing, 2004), p. 30.

"There really was nothing to lose" Pete Hamill, *Why Sinatra Matters,* p. 99.

"Thank you for letting me sing" Shirley MacLaine, *My Lucky Stars,* p. 89.

22 "if the local orchestras" Nancy Sinatra, *Frank Sinatra: An American Legend,* p. 25.

"What I finally hit on" CBS News, *Sinatra Off the Record,* hosted by Walter Cronkite, 1965; Frank Sinatra, "Me and My Music," *Life,* April 23, 1965.

23 "So I started becoming" Pete Hamill, *Why Sinatra Matters,* p. 94.

"Someday that's gonna be me" Will Friedwald, *Sinatra! The Song Is You,* pp. 146–147.

25 "I'm Frank—I'll speak for the group" *The Original Amateur Hour*, DVD, 2005.
26 "We didn't realize that we were hurting anyone at the time" Nancy Sinatra, *Frank Sinatra: An American Legend*, p. 27.
"They're good boys" *Person to Person with Edward R. Murrow*, CBS Television, 1956.
27 "mind-numbing thirty-five shows per week" *The Original Amateur Hour*, DVD, 2005.
"Sinatra utilized the family connection of cousin Ray Sinatra" Scott Allen Nollen, *The Cinema of Sinatra*, p. 21.

Boy Singer

29 "I walked up" Bill Zehme, *The Way You Wear Your Hat: Frank Sinatra and the Lost Art of Livin'* (New York: HarperCollins, 1997), p. 225.
30 "I said 'no way, baby'" Pete Hamill, *Why Sinatra Matters*, p. 38.
"I stood in the snow" Nancy Sinatra, *Frank Sinatra: An American Legend*, p. 42.
"Fear is the enemy of logic" Frank Sinatra with Joe Hyams, *Playboy*, February 1963.
"What did I learn from T-Bone Dorsey?" Frank Sinatra on *A Man and His Music*, LP released November 1965.
31 "If Harry James instilled" Will Friedwald, *Sinatra! The Song Is You*, p. 85.
"The slow tempo" Will Friedwald and William Ruhlmann, *Tommy Dorsey, Frank Sinatra: The Song Is You* (RCA66363), p. 24
34 "He sings prettily" George Simon, *Metronome* as cited in Daniel O'Brien, *The Frank Sinatra Film Guide*, p. 204.
37 "Frank Sinatra's singing" Scho, *Variety*, April 1942, as quoted in Nancy Sinatra, *Frank Sinatra: An American Legend*, p. 50.
"Had he been a healthier" Tina Sinatra, *My Father's Daughter*, p. 160.
"so desperate had Sinatra been" Nancy Sinatra, *Frank Sinatra: An American Legend*, p. 50.
"Dorsey refused, agreeing to release Sinatra" Nancy Sinatra, ibid.
38 "I hope you fall on your ass" Nancy Sinatra, *Frank Sinatra: An American Legend*, p. 51.
"Sinatra himself requested his file" Irwin Molotsky, "FBI Released Its Sinatra Files with Tidbits Old and New," *The New York Times*, December 9, 1998.
39 "And then I said" Nancy Sinatra, *Frank Sinatra: An American Legend*, p. 51.
"What the fuck" Pete Hamill, *Why Sinatra Matters*, p. 91.
40 "Frank believed in the *words*" Connie Haines as quoted in *Sinatra: The Life*, Anthony Summers and Robbyn Swan (New York: Alfred A. Knopf, 2005), p. 67.
"obsessed bobby-soxer Rosemary Clooney" Rosemary Clooney, *Girl Singer* (New York: Doubleday, 1999), p. 16.
"grossing $3 million" Richard Havers, *Sinatra*, p. 77.
"Interestingly, Sinatra received only one thousand dollars" ibid., p. 71.
42 "Night and Day" music and lyrics by Cole Porter.
"a slight young man" John T. McManus *PM* as quoted in Gene Ringgold and Clifford McCarty, *The Films of Frank Sinatra*, p. 33.

The Boy Next Door

44 "when asked if" Charles Pignone, *The Sinatra Treasures* (New York: Bullfinch Press, 2004), p. 82.
"RKO filed suit" Gene Ringgold and Clifford McCarty, *The Films of Frank Sinatra*, p. 250.
45 "I feel badly" "Army Classifies Sinatra in 4F Because of Punctured Eardrum," *New York Herald Tribune*, December 10, 1943.
"'running ear' and 'head noises'"; "neurotic, afraid to be in crowds" Tom and Phil Kuntz, eds. *The Sinatra FBI Files: The Secret FBI Dossier* (New York: Three Rivers Press, 2000), p. 21.
"not acceptable material . . . undue unpleasantness" Tom Kuntz, "From 4F to Eternity," *The New York Times*, August 12, 2000.

"at least 25 percent of the reports"   Anthony Summers and Robbyn Swan, *Sinatra: The Life,* pp. 102–103.

50   "this visual is all that remains"   Daniel O'Brien, *The Frank Sinatra Film Guide,* p. 15.

51   "It was almost as though your power"   Shirley MacLaine, *Newsweek,* May 25, 1998.

52   "an effect which can only"   Chris Ingham, *The Rough Guide to Frank Sinatra,* p. 282.

"Frankie is no Gable or Barrymore"   Bosley Crowther, *The New York Times,* as quoted in Kitty Kelley, *His Way: The Unauthorized Biography of Frank Sinatra* (New York: Bantam, 1987), p. 90.

"The crooner certainly doesn't fulfill"   *Los Angeles Times,* December 1943, as quoted in Gene Ringgold and Clifford McCarty, *The Films of Frank Sinatra,* p. 36.

53   "Already I was being prepared"   Nancy Sinatra, *Frank Sinatra: An American Legend,* p. 21.

56   "Sinatra's demand that the close-in-height DeHaven"   Scott Allen Nollen, *The Cinema of Sinatra,* p. 39.

57   "I don't want any more movie acting"   "Sinatra Quits Screen," *The New York Times,* September 10, 1944.

"an electric contagion of excitement"   *The New Republic* as cited in Anthony Summers and Robbyn Swan, *Sinatra: The Life,* p. 83.

59   "consensual American culture"   T. H. Adamowski, "Love in the Western World," in *Frank Sinatra and Popular Culture: Essays on an American Icon,* Leonard Mustazza, ed. (Westport, CT: Praeger, 1998), p. 29.

61   "I guess the way I sang it"   Nancy Sinatra, *Frank Sinatra: An American Legend,* p. 59.

"payment of $130,000,"   Daniel O'Brien *The Frank Sinatra Film Guide,* p. 20.

62   "due regard to public conventions"   *Sinatra: His Life and Loves Decade by Decade,* collector's edition, eds. Sheila and J. P. Cantillon, (Los Angeles: LFP, 1990), p. 50., as cited in Anthony Summers and Robbyn Swan, *Sinatra: The Life,* p. 126.

63   "If you're not there Monday"   Nancy Sinatra, *Frank Sinatra: An American Legend,* p. 62.

64   "Because I didn't think I was as talented"   ibid., p. 61.

65   "We rehearsed *Anchors Aweigh*"   Arnold Shaw, *Sinatra: The Entertainer,* p. 90.

"In a measure"   Richard Havers, *Sinatra,* p. 104.

66   "from lousy to adequate"   Anthony Summers and Robbyn Swan, *Sinatra: The Life,* p. 83.

67   "with an entourage of no less than eight men"   Daniel O'Brien, *The Frank Sinatra Film Guide,* p. 22.

68   "The two figures were optically linked"   Jeanine Basinger, *Pyramid Illustrated History of the Movies* (New York: Pyramid, 1976), p. 46.

69   "Sock artists"   Louella Parsons, *Los Angeles Examiner,* as quoted in Gene Ringgold and Clifford McCarty, *The Films of Frank Sinatra,* p. 44.

71   "The House I Live In," music by Earl Robinson, lyrics by Lewis Allan.

72   "I'm always for the little guy"   Tina Sinatra, *My Father's Daughter,* p. 67.

73   A lot of people were talking"   George Murphy, 18th Annual Academy Awards, Grauman's Chinese Theater, Hollywood, CA, March 7, 1946.

A Paesano Onscreen

74   "Then I discovered at—what?"   Pete Hamill, *Why Sinatra Matters,* p. 38.

"hate myself for laughing"   ibid., pp. 48–49.

77   "I don't believe any more"   Ralph Gleason in *Rolling Stone* as quoted in Arnold Shaw, *Sinatra: The Entertainer,* p. 118.

"cloak himself in respect and dignity"   Tommy Thompson as quoted in ibid.

78   "one key to Frank"   Tommy Thompson, "Understanding Sinatra," *McCall's Magazine,* October 1974.

"a kindness that was also an assertion"   Ruth Conte as quoted in John Lahr, *Sinatra's Song,* June 1, 1998.

All Over the Map

80 "It looks as though Mr. Sinatra" Bosley Crowther, *The New York Times* review of *It Happened in Brooklyn,* March 14, 1947.
"The trouble with Frankie is" *Screen Album,* Fall 1947.
"Ol' Man River," music by Jerome Kern, lyrics by Oscar Hammerstein II.
84 "You had to write your own material" Tony Bennett as quoted in John McDonough, "Tony Bennett—Survival by Song," *Downbeat,* October 2006.
"a high point in bad taste" *Life,* 1946, as quoted in Daniel O'Brien, *The Frank Sinatra Film Guide,* p. 204.
"Both versions are creditably done" *Variety* as quoted in Gene Ringgold and Clifford McCarty, *The Films of Frank Sinatra,* p. 50.
"He is at his most ludicrous" Pete Hamill, *Why Sinatra Matters,* p. 69.
"My idea with that song" Jerome Kern as quoted by Amy Porter, *Collier's Magazine,* as quoted in Gene Ringgold and Clifford McCarty, *The Films of Frank Sinatra,* p. 50.
86 "Durante can upstage anyone" Daniel O'Brien, *The Frank Sinatra Film Guide,* p. 27.
87 "How About You," music by Burton Lane, lyrics by Ralph Freed.
90 "Production memos reveal" Chris Ingham, *The Rough Guide to Frank Sinatra,* p. 285.
"Mr. Sinatra the self-confessed savior" Robert Ruark as quoted in Pete Hamill, *Why Sinatra Matters,* p. 144.
91 "I was brought up" ibid., p. 145.
"It was one of the dumbest" ibid.
" 'grinning' Sinatra acknowledged" *New York Herald Tribune,* April 10, 1947.
"In the end Sinatra paid" *New York Herald Tribune,* June 4, 1947.
"I have received satisfaction" ibid.
"physical bout in my lifetime" Pete Hamill, *Why Sinatra Matters,* p. 139.
"it was a critical mistake" ibid.
92 "promise him that she would never let granddaughter A. J." Nancy Sinatra, *Frank Sinatra: An American Legend,* p. 87.
93 "Evidently Benedek" Daniel O'Brien, *The Frank Sinatra Film Guide,* p. 32.
95 "Siesta" by Earl K. Brent, Nacio Herb Brown.
96 "While his songs aren't bad" Justin Gilbert, *Los Angeles Mirror* as cited by Kitty Kelley, *His Way: The Unauthorized Biography of Frank Sinatra* (New York: Bantam Books, 1987), p. 130.
"I hated reading the script" Pete Hamill, *Why Sinatra Matters,* p. 138.
97 "an ABC radio poll" Scott Allen Nollen, *The Cinema of Sinatra,* p. 73.
98 "when the non-English-speaking mother" ibid.
100 "Ever Homeward," by Kasimierez Lubomirski, adapted by Jule Styne and Sammy Cahn.
"I never sing a song" Frank Sinatra in *Liner Notes, Frank Sinatra: The Hollywood Years 1940–1964,* p. 17.
"The picture can be reasonably described" *Cue* magazine review of *The Miracle of the Bells,* as quoted in Daniel O'Brien, *The Frank Sinatra Film Guide,* p. 38.
"Sinatra wisely doesn't attempt" Philip K. Scheuer, *Los Angeles Times,* as quoted in Gene Ringgold and Clifford McCarty, *The Films of Frank Sinatra,* p. 56.
"a hunk of religious baloney" Hedda Hopper as quoted in Richard Havers, *Sinatra,* p. 133
101 "at the time of filming" Scott Allen Nollen, *The Cinema of Sinatra,* p. 79.
102 "the fledgling screenwriters received" Sheridan Morley and Ruth Leon, *Gene Kelly: A Celebration* (London: Pavilion Books Limited, 1996), p. 86.
103 "Frank worked hard" Betty Garrett as quoted in Kitty Kelley, *His Way,* p. 130.
104 "The Right Girl for Me," music by Roger Edens, lyrics by Betty Comden and Adolph Green.
105 "Sinatra sings and gags his way through" *Hollywood Reporter* review of *Take Me Out to the Ball Game,* as quoted in Gene Ringgold and Clifford McCarty, *The Films of Frank Sinatra,* p. 62.
"*Take Me Out to the Ball Game* is a lazy" *Time* review of *Take Me Out to the Ball Game,* as quoted in ibid.
106 "I really believed it would be a milestone" Clive Hirschhorn, *Gene Kelly* (London: WH Allen), p. 182.

107 " 'smutty' " and " 'Communistic' "   ibid., p.180.
"As a result of that investment"   Stephen Silverman, *Dancing on the Ceiling: Stanley Donen and His Movies* (New York: Alfred A. Knopf, 1996), p. 108.
"But that f——ing Arthur Freed"   Frank Sinatra in *Liner Notes, Frank Sinatra: The Hollywood Years 1940–1964,* p. 7.
108 "Munshin was so phobic"   Stephen Silverman, *Dancing on the Ceiling,* pp. 114–115.
109 "demanded that the original lyric"   ibid., p. 112.
110 "You're Awful," music by Roger Edens, lyrics by Betty Comden and Adolph Green.
"The still-skinny Sinatra"   Richard Havers, *Sinatra,* p. 145.
112 "front office suits could"   Daniel O'Brien, *The Frank Sinatra Film Guide,* p. 46.
"He didn't fall off a horse"   Scott Allen Nollen, *The Cinema of Sinatra,* p. 88.
"I wish I could take that back"   Nancy Sinatra, *Frank Sinatra: An American Original,* p. 95.
"That's not a very nice thing to do"   ibid.
"As a freelance artist"   MGM press release as quoted in Daniel O'Brien, *The Frank Sinatra Film Guide,* p. 48.
113 "*On the Town* brings airy imagination"   *Time* review of *On the Town* as quoted in Gene Ringgold and Clifford McCarty, *The Films of Frank Sinatra,* p. 66.
114 "A TV set cannot"   Wilfrid Sheed, *The House That George Built,* (New York: Random House, 2007), p. 306.
"Sinatra walked off the TV high end"   Chris Ingham, *The Rough Guide to Frank Sinatra,* p. 326.
"The delay occurred at the behest of RKO boss Howard Hughes"   Daniel O'Brien, *The Frank Sinatra Film Guide,* p. 49.

Ava and the Downfall

117 "His voice and his woman"   Bill Zehme, *The Way You Wear Your Hat: Frank Sinatra and the Lost Art of Livin',* p. 75.
"There isn't a building"   ibid., p. 160.
"the couple's first date"   Lee Server, *Ava Gardner: Love Is Nothing* (New York: St. Martin's Press, 2006), pp. 175–176.
"The blue eyes"   Ava Gardner, *Ava: My Story* (New York: Bantam Books, 1990), p. 124.
118 "that escalated so rapidly"   Lee Server, *Ava Gardner,* p. 248.
"always an edge"   Ava Gardner, *Ava,* p. 162.
"a bullshit story"   Lee Server, *Ava Gardner,* p. 225.
"Ava taught him"   Pete Hamill, *Why Sinatra Matters,* p. 177.
119 "I am very much surprised"   ibid., p. 125.
"Oh God, it was magic"   Lee Server, *Ava Gardner,* p. 128.
120 "Unfortunately, we never had any trouble"   Ava Gardner, *Ava,* p. 128.
"it is a kind of"   Lee Server, *Ava Gardner,* p. 187.
"Something's Gotta Give," music and lyrics by Johnny Mercer.
"Get off that"   Ava Gardner, *Ava,* pp. 154–155.
121 "He looked so pained"   Mia Farrow, *What Falls Away,* p. 95.
"the locks were changed"   Lee Server, *Ava Gardner,* p. 183.
"I did it"   Frank Sinatra as quoted in Bill Zehme, *The Way You Wear Your Hat,* p. 218.
122 "I was never so panic stricken"   Nancy Sinatra, *Frank Sinatra: An American Legend,* p. 95.
"wasn't as tumultuous"   Lee Server, *Ava Gardner,* p. 200.
"dark period I went through"   Frank Sinatra to Edward R. Murrow, *Person to Person,* CBS Television, 1956.
"my voice ran away"   *Frank Sinatra: A Man and His Music,* Reprise Records, 1965.
123 "Nancy received"   Lee Server, *Ava Gardner,* p. 214.
"so dire"   ibid., p. 236.
125 "Sinatra was like a lightning rod"   John Rockwell, *Sinatra: An American Classic* (New York: Random House, 1984), pp. 131–132.
127 "the mutual dislike"   Richard Havers, *Sinatra,* p. 155.

128 "But the sighs and screeches" *The New York Times,* March 27, 1952, p.34.
129 "Gone on Frankie in '42" *World Telegram and Sun,* March 27, 1952.
"Apart from romantic and melodramatic trimmings" *Time,* as quoted in Gene Ringgold and Clifford McCarty, *The Films of Frank Sinatra,* p. 73.
"title role is tailor-made for Sinatra" Brog, *Variety,* January 16, 1952.

The Comeback

130 "Don't despair" Bill Zehme, *The Way You Wear Your Hat,* p. 216.
"I showed those mothers" ibid., p. 221.
131 "For the first time" Nancy Sinatra, *Frank Sinatra: An American Legend,* p. 106.
"More than a book" ibid., p. 115.
"His fervor" ibid., p. 114.
132 "The horse's head" ibid., p. 110.
"As for Sinatra himself" ibid., p. 50.
133 "You must be out of" Harry Cohn as quoted in Earl Wilson, *Sinatra: An Unauthorized Biography* (New York: Macmillan, 1976), p. 108.
"You know who's right" Nancy Sinatra, *Frank Sinatra: An American Legend,* p. 115.
"What confuses the matter" Lee Server, *Ava Gardner,* p. 244.
"next to the bed" Nancy Sinatra, *Frank Sinatra: An American Legend,* p. 106.
134 "derogatory to a sister service" Richard Havers, *Sinatra,* p. 180.
136 "The way he pitched" Daniel O'Brien, *The Frank Sinatra Film Guide,* p. 63.
137 "As a singer . . ." J. Randy Taraborelli, *Sinatra: Behind the Legend,* p. 160.
138 "With due respect" Fred Zinnemann, *A Life in the Movies: An Autobiography* (New York. Scribner, 1992), p. 124.
139 "Lancaster related" Nancy Sinatra, *My Father* (New York: Pocket Books, 1985), pp. 97–98.
"See his head don't bump" Daniel O'Brien, *The Frank Sinatra Film Guide,* p. 65.
140 "Simply superb" *Los Angeles Herald Examiner* review of *From Here to Eternity* as quoted in Gene Ringgold and Clifford McCarty, *The Films of Frank Sinatra,* p.79.
"As you can see" *The New Yorker,* as quoted in ibid.
"He was very, very good" Fred Zinnemann as quoted in John Howlett, *Frank Sinatra* (Philadelphia: Courage Books, 1980), p. 71.
142 "Above all, though, Tommy taught me" Frank Sinatra on *A Man and His Music* LP, released November 1965.
143 "even on the classic torch albums" Pete Hamill, *Why Sinatra Matters,* p. 177.
"I think I get an audience involved" Frank Sinatra with Joe Hyams, *Playboy,* February 1963.
"Italians tend to break down" Gene di Novi as quoted in Gene Lees, *Singers and the Song II* (New York: Oxford University Press, 1987, 1998), p. 91.
"He cut his left wrist" Lee Server, *Ava Gardner,* p. 273.
144 "a previous suicide attempt" Nancy Sinatra, *Frank Sinatra: An American Legend,* p. 105.
"Dad's days with Ava were numbered" Tina Sinatra, *My Father's Daughter,* p. 27.
146 "You're the Top," music and lyrics by Cole Porter.
147 "As simple and startling as a good scream" Gene Ringgold and Clifford McCarty, *The Films of Frank Sinatra,* p. 82.
149 "He tenses" M. A. Schmidt, *The New York Times,* May 9, 1954.
151 "Around 1970, Sinatra discovered" Daniel O'Brien, *The Frank Sinatra Film Guide,* p. 76.
152 "*Suddenly* provides an excellent" Gene Ringgold and Clifford McCarty, *The Films of Frank Sinatra,* p. 83.

The Peak Years

155 "He was a natural personality" George Sidney as quoted in J. Randy Taraborelli, *Sinatra: Behind the Legend,* p. 204.

156 "From the very beginning" A. E. Hotchner, *Doris Day: Her Own Story* (New York: William Morrow, 1976), p. 146.

"Some days when he missed" ibid., p. 148.

"I don't think Frank was concerned" ibid.

"Lang was a painstaking craftsman" ibid., p. 147.

158 "Despite Frank's sure and cocky exterior" ibid., p. 148.

161 "Day herself theorized" A. E. Hotchner with Doris Day, *Doris Day: Her Own Story*, pp. 146–147.

162 "there was an inevitability" ibid., p. 145.

168 "Sinatra, who seems to become a better actor" Jack Moffitt, *The Hollywood Reporter*, as quoted in Gene Ringgold and Clifford McCarty, *The Films of Frank Sinatra*, p. 90.

169 "Interestingly, Goldwyn's first choice for the part" Daniel O'Brien, *The Frank Sinatra Film Guide*, p. 79.

171 "*Guys and Dolls* was not a particularly" ibid., p. 80.

"another time we laughed at *Guys and Dolls*" Tina Sinatra, *My Father's Daughter*, p. 265.

"Frank Sinatra . . . never forgave" Wilfried Sheed, *The House That George Built*, p. 275.

175 "is always a man" Jack Moffitt, *The Hollywood Reporter*, as quoted in Gene Ringgold and Clifford McCarty, *The Films of Frank Sinatra*, pp. 98–99.

"Faithful in detail" *Time*, as quoted in Daniel O'Brien, *The Frank Sinatra Film Guide*, p. 81.

"Colorful as a bright new lipstick" *The Hollywood Reporter* as quoted in Daniel O'Brien, *The Frank Sinatra Film Guide*, p. 84.

176 "Everything is ahead of me" *The New York Times,* October 2, 1955, "Sinatra Sitting On Top of the World."

179 "willed nonchalance" T. H. Adamowski, "Love in the Western World," in *Frank Sinatra and Popular Culture: Essays on an American Icon,* Leonard Mustazza, ed. (Westport: Praeger, 1998), p. 29.

181 "very difficult" Debbie Reynolds as quoted in Nancy Sinatra, *Frank Sinatra: An American Legend,* p. 124.

182 "You're not getting two Sinatras" Michael Freedland, *All the Way: A Biography of Frank Sinatra*, (New York: St. Martin's Press, 1997), p. 249.

"So, when he saw two cameras" *Frank Sinatra Memorial,* DVD (Passport Video 9011), 1999.

188 "John Garfield who originally bought the film rights" Scott Allen Nollen, *The Cinema of Sinatra,* p. 132.

"for a salary of $100,000" Daniel O'Brien, *The Frank Sinatra Film Guide,* p. 85.

"Costar Eleanor Parker" Foster Hirsch, *Otto Preminger: The Man Who Would Be King* (New York: Alfred A. Knopf, 2007), p. 237.

189 "Sinatra arrived for work each day" Daniel O'Brien, *The Frank Sinatra Film Guide,* p. 86.

"was surprised to discover" Otto Preminger, *Preminger: An Autobiography* (New York: Doubleday, 1977), p. 112.

193 "She was terrified" ibid., p. 113.

"has a chip" Foster Hirsch, *Otto Preminger,* p. 237.

"Ironically, the film received" ibid.

195 "forty seconds . . . the most frightening" J. Randy Taraborelli, *Sinatra: Behind the Legend,* p. 188.

"I thought I won" Nancy Sinatra, *Frank Sinatra: An American Legend,* p. 125.

196 "thin, unhandsome one-time crooner" Arthur Knight, *The Saturday Review,* as quoted in Gene Ringgold and Clifford McCarty, *The Films of Frank Sinatra,* p. 104.

198 "with the loosening" William K. Everson, *The Hollywood Western* (New York: Citadel Press, 1969, 1992), p. 18.

201 "then-Sinatra-girlfriend Gloria Vanderbilt" Scott Allen Nollen, *The Cinema of Sinatra,* p. 139.

203 "Mr. Sinatra, the actor" Bosley Crowther, *The New York Times*, August 16, 1956.

208 "Well, Did You Evah!" music and lyrics by Cole Porter.

209 "song, dance, hit their camera marks" Jeanine Basinger, *The Star Machine,* (New York: Knopf, 2007), p. 5.

212 "Mr. Todd . . . wasn't making" Bosley Crowther, *The New York Times,* as quoted in Gene Ringgold and Clifford McCarty, *The Films of Frank Sinatra,* p. 122.

214 "Stanley Kramer runs for office" Pauline Kael, "The Intentions of Stanley Kramer," *Kiss Kiss, Bang Bang* (Boston: Atlantic–Little, Brown, 1968), pp. 209–213, as quoted in Mark Harris, *Pictures at a Revolution* (New York: Penguin Group, 2008), p. 113.
"Stanley was a better producer" Harris, ibid., p. 112.

216 "Sinatra insisted on staying" Thomas M. Pryor, "Rise, Fall, and Rise of Sinatra," *The New York Times,* February 10, 1957.
"contractually required twenty-five dollars" Kitty Kelley, *His Way,* p. 231.

217 "How do you handle" George Stevens Jr., *Conversations with the Great Moviemakers of Hollywood's Golden Age* (New York: Vintage Books, 2007), pp. 569–570.
"The incident also reaffirmed" Daniel O'Brien, *The Frank Sinatra Film Guide,* p. 96.
"If Sinatra really wanted to work" Richard Havers, *Sinatra,* p. 229.
"Spencer Tracy liked Frank Sinatra" Stanley Kramer, "Spencer Tracy: He Could Wither You with a Glance" in *Close-Up: The Movie Star Book,* Danny Peary, ed. (New York: Workman, 1978), p. 516.

218 "Frank fascinates the curious" Cary Grant as quoted in Nancy Sinatra, *Frank Sinatra: An American Legend,* p. 265.

219 "Not since *The Ten Commandments*" Bosley Crowther, *The New York Times,* June 25, 1957.

220 "He was on her mind" Lee Server, *Ava Gardner,* p. 335.

221 "It was a chilling moment" Ava Gardner, *Ava,* p. 191.
"He was always calling her up" ibid., p. 287.
"She had come to think of him" Lee Server, *Ava Gardner,* p. 374.
"Yes, yes, I know" ibid., pp. 404–405.
"I took one look" Ava Gardner, *Ava,* pp. 149–150.

222 "You know you two kids" Lee Server, *Ava Gardner,* p. 266.
"She loved him" Ava Gardner, *Ava,* p. 287.
"Ava didn't like" Lee Server, *Ava Gardner,* p. 409.
"was a deep affront" ibid., p. 410.
"I'd say he's both" Lauren Bacall as quoted in Barbara Grizzuti Harrison "Terrified and Fascinated by His Own Life," *The New York Times,* November 2, 1986.

223 "Having bought the rights" Chris Ingham, *The Rough Guide to Frank Sinatra,* p. 302.
"with Frank himself collecting" Thomas Pryor, "Rise, Fall, and Rise of Sinatra," *The New York Times,* February 10, 1957.

225 "When Lewis, highball in hand" Philip K. Scheuer, *Los Angeles Times,* as quoted in Gene Ringgold and Clifford McCarty, *The Films of Frank Sinatra,* p. 131.

228 "Sinatra is the greatest natural actor" Thomas Pryor, "Rise, Fall, and Rise of Sinatra," *The New York Times,* February 10, 1957.
"But sometime between the start of the picture" William R. Weaver, *Motion Picture Herald,* as quoted in Gene Ringgold and Clifford McCarty, *The Films of Frank Sinatra,* pp. 131–134.
"You had more fun" Chris Ingham, *The Rough Guide to Frank Sinatra,* p. 302.

229 "It's not just that he didn't care" Kitty Kelley, *His Way,* pp. 250–251.

230 "MGM's loan-out price for Kelly" Scott Allen Nollen, *The Cinema of Sinatra,* p. 165.
"Essex Productions, negotiated a deal" ibid., p. 166.

231 "It's your world" Dean Martin as quoted in ibid., p. 246.

233 "Zip," music by Richard Rodgers, lyrics by Lorenz Hart.

234 "insolent caress" Derek Jewell, *Frank Sinatra: A Celebration* (Boston: Little, Brown, 1985), p. 165.

236 "Bewitched, Bothered and Bewildered," music by Richard Rodgers, lyrics by Lorenz Hart.

238 "the story has a 'happy ending' " *Look,* as quoted in Gene Ringgold and Clifford McCarty, *The Films of Frank Sinatra,* p. 138.

240 "After an hour" Will Friedwald, *Sinatra! The Song Is You,* p. 379.

242 "You must learn" Nancy Sinatra, *Frank Sinatra: An American Legend,* p. 136.
"Say your lines" George Jacobs, *My Life with Mr. S.,* p. 76.

244   "In order to secure Wood's participation"   Daniel O'Brien, *The Frank Sinatra Film Guide*, p. 106.
246   "The movie *Kings Go Forth* doesn't come close"   *Los Angeles Mirror-News*, as quoted in Gene
        Ringgold and Clifford McCarty, *The Films of Frank Sinatra*, p. 143.
        "may not be the best actor"   Wanda Hale, *New York Daily News*, as quoted in Daniel O'Brien,
        The Frank Sinatra Film Guide, p. 108.
247   "underprivileged children"   Scott Allen Nollen, *The Cinema of Sinatra*, p. 236.
        "raised over one billion"   *Frank Sinatra Memorial*, DVD (Passport Productions, 1999).
250   "the Italians . . . had a more apt word"   Shirley MacLaine, *My Lucky Stars*, p. 41.
        "He *cannot* communicate"   Nick Tosches, *Dino* (New York: Doubleday, 1999), p. 256
251   "the cuteness, the strength, the humor"   Michael Freedland, *All the Way*, p. 52.
253   "Nature Boy," music by eden ahbez, lyrics by Kalan Porter.
        "too precious"   Shirley MacLaine, *My Lucky Stars*, p. 74.
        "towering rages"   Vincente Minnelli, *I Remember It Well* (New York: Doubleday, 1974), p. 328.
        "of course, he's prone"   Vincente Minnelli, ibid., p. 328.
        "Oh, I just wish"   Shirley MacLaine, *My Lucky Stars*, p. 87.
254   "The camera wouldn't"   Vincente Minnelli, *I Remember It Well*, p. 329.
        "tearing a telephone"   Daniel O'Brien, *The Frank Sinatra Film Guide*, p. 112.
        "shoving match"   ibid.
        "He gave me everything"   Vincente Minnelli, *I Remember It Well*, p. 329.
255   "the freedom of choice"   Shirley MacLaine, *My Lucky Stars*, p. 76.
        "Performers work better"   Vincente Minnelli, *I Remember It Well*, p. 327.
256   "He was my brother"   Michael Freedland, *All the Way*, p. 422.
258   "Sinatra's insistence"   Shirley MacLaine, *My Lucky Stars*, p. 76.
        "an unforgettable vignette"   *Life* review of *Some Came Running*, as quoted in Vincente Minnelli,
        I Remember It Well, p. 329.
        "Yet as bromide follows bromide"   *Time*, as quoted in Gene Ringgold and Clifford McCarty,
        The Films of Frank Sinatra, p. 147.
259   "would grant star and director equal vote"   Frank Capra, *The Name Above the Title*, p. 449.
        "It's not the Hollywood"   ibid., p. 447.
260   "The excitement of moving"   ibid., p. 455.
        "once you're on that record"   Robin Douglas-Home interview with Frank Sinatra as quoted in
        Gay Talese, "Frank Sinatra Has a Cold," originally published in *Esquire*, reprinted in *The Frank
        Sinatra Reader*, Steven Petkov and Leonard Mustazza, eds. (New York: Oxford University Press,
        1995), p. 127.
261   "one of the fastest and best"   Frank Capra, *The Name Above the Title*, p. 462.
263   "I don't believe in exhausting myself"   Michael Freedland, *All The Way*, p. 257.
        "based on his belief that Sinatra"   Frank Capra, *The Name Above the Title*, p. 462.
        "mostly unspoken"   ibid.
264   "High Hopes," music by Jimmy Van Heusen, lyrics by Sammy Cahn.
267   "A soap-opera plot if ever there was one"   *Newsweek*, as quoted in Gene Ringgold and Clifford
        McCarty, *The Films of Frank Sinatra*, p. 153.
        "he has not performed any major miracles"   Philip K. Scheuer, *Los Angeles Times* in ibid.
269   "the basic questions any war film"   Jeanine Basinger, *The World War II Combat Film: Anatomy of
        a Genre* (New York: Columbia University Press, 1986), p. 80.
270   "Talent is not an excuse"   *The Sammy Davis Jr. Reader*, Gerald Early, ed., (New York: Farrar,
        Straus and Giroux, 2002), p. 25.
        "Davis offers a different scenario"   Sammy Davis Jr., *Hollywood in a Suitcase* (New York:
        William Morrow, 1980), pp. 88–89.
273   "Not merely an entertainer"   Richard Gehman, *Good Housekeeping*, July 1960, as quoted in
        Nancy Sinatra, *Frank Sinatra: An American Legend*, p. 147.
        "with Frank receiving a fee of $200,000"   Daniel O'Brien, *The Frank Sinatra Film Guide*, p. 124.
275   "Supposedly it was MacLaine who talked Sinatra out of"   Scott Allen Nollen, *The Cinema of
        Sinatra*, p. 201.
        "required Fox to buy out MacLaine's contract"   Daniel O'Brien, *The Frank Sinatra Film Guide*,
        p. 124.

277 "Ira Gershwin and Sammy Cahn supplied" Scott Allen Nollen, *The Cinema of Sinatra*, pp. 201–202.

"Let's Do It," music and lyrics by Cole Porter.

278 "It's All Right with Me," music and lyrics by Cole Porter.

279 "lascivious, disgusting and immoral" Daniel O'Brien, *The Frank Sinatra Film Guide*, p. 126.

280 "His potential is fantastic" Shirley MacLaine, as quoted in Kelley, *His Way*, p. 253.

"I think this" Billy Wilder, as quoted in Kelley, *His Way*, pp. 252–253.

281 "His first take" George Sidney as quoted in Nancy Sinatra, *Frank Sinatra: An American Legend*, p. 325.

The Rat Pack

283 "The Rat Pack depended" T. H. Adamowski, "Love in the Western World," in *Frank Sinatra and Popular Culture: Essays on an American Icon*, Leonard Mustazza, ed., p. 36.

"If I had to choose between" *Frank Sinatra: A Man and His Music*, Reprise Records, 1965.

284 "Having heard from aspiring director" Daniel O'Brien, *The Frank Sinatra Film Guide*, p. 128.

"then-presidential-candidate Kennedy turned up" *The Ocean's Eleven Story*, DVD, 2002.

"One-sixth a bonanza" Scott Allen Nollen, *The Cinema of Sinatra*, p. 205.

"preferred a noon–until–seven shooting day" Daniel O'Brien, *The Frank Sinatra Film Guide*, p. 129.

285 "When Frank isn't actually acting himself" Michael Freedland, *All The Way*, p. 287.

"Of course, they're not great movies" Chris Ingham, *The Rough Guide to Frank Sinatra*, p. 310.

286 "The Sands turned down eighteen thousand requests" *Ocean's Eleven*, DVD, audio commentary by Frank Sinatra Jr.

"The Rat Pack is the Mount Rushmore" James Wolcott, *Vanity Fair*, May 1997.

"When you have a Daddy" Nancy Sinatra in *Frank Sinatra: Off the Record*, CBS Television, 1965.

287 "He gave himself fully" Tina Sinatra, *My Father's Daughter*, p. 106.

"Don't be a pain in the ass" ibid.

288 "I'm for anything" Mia Farrow, *What Falls Away*, pp. 99–100

"Bishop actually wrote most of the 'ad-libbed' jokes" *The Ocean's Eleven Story*, DVD, 2002.

"The Summit members" Daniel O'Brien, *The Frank Sinatra Film Guide*, p. 131.

291 "How wonderful it is" James Kasher, "A Legend with Legs," *Vanity Fair*, January 2008.

294 "Milestone said, 'I saw that happen once'" Frank Sinatra as guest host on *The Tonight Show*, *Ocean's Eleven*, DVD.

"something you should keep your children away from" *Los Angeles Herald Examiner*, August 11, 1960.

"We're not setting out to make *Hamlet*" Sammy Davis Jr., *Hollywood in a Suitcase*, p. 84.

495 "Sinatra land the number-six spot" Daniel O'Brien, *The Frank Sinatra Film Guide*, p. 133.

"Laboring under the handicaps of a contrived script" Tube, *Variety*, August 10, 1960.

296 "served to heighten Giancana's wrath" Nick Tosches, *Dino*, p. 328.

"muscling support" Scott Allen Nollen, *The Cinema of Sinatra*, p. 217.

"'What have I done?'" Tina Sinatra, *My Father's Daughter*, p. 77.

297 "an FBI wiretap" ibid.

"settling of the debt" Scott Allen Nollen, *The Cinema of Sinatra*, p. 219.

300 "Since I will produce and direct" *Daily Variety*, March 28, 1960.

"I do not ask the advice" ibid.

301 "an unrepentant enemy" Patricia Seaton Lawford with Ted Schwarz, *The Peter Lawford Story* (New York: Carroll and Graf, 1988), p. 199.

"he would not fire Maltz" Tina Sinatra, *My Father's Daughter*, p. 68.

"In view of the reaction of my family" *The New York Times*, April 9, 1960.

302 "carrying papers and people alike" Tina Sinatra, *My Father's Daughter*, p. 143.

"released no fewer than six" Richard Havers, *Sinatra*, p. 260.

"first-class but minor" Whit, *Variety* review of *The Devil at 4 O'Clock*, October 1961.

"Nobody had his power" Nancy Sinatra, *Frank Sinatra: An American Legend*, p. 157.

309 "He'd come in at eleven" Michael Freedland, *All the Way,* p. 289.
310 "Somewhere east of Suez" Hazel Flynn, *The Hollywood Citizen-News*, as quoted in Gene Ring-gold and Clifford McCarty, *The Films of Frank Sinatra,* p. 180.
"His Cub Scout troupe" *Variety* review of *Sergeants 3* as quoted in Richard Havers, *Sinatra,* p. 267.
311 "In this letter regarding gambling" Antoihette Giancana and Thomas C. Renner, *Mafia Princess* (New York: Willam Morrow, 1984) p. 248.
"According to FBI agent" ibid.
"overtures" ibid.
"You know Pierre Salinger" ibid., p. 249.
"as a result, the proposed roles" Daniel O'Brien, *The Frank Sinatra Film Guide,* p. 148.
312 "He didn't tear any walls" Tina Sinatra, *My Father's Daughter,* p. 79.
315 "Sinatra met with President John Kennedy" ibid., p. 82.
316 "It's worth noting" Cindy De La Hoz, *Lucy at the Movies* (Philadelphia: Running Press Book Publishers, 2007), p. 353.
317 "Keeping the need for retakes" Daniel O'Brien, *The Films of Frank Sinatra,* p. 234.
318 "We filmed this scene" *The Manchurian Candidate,* DVD, commentary by John Frankenheimer, 1988.
319 "edited . . . at random" ibid.
320 "This is the kind of scene" ibid.
323 "In a nice touch of irony" Anthony Summers and Robbyn Swan, *Sinatra: The Life*, p. 300.
324 "It's important to know that" *The Manchurian Candidate*, DVD, commentary by John Franken-heimer, 1988.
326 "it all had to do with the way" *The Manchurian Candidate*, DVD, commentary by Angela Lans-bury, 1988.
"This is the film" Angela Lansbury, *Playbill,* May 2007.
327 "Every once in a rare while" *Variety* review of *The Manchurian Candidate*, October 16, 1962.
"The acting is all" *The New Yorker* review of *The Manchurian Candidate* as quoted in Gene Ringgold and Clifford McCarty, *The Films of Frank Sinatra,* p. 187
"We just set out" *The Manchurian Candidate,* DVD, commentary by Frank Sinatra, 1988.
"I thought this might be something extraordinary" *The Manchurian Candidate,* DVD, commen-tary by Angela Lansbury, 1988.
"Frank wasn't the easiest person" ibid.
"I remember a wonderful enthusiasm" *The Manchurian Candidate,* DVD, commentary by Frank Sinatra, 1988.
328 "I didn't know we owned the rights" Nancy Sinatra, *Frank Sinatra: An American Legend,* p. 168.
329 "According to Jan Merlin" Tom Weaver, *Earth vs. the Sci-Fi Filmmakers: Twenty Interviews* (Jef-ferson, NC: McFarland & Co., 2005), p. 286.
333 "walked the block" Michael Freedland, *All the Way,* p. 301.
"like singing a song twice" Peter Bogdanovich, "I'll Be Around," *New York Observer*, May 25, 1998.
335 "a feeling of vapid boredom . . . He appears so indifferent" Bosley Crowther, *The New York Times,* June 5, 1963.
"Frankie tries harder this time" Philip K. Scheuer, *Los Angeles Times*, as quoted in Gene Ring-gold and Clifford McCarty, *The Films of Frank Sinatra,* p. 190.
336 "when Laszlo's time-consuming setups" Daniel O'Brien, *The Frank Sinatra Film Guide,* p. 154.
339 "So intense were the arguments" ibid.
340 "you can be the most artistically perfect" Frank Sinatra with Joe Hyams, *Playboy*, February 1963.
"one of those pictures that are known in Hollywood" *Time* review of *4 for Texas,* as quoted in Gene Ringgold and Clifford McCarty, *The Films of Frank Sinatra,* p. 197.
"Shortly after the release" Nancy Sinatra, *Frank Sinatra: My Father,* p. 173.
"big money, real security" ibid.
"making him amongst the highest paid" Anthony Summers and Robbyn Swan, *Sinatra: The Life,* p. 300.

341 "it was thought for a while"　Nancy Sinatra, *Frank Sinatra: My Father*, p. 173.
　　"partial owner's stake"　Arnold Shaw, *Sinatra: The Entertainer*, p. 110.
　　"he also increased his share"　Scott Allen Nollen, *The Cinema of Sinatra*, p. 224.
　　"Giancana sojourned"　Antoinette Giancana and Thomas C. Renner, *Mafia Princess*, p. 226.
342 "vile, intemperate"　ibid., p. 227.
　　"had an interest in the casino"　ibid., p. 107.
　　"although Frank was to publicly state"　ibid., p. 113.
　　"would not allow"　Nancy Sinatra, *Frank Sinatra: An American Legend*, p. 154.
　　"In my mind"　ibid., pp. 154–155.
343 "Then came the ridiculous accusations"　*Frank Sinatra: Off the Record*, CBS television interview with Walter Cronkite, 1965.
　　"The fact that I used to be"　ibid.
　　"I never reacted beyond"　Tina Sinatra, *My Father's Daughter*, p. 74.
344 "kept telling Howard Koch"　Clive Hirschhorn, *Gene Kelly*, p. 277.
345 "Preminger went so far"　Daniel O'Brien, *The Frank Sinatra Film Guide*, p. 208.
346 "According to a 1996 profile"　Douglas Thompson, "Barbara Sinatra Interview," 1996.
347 "the graveyard scene . . . Sinatra wandered off"　*Robin and the 7 Hoods*, DVD, commentary by Frank Sinatra Jr.
348 "The spell had kind of been broken"　ibid.
　　"Then there were a lot of delays"　Nancy Sinatra, *Frank Sinatra: My Father*, p. 324.
350 "producer Sinatra made a decision"　*Robin and the 7 Hoods*, DVD, commentary by Frank Sinatra Jr.
　　"according to lyricist Cahn"　Richard Havers, *Sinatra*, p. 282.
353 "*Robin and the 7 Hoods* is the latest"　James Powers, *The Hollywood Reporter*, June 25, 1964.
　　"to its members"　T. H. Adamowski, "Love in the Western World," in *Frank Sinatra and Popular Culture: Essays on an American Icon*, Leonard Mustazza, ed., p. 36
354 "the greatest loneliness lies in disillusion"　Donald Clarke, *All or Nothing at All*, p. xii.
　　"When I first came across that river"　Pete Hamill, *Why Sinatra Matters*, p. 179.
　　"The same thing that made me think"　Joe Hyams, "Sinatra Sitting on Top of the World," *New York Herald Tribune*, October 2, 1955.
357 "saved Sinatra's life"　"Sinatra Rescued in Surf as Undertow Traps Him," *The New York Times*, June 17, 1964.
360 "directing's my favorite medium"　Daniel O'Brien, *The Frank Sinatra Film Guide*, p. 165.
　　"I'm well aware"　Peter Bart, "Sinatra Swings Upward," *The New York Times*, April 18, 1966.
362 "the band days with Tommy"　Mia Farrow, *What Falls Away*.
　　"Although the armies of his heart and mind"　ibid., p. 121.
　　"got along so well"　ibid., p. 104.
363 "and a salary of $250,000"　Scott Allen Nollen, *The Cinema of Sinatra*, p. 261.
　　"Robson was the only director"　Richard Havers, *Sinatra*, p. 292.
364 "Having weathered Marlon Brando's tantrums"　Daniel O'Brien, *The Frank Sinatra Film Guide*, p. 167.
365 "as the steely-eyed, curt American officer"　Abe Greenberg, *Hollywood Citizen-News*, as quoted in Gene Ringgold and Clifford McCarty, *The Films of Frank Sinatra*, p. 207.

A Waste of Talent

367 "He has an insatiable desire"　Brad Dexter as quoted in Gene Ringgold and Clifford McCarty, *The Films of Frank Sinatra*, p. 19.
　　"Sinatra eventually enlisted well-known attorney"　Scott Allen Nollen, *The Cinema of Sinatra*, p. 266.
372 "Mr. Sinatra is his usual uncannily confident self"　*The New Yorker*, September 1965, as quoted in Gene Ringgold and Clifford McCarty, *The Films of Frank Sinatra*, p. 211.
375 "But this is that true movie rarity"　Richard Schickel, *Life*, February 1966, as quoted in ibid., p. 218.

"wrote in his autobiography" Tony Bennett (with Will Friedwald), *The Good Life* (New York: Simon & Schuster, 1998), p. 185.

377 "It might have been better" Michael Freedland, *All the Way,* p. 322.

378 "Frank Sinatra, looking all of 28 years old" Clyde Leech, *Los Angeles Herald Examiner,* as quoted in Gene Ringgold and Clifford McCarty, *The Films of Frank Sinatra,* p. 215.
"*Cast a Giant Shadow* is an embarrassing movie" Brendan Gill, *The New Yorker,* as quoted in ibid., p. 214.
"Another exercise in movie biography" *Time,* as quoted in ibid., p. 215.

380 "To me he was always a symbol" *Assault on a Queen* Pressbook (Paramount Pictures: 1966), p. 2.
"If they'd had Virna in the Mafia" ibid., p. 4.

381 "Just about as enthralling" *Monthly Film Bulletin* as quoted in Chris Ingham, *The Rough Guide to Frank Sinatra,* p. 317.

384 "It is curious how" Bosley Crowther, *The New York Times,* as quoted in Arnold Shaw, *Sinatra: The Entertainer,* p. 36.

386 "Mr. S. hated London" George Jacobs with William Stadiem, *Mr. S.,* p. 7.
"In the further recounting of Brad Dexter" Daniel O'Brien, *The Frank Sinatra Film Guide,* p. 180.
"*The Naked Runner* might be a good movie" Pauline Kael, *The New Republic,* as quoted in Gene Ringgold and Clifford McCarty, *The Films of Frank Sinatra,* p. 226.
"Of Sinatra, it must be said" Charles Champlin, *Los Angeles Times,* July 1967, as quoted in Gene Ringgold and Clifford McCarty, *The Films of Frank Sinatra,* p. 226.

388 "My Way," music by Claude François and Jacques Revaux, French lyrics by Claude François and Gilles Thibaut, English lyrics by Paul Anka.

Knight-Errant

389 "I believe in complete honesty" Frank Sinatra, as quoted in Bill Zehme, *The Way You Wear Your Hat,* p. 228.

390 "That's Life," by Dean Kay and Kelly Gordon.

391 "Tony Rome," music and lyrics by Lee Hazlewood.

393 "at the time of filming" Daniel O'Brien, *The Frank Sinatra Film Guide,* p. 184.
"He's a restless actor" Aaron Rosenberg as quoted in ibid.

395 "By fadeout" Murf, *Variety,* November 8, 1967.
"It is provoking" Bosley Crowther, *The New York Times,* November 10, 1967.
"That did it" ibid.
"Frank Sinatra has been a talent" Hollis Alpert, *The Saturday Review,* as quoted in Gene Ringgold and Clifford McCarty, *The Films of Frank Sinatra,* p. 230.

397 "had an obligation" Tina Sinatra, *My Father's Daughter,* p. 119.

398 "If Frank wanted a divorce" Mia Farrow, *What Falls Away,* p. 124.
"I had come to Frank Sinatra" ibid., p. 129.
"I don't know, maybe we'll only have" Nancy Sinatra, *Frank Sinatra: An American Legend,* p. 199.
"Just your respect" Tina Sinatra, *My Father's Daughter,* p. 122.
"had been speaking with him" Peter Bogdanovich, "I'll Be Around," *New York Observer,* May 25, 1998.

399 "There was . . . no return" Lee Server, *Ava Gardner,* p. 453.
"when Ava felt well enough to travel" ibid., p. 467.
"I love you, baby" ibid., p. 488.
"Ava was a great lady" ibid., p. 498.
"Frank went into his room" ibid., p. 499.

406 "I used to chat with" Frank Sinatra on *Live with Larry King,* May 13, 1988.

000 "best performance since" Ray Loynd, *The Hollywood Reporter,* as quoted in Gene Ringgold and Clifford McCarty, *The Films of Frank Sinatra,* p. 234.

408 "consistently crude" Vincent Canby, *The New York Times,* November 21, 1968, p. 41.

"fun at its own expense" John Mahoney, *The Hollywood Reporter,* as quoted in Gene Ringgold and Clifford McCarty, *The Films of Frank Sinatra,* p. 237.

"He projects the ex-cop turned private shamus" Charles Champlin, *Los Angeles Times,* November 20, 1968.

"same desires as the Governor" "Sinatra, a Backer of Kennedys, Plans to Support Reagan," *The New York Times,* July 9, 1970.

"an honorable person" *The New York Times,* February 26, 1981.

"I never invited Mr. Giancana" ibid.

409 "key employee license . . . chastised the news media" ibid.

410 "When his father died" Nancy Sinatra, *Frank Sinatra: An American Legend,* p. 200.

"he needed this silliness" ibid., p. 214.

"he gave up his $1 million film fee" Daniel O'Brien, *The Frank Sinatra Film Guide,* p. 197.

"As a person I look pretty bad" *Dirty Dingus Magee* Pressbook (Metro-Goldwyn-Mayer Pictures, 1970), p. 4.

"the old time comedians like Chaplin" ibid., p. 5.

414 "disgusting" Kevin Thomas, *Los Angeles Times,* as quoted in Gene Ringgold and Clifford McCarty, *The Films of Frank Sinatra,* p. 239.

"seems ineffably bored" Arthur Knight, *The Saturday Review,* as quoted in Arnold Shaw, *Sinatra: The Entertainer,* p. 38.

"a dreadful parody" Roger Greenspun, *The New York Times,* November 19, 1970, p. 42.

415 "a condition called Dupuytren's contracture" Tina Sinatra, *My Father's Daughter,* p. 124.

"Frank's testimony before a committee" "Reputed Mafia Chief Testifies He Never Met Sinatra," *The New York Times,* July 20, 1972.

"alternately bellicose and bored" ibid.

"This bum went running off" Nan Robertson, *The New York Times,* July 19, 1972, "Sinatra Berates House Unit for Letting Felon Link Him to Mafia."

416 "There is a form of bigotry" Frank Sinatra, "We Might Call This the Politics of Fantasy," *The New York Times,* July 24, 1972.

"be extremely cruel" Fred Ebb as quoted in *Colored Lights,* John Kander and Fred Ebb as told to Greg Lawrence (New York: Faber and Faber, 2003), p. 105.

"I'm more at home" ibid., p. 106.

"Frank was not ungracious" ibid.

"I've turned on it" ibid., p. 107.

421 "This isn't nostalgia, it's history" Nora Sayre, *The New York Times,* June 21, 1974.

"They are bums and parasites" "Sinatra In Encore Calls Unions' Ban Ridiculous," *The New York Times,* July 15, 1974.

"buck-and-a-half hookers" ibid.

422 "because my husband's from" Nikki Finke, "Doing It Her Way," *Los Angeles Times,* February 28, 1988.

"Because of the way they are" Dinah Shore as quoted in ibid.

423 "With his last try" Tina Sinatra, *My Father's Daughter,* p. 161.

"self-serving, rough and ready" ibid.

"Although Barbara Sinatra had a six-figure" ibid., p. 199.

426 "In two days he will not" Stephen Silverman, *Dancing on the Ceiling,* p. 325.

"Did I know those guys" Pete Hamill, *Why Sinatra Matters,* p. 146.

427 "They'd fought through his childhood" Nancy Sinatra, *Frank Sinatra: My Father,* p. 257.

"I saw Duke recently" *TV Guide,* November 19–26, 1977, p. 14.

430 "10th-rate Kojak" ibid., "This Week's Movies."

"From Mr. Sinatra on down" John J. O'Connor, *The New York Times,* as quoted in Gene Ringgold and Clifford McCarty, *The Films of Frank Sinatra,* p. 243.

431 "You gotta love livin', baby" *London Daily Mirror,* May 16, 1998.

435 "Roxie," from the musical *Chicago,* music by John Kander, lyrics by Fred Ebb.

437 "the first one in some time" Cart, *Variety,* October 22, 1980.

438 "supposedly worked for a grand total" Daniel O'Brien, *The Frank Sinatra Film Guide,* p. 205.

"Frank's appearance actually came about" Ibid.

"In producer Albert Ruddy's version" Ibid.

440 "Sinatra showed up early" *The Cannonball Run II*, DVD, commentary by Hal Needham.

441 "If you don't want to do it" Nick Tosches, *Dino*, p. 430.

442 "helpless and frail" Tina Sinatra, *My Father's Daughter*, p. 190.

443 "Working with him is real interesting" *TV Guide*, May 30–June 5, 1988.

444 "He was an incredible actor" Quincy Jones, liner notes, *Sinatra: Vegas*, four-CD compilation released December 2006, p. 39.

"Conducting Frank Sinatra" *Vanity Fair*, July 2007.

"Having arranged and conducted the live album" Quincy Jones, liner notes, *Sinatra: Vegas*, p. 39.

445 "Possibly the most exciting engagement" *Listen Up: The Lives of Quincy Jones*, released October 1990.

"constantly running . . . Quincy had a key" ibid.

That's Life

447 "I never studied, you know" Television interview, *Live with Larry King*, May 13, 1988.

"Later on in Frank's life" Shirley MacLaine, *Sage-ing While Age-ing* (New York: Atria Books, 2007), p. 30.

448 "This must be one stupid broad" Joe Del Priore, "Spank Me, Frankie" *The Village Voice*, September 11, 1990.

449 "The tragedy of fame" Frank Sinatra, "Letter to the Editor," *Los Angeles Times*, September 16, 1990.

"I could fill volumes" Warner Bros. press release for *Sinatra*, Warner Bros. Television miniseries, 1992.

450 "will never happen because" Marilyn Beck and Stacy Jewel Smith, *New York Daily News*, May 19, 1998.

"Good idea. You do it" Warner Bros. press release for *Sinatra*, Warner Bros. Television miniseries, 1992.

"Dad should have watched" Tina Sinatra, *My Father's Daughter*, p. 227.

451 "I go to too many" Pete Hamill, *Why Sinatra Matters*, p. 180.

"My Way," music by Claude François and Jacques Revaux, French lyrics by Claude François and Gilles Thibaut, English lyrics by Paul Anka.

452 "Rock and roll people love Sinatra" Will Friedwald, "Style and Swagger Pop's Big Bang," *The New York Times*, May 24, 1998.

453 "I started my career" Tina Sinatra, *My Father's Daughter*, p. 242.

"Dad seemed a foot taller" ibid., pp. 242–243.

"I could tell he hated" ibid., p. 246.

454 "And I'd do it all again" Frank Sinatra as related by Frank Sinatra Jr., New York, May 13, 2008.

455 "I'm losing" Scott Allen Nollen, *The Cinema of Sinatra*, p. 311.

"His music and movies" *All Politics*, May 15, 1998, as quoted in Scott Allen Nollen, *The Cinema of Sinatra*, p. 313.

"He was an idol of mine" *Sinatra: A Tribute*, CD (BDD Audio), as quoted in ibid.

457 "There were no heights" J. Randy Taraborelli, *Sinatra: Behind the Legend*, p. 204.

"I made some pretty good pictures" Nancy Sinatra, *Frank Sinatra: An American Legend*, p. 329.

"sadistic form of torture" ibid., p. 87.

Bibliography

Of the now more than one hundred books that deal with the life and career of Frank Sinatra, I found three books to be particularly helpful in terms of background information: *The Cinema of Sinatra,* by Scott Allen Nollen, which provides an extraordinarily detailed chronology of Sinatra's film and, especially, recording careers; Daniel O'Brien's *The Frank Sinatra Film Guide,* which presents interesting and thorough information regarding the production background of Sinatra's movies; and *The Films of Frank Sinatra,* by Gene Ringgold and Clifford McCarty, the single best compendium of critical reaction to Sinatra's feature film career. Although all three books utilize a different approach to Sinatra's film legacy than that which I have undertaken, they were especially helpful to me in writing my own study.

As concerns background about the personal life of Frank Sinatra, the three most helpful and insightful sources remain the brief but beautifully written *Why Sinatra Matters,* by Pete Hamill, and the loving yet remarkably honest books by his daughters Nancy—*Frank Sinatra: An American Legend*— and Tina—*My Father's Daugher.*

Bacall, Lauren. *By Myself.* New York: Alfred A. Knopf, 1979.
Basinger, Jeanine. *A Woman's View.* New York: Alfred A. Knopf, 1993.
———. *Pyramid Illustrated History of the Movies: Gene Kelly.* New York: Pyramid Communications, 1976.
———. *The Star Machine.* New York: Alfred A. Knopf, 2007.
———. *The World War II Combat Film: Anatomy of a Genre.* New York: Columbia University Press, 1986.
Bloom, Ken. *The American Songbook: The Singer, the Songwriters, the Songs.* New York: Black Dog and Leventhal Publishers, 2005.
Bosworth, Patricia. *Montgomery Clift: A Biography.* New York: Arbor House, 1977.
Britt, Stan. *Sinatra: A Celebration.* New York: Simon & Schuster, 1995.
Capra, Frank. *The Name Above the Title.* New York: Macmillan, 1971.
Clarke, Donald. *All or Nothing at All: A Life of Frank Sinatra.* London: Macmillan, 1997.
Clooney, Rosemary. *Girl Singer.* New York: Doubleday, 1999.
Davis Jr., Sammy, Jane Boyar, and Burt Boyar. *Why Me?* New York: Farrar, Straus and Giroux, 1989.
De La Hoz, Cindy. *Lucy at the Movies.* Philadelphia: Running Press Book Publishers, 2007.
Douglas-Home, Robin. *Sinatra.* New York: Grosset & Dunlap, 1962.
Evans, Richard. *Sinatra.* New York: DK Publishing, 2004.
Early, Gerald (ed.). *The Sammy Davis Jr. Reader.* New York: Farrar, Straus and Giroux, 2001.
Everson, William K. *The Hollywood Western.* New York: Citadel Press, Carol Publishing Group, 1969, 1992.
Fallaci, Oriana. *The Egotists: Sixteen Surprising Interviews.* Chicago: Regnery Publishing, 1968.

Farrow, Mia. *What Falls Away*. New York: Doubleday, 1997.

Feinstein, Michael. *Nice Work If You Can Get It: My Life in Rhythm and Rhyme*. Hyperion, New York 1995.

Freedland, Michael. *All the Way: A Biography of Frank Sinatra*. New York: St. Martin's Press, 1997.

Friedwald, Will. *Jazz Singing: America's Great Voices from Bessie Smith to Bebop and Beyond*. New York: Scribner, 1990.

———. *Sinatra! The Song Is You: A Singer's Art*. New York: Scribner, 1995.

Gardner, Ava. *Ava: My Story*. New York: Bantam Books, 1990.

Gehman, Richard. *Sinatra and His Rat Pack*. New York: Belmont, 1961.

Giancana, Antoinette, and Thomas C. Renner. *Mafia Princess: Growing Up in Sam Giancana's Family*. New York: William Morrow, 1984.

Granata, Charles. *Sessions with Sinatra*. Chicago: A Cappella Books, 1999.

Hamill Pete. *Why Sinatra Matters*. New York: Little, Brown, 1998.

Harris, Mark. *Pictures at a Revolution*. New York: Penguin Press, 2008.

Havers, Richard. *Sinatra*. New York: DK Publishing, 2004.

Hirsch, Foster. *Otto Preminger*. New York: Alfred A. Knopf, 2007.

Hirschhorn, Clive. *Gene Kelly: A Biography*. London: WH Allen, 1974.

Hotchner, A. E., with Doris Day. *Doris Day: Her Own Story*. New York: William Morrow, 1975.

Howlett, John. *Frank Sinatra*. Philadelphia: Courage Books, 1980.

Ingham, Chris. *The Rough Guide to Frank Sinatra*. New York: Penguin Group, 2005.

Jacobs, George, with William Stadiem. *Mr. S: My Life with Frank Sinatra*. New York: HarperCollins, 2003.

Jewell, Derek. *Frank Sinatra: A Celebration*. Boston: Little, Brown, 1985.

Kahn Jr., E. J. *The Voice*. New York: Harper Bros., 1947.

Kander, John, and Fred Ebb, as told to Greg Lawrence. *Colored Lights*. New York: Faber and Faber, 2003.

Katz, Ephraim. *The Film Encyclopedia*, Fourth Edition. New York: HarperCollins, 2001.

Kelley, Kitty. *His Way: The Unauthorized Biography of Frank Sinatra*. New York: Bantam Books, 1987.

Kuntz, Tom, with Phil Kuntz. *The Sinatra Files: The Secret FBI Dossier*. New York: Three Rivers Press, 2000.

Lahr, John. *Sinatra: The Artist and the Man*. New York: Random House, 1997.

Lawford, Patricia Seaton, with Ted Schwarz. *The Peter Lawford Story*. New York: Carroll and Graf, 1988.

Lees, Gene. *Singers and the Song*. New York: Oxford University Press, 1987.

———. *Singers and the Song II*. New York: Oxford University Press, 1999.

Levy, Shawn. *Rat Pack Confidential*, New York: Doubleday, 1998.

Liner Notes, *Frank Sinatra: The Hollywood Years 1940–1964*. Bristol Productions Limited Partnership under exclusive license to Reprise Records, 2002.

Liner Notes, *The Song Is You: Tommy Dorsey, Frank Sinatra*, RCA Records 66363, distributed by BMG Music, 1994.

Lonstein, Albert I. (ed.), reedited by Gene Frank. *Sinatra: An Exhaustive Treatise Compilation/Comments*. New York: Musicprint Corp. 1983.

MacLaine, Shirley. *My Lucky Stars*. New York: Bantam Books, 1995.

———. *Sage-ing While Age-ing*. New York: Atria Books, 2007.

Mann, William J. *Kate*. New York: Picador, 2006.

Minnelli, Vincente. *I Remember It Well*. New York: Doubleday, 1974.

Morley, Sheridan, and Ruth Leon. *Gene Kelly: A Celebration*. London: Pavilion Books Limited, 1996.

Mustazza, Leonard. *Frank Sinatra and Popular Culture: Essays on an American Icon*. Westport, CT: Praeger Press, 1998.

    "Love in the Western World." T. H. Adamowski. pp. 26–37.

    "The Swinger and the Loser: Sinatra, Masculinity and Fifties Culture." Roger Gilbert. pp. 38–49.

    "The Composition of Celebrity." Gilbert L. Gigliotti. pp. 69–82.

    "Psychiatric Musings." Lloyd L. Spencer, pp. 94–105.

————. *Ol' Blue Eyes: A Frank Sinatra Encyclopedia.* Westport, CT: Greenwood Press, 1998.

————. *Sinatra: An Annotated Bibliography, 1938–1999.* Westport, CT: Greenwood Press, 1999.

Nollen, Scott Allen. *The Cinema of Sinatra.* Baltimore: Luminary Press, 2003.

O'Brien, Daniel. *The Frank Sinatra Film Guide.* London: Butler & Tanner, 1998.

Petkov, Steven, and Leonard Mustazza (eds.). *Frank Sinatra Reader.* New York: Oxford University Press, 1995.

 "Frank: Then and Now." Ralph J. Gleason. pp. 225–227.

Peary, Danny (ed.). *Close-Ups: The Movie Star Book.* New York: Workman, 1978.

Pickard, Ray. *Frank Sinatra at the Movies.* New York: Robert Hale & Co., 1999.

————. *Remembering Sinatra: A Life in Pictures.* New York: Time, Inc. 1998.

Pignone, Charles. *The Family Album.* New York: Little, Brown, 2007.

————. *The Sinatra Treasures.* New York: Bulfinch Press, 2004.

Quirk, Lawrence J., and William Schoell. *The Rat Pack: Neon Nights with the Kings of Cool.* New York: Harper, 2003.

Ringgold, Gene, and Clifford McCarty. *The Films of Frank Sinatra.* Secaucus, NJ: Carol Publishing Group, 1971, 1993.

Rockwell, John. *Sinatra: An American Classic.* New York: Random House, 1984.

Schickel, Richard. *The Stars.* New York: Dial Press, 1962.

Sennett, Ted. *Hollywood Musicals.* New York: Harry N. Abrams, 1981.

Server, Lee. *Ava Gardner: Love Is Nothing.* New York: St. Martin's Press, 2006.

Shaw, Arnold. *Sinatra: The Entertainer.* New York: Delilah Books, 1982.

Sheed, Wilfrid. *The House That George Built.* New York: Random House, 2007.

Silverman, Stephen M. *Dancing on the Ceiling: Stanley Donen and His Movies.* New York: Alfred A. Knopf, 1996.

Simon, George T. *The Big Bands.* New York: Schirmer Books, 1981.

Sinatra, Nancy. *Frank Sinatra: An American Legend.* Santa Monica, CA: General Publishing Group, 1995.

————. *Frank Sinatra, My Father.* New York: Doubleday, 1985.

Sinatra, Tina, with Jeff Coplon. *My Father's Daughter.* New York: Simon & Schuster, 2000.

Spada, James. *Peter Lawford: The Man Who Kept the Secrets.* New York: Bantam Books, 1991.

Stevens Jr., George. *Conversations with the Great Moviemakers of Hollywood's Golden Age.* New York: Vintage Books, 2007.

Summers, Anthony, and Robbyn Swan. *Sinatra: The Life.* New York: Alfred A. Knopf, 2005.

Talese, Gay. *Fame and Obscurity.* New York: Dell, 1981.

Taraborelli, J. Randy. *Sinatra: Behind the Legend.* New York: Citadel Press/Kensington Publishing Corp., 1997.

Thomson, David. *A Biographical Dictionary of Film.* New York: William Morrow, 1976.

Tosches, Nick. *Dino: Living High in the Dirty Business of Dreams.* New York: Doubleday, 1999.

Turner, Lana. *Lana.* New York: E. P. Dutton, 1982.

Walker, Leo. *The Wonderful Era of the Great Dance Bands.* New York: Da Capo Press, Inc., 1990.

Weaver, Tom. *Earth vs. the Sci-Fi Filmmakers: Twenty Interviews.* Jefferson, NC: McFarland & Co, 2005.

Wilson, Earl. *Sinatra: An Unauthorized Biography.* New York: Macmillan, 1976.

Yudkoff, Alvin. *Gene Kelly: A Life of Dance and Dreams.* New York: Backstage Books, 1999.

Zehme, Bill. *The Way You Wear Your Hat: Frank Sinatra and the Lost Art of Livin'.* New York: HarperCollins, 1997.

Zinnemann, Fred. *A Life in the Movies: An Autobiography.* New York: Scribner, Maxwell Macmillan International, 1992.

Archives

Billy Rose Theatre Collection, Lincoln Center Library for the Performing Arts, New York.
The Paley Center for Media, New York.

Documentaries

Frank Sinatra: The Voice of Our Time. PBS Broadcasting.
Sinatra: Off the Record. CBS Television, 1965.

Magazines, Periodicals, and Newspapers

The Advocate: June 23, 1998, Tony Kushner, "Last Word: Remembering Frank."
The American Weekly: December 26, 1950, Harrison Carroll, "Nancy Sinatra's Story."
Atlantic City Press: September 12, 1963, "Sinatra Is Accused of Hosting Mobster; D'Amato Under Fire."
Bandleader: July 1944, Gretchen Weaver, "Our Frankie."
Billboard: December 5, 1960, "Sinatra Label Ready for February Debut."
Christian Science Monitor: May 21, 1998, Gloria Goodale, "Why Three Generations Swooned to the Sultan."
Daily Variety: March 8, 1963, "Sinatra, Dean Un-Harnessed, Attys. Report"; May 18, 1998, Steven Gaydos, "A Frank Approach to Cinematic Greatness"; May 18, 1998, Richard Natale and Timothy M. Gray, "The Voice Is Silenced."
Downbeat: October 2006, John McDonough, "Tony Bennett—Surviving by Song"
Entertainment Weekly: Fall 1996, "100 Greatest Movie Stars of All Time: Special Collector's Edition."
Hofstra University Program for "The Conference—Frank Sinatra: The Man, the Music, the Legend," November 12–14, 1998.
The Hollywood Reporter: May 18, 1998, Duane Byrge, "From Bar Stool to Big Screen."
Houston Post: January 11, 1993, Joe Leyden, "Friends, Colleagues Salute Frank Sinatra at Film Festival."
Las Vegas Review Journal and Las Vegas Sun: May 15, 1998, "Frank Sinatra 1915–1998."
The London Observer: May 17, 1998, Stuart Nicholson, "Sinatra's Final Days."
London Sunday Express: Douglas Thompson, "Frank's Lucky Lady," 1996.
Los Angeles Examiner: August 11, 1960, "Ocean's 11."
Los Angeles Times: February 28, 1988, Nikki Finke, "Doing It Her Way"; September 16, 1990, Frank Sinatra "Letter to the Editor"; July 4, 1991, Frank Sinatra, "Op-Ed"; May 15, 1998, George Custen, "On Screen: Always the Hoboken Kid"; May 21, 1998, Carla Hall, "Saying Farewell to the Voice."
McCall's Magazine: October 1974, Tommy Thompson, "Understanding Sinatra."
The New Jersey Star Ledger: May 17, 1998, Matt Zoller Sertz, "Francis Albert Sinatra Issue: It Was a Very Good Life."
The New Republic: November 6, 1944, "The Voice and the Kids."
New York Daily News: December 26, 1963, "Movies: Frank & Dean Overdo Lines in Texas Tale"; June 12, 1966, Florabel Muir, "New Sinatra Brawl: Exec in a Coma"; August 13, 1983, "Dino & Frank Will Duet Here"; April 27, 1988, "Frank, Sammy & Liza Too!"; May 17, 1998, "Frank's New York"; May 18, 1998, "Frank Sinatra, Great Raconteur and a Great Friend"; May 19, 1998, Marilyn Beck and Stacy Jewel Smith, "Frank Sinatra"; May 21, 1998, Michelle Carusa and Ana Figueroa, "Last Goodbye to the Voice"; May 21, 1998, Sidney Zion, "Sinatra, Wells vs. Media Calvinists"; September 22, 1998, "Godfather Sinatra."
New York Herald Tribune: December 10, 1943, "Army Classifies Sinatra in 4-F Because of Punctured Eardrum"; October 3, 1944, "30,000 Sinatra Fans Lay Siege to Theatre with 3500 Seats"; March 4, 1945, "Sinatra Found Unfit for Army, Held 'Necessary' to the Nation"; October 30, 1945, "Sinatra to Talk at School"; November 2, 1945, "Town Hall Rally for Tolerance Honors Sinatra"; April 10, 1947, "Sinatra Slugs Lee Mortimer at Night Club"; June 4, 1947, Sinatra–Mortimer Fracas Is Settled"; May 3, 1950, "Sinatra Ordered to Rest, Has Throat Hemorrhage"; September 23, 1950, "Sinatra to Give His Wife Third of Income for Life"; August 10, 1951, "Sinatra in Reno to Wed Ava Gardner after Decree"; April 23, 1955, "Sinatra Lists 'One Way Out' as First Independent Film"; June 12, 1955, Myer P. Beck, "If Sinatra Fad Ended, Who's That Big Star"; October 2,

1955, "Sinatra Sitting on Top of the World"; October 30, 1955, Don Ross, "Sinatra: Phoenix of Film"; July 1, 1958, Art Buchwald, "A Guide to Sinatra"; December 8, 1960, "Lawford, Sinatra Show to Clear Democrat Deficit"; October 23, 1963, "State of Nevada Deals Sinatra Out."

The New York Observer: May 25, 1998, Peter Bogdanovich, "I'll Be Around."

New York Post: January 23, 1959, Archer Winsten, "Reviewing Stand: *Some Came Running*"; May 15, 1998, Rod Drecher, "Actor Frank Became Star of Noir"; May 16, 1998, "Sinatra Special"; May 16, 1998, John Leo, "Sinatra's Double Life"; May 17, 1998, Jami Bernard, "The Singer and Cinema"; May 18, 1998, Bill Hoffman, "Longtime Pal Shirley Gives Skinny on Frank"; May 20, 1998, Michael Kelly, "How Sinatra Ruined America"; May 25, 1998, Gay Talese, "The Man Who Knew How to Say Goodbye."

The New York Review of Books: June 25, 1998.

The New York Sun: September 29, 1944, "Sinatra Wasn't Asked to Sing."

The New York Times: October 10, 1944, "Sinatra Quits Screen"; August 25, 1953, "Sinatra Quits Film Site"; November 4, 1955, Bosley Crowther, "Featuring Frankie"; February 10, 1957, Thomas M. Pryor, "Rise, Fall, and Rise of Sinatra"; May 7, 1957, "Sinatra Charges $2,3000,000 Libel"; July 15, 1960, "Sinatra, Dean Martin Apply to Buy a Casino"; May 11, 1964, "Sinatra Rescued in Surf as Undertow Traps Him"; June 17, 1964, "Sinatra to Lease Nevada Club"; July 9, 1965, Richard F. Shepard, "Sinatra and Basie Charm 15,000 in Forest Hills"; July 10, 1965, Gay Talese, "Sinatra Means a Jumping Jilly's"; October 18, 1965, Charles Van Deusen, "Sinatra-at-Sea"; January 12, 1966, "Sinatra Opponent Gains after Brawl"; April 18, 1966, Peter Bart, "Sinatra Swings Upward"; June 11, 1966, Peter Bart, "Sinatra Involved in Brawl in Bar"; July 14, 1966, "Frank Sinatra Will Marry, Mia Farrow, 21, This Year"; July 20, 1966, "Frank Sinatra Marries Mia Farrow in Las Vegas"; August 6, 1967, "Mexico Lifts Ban on Sinatra for Film Gibing at Divorce"; October 15, 1969, "Sinatra Arrest Sought in New Jersey as He Fails to Appear at Inquiry"; February 18, 1970, "Sinatra Testifies in Jersey Inquiry"; February 19, 1970, Ronald Schvar, "Sinatra Hearing: Show of Strength"; May 9, 1970, "Sinatra Enthralls 3,000 with a Concert in London"; July 9, 1970, "Sinatra, a Backer of Kennedys, Plans to Support Reagan"; March 24, 1971, "Sinatra Bows Out of Show Business after 3 Decades"; June 8, 1972, "Sinatra to Shun Inquiry on Crime"; July 19, 1972, Nan Robertson, "Sinatra Berates House Unit for Letting Felon Link Him to Mafia"; July 24, 1972, Frank Sinatra, "We Might Call This the Politics of Fantasy"; July 20, 1972, "Reputed Mafia Chief Testifies He Never Met Sinatra"; August 10, 1973, Wallace Turner, "Agnew Host, Sinatra Now GOP Insider"; December 2, 1973, John J. O'Connor, "Frank Sinatra Came Back, and the Rest Was Music"; March 12, 1974, Russell Baker "Observer: 1974 Nice Guy Awards"; July 15, 1974, "Sinatra in Encore Calls Unions' Ban 'Ridiculous' "; October 3, 1974, Martha Weinman Lear, "The Bobby Sox Have Wilted, But"; April 10, 1975, "At Oscar Awards, Backstage Drama"; July 16, 1975, "Martin Joins Sinatra in Supporting Reagan"; July 12, 1976, "Sinatra Wed in Palm Springs: Reagan, Agnew Among Guests"; November 10, 1976, Charlotte Curtis, "New Yorkers, etc.: 'For Barbara Sinatra, Every Day Has Become Christmas' "; January 8, 1977, "Sinatra's Mother on Jet Missing and Presumed Crashed on Coast"; May 19, 1977, Robert Palmer, "Sinatra and Martin, Rock Stars"; July 21, 1977, Molly Ivins, "Cuomo Meets with Sinatra in Little Italy"; April 15, 1980, "Possible Sinatra Tie to Theatre Scheme Is Studied"; February 2, 1984, "Gangster's Daughter Disputes Sinatra on Tie"; August 30, 1984, "Jersey Official Sees 'Tantrum' in Sinatra Cancellation"; November 2, 1986, Barbara Grizzuti Harrison, "Terrified and Fascinated by His Own Life" Book Review; July 28, 1989, "Frank Sinatra Latest Hero of Soviet Socialist Republic"; October 10, 1992, "Sinatra and MacLaine: Stoic and Feisty Nostalgia"; November 22, 1994, Evelyn Nieves, "Sinatra Library? Hoboken Ho-Ho-Holds Its Breath"; December 14, 1995, John J. O'Connor, "Stars Honor a Legend at 80"; May 16, 1998, Janny Scott, "Even Scholars Say It's Witchcraft"; May 16, 1998, Frank Rich, "Sinatra Without Tears"; May 16, 1998, Gay Talese, "The Firefighter's Son"; May 16, 1998, Stephen Holden, "Frank Sinatra Dies at 82; Matchless Stylist of Pop"; May 17, 1998, Stephen Holden, "Sinatra's Lasting Image: The Voice or the Vices": May 21, 1998, "Family and Friends Bid Sinatra Farewell"; May 24, 1998, "Sinatra's Legacy: The Singing Itself"; May 24, 1998, Will Friedwald, "Style & Swagger Pop's 'Big Bang' "; May 27, 1998, Joyce Wadler, "A Very Public Case of Sinatra Fascination"; June 1, 1998, Margo Jefferson, "Sinatra Not a Myth But a Man, and One Among Many"; August 21, 1998, Stephen Holden, "From Fluff to Eternity: The Many Faces of Sinatra on Screen"; November 13, 1998, "Sinatra Is Now Big Man on Campus"; December 10, 1998, "Swooning over a Crooner's File"; December 18, 1998, Irwin Molotsky, "FBI Releases Its Sinatra Files with Tidbits Old and New"; February 6, 2000, "Don't Put Sinatra on Pedastal, Some Say"; August 13, 2000, "From 4F to Eternity"; June 30, 2002, "Four Years After His Death Sinatra Brings Down the House"; October 5, 2003, John Rockwell, "It Wasn't the Final Curtain After All"; October 17, 2003, Stephen Holden, "Reincarnation of Sinatra Under Radio City Big Top."

The New Yorker: October 4, 1982, "Jazz King Again"; May 25, 1998, "Talk of the Town: 'Eighty-Two Very Good Years' "; June 1, 1998, John Lahr, "Department of Send-offs."

Newsday: October 3, 1988, Tim Page, "Aging Enfant Terrible"; December 9, 1990, Terry Kelleher, "Sinatra on Video"; December 9, 1990, Murray Kempton, "Talent for Intimacy"; December 9, 1990, Wayne Rolins, "A New Generation Turns to Ol' Blue Eyes"; December 9, 1990, Gene Seymour, "The Ugly Rumors"; May 15, 1998, Gene Seymour, "His Movies in Hollywood—Some Very Good Years"; May 16, 1998, "His Life, His Music and More"; May 17, 1998, Jimmy Breslin, "It Was a Life Sinatra Was Born to Live"; May 21, 1998, "The Final Curtain."

Newsweek: Frank Sinatra, Interview by Betty Voigt, July 1959.

Playbill: May 2007.

Playboy: "Frank Sinatra," Interview by Joe Hyams, February 1963.

Souvenir Program: 1976, Frank Sinatra Concert Tour.

Sunday Mirror: March 8, 1970, Jack Bentley, "The Ballad of Frankie and Mia."

Time Out London: August 24–31, "Clive James Finally Meets Frank Sinatra."

TV Guide: May 30–June 5, 1988, Special Issue: Dan Wakefield, "Forever Frank"; Will Friedwald, "Frank Sinatra."

Vanity Fair: May 1997, James Wolcott, "When They Were Kings"; July 2007, "Proust Questionnaire with Quincy Jones"; January 2008, Sam Kasher, "A Legend with Legs."

Variety: June 29, 1960, "Sinatra, Martin, A.C.'s D'Amato Teaming for Buy-Up of Cal-Neva Club"; September 14, 1960, "Sinatra Group's Cal-Neva Buy Gets Nev. Okay"; June 24, 1964, (Review of) *Robin and the Seven Hoods*; September 22, 1965, Whit, (Review of) *"Marriage on the Rocks";* October 19, 1977, Obituary, Bing Crosby; July 11, 1984, Loyn, (Review of) *Cannonball Run II*; March 15, 1988, Herb Michaelson, "Rat Pack Tour Gets Underway; Could Gross 420 Mil by Autumn"; June 16, 2003, Peter Bart, "A Black Eye for Old Blue Eyes."

The Village Voice: July 27, 1972, "Chairman of the Board Plays His Flip Side"; April 21, 1980, Gary Giddins, "The Once and Future Sinatra"; September 28, 1982, Jonathan Schwartz, "Sinatra and Torme"; September 11, 1990, Joe Del Priore, "Spank Me, Frankie"; May 26, 1998, Gary Giddins, "The Last Crooner."

Wall Street Journal: May 18, 1998, "Hoboken Homeboy."

World Journal Telegram: May 3, 1967, Hy Gardner, "Sinatra to Head US–Italian ADL"; May 4, 1967, "Sinatra Vows Active Bias Fight."

Index